Ius Comparatum – Global Studies in Comparative Law

Volume 28

Series Editors
Katharina Boele-Woelki, Bucerius Law School, Hamburg, Germany
Diego P. Fernández Arroyo, Institut d'Études Politiques de Paris, Sciences Po, Paris, France

Founding Series Editors
Jürgen Basedow, Max Planck Institute for Comparative and International Private Law, Germany
George Bermann, Columbia University School of Law, USA

Editorial Board
Bénédicte Fauvarque-Cosson, Université Panthéon-Assas, Paris 2, France
Joost Blom, University of British Columbia, Canada
Giuseppe Franco Ferrari, Università Bocconi, Milan, Italy
Toshiyuki Kono, Kyushu University, Fukuoka, Japan
Marek Safjan, Court of Justice of the European Union, Luxembourg
Jorge Sanchez Cordero, Mexican Center of Uniform Law, Mexico
Ulrich Sieber, Max Planck Institute for Foreign and International Criminal Law, Germany

More information about this series at http://www.springer.com/series/11943

Académie Internationale de Droit Comparé
International Academy of Comparative Law

Marie Mercat-Bruns • David B. Oppenheimer •
Cady Sartorius
Editors

Comparative Perspectives on the Enforcement and Effectiveness of Antidiscrimination Law

Challenges and Innovative Tools

Editors
Marie Mercat-Bruns
Sciences Po Law School
Paris, France

David B. Oppenheimer
Berkeley Law
Berkeley, CA, USA

Cady Sartorius
Berkeley Law
Berkeley, CA, USA

ISSN 2214-6881   ISSN 2214-689X   (electronic)
Ius Comparatum – Global Studies in Comparative Law
ISBN 978-3-319-90067-4   ISBN 978-3-319-90068-1   (eBook)
https://doi.org/10.1007/978-3-319-90068-1

Library of Congress Control Number: 2018947638

© Springer International Publishing AG, part of Springer Nature 2018
This work is subject to copyright. All rights are reserved by the Publisher, whether the whole or part of the material is concerned, specifically the rights of translation, reprinting, reuse of illustrations, recitation, broadcasting, reproduction on microfilms or in any other physical way, and transmission or information storage and retrieval, electronic adaptation, computer software, or by similar or dissimilar methodology now known or hereafter developed.
The use of general descriptive names, registered names, trademarks, service marks, etc. in this publication does not imply, even in the absence of a specific statement, that such names are exempt from the relevant protective laws and regulations and therefore free for general use.
The publisher, the authors and the editors are safe to assume that the advice and information in this book are believed to be true and accurate at the date of publication. Neither the publisher nor the authors or the editors give a warranty, express or implied, with respect to the material contained herein or for any errors or omissions that may have been made. The publisher remains neutral with regard to jurisdictional claims in published maps and institutional affiliations.

Printed on acid-free paper

This Springer imprint is published by the registered company Springer International Publishing AG part of Springer Nature.
The registered company address is: Gewerbestrasse 11, 6330 Cham, Switzerland

Contents

Part I Introduction and General Report

Enforcement and Effectiveness of Antidiscrimination Law: Global Commonalities and Practices 3
Marie Mercat-Bruns, David B. Oppenheimer, and Cady Sartorius

Part II National Reports

Argentina 17
Ursula Cristina Basset, Alejandra Rodriguez Galán, and Alfredo M. Vítolo

Australia 31
Beth Gaze and Dominique Allen

Belgium 43
Emmanuelle Bribosia and Isabelle Rorive

Brésil (Brazil) 63
Elton Venturi

Canada 83
Colleen Sheppard

Canada 111
Stéphane Beaulac

Croatia 129
Emilia Mišćenić and Dijana Kesonja

Czech Republic 153
Markéta Selucká, Martina Grochová, and Jana Komendová

Denmark 175
Pia Justesen

France: le jeu des acteurs 189
Sophie Latraverse

Discrimination Et Matiere Penale En France 215
Dominique Viriot-Barrial

France and the Netherlands: Toward Convergence? 239
Réjane Sénac, Janie Pélabay, and Lisa Ammon

Germany 257
Malte Kramme

Greece 283
Antonia Papadelli

India 295
Maithili Pai and Nupur Raut

Israel 311
Tamar Kricheli Katz and Donna Zamir

Italy 335
Marzia Barbera and Alberto Guariso

Japan 353
Akiko Ejima

Republic of Korea 369
Jean Ahn

Liban (Lebanon) 383
Maan S. Bou Saber

Portugal 393
Ana Maria Guerra Martins

Romania 415
Irina Moroianu Zlătescu and Petru Emanuel Zlătescu

South Africa 431
Debbie Collier

Spain 457
María José Gómez-Millán Herencia

Turkey 475
Nurhan Süral

United Kingdom 493
Colm O'Cinneide

The United States 513
Julie C. Suk and Fred L. Morrison

Part III Regional Reports

European Convention of Human Rights/Council of Europe 531
Mathias Möschel

The Inter-American Court of Human Rights 543
Anne-Claire Gayet

Appendix A: Questionnaire 563

Appendix B: Meet the Editors 565

Part I
Introduction and General Report

Enforcement and Effectiveness of Antidiscrimination Law: Global Commonalities and Practices

Marie Mercat-Bruns, David B. Oppenheimer, and Cady Sartorius

> As long as poverty, injustice and gross inequality persist in our world, none of us can truly rest.—Nelson Mandela

1 Introduction

Almost every nation in the world embraces the principle of equality and non-discrimination, in theory if not in practice. The bases that find protection are broader in some countries, narrower in others. The sources of the principle vary considerably. The methods of enforcement and remedies available cover a panoply of approaches. And the effectiveness of enforcement ranges broadly. But the principle is nearly universal.

How then, do we define, limit, and enforce the antidiscrimination principle. What works, where, and what doesn't? Is there a universal answer to a universal principle? This report explores the enforcement and effectiveness of antidiscrimination law from 23 nations, found on 6 continents, and 3 international or regional bodies. In French and English, from legal scholars and scholar/practitioners, we examine national, regional and international systems looking for common practices, and innovative approaches to long-standing problems.

What are the sources of antidiscrimination law? International and regional treaties and conventions; national constitutions; civil and criminal codes; administrative

M. Mercat-Bruns (✉)
Sciences Po Law School, Paris, France

D. B. Oppenheimer · C. Sartorius
Law School, University of California, Berkeley, CA, USA

regulations; common law; religious law; natural law; municipal law; tradition; custom; private contracts; community practices; and more.

How is antidiscrimination law enforced? Through criminal prosecution; civil prosecution by the state, including but not limited to its equality bodies and ombudspersons; individual and class-wide civil lawsuits; administrative claims, including claims for rights of related wrongs; actions by unions and NGOs (non-governmental organizations); actions in religious courts; with claims for damages, changes in behavior, training, apologies, imprisonment, or fines; by arbitration, conciliation, mediation, meditation, and community resolution processes; with interventions by elders or neighbors or friends; and most often not at all.

Which of these methods of enforcement are effective? Compared to what? By any comparison, some countries experience far more success than others, and often in unexpected ways. In some places, there is hardly any success at all.

Moreover, we recognize that there is no single objective measure by which we can assess effectiveness. Effectiveness varies with legal and social cultures, expectations, and goals. If there were any doubt that there is no single measure of effectiveness, we need only turn to the two leading indexes of inclusiveness, each of which attempts to compare and rank states by their success at inclusion.

The first, the 2016 Inclusiveness Index for Measuring Inclusion and Marginality,[1] published by the Haas Institute for a Fair and Inclusive Society, ranks the Netherlands as the most inclusive nation-state in the world while ranking Canada as number ten. By contrast, the Migrant Integration Policy Index,[2] produced by the Migration Policy Group, ranks Canada first in the world in antidiscrimination practice and policy, while ranking the Netherlands number fourteen.

To examine the enforcement and effectiveness of antidiscrimination law we asked 27 national and regional reporters, representing 24 nations (including two reports from Canada, one in French, one in English), to address thirteen questions, which follow this introduction. Their reports are reproduced herein.

These enriching national and international reports, in unison, highlight the need for more creative, concrete and coordinated means of enforcement to ensure the effectiveness of antidiscrimination law, regardless of the legal tradition concerned, but in light of these traditions. We found each report remarkable, and learned something new and interesting from every report. We hope you will as well.

In attempting to synthesize the reports, five important themes emerged. First, the response to the enforcement and effectiveness of equality norms is ambivalent in every part of the world. Second, the enforcement and effectiveness of antidiscrimination law depends on a variegated treatment of the grounds of discrimination. Third, the laws of procedure and evidence are decisive to the enforcement of antidiscrimination law and access to justice. Fourth, resistance to effective remedies in antidiscrimination law is common. Finally, there is a shared concern as to whether

---

[1] See http://haasinstitute.berkeley.edu/sites/default/files/haasinstitute_2016inclusiveness_index_publish_sept26.pdf

[2] See http://www.mipex.eu/antidiscrimination

or how antidiscrimination law is transformative to further substantive equality today and in the future.

2 Enforcement, Effectiveness and the Ambivalent Reception of Antidiscrimination Law (Theme 1)

The most striking commonality in the reports from around the world is, on the one hand, the value of antidiscrimination law, and on the other the ambivalence and resistance to its enforcement. Nearly every reporter pointed to the constitutional and international foundations of antidiscrimination law, the extent of the antidiscrimination norm across the globe, and the often broad scope of antidiscrimination law. Yet there is also wide resistance to antidiscrimination law, varied in nature and in origin; resistance finds its strength in historical, institutional, cultural, political, and economic structures. This ambivalent reception to antidiscrimination law sets the stage for the general framework needed to evaluate globally the enforcement and effectiveness of antidiscrimination law.

In the European, South American and Asian reports, antidiscrimination prevails as a constitutional principle in most countries, coined as a fundamental right in countries like Argentina, Germany, Brazil, the Czech Republic, Israel, Spain, Japan, and India. A number of reports acknowledge the value of these higher norms for the reception and incorporation of antidiscrimination law that pervades the core of the rules of most legal systems. The important transnational dimension of this field of law puts it on a par with other human rights principles like liberty or dignity in Brazil, France, Canada, and Israel, among others, setting the stage for decisive interpretation by the Inter-American Court of Human Rights, the European Court of Human Rights (ECtHR) and the International Court at The Hague. This formal and imposing recognition justifies the broad scope of the antidiscrimination norm, which can cover civil and administrative law targeting illegal practices in housing, employment, education, or access to public and private spaces, for instance, in South Africa and the United States. Criminal sanctions exist in Turkey, Croatia, India, France, Korea, and Brazil, among others.

However, the laws' extensive scope in some countries does not prevent persistent hostility towards antidiscrimination law or resistance to its full implementation. Outside of strong explicit support for antidiscrimination in Canada, Portugal, and Brazil (defending a "racial democracy" and where "exclusion is harmful to all"), or high awareness of discrimination issues in the United States, South Africa, or Canada, the forms of resistance vary. Judicial hostility exists in countries like Australia and Croatia that consider antidiscrimination norms a threat to social cohesion, and in France where these norms are a menace to the Republican idea of equality. They are seen as infringing on the freedom of contract law in the Czech Republic. Specific groups also rally against discrimination law, from right wing political groups in Denmark and France, to religious opposition in Lebanon, Italy, and Brazil. Economic interests also seem to thwart enforcement of antidiscrimination law that favors indigenous people in Brazil, or full application in the employment context when corporations attempt to resist its hold, as is the case in the United States.

3 Enforcement and the Disparate Treatment of Grounds of Discrimination (Theme 2)

Antidiscrimination law is highly contextual. Based on unequal treatment in the different countries, it refers most often to a specific list of grounds rather than an open-ended list, as is found in the ECHR Convention. A closer look at this ambivalent reception of antidiscrimination law in different countries reveals that the enforcement and effectiveness of antidiscrimination depends on how a specific ground of discrimination is protected. The ban on disability discrimination is vigorously enforced in Korea, for example, whereas in Argentina, women and transgender groups seem to benefit more from action against discrimination. Countries do not necessarily determine a hierarchy of grounds, though race and sex are often the focus of national policies, for example in Denmark for race. Coverage of a ground does not mean successful enforcement for certain particularly vulnerable groups like the Roma in Europe, gay, lesbian and transsexual people (LGBT) groups in Croatia, indigenous people in Brazil, migrants in the Czech Republic, or women in Lebanon. Some grounds do not benefit from the same legal protection. Exceptions exist for age, for example, in Europe or Quebec, and exemptions restrict the prohibition of religious discrimination, for instance, in the United States.

Among the recurring questions, does efficient enforcement justify covering a large number of grounds like in South Africa, Turkey, Australia, or Israel? In this regard, France recently added socio-economic status or place of residence as prohibited grounds. Some countries still do not cover sexual orientation discrimination (such as federal law in the United States) or encounter difficulties in enforcing the age discrimination prohibition (as in Spain and Portugal). Others fail to protect certain religions, such as Islam in the Czech Republic and France. Intersectional discrimination poses a challenge in terms of proving the effect of discrimination based on a combination of grounds, which the Inter-American Court report highlights.

4 Enforcement of Antidiscrimination Law, Evidence, and Procedural Rules (Theme 3)

Access to justice is a challenge in every country. All reports mention the effect of procedural rules and issues of evidence that apply to discrimination law. Some procedural norms are specific to antidiscrimination law, while others are general rules that apply to all litigation. Some countries like Denmark, Japan, the Netherlands, and Israel note, for example, that it is difficult for victims to resort to the courts due to the high cost of representation in Denmark, court fees in the Czech Republic, or the need for an attorney in cases of racist insults in Israel. Other reports state that antidiscrimination law requires judicial action, which is often slow in places like Brazil. Proper enforcement of antidiscrimination law is sometimes hindered by a strong deference of the judiciary to the legislative power, as it is the case in Japan, or the will of the judges to avoid trial altogether and impose summary judgment, as is increasingly the case in the United States.

Other procedural issues raised in the reports are linked to the nature of discrimination itself. Some countries confine their enforcement to responding to individual action. Others have developed collective mechanisms like class actions to deal with systemic discrimination, including the United States, Brazil, Denmark, Canada, and France (with a new class action law recently adopted). Others, including Croatia and the Czech Republic, do not offer this tool for litigation.

What is equally at stake in discrimination law is how litigation or other means of conflict resolution may or may not demand proof of a discriminatory motive in the conscious or unconscious mind of the perpetrator. A key issue in antidiscrimination law and its effectiveness is the question of the allocation of the burden of proof of discrimination. European Union (EU) Member States report that the shift of the burden of persuasion to the defendant in these cases, as required by the EU directives, has facilitated better enforcement of law, as explained in the reports from France, Italy, the United Kingdom, and the Czech Republic. Yet it is criticized by legal doctrine in the latter country. The French report explains that this shift does not apply to criminal law because of the presumption of innocence favoring the defendant. Some countries have no shift of the burden of proof, like Australia, or a less favorable shift, like the United States, where in most disparate treatment cases only the burden of production shifts to the defendant. In certain legal systems, as exposed in the United States report, a useful rule of discovery generally requires the parties to disclose a copy of all documents, information, and objects that the disclosing party has in its possession, custody, or control that the producing party may use to support its claims or defenses. Perhaps because these initial disclosures help lawyers fully evaluate the likely outcome of their cases at an early point, most claims confidentially settle instead of going to trial. Under French law, by contrast, such disclosures cannot be used as evidence by civil courts, but the Defender of Rights can engage in an investigation, which may be useful for the plaintiff.

5 Enforcement and Variable Resistance to Effective Remedies in Antidiscrimination Law (Theme 4)

The challenge of effective enforcement also requires insight on the remedies awarded to victims of discrimination. In most countries, obtaining generous monetary compensation in court is often difficult, for example in France, Belgium, the

Czech Republic, and Denmark. There is a cap on the amount of compensation allowed in Turkey. Notable exceptions are Canada/Quebec, the United States, Spain, Israel, the United Kingdom, and South Africa. The limited amount of compensation awarded in most countries is a common concern among international courts, as described in the ECHR report.

The resistance to effective remedies also lies in the courts, which can reflect judicial hostility to antidiscrimination law, as the report on Croatia suggests. Fewer claims are introduced in civil courts, as in the Netherland and Denmark, where the preference is for Alternative Dispute Resolution (ADR). Numerous claims confidentially settle in the United States and Canada/Quebec or are abandoned in Australia. Criminal sanctions are available but rarely applied in Turkey, Croatia, France, and Brazil, with incarceration especially rare. In France, fines are mostly symbolic and often involve hate speech.

Effective remedies can depend on the ground of discrimination. Claims can be introduced more frequently for certain grounds like pregnancy, age, military reserve duty, and nationality, and discrimination based on family responsibility in Israel, and less frequently for other grounds like sexual orientation. For example, LGBT persons are subject to persistent discrimination in Brazil.

Constructive forms of sanctions and useful remedies exist in some countries. For example, decisions, recommendations, or investigations by equality bodies are reported as playing a significant role in obtaining successful compensation for victims of discrimination in many countries. Among the creative remedies reported, in Brazil injunctions to stop discriminating constitute an efficient alternative, and remedies for ethnic discrimination are allocated to a new fund for policies to promote ethnic equality. In the United States, public contracts require proper compliance with antidiscrimination law, and a specific public agency oversees contract compliance.

6 A Way Forward: Antidiscrimination Law as Transformative Law? (Theme 5)

The reports reveal a great diversity of enforcement tools to make antidiscrimination law more efficient, through strategies that involve many actors, including NGOs, public authorities, judges, equality bodies and unions.

To move forward, the common query in the reports, beyond acknowledging the quantitative or qualitative means of enforcement, is to wonder what exact role antidiscrimination law is meant to play in achieving substantive equality. If the goal is only to increase the number of successful claims or sanctions, the reports show the scope but also the limits of a constant battle to eradicate all forms of discrimination, regardless of the grounds, once the arbitrary treatment is revealed. Persistent criticism of antidiscrimination laws' effectiveness exists in certain countries such as the United States, France, India, Korea, and Australia. Eradicating individual biases is sometimes seen as perpetuating the status of victims of those who should benefit from its application, instead of investing energy and money in traditional labor and social policies to further social and economic equality for all groups.

In light of the strong international consensus to support all fundamental rights, and despite cultural and economic resistance to antidiscrimination law in some countries, the reports disclose an increase in the number of alternatives to traditional modes of enforcement (namely through the court system).

To appreciate the effectiveness of these alternatives, consider whether these countries believe antidiscrimination law can be *transformative* for the individuals involved, keeping in mind the structural barriers which perpetuate discrimination in all areas including housing, education, health, public and private services, or employment.

The reports produce an inventory of the ways in which reform can affect the structural causes of discrimination through (1) procedural rules favoring Alternative Dispute Resolution (ADR), (2) preventive measures before discrimination arises, (3) systemic solutions based on affirmative action, (4) better detection of direct and indirect discrimination through monitoring or education, and (5) reasonable accommodation across the board for people with disabilities, parents, senior citizens, and members of religious minorities. A preliminary illustration of the diverse nature of these different actions is necessary. (1) Often public enforcement authorities do not exclusively favor litigation against discrimination. This is true in Australia, France, and Canada. The Canadian Human Rights Commissions diversify their mission to investigate, conciliate, mediate, and prosecute before special administrative tribunals. (2) The Japanese legal system approach to discrimination seems to favor a "soft approach" based on awareness-raising. (3) In Argentina, structural initiatives are sought by the Women's Office, created in 2009, which has promoted a comprehensive process for mainstreaming gender views in institutional planning and internal processes to achieve gender equality both in the judiciary and for those who use the justice system. In South Africa, there is a strong and explicit emphasis on affirmative action programs. (4) The Israeli Ministry of Justice focuses on racism: raising awareness with an information center for victims and giving legal tools and intensification of labor law enforcement especially in the area of antidiscrimination law. (5) The Czech Republic, through its Public Defender or the United States through its Equal Employment Opportunity Commission, among others, targets reasonable accommodation for people with disabilities.

Affirmative action is most present in South Africa, Brazil, the United States, Canada, India, and Turkey, even though it is often regarded as divisive and has been contested with variable success (for example, in the United States with regard to race). Brazil, South Africa, and India have racial quotas (called "reservations" in India), and the government is widely engaged, supporting social inclusion for all vulnerable groups. Other countries, such as Australia, do not allow affirmative action. Positive action based on disability and sex is less prone to criticism, for example in Spain and France, which both have rules on parity for women in elected office and for people with disabilities in the workforce.

In Lebanon, the emphasis is on developing training for judges to raise awareness about direct discrimination, not on indirect and systemic discrimination. The two reports on Canada emphasize how the government has made the fight against systemic discrimination one of its main goals. Mandatory or contractually binding ADR through arbitration can be found respectfully in Australia and the United States, as well as Germany, Greece, Portugal, and through a new reform (the multi-door courthouse system) in Brazil. As long as ADR does not prevent access to litigation (which is a current risk in the United States), it can be a positive alternative to litigation. Japan prefers measures like education to address hate speech against Koreans. Other countries such as Greece, Spain, and Portugal see either NGOs or unions as strong actors to promote antidiscrimination law and represent individuals and groups.

Institutional change can come from the administrative equality bodies' work in the United States and Spain, general human rights bodies in France (Defender of Rights) and the Netherlands (Human Rights Commission), the National Human Rights Commission in Korea, the Romanian Institute for Human Rights in Romania, the Ombudsman in Portugal and Australia, and the public defenders in the Czech Republic and Brazil. Some more specialized enforcement agencies exist like the National Institute Against Discrimination, Xenophobia and Racism in Argentina. These public authorities have a specific mandate on the question of discrimination and can often work from different angles (litigation, ADR, education) to combat inequalities. Courts often follow their rulings, as in Denmark and France. French authorities interviewed for the French-Dutch report, as well as Japanese authorities, seem keen on developing soft-law charters and codes of best practices, though none presently exist. Reports in some countries, like Denmark, confirm that there is generally a crucial need for more systematic statistical accounts on enforcement.

A major difficulty is to coordinate, without a global antidiscrimination policy, the more in-depth work on causes of discrimination before it arises in education, housing, health, and employment sectors, concludes the comparative French-Dutch political science study. Outside of awareness-raising in information centers for victims, local agencies or equal opportunity boards are not always equipped to deal with the more subtle forms of discrimination, for example in the Netherlands, where indirect discrimination is rarely detected.

The French-Dutch report, citing Dworkin, recommends "taking rights seriously" in matters of discrimination. This does not only depend on the nature of the legal system involved but the political impetus to implement coherent and diversified policies engaging public authorities, civil society, and judges, targeting both individual and systemic levels. Italy seems to embrace various scales of intervention. From early education to retirement policies, there is a need to mainstream the question of the risk of inequality when reflecting on any new public or private action. From the start, all tools of discrimination law (prevention, sanction, education, positive action) can contribute to social cohesion like any other policy (health, education, or labor). Yet schools, companies, and social services do not consider equality law as a top priority. This might be less true with disability, which generates positive policies of reasonable accommodation to avoid discrimination, as the Quebec report demonstrates. On the other hand, racial, ethnic, and religious discrimination are still reported as prevalent in every country in the world from which a report was submitted.

7 Conclusion: From Enforcement to Effectiveness?

While every national and regional report points to widely adopted policies against discrimination, and myriad legal and social tools are deployed for the enforcement of antidiscrimination law, the work of antidiscrimination law is incomplete. The reports that follow bolster our conclusion that nation states and regional actors can learn through comparison, taking note of how legal and social systems will inevitably privilege some forms of enforcement over others, often at the expense of effectiveness. Lawyers, scholars, and policy makers should, at a minimum, consider the likely effectiveness within their systems of administrative enforcement, affirmative action, Alternative Dispute Resolution, civil litigation, conciliation, criminal enforcement, empowering NGOs and unions, equality bodies, mediation, and ombudspersons. And none should be self-satisfied in light of the continuing challenge. Bridging the enforcement gap is a recurring challenge of many fields of law but here especially we feel we must add a few final words on the notion of effectiveness of antidiscrimination, given that the fight for equality triggers such ambivalence.

There are several ways to understand the effectiveness of antidiscrimination law: from a narrow to a broader perspective, depending on the nature of the laws promoting equality.

Effectiveness of a law can be measured by the degree of compliance.[3] The degree of compliance depends on the type of law. "If the law is preventive, designed to discourage behavior which is disapproved of, the goal is to see if the behavior is diminished or absent."[4] Our first observation would be that overt discrimination is probably less prevalent in certain countries even though its nature has also changed: in those countries, it can take a subtler form.

Thus, if our measure is compliance, the twenty-nine reports reveal a degree of effectiveness, in the reduction of overt discrimination. But they also reveal nearly universal resistance, though the form of resistance varies considerably. They also reveal an unwillingness to accept the central premise of the need for antidiscrimination law—that in every one of our reports we see the recurring problem of reports of denial of discrimination as a systemic problem. Before we can measure success by compliance, there is still much to be done.

"If the law is curative, operating ex post facto to rectify some failing or injustice or dispute, the goal is to see if the law serves to achieve these ends."[5] In most

---

[3] Allott (1991), p. 234.
[4] Allott (1991), p. 234.
[5] Allott (1991), p. 234.

countries, disputes arise to react to discrimination, and litigation or mediation takes place. Does a rise in disputes triggered by violations of antidiscrimination law reflect an increase of its effectiveness? Not necessarily. But an increase in claims-making does suggest that there is an increasing belief that antidiscrimination law has curative power.

Lastly, "if the law is facilitative, providing formal recognition, regulation and protection for an institution of the law, such as marriage or contract, the measure of effectiveness is the extent to which the institution so regulated is in fact insulated from attack."[6] Equality laws have extended the scope of institutions like marriage, parental rights, and labor law to benefit certain groups, but it has also questioned the very nature of these institutions. And our observation that overt discrimination is reportedly far less common suggests that we have indeed given recognition to a social commitment to non-discrimination as an institution itself, albeit one to which we see continuing resistance.

So, all in all, the effectiveness of antidiscrimination law might have to be considered according to its inherent nature, its inherent logic. It is a useful vehicle to uphold fundamental rights but also to question indefinitely those in power (in the public and private spheres) who, consciously or unconsciously, do not promote inclusion as a beacon of democracy. And its progress moves in fits and starts, but it continues to spread and gain acceptance that outweighs its resistance. Thus, while we recognize that there is much work to be done and much progress to be made, we think we are justified in joining with Bishop Desmond Tutu of South Africa, who has famously described himself as 'a prisoner of hope.' As are we.

Reference

Allott A (1991) The effectiveness of law. Valparaiso Univ Law Rev 15:234

Marie Mercat-Bruns is an Affiliated Professor at Sciences Po Law School and a tenured Associate Law Professor at the Conservatoire National des Arts et Métiers where she copilots the Gender Program (LISE,CNRS). She holds an LLM from the University of Pennsylvania Law School and a prize winning, comparative PhD on Law and Aging from the University of Paris West Nanterre. She is the author of "Discrimination at Work: Comparing European, French, and American Law" UC Press, 2016. Her more recent articles cover systemic discrimination and racial harassment.

---

[6]Allott (1991), pp. 234–235.

David B. Oppenheimer is a Clinical Professor of Law at the University of California, Berkeley. He holds a JD from Harvard University and a BA from the University Without Walls, Berkeley. He is the author of several books and numerous articles on antidiscrimination law, civil rights history, and comparative antidiscrimination law.

Cady Sartorius was a sign language interpreter in New Mexico before attending law school at the University of California, Berkeley. She now practices law at the California Civil Rights Law Group—a plaintiff-side firm fighting workplace discrimination and civil rights violations.

Part II
National Reports

Argentina

Ursula Cristina Basset, Alejandra Rodriguez Galán, and Alfredo M. Vítolo

1 Introduction

This paper analyses the characteristics of the Argentine antidiscrimination laws and their enforcement in the context of the demand for equality, and the way in which such laws have been enforced from several perspectives. We begin this analysis with a section that introduces the basic principles underlying the subject.

The term "discrimination" came up in the international human rights texts only in the last century. The Universal Declaration of Human Rights of 1948, adopted in the context of the world's (late) reaction to the Holocaust, and developing one of the core purposes set out in the United Nations Charter of *"promoting and encouraging respect for human rights and for fundamental freedoms for all without distinction as to race, sex, language, or religion,"*[1] in its Article 7 states that *"All are equal before the law and are entitled without any discrimination to equal protection of the law. All are entitled to equal protection against any discrimination in violation of this Declaration and against any incitement to such discrimination."*

---

[1] United Nations Charter, Article 1.3.

U. C. Basset (✉)
Universidad Austral, School of Law, Buenos Aires, Argentina

Pontifical Catholic University, School of Law, Buenos Aires, Argentina
e-mail: ubasset@austral.edu.ar

A. Rodriguez Galán
Universidad de Buenos Aires, School of Law, Buenos Aires, Argentina
e-mail: alejandrarodriguezgalan@derecho.uba.ar

A. M. Vítolo
National University of Buenos Aires, School of Law, Buenos Aires, Argentina
e-mail: avitolo@derecho.uba.ar

© Springer International Publishing AG, part of Springer Nature 2018
M. Mercat-Bruns et al. (eds.), *Comparative Perspectives on the Enforcement and Effectiveness of Antidiscrimination Law*, Ius Comparatum – Global Studies in Comparative Law 28, https://doi.org/10.1007/978-3-319-90068-1_2

It is in the International Labor Organization' Discrimination (Employment and Occupation) Convention—C111, adopted in 1958, where the term "discrimination" is defined for the first time in an international instrument. This Convention states in Article 1 that:

1. For the purpose of this Convention the term "discrimination" includes:

(a) Any distinction, exclusion or preference made on the basis of race, colour, sex, religion, political opinion, national extraction or social origin, which has the effect of nullifying or impairing equality of opportunity or treatment in employment or occupation;

(b) Such other distinction, exclusion or preference which has the effect of nullifying or impairing equality of opportunity or treatment in employment or occupation as may be determined by the Member concerned after consultation with representative employers' and workers' organisations, where such exist, and with other appropriate bodies.[2]

The same conceptual argument appears in other international instruments, among other, in the Convention against Discrimination in Education (1960),[3] the International Convention on the Elimination of all Forms of Racial Discrimination (1965)[4]; the Convention on the Elimination of all Forms of Discrimination against Women (CEDAW, 1979).[5]

Claudio Kiper, argentine jurist, author of a book on discrimination against minorities[6] distinguishes a popular use of the term discrimination, which consists of a distinction in favor of or against a person based on the group, class or category to which a person belongs, rather than on its own merits. But, he also states that there is a sociological sense of the term, where hostility in relations among people, directed against a group of them or against each of its members. This is the most pervasive use of the term.

The Argentine author Julio Martinez Vivot[7] points out that discrimination can be direct or indirect. Direct discrimination is linked to the difference in consideration or treatment without an objective circumstance or situation that justify or explain, injuring with such conduct dignity of the person and his guaranteed human rights. The concept of indirect discrimination, however, is related with the adverse effect, where the measure itself does not appear as discriminatory, but not doubt that entails that intention.

In Argentina, its Constitution, adopted in 1853, as most constitutions of its time, recognizes the principle of equality under law, without making any express reference to the term discrimination. Its Section 16 provides that:

---

[2]Discrimination (Employment and Occupation) Convention, 1958 (C No. 111)—adopted on 25 June 1958 by the General Conference of the International Labour Organisation at its forty-second session; entry into force on 15 June 1960.
[3]Convention against Discrimination in Education (1960), Article 1.1.
[4]International Convention on the Elimination of all Forms of Racial Discrimination (1965), Article 1.1.
[5]Convention on the Elimination of all Forms of Discrimination against Women (CEDAW) (1979), Article 1.
[6]Kiper (1998).
[7]Martínez Vivot (1981, 2000).

The Argentine Nation admits neither blood nor birth prerogatives: there are neither personal privileges nor titles of nobility. All its inhabitants are equal before the law, and admissible to employment without any other requirement than their ability. Equality is the basis of taxation and public burdens.

Section 20, moreover, provides,

Foreigners enjoy within the territory of the Nation all the civil rights of citizens; they may exercise their industry, trade and profession; own real property, buy and sell it; navigate the rivers and coasts; practice freely their religion; make wills and marry under the laws. They are not obliged to accept citizenship nor to pay extraordinary compulsory taxes.

The equality principle has been early defined by the federal Supreme Court. In a case decided in 1875, the highest court of the country indicated that it required that the law *"does not establish privileges or distinctions that exclude someone from what is given to others in similar circumstances."*[8]

The constitutional amendment of 1994 added new contents to the concept, in line with international developments. The new Section 75 §22 gives most international conventions on human rights constitutional hierarchy, thus incorporating their provisions regarding the prohibition on discrimination; Section 75 §19 entrusts Congress with the task of promoting *the equality of opportunities and means without any discrimination whatsoever*; while §23 requires Congress, *"to legislate and promote proactive measures that guarantee true equality of opportunity and treatment, and the full enjoyment and exercise of the rights recognized by this Constitution and by current international treaties on human rights, in particular with respect to children, women, the elderly and people with disabilities."*

As regards political rights, Section 37 states, *"This Constitution guarantees full enjoyment of political rights, in accordance with the principle of popular sovereignty and with the laws dictated pursuant thereto. Suffrage is universal, equal, secret and mandatory. True equality of opportunity between men and women in running for elected and party offices shall be guaranteed through affirmative actions in the regulation of political parties and in the electoral system,"* which substantially increased the level of protection by establishing a much stricter criteria for equality.

The federal Constitution also protects religious freedom by granting all residents, either nationals or not, the right *"to freely profess their faith,"*[9] notwithstanding that the federal government *"supports the Roman Catholic Apostolic Faith."*[10] Prominent social leaders took positive steps to promote religious freedom and interreligious dialogue. Certain constitutional regulations that could be viewed as limiting religious freedom, such as the requirement for the President to be Catholic, or the mandate to Congress to promote the conversion of Indians to Catholicism, were abrogated by the 1994 constitutional amendment.

Based on these, it can be said that Argentina vigorously recognizes the principle of equality before law, and its Constitution and implementing laws (including

---

[8] Argentine Supreme Court, *Guillermo Olivar*, Fallos 16:156 (1875).
[9] Argentine Constitution, Sections 14 and 20.
[10] Argentine Constitution, Section 2.

affirmative actions) are directed towards achieving the principle of equal opportunities for all, eradicating discrimination at all stages.

2 The Antidiscrimination Act

Notwithstanding several isolated laws provided grounds to attack discrimination, it wasn't until the return of the country to democratic rule in 1983, which inaugurated a period of consolidation of democratic institutions and observance of constitutional guarantees, that the first specific law on discrimination was enacted, Law 23.592, passed in 1988. This Act—still in force—guarantees the right of all persons in the country to live in a plural and equal society, consistent with the principles of the Constitution, and sanctions the discriminatory acts that are motivated by religious or racial causes, nationality, ideological, sex and political opinion bias.[11]

The enactment of this law opened the question of discrimination in Argentina, as it involves the recognition of the State's obligation to provide answers to certain discriminatory practices.

3 The Scope of the Antidiscrimination Laws in Argentina

As mentioned earlier in this work, Argentina has adopted and became a party to the main international treaties dealing with antidiscrimination, some of which bear the same force as our Constitution, since they have been expressly named in Section 75 §22. As a consequence, every individual within Argentina benefits from and may demand compliance with antidiscrimination law because of the general prohibitions that can be found in documents such as the Universal and American Declarations on Human Rights, the International Covenant on Civil and Political Rights, the International Covenant on Economic, Social and Cultural Rights and the American Convention on Human Rights.

Section 75 §22 of the federal Constitution, also granted constitutional hierarchy to some conventions focused on vulnerable members of our society, thus increasing the scope of protection against discrimination. This is the case of women[12] and

---

[11]Law 23.592, *"Article 1 Whoever arbitrarily impedes, obstructs, restricts or in any way impairs the full exercise on an equal basis of the fundamental rights and guarantees recognized in the Constitution, shall be obliged, at the request of the victim, to repeal the discriminatory act or cease to perform and to repair the moral and material damage caused. For the purposes of this Article, certain discriminatory acts or omissions on grounds such as race, religion, nationality, ideology, political or union opinion, sex, economic status, social status or physical characteristics shall be particularly taken into consideration".*

[12]Convention on the Elimination of All Forms of Discrimination against Women (CEDAW, 1979).

children[13] and those who might be targeted by racial discrimination[14] or genocide.[15]

Argentina also subscribed the International Convention on the Rights of Persons with Disabilities (2007)[16] and the Inter-American Convention on the Rights on the Elimination of All Forms of Discrimination against Persons with Disabilities.[17] On the other hand, concerning women, Argentina passed a law in order to ratify the Inter-American Convention on the Prevention, Punishment and Eradication of Violence against Women "Convention of Bélem do Pará."[18] Migrant workers are also beneficiaries of a special treatment, since Argentina ratified the International Convention on the Protection of the Rights of All Migrant Workers.[19] All of these International Treaties have in our legal system—by constitutional mandate—superiority over federal and state law. In case of inconsistencies, they would prevail. Notwithstanding Argentina being a federal country, federal law is enforceable against the different components of the federation, the provinces.

Finally, we note that Argentina addressed in its laws several categories of vulnerabilities that might be subject to discrimination in order to provide protection against it.

At a systemic level, it is possible to identify the more vulnerable groups in the very sense define in the United States Supreme Court oft-cited case *"United States v. Carolene Products Co.* (304 U.S. 144 (1938)), footnote n°4 *"Nor need we enquire whether similar considerations enter into the review of statutes directed at particular religious, or national, or racial minorities: whether prejudice against discrete and insular minorities may be a special condition, which tends seriously to curtail the operation of those political processes ordinarily to be relied upon to protect minorities, and which may call for a correspondingly more searching judicial inquiry"* (citations omitted).

In Argentina, indigenous peoples, immigrants from border countries, senior citizens and women, disabled, among others, qualify under these groups.

Women are probably the most benefitted category. Law 26.171 adhered to the Additional Protocol of the CEDAW (1999), which permitted the Committee on the Elimination of Discrimination against Women to receive and consider communications from victims of a violation of any of the rights set forth in the Convention. More recently, Congress passed a specific antidiscrimination act to prevent, eradicate and punish any form of violence against women.[20] Moreover, in order to

---

[13]Convention on the Rights of the Child (1989).

[14]International Convention on the Elimination of all Forms of Racial Discrimination (adopted and opened for signature and ratification by General Assembly resolution 2106 of 21 December 1965; entry into force on 4 January 1969).

[15]International Convention on the Prevention and Punishment of Genocide (1948).

[16]Ley 26.378.

[17]Ley 25.280.

[18]Ley 24.632.

[19]Ley 26.202.

[20]Ley 26.485.

prevent gender-biased violence, a law required schools to dedicate a full day to reflect about gender violence and discrimination against women,[21] and a body of experienced practitioners was created in order to provide legal counseling and defend women victims of gender violence.[22] Argentina also became member of the ILO Convention C156 about Workers with Family Responsibilities, which concerns equal opportunities and equal treatment for men and women workers.[23] Finally, besides the special provisions in labor law concerning the dismissal of pregnant women, Argentina passed a law banning the exclusion of pregnant adolescents from high school.[24]

Another group that benefitted from the Argentine legislation are transgender people. A wide-scope law was enforced to recognize them not only for access to free public health and free health care by private health care services,[25] but also requiring to change the public records of their sexual assignation without having to undergo any kind of surgery to alter their secondary sexual characteristics.[26]

Children are probably the group that benefits least from direct antidiscrimination laws, despite the fact that the Convention on the Rights of the Child enjoys constitutional hierarchy. Federal law bans any form of discrimination against children. However, since school, as we will see below, is a space where discrimination practices may arise, we should attend to the application of two relatively new legal devices: a law to regulate conflicts within an educational establishment and the creation of a day of reflection on discrimination and violence.[27]

To sum up, from the standpoint of its legal protection against discrimination, Argentina has strong general clauses, but when it comes specific provisions in order to protect special groups, its approach is limited to women, transgender people, persons with disabilities, migrant workers and children at school.

4 Problems

The enforcement of antidiscrimination law in Argentina conflicts mainly with the rights of companies and business enterprises, educational establishments, particularly if they have certain restrictions, according to their ethos, and private and public health care services. Companies have eventually complained of having to reinstate a dismissed worker who they claim is not adapted to their particular needs. In a recent case against a bus company, to ensure positive measures to engage women as

---

[21] Ley 27.234.
[22] Ley 27.210.
[23] Ley 23.451.
[24] Ley 25.584.
[25] Decreto 903/2015.
[26] Ley 26.743.
[27] Ley 26.892.

drivers, the Supreme Court of Salta (a Province in Argentina) ruled as discriminatory the preference for men drivers; the same happened in connection with ice cream parlours. Transgender people may affect the ethos of educational establishments when they pretend to teach in private schools. Private and public health care services are said to be overloaded, since antidiscrimination law forces them to cover entirely in vitro fertilization treatments, expensive disability treatments or sex reassignment surgeries without any cost to be charged to the person who requires them. The issue becomes particularly sensitive when it comes to certain practices which might raise ethical concerns to the particular persons having to offer those practices, to the institutions if they have certain shared principles on the matter (e. g, if they have a religious adscription), or the society as a whole o to the members of a certain institution, if they have to pay ultimately for the services that others, because of their personal choices and notwithstanding their personal wealth, obtain freely.

5 Enforcement: The INADI and Other Agencies—Civil Society

The enforcement of antidiscrimination laws falls on the judiciary (who can only act upon a case is brought to them by an affected party) and on the administrative sanctions applicable by the INADI, the National Institute against Discrimination, Xenophobia and Racism, a federal decentralized agency created in 1995 by Law 24.515. Since 2005, the INADI functions within the orbit of the Ministry of Justice and Human Rights. This agency began its work in 1997, and is entrusted by the law to prepare reports and proposals in connection with discrimination, xenophobia and racism; prepare public awareness campaigns on the matter; receive denounces of violations of the requirements of Law 23.592; provide assistance to victims of discrimination, xenophobia or racism; and act before the judicial courts in the defense of victims. For these purposes, INADI has established agencies in the different provinces of our country.[28]

As part of its functions, the INADI targets several forms of discrimination by the creation of observatories and special public policies. As it arises from several reports published during the present year (2016),[29] we should note:

a) One of the main concerns in Argentina is the discrimination of migrant workers, which leads in turn to educational and social discrimination and poverty. Mostly against workers and their families and children coming from neighbour countries such as Bolivia and Paraguay, but also against those migrating from Peru.

---

[28] More information on INADI's functions can be found at www.inadi.gob.ar.
[29] See http://www.inadi.gob.ar/mapa-discriminacion/documentos/mapa-de-la-discriminacion-segunda-edicion.pdf.

There are several stereotypes of each of those migrants. Argentina is designing devices to target and combat such discrimination.
b) As regards discrimination against women, one of the main concerns is not only gender violence, but also the distribution of work and family responsibilities. Women continue to be the main carers in a family when there are children, family members with disabilities, diseased or aged persons. On the other hand, lot of progress has been made concerning the involvement of women in the labour market. However, those advancements conspire ultimately against equality because no adjustment has been made in order to give an answer to the special caring tasks women spontaneously assume. Divorce laws that have come to the point to treat equally men and women, despite their gender or sexual orientation, now face new inequalities, precisely because of women's caring position, they are disadvantaged. Women are also subject to stereotypes concerning their physical appearance (their weight, their age) that in turn leads to trauma and to illnesses such as anorexia, bulimia, and psychological trauma.
c) A subject yet needing to be addressed, is the maltreatment of older persons under the care of third parties.
d) Argentina has made enormous advancement on the protection of the rights of indigenous communities, however, their integration in society is not always exempt of tensions and stereotypes.
e) Persons with disabilities are often the target of several forms of discrimination, which need to be addressed taking into consideration the particularity of their disabilities, their needs and characteristics.
f) Discrimination studies should not be focused only on the group of persons that are suffering discrimination, but on the context where such discrimination takes place. INADI statistics show that discrimination occurs mostly in school and at work. Therefore, it realizes it should focus its work on promoting awareness in order to prevent such discrimination in those two frames.
g) Finally, the INADI has created three observatories in order to monitor compliance with antidiscrimination laws: the Observatory of Radio and TV Shows,[30] a Platform for an Internet Free of Discrimination[31] and the Observatory of Discrimination in Sports.[32]

Since 2001, Argentina took a commitment to prepare a national plan to fight discrimination, along the lines of the Declaration and Plan of Action of the Durban Conference, held the same year. In March 2004, the Ministry of Foreign Affairs, INADI and the United Nations Development Program (UNDP) signed and adopted the ARG/02/024 project entitled *Plan Nacional de Lucha contra la Discriminación*

---

[30] See http://www.inadi.gob.ar/politicas/observatorios-discriminacion/observatorio-radio-television/.

[31] See http://www.inadi.gob.ar/politicas/observatorios-discriminacion/plataforma-internet/.

[32] See http://www.inadi.gob.ar/politicas/observatorios-discriminacion/observatorio-deporte/.

(National Plan against Discrimination). On these basis, the document entitled "Towards a National Plan against Discrimination-Discrimination in Argentina. Diagnosis and proposals" was approved, which included a national call for discussion to different sectors of civil society, vulnerable groups, universities, parliamentary committees and the governmental areas involved.[33] This program commended INADI the task of coordinating the implementation of proposals designed therein. Since then, INADI has been developing updated versions of Maps of Discrimination showing patterns of discrimination in different areas such as Bolivian migrants, disadvantaged socioeconomic sectors, the overweight/obesity condition, LGBT, school and disco bullying, etc.

NGOs are active in promoting the antidiscrimination agenda among the community at large, as well as in lobbying government for the enactment of regulations on these long demanded claims.

This type of interaction between legal and institutional developments and the claims of social groups crystallized in measures such the creation of the National Program of Comprehensive Sex Education (Law 26.150); the Law for the eradication of violence against women (Law 26.485); the Law on Equal Marriage (Law 26.618); the Protection of Mental Health (Law 26.657). Similarly, instruments of relevant international importance, such as the Convention on the Rights of Persons with Disabilities (ratified by Argentina by Law 26.378) and the current discussion on the Convention on the Rights of the adult/senior citizens that have been formulated from the human rights and antidiscrimination perspective.

Besides INADI, other agencies are entrusted with the task of promoting equality and enforcing different laws regarding discriminatory practices and acts. The National Institute of Social Services for Pensioners, better known as PAMI—*Plan Asistencial Médico Integral*—(1971), was created to provide medical, social and welfare care for a specific group, the elderly.

In 2009, the Supreme Court created within its orbit, the *Oficina de la Mujer* (Women's Office).[34] Since its inception, this Office has promoted a comprehensive process for mainstreaming gender views in institutional planning and internal processes to achieve gender equality both in the judiciary and in those who use the justice system.

6 Enforcement: Case Law

As regards judicial enforcement of the antidiscrimination laws, it should be noted that, as mentioned, our Supreme Court has established the principle that the equality principle does not prevent the legislator to contemplate differently different situations, as far as there is not an arbitrary discrimination or unlawful persecution or

---

[33]Decree 1086 of 27 September 2005.
[34]Argentine Supreme Court, Acordada 13/2009.

undue privilege given to individuals or groups of people, although the foundation of the distinction may be debatable. In this area, Argentine courts have shown—in principle—great deference to the legislative criteria.[35] Notwithstanding deferential treatment, the Supreme Court has more recently stated that, unequal treatment will be declared illegitimate as long as those who defend its validity cannot establish the justification that merely responds to achieve that aim, subjecting these cases to the strictest level of scrutiny.[36]

In the same case, it has set out a very strong principle regarding the limits of state tolerance on discriminatory conduct. In rejecting recognition to a filo-Nazi political party whose rallies and activities foresee specific acts of discrimination, it indicated, *"a political program that includes discrimination based on sex, race and origin turns out to be paradigmatically antisocial."*[37]

We will try to summarize some of the cases.

6.1 Sexual Orientation

In 1991, in the case *Comunidad Homosexual Argentina* (CHA), the decision of the General Inspectorate of Justice to deny legal status to the entity because of the sexual orientation of its members and its relationship with the association's purpose according to its by-laws was upheld by a divided Supreme Court. However, the case made way to a review of the procedures and the dissent's principles became holding in the 2005 case *Asociación Lucha por la Identidad Travesti Transexual.*[38]

6.2 People with Disabilities

A recent decision (June 2016) in the case *I, J.M s/Proteccion Especial*, where the rights of a mother with disabilities regarding her son were discussed, the Supreme Court recognized the right of the mother to raise her infant son despite her disability, with State's support and assistance, based on that that the Convention on the Rights of Persons with Disabilities (ratified by Law 27.044)—that specifically protects individual autonomy and non-discrimination—, involves reasonable adjustments to be adopted at State's expense.

---

[35] See, Vitolo (1989).

[36] Argentine Supreme Court, *Partido Nuevo Triunfo*, Fallos 332:433 (2009).

[37] Argentine Supreme Court, Partido Nuevo Triunfo, Fallos 332:433 (2009), Justice Fayt concurring opinion.

[38] Argentine Supreme Court, Fallos 329:5266 (2006).

6.3 Gender Discrimination in Employment

With regard to employment discrimination, in the case S*isnero Mirtha Graciela y otros c/Taldelva SRL y otros s/amparo* (20/05/2014), the Supreme Court ordered the cessation of discrimination on grounds of gender, requiring public transport companies to hire female staff up to thirty percent of the total drivers. In doing so, it rejected the defenses presented by the companies as inadmissible to rebut the presumption that the defendants have engaged in discriminatory behaviors and practices against women in general and the plaintiff in particular.[39]

6.4 Nationality

Following the path started in 1988 in the case *Repetto*,[40] where the Supreme Court considered the nationality requirement for the appointment of a teacher to violate the equality principle, the Court considered nationality to be a suspect classification and subject it to the strictest constitutional scrutiny in several other cases.[41]

7 Towards a More Equal Society

The fact that National Constitution vigorously protect equality before the law and equal opportunities, strengthened by positive action to avert discrimination, is a strong signal that the implementation of antidiscrimination laws is something different from the one of laws of other nature. The fight against discrimination may be advanced through different channels.

On the one hand, by ensuring the validity of constitutional provisions concerning affirmative action and equal protection clause and related public policies. In this sense, Congress has receive a constitutional mandate *"To enact laws referring to the organization and basis of education consolidating national unity and respecting provincial and local characteristics; which ensure the state responsibility that cannot be delegated, family and society participation, the fostering of democratic values and equal opportunities and possibilities with no discrimination whatsoever; and which guarantee the principles of free and equitable State public education as well as the autonomy and autarky of national universities."*[42] It is understood that

---

[39]Fallos: 337: 611 (2014).
[40]Fallos 311:2272 (1988).
[41]Access to the Judiciary (*Hooft*, Fallos 327: 5118 (2004); *Gottschau*, Fallos: 329: 2986 (2006); Public employment (*Mantecón Valdez*, Fallos: 331: 1715 (2008); *Pérez Ortega*, Fallos 336:131 (2013).
[42]Argentine Constitution, Section 75 §19.

this mandate also applies to the Executive branch and its agencies, as well as to the provincial governments. As a good example of affirmative action in the quest for equality in political representation, Law 24.012 seeks to increase representation of women in politics through minimum female quotas in the lists of candidates presented by the parties in federal elections.

On the other hand, the courts scrutiny regarding the enforcement of antidiscrimination law must be far more rigorous than in other fields of law. While the Supreme Court had applied minimal scrutiny to the economic regulation cases, stricter standards of review are required in antidiscrimination cases, assuming that its very nature justifies a delicate standard of judicial review. This idea has significantly influenced equal protection jurisprudence and judicial review in Argentina.

In the last analysis, the enforcement of antidiscrimination law also requires a collective point of view based upon moral reasons followed by a social reprisal of these misbehaviours.

In this sense, education is an extraordinary tool to create and promote awareness in children and youth to value others who are perceived as different. The first tier of education is received at home where children learn the most significant values for life including non-discrimination and respect, without distinction. In this very sense, actions oriented towards achieving inclusive behaviours are significant steps that will bear fruit in time. It is central to introduce the antidiscrimination perspective early in life, at school, within the neighbourhoods, etc.

The effectiveness of antidiscrimination laws depends on the adequate information by the people on the rights and duties arising from them. Ordinary people are entitled to a wide access to information that should be adequately broadcasted by mass media, advertising campaigns and cultural dissemination. To this end, the acts of reflection for children and adolescents at school might be a good start to increase public awareness.

8 Conclusion

This work has the purpose of analysing the issue of discrimination in Argentina from a general perspective related to possible cases that often occur at different levels in our society. In this sense we have first considered necessary to take a generic view of the problem, and to deal more closely with some of those discriminations that may occur more frequently, or which may have had greater public attention. Strictly speaking, the range of situations in this matter is multiple, and the answer of the legislation, administrative agencies and the courts of law varies upon the degrees of protection but with the very same aim to enforce antidiscrimination policies both at systemic and individual levels. Also, it has been interesting to present how International Law has upheld legislation to fight discrimination in social relations.

The Argentine legal system is rapidly progressing with recognizing antidiscrimination rules, yet intervention of the State is necessary to answer the multidimensional phenomena of discrimination at different levels. By virtue of the effective enforcement of active antidiscrimination policies and the Federal government's commitment to fulfill them, regardless the party in power, Argentina is oriented to establish a broader inclusion frame to combat structural sources of discrimination and to build a more just society with better opportunities for all.

Finally, state action aimed to overcome situations of discrimination must be complemented with the conviction by citizens that effective validity of the principle of equality before the law demands full respect for all people, regardless of race, colour of the skin, gender, orientation sex, religion, political opinion, social origin or disability, among others.

References

Kiper CM (1998) Derechos de las minorías ante la discriminación. Hammurabi, Buenos Aires
Martínez Vivot J (1981) Las mujeres y los menores ante el derecho del trabajo. Astrea, Buenos Aires
Martínez Vivot J (2000) La discriminación laboral. Despido discriminatorio. USAL, Buenos Aires
Vitolo AM (1989) Regulation and restriction of constitutional rights, a comparative analysis. Paper presented in compliance of the requirements for the LLM degree, Harvard Law School. http://id.lib.harvard.edu/aleph/001706039/catalog

Ursula Cristina Basset is a Professor of Law at the Universidad Austral in Buenos Aires, Argentina. She holds a Ph.D. from Pontifical Catholic University of Buenos Aires. She is Director of the Department of Interdisciplinary Research on Family Relations. She is author of several books and articles on the field of Family Law and Human Rights and took part in the drafting commissions of Argentina's new Civil and Commercial Code. She writes and teaches in the field of Comparative Family Law and Human Rights.

Alejandra Rodriguez Galán is a Professor of Constitutional Law at the Universidad de Buenos Aires (UBA) and at the University of El Salvador (USAL). She holds a Masters degree in Political Science from the City University of New York, New York, USA (CUNY). She is member of the International Academy of Comparative Law, the Argentine Association of Constitutional Law; the Constitutional Law Institute of the National Academy of Law of Buenos Aires, and of the Institute of Constitutional Politics of the National Academy of Moral and Political Sciences. She was advisor at the Constitutional Convention for the Reform of the National Constitution and Secretary General of the Argentine Association of Comparative Law. Currently she works at the Argentine Supreme Court of Justice. She is author of several articles in its field and collaborated as a co-author in collective books, and participated in conferences and seminars related to topics on her specialty.

Alfredo M. Vítolo is a Professor of Law at the National University of Buenos Aires Law School. He holds a J.D. from the same university and an LL.M. from Harvard Law School. He is currently Legal Advisor to the Argentine Secretariat on Human Rights. Mr. Vítolo writes and teaches in the fields of Constitutional Law and Human Rights.

Australia

Beth Gaze and Dominique Allen

1 Introduction

In Australia, laws prohibiting discrimination have been passed by both the federal government and by the governments in the six states and two territories, as listed below. These two schemes operate in parallel to one another and are somewhat similar.

Discrimination is prohibited across a range of attributes (such as race, sex, age and disability) in employment and non-employment. Both direct and indirect discrimination are prohibited. Broadly, direct discrimination is unfavorable treatment because of an attribute and indirect discrimination is a requirement, condition or practice which has a disadvantageous effect on someone because of their attribute and which is not reasonable. The legislation allows for the application of special measures to achieve equality and some requires employers and service providers to reasonably accommodate a person with a disability.

Statutory agencies in each jurisdiction are responsible for receiving complaints about discrimination and attempting to resolve them using Alternative Dispute Resolution ("ADR") before the individual who was subject to discrimination can proceed to court. As we discuss in detail in our report, the individual who has experienced discrimination is largely responsible for enforcing the law. The statutory

---

B. Gaze (✉)
Law School, University of Melbourne, Melbourne, VIC, Australia
e-mail: egaze@unimelb.edu.au

D. Allen
Department of Business Law and Taxation, Monash Business School, Monash University, Caulfield, VIC, Australia
e-mail: dominique.allen@monash.edu

agencies have been limited powers and their primary responsibility is to educate the public about the law and offer dispute resolution services.

Since 2009, federal industrial relations laws have prohibited discrimination in the workplace. This Act is enforced separately from the older antidiscrimination laws, as we discuss below.

2 Is Antidiscrimination Law Enforced?

The federal government has enacted four pieces of legislation which prohibit discrimination in employment and outside employment: the *Racial Discrimination Act 1975* (Cth[1]); the *Sex Discrimination Act 1986* (Cth); the *Disability Discrimination Act 1992* (Cth); and the *Age Discrimination Act 2004* (Cth). The *Australian Human Rights Commission Act 1986* (Cth) establishes the federal statutory agency, the Australian Human Rights Commission, and regulates the process of making a complaint and having it resolved, which we discuss below. In addition, § 351 of the *Fair Work Act 2009* (Cth) prohibits an employer from taking adverse action (which includes dismissal, injuring or altering employment and discrimination) against an employee or prospective employee because of a listed attribute. It is enforced separately from the older antidiscrimination laws.

Each state and territory government has also passed antidiscrimination laws that operate in parallel to the federal schemes:

- *Antidiscrimination Act 1977* (New South Wales)
- *Antidiscrimination Act 1992* (Northern Territory)
- *Antidiscrimination Act 1991* (Queensland)
- *Antidiscrimination Act 1998* (Tasmania)
- *Equal Opportunity Act 1984* (South Australia)
- *Equal Opportunity Act 1984* (Western Australia)
- *Equal Opportunity Act 2010* (Victoria)
- *Discrimination Act 1991* (Australian Capital Territory)

The state and territory laws are not consistent with the federal laws in terms of coverage, exceptions or how discrimination is defined. However, each uses a similar two-stage enforcement process, which we discuss in detail below. Essentially, the person who has experienced discrimination is required to lodge their complaint at a statutory antidiscrimination agency that will attempt to resolve it using ADR and if that is not successful, the individual can lodge the complaint in a civil court where it will be adjudicated.

---

[1] "Cth" refers to Commonwealth and is the accepted format for referring to federal laws in Australia.

3 How Is Antidiscrimination Law Enforced?

The individual who has experienced discrimination primarily enforces antidiscrimination law through a two-stage process. Unions and other associations can also bring claims on behalf of their members and some jurisdictions allow for representative complaints, but the majority of complaints are made by an individual.

They do so by lodging a written complaint at the statutory antidiscrimination agency in their state and territory or at the federal Australian Human Rights Commission. Provided that the complaint has substance and falls within the agency's jurisdiction, it will attempt to resolve it informally using ADR. The vast majority of complaints are resolved this way or they are withdrawn. The process of resolving a complaint through ADR is confidential and the settlements usually include a confidentiality clause so it is difficult to know what complaints are being made about, who they are against and the terms of settlement.

If the complaint is not settled, the individual complainant can ask the agency to refer the matter to the civil tribunal in their jurisdiction or to the Federal Courts if it is a federal complaint. Courts and tribunals regularly require the parties to undertake ADR and attempt to settle the complaint but if they are unable to do so, the court or tribunal will hear the matter. The exception is Victoria, where the complainant has direct access to the civil tribunal and does not have to use the agency's ADR's services, though many still do.

Discrimination complaints made under industrial relations laws are enforced in much the same way except they are only required to undertake ADR (which is provided by the Fair Work Commission) if there was a dismissal; otherwise it is optional.

4 Who Enforces Antidiscrimination Law?

The individual who experienced discrimination is responsible for enforcing antidiscrimination law. The statutory antidiscrimination agencies do not have the power to do so; as we discuss further below, their powers are limited. The exception is complaints made under the industrial relations laws. The federal Fair Work Ombudsman is able to receive complaints, investigate them and if it forms the belief that discrimination has occurred, it can seek an enforceable undertaking from the employer to remedy the breach, issue a compliance notice or enforce the law in the federal courts and seek the imposition of civil penalties.

5 Who Benefits from the Enforcement of Antidiscrimination Law?

It may be said that the individual who experienced discrimination is the only one who benefits from the enforcement of antidiscrimination law given that the vast majority of complaints are settled with a confidential agreement between the parties, which usually includes an individual remedy such as the payment of compensation. When a complaint is settled, though, the parties sometimes agree to wider remedies, such as changes to policies and practices and giving access to goods and services to people with a disability, so the settlement of complaints will benefit others, though the extent of this is difficult to measure because settlements are confidential.

The high rate of settlement and the focus on individual complaints makes it difficult to argue that society benefits to a great degree from the enforcement of antidiscrimination law or even that those in a similar situation to the individual complaint benefit, because they will not normally be aware that a complaint has been made unless it proceeds to a public hearing by a court. However, when a complaint is heard by the court and results in a favorable outcome, the benefit is much broader. Society may then become aware of the case through media coverage and subsequent complainants will benefit from the precedent set. The body of antidiscrimination law is small, particular from superior courts, so a favorable decision from a superior court may well be used in other jurisdictions in the country.

6 Who Is Harmed by the Enforcement of Antidiscrimination Law?

The individual perpetrator and/or respondent employer or service provider are the only ones harmed by the enforcement of antidiscrimination law since they are the only ones who will be aware that a complaint has been made (unless it proceeds to court). They will have to respond to the claims and may ultimately have to pay compensation.

7 What Remedies Are Provided by the Enforcement of Antidiscrimination Law?

The predominant remedy is compensation (damages), which is usually awarded or negotiated at very modest amounts. In some jurisdictions, the court can order the respondent to do something to address the effect of the discrimination but this is rarely ordered, while in others the court can order the respondent to make a public or private apology.

In a recent sexual harassment case, the Federal Court of Appeal held that the amounts awarded for compensation for pain and suffering in serious cases were too low by community standards, so awards may increase to some extent in the next few years. However, it has also been observed that in a strong case, a better result can be obtained when a matter is settled at conciliation than by going to court. The court's powers to awards remedies largely focus on the particular case. But when a case is settled by agreement there are no such limits, so the parties can agree on systemic remedies such as adopting or revising policies, or providing training for employees, managers, or senior managers, which could not be obtained in court.

In the federal industrial relations sphere, the remedies are compensation and reinstatement, plus the respondent employer may also be required to pay a civil penalty (fine) of an amount determined by the court.

8 Who Supports the Enforcement of Antidiscrimination Law?

Primarily, affected individuals—either alone or through group legal actions—undertake to enforce the law in Australia. Antidiscrimination agencies and legal aid bodies of the various governments provide support for enforcement, as do organizations and support groups for people affected.

The antidiscrimination agencies do not have powers to enforce the law by bringing actions themselves, but they do have powers to act as amicus curiae and/or interveners in litigation under the laws brought by other parties. Courts or tribunals can give the agency leave to appear as amicus curiae ('friend of the court') to assist the court 'by drawing attention to some aspect of the case which might otherwise be overlooked.'[2] An amicus curiae may offer the court a submission on law or relevant fact which will assist the court in a way in which the court would not otherwise have been assisted. This role does not extend to introducing evidence to the court [...] [a]n amicus curiae is not a party to the proceedings and is not bound by the outcome of the proceedings.[3]

For example, the Victorian Equal Opportunity and Human Rights Commission regularly presents arguments about how the provisions of the Act should be interpreted. In contrast, an intervener becomes a party to the case, bound by its outcome, and may be affected by a costs order. An intervener can do more than present argument—it can also present witnesses and undertake cross-examination. This power is less frequently used by the agencies because of the costs risks involved.

---

[2] Australian Law Reform Commission (2014), p. 15. New Regulatory Mechanisms at https://www.alrc.gov.au/publications/15-new-regulatory-mechanisms/amicus-curiae-and-intervener-roles-australian-information (accessed 17 December 2015).
[3] Ibid.

Legal aid support for enforcement comes from several sources. Each government has a legal aid body that conducts litigation for clients in house, funds legal work by private lawyers for clients who meet its criteria for assistance, and supports community legal centres that may specialize in particular areas of law or be a general community based service. Legal aid criteria require very low incomes to qualify for assistance, and prioritize criminal and family law matters, so assistance available in antidiscrimination matters is much less than the demand. Some of the gap is covered by the efforts of community legal services and pro bono services of the larger law firms, although assistance is quite limited, and generally extends to preparatory advice but not to legal representation at court, so many complainants and a lower number of respondents appear unrepresented. Some specialist community legal centers have been able to support selected actions for enforcement on behalf of important client groups, such as workers with intellectual disabilities in government supported employment. Such actions are, in general, also supported by organizations for the groups in question, some of which also receive government funding to cover their administrative and activity costs. Disability groups are the best example of such support in action, working with specialist disability employment legal services.

9 Who Opposes the Enforcement of Antidiscrimination Law?

The cost of effective enforcement of antidiscrimination laws falls on the respondents who at present benefit by ineffective or under-enforcement of the law. This includes employers and many service providers, whether private, public, or outsourced by government. It includes those who are actually respondents to a claim, as well as others in a similar position whose liabilities would be affected by the precedent effect of a decision.

For example, in a recent case, the Sydney Rail Corporation, which runs the train service in metropolitan Sydney, was held to be in breach of the Disability Discrimination Act and Disability Standards for Public Transport for failing to ensure that announcements on trains were both audible and working effectively almost all the time. By failing to comply with the law, it had saved expenditure on maintenance and monitoring its services. In some cases, organizations may spend much more on legal costs in defending a claim than it would have taken to comply with the law in the first place. In other cases, however, claims are strongly and even aggressively defended because of the potential for substantial costs if compliance is ordered. For example, in a series of cases, parents of children with disabilities have brought claims against state education departments seeking more effective and better staffed provision of integration aides or other adjustments. Success in a claim would potentially cost the states a substantial amount to increase funding for the service. However, to date none of these cases have been successful, partly because of the vast disparity in power that exists in antidiscrimination law litigation. The cases are defended extremely strongly because of the potential costs involved for governments.

At a political level, employer organizations are the most vocal opponents of reform to antidiscrimination laws that might strengthen the laws and make them more effective. When reform and consolidation of the Commonwealth laws into one piece of legislation was proposed in 2012, including a proposal to create a shifting onus of proof in direct discrimination claims, a very strong employer campaign was mobilized by several peak employer bodies, such as the Australian Industry Group and the Australian Chamber of Commerce and Industry. These campaigns, which included advertising and public relations elements, were successful, increasing the political costs for the government of proceeding with the reforms to the extent that the Bill was dropped and has not been proceeded with. However, reforms were adopted in Victoria in 2010 despite dissent by employer bodies, so whether reform proceeds depends on the commitment of those in government with an interest in the process.

10 How Broad Is the Coverage of Antidiscrimination Law?

The laws vary in detail but in general the coverage is fairly consistent. The breadth of the law is in two directions. First is the range of attributes protected. The four major areas protected are those included in all laws, Commonwealth, state and territory. They include race (including ethnicity, national origin, color and descent), sex (including marital or relationships status, pregnancy, potential pregnancy, breastfeeding, family responsibilities, intersex status, gender identity and sexual orientation), disability (defined widely to include most malfunctions of the body or mind, including intellectual disability, mental illness and physical disability, with no minimum required level, and also extending to assistance animals and aides) and age. These attributes are usually expressed to include characteristics that are generally attributed to or generally appertain to persons with that characteristic (to cover stereotyping and over generalizations) and persons who are associated with a person with that characteristic (such as a carer for a person with a disability). In addition, most, but not all, state and territory laws protect attributes such as industrial activity, employment activity, political belief or activity, and religious belief or activity, or religious appearance or dress. In addition, some laws also provide protection in relation to physical features, irrelevant criminal record, irrelevant medical record, lawful sexual activity, profession, trade, occupation or calling, and publication of details on a fines enforcement website.

The second dimension of the coverage of the laws is in relation to the activities to which they apply. This is fairly consistent across all the laws, and extends to most activities that would be regarded as public activities, such as employment (defined widely to include work under a contract of service, commission work and agency hire work), education, provision of goods and services, government administration, and a range of other areas. There are exceptions for special measures to achieve equality, for genuine and reasonable requirements in some laws, inherent requirements of the job, for religious organizations and schools, and so on.

11 Does the Enforcement of Antidiscrimination Law Vary According to the Ground of Discrimination?

In Australia, the enforcement processes are quite similar in most jurisdictions and follow the two-stage pattern described above. The enforcement processes are specified in each antidiscrimination law, so that where a law covers several attributes, the same enforcement process will apply to all. Enforcement differs for attributes covered by different laws that have different enforcement processes. The main differences are between the Commonwealth laws and the state and territory laws, and between the antidiscrimination laws and claims of employment discrimination brought under the national workplace laws (*Fair Work Act*).

Attributes that are covered by federal laws (race, sex, disability and age) are enforced through court proceedings in the Federal Courts where the loser is usually required to pay the legal costs of the winner in addition to any compensation that is awarded. This makes enforcing these laws high risk unless the claim is strong. By contrast, under the state and territory laws, any enforcement action is taken in a tribunal in which the rule generally is that no costs are awarded and each party pays their own legal costs whether they win or lose. While this approach minimizes the risks of litigating, it also often leaves a party that has won their case undercompensated, as they are not awarded their own legal costs and have to pay those out of any compensation awarded. Compensation is awarded for proved loss ("special damages") and for pain and suffering ("general damages"). The latter is often quite a small amount, as discussed above.

Enforcement is different under the national employment law, where a discrimination-type claim can be brought as a claim of "adverse action" taken by an employer on a prohibited ground. These actions can be settled by conciliation, but if they have to be resolved in court, then the litigation takes place in the federal courts. But the *Fair Work Act* provides that costs are generally not awarded in such cases. In addition, under the *Fair Work Act*, there is a public agency, the Fair Work Ombudsman, that can play an active role in enforcement.

12 What Is the Relationship Between the Enforcement of Antidiscrimination Law and the Quest for Equality on Both an Individual and Systemic Level?

Officially, the focus of the quest for equality in Australia is the antidiscrimination laws, which are the main general legal approach to seeking equality. All antidiscrimination laws include an exception for special measures to advance equality, but none actually require such measures to be taken. The only requirement for positive action is that in the *Workforce Gender Equality Act 2012* (Cth), which requires all private sector employers of 100 or more staff to monitor and report annually on a set of gender equality indicators, including gender pay equity, in their workforce. The Act does not require any particular actions be taken apart from reporting the data, implicitly relying on the publication of the information creating pressure to act.

There are, in practice, many other initiatives that contribute substantially to achieving greater social equality. These include such broad areas as the social welfare and taxation systems. Australia has a non-contributory pension and social security scheme and an effective social welfare system, although governments attempt to reduce payment levels on a regular basis. The government pays for maternity leave at the minimum wage for around 3 months, but many employers have their own more generous maternity leave schemes.

Beyond that, specific programs are active in certain areas. The National Disability Insurance Scheme is currently being set up around the country and will provide services on a no-fault basis to people with disabilities. Services for the indigenous community are similarly provided though separate programs, although they are not adequate, and in recent times there has been criticism of the government's interventions into indigenous welfare in the Northern Territory and subsequently throughout the country. However, in 2015, the government set up the first indigenous employment contract compliance scheme that requires companies contracting with the government to ensure that a certain proportion of the work goes to indigenous owned and run businesses.

13 Is the Enforcement of Antidiscrimination Law Regarded as Different from the Enforcement of Other Laws?

Yes, antidiscrimination law is treated differently to other areas of law in terms of enforcement. We have already referred to the fact that litigation in the federal courts under the *Fair Work Act* is supported by a powerful regulator and does not attract the costs rules, unlike litigation in the very same courts under federal antidiscrimination laws. Not only is the enforcement of antidiscrimination law weaker structurally and institutionally than employment law, but also it is weaker than areas of law such as occupational health and safety law and even consumer law. In those areas, a regulator has power to enforce the law in recognition of the weakness of aggrieved parties compared to the often large corporations that exist in the industry. Even in these areas, enforcement can be difficult, as the regulator cannot be active in every area.

But in antidiscrimination law, none of these capacities are available. Thus antidiscrimination law is less easy to enforce and less enforced than the comparable areas such as employment, health and safety at work, or consumer laws. Although difficulties of enforcing antidiscrimination laws have been well publicized for more than a decade, little action has been taken to remedy this, which suggests that the politicians do not see this as a priority. One state government, in Victoria, did adopt some regulatory powers for its antidiscrimination agency when its law was reformed in 2010, including power to issue compliance notices and to enter into enforceable undertakings without the need for litigation. However, those powers were repealed by a succeeding government before they commenced, indicating that the conservative parties do not see strengthening enforcement as a priority, and may prefer not to do so.

14 What Does the Enforcement of Antidiscrimination Law Reveal About the Nature of Your Legal System or About the Enforcement of Laws in Your Legal System?

In general, the scope of Australian antidiscrimination law is broad. Governments have been willing to broaden the scope of the law's coverage by extending it to protect additional attributes. The range of attributes protected is wide and comprehensive, although arguments for improved coverage remain, for example to include protection for victims of family violence or broad coverage of irrelevant criminal or medical record discrimination.

Greater concerns exist about the reluctance of governments to improve the enforceability of the laws to make enforcement easier and more effective in achieving the Acts' objectives. For example, none of the Australian laws provide for a shifting onus of proof in relation to direct discrimination claims, and none allow for an agency to enforce a claim on behalf of an aggrieved party. None of the antidiscrimination agencies have regulatory powers to enforce the laws, such as powers to monitor compliance and to issue compliance notices or enforce the law. In the absence of actions to make the enforcement of the laws more effective, protection against discrimination can appear to be rather illusory.

Because enforcement is difficult, expensive and risky, there is limited litigation and precedents are often favorable to respondents, meaning the laws have had limited effect in changing practices. As a consequence, lawyers do not treat these laws as fundamental to all activities and good knowledge about them tends to be confined to a few experts and not broadly spread. Because antidiscrimination law is an optional subject in law school, many lawyers (and judges) are uneducated about these laws. There is a clear need for legislative change to improve the laws in the ways highlighted above and to ensure much broader knowledge and understanding of the principles of discrimination and equality and how the law contributes to their achievement.

15 Conclusion

Enforcement of antidiscrimination law in Australia is difficult and risky, as it relies entirely on litigation by the victims of discrimination with limited support from the government or legal aid. While the scope of the law is quite broad, and governments have been willing to extend the law to protect many groups, the mechanisms for enforcement are narrow. This includes aspects such as the absence of a shifting onus of proof in direct discrimination, and the inability of antidiscrimination agencies to conduct or assist in enforcing the law. By contrast with workplace laws or areas such as consumer law, antidiscrimination law's enforcement is relatively ineffective.

Reference

Australian Law Reform Commission (2014) Serious invasions of privacy in the digital era. ALRC Discussion Paper 80, p 15

Beth Gaze is Professor of Law at the University of Melbourne. She holds a PhD (Monash University), LLM (University of California (Berkeley)), LLB (Hons) (Monash) and B Sc (University of Melbourne). She has taught antidiscrimination law for many years and has published extensively in the area. Her most recent book is Equality and Discrimination Law in Australia: An Introduction (2017, Cambridge University Press, with Associate Professor Belinda Smith of the University of Sydney). She has acted as a consultant to the Victorian government and parliament, Australian human rights agencies, and the International Labour Organisation.

Dominique Allen is a Senior Lecturer at Monash University. She hold a PhD (University of Melbourne), LLB (Hons) (the Australian National University) and B Comm (the University of Canberra). She has published widely on antidiscrimination law and dispute resolution in Australia and internationally. With Neil Rees and Simon Rice, she is the author of 'Australian Anti-Discrimination and Equal Opportunity Law' (Federation Press, 2018).

Belgium

Emmanuelle Bribosia and Isabelle Rorive

1 Introduction

Belgium has been a part of the European Union (EU) from the very beginning of the European Communities. From the outset, antidiscrimination has been a key element of a European integration relying on free movement and eager to avoid distortions of competition between Member States. At the end of the 1990s, the emerging concept of EU citizenship and the EU's need for more popular legitimacy fostered broader equal opportunities policies and new legislative powers "to combat discrimination based on sex, racial or ethnic origin, religion or belief, disability, age or sexual orientation."[1] This, in turn, had a profound impact on Belgian antidiscrimination law.

The country's government type is that of a representative democracy. The official head of the State is the King who has mainly formal functions. The Prime Minister is the head of the federal government, which always consists of a coalition of different

---

This research has been funded by the Interuniversity Attraction Poles Programme (IUAP), initiated by the Belgian Science Policy Office (BELSPO). More particularly, this paper has been written in the framework of the IUAP project *The Global Challenge of Human Rights Integration: Towards a Users' Perspective* (2012–2017): www.hrintegration.be/. Note that this paper was written in December 2015 and was slightly updated in March 2017.

[1] Article 13 inserted in the EC treaty in 1997 (in force, 1999) and now enshrined in Article 19 TFEU.

E. Bribosia (✉)
ULB (Free University of Brussels), Faculty of Law, Centre for European Law, Brussels, Belgium
e-mail: emmanuelle.bribosia@ulb.ac.be

I. Rorive (✉)
ULB (Free University of Brussels), Faculty of Law, Perelman Centre for Legal Philosophy, Brussels, Belgium
e-mail: irorive@ulb.ac.be

political parties since usually several parties get elected into parliament. Belgium is a federal State with three Communities[2] and three Regions[3] which have exclusive fields of competence and are not subordinate to the federal State. In the Belgian federal system, the competence to legislate on discrimination in the areas covered by the EU Directives (the Racial Equality Directive,[4] the Employment Equality Directive[5] and the Gender Equality Directives[6]) is divided between the federal State, the Communities and the Regions.

The federal structure of the country has been, and still is, a complicating factor in the implementation of antidiscrimination law, not only because of the uncertainties concerning the division of competences between the federal State, the Regions and the Communities, but also because the sociological and political context is different in each part of the country. While the French-speaking part (the French Community, the Walloon Region and, to a large extent, the Brussels-Capital Region) has traditionally chosen a more formal and individual model of combating discrimination which is closer to the French model, the Dutch-speaking part (the Flemish Region and Community) has been more willing to seek inspiration from the United Kingdom or the Netherlands. These countries used to have a more multiculturalist approach implying, for instance, a greater willingness to promote equal treatment through statistical monitoring and allowing for affirmative action schemes. The stakes are also higher in the Flemish Region/Community, because of the significance in that part of the country of populist parties. Their representation in parliament and, for the N-VA (*Niew Vlaams Allientie*—New Flemish Alliance), in the Flemish and the federal governments allow them to influence the debates on issues such as the integration of migrants or the wearing of headscarves by Muslim women in schools or in employment.

---

[2]The French-speaking Community (*Communauté française*), which is referred to as the Federation Wallonia-Brussels (Fédération Wallonie-Bruxelles) in the political and media discourse, the Flemish Community (*Vlaamse Gemeenschap*), the German-speaking Community (*deutschsprachigen Gemeinschaft*).

[3]The Walloon Region (*Région wallonne*), the Flanders (*Vlaams Gewest*) and the Brussels-Capital Region (*Région de Bruxelles-capitale*). In contrast to the French-speaking part of Belgium, the Region and the Community are merged in the Flemish part.

[4]Council Directive 2000/43/EC of 29 June 2000 implementing the principle of equal treatment between persons irrespective of racial or ethnic origin, OJ L 180 of 19 July 2000, pp. 22–26.

[5]Council Directive 2000/78/EC of 27 November 2000 establishing a general framework for equal treatment in employment and occupation, OJ L 303 of 2 December 2000, pp. 16–22.

[6]Primarily, Directive 2006/54/EC of the European Parliament and of the Council of 5 July 2006 on the implementation of the principle of equal opportunities and equal treatment of men and women in matters of employment and occupation (recast), OJ L 204 of 26 July 2006, pp. 23–36 and Council Directive 2004/113/EC of 13 December 2004 implementing the principle of equal treatment between men and women in the access to and supply of goods and services, OJ L 373 of 21 December 2004, pp. 37–43.

2 Is Antidiscrimination Law Being Enforced?

Belgium is party to most of the important international agreements relevant for counteracting discrimination. However, it has not yet ratified Protocol no. 12 to the European Convention on Human Rights and the Council of Europe Framework Convention for the Protection of National Minorities. After ratification, these international instruments are part of the domestic legal order and can be applied directly by domestic courts if the provision at stake is sufficiently clear and precise for direct application.

Articles 10 and 11 of the Constitution which prohibit discrimination are applicable generally, without any restriction either as to the grounds on which the discrimination is based (they require that the principle of equality be respected in relation to all grounds) or as to situations concerned (they apply to all contexts and not only employment and occupation, but also to the scope of the Racial Equality Directive). However, they are rarely invoked in private relationships because of their very general formulation and the delicate issues which would be entailed by their application in this context, for instance to protect an individual from private acts of discrimination by an employer. These constitutional provisions have been most effective when invoked against either legislative norms or administrative acts. In this respect, the Constitutional Court and the Council of State, the highest administrative court, have developed a very extensive jurisprudence.

Today, the major antidiscrimination legislation at federal level is embodied in three Acts adopted on 10 May 2007. First, there is the federal Act amending the Act of 30 July 1981 criminalising certain acts inspired by racism or xenophobia (hereafter the Racial Equality Federal Act).[7] This Act aims at implementing both the Racial Equality Directive and the 1965 International Convention on the Elimination of All Forms of Racial Discrimination in one single legislation prohibiting discrimination on grounds of alleged race, colour, descent, national or ethnic origin, and nationality. It marks a turning point as the federal Act of 30 July 1981 originally formed part of criminal legislation. The evidentiary burdens facing the prosecution in that context—or, indeed, an alleged victim of discrimination—have most of the time appeared insuperable because the perpetrator's intent had to be established.

Secondly, there is the Federal Act pertaining to the fight against certain forms of discrimination (hereafter the General Antidiscrimination Federal Act),[8] which covers age, sexual orientation, civil status, birth, property, religious or philosophical belief, actual or future state of health, disability, physical characteristic, political opinion, trade union opinion, language, genetic characteristic and social origin. The third Federal Act concerns the fight against discrimination between women and men (hereafter the Gender Equality Federal Act),[9] which relates to gender and related

---

[7]OJ (*Moniteur belge*), 30 May 2007, modified subsequently.
[8]OJ (*Moniteur belge*), 30 May 2007, modified subsequently.
[9]OJ (*Moniteur belge*), 30 May 2007, modified subsequently.

grounds including pregnancy, childbirth, maternity, gender reassignment, gender identity and gender expression.

Apart from the federal legislator, the Regions and Communities have also taken action in their respective and vast fields of competence (such as education, housing, healthcare, vocational training, placement of workers, policies for the professional integration of the unemployed, social aid, public transports apart from the national airport and public railway).[10] These attempted to harmonize the content of their statutory law to the Federal Antidiscrimination Acts.

This large body of international, European and domestic law is not only a law on paper. Antidiscrimination law is, to a certain extent, applied and enforced in practice. However, judicial precedents show a mixed picture.[11] With regard to the enforcement of new legal concepts for instance, one might point to very promising precedents in disability cases although reasonable accommodation was unknown in Belgian law before the Employment Equality Directive. Conversely, a fair amount of cases decided in court show that there is still a noticeable lack of knowledge of antidiscrimination law by the professionals in charge of its implementation, especially with a view to the notion of indirect discrimination.

Barometers supported by the Inter-federal Centre for Equal Opportunities (ICEO, named UNIA since 2016) provide data and statistics that are crucial to address discrimination issues (these include the Socio-economic Monitoring, the Diversity Barometer in Employment and the Diversity Barometer in Housing). These barometers show that there are still many discriminatory practices in employment and housing. A Diversity Barometer in Education is expected in 2018. It is well-documented that structural instances of discrimination remain unsolved. For instance, the European Committee of Social Rights (ECSR) condemned Belgium twice in recent years in major cases. One case related to the lack of social services available to highly dependent persons with disabilities[12] and the other to the breach

---

[10]Framework Decree for the Flemish equal opportunities and equal treatment policy of 10 July 2008 (OJ (*Moniteur belge*), 23 September 2008, modified subsequently; Decree of the French Community of 12 December 2008 on the fight against certain forms of discrimination (OJ (*Moniteur belge*), 13 January 2009, modified subsequently; Decree of the Walloon Region of 6 November 2008 on the fight against certain forms of discrimination, including discrimination between women and men in the fields of economy, employment and vocational training (OJ (*Moniteur belge*), 19 December 2008, modified subsequently; Decree of the German-speaking Community of 19 March 2012 aiming at fighting certain forms of discrimination, OJ (*Moniteur belge*), 5 June 2012; Ordinance of the Region of Brussels-Capital of 4 September 2008 relating to the fight against discrimination and equal treatment in the employment field, OJ (*Moniteur belge*), 16 September 2008, modified subsequently; Decree of the *Commission communautaire française* of 9 July 2010 on the fight against certain forms of discrimination and on the implementation of the principle of equal treatment, OJ (*Moniteur belge*), 3 September 2010; modified subsequently.

[11]Charlier and Ringelheim (2015), p. 121.

[12]ECSR, *International Federation of Human Rights Leagues (FIDH) v. Belgium*, complaint no. 75/2011, decision adopted on 18 March 2013 (published on 29 July 2013).

of the right of housing in the context of unfair treatment of Travellers and Roma.[13] Moreover, in 2014, the UN Committee for the Protection of Persons with Disabilities expressed its concern about the "poor accessibility for persons with disabilities, the absence of a national plan with clear targets and the fact that accessibility is not a priority."[14] The Committee also noted "the low number of persons with disabilities in regular employment" and "the Government's failure to reach targets for the employment of persons with disabilities within its own agencies, as well as the lack of a quota in the private sector."[15] Regarding Travellers, in 2014 concerns were also raised by the European Commission against Racism and Intolerance (ECRI)[16] and by the Committee on the Elimination of Racial Discrimination.[17] There is still a shortage of properly equipped transit sites for Travellers, in particular in the Walloon Region and in the Brussels-Capital Region. Furthermore, the numerous judicial rulings involving the highest courts in Belgium (such as the Constitutional Court or the Council of State) show that the issue of religious symbols (and actually, the wearing of the Islamic veil known as the *hidjab*) remains a very controversial one in Belgium. There is, for instance, much confusion in the case law about profit companies which invoke the respect of neutrality in their brand so as to justify the dismissal of female workers wearing the *hijab*.[18] The anti-terrorist climate at the end of 2015 has already led to numerous police abuses against Muslim persons (or those perceived as such).[19]

3 How Is Antidiscrimination Law Enforced?

The statutory reform of 2007 aimed not only at implementing EU law but also at addressing the deficiencies of Belgian antiracism law. The 1981 Moureaux Act was the first piece of legislation to address ethnic discrimination.[20] A legal provision

---

[13]ECSR, *International Federation of Human Rights Leagues (FIDH) v. Belgium*, complaint no. 62/2010, decision adopted on 21 March 2012 (published on 31 July 2012).

[14]Committee on the Rights of Persons with Disabilities, concluding observations on the initial report of Belgium adopted by the Committee at its twelfth session (15 September–3 October 2014), paras 22–23.

[15]Committee on the Rights of Persons with Disabilities, concluding observations on the initial report of Belgium adopted by the Committee at its twelfth session (15 September–3 October 2014), paras 38–39.

[16]2014 ECRI report on Belgium.

[17]CERD/C/BEL/CO/16–19, 14 March 2014, paras 18–19.

[18]See, however, the recent ruling of the CJEU, case C-157/15, *Achbita*, ECLI:EU:C:2017:203.

[19]P. Charlier, co-director of the Inter-federal Centre for Equal Opportunities, Protéger nos libertés et garantir notre sécurité, carte blanche in the *Libre de Belgique*, 7 December 2015.

[20]Act of 30 July 1981 criminalising certain acts inspired by racism or xenophobia, OJ (*Moniteur belge*), 8 August 1981.

criminalising discrimination in the labour market was adopted in 1994.[21] However, no case was successful in court despite several scientific studies showing a high level of ethnic discrimination in employment.[22] According to the Belgian equality body, then the Centre for Equal Opportunities and Opposition to Racism (CECLR), this was to a large extent due to the weight of the burden of proof. It is highly difficult to prove that an employer's decision to not hire or to dismiss a person is based on considerations of race or ethnic origin. Employers do not have to give reasons for their actions and other workers are rarely ready to testify against their employer. In addition, many barriers contributed to the inefficiency of the Moureaux Act such as the failure of the police to register discrimination complaints or to draw up official reports and the prosecutor's reluctance to take legal action.

Thus, one of the major changes of Belgian law at the beginning of the twenty-first century was to develop a civil protection device applicable beyond racial or ethnic grounds. This has allowed the equality bodies—which do not have the status of quasi-judicial bodies—to develop non-binding procedures in their assistance to victims to reach an amicable settlement. In this vein, the Inter-federal Centre for Equal Opportunities has built up a system of informal conciliation and mediation, which is one of the usual paths through which antidiscrimination law is enforced at the individual level. The "amicable settlements" (*solutions négociées*) are published on its website in a way that ensures the anonymity of the parties.

4 Who Enforces Antidiscrimination Law?

In Belgium, there are two bodies for the promotion of equal treatment: the Interfederal Centre for Equal Opportunities (ICEO, named UNIA since 2016) and the Institute for Equality between Women and Men.

The former was created in 1993, initially called Centre for Equal Opportunities and Opposition to Racism.[23] Until 2014, it was a federal Centre, only competent in the implementation of the Racial Equality Federal Act and the General Antidiscrimination Federal Act. By now it has become an inter-federal Centre with a main office in Brussels and decentralized contact points in Flanders and in Wallonia, competent to promote equal opportunities and fight any kind of distinction, exclusion or restriction based on the prohibited grounds contained in various antidiscrimination instruments adopted at both regional and federal levels.[24] For

---

[21]Article 2*bis* of the Moureaux Act inserted by an Act of 12 April 1994, OJ (*Moniteur belge*), 14 May 1994.

[22]See, among others, Arrijn et al. (1998) and Martens et al. (2005).

[23]The Centre for Equal Opportunities and Opposition to Racism was created by a Federal Act of 15 February 1993 (OJ (*Moniteur belge*), 19 February 1993).

[24]Apart from language to avoid to trap the Centre in linguistic disputes which are at the forefront of many political debates in Belgium.

political and policy reasons, the federal Institute for Equality between Women and Men (created in 2002)[25] is competent to tackle discriminations based on gender and related grounds (pregnancy, childbirth, maternity, gender reassignment, gender identity and gender expression). However, such an institutional setup does not facilitate the development of policies against multiple or intersectional discriminations when gender is at stake.

Both equality bodies are autonomous public services. Their independence is guaranteed by legislation and, in practice, they fulfil their mandate in an independent fashion with an annual budget, which has not been cut following the financial crisis of 2008. The ICEO and the Institute issue reports and recommendations within their mandate. They also assist victims of discrimination and they may file judicial actions. In 2015, the Centre received 4554 complaints; it opened a file in 1596 cases and it launched lawsuits in 14 cases. The low number of cases relative to the opened files is partly due to the capacity of the Centre to reach amicable settlement through mediation. Of course, victims can file a complaint on their own before civil courts or where an employment relationship is concerned before employment tribunals (*tribunaux du travail*). They might need to instruct a lawyer and even if the Judicial Code provides for legal aid in favour of claimants with low incomes, there are increasingly restrictive conditions attached.

Seeing the limited scope of this paper and the fact that the action of the Institute for Equality between Women and Men is more confidential, we focus here on the action of the ICEO. It receives discrimination reports on a daily basis either directly or through local contact points. A large number of requests for intervention can be dealt with quickly by providing information or by making a referral to other authorities or organisations. Other issues require more investigation: racist or homophobic attacks, conflicts between employer and employee, discrimination in domestic leases, racist remarks and incitement to hatred on the Internet, etc. In the new inter-federal structure, there are 25 persons working in the department in charge of processing individual reports. Moreover, the Centre collaborates on a regular basis with NGOs as well as Belgian or European universities and institutions such as the King Baudouin Foundation. The Centre is an early member of the European Network of Equality Bodies (Equinet). In the framework of this cooperation, it organises trainings, seminars and programs for the exchange of information and practical experience. The Centre publishes recommendations and provides expertise to all levels of government on how to improve legislation and to develop action plans or new policies.

Social partners have also been actively involved in dissemination activities. The ICEO regularly organized training sessions in cooperation with employers' and workers' organizations. Some major Collective Agreements (as made compulsory through regulation) foster antidiscrimination policies. Moreover, social partners are involved in specific task forces promoting equality that are directly linked to Federal

---

[25]The Institute for Equality between Women and Men was created by a Federal Act of 16 December 2002 (OJ (*Moniteur belge*), 31 December 2002).

Public Services (Ministries).[26] At the regional level for instance, the Flemish Government concluded a number of agreements with businesses at the sectorial level that encourage diversity, promote specific measures for the integration of migrant workers, and provide for codes of conduct in favour of diversity and against discrimination at the level of companies. In addition, a range of initiatives has been taken to actively promote the employment of members of (traditionally under-represented) "target groups," in particular persons of foreign origin (*allochtones*) and persons with disabilities. The "Jobkanaal" project, for instance, launched within the Flemish network of undertakings VOKA, or the "diversity" focal point of the UNIZO (association of small and middle-size enterprises), contribute to promoting diversity in employment.

5 Who Benefits from the Enforcement of Antidiscrimination Law?

It is difficult to define who specifically benefits from the enforcement of antidiscrimination law. Federal antidiscrimination legislation of 2007 should have been assessed after 5 years but the process will only been completed in 2017. The annual report of the ICEO provides some figures that are not more than the tip of the iceberg and which do not take into account gender discriminations. In 2015, on almost all discrimination grounds, the number of cases dealt with by the ICEO increased. The main grounds (as of 2013 and 2014) were race and ethnicity (38% of all cases), disability (21%) and religious and philosophical belief (19%) followed by age (5%), sexual orientation (5%), property (4%) and health status (4%). The main social areas concerned were (again as of 2013 and 2014) goods and services (24% of all files, among which many relate to housing), employment and the labour market (22%), and media (23%) followed by education (11%) and life in society that concerns neighbourhood conflicts or disputes in the public space (10%).[27]

6 Who Is Harmed by the Enforcement of Antidiscrimination Law?

We are not aware of any detailed studies which discuss who has been "harmed" by the enforcement of antidiscrimination law in Belgium. Recent interdisciplinary analyses that rely on Belgian law and the social sciences are too general to provide

---

[26]See for instance, the "Multicultural Business Unit" (*Cellule Entreprise Multiculturelle*), set up within the Federal Public Service (Ministry) of Employment.

[27]*Le travail d'UNIA exprimé en chiffres pour l'année 2015*, report issued in June 2016, available on its website (www.unia.be).

well-defined answers. Among the unintended effects of antidiscrimination law, they point to the shift of discrimination and the concealment of discrimination. Institutions and organizations put internal legal structures in place that are designed to symbolize the respect for the law. The protection framework becomes managerial. The violation of a right is framed as a misunderstanding that should be sorted out within the organization.[28]

What is sure is that, while Belgium has a fairly good antidiscrimination law on paper, discrimination in major fields such as employment, housing or education remains pervasive.

7 What Remedies Are Provided by the Enforcement of Antidiscrimination Law?

Under the antidiscrimination law adopted at the federal level and by the Regions and the Communities, the victim of discrimination may either seek damages according to the usual principles of civil liability or may opt for a payment of lump sums defined in the law. Damages are payable each time a discriminatory practice is proven to have occurred (in line with the general rule in non-contractual civil liability enshrined in Article 1382 of the Civil Code which provides for compensatory damages). The shift of the burden of proof is provided in all jurisdictional procedures except criminal ones. However, some judicial precedents show that courts are still struggling with this device. Providing for the choice of the victim to seek the payment of damages on the basis of the "effective" damage or on the basis of the lump sums defined in the law aims to ensure the effectiveness of the sanctions provided for instances of discrimination.

The victim can also request that (1) the court rules that the discriminatory provisions enshrined in a contract are null and void; (2) the court delivers an injunction ordering the immediate cessation of the discriminatory practice under the threat of financial penalties (*astreintes*); (3) the court imposes the publicity of the judgment finding discrimination by posting the judicial decision on the premises where discrimination occurred or by the publication of the judicial decision in newspapers.

The decisions handed down by the Commercial Court and the Court of Appeal of Ghent in the case *Centre for Equal Opportunities and Opposition to Racism v. B.V. B.A. Kuoni Travel Belgium*[29] provide a good example of the sanctions applicable in Belgian law. The case concerns a deaf man used to self-sufficient travelling who called upon the services of a travel agency to book a package tour in Jordan. Believing that his security would not be correctly insured because of his difficulties

---

[28]See, for instance, Vrielink (2015), pp. 51–66.

[29]Judgment no. 7302 of 29 September 2010 of the Commercial Court of Ghent and Decision of 20 January 2011 of the Court of Appeal of Ghent.

communicating with the local population, the travel agency refused to offer its services unless an independent guide accompanied the deaf man at his own expense. After several mediation attempts, the ICEO brought an action before the Commercial Tribunal of Ghent, alleging that simple adjustments should have been admitted by the travel agency. The Commercial Court of Ghent ruled in favour of the ICEO and sentenced the travel agency for its failure to provide reasonable accommodation to the victim and to have refused him the package tour in Jordan. The travel agency was condemned to pay a lump sum of EUR 650 and a civil fine (*astreinte*) of EUR 1000 for every possible new offence noticed and per diem if the offence continued. Furthermore the travel agency had to advertise the judgment in its Ghent's branch and on its website, and to publish it at its own expenses in the media. In a decision of 20 January 2011, the Court of Appeal of Ghent confirmed the judgment of the Commercial Court of Ghent, but decided to condemn the travel agency to pay a lump sum of EUR 1300 (and not only EUR 650 as it was decided in first instance).

The famous *Feryn* case is another good example.[30] After the decision of the Court of Justice of the European Union (CJEU), the Labour Appeal Court ruled that Mr. Feryn, by publicly declaring that his firm was not recruiting any employees of Moroccan origin, was engaging in direct discrimination. It ordered the cessation of the discriminatory practice and the publication of the judicial injunction in several newspapers.[31]

In addition, due to the insistence of certain non-governmental organizations, a limited range of discriminatory acts (such as racial discrimination in the provision of goods or services and in employment) is also criminally punishable. These offences may lead to imprisonment (one month to a year), fines (EUR 250–5000), a combination of the two, or even the loss of civil and political rights for a certain time (meaning that during this time the offender cannot be a civil servant, nor be elected, nor sit in representative bodies). Moreover, the victim has the option of claiming compensation for the damage caused by the offence. Actually, these criminal offences have been very rarely prosecuted and have led to very few convictions because of the difficulties in finding a person criminally liable (the burden of proof issue).

Still, on the terrain of criminal law, the incitement to commit discrimination or the incitement to hatred or violence against a group defined by certain characteristics is a criminal offence, if it is done under the conditions of publicity defined by Article 444 of the Penal Code. Civil servants who, in the exercise of their functions, commit discrimination may be criminally charged. And, when certain offences defined in the Penal Code are committed with an "abject motive," i.e. with discriminatory intent

---

[30]CJEU, case C-54/07, *Centrum voor gelijkheid van kansen en voor racismebestrijding v. Firma Feryn* NV, ECLI:EU:C:2008:397, developed below in Sect. 7.

[31]Judgment of 28 August 2009 of the Labour Appeal Court of Brussels after the preliminary ruling of the Court of Justice of the European Union of 10 July 2008 (case C-54/07).

(hate crimes), this might be held as an aggravating circumstance.[32] In this respect, the murder of a young homosexual man in May 2012 was the first murder to be treated as a homophobic hate crime by the Belgian judicial authorities under new antidiscrimination law.[33] In a recent case where about fifteen people—mainly undocumented migrants and homeless people—were victims of violent and degrading treatment by railway police officers, the perpetrators were brought before the Court of First Instance of Brussels (criminal section) by the public prosecutor. They were notably charged with the use of illegitimate violence committed with a discriminatory intent (hate crimes). On 26 February 2014, the Court of First Instance of Brussels (Criminal section) convicted eleven out of fourteen defendants. The nature and the degree of the sentences varied depending on the role of the perpetrators in the violent acts at stake and some of their former criminal convictions but included community service of 60 h, prison sentences of 1 year to 40 months with probation that was combined, in some cases, with a fine between 500 and 600 euros. It is worth noting that the abject motive (discriminatory intent) was retained against the four police officers in the cases in which the ICEO intervened.[34]

The 2007 Federal Antidiscrimination Acts significantly improve the system of sanctions available to victims of discrimination, bringing Belgium closer to a situation where discrimination leads to "effective, proportionate and dissuasive" sanctions as required by EU law.

8 Who Supports the Enforcement of Antidiscrimination Law?

Antidiscrimination law provides for the legal standing of the ICEO, the Institute for Equality between Women and Men, and organizations with a legal interest in the protection of human rights or in combating discrimination (at least 3 years after their creation) and trade unions. They may file a suit (civil or criminal) on the basis of the antidiscrimination legislation. However, where the victim of the alleged discrimination is an identifiable (natural or legal) person, her consent determines the

---

[32]These offences, which may lead to stronger convictions if driven by such an "abject motive," are: rape and sexual assault (Articles 372–375 of the Penal Code); homicide (Articles 393–405*bis* of the Penal Code); refusal to assist a person in danger (Articles 422*bis* and 422*ter* of the Penal Code); deprivation of liberty (Articles 434–438 of the Penal Code); harassment (Article 442*bis* of the Penal Code); attacks against the honour or the reputation of an individual (Articles 443–453 of the Penal Code); putting a property on fire (Articles 510–514 of the Penal Code); destruction or deterioration of goods or property (Articles 528–532 of the Penal Code). Except for the offence of harassment, these situations are not normally met in the field of employment and occupation.

[33]Courts of Azzize of Liège, 22 December 2014, *Ihsane Jarfi* case.

[34]Judgment of the Court of First Instance of Brussels (Criminal section) of 26 February 2014, available on the website of the ICEO renamed UNIA (www.unia.be).

admissibility of the claim. Class action is not allowed and instances of strategic litigation are not frequent but often successful.

To give a few examples, in the *Feryn* case, the ICEO initiated the first case of ethnic discrimination before the CJEU.[35] It is a topical instance where the ICEO acted on its own behalf to denounce a breach of the antidiscrimination legislation, as there was no identified victim. The ICEO pressed for a referral to the CJEU to decide that, in case an employer declares publicly that he will not recruit employees of a certain ethnic or racial origin, it is likely to deter applicants from this ethnic minority. This practice hinders their access to the labour market and constitutes a direct discrimination in respect of recruitment within the meaning of the Racial Equality Directive. The issue of the shift of the burden of proof was also at the core of the *Feryn* case. Similarly, the ICEO has been working for many years to address the policy of profit companies that include the respect of neutrality in their brand so as to justify the dismissal of female workers wearing the *hijab* and bypass antidiscrimination law. After initially unsuccessful attempts,[36] the ICEO finally managed to convince the Court of Cassation, the highest court in the judiciary, to make a reference for a preliminary ruling in the *Achbita* case.[37] Again, this led to one of the first European Court of Justice (ECJ) ruling related to the ground of religion.[38]

The *Adecco* case is a good example of (transnational) strategic litigation pursued by a trade union.[39] The multinational temp agency Adecco was listing job seekers depending on their race and ethnic origin. Native Belgian people without foreign roots were registered in the computer system under the code BBB, by reference to the Belgian breed of Cattle *Blanc Bleu Belge* ("White Blue Belgian"). The system was put in place to please certain clients. In 2009, the French NGO "SOS Racisme," which was involved in another procedure in France against Adecco for similar facts and a Belgian leftist trade union organisation (the FGTB), launched a procedure before the Court of First instance of Brussels. They claimed that thousands of job seekers had been discriminated against on the grounds of their race and ethnic origin. The Tribunal acknowledged the discrimination and sentenced Adecco to pay EUR 25,000 damages to the first applicant and a symbolic EUR 1 to the second applicant. On 10 February 2015, the Appeal Court of Brussels rejected the argument brought

---

[35]CJEU, case C-54/07,*Centrum voor gelijkheid van kansen en voor racismebestrijding v. Firma Feryn NV*, ECLI:EU:C:2008:397.

[36]See, for instance, Labour Court (*Arbeidsrechtbank*) of Tongres (Flanders), 2 January 2013, *Joyce V.O.D.B. v. R.B.NV and H.B.BVBA,* judgment no. A.R. 11/2142/A, available on the website of the ICEO renamed UNIA (www.unia.be).

[37]Samira Achbita, *Centrum voor gelijkheid van kansen en voor racismebestrijding v. G4S Secure Solutions NV,* case C-157/15, request for a preliminary ruling lodged by the Belgian Court of Cassation on 3 April 2015.

[38]CJEU, case C-157/15, *Achbita*, ECLI:EU:C:2017:203. See also, CJEU, case C-188/15, *Asma Bougnaoui and Association de défense des droits de l'homme (ADDH) v Micropole SA*, ECLI:EU:C:2017:204 (on a request for a preliminary ruling lodged by the French Court of Cassation on 24 April 2015).

[39]Appeals Court of Brussels, 10 February 2015, available on the website of UNIA (www.unia.be).

forward by Adecco according to which there would be a lack of interest of the French NGO "SOS Racism" because its interest would be restricted to discrimination occurring in France. Interpreting Article 32, 1° of the Racial Equality Federal Act (associations willing to claim damages on behalf or in support of complainants, in case of violation of the antidiscrimination legislations, must have a legal personality for at least 3 years and a legal interest in the protection of human rights or in combating discrimination) in the light of European law, the Court held that there was no territorial requirement and that an association could bring a non-discrimination claim irrespective of the location of its head office in the European Union. As to the merits of the case, the Court upheld the decision of the Tribunal of first instance in holding Adecco liable of discrimination. The liability was assessed under a Provision of the Civil Code (Art. 1384, al. 3) according to which an employer is liable for his/her employee's civil wrongs committed during the employment relationship (irrebuttable presumption of liability). The Appeal Court of Brussels condemned Adecco to a much heavier compensation (EUR 25,000 to both applicants), stressing that a mere symbolic sentence does not meet the requirement of effective and deterrent sanction as imposed by European Law. Although it was the first time that a multinational in Belgium was convicted for racial discrimination on a wide scale, one should not forget that direct responsibility of the company was not established but only the responsibility for the discriminatory acts of its employees. Beyond this specific case, it is striking that there is still a lot of racism in the field of temporary employment in Belgium. On 23 February 2015, ICEO published an article where it called on Belgian governments to take measures to cease the illegal practices of discrimination in the sector of "service vouchers" (*titres services*).[40] Indeed, according to a study of the NGO *Minderhedenforum*, two out of three service vouchers companies in the Flemish part of Belgium still accommodate the wish of their clients when they ask for workers with no foreign roots.

Finally, the French-speaking Human Rights League (LDH) ran two successful antidiscrimination cases before the ECSR. The first case concerned the breach of the right of housing in the context of unfair treatment of Travellers and Roma.[41] The second case dealt with the lack of social services available to highly dependent persons with disabilities.[42]

---

[40] The "service vouchers sector" is a system of temporary employment in the field of domestic work.

[41] ECSR, *International Federation of Human Rights Leagues (FIDH) v. Belgium*, complaint no. 62/2010, decision adopted on 21 March 2012 (published on 31 July 2012), developed above in Sect. 1.

[42] ECSR, *International Federation of Human Rights Leagues (FIDH) v. Belgium*, complaint no. 75/2011, decision adopted on 18 March 2013 (published on 29 July 2013), developed above in Sect. 1.

9 Who Opposes the Enforcement of Antidiscrimination Law?

The political context in Belgium is highly volatile due to fierce linguistic disputes rooted in historical and economic differences. This does not favour antidiscrimination policies as the ECRI pointed out in 2014:

> [...] since its fourth report on Belgium a number of leaders of and militants from extremist parties have continued making statements in public against the other linguistic Community in the name of extreme nationalism combined with intolerant and xenophobic arguments against foreigners and minority groups. ECRI considers that this exploitation of the climate of political tension that exists between the linguistic Communities is particularly deplorable as it not only encourages inter-Community prejudice and stereotyping but can fuel hatred also against ethnic minorities and migrants.[43]

This statement is mirrored in recent developments. Over the last years, politicians of the Dutch-Speaking Nationalist Flemish Party (N-VA) repeatedly issued statements with racist connotations. There is much political concern about this issue as this is the most influential party in the Flemish part of Belgium. After the elections of May 2014, it has been, for the first time, become part of the Federal Government. In this line, it became public that the current Secretary of State for Asylum, Migration and Administrative Simplification, Theo Francken, wrote on Facebook: "I acknowledge the added value of the Jewish, Chinese and Indian Diasporas but I don't recognize the added value of the Moroccan, Congolese and Algerian Diasporas." In March 2015, Bart De Wever, the President of the NVA and Mayor of the major Flemish city (Antwerp) stated that "racism is a relative concept and is used too frequently as an excuse of personal failure by some communities such as Moroccans, especially Berbers."[44] Such controversial statements initiated an awkward debate as to whether this is racism or not according to the Racial Equality Federal Act. Some organizations and citizens lodged a complaint for racism against Bart De Wever. Even if the applicability of the Racial Equality Federal Act is questionable, it is highly problematic that politicians of high profile stigmatize ethnic minorities whose members have been facing discrimination in Belgium for many years. In addition, despite the repeated calls of the ICEO for an Inter-federal Action Plan against Racism, the 2014 federal Governmental Agreement enshrines no commitment in this respect. Belgium is still failing to keep a promise made during the World Conference against Racism held in Durban in 2001.

The appointment of Prof. Matthias Storme at the Board of Directors of the new Inter-federal Centre for Equal Opportunities in 2014 is also controversial. This lawyer and law professor is well known as a fierce opponent of the equal treatment legislations and the equality body in charge of their implementation. He was the one who launched the actions in annulment against almost all the provisions of the Federal Antidiscrimination Acts of 10 May 2007 (the Racial Equality Federal Act,

---

[43]Para 51 of the 2014 ECRI report on Belgium.

[44]See the press article available on the website of the newspaper *Le Soir* (www.lesoir.be).

the General Antidiscrimination Federal Act and the Gender Equality Federal Act), which were rejected by the Constitutional Court on 12 February 2009.[45] In addition, in 2004, he publicly stated that the conviction for racism of the *Vlaams Blok*, an extreme-right party now renamed *Vlaams Belang*, almost morally obliged him to vote for the extreme-right and that antidiscrimination law was a "blunder and an attack against democracy."[46] Still on a libertarian tone, he also stated that "discriminating is a fundamental freedom."[47]

Beside the political context, opposition against antidiscrimination law comes at times from employers, landlords or insurance companies. For instance, when conditions of admissibility of situation testing in court were discussed at the federal level in 2005, the VLD (a Flemish right-wing party which was part of the coalition government) relayed criticism by employers' organizations and the National Office for Landlords (*Office national des propriétaires*). In a major daily newspaper, the party refused "to set up a team of spies, send moles to infiltrate companies, open informer hotlines and sanction Big Brother."[48] The Prime Minister himself did not shy away from calling the testers "infiltrators" and "informers," adding: "you do not send a naked woman to a man to see if he is adulterous."[49] And, after the ECJ ruling in the *Test-achats* case[50] (which originated from Belgium), the insurance companies were very clear that they will rely on other grounds than gender (such as the state of health) to assess risk and define premium for life insurances.

10 How Broad Is the Coverage of Antidiscrimination Law?

The coverage of antidiscrimination law is very broad in Belgium. On the one hand, it concerns 19 explicit grounds: alleged race, colour, descent, national or ethnic origin, nationality, age, sexual orientation, civil status, birth, property, religious or philosophical belief, actual or future state of health, disability, physical or genetic characteristic, political opinion, language, social origin, trade union opinion, gender and related grounds (pregnancy, childbirth, maternity, gender reassignment, gender identity and gender expression). It also provides for protection in large areas of public life: the provision of goods or services when these are offered to the public;

---

[45] Ruling no. 17/2009.

[46] "Le N-VA Matthias Storme nommé administrateur du Centre interfédéral pour l'Egalité des Chances," *Le Soir*, 25 October 2014, available on the website of the newspaper *Le Soir* (www.lesoir.be).

[47] "La N-VA a nommé Matthias Storme au poste d'administrateur de l'institution. Ses partenaires n'y voient rien à redire," *Le Soir*, 27 October 2014, available on the website of this newspaper (www.lesoir.be).

[48] *Le Soir*, 26, 27 and 28 March 2005.

[49] *De Standaard*, 25 March 2005.

[50] CJEU, case C-236/09, *Association Belge des Consommateurs Test-Achats ASBL and Others v Conseil des ministres*, ECLI:EU:C:2011:100.

access to employment, promotion, conditions of employment, dismissal and remuneration, both in the private and in the public sector; the nomination of a public servant or his/her assignment to a service; the mention in an official document of any discriminatory provision; and access to and participation in, as well as exercise of an economic, social, cultural or political activity normally accessible to the public.

Regrettably, some uncertainties remain with a view to the precise delimitation of the powers held respectively by the Federal State and the Regions and Communities in this field, which has constituted an obstacle in the process of implementation and is still tricky with respect to enforcement.

11 Does the Enforcement of Antidiscrimination Law Vary According to the Ground of Discrimination?

Contrary to EU law, the material scope of protection is the same with respect to the 19 protected grounds. The legal coverage is, however, not entirely the same. First, differential treatment based on a ground not covered by EU law (such as civil status, birth, property, actual or future state of health, physical characteristic, political opinion, trade union opinion, language, genetic characteristic, social origin and nationality) can be more easily justified. In addition, specific tools apply only to some grounds protected in EU law (i.e. reasonable accommodation duty limited to disability, ethos-based organization exception related to direct discrimination based on religion or belief, genuine and determining professional requirement, etc.). Second, although it is one of the guiding principles of the 2007 federal reform that there should be no hierarchy between grounds, criminal offences were chiefly upheld in the Racial Equality Federal Act (discrimination in the provision of goods or services, in access to employment, vocational training or in dismissal procedure).

In practice, as we saw above, the files opened by the ICEO show important disparities between grounds. In addition, some discrimination grounds might get a higher priority based on the political agenda. For instance, due to European pressure, a Task Force on Roma was set up and led to the adoption of a "National Strategy for Roma Integration" in March 2012. Significant acts of violence against LGBT people led to the drafting of an Inter-federal Action Plan preventing and fighting homophobic and transphobic violence in 2013. One year later, the UN Committee for the Protection of Persons with Disabilities expresses its concern about the "poor accessibility for persons with disabilities, the absence of a national plan with clear targets and the fact that accessibility is not a priority."[51] The ICEO is clearly pushing the political agenda in this sense.

---

[51]Committee on the Rights of Persons with Disabilities, concluding observations on the initial report of Belgium adopted by the Committee at its 12th session (15 September–3 October 2014), paras 22–23.

Finally, judicial rulings also show some disparities. For instance, decisions from the highest courts in Belgium (such as the Constitutional Court or the Council of State) show that the issue of religious symbols (and actually, the wearing of the *hidjab*) is still a very controversial one in Belgium.

12 What Is the Relationship Between the Enforcement of Antidiscrimination Law and the Quest for Equality on Both an Individual and Systemic Level?

The path chosen by the ICEO illustrates a will to tackle structural discrimination. In its 2014 report, it stressed that more and more people are facing exclusion and that discrimination is most often taking a "structural form."[52] It insists on the need of carrying on to develop socio-economic devices such as the diversity barometers. In the opinion of the ICEO, promoting equal opportunities is based on at least three pillars: employment, education and housing, to which one should add access to culture and access to health care. Cross policies between the too numerous and scattered competent public authorities is one of the main challenges for the future.[53]

However, one should keep in mind that there are no specific sanctions (such as desegregation plans) to tackle the issue of structural discrimination. In addition, the Federal State, the Regions, and the Communities are very reluctant to foster measures of positive action, which, at this stage, are still very limited on the ground.[54]

13 Is the Enforcement of Antidiscrimination Law Regarded as Different from the Enforcement of Other Laws?

As the issue of effectiveness has been troublesome with respect to antidiscrimination law, some legal tools derogatory to civil procedure and the law of evidences were implemented. In line with EU law, the shifting of the burden of proof where a *prima facie* case is made out is provided for. In addition, the claimant in a discrimination claim might ask the court to deliver an injunction ordering the immediate cessation of the discriminatory practice under the threat of financial penalties (*astreintes*). This injunction is made as if there were emergency proceedings but the court ruling is definitive (and not an interim decision). Such a specific procedure (*comme en référé*) only applies in particular fields as, for instance, environmental law, intellectual property rights or family law issues.

---

[52]ICEO, *Rapport annuel 2014. Une année charnière qui ouvre des portes*, issued on p. 68.

[53]ICEO, *Rapport annuel 2014. Une année charnière qui ouvre des portes*, p. 69.

[54]ICEO, *Rapport annuel 2014. Une année charnière qui ouvre des portes*, p. 69.

The actors in charge of the enforcement of antidiscrimination law are also playing a major role. With their broad mandate,[55] the two equality bodies are the key players in this field. But they are not the only ones to have received legal standing. Organizations with a legal interest in the protection of human rights or in combating discrimination, established for at least 3 years, and trade unions, are also entitled to file a suit (civil or criminal) in antidiscrimination cases.

Finally, the Ministerial Circular (*circulaire commune*) for an efficient policy of monitoring and prosecution of any type of discrimination, adopted on 16 December 2013, is another legal tool. The Circular aims at strengthening the cooperation between the Justice departments and the Police departments to ensure a better registration and prosecution of all forms of discrimination and hate crimes, including homophobic discrimination and cyberhate. In criminal matters, this Circular compels the prosecution departments and the police services to register all criminal cases implying a discriminatory intent. Moreover, this Circular provides for the appointment of a "coordinator prosecutor" (*magistrat coordinateur*) who is in charge of its implementation. This prosecutor is the contact person for the ICEO. Other prosecutors and labour auditors are in charge of discrimination issues in their respective departments (prosecution department and labour department) as well as public servants in police services.

14 What Does the Enforcement of Antidiscrimination Law Reveal About the Nature of Your Legal System or About the Enforcement of Laws in Your Legal System?

The enforcement of antidiscrimination law in Belgium illustrates one of the pitfalls of the complex federal structure. The Council of State has failed to provide clear guidelines concerning the division of tasks between the federal level, the Regions and the Communities in the implementation of the European directives.[56] In some respect it could lead to situations in which competence disputes supersede the objective of respecting and promoting equality and non-discrimination. This is also the case for other fundamental rights, which have to be enforced by public authorities at different levels (federal, Regions and Communities) and is more broadly the current situation in the institutional framework of Belgium.

For almost 10 years, the lack of a strong coordination between the different levels of the state was certainly the most serious obstacle to achieving full compliance with

---

[55]See above, in Sect. 3.

[56]Council of State, opinions no. 40.689/AG, 40.690/AG, and 40/691/AG, of 11 July 2006. These opinions were appended to the governmental bill presented to the House of Representatives on 26 October 2006 (doc. No. 51 2720/001). Following a number of changes to the original bill, a second text was presented to the Council of State on 2 October 2006. However, the second opinion did not re-examine the question of the division of competences.

EU law. There have been significant improvements in this respect as the Regions and Communities managed to harmonise their statutory law with federal legislation. Moreover, the Federal State, the Regions and the Communities approved a Cooperation Agreement on 12 June 2013 to turn the Centre for Equal Opportunities and Opposition to Racism into an Inter-federal Centre, which has been operational since March 2014. The Institute for Equality between Women and Men is likely to remain a federal organization.

15 Conclusion

Belgium is at a crossroads. The legal reforms instilled by the EU are mostly implemented on paper. On the ground, the scope of discriminatory practices in employment, housing, education is large and major structural instances of discrimination remain unsolved.

A fair amount of cases decided in court show that there is still a noticeable lack of knowledge of the antidiscrimination law by the professionals in charge of its implementation. Indeed, antidiscrimination law is tough to master. It is highly technical with some legal devices originating from common law legal systems. It crosses the classical branches of the law (such as civil law, labour law, social security, constitutional law, human rights law, criminal law) on which the field of competences of lawyers are built. It is also scattered between different institutions, public authorities and legal texts. More resources should be allocated to properly train judges and lawyers. Strategic litigation is often well thought of by the ICEO or NGOs such as the LDH, which have used the European Courts and bodies (ECSR) to develop judicial precedents. But litigation is not enough. The follow up of judicial achievements should be closely designed. And while the ICEO and the Institute for Equality between Women and Men are carrying on antidiscrimination campaigns, it seems that there is never going to be enough information and education to deconstruct stereotypes, reduce personal prejudices and bridge the distances between "Us" and "Them."

References

Arrijn P, Feld S, Nayer A (1998) La discrimination à l'accès à l'emploi en Belgique en raison de l'origine étrangère. International Labour Office
Charlier P, Ringelheim J (2015) Les lois belges de 2007 et la lutte contre la discrimination: l'épreuve de la pratique. In: Ringelheim J, Herman G, Rea A (dir) Politiques antidiscriminatoires. de Boeck, Louvain-la-Neuve
Martens A, Ouali N et al (2005) Discriminations des étrangers et des personnes d'origine étrangère sur le marché du travail de la Région de Bruxelles-Capitale. Université Libre de Bruxelles and Katholieke Universiteit Leuven, ORBEM

Vrielink J (2015) Le droit de l'égalité fait-il la différence? Les effets du droit antidiscriminatoire à la lumière des recherches en sciences sociales. In: Ringelheim J, Herman G, Rea A (dir) Politiques antidiscriminatoires. de Boeck, Louvain-la-Neuve

Emmanuelle Bribosia is a Professor of Law at the ULB (Free University of Brussels) and the Director of the Centre for European Law (ULB). She holds a Ph.D. from ULB. She serves as an expert in the European Equality Law Network. Ms Bribosia writes and teaches in the fields of Human Rights Law, Antidiscrimination Law and EU Law. With Isabelle Rorive, she founded the Equality Law Clinic (ELC) in 2014.

Isabelle Rorive is a Professor of Law at the ULB (Free University of Brussels) and the Director of the Perelman Centre for Legal Philosophy. She holds a Ph.D. from ULB and a Master of Studies in Legal Research from the University of Oxford. She serves as an expert in the European Equality Law Network. Ms. Rorive writes and teaches in the fields of Antidiscrimination Law, Comparative Law and Human Rights. With Emmanuelle Bribosia, she founded the Equality Law Clinic (ELC) in 2014.

Brésil (Brazil)

Elton Venturi

1 Introduction

Afin de comprendre et de contextualiser les défis rencontrés par le Brésil concernant l'affirmation et la protection des droits de l'homme, la planification et la mise en œuvre des politiques antidiscriminatoires, il me semble important d'évoquer quelques brèves informations sur sa population, son territoire et son économie, selon les informations traitées par l'IBGE (Institut brésilien de géographie et de statistique) en 2010.[1]

Le Brésil est le cinquième pays dans le monde par son étendu (8.515.767.049 km^2), comptant actuellement une population d'environ 205 millions d'habitants, composé de blancs (47,7%), de métis (*pardos*) (43,1%), de noirs (7,6%), d'asiatiques jaunes (1,1%) et d'Indiens (0,4%). Les femmes constituent la majorité comptant 51,4% de la population. Ceux qui se déclarent catholiques atteignent 64,6%, suivis par les évangéliques (22,2%), les irréligieux (8%) et les spirites (2%). Environ 45,6 millions de personnes ont une certaine forme de handicap, ce qui représente 23,9% de la population brésilienne.

L'économie brésilienne se trouve parmi les dix plus importantes au monde, et son produit intérieur brut (PIB) a atteint en 2015 US$ 1,8 milliard de milliards. Cependant, le pays possède encore un faible indice de développement humain (IDH 0,755), ne se trouvant qu'en 75e position parmi les pays évalués par le Programme des Nations Unies pour le développement (PNUD). Le salaire minimum mensuel actuel (2017) est un peu plus de US$ 300,00.

---

[1]Source http://censo2010.ibge.gov.br/.

E. Venturi (✉)
Federal University of Paraná, Paraná, Brazil
e-mail: eventuri@uol.com.br

Après plus de deux décennies de dictature militaire (initiée par le coup d'État militaire en 1964), une Assemblée nationale constituante a adopté une nouvelle Constitution fédérale en 1988, qui visait à présenter les attentes nationales de redémocratisation et de construction d'un État social-démocratique de droit. En conséquence, la constitution est riche des dispositions sur l'engagement du pays à la protection des droits fondamentaux, de l'égalité et du respect de la diversité.

La Constitution fédérale définit le Brésil comme un «État démocratique, destiné à garantir l'exercice des droits sociaux et des droits individuels, la liberté, la sécurité, le bien-être, le développement, l'égalité et la justice comme des valeurs suprêmes d'une société fraternelle, pluraliste et sans préjugés». La dignité de la personne humaine est expressément mentionnée comme le fondement de l'État brésilien (art. 1, III), ayant pour objectifs fondamentaux «promouvoir le bien de tous, sans préjugés raciaux d'origine, de sexe, de couleur, d'âge et d'autres formes de discrimination» (art. 3, IV), étant régie dans ses relations internationales par «le refus du terrorisme et du racisme» (art. 4, VIII). En ce qui concerne les droits et garanties fondamentaux, le texte constitutionnel exprime (art. 5, caput) que «tous sont égaux devant la loi, sans distinction d'aucune sorte», déterminant au législateur ordinaire la mise en œuvre des lois qui punissent «toute discrimination préjudiciable aux droits et libertés fondamentaux» (art. 5, XLI).

À partir de ces dispositions constitutionnelles, les Pouvoirs législatif, exécutif et judiciaire tentent d'affirmer et d'appliquer progressivement les droits fondamentaux, comptant à la fois sur l'aide des institutions publiques indépendantes (telles que le Ministère Public et la Défense Publique/*Defensoria pública*) et des organismes sociaux non-gouvernementaux.

Toutefois, en ce qui concerne la voie de la protection des droits fondamentaux et de la mise en œuvre des politiques publiques antidiscriminatoires, le Brésil doit encore surmonter de grandes barrières socio-culturelles, politiques et économiques qui entravent la réalisation de l'égalité substantielle et le droit à la diversité. Ce rapport est donc limité à dépendre avec l'objectivité et la concision nécessaires quelques-unes des données les plus importantes concernant la concrétisation du droit antidiscriminatoire au Brésil.

2 Le droit antidiscriminatoire est-il mis en œuvre?

Avant de donner une réponse sur la mise en œuvre du droit antidiscriminatoire au Brésil, il faudrait signaler que le traitement législatif des politiques antidiscriminatoires est caractérisé par la casuistique et donc par l'absence de systématisation. La fragmentation des statuts de protection des diverses catégories de personnes vulnérables obscurcit la compréhension de l'existence d'un droit antidiscriminatoire.

La Constitution brésilienne non seulement reconnaît mais assure l'exercice du droit à l'égalité et à la diversité des individus et des groupes d'individus particulièrement vulnérables à toute forme de discrimination (comme les Indiens, les Afro-descendants, les femmes, les homosexuels, les personnes âgées et les personnes handicapées).

Les statuts antidiscriminatoires existants au Brésil fonctionnent à partir de l'imposition normative des actions positives (sens positif) pour la mise en œuvre des politiques publiques en faveur des personnes vulnérables dans les domaines de l'éducation, de l'accessibilité, de la santé, du travail et du bien-être. D'autre part, ces statuts ont également l'intention de limiter des comportements discriminatoires (sens négatif) et les punir dans les domaines administratif, civil et éventuellement pénal.

Cependant, en dépit des garanties constitutionnelles et de l'existence de statuts juridiques qui criminalisent la discrimination, en dépit des politiques publiques antidiscriminatoires et de la protection juridictionnelle promise aux victimes, les statistiques récentes ne nous permettent pas d'ignorer ou de sous-estimer la gravité de la réalité de la discrimination au Brésil.

Démystifiés certains mythes qui historiquement ont créé les stéréotypes de la société du pays – tel que celui de la «cordialité du peuple brésilien»[2] et celui de la «démocratie raciale»[3] – le débat sur le racisme, l'homophobie, la xénophobie, l'habituelle inégalité entre les hommes et les femmes, la misérabilité et le mépris vis-à-vis des communautés indigènes et quilombolas[4] commence à être valorisé non seulement dans le milieu universitaire, mais également au sein des mouvements sociaux, du Parlement et du pouvoir judiciaire.

Les groupes particulièrement vulnérables à la discrimination ont maintenant une plus grande visibilité et aussi, une meilleure protection de l'État.

Comme on cherche à nuancer les réponses fournies dans le présent rapport, la résolution plus globale des conflits sociaux au Brésil est encore très dépendante du pouvoir judiciaire, notamment de la légendaire culture de l'adjudication publique. Ainsi, les problèmes liés à la non-application de la législation et des politiques publiques contre la discrimination finissent par être renvoyés au système juridictionnel qui, outre son extrême lenteur, se montre inefficace ou insuffisant pour les garantir.

Les réformes récentes du système de justice (le nouveau code de procédure civile, la nouvelle loi sur la médiation et l'amélioration du droit de l'arbitrage) promettent toutefois d'inaugurer dans le pays un système de *résolution à portes multiples*,[5] pour lequel doivent contribuer les mécanismes consensuels et extrajudiciaires tels que la médiation, la conciliation et l'arbitrage.

Dans quel sens ira cette réforme du système de justice pour d'"améliorer la mise en œuvre du droit antidiscriminatoire? Il s'agit d'une question dont la réponse est encore difficile et incertaine.

---

[2]Holanda (2015).
[3]Freyre (2004).
[4]Communautés de descendants des esclaves africains.
[5]Le *Multi-door Courthouse System* propose qu'après un triage réalisé par un professionnel spécialisé, la partie soit conduite a la "porte" la plus adéquate pour résoudre la controverse. Il s'agit d'une approche à "porte multiples" d'accès à la justice.

3 Comment le droit antidiscriminatoire est-il appliqué?

Il semble évident que les normes juridiques de non-discrimination - tels que le système normatif en général - devraient être fidèlement observées et respectées par ses destinataires. Ainsi, par exemple, les employeurs devraient respecter les quotas destinés aux employés handicapés. Les écoles publiques et privées devraient se conformer à la législation qui garantit l'inclusion des élèves handicapés. Les établissements commerciaux devraient respecter la priorité aux personnes âgées. L'administration Publique devrait garantir des conditions minimales de dignité et de réinsertion sociale des détenus. Les institutions d'enseignement moyen et fondamental[6] devraient inclure dans leurs programmes d'études l'histoire de la population noire au Brésil. Le gouvernement fédéral aurait déjà dû délimiter et régler toutes les terres traditionnellement occupées par des communautés indigènes dans le pays.

Le non-respect systématique de la loi – et en particulier des règles de mise en œuvre des politiques antidiscriminatoires – est cependant l'un des problèmes les plus complexes et les plus graves auquel la société brésilienne doit faire face et qui suscite donc l'intervention administrative et juridictionnel de l'État.

La mise en œuvre des différents statuts légaux antidiscriminatoires est donc réalisée au Brésil essentiellement par le Pouvoir Judiciaire et par l'Administration Publique.

Le Pouvoir Public est chargé, tout d'abord, non seulement de la promotion des actions positives en vue de faciliter l'intégration sociale des personnes vulnérables mais aussi de contrôler simultanément sa conformité. Plusieurs organismes et agences de réglementation sont chargés de surveiller la mise en œuvre des politiques publiques et la conformité aux statuts antidiscriminatoires, en appliquant des sanctions administratives aux personnes responsables de sa violation. Elle peut donner lieu à des amendes, la suspension ou la révocation des licences d'exploitation des entités publiques et privées.

Cependant, c'est le gouvernement lui-même qui omet souvent le devoir constitutionnel et juridique de contrôler le respect des droits et des politiques antidiscriminatoires.

En outre, la concrétisation du droit antidiscriminatoire au Brésil finit souvent par être implantée par voie juridictionnelle, dans la mesure où le pouvoir judiciaire est chargé du contrôle définitif de l'interprétation et l'application des lois dans le pays. Selon la Constitution Fédérale (art. 5, XXXV), tout citoyen qui se sente menacé, lésé ou empêché d'exercer ses droits, peut avoir accès au système juridictionnel, à travers le dépôt des actions individuelles.

L'accès individuel au système juridictionnel, le système national de justice a également recours aux actions collectives ou aux actions de classe qui, étant dotées d'efficacité «erga omnes» en cas d'accueil de la demande, assurent un rempart non négligeable la protection obtenue auprès des tribunaux.

---

[6]En France, équivalent respectivement du lycée et de l'école primaire et du collège.

C'est la raison pour laquelle précisément la création et le contrôle de la mise en œuvre des politiques publiques destinées à lutter contre la discrimination et à assurer l'inclusion sociale ont été prévues dans le pays par voie de dépôt de recours collectifs, dont beaucoup proposent des actions positives essentielles à la concrétisation de l'égalité formelle et substantielle des personnes vulnérables dans les relations de travail, l'accessibilité urbaine, les services publics, les relations de consommation, dans la santé et l'éducation.

4 Qui exécute le droit antidiscriminatoire?

Au Brésil, le pouvoir judiciaire joue un rôle de premier plan dans la concrétisation des politiques antidiscriminatoires par voie d'un important activisme des magistrats dans la mise en œuvre des droits fondamentaux.

Bien qu'au long de ces dernières décennies, l'assemblée législative ait approuvé d'importants statuts juridiques protectifs de groupes traditionnellement vulnérables à la discrimination dans plusieurs domaines, le caractère notoirement contre-majoritaire d'une grande partie des politiques antidiscriminatoires, conduisent à l'activisme judiciaire au Brésil, considéré par beaucoup comme le seul moyen efficace de concrétisation des garanties constitutionnelles d'égalité et la primauté des droits fondamentaux dans le pays.[7]

Parmi les entités responsables du dépôt des actions visant à l'imposition de politiques antidiscriminatoires, on signale le ministère public (MP), une institution indépendante qui ne trouve aucun parallèle des autres institutions publiques dans le monde entier. Il est responsable de la défense de l'ordre juridique, du régime démocratique et des intérêts sociaux et individuels indisponibles. En plus de la légitimité exclusive pour le dépôt de la procédure pénale publique, le Ministère Public est également responsable de la promotion de la tutelle juridictionnelle des droits «transindividuels (diffus et collectifs)» devant la justice civile, en utilisant un remarquable système procédural d'actions collectives - parmi lesquelles, les «class actions» - considéré comme l'un des plus avancés parmi les pays de droit civil (civil law).

Tant le Ministère Public que d'autres organismes publics incarnent aussi le droit antidiscriminatoire à travers les engagements dits «d'ajustement des conduites». Il s'agit d'un instrument par lequel s'établit une forme particulière de transaction extrajudiciaire auprès des responsables de la violation des obligations et des devoirs inhérents à la non-discrimination, afin d'obtenir l'exécution fidèle des règles d'inclusion pour éviter ou éliminer d'éventuelles poursuites judiciaires.

On signale également une autre institution qui joue de manière croissante le rôle de provocatrice de la Juridiction visant à la concrétisation du droit de la non-discrimination: la *Defensoria Pública*/la Défense Publique. Celle-ci est l'entité

---
[7]Miragem (2015), p. 72.

qui, comme t Ministère Public, est constitutionnellement orientée vers la protection des droits sociaux, notamment la protection des individus ou groupes d'individus considérés insatisfaits - tel qu'on peut qualifier ceux qui sont traditionnellement vulnérables à toute sorte de discrimination.

Enfin, le rôle joué directement par l'Administration Publique n'est pas négligeable. Parmi les initiatives gouvernementales, on signale : le programme *Bolsa Família/ Bourse familiale* – créé en 2003 et ayant pour but de lutter contre la pauvreté et l'inégalité au Brésil; le Programme national des droits de l'homme (PNDH) – qui vise à mettre en œuvre les programmes du gouvernement fédéral et les traités internationaux ratifiés par le Brésil sur les droits de l'homme; et le Conseil national de lutte contre la discrimination et la promotion des droits des lesbiennes, gays, bisexuels, travestis et transgenres (CNCD/LGBT) – qui intègre le Secrétariat des droits de l'homme, composé de représentants du gouvernement et de la société civile afin d'agir pour la proposition et le suivi des politiques publiques impliquées dans la défense des droits sociaux et individuels des victimes de discrimination raciale ou d'autres formes d'intolérance.

5 Qui bénéficie de la mise en œuvre du droit antidiscriminatoire?

Le Brésil a actuellement plusieurs statuts légaux de protection des individus ou groupes d'individus particulièrement vulnérables à la discrimination. Ces statuts visent à générer des protections préventives et répressives dans les juridictions pénales, administratives et civiles, à partir de la reconnaissance de la vulnérabilité par des critères d'âge, de sexe, d'orientation sexuelle, de race, de croyance et d'origine sociale.

En ce qui concerne le critère de l'âge, le Statut de l'enfant et de l'adolescent (Loi n °8069/1990) prévoit que «Aucun enfant ou adolescent ne sera soumis à une forme quelconque de négligence, de discrimination, d'exploitation, de violence, de cruauté et d'oppression, puni conformément à la loi tout attentat par acte ou omission, de leurs droits fondamentaux» (art. 5). Le Statut des personnes âgées (Loi n°10.741/ 2001) établit un ensemble de règles administratives, civiles et pénales de protection et des soins aux personnes âgées de 60 ans ou plus. Selon ce statut «Aucune personne âgée ne sera l'objet d'une forme quelconque de négligence, de discrimination, de violence, de cruauté ou d'oppression, et toute violation de leurs droits, par acte ou omission, sera puni conformément à la loi» (art. 4).

En ce qui concerne le critère du sexe, la loi Maria da Penha (Loi n°11.340/2006) a représenté une étape importante dans la protection des femmes, grâce à la création de mécanismes visant à refréner la violence familiale à laquelle elles sont soumises. Conformément à l'art. 2, « chaque femme, sans distinction de classe, de race, d'origine ethnique, d'orientation sexuelle, de revenu, de culture, de niveau d'éducation, d'âge et de religion, jouit des droits fondamentaux inhérents à la personne humaine et on doit lui assurer les opportunités et les facilités pour vivre sans violence, préserver sa santé physique et mentale et son perfectionnement moral, intellectuel et social». La Loi n°13.104/2015 a aggravé la peine du crime d'homicide lorsqu'il a été commis contre la femme «pour des raisons de la condition du sexe féminin lorsque le crime implique la violence domestique et familiale, le mépris ou la discrimination à la condition de la femme». Il faudrait encore souligner le Projet de Loi n°5002/2013, concernant le droit à l'identité de genre.

Bien que le Brésil ne compte pas encore sur une loi spécialement conçue pour garantir la liberté de l'orientation sexuelle, le Tribunal Suprême Fédéral (*Supremo Tribunal Federal – STF*) a établi un précédent important en 2011, quand il a reconnu l'union stable homo-affective. De ce jugement, les couples homosexuels ont maintenant différents droits reconnus, jusqu'alors acquis seulement par les couples hétérosexuels.

En 2010, la Loi n°12288 a introduit dans le pays ce que l'on appelle le «Statut de l'égalité raciale», pour garantir à la population noire la réalisation de l'égalité des chances, la protection des droits ethniques individuels, collectifs et diffus et la lutte contre la discrimination et contre d'autres formes d'intolérance ethnique. Cette législation définit la discrimination raciale ou ethno-raciale comme «toute distinction, exclusion, restriction ou préférence fondée sur la race, la couleur, la descendance ou l'origine nationale ou ethnique qui a pour but d'annuler ou de restreindre la reconnaissance, la jouissance ou l'exercice, sur un pied d'égalité, les droits de l'homme et les libertés fondamentales dans les domaines politique, économique, social, culturel ou dans tout autre domaine de la vie publique ou privée» (art. 1, par. unique, I).

L'un des plus récents statuts antidiscriminatoires brésiliens concerne les personnes handicapées. En 2015, la Loi n°13.146 établit le Statut de la personne handicapée, afin d'assurer et de promouvoir, sur un pied d'égalité, l'exercice des droits et des libertés fondamentales pour les personnes handicapées, visant à leur inclusion sociale et à la citoyenneté.

6 Qui est concerné par la mise en œuvre du droit antidiscriminatoire?

Le projet d'inclusion sociale consolidé grâce à la mise en œuvre des politiques antidiscriminatoires produit d'importants effets culturels, sociaux, politiques et économiques. Ainsi, les différents segments de la société pourraient être considérés comme affectés par la concrétisation effective du droit antidiscriminatoire.

L'analyse de la mise en œuvre des politiques publiques liées aux différents systèmes de quotas d'accessibilité à l'enseignement supérieur public et aux fonctions publiques représente un bon exemple de ce qui vient d'être dit. La Loi n°12.711/2012 (Loi des quotas) a établi la réserve de 50% des places dans l'enseignement supérieur des institutions fédérales aux étudiants issus intégralement de lycées publics, parmi lesquels les étudiants noirs, métis et les Indiens. La loi n° 12990/2014 a établi une réserve aux noirs de 20% des places offertes dans les concours publics fédéraux. Cette loi a été déclarée constitutionnelle par Le Tribunal Suprême Fédéral au jugement du 08/06/2017 (ADC N° 41), à un moment où la cour suprême a affirmé que la désquiparación promue par la politique d'action positive en question est conforme au principe d'isonomie, ne viole pas les principes du concours public et l'efficacité et observe le principe de proportionnalité.

En outre, au niveau fédéral, la Loi n°8112/90 (art. 5, paragraphe 2) a réservé aux personnes handicapées jusqu'à 20% des places offertes dans les concours publics fédéraux.

La mise en œuvre de ces systèmes de quotas génère encore un grand débat national. Le différend de ces places oppose les intérêts des groupes vulnérables bénéficiaires et les intérêts d'une grande partie de la société qui estime que les quotas sont contraires au principe de l'égalité et produisent des préjugés au détriment des bénéficiaires des quotas. On argumente également qu'en raison des systèmes de quotas la classe moyenne brésilienne – notamment blanche et plus accablée par le fardeau fiscal du pays – non seulement souffrirait d'une concurrence accrue pour ses enfants mais serait encore tenue de payer indûment une dette historique supposée qui ne lui appartient pas. Malgré cela, le Tribunal Suprême Fédéral a déjà déclaré la constitutionnalité des actions positives qui ont mis en œuvre la réserve des quotas raciaux pour l'accès à l'université publique (ADPF n°186, en 2012).

Au sein des entreprises privées, l'intervention de la législation antidiscriminatoire génère une réaction contraire de la part des employeurs. La Loi n°8.213/91 a mis en place l'obligation d'engager des travailleurs handicapés pour les entreprises de plus de 100 employés (2% à 5% du total des salariés). Certains considèrent cependant que cet avantage ne serait applicable qu'aux personnes handicapées «réhabilitées» ou «qualifiées» comme telles dans les registres du gouvernement.

Le tout récemment édité Statut des personnes handicapées a déterminé l'obligation des écoles privées de recevoir des élèves handicapés (art. 28, § 1, et l'art. 30, caput). Contre ce dispositif, la Confédération nationale des établissements d'enseignement (Confenen) a plaidé auprès du Tribunal Suprême Fédéral la déclaration d'inconstitutionnalité d'une telle disposition (ADI 5.357), au motif que ce serait une violation du droit à la propriété, à sa fonction sociale et à la liberté d'initiative, outre le fait que l'éducation d'une personne handicapée serait une obligation exclusive de l'État et de la famille.

7 Quels recours juridiques sont-ils disponibles afin de mettre en œuvre le droit antidiscriminatoire?

Afin d'imposer l'application du droit antidiscriminatoire, le Brésil dispose de procédures administratives et juridictionnelles qui peuvent être déclenchées soit par les individus affectés eux-mêmes, soit par des entités publiques et privées représentatives des intérêts collectifs ou individuels des victimes.

Dans les cas où il y a la classification pénale pour des comportements discriminatoires – comme dans les cas de pratique du racisme ou d'injure raciale et de féminicide – l'enquête policière est effectuée au moyen d'enquêtes administratives qui, une fois achevées, sont envoyées à l'analyse du Ministère Public – institution chargée de proposer des poursuites publiques (relativement à des infractions considérées comme plus graves).

Toutefois, les crimes liés à la discrimination n'arrivent même pas à être signalés par les victimes ou officiellement enregistrés par les organismes d'enquête et de poursuite. Un autre problème majeur jaillit des poursuites pénales (y compris l'enquête et la procédure judiciaire) sont chronophages au Brésil, ce qui provoque parfois même une limitation de la répression en vertu de sa prescription. En outre, la Constitution garantit que la présomption d'innocence des accusés par la pratique de crimes ne serait surmontée qu'avec la condamnation passée en force de chose jugée. Ainsi, en principe, l'exécution des sanctions pénales ne peut commencer qu'après de longues années après les crimes – ce qui crée un grand sentiment d'impunité au sein de la société.

Dans le cadre de la justice civile, à la fois les actions individuelles et les actions collectives peuvent être utilisées pour la mise en œuvre des politiques antidiscriminatoires. Grâce à ces actions, les personnes impliquées peuvent exiger l'application spécifique des droits antidiscriminatoires et la punition des responsables de sa violation versant une indemnité pour les dommages matériels et moraux.

La forme la plus efficace de protection juridictionnelle des droits est celle qui permet sa tutelle spécifique. Ainsi, le système juridique brésilien autorise l'émission d'ordonnances judiciaires qui soient prédisposées à demander l'exécution spécifique des obligations ou des devoirs légaux à faire et à ne pas faire (comportement par omission ou par action), ou l'obtention de résultats pratiques équivalents. Quand les magistrats expédient ces ordres, ils sont autorisés à utiliser – le cas échéant – tout mécanisme de soutien afin que ces ordres deviennent efficaces, telle que l'imposition d'amendes pour retard dans le respect de la décision et, exceptionnellement, même des détentions.

Lorsque la mise en œuvre spécifique du droit antidiscriminatoire se voit entravée, il est toujours possible de présenter la solution de réparation matérielle au Brésil, est conçue dans les cadres patrimoniaux et extrapatrimoniaux, et calculée en fonction de l'étendue des dégâts produits.

En cas de dépôt de recours collectifs relatifs aux dommages indivisiblement causés à des droits ou à des intérêts diffus ou collectifs dans l'hypothèse d'une réparation matérielle, l'argent doit être adressé à des fonds sociaux réparateurs – comme le fonds nouvellement créé pour financer les politiques d'égalité ethnique.[8]

---

[8]Comme prévu par la loi n° 12.288/2010, tous les accords ou condamnations judiciaires en raison de dommages causés par un acte de discrimination ethnique doivent être utilisées pour le fond diffus, étant utilisés pour des actions visant à promouvoir l'égalité ethnique.

Bien que le Brésil n'ait pas encore de tradition des modes alternatifs de résolution des conflits, la dernière édition d'un nouveau Code de Procédure civile, la nouvelle Loi sur la médiation et les changements dans la Loi sur l'arbitrage promettent d'orienter le pays dans ce sens – y compris pour des solutions possibles de conflits découlant de la non-exécution du droit antidiscriminatoire.

8 Qui soutient la mise en œuvre du droit antidiscriminatoire au Brésil?

La mobilisation de la société civile brésilienne a été en grande partie responsable de la pression sur les pouvoirs publics concernant l'adoption de politiques antidiscriminatoires.

Les organisations non-gouvernementales, les associations civiles, les centrales syndicales et d'autres mouvements sociaux jouent un rôle fondamental en ce qui concerne non seulement l'appui, mais aussi la véritable construction de l'action positive dans plusieurs domaines.

Signalons parmi ces mouvements, les groupes de défense des droits des Afro-descendants, les femmes, les personnes handicapés, les personnes âgées, les gays, les lesbiennes, les transsexuels et les travestis. Voici les entités nationales composées des représentants de la société civile qui appartiennent au Conseil national des droits de l'homme (CNDH): Association brésilienne des lesbiennes, gays, bisexuels, travestis et transsexuels (ABGLT), Collectif national de la jeunesse noire (ENEGRECER[9]), Conseil Fédéral de Psychologie (CFP), le Conseil indigéniste missionnaire (CIMI), Intervozes – Collectif Brésil de Communication sociale, Mouvement national de la population de rue (MNPR), Mouvement national des droits de l'homme (MNDH), Plateforme pour les droits de l'homme – Dhesca Brésil et Réseau national féministe de la santé, des droits sexuels et des droits reproductifs.

Les organisations internationales soutiennent également de façon vigoureuse les politiques antidiscriminatoires au Brésil. Parmi ces organisations, la plus importante est sûrement l'Organisation des Nations Unies (ONU).[10] Ayant une représentation fixe au Brésil depuis 1947, l'organisation soutient fortement la mise en œuvre des projets antidiscriminatoires et des actions positives dans le pays.[11] Ses diverses agences thématiques développent des projets en partenariat à la fois avec le

---

[9]"Devenir Noir".

[10]See https://nacoesunidas.org/onu-no-brasil/.

[11]Par exemple, la publication "Guia de orientação das Nações Unidas no Brasil para denúncias de discriminação étnico-racial" (http://www.pnud.org.br/pdf/GuiaDenunciasDiscriminacaoRacial.pdf).

gouvernement brésilien (dans les cadres fédéral, étatique et municipal) ainsi qu'avec le secteur privé, les établissements d'enseignement, les ONG et la société civile.

On ne peut malheureusement pas dire qu'en règle générale les entrepreneurs soutiennent les politiques antidiscriminatoires au Brésil. Si d'une part il est exagéré de les percevoir comme des adversaires de ces politiques, il est vrai que peu d'initiatives sont prises pour favoriser l'inclusion sociale des personnes vulnérables.

Au moins c'est ce qui montre une étude récemment publiée, qui impliquait l'analyse des 500 plus grandes entreprises brésiliennes. Les diagnostics ont montré que la plupart des entreprises ne disposent d'aucune action positive qui favorise la présence des femmes et des Noirs dans les cadres d'employés. L'enquête a révélé que, dans les conseils d'administration des entreprises, la participation des femmes n'est que de 13,6% et celle des Noirs ne dépasse 4,7%.[12]

9 Qui s'oppose à la mise en œuvre du droit antidiscriminatoire?

L'opposition à la mise en œuvre concrète l du droit antidiscriminatoire au Brésil provient de divers segments de la société, tantôt fondée sur les intérêts économiques et politiques, tantôt fruit de l'ignorance, de la pure haine ou de la révolte contre le droit à l'égalité et à la diversité.

Quoique le Brésil soit le 5ème plus grand pays du monde par son étendu, le problème foncier est encore l'un des principaux défis à surmonter, ayant des répercussions très graves, par exemple, dans la réalisation des droits des communautés indigènes et quilombolas - traditionnellement vulnérables à la discrimination ethnique.

Bien que la Constitution Fédérale garantisse aux Indiens «les droits originaires sur les terres qu'ils occupent traditionnellement» (art. 231), plusieurs groupes intéressés par l'appropriation et l'exploitation de ces terres (*les ruralistes,* les *posseiros,* les *fazendeiros,*[13] les mineurs qui exploitent des gisements et les exploitants forestiers, entre autres) agissent directement – et invariablement de manière violente – afin de compromettre la reconnaissance et la délimitation des réserves indigènes. Au niveau parlementaire mais à la différencedes Indiens, ces groupes mentionnés sont habituellement très bien représentés.[14] Ceci rend le

---

[12]"Perfil social, racial e de gênero das 500 maiores empresas do brasil e suas ações afirmativas" (www3.ethos.org.br/wp-content/uploads/2016/05/Perfil_Social_Tacial_Genero_500empresas.pdf).

[13]Respectivement les grands agriculteurs, ceux qui cultivent la terre sans droit de propriété et les grands propriétaires de terres.

[14]Depuis le début du processus de démocratisation au Brésil (1984), les 817.000 Indiens ne disposent pas d'un représentant au Congrès. D'autre part, aux dernières élections législatives (2014), le grands agriculteurs e les grands propriétaires de terres a maintenant environ 250 députés et 16 sénateurs (www.cartacapital.com.br/sociedade/indios-ocupam-brasilia-para-serem-enxergados-pelo-governo-7001.html).

processus de réalisation des droits des communautés indigènes sur leurs terres extrêmement complexe.[15]

Parfois, la discrimination contre les communautés indigènes découle d'une perception erronée du processus d'«acculturation» auquel elles ont été contraintes de subir finirait par les disqualifier en tant que groupes dignes de protection spéciale de l'État, soit à des fins d'adoption de politiques publiques protectives, soit pour la reconnaissance pure du droit aux terres traditionnellement occupées par ces communautés.

De surcroit, l'existence d'interdiction constitutionnelle relative à toute forme de discrimination fondée sur le sexe n'a pas encore été suffisante pour engendrer la criminalisation de l'homophobie.[16] Si le Brésil n'a toujours pas d'interdiction légale du statut légal discrimination sexuelle, cela est dû en grande partie à la pression exercée au Parlement brésilien par des groupes politiques et religieux opposésà la reconnaissance du droit à la liberté d'orientation sexuelle. L'opposition à la réalisation du droit à la liberté sexuelle peut être mesurée au Brésil, par exemple, par les traitements thérapeutiques publics proposés visant à la réversion ou à la conversion de l'homosexualité (la soi-disant «cure des gays »). De même, la perception de la transidentité comme pathologie reflète sur la désinformation ou le préjugé qui mine encore la société brésilienne quant à la reconnaissance des droits sexuels.

10 Quelle est l'ampleur de la couverture du droit antidiscriminatoire?

Il y a plusieurs avantages générés aux personnes vulnérables par les statuts antidiscriminatoires au Brésil afin de leur fournir l'inclusion sociale par des facilitations d'accessibilité à l'emploi, à la santé, au logement, aux services publics, au sport, à la culture de loisirs et au bien-être social. La couverture du droit antidiscriminatoire dans le pays se révèle ainsi, au moins en théorie, ample et générale comme on illustre ci-après.

En ce qui concerne les personnes handicapées, la législation brésilienne prévoit, entre autres choses, le devoir de construire dans l'immobilier public ou privé, des rampes accessibles aux utilisateurs de fauteuils roulants, des salles de bains et des toilettes munies d'adaptations spéciales et des emplacements dans les stationnements

---

[15]Un amendement constitutionnel proposé au Brésil (PEC 215) vise à transférer au Congrès la décision finale sur la démarcation des terres d'Indiens, les territoires quilombolas et les unités de conservation de l'environnement. Par ailleurs, le Projet interdit l'expansion des terres autochtones déjà délimitées et fixe un calendrier limite (1988) pour la reconnaissance de terres traditionnellement occupées par des communautés indigènes dans le pays.

[16]La conception du Projet de Code Penal - qui est toujours en suspens au Congrès national -, criminalise les préjugés contre les homosexuels, les transsexuels et transgenres. De même, le Projet assimile les préjugés contre les femmes et les préjugés fondés sur l'origine régionale au crime de racisme, qui est considéré imprescriptible.

réservés aux personnes handicapées. Dans la fonction publique, il est prévu qu'un pourcentage des places soit réservé à l'approvisionnement de postes publics. Les entreprises privées sont tenus de se conformer aux quotas pour les personnes handicapées parmi leurs employés. La Loi n°10.436/2002 (Loi de *Libras*/Loi des Signes) a déterminé l'obligation de l'enseignement de la langue brésilienne des signes dans des cours de formation en éducation spéciale, en orthophonie et au cours de formation d'enseignants (*magistério*). Il y a aussi selon le type et le degré d'invalidité, des exonérations fiscales pour l'achat de véhicules.

Quant aux personnes âgées, outre les emplacements de stationnement privilégiés et un traitement préférentiel dans les établissements privés et dans les services publics, il leur est encore garanti le libre accès ou des tarifs spéciaux pour la circulation par les transports en commun et la priorité pour recevoir le remboursement d'impôts sur le revenu et s'appliquant notamment aux procédures judiciaires et administratives dans lesquelles la personne âgée constitue la partie ou l'intéressée.

Tant pour les personnes âgées que pour les personnes handicapées qui n'ont pas des conditions d'existence minimales, la Loi n° 8.742/93 établit également le Bénéfice de la prestation continue, qui consiste à leur transférer un salaire minimum mensuel.

Il est garanti aux jeunes âgés de 15-29 ans à faible revenu, aux personnes handicapées et à leurs accompagnateurs (si nécessaire) et aux personnes âgées l'accès aux salles de cinéma, aux ciné-clubs, aux théâtres, aux concerts, à des spectacles de cirque, à des événements éducatifs, sportifs, à des activités de loisirs et de divertissement, sur tout le territoire national, réalisés par toute entité dans des établissements publics ou privés sur paiement de la moitié du prix de la place réellement facturée auprès du grand public (Loi n° 12.933/2013).

Le congé maternité dans le secteur privé est de 120 jours, ce qui laisse l'employeur responsable du paiement de l'indemnité maternité, au-delà du salaire mensuel. En plus de fixer la période de 180 jours de congé maternité pour les fonctionnaires, La Loi n° 11.770/2008 crée également des incitations fiscales aux entreprises qui étendent le congé maternité de 120 jours à 180 jours.

Afin d'accroître la représentation politique des femmes, la législation électorale brésilienne prévoit obligatoirement qu'au moins 30% des candidats soient des femmes.[17]

Au moyen du Décret n°8727/2016 on a accordé l'utilisation du *nom social* et la reconnaissance de l'identité de genre des personnes travesties et des transsexuelles au sein de l'Administration publique fédérale directe, des organismes autonomes et des fondations.

---

[17]Cette politique publique, cependant, a généré une croissance de seulement trois points de pourcentage à la participation des femmes au Congrès (7% en 1997 à 9,9% en 2015), ce qui rend le Brésil la position 116ème dans le classement de la représentation féminine à l'Assemblée législative - derrière des pays qui restreignent les droits des femmes comme l'Arabie Saoudite, la Somalie et la Jordanie (source: www.conjur.com.br/2016-jun-05/cotas-mulheres-legislativo-aumentam-igualdade-politica)

11 La mise en œuvre du droit antidiscriminatoire varie selon le degré de discrimination?

Les diverses statuts antidiscriminatoires brésiliens comprennent diverses sanctions concernant les pratiques discriminatoires qui varient selon le degré et l'intensité de la violation.

Dans le domaine civil, une éventuelle indemnisation pour les dommages patrimoniaux et extrapatrimoniaux à être déterminée par infraction discriminatoire sera évaluée par la règle générale selon laquelle «la réparation est mesurée à la hauteur de l'étendue des dégâts». Le degré de culpabilité des agresseurs d'autre part, peut se mesurer à l'aune du principe de la proportionnalité et du caractère raisonnable de la sanction pécuniaire à appliquer.

En outre, si le comportement discriminatoire offense non seulement un individu, mais tout un groupe, classe ou catégorie de personnes vulnérables, le système judiciaire national conçoit la possibilité de condamner les contrevenants à payer une indemnité pour «préjudice moral collectif» qui sert à compenser socialement le groupe offensé.

Cependant, l'impact que la variation du degré de la discrimination génère dans la sanction du contrevenant est cependant plus visible dans le cadre pénal.

La définition des crimes d'injures raciales et de racisme illustre une des figures juridiques qui génèrent encore une certaine confusion dans le système national de justice.

L'injure raciste – dont la peine prévue par l'art. 140, paragraphe 3 du Code pénal est la réclusion d'un à trois ans et une amende – est l'atteinte à l'honneur ou à la dignité d'une personne en vertu de la référence à la race, à la couleur, à l'origine à l'ethnie, à la religion ou à l'origine ou à la condition des personnes âgées ou handicapées. Les poursuites pénales pour le traitement de ce crime sont publiques (proposées par le ministère public), sous réserve de la représentation de la victime.

D'autre part, le crime de racisme – prévu par la loi n°7716/1989 et passible de peine d'emprisonnement de deux à cinq ans et d'une amende – atteint une collectivité indéterminée d'individus, discriminant l'intégralité des catégories, des groupes ou des classes sociales en fonction de la race, de l'ethnie, de la religion ou de l'origine. L'action pénale, dans ces cas, doit être déposée par le ministère public indépendamment de la représentation de la victime. Classé en tant que crime odieux, est imprescriptible et le crime n'est pas assorti de caution possible.

12 Quelle est la relation entre la mise en œuvre du droit antidiscriminatoire et la recherche de l'égalité à la fois individuelle et collective?

Le droit antidiscriminatoire est essentiellement un droit d'inclusion sociale des vulnérabilités. Toutes les formes de discrimination raciale, religieuse, sexuelle, de genre, ou fondées sur la nationalité provoque un déséquilibre illégitime et illégal entre les citoyens, produisant de graves pressions sociales, politiques et économiques.

En conséquence, la violation du principe de l'égalité – le fondement principiel de toute politique antidiscriminatoire – ne peut être comprise que comme préjudiciable aux victimes particulièrement vulnérables dont les droits ou les intérêts les divers statuts nationaux et internationaux antidiscriminatoires visent à protéger.

En fin de compte, «à qui l'égalité rend service? La référence aux avantages de l'égalité – y compris celle qui impose des traitements différenciés – ne serait pas complète si elle ne comprenait pas, outre ceux qui en bénéficient, nous tous qui avons le droit de vivre avec nos semblables/différents et partager les expériences de la diversité dans un esprit démocratique (participatif) et solidaire. L'exclusion est préjudiciable à tous.»[18]

Tant le devoir de ne pas discriminer (les égaux) que le devoir de discriminer (les différents) jouent un rôle absolument essentiel dans l'État constitutionnel dans la garantie des droits fondamentaux et du soi-disant «minimum existentiel», soit au niveau individuel, soit au niveau collectif.

L'affirmation du droit antidiscriminatoire au Brésil représente la lutte pour la reconnaissance non seulement de l'égalité formelle de tous devant la loi, mais aussi une égalité matérielle qui, à son tour, ne se réduit pas à une intention de justiciabilité socio-économique entre les citoyens. L'égalité matérielle est bien plus que cela. Elle représente le droit à la «reconnaissance des identités propres, distinctes des groupes hégémoniques», guidée par des critères de genre, d'orientation sexuelle, d'âge, de race, d'ethnie et de nationalité entre autres.[19]

C'est dans cette perspective que la mise en œuvre des lois antidiscriminatoires au Brésil a été principalement conçu par les actions positives, considérées comme des mesures nécessaires et légitimes «afin de soulager, de guérir et de transformer l'héritage d'un passé discriminatoire. Elles doivent être comprises non seulement par le biais rétrospectif – afin d'alléger le fardeau d'un passé discriminatoire – mais également prospectif – afin de favoriser le changement social et par conséquent la création d'une nouvelle réalité, sous l'inspiration du droit à l'égalité matérielle et substantive».[20]

En ce sens, au cas où les politiques antidiscriminatoires ne se réaliseraient pas de façon raisonnable, le Brésil continuera à présenter des statistiques sociales infamantes dans les domaines de l'éducation, de la santé, de la sécurité publique, du travail et du bien-être social.

---

[18]Rothenburg (2009), p. 347.
[19]Ramos (2016), p. 505.
[20]Ramos (2016), p. 505.

13 La mise en œuvre du droit antidiscriminatoire est-elle comprise comme différente de l'exécution d'autres droits?

Dans la mesure où la mise en œuvre du droit antidiscriminatoire est essentielle à la réalisation des droits fondamentaux telles que l'égalité et la dignité humaine, la Constitution fédérale brésilienne confère un statut différencié à l'interprétation et à l'application des règles antidiscriminatoires par rapport à d'autres statuts juridiques.

Conformément au §3° de l'art. 5° de la Constitution Fédérale, lorsque les traités et les conventions internationales sur les droits de l'homme sont assimilés dans le pays - par le truchement de l'approbation par le Congrès national - ils seront considérés comme équivalant aux amendements constitutionnels.

Lorsqu'on discute au contentieux de toute violation des règles antidiscriminatoires, compte tenu de la présomption de l'existence d'intérêts diffus, collectifs ou individuels indisponibles, le ministère public intervient obligatoirement – organisme chargé de la supervision de l'adéquate protection de cette intervention par la participation selon les coûts.

L'indisponibilité du droit objet du litige implique, en principe, l'impossibilité d'utiliser des moyens extrajudiciaires de règlement des conflits, comme l'arbitrage, la médiation et la conciliation. Le système de justice brésilienne est encore très lié au dogme de l'adjudication publique des conflits portant sur des droits inaliénables.

La plus importante distinction trouvée dans l'application des règles antidiscriminatoires devient évidente toutefois dans le droit pénal - en particulier dans les cas de crimes de racisme et de féminicide.

La Loi n°7716/1989 a institué le délit de racisme comme celui résultant de la discrimination ou des préjugés fondés sur la race, la couleur, l'origine ethnique, la religion ou l'origine nationale. Loi n°13104/2015 prévoit le féminicide comme une circonstance de qualification d'homicide (lorsqu'il est pratiqué contre les femmes en raison de la condition de sexe féminin). La loi brésilienne qualifie tous les deux crimes comme des crimes odieux, c'est-à-dire, des crimes non-susceptibles d'avantages tels que l'amnistie, la grâce, l'indult ou la caution. L'application des dispositions pénales de la peine dans ces cas doit se faire dans ce cadre initialement fermé. La Loi n°13.285/2016 a récemment conféré le régime de préférence dans le traitement des affaires pénales impliquant des crimes.

En matière civile, d'autre part, bien que la mise en œuvre des mesures antidiscriminatoires ne possède aucun régime spécial, elle est soumise au caractère extraordinairedes moyens d'exécution, notamment ce la possibilité de l'utilisation de toute action, technique ou mécanisme dans l'obtention de la réalisation spécifique du devoir ou de l'obligation, ou même dans l'obtention du résultat pratique équivalent.

14 Qu'est-ce que l'exécution du droit antidiscriminatoire révèle à propos de la nature de son système légal ou à propos de l'exécution des lois dans son système légal?

La frustration concernant l'effectivité des règles antidiscriminatoires au Brésil mène à une conclusion claire: il existe un énorme fossé entre le discours théorique et constitutionnel, facile et attrayant, et la réalité empirique de la mise en œuvre des politiques antidiscriminatoires. On conclut encore que le système de justice brésilien n'est pas efficace pour assurer le plein exercice des droits fondamentaux.

Par exemple, le Brésil est considéré par les recherches récentes le pays ayant le plus grand nombre de meurtres de travestis et de transsexuels dans le monde. Entre janvier 2008 et décembre 2015, 802 décès ont été enregistrés dans le pays.[21]

Quant aux homosexuels, selon le rapport annuel publié par le Grupo Gay da Bahia (GGB/Groupe gay de l'état de Bahia) – la plus ancienne organisation du genre au Brésil – 318 personnes ont été tuées en 2015 en raison de leur orientation sexuelle. Sur le total des victimes, 52% étaient des hommes homosexuels, 37% de travestis, 16% de lesbiennes et 10% de bisexuels. En 2014, ce rapport souligne l'assassinat de 326 personnes des groupes mentionnés.[22]

En ce qui concerne les Afro-descendants, un rapport récent de l'ONU a conclu que le Brésil a tout simplement échoué dans la mise en place de ses politiques d'égalité raciale. Certaines données parlent par soi-même. Sur les quelques 16,2 millions de personnes vivant dans l'extrême pauvreté dans le pays, 70,8% sont des Afro-descendants. Les salaires moyens versés aux Noirs au Brésil sont environ 2,4 fois inférieurs à ceux payés aux Blancs. Environ 80% des Brésiliens analphabètes sont noirs et 64% d'entre eux n'a pas terminé l'enseignement de base. Le Brésil ne compte que 15,7% des juges noirs et au Congrès, seulement 8,5% des députés sont noirs. Sur les 56.000 homicides enregistrés au Brésil par an, 30.000 impliquent les 15-29 ans, dont 77% étaient des garçons noirs. On estime que 75% de la population carcérale au Brésil est composée d'Afro-descendants.[23]

Bien qu'en vigueur depuis 20 ans, la Loi 7.716/89, qui classe le racisme comme un crime non-sujet à caution, punissable d'emprisonnement pouvant aller jusqu'à cinq ans et amende, est rarement appliquée. La plupart des cas de discrimination raciale est encadrée dans l'article 140 du Code pénal (Décret-Loi 2.848/40), comme injure, prévoyant une peine plus clémente: un mois à six mois de prison et une amende. Cela signifie que, dans la pratique, la peine finit par être convertie en panier alimentaire de base (*cesta básica*) ou en prisons de quelques jours, lorsque l'agresseur est pris en flagrant délit.

---

[21]Source http://tgeu.org/transgender-day-of-visibility-2016-trans-murder-monitoring-update/.

[22]Source https://grupogaydabahia.com.br/2016/01/28/assassinato-de-lgbt-no-brasil-relatorio-2015.

[23]Rapport de la Commission des Nations Unies sur les droits de l'homme (14/3/2016), synthétisé dans l'édition du journal Estado de São Paulo (source http://brasil.estadao.com.br/noticias/geral, politicas-de-igualdade-racial-fracassaram-no-brasil--afirma-onu).

Toutes les 17 plaintes de racisme au Brésil, une seule génère la punition. Dans 92% des actions qui ont concerné la pratique du crime raciste entre 2005 et 2007, la qualification pénale retenue devant les juridictions a été l'injure, même si le crime dénoncé dans son origine était sans caution possible.[24]

Au Brésil, le taux de féminicides est de 4,8 à 100.000 femmes – le cinquième plus grand dans le monde, selon l'Organisation mondiale de la santé (OMS).[25]

Selon la dernière Recherche nationale par échantillon de domicile (PNAD), de l'IBGE,[26] concernant l'année 2014, le revenu moyen des femmes au Brésil équivalait à 74,5% de celui perçu par les hommes.

15 Conclusion

Le Brésil connaît un processus de reconnaissance progressive des vulnérabilités sociales et de construction de politiques publiques visant à lutter contre toutes les formes de discrimination.

L'efficacité de la loi antidiscriminatoire est cependant loin de compter uniquement sur la reconnaissance législative ou judiciaire. La création de nouveaux status légaux de protection des catégories de personnes vulnérables plus élaborés ou même la reconnaissance de la valeur constitutionnelle des politiques publiques par les tribunaux nationaux ne garantit pas, de manière pragmatique, sa réalisation complète et adéquate.

Le manque de contrôle et l'absence de sanctions efficaces, capables d'imprimer non seulement la punition efficace, mais aussi de générer une prévention globale en ce qui concerne les pratiques discriminatoires se révèlent être les principaux problèmes pour la mise en œuvre du droit antidiscriminatoire dans le pays.

D'autre part, l'accent mis sur la sanction pénale, quoiqu'elle se prête potentiellement à inhiber des comportements discriminatoires plus graves, n'est sûrement pas propice à la mise en œuvre des droits et obligations incidents sur l'Administration publique, sur les sociétés privées et sur les citoyens, pour l'efficacité des politiques publiques d'inclusion sociale de divers groupes vulnérables.

Si la prévention et la répression aux comportements discriminatoires, ainsi que le développement et la mise en œuvre des politiques publiques en faveur de l'inclusion sociale sont à la charge surtout des organismes de l'État, la responsabilité de la société civile ne peut pas être démesurée.

Le Tribunal suprême fédéral a déjà reconnu que le respect et la réalisation des droits de l'homme relèvent de la responsabilité tant du secteur public que du secteur privé. Ainsi, la discussion sur la mise en œuvre du droit antidiscriminatoire ne peut

---

[24]Santos (2013).
[25]Source http://www.onumulheres.org.br.
[26]Institut brésilien de géographie et de statistique.

pas servir tout simplement d'arène pour les critiques de l'inefficacité de l'administration publique ou du pouvoir judiciaire.

La lutte contre la discrimination et les préjugés, ainsi que le devoir d'inclusion sociale des femmes, des Noirs, des personnes handicapés physiques, des personnes âgées, des Indiens et des Quilombolas, des non-nationaux, des homosexuels et des transsexuels, qui font partie des groupes traditionnellement considérés comme vulnérables incombent à chacun et à tous les êtres humains, en tout temps et en tout lieu.

References

Freyre G (2004) Casa - grande & Senzala: formação da família brasileira sob o regime da economia patriarcal, 49ª Ed. Global, São Paulo

Holanda S (2015) Buarque de, Raízes do Brasil, 26ª ed. Companhia das Letras, São Paulo

Miragem B (2015) Direito à diferença e autonomia: Proteção da diversidade no direito privado em relação ao exercício individual das liberdades sexual e religiosa. In: Direito à diversidade. Editora Atlas, São Paulo, p 72

Ramos AdC (2016) Curso de direitos humanos, 3ª ed. Saraiva, São Paulo, p 505

Rothenburg WC (2009) Igualdade. In: Direitos fundamentais e estado constitucional – estudos em homenagem a J. J. Canotilho (coord. Leite e Sarlet). Editora Revista dos Tribunais, São Paulo, p 347

Santos IAAD (2013) Direitos humanos e as práticas de racismo. Câmara dos Deputados, Edições Câmara, Brasília

Elton Venturi is a Professor of Law at the Federal University of Paraná (Brazil) and a Federal Prosecutor. He holds a Ph.D and a LLM from Catholic University of São Paulo (Brazil). In 2015, he researched at Columbia Law School and at Berkeley Law School as a visiting scholar. Mr. Venturi writes and teaches in the field of Civil Procedure Law and Class Actions.

Canada

Colleen Sheppard

1 Introduction

> Interpreting human rights legislation primarily in terms of formal equality undermines its promise of substantive equality and prevents consideration of the effects of systemic discrimination [...]
>
> Chief Justice Beverley McLachlin, Supreme Court of Canada[1]

Legal protections against discrimination began to emerge in the post-World War II era in Canada, with specific legislative enactments prohibiting exclusions based on race, sex, national or ethnic origin and religion in employment, housing and access to public services.[2] More expansive and comprehensive statutory protections were introduced in the 1960s and 1970s in provinces and territories across Canada and at the federal level.[3] Constitutional protections for equality and non-discrimination were entrenched in the 1980s and the Supreme Court of Canada has repeatedly affirmed a substantive approach to equality in its constitutional rulings.[4] In addition,

---

[1]*British Columbia (Public Service Employee Relations Commission) v. BCGSEU*, [1999] 3 SCR 3 at para 41 [*BCGSEU*].

[2]Tarnopolsky (1982), Sheppard (2010), Dominique Clément & Canadian Human Rights Commission (2012).

[3]Dominique Clément & Canadian Human Rights Commission (2012). For a full enumeration of current protections, see Appendix.

[4]Canadian Charter of Rights and Freedoms, Part I of the *Constitution Act, 1982*, being Schedule B to the Canada Act 1982 (UK), 1982, c 11 [Canadian Charter]; Andrews v. Law Society of British Columbia, [1989] 1 SCR 143, 56 DLR (4th) 1; Law v. Canada (Minister of Employment and Immigration), [1999] 1 SCR 497, 170 DLR (4th) 1; R. v. Kapp, 2008 SCC 41, [2008] 2 SCR 483.

C. Sheppard (✉)
Faculty of Law, McGill University, Montreal, QC, Canada
e-mail: colleen.sheppard@mcgill.ca

Canada has ratified numerous international human rights conventions.[5] Thus, the most pressing challenge today is ensuring a broad and robust interpretation of these legal protections, and securing their effective enforcement.

2 The Enforcement of Antidiscrimination Law

2.1 Antidiscrimination Statutes and Complaints-based Enforcement

The major approach to enforcing antidiscrimination statutes (referred to as human rights codes or acts) in Canada is a retroactive complaints model. In most jurisdictions across Canada, individuals or groups file human rights complaints with the relevant human rights commission in their province/territory or with the federal human rights commission. Human rights commissions were set up in tandem with the passage of antidiscrimination laws to provide publically-funded support to individuals in making claims of discrimination. Upon receipt of a complaint of discrimination, most commissions assume responsibility for investigating allegations of discrimination. Following investigation, where evidence of discrimination is obtained, commissions often seek to conciliate or mediate a settlement between the parties. If no settlement is negotiated, commissions may pursue legal remedies before a specialized human rights administrative tribunal.[6] In many jurisdictions across Canada, human rights commissions have important "gatekeeping" functions, which accords them a degree of discretion (subject to judicial review) to decide whether or not to take a case to adjudication. The fundamental *raison-d'être* of the human rights commissions was to enhance access to justice for individuals by assuming public responsibility for investigation and legal representation in the adjudication of antidiscrimination complaints.[7] Human rights commissions also have research, public education, and prevention mandates in many jurisdictions.

Despite the promise and successes of the human rights commission model, it has encountered difficulties, most notably, significant time delays.[8] As a result of these concerns, some jurisdictions in Canada have reformed the human rights complaint process. In the province of British Columbia, the human rights commission was abolished in 2003 and individuals now file claims directly with a specialized human rights tribunal.[9] In lieu of a human rights commission, British Columbia established

---

[5]See below, section 1.4.

[6]For a recent decision affirming the importance of deference by courts to specialized human rights tribunals, see *Mouvement laïque québécois v. Saguenay (City)*, [2015] 2 SCR 3, paras 37–44.

[7]Eliadis (2014), pp. 26, 153.

[8]Eliadis (2014), pp. 75–78, 51–52.

[9]Eliadis (2014), p. 91; British Columbia, *BC Human Rights Tribunal*, online: < www.bchrt.bc.ca/>. Recently, British Columbia has announced its intention to re-establish a human rights commission:

a Human Rights Clinic to provide free legal support to complainants. In Ontario, a direct access model has also been introduced. While the human rights commission was retained, as of 2008, individuals file complaints directly with the Ontario Human Rights Tribunal.[10] In 2008, the Ontario government also set up a Human Rights Legal Support Centre, which provides representation and information to members of the public wishing to file a complaint in the province. Nevertheless, recent studies reveal that a significant majority of complainants in Ontario are self-represented before the Ontario Human Rights Tribunal.[11] The Ontario Human Rights Commission has now shifted its focus to policy and education work and legal intervention in complex, systemic discrimination cases before the tribunal.[12] At the federal level, the Canadian Human Rights Commission reorganized its approach to reduce its involvement in individual human rights complaints, while maintaining a role in more complex, systemic cases.[13] In Quebec, individuals have the choice of filing a complaint with the Quebec Human Rights and Youth Rights Commission or of seeking redress in the regular court system.[14] Finally, the territory of Nunavut has a direct access system. An individual or group of individuals can file a notification with the Nunavut Human Rights Tribunal when they allege that their rights have been infringed.[15]

2.2 Proactive Legislative Initiatives

While the legal definitions of discrimination and equality have expanded over the past 30 years to encompass indirect and systemic discrimination,[16] governments have also recognized that an individualized retroactive litigation (or complaints-based) approach to compliance is insufficient. Proactive legislative initiatives to advance workplace equality emerged in the 1980s, including the Federal *Employ-*

---

see *A Human Rights Commission for the 21st Century: British Columbians Talk about Human Rights*, https://engage.gov.bc.ca/app/uploads/sites/213/2017/12/HRC-Final-Report-accessible-PDF.pdf

[10]For a review, see Pinto (2013); see also Flaherty (2013), p. 169.

[11]Flaherty (2013), p. 181.

[12]Eliadis (2014), p. 100.

[13]Canada, Canadian Human Rights Commission, online: <www.chrc-ccdp.gc.ca>.

[14]Brunelle (2015), p. 11; Quebec (Commission des droits de la personne et des droits de la jeunesse) v. Communauté urbaine de Montréal, 2004 SCC 30, para 13, [2004] 1 SCR 789.

[15]Human Rights Act, SNu 2003, c 12, s 21 [Nunavut Human Rights Act].

[16]On indirect or adverse effect discrimination, see: *Ont. Human Rights Comm. v. Simpsons-Sears*, [1985] 2 SCR 536, at para 18; Andrews v. Law Society of British Columbia, [1989] 1 SCR 143, 56 DLR (4th) 1, 165; On systemic discrimination, see *CN v. Canada (Canadian Human Rights Commission)*, [1987] 1 SCR 1114 at 1138 [*CN*]; See also Sheppard, *Inclusive Equality*, supra, note 2 at 19.

ment Equity Act and Federal Contractors Program,[17] as well as provincial pay and employment equity legislation.[18] More recently, some provinces have introduced proactive disability rights, anti-harassment and anti-racism legislation.[19] These initiatives are an innovative response to the perceived inadequacies of retroactively enforced antidiscrimination guarantees. Designed to redress systemic problems of exclusion and discrimination, proactive legislative initiatives shift the focus of enforcement of antidiscrimination protections towards prevention. They engage public and private actors in identifying inequities and putting in place policies and programs to redress them, rather than relying on a retroactive complaints approach. While they are critical to ensuring effective and transformative approaches to the challenges of systemic inequality and social exclusion, difficulties in their enforcement and implementation have been encountered.[20]

2.2.1 Employment Equity

The first significant foray into proactive legislation was federal *Employment Equity Act,* (enacted in 1986, and significantly amended in 1995) and the Federal Contractors Program (FCP).[21] These initiatives were a response to recommendations included in the 1984 *Royal Commission Report on Equality in Employment*. The Commission was established "to explore the most efficient, effective, and equitable means of promoting equality in employment" for four designated groups: women, Indigenous people, persons with disabilities and racialized communities.[22] In her Report, Judge Rosalie Silberman Abella (now a Justice at the Supreme Court of

---

[17] *Employment Equity Act*, SC 1995, c 44 [*Employment Equity Act*]; For an overview of the Federal Contractors Program, see, Canada, Employment and Social Development Canada, "Federal Contractors Program", (7 May 2013), online: <www.labour.gc.ca/eng/standards_equity/eq/emp/fcp/index.shtml> [Canada, *Federal Contractors Program*].

[18] See, e.g. *Quebec Charter of Human Rights and Freedoms*, CQLR c C-12, arts 86-92 [*Quebec Charter*]; *An Act Respecting Equal Access to Employment in Public Bodies*, CQLR c A-2.01; *Pay Equity Act*, CQLR c E-12.001 [*Quebec Pay Equity Act*]; *Pay Equity Act*, RSO 1990, c P.7 [*Ontario Pay Equity Act*]; *Pay Equity Act*, CCSM c P13; *Pay Equity Act*, SNB 2009, c P-5.05; *Pay Equity Act*, RSNS 1989, c 337; *Pay Equity Act*, RSPEI 1988, c P-2.

[19] See *Ontarians with Disabilities Act*, SO 2001, c 32 [*Ontarians with Disabilities Act*]; *Vulnerable Persons Living with a Mental Disability Act*, CCSM c V90; *An Act to Secure Handicapped Persons in the Exercise of Their Rights with a View to Achieving Social, School and Workplace Integration*, CQLR c E-20.1. See also, *Sexual Violence and Harassment Action Plan Act (Supporting Survivors and Challenging Sexual Violence and Harassment)*, S.O. 2016 C.2 and the very recent *Anti-Racism Act*, S.O. 2017 C.15. See also, *An Act to prevent and fight sexual violence in higher education institutions*, S.Q. 2017, chapter 32.

[20] See, e.g. Agócs (2014).

[21] *Employment Equity Act, supra* note 17; *Canada, Federal Contractors Program, supra* note 17. Note that in 2013, the Federal Contractors Program limit was raised from $200,000 in annual federal grants or contracts to $1 million.

[22] Canada and Abella (1984), p. v. (The terminology used in the report for Indigenous people was "native people" and the term for racialized communities was "visible minorities.") [*Abella Report*].

Canada) recommended that the federal government enact proactive affirmative action initiatives.[23] Rather than using the term "affirmative action," the term used in the United States, she proposed a new term—"employment equity" to describe proactive initiatives to identify and eliminate systemic discrimination in employment.[24]

In implementing her recommendations, the federal government introduced the *Employment Equity Act,* which requires employers to implement employment equity by "identifying and eliminating employment barriers against persons in designated groups" and "instituting such positive policies and practices and making such reasonable accommodations as will ensure that persons in designated groups" have greater representation in the workplace.[25] Employers have reporting obligations under the legislation. The Canadian Human Rights Commission is responsible for ensuring that employers fulfill their obligations under the Act. It also undertakes compliance audits and may issue compliance orders to employers. Disputes regarding compliance are adjudicated by an Employment Equity Review Tribunal.[26]

These proactive employment equity initiatives, however, apply to only a small part of the Canadian workforce.[27] Most provinces have not introduced general employment equity laws; some have legislated obligations to establish employment equity programs with respect to provincial public sector employees.[28]

2.2.2 Pay Equity

Beginning in the late 1980s, provincial governments began enacting pay equity laws—designed to proactively assess equal pay for work of equal value (or comparable work) and in so doing to eliminate gender-based wage discrimination. The provinces of Ontario and Quebec have pay equity laws that apply to both public and private sector employers[29]; four other provinces have public sector pay

---

[23] *Ibid* at 9.

[24] *Ibid* at 7 (She noted that the term *affirmative action* was often associated with quotas and its use might prompt "intellectual resistance and confusion").

[25] *Employment Equity Act, supra* note 17, s 5.

[26] *Ibid,* Part II. (Monetary penalties for non-compliance are also included in the Act, see Part III.).

[27] Coverage extends to about 13–14% of the Canadian workforce. See Evaluation Directorate Strategic Policy and Research Branch Human Resources and Skills Development Canada, *Strategic Evaluation of the Employment Equity Programs,* (Ottawa: HRSDC, November 2012) at 2–3; Population of the Federal Public Service data: https://www.canada.ca/en/treasury-board-secretariat/services/innovation/human-resources-statistics/population-federal-public-service.html.

[28] See, e.g. in Quebec, *An Act Respecting Equal Access to Employment in Public Bodies, supra* note 18. See also, Bakan and Kobayashi (2000).

[29] See *Ontario Pay Equity Act, supra* note 18 (first enacted in 1987); *Quebec Pay Equity Act, supra* note 18 (introduced in 1996). Of note is the absence of proactive pay equity legislation at the federal level: see Andrée Côté & Julie Lassonde, "Status report on pay equity in Canada" (2007) National Association of Women and the Law, Final Report of the Workshop on Pay Equity (Ottawa); House of Commons, Special Committee on Pay Equity, *It's Time to Act* (June 2016) (Chair: Anita Vandenbeld).

equity laws, and three have adopted policy frameworks for pay equity.[30] Pay equity legislative schemes also include complaints mechanisms to address allegations of non-compliance with statutory obligations. Despite these important legislative initiatives, enforcement of pay equity has been difficult and progress has been slow.[31] As noted in the Committee Report of the Office of the United Nations High Commissioner for Human Rights:

The Committee is concerned about the persisting inequalities between women and men. In particular, the Committee is concerned about (a) the high level of the pay gap, which is more pronounced in some provinces such as Alberta and Nova Scotia, and disproportionately affects low-income women, in particular minority and indigenous women.[32]

2.2.3 Proactive Disability Rights

The rights of persons with disabilities have been the focus of a significant proportion of individual complaints with human rights commissions; however, more proactive regulatory initiatives have also been introduced. The province of Ontario has been at the forefront of these initiatives with its 2001 *Ontarians with Disabilities Act* and its more recent *Accessibility for Ontarians with Disabilities Act* in 2005.[33]

2.2.4 Sexual Violence, Harassment and Anti-Racism Initiatives

In an effort to prevent sexual violence and harassment, the provinces of Ontario and Quebec have introduced laws aimed at preventing sexual violence and harassment, including, for example, provisions requiring colleges and universities to develop proactive sexual violence policies.[34]

---

[30]Equal Pay Coalition, "Other Provinces", online: <www.equalpaycoalition.org/history/other-prov inces/>.

[31]Mary Cornish and Jan Borowy, "Brief to the Parliamentary Special Committee on Pay Equity", Ontario Equal Pay Coalition (May 2016) (noting some narrowing of the pay gap); Singh and Peng (2010), p. 570; Armstrong (2007), p. 11; England and Gad (2002), p. 281; See also, Fudge (2007), p. 235.

[32]See United Nations Office of the High Commissioner for Human Rights, "Concluding Observations of the Sixth Periodic Report of Canada" (2015), at 2: online: http://tbinternet.ohchr.org/_layouts/treatybodyexternal/Download.aspx?symbolno=CCPR%2FC%2FCAN%2FCO%2F6&Lang=en.

[33]*Ontarians with Disabilities Act*, supra note 19; *Accessibility for Ontarians with Disabilities Act*, SO 2005, c 11; For an overview of the Ontario disability rights protections, see Mayo Moran, *Legislative Review of Accessibility for Ontarians with Disabilities Act*, 2014, online: <www.ontario.ca/document/legislative-review-accessibility-ontarians-disabilities-act>.

[34]*Supra*, note 19. For an overview of the legislation, see online: https://www.labour.gov.on.ca/english/hs/pubs/wpvh/index.php.

Two important recent initiatives seek to address racism proactively. The *Ontario Anti-Racism Act* requires the provincial government "to maintain an anti-racism strategy [...] to eliminate systemic racism and advance racial equity [...] as well as targets and indicators to measure the strategy's effectiveness."[35] At the federal level, a recent non-binding motion was adopted in the House of Commons condemning "Islamophobia and all forms of systemic racism and religious discrimination" and calls on the government "to develop whole-of-government approach to reducing or eliminating systemic racism".[36]

2.3 Constitutional Equality Rights and Protections Against Discrimination

The major source of constitutional protection against discrimination is the *Canadian Charter of Rights and Freedoms*. Enacted in 1982, with a 3 year implementation delay for the equality rights and antidiscrimination section, the *Charter* extended protection against discrimination to government action and laws at all levels of governance (i.e. federal, provincial, territorial, municipal).[37] The earlier, quasi-constitutional and narrowly interpreted *Canadian Bill of Rights* (which only applies to federal laws and government action) is still in force, though rarely used.[38] The Supreme Court of Canada has also recognized "minority rights" as a fundamental constitutional principle.[39]

The *Canadian Charter of Rights and Freedoms* includes important protections for equality and non-discrimination.[40] In the constitutional domain, an expansive interpretation of discrimination that includes both direct and indirect discrimination has been endorsed and a substantive rather than formal approach to equality adopted.[41] The constitutionality of affirmative action initiatives is explicit in the

---

[35] See *Bill 114, Anti-Racism Act, 2017 Explanatory Note*: http://ontla.on.ca/web/bills/bills_detail.do?locale=en&Intranet=&BillID=4694.

[36] Private Member's Motion M-103, Federal House of Commons, Canada, 23 March 2017: http://www.ourcommons.ca/Parliamentarians/en/members/Iqra-Khalid(88849)/Motions?documentId=8661986%2520&sessionId=152.

[37] *Canadian Charter*, supra note 4.

[38] *Canadian Bill of Rights*, SC 1960, c 44.

[39] *Reference re Secession of Quebec*, [1998] 2 SCR 217, 161 DLR (4th) 385 [*Secession Reference*]; Other constitutional protections extend rights to groups and communities, such as minority language groups (see *Canadian Charter*, §§ 16–23) and Aboriginal peoples (*Constitution Act, 1982*, being Schedule B to the *Canada Act 1982* (UK), 1982, c 11, s 35 [*Constitution Act 1982*]); See Sheppard (2006a), p. 463.

[40] See *Canadian Charter*, §§ 2(a), 15, 16–23, 27, 28; *Constitution Act 1982*, ibid, s 35.

[41] Andrews v. Law Society of British Columbia, [1989] 1 SCR 143, 56 DLR (4th) 1; Law v. Canada (Minister of Employment and Immigration), [1999] 1 SCR 497, 170 DLR (4th) 1; R. v. Kapp, 2008 SCC 41, [2008] 2 SCR 483.

text of the *Charter*.[42] Enforcing and applying constitutional guarantees of equality and non-discrimination in modern regulatory state contexts has nonetheless proved challenging. It has been difficult to assess the fairness of complex legislative schemes that contain numerous regulatory classifications and distinctions. Moreover, the costs and time delays associated with litigating constitutional rights claims have undermined access to justice in the constitutional domain.

Constitutional protections are subject to judicial and administrative adjudicative enforcement.[43] Discrimination in both the administration and the substance of laws may be challenged in the courts and in some administrative tribunals.[44] Unlike initiatives to create a public infrastructure for the enforcement of statutory antidiscrimination laws, constitutional antidiscrimination protections are enforced through regular litigation channels. In 1994, a Court Challenges Program was established to help fund equality and minority language rights claims; in 2006, funding for equality rights challenges was discontinued.[45] This year the program was re-instated and a parliamentary committee has since submitted a report recommending several changes to the program to ensure its sustainability.[46]

2.4 International Protection

A final important source of protection against discrimination in Canadian law is the panoply of international conventions to which Canada is a party.[47] These

---

[42]See *Canadian Charter,* s 15(2); R. v. Kapp, 2008 SCC 41, [2008] 2 SCR 483.

[43]See Sharpe and Roach (2017), ch. 2. See also, *R. v. Conway*, 2010 SCC 22 at paras 20–22, [2010] 1 SCR 765 ("...the principles governing remedial jurisdiction under the Charter apply to both courts and administrative tribunals".).

[44]Administrative tribunals form an integral part of Canada's dispute resolution system. These tribunals are less formal and do not form part of the court system, however their decisions may be reviewed in court. Administrative tribunals that address discrimination cases include human rights tribunals and labour arbitration boards. See Government of Canada, Department of Justice, "Courts and other Bodies under Federal Jurisdiction", online: <www.canada.justice.gc.ca/eng/csj-sjc/ccs-ajc>.

[45]Court Challenges Program, "About CCP", online: <www.ccppcj.ca/en/about.php>.

[46]Court Challenges Program, "Reinstatement News", online: <www.ccppcj.ca/en/news/php>; To access the full report, see, House of Commons, Standing Committee on Justice and Human Rights, *Access to Justice Part 1: Court Challenges Program: Report of the Standing Committee on Justice and Human Rights* (September 2016) (Chair: Anthony Housefather).

[47]See, e.g. *International Covenant on Civil and Political Rights*, 19 December 1966, 999 UNTS 171, s 26 (entered into force 23 March 1976, accession by Canada 19 May 1976); *Convention on the Elimination of All Forms of Discrimination against Women*, 18 December 1979, 1249 UNTS 13, Can TS 1982 No 31, 19 ILM 33 (entered into force 3 September 1981, ratification by Canada 10 December 1981); *International Convention on the Elimination of All Forms of Racial Discrimination*, 7 March 1966, 660 UNTS 212 (entered into force 4 January 1969, ratified by Canada 13 November 1970); *Convention on the Rights of Persons with Disabilities*, 30 March 2007, 2515 UNTS 3 (entered into force 3 May 2008, accession by Canada 11 March 2010).

international conventions, however, require legislative implementation at the domestic level.[48] In certain cases, once domestic remedies have been exhausted, individuals may pursue their complaints with international adjudicative bodies.[49] In the Canadian context, an important historic example of this strategy towards effective enforcement was the Sandra Lovelace case—an Indigenous woman who took her allegations of discrimination against the Canadian government to the International Human Rights Committee under the Covenant on Civil and Political Rights.[50]

3 Scope of Protection: Grounds and Contexts

3.1 Scope of Protection: Protected Grounds of Discrimination

3.1.1 Antidiscrimination Statutes: Grounds of Discrimination

Antidiscrimination laws in Canada (commonly referred to as human rights laws) provide fairly comprehensive grounds-based protection against discrimination (i.e. race, national or ethnic origin, religion, sex, sexual orientation, mental or physical disability, age) in specific contexts (i.e. employment, housing, access to public services). The antidiscrimination laws in each province-territory and the legislation at the federal level only apply to the specific enumerated grounds of discrimination, which are exhaustive. Hence, people who fall into these categories benefit from the protection and enforcement of antidiscrimination law in Canada.

In all jurisdictions, protected grounds include: sex, race, colour, ethnic origin (or ancestry), religion, sexual orientation, disability (including mental and physical disability) and age. With respect to other grounds, there is considerable variability. In some jurisdictions, additional grounds are protected, such as: citizenship, cultural identity, place of origin, gender identity or expression, pregnancy, language, civil status, family status, marital status, social condition, source of income, political belief, political activity, political convictions, disfigurement, Aboriginal origin,

---

[48] See Catherine Morris, Implementation of human rights treaties in Canada, Briefing Note, 1 March 2014, Lawyers' Rights Watch Canada: online: <www.lrwc.org/implementation-of-human-rights-treaties-in-canada-briefing-note/>.

[49] For an overview of the individual complaints mechanisms pursuant to international treaties, see UN, Office of the High Commissioner for Human Rights, "Human Rights Bodies - Complaint Procedures", online: <www.ohchr.org/EN/HRBodies/TBPetitions/Pages/HRTBPetitions.aspx#individualcomm>; See also Canada (2002).

[50] *Sandra Lovelace v. Canada,* Communication No. R.6/24, U.N. Doc. Supp. No. 40 (A/36/40) at 166 (1981).

conviction of an offence for which a pardon has been granted or in respect of which a record of suspension has been ordered, an irrational fear of contracting an illness or disease, and receipt of public assistance (see Appendix).

When new problems of discrimination emerge, an expansive interpretation of existing grounds will often ensure antidiscrimination protection. In some cases, however, advocates seek legislative amendments to recognize new grounds of discrimination. Debates regarding "genetic discrimination" and "transgender discrimination" illustrate these trends.[51] Genetic discrimination may be protected under the rubric of disability or perceived disability.[52] Transgender discrimination has been protected under sex discrimination.[53] Nonetheless, some have maintained that "genetic discrimination" should be accorded explicit protection; similarly, some argue that "gender identity or expression" should be expressly protected.[54]

While there has been fairly comprehensive grounds-based protection in Canada, there have been important critiques of the categorical rigidities of grounds-based approaches and the inability of grounds-based protections to recognize and remedy intersectional, multiple or intragroup discrimination.[55]

3.1.2 Constitutional Protections: Enumerated and Analogous Grounds

Constitutional protections against discrimination are more open-ended and the enumerated list of grounds is not exhaustive. The key equality rights section provides:

> 15(1) Every individual is equal before and under the law and has the right to the equal protection and equal benefit of the law **without discrimination and, in particular,** without discrimination based on race, national or ethnic origin, colour, religion, sex, age or mental or physical disability.[56]

---

[51]Canada, Parliament of Canada, *Genetic Discrimination and Canadian Law,* by Julian Walker, (September 2014) online: <www.parl.gc.ca/Content/LOP/ResearchPublications/2014-90-e.html> [*Walker*].

[52]*Ibid*, at 6.

[53]See, e.g., *XY v. Ministry of Government and Consumer Services* [2012] HRTO 726 (CanLII); *M. L. et Commission des droits de la personne* (1998) CanLII 28 (QC TDP).

[54]See, for e.g., Canadian Coalition for Genetic Fairness, online: <ccgf-cceg.ca/en/home/>. See, for e.g., *An Act to amend the Canadian Human Rights Act and the Criminal Code*, S.C., c. 13, (Royal assent, 19 June 2017), adding gender identity and gender expression as prohibited grounds of discrimination under the *Canadian Human Rights Act*.

[55]See Iyer (1993), p. 179; Sheppard (2001a), p. 893; Réaume (2002), p. 113.

[56]For a concise overview of *Charter* equality and antidiscrimination cases, see Mary C. Hurley, *Charter Equality Rights: Interpretation of Section 15 in Supreme Court of Canada Decisions* (2007), online: <www.parl.gc.ca/content/lop/researchpublications/bp402-e.htm>.

Courts have recognized additional grounds, including "citizenship,"[57] "sexual orientation,"[58] and "marital status."[59] Of particular note is the non-recognition to date of "marginalized economic status or poverty" as an analogous ground.[60]

Another significant feature of the *Charter* is section 15(2) which provides explicit grounds-based protection for "any law, program or activity that has as its object the amelioration of conditions of disadvantaged individuals or groups including those that are disadvantaged because of race, national or ethnic origin, colour, religion, sex, age or mental or physical disability." This provision has been relied upon to protect affirmative action initiatives and special programs from "reverse discrimination" challenges.[61]

3.2 Scope of Protection: In What Context and Sectors Are Individuals and Groups Protected?

3.2.1 Protected Contexts and Sectors: Antidiscrimination Statutes (see Appendix)

Most provincial laws are restricted to certain sectors (mainly employment, services offered to the general public, housing and accommodation, and education). The majority of antidiscrimination cases arise in the employment context, although there have also been a significant number of complaints in educational and health services, housing, as well as access to services normally offered to the public. Explicit statutory protection has also been provided for grounds-based harassment, which has also been understood to constitute a form of discrimination.[62]

It is significant to note the more extensive reach of some provincial human rights legislation.[63] The *Quebec Charter of Human Rights and Freedoms* goes beyond many other provincial human rights codes and provides protection for fundamental rights and freedoms, including the safeguarding of freedom of expression, religion, private life, human dignity, as well as enumerating key economic and social rights.

---

[57] See *Andrews, supra* note 4.

[58] *Egan v. Canada*, [1995] 2 SCR 513.

[59] *Miron v. Trudel*, [1995] 2 SCR 418. Other analogous grounds that have been recognized include: "off reserve Aboriginality residence (*Corbiere v. Canada (Minister of Indian and Northern Affairs)*, [1999] 2 SCR 203).

[60] See *Gosselin v. Québec (Attorney General)*, 2002 SCC 84, [2002] 4 SCR 429 [*Gosselin*]—but in *Falkiner v. Ontario (Minister of Community and Social Services)*, 59 OR (3d) 481 the Court of Appeal of Ontario ruled that "receipt of social assistance" was an analogous ground.

[61] See *Kapp, supra* note 4; *Lovelace v. Ontario*, 2000 SCC 37, [2000] 1 SCR 950; See Sheppard (1993) [Sheppard, *Equity and Equality*].

[62] See *Janzen v. Platy Enterprises Ltd.*, [1989] 1 SCR 1252 [*Janzen*].

[63] See *Quebec Charter, supra* note 18. See also, *Saskatchewan Human Rights Code*, SS 1979, c S-24.1, §§ 4–8 [*Saskatchewan Human Rights Code*].

The *Saskatchewan Human Rights Code* also contains a bill of rights, which provides protection for fundamental freedoms, in addition to antidiscrimination protections.

There are some limitations to the scope of protection. For example, in the province of Quebec, protection against discrimination on the basis of past convictions is not included in the general antidiscrimination protection, but accorded protection only with respect to employment.[64] In Ontario, protection against discrimination on grounds of being in receipt of public assistance is only available with respect to occupancy of accommodation and the right to be free from harassment from one's landlord.[65] Similarly, some specific exemptions reduce protection for certain groups. For example, in Quebec, discrimination based on "age, sex or civil status" in an "insurance or pension contract, a social benefits plan, a retirement, pension or insurance plan, or a public pension or public insurance plan" is deemed non-discriminatory when it is based on actuarial data.[66] In these contexts, "the use of health as a risk determination factor does not constitute discrimination," thus reducing the extent of protection accorded to disability-related discrimination.[67] In British-Columbia, the discriminatory ground "political belief" is only applicable to employment contexts.[68]

In jurisdictions across Canada, the scope of protection is limited by standard statutory defenses, such as *bona fide* qualifications or requirements.[69] Of significance in the Canadian context as well is the commitment to the duty to accommodate to the point of undue hardship, both with respect to direct and indirect discrimination.[70]

3.2.2 The Scope of Constitutional Protections

The *Canadian Charter of Rights and Freedoms* has a broad scope of application to all laws and governmental acts at the federal, provincial and municipal levels of government.[71] As a comprehensive guarantee for equality and non-discrimination, it

---

[64]See *Quebec Charter, supra* note 18 which provides in art 18.2: "No one may dismiss, refuse to hire or otherwise penalize a person in his employment owing to the mere fact that he was convicted of a penal or criminal offence, if the offence was in no way connected with the employment or if the person has obtained a pardon for the offence."

[65]*Human Rights Code*, RSO 1990, c H.19, s 2 [*Ontario Human Rights Code*].

[66]*Quebec Charter, supra* note 18, art 20.1 para 1.

[67]*Ibid*, art 20.1 para 2.

[68]*Human Rights Code*, RSBC 1996, c 210, ss 11, 13–14 [*BC Human Rights Code*].

[69]See *BCGSEU, supra* note 1.

[70]*Ibid*; see also Sheppard (2001b), p. 533; Lepofsky (1993), p. 1. For an explanation of "undue hardship", see, *Council of Canadians with Disabilities v. VIA Rail Canada Inc.*, 2007 SCC 15 at paras 122–123, [2007] 1 SCR 650. The principle of "undue hardship" imposes a duty to accommodate until the burden to accommodate becomes unreasonable.

[71]See *Canadian Charter*, s 32; *RWDSU v. Dolphin Delivery Ltd.*, [1986] 2 SCR 573 at paras 34, 39. The *Canadian Charter* does not apply to interactions between individuals.

can apply to a diverse range of contexts and all sectors of government regulation. Many of the *Charter* equality cases have involved challenges to government benefits schemes and programs.[72] The *Charter* may also be used to challenge limitations, exemptions and exclusions in statutory antidiscrimination laws.[73]

4 Remedies

4.1 *Remedies Under Antidiscrimination Statutes*

Antidiscrimination statutes authorize human rights tribunals to provide an extensive range of remedies in the face of findings of discrimination, including remedies designed to redress past discrimination and those aimed at preventing its recurrence in the future.[74]

4.1.1 Remedies for Past Discrimination

First, human rights tribunals may make orders to cease the discriminatory practice.[75] Second, damages may be ordered to compensate an individual or group of individuals for the harms associated with discrimination. Such compensation may redress tangible material losses (e.g. lost earnings)[76] and/or more intangible moral damages linked to pain and suffering, or injury to dignity, feelings and self-respect.[77] Beyond

---

[72] See, e.g., Law v. Canada (Minister of Employment and Immigration), [1999] 1 SCR 497, 170 DLR (4th) 1; *Gosselin, supra* note 61; *Eldridge v. British Columbia (Attorney General)*, [1997] 3 SCR 624 [*Eldridge*].

[73] See, e.g. *Vriend v. Alberta*, [1998] 1 SCR 493 [*Vriend*]; *Re Blainey and Ontario Hockey Association*, 54 OR (2d) 513 [*Blainey*].

[74] See *Canadian Human Rights Act*, RSC 1985, c H-6, s 53 [*Canadian Human Rights Act*]; *Alberta Human Rights Act*, RSA 2000, c A-25.5, s 32; *BC Human Rights Code, supra* note 67, s 37; *Human Rights Code*, CCSM c H175, s 43 [*Manitoba Human Rights Code*]; *Human Rights Act*, RSNB 2011, c 171, s 23(7) [*NB Human Rights Act*]; *Human Rights Act, Human Rights Act, 2010*, SNL 2010, c H-13.1, s 39 [*NL Human Rights Act*]; *Human Rights Act*, SNWT 2002, c 18, s 62 [*NWT Human Rights Act*]; *Human Rights Act*, RSNS 1989, c 214, s 34(8) [*NS Human Rights Act*]; *Ontario Human Rights Code, supra* note 63, §§ 45.2 and 45.3; *Quebec Charter, supra* note 18, art 49; *Human Rights Act*, RSY 2002, c 116, s 24 [*Yukon Human Rights Act*].

[75] See, e.g. *First Nations Child and Family Caring Society of Canada et al. v. Attorney General of Canada (for the Minister of Indian and Northern Affairs Canada)*, 2016 CHRT 2 at paras 474–484 [*First Nations Caring Society*].

[76] See, e.g., *Denise Seeley c La compagnie des chemins de fer nationaux du Canada*, 2010 TCDP 23 [*Seeley*]; *Whyte v. Canadian National Railway*, 2010 CHRT 22 [*Whyte*].

[77] *Commission des droits de la personne et des droits de la jeunesse c Bathium Canada inc.*, 2015 QCTDP 13 [*Bathium*]; *Commission des droits de la personne et des droits de la jeunesse c 9209-9829 Québec inc.*, 2015 QCTDP 1 [*9209-9829 Québec inc*].

compensatory damages, punitive damages[78] or damages for wilful or reckless conduct may be provided.[79] One recurrent concern with respect to damage awards in antidiscrimination law in Canada is their low monetary value.[80] In some jurisdictions, damages award limits are set by statute.[81] Thirdly, human rights tribunals may make positive orders to remedy the effects of discrimination, including reinstatement orders or other remedies related to the specific case circumstances.[82]

One key theme in Canadian antidiscrimination law is that the primary objective of human rights laws is to compensate the victims (or survivors) of discrimination rather than to punish the perpetrators. As Justice La Forest explained in an important decision imposing employer liability for workplace sexual harassment, "[t]he legislative emphasis on prevention and elimination of undesirable conditions, rather than on fault, moral responsibility and punishment, argues for making the Act's carefully crafted remedies effective."[83]

4.1.2 Systemic Remedies: Proactive and Preventive

Despite reticence on the part of courts and tribunals, human rights legislation across Canada authorizes human rights adjudicators to order remedies that are directed towards prevention of future problems of discrimination.[84] More proactive orders may include mandated policy changes (e.g. selection criteria, recruitment practices and advertising)[85]; sensitivity and antidiscrimination training for managers, supervisors and/or employees,[86] and the setting up of a committee to monitor the implementation of antidiscrimination measures.[87]

---

[78]*Ibid.*

[79]*Seeley, supra* note 77; *Whyte, supra* note 77.

[80]See, e.g. *Pinto, supra* note 10 at 71.

[81]See, e.g. *Canadian Human Rights Act, supra* note 74, s 53(3) ($20,000).

[82]See, e.g., "restore the Complainant's pension benefits to the position they were in at the time of her layoff" (*Grant v. Manitoba Telecom Services Inc.*, 2012 CHRT 20); "Ms. Nicolosi is to be placed at the top of the VGHC waiting list and offered the next two-bedroom unit that becomes available. The Board will consider Ms. Nicolosi's application on the basis that the Membership Committee has recommended her and that all references have been successfully checked" (*Nicolosi v. Victoria Gardens Housing Co-operative and another (No. 2)*, 2013 BCHRT 1).

[83]*Robichaud v. Canada (Treasury Board)*, [1987] 2 SCR 84 at para 15.

[84]See *CN, supra* note 16 at 1142.

[85]*Commission des droits de la personne et des droits de la jeunesse c Gaz métropolitain inc.*, 2008 QCTDP 24 (confirmed by the QCCA) [*Gaz métropolitain*]; *National Capital Alliance on Race Relations v. Canada (Department of Health & Welfare)*, 1997 CanLII 1433 (CHRT) [*NCARR*]; *Action Travail des Femmes v. Canadian National Railway*, 1984 CanLII 9 (CHRT) (confirmed by [1987] 1 SCR 1114).

[86]*Gaz métropolitain, Ibid; NCARR, ibid.*

[87]See *CN, supra* note 16; *Gaz métropolitain, supra* note 86; *NCARR, supra* note 86.

In many jurisdictions, antidiscrimination statutes also specifically authorize human rights tribunals to order employers to develop a pay equity plan[88] and/or an affirmative action or employment equity program.[89] In the leading Supreme Court of Canada decision affirming the authority of human rights tribunals to order affirmative action programs, Chief Justice Dickson explained that, "[s]ystemic remedies must be built upon the experience of the past so as to prevent discrimination in the future."[90] In a more recent case, however, which involved discrimination and learning disabilities in schools, the Supreme Court of Canada was more reticent to endorse proactive systemic remedies. In finding the systemic remedies too remote, the Court indicated that human rights tribunals should ensure that the remedies they order are closely linked to the circumstances of the individual case.[91]

4.2 Constitutional Remedies

In cases involving constitutional violations of discrimination, remedies may be provided to individuals directly affected by the discriminatory application, implementation or enforcement of the law. These remedies may include declaratory relief, injunctive relief, and/or damages.[92] Constitutional equality rights challenges may also result in a finding that the substance of the law is discriminatory, in which case, remedies may include striking down the law in whole or in part.[93]

---

[88] *Newfoundland and N.A.P.E., Re,* 2004 SCR 3; *Public Service Alliance of Canada v. Canada (Treasury Board),* 1991 CanLII 387 (CHRT).

[89] *Commission des droits de la personne du Québec c Commission scolaire régionale Chauveau,* 1993 CanLII 7 (QCTDP); *Gaz métropolitain, supra* note 86.

[90] *CN, supra* note 16 at 1145.

[91] See *Moore v. British Columbia (Education),* [2012] 3 SCR 360 [*Moore*]. While the Supreme Court of Canada noted at para 55 that the remedial order of an administrative tribunal should only be overturned if "patently unreasonable," it found at para 57 that the systemic remedies were not warranted. See also, Vizkelety (2015), p. 43. See also, Brodsky et al. (2017), p. 1.

[92] See *Canadian Charter,* s. 24(1); See *Nelles v. Ontario,* [1989] 2 SCR 170; *Little Sisters Book and Art Emporium v. Canada (Minister of Justice),* [2000] 2 SCR 1120; For an overview of *Charter* remedies, see Roach (2013), p. 473.

[93] See *Constitution Act 1982,* s. 52(1).

5 Public Responsibility, Civil Society and the Role of Private Actors

The general principles of equality and non-discrimination are widely endorsed in Canadian society. Indeed, the Supreme Court of Canada has indicated that the protection of minority rights is "an independent principle underlying our constitutional order."[94] The initial regulatory model of antidiscrimination enforcement contemplated publically funded human rights commissions receiving retroactive complaints and ensuring access to justice by investigating and assuming responsibility for the carriage of these complaints to a specialized human rights tribunal. As this system became mired in delay and underfunding, community-based civil society organizations became increasingly implicated in supporting individuals in taking cases to human rights commissions and tribunals, and in ensuring more effective enforcement.[95] In the constitutional context, where the costs of challenging laws and government acts are formidable, advocacy organizations and also labour unions (in many employment-related cases) have played a critically important role.[96] There have also been debates about the fairness of affirmative action measures in Canada, although to a much lesser degree than in many other countries. In part, this is due to the express protection granted to affirmative action in both the constitution and antidiscrimination laws.[97]

In key constitutional equality rights cases, civil society organizations have also intervened to ensure a wide range of perspectives and arguments are presented.[98] Such cases have also prompted the legal intervention of civil society organizations that oppose the arguments advanced by equality-seeking groups.[99]

---

[94]See *Secession Reference, supra* note 40 at para 80; See generally, paras 79–82.

[95]See, e.g., Centre de Recherche-Action sur les Relations Raciales, online: <www.crarr.org>; Canadian Civil Liberties Association, online: <https://ccla.org/>; Egale Canada Human Rights Trust, online: <http://egale.ca/>.

[96]See Sheppard, *Inclusive Equality, supra* note 2.

[97]*Canadian Charter*, s. 15(2); *Quebec Charter, supra* note 18, arts 86–92; *An Act Respecting Equal Access to Employment in Public Bodies, supra* note 18; *Employment Equity Act, supra* note 17; *Canadian Human Rights Act, supra* note 75, §§ 16–17; See Sheppard, *Equity and Equality, supra* note 62.

[98]See, e.g., Women's Legal Education and Action Fund, online: <http://www.leaf.ca/>; Canadian Doctors for Refugee Care, online: <www.doctorsforrefugeecare.ca>; Action travail des femmes, online: <www.atfquebec.ca>.

[99]See, for e.g., same sex marriage opponents such as Real Women of Canada, online: <www.realwomenofcanada.ca>.

6 Effective Enforcement and Different Grounds of Protection

In both the statutory and the constitutional context, the degree of protection and legal processes for implementation and enforcement are the same, regardless of which ground (or combination of grounds) of discrimination is being advanced. Human rights commissions are also mandated to provide protection for all of the enumerated grounds included in the relevant statutory provisions for their jurisdiction. While judges, adjudicators and legislators have recognized compound and intersectional discrimination, there remains a tendency in actual cases to focus on single grounds rather than adopting an intersectional analysis.[100] There is still, therefore, a risk that some more complex forms of discrimination may fail to be recognized by Canadian courts and tribunals.[101]

In terms of which types of discrimination tend to be the focus of discrimination complaints and/or *Charter* challenges, data from human rights commission and tribunal annual reports provide us with some important insights.[102] The vast majority of the statutory human rights complaints arise in the employment context. A large number concern race and sex discrimination, including sexual harassment. It is noteworthy that many discrimination complaints deal with disability, though in many cases, it is not the most vulnerable members of the community of persons with disabilities who bring complaints, but rather those who are involved in employment or educational institutions. There are relatively few complaints alleging discrimination based on sexual orientation, marital status and religious discrimination.

In the constitutional context, there have been a few very high profile and successful cases dealing with discrimination on the basis of sexual orientation,[103] as well as discrimination based on disability and religion.[104] There have been very

---

[100] See Bilge and Roy (2010), p. 1.

[101] *Ibid*; See also, Iyer (1993), p. 179; Ontario, Ontario Human Rights Commission, "An Intersectional Approach to Discrimination: Addressing Multiple Grounds in Human Rights Claims", Policy and Education Branch (Toronto: Ontario Human Rights Commission, 9 October 2001).

[102] Canada, Canadian Human Rights Commission, *2014 Annual Report*, (Minister of Public Works and Government Services, 2015); Ontario, Social Justice Tribunals Ontario, *2013–2014 Annual Report*; Quebec, Tribunal des droits de la personne, *Bilan d'activités 2013–2014*, (Mars 2015); British Columbia, BC Human Rights Tribunal, *Annual Report 2014–2015*, (June 2015); Alberta, Alberta Human Rights Commission, *Annual Report 2013–2014;* Manitoba, Manitoba Human Rights Commission, *Annual Report 2013*; New Brunswick, New Brunswick Human Rights Commission, *Annual Report 2013–2014,* (September 2014); Newfoundland and Labrador, Newfoundland Labrador Human Rights Commission, *Annual Report 2014–2015*; Prince Edward Island, Prince Edward Island Human Rights Commission, *Annual Report 2013–2014*; Saskatchewan, Saskatchewan Human Rights Commission, *Annual Report 2013/2014*.

[103] *Halpern v. Canada (AG)*, 65 OR (3d) 161; *Vriend, supra* note 74.

[104] See *Eldridge, supra* note 73; *Eaton v. Brant County Board of Education*, [1997] 1 SCR 241; *Multani v. Commission scolaire Marguerite-Bourgeoys*, [2006] 1 SCR 256.

few gender-based equality rights cases and even fewer cases dealing with racial discrimination.[105]

In interpreting these observations, it is important to take into account a number of factors that may influence the number of complaints brought by different groups, including, (1) the actual incidence of discrimination against particular groups in society; (2) the degree of vulnerability of different group(s) and the extent to which they are able to access the legal system; (3) the extent to which it is more or less difficult to prove some forms of discrimination, making it more or less likely that a group will seek vindication through legal channels. In considering these factors, it is extremely troubling, for example, when there is a high incidence of discrimination and a low number of complaints. Indeed, this would appear to be the case with respect to Indigenous people in Canada, and certain religious minority groups.[106] Similarly, some types of discrimination (e.g. racial profiling, unconscious bias, systemic discrimination) are difficult to prove, making it less likely for complaints to proceed or succeed.[107]

7 Individual Versus Systemic Approaches

One critical underlying assumption of more traditional antidiscrimination law, with its focus on retroactive individual complaints, is that the institutional and social *status quo* is generally fair and equitable; retroactive redress is required only for aberrant and exceptional instances of discrimination. As it becomes increasingly apparent that many problems of discrimination are not isolated incidents, but rather pervasive and often embedded in apparently neutral rules, practices and policies, the adequacy of the traditional model comes into question. Thus, the expansion in conceptions of discrimination to embrace indirect and systemic discrimination has raised questions about the inadequacy of a retroactive individual complaints approach to enforcement. At the same time, individual complaints have an increased potential to lead to greater institutional and structural change in a legal context where we are witnessing expanding definitions of discrimination and more proactive remedies.

For example, legal recognition of adverse effects discrimination brought into question apparently neutral institutional rules, policies and laws. The remedial response includes either the elimination of the rule, policy or law, or some kind of individual or group accommodation (or legal exemption) to address the negative effects of the facially neutral rule or policy. Thus, recognition of adverse effects

---

[105] See, e.g., Rodgers et al. (2006), Faraday et al. (2006), Tanovich (2008), p. 655.

[106] See, e.g., Canada, Canadian Human Rights Commission (2014).

[107] See, e.g., *Peel Law Association v. Pieters*, 2013 ONCA 396 (Can LII), 116 OR (3d) 81; *Shaw v. Phipps*, 2012 ONCA 155 (Can LII); *Radek v. Henderson Development (Canada) Ltd*, 2005 BCHRT 302.

discrimination moves us in the direction of systemic institutional and legal change. This shift may occur even in the wake of an individual complaint.[108]

Although it has proven very difficult to litigate, the concept of systemic discrimination in individual cases attests even more to the potential for individual or group-based complaints to lead to broader systemic change. As Justice Abella explained in her *Equality in Employment Report*, "[s]ystemic discrimination requires systemic remedies. Rather than approaching discrimination from the perspective of the single perpetrator and the single victim, the systemic approach acknowledges that by and large the systems and practices we customarily and often unwittingly adopt may have an unjustifiably negative effect on certain groups in society".[109]

The concept of systemic discrimination allows us to understand new forms of discrimination, which are impossible to see if we only use an individual discrimination framework. Moreover, to remedy systemic discrimination effectively, broader institutional and societal change is needed.

In addition to understanding how an expansive interpretation of the concept of discrimination provides a greater likelihood that individual cases will lead to broader systemic change, it is also important to highlight the important connections between the legal meaning of equality and discrimination. Most notably, the concept of substantive equality in Canadian law (with its recognition that equitable outcomes may require differential treatment and its concern for the adverse effects of apparently neutral laws and policies) is closely linked to expansive definitions of discrimination.[110] The inclusion of explicit antidiscrimination protections in the constitutional equality rights section may explain the interplay between these two concepts.[111] In relation to the broader goals of equality, as the legal concept of discrimination expanded, a conceptual convergence emerged between the goals of antidiscrimination law and the ideals of societal equality.[112] This is particularly the case to the extent that discrimination in government policies and laws may be contested.

Overlap between the statutory and constitutional domains is also apparent in relation to section 15(2), which endorses the constitutionality of special group-based programs. Such a provision is in line with antidiscrimination statutes that also include explicit protection for affirmative action remedies and special programs.[113] Section 15(2) has also been interpreted as a provision that reinforces the substantive conception of equality in Canadian law.[114] The Supreme Court of Canada has

---

[108] See, e.g. *Eldridge, supra* note 73; *Moore, supra* note 92.

[109] *Abella Report, supra* note 23.

[110] See, e.g. *First Nations Caring Society, supra* note 76.

[111] Andrews v. Law Society of British Columbia, [1989] 1 SCR 143, 56 DLR (4th) 1 (importance of discrimination in section 15).

[112] Sheppard (2012), pp. 1–2.

[113] See, e.g., *Ontario Human Rights Code, supra* note 65, s 14(1); *Quebec Charter, supra* note 18, art 86.

[114] See R. v. Kapp, 2008 SCC 41, [2008] 2 SCR 483.

explained that the affirmative action provision in the Canadian Charter "is aimed at permitting governments to *improve* the situation of members of disadvantaged groups that have suffered discrimination in the past, in order to enhance substantive equality."[115]

Canadian antidiscrimination and equality rights law, however, has done little to address systemic socio-economic inequalities. Although some provincial human rights laws include "social condition" or "receipt of social assistance" as grounds of discrimination, poverty has generally not been recognized as a ground of discrimination.[116] There has been resistance to acknowledging economic inequalities as discrimination perhaps in part due to the very pervasiveness of such inequities. The appropriate limits of the judiciary in relation to resource allocation issues, and concerns about positive rights, have been raised in cases involving allegations of economic inequality and discrimination. Legal responses to poverty and economic inequality, therefore, have been limited to instances where poverty is linked to other grounds of discrimination (e.g. feminization of poverty, elderly poor, persons with disabilities, Aboriginal people). Indeed, poverty is disproportionately experienced by many of the groups targeted by antidiscrimination law; it remains one of the most significant and deleterious effects of discrimination.[117]

8 The Challenges and Specificity of Enforcing Antidiscrimination Law

Antidiscrimination laws enjoy a special status in Canada. The Supreme Court of Canada "has repeatedly reiterated the view that human rights legislation has a unique quasi-constitutional nature and ought to be interpreted in a liberal and purposive manner in order to advance the broad policy considerations underlying it".[118] As noted above, concerns about facilitating access to justice were reflected in the establishment of human rights commissions and specialized human rights tribunals.

Despite this juridical endorsement of antidiscrimination law and political support for human rights infrastructures to enhance timely and inexpensive access to justice, securing the effective enforcement of human rights laws in Canada has proven difficult. Significant erosion in public funding of human rights infrastructures has been documented and extensive delays in the human rights commission process has prompted widespread concern.[119] Moreover, effective enforcement continues to be a challenge, not only in relation to individual complaints of discrimination, but also

---

[115]*Ibid.* at para 40 (emphasis added).

[116]See, e.g., *Quebec Charter, supra* note 18; *Ontario Human Rights Code, supra* note 66; See Appendix.

[117]See Sheppard (2015), p. 225, online: <opo.iisj.net/index.php/osls/article/view/439/561>.

[118]*B v. Ontario (Human Rights Commission)*, [2002] 3 SCR 403 at para 44.

[119]See Eliadis (2014).

with respect to proactive legislative and policy initiatives.[120] For example, the federal government's 2014 progress report on the implementation of employment equity by federally-regulated private sector employers reveals very slow progress, particularly for persons with disabilities.[121] In Quebec, research reveals inadequate enforcement of employment equity over the past 25 years.[122] In its 2015 study of the Quebec police force, the Quebec Human Rights and Youth Rights Commission reported that little or no progress has been made in increasing the representation of diverse groups, including women, racialized minorities, Aboriginal peoples and persons with disabilities.[123] As discussed above, the enforcement of pay equity has also been difficult and very little progress made in closing the wage gap.[124]

In addition to weaknesses in government enforcement of antidiscrimination laws and proactive equity laws, Canada has also experienced resistance to the potential transformative effects of equality rights.[125] The media has at times been a forum for the expression of discontent with human rights laws, particularly employment equity initiatives.[126] In a world of both overt and unconscious bias, the challenge to secure greater equity and inclusion in Canadian society continues.[127]

---

[120] See Agócs, *supra*, note 21.

[121] Canada, Employment and Social Development Canada (2014).

[122] *Ibid.* at 97.

[123] Quebec, Quebec Human Rights and Youth Rights Commission, *L'accès à l'égalité en emploi: rapport sectoriel sur les effectifs policiers de la Sûreté du Québec: Loi sur l'accès à l'égalité en emploi dans des organismes publics* (2015).

[124] See *supra*, s. 1.2.2.

[125] See Sheppard (2006b), p. 251.

[126] See, e.g. Mathieu Bock-Côté, "Abolir la Commission des droits", *Le Journal de Montréal*, (1 August 2015), online : <www.journaldemontreal.com/2015/08/01/abolir-la-commission-des-droits>; Patrick Lagacé, "Jérémy Gabriel c. Mike Ward", *La Presse*, (26 September 2015), online : <www.lapresse.ca/debats/chroniques/patrick-lagace/201509/23/01-4903096-jeremy-gabriel-c-mike-ward.php>; Chris Doucette, "White worker says Canada Revenue Agency discriminated against him", Toronto Sun, (28 October 2015), online: <www.torontosun.com/2015/10/28/white-worker-sues-canadarevenue-agency-for-discrimination> (A white man took his unsuccessful human rights complaint to federal court claiming that the employment equity laws were subjecting him to discrimination); Catherine Girouard, "Cachez cette grossesse que je ne saurais voir...", Journal Métro, (29 November 2015), online: <journalmetro.com/plus/carrieres/882353/cachez-cette-grossesse-que-je-ne-sauraisvoir/>.

[127] See, e.g. Oreopoulos and Dechief (2011).

9 Conclusion: Canadian Law and Society Through the Lens of Antidiscrimination Law

As in many countries around the world, Canada has fairly comprehensive antidiscrimination protection secured in both its legislative and constitutional law. At the same time, the effective enforcement of antidiscrimination laws and proactive equity initiatives has proven to be a formidable challenge. Access to justice, especially for the most vulnerable members of protected groups, continues to be limited. Increasingly, individuals need the support of civil society or community-based organizations to advance antidiscrimination claims, particularly in the constitutional domain. The shift to proactive equity strategies in the employment domain is a promising and important response to the limitations of the retroactive individual complaints approach, but results are disappointing and enforcement is slow. Progress is no doubt further impeded by changing social, political and economic realities—economic downturns thwart new hiring, prompt layoffs and create the social conditions for the emergence of heightened backlash against equity and diversity.[128] The invisibility of privilege in the institutional *status quo* continues and is embedded in the unconscious bias of myriad everyday decisions.[129]

Despite continuing challenges, there have been some critical advances and important victories. Antidiscrimination laws and constitutional protections for equality and non-discrimination provide an essential vehicle for raising concerns about social injustice and seeking remedies in the legal system. Such an approach to vindicating and advancing the rights of historically disadvantaged groups and communities resonates with a deep commitment to the rule of law—both in terms of retroactive complaints and proactive legislative reform.

Acknowledgements I wish to thank Vanessa Clermont-Isabelle, Shereen Aly and Rebecca Jones for their excellent research assistance. I also wish to acknowledge support from the Social Sciences and Humanities Research Council of Canada, through its funding of my research project on systemic discrimination.

---

[128] See Otobe (2011).

[129] Sheppard (2013), pp. 107–110.

Appendix

Federal—*Canadian Human Rights A*ct, RSC 1985, c H-6	
Protected grounds	Race—National or ethnic origin—Colour—Religion—Age—Sex—Sexual orientation—Marital status—Family status—Disability—Conviction for an offence for which a pardon has been granted or in respect of which a record suspension has been ordered—Gender identity or expression
Protected areas	Denial of good, service, facility or accommodation (s.5)—Denial of commercial premises or residential accommodation (s.6)—Employment (s.7, 8, 9, 10)—Equal wages (s. 11)—Publication of discriminatory notices, etc. (s.12)—Harassment (s.14)
Ontario—*Human Rights Code*, RSO 1990, c H.19	
Protected grounds	Age—Ancestry, colour, race—Citizenship—Ethnic origin—Place of origin—Creed—Disability—Family status—Marital status (including single status)—Gender identity, gender expression—Receipt of public assistance (in housing only)—Record of offences (in employment only)—Sex (including pregnancy and breastfeeding)—Sexual orientation
Protected areas	Services (s.1)—Accommodation (s.2)—Contracts (s.3)—Employment (s.5)—Vocational association (s.6)—Sexual harassment (s.7)
Quebec—*Charter of human rights and freedoms*, CQLR c C-12	
Protected grounds	Race—Colour—Sex—Pregnancy—Sexual orientation—Civil status—Age except as provided by law—Religion—Political convictions—Language—Ethnic or national origin—Social condition—A handicap or the use of any means to palliate a handicap
Protected areas	Harassment (s. 10.1)—Notice, symbol or sign (s. 11)—Juridical act (s.12, s.13)—Access to public space (s.15)—Employment (s.16, 18, 18.1, 18.2—criminal offence)—Discriminatory association (s.17)
British Columbia—*Human Rights Code*, RSBC 1996, c 210	
Protected grounds	Race—Colour—Ancestry—Place of origin—Religion—Marital status—Family status (except in purchase of property)—Physical or mental disability—Sex—Sexual orientation—Age—Criminal conviction (only in employment and membership in a union or occupational association)—Political belief (only in employment, employment advertisements, and membership in a union or occupational association)—Source of income (only in tenancy)
Protected areas	Publication (s.7)—Accommodation, service and facility (s.8)—Purchase of property (s.9)—Tenancy premises (s.10)—Employment advertisements (s.11)—Wages (s.12)—Employment (s.13)—/unions and associations (s.14)
Alberta—*Alberta Human Rights Act*, RSA 2000, c A-25.5	
Protected grounds	Race—Religious beliefs—Colour—Gender—Physical disability—Mental disability—Ancestry—Age (except in tenancy and goods, services, accommodation)—Place of origin—Place of birth—Marital status—Source of income—Family status—Sexual orientation
Protected areas	Publications, notices (s.3)—Goods, services, accommodation, facilities (s.4)—Tenancy (s.5)—Employment practices (s.7)—Applications and advertisements re employment (s.8)—Membership in trade union, etc. (s.9)
Manitoba—*The Human Rights Code*, CCSM c H175	
Protected grounds	Ancestry, including colour and perceived race—Nationality or national origin—Ethnic background or origin—Religion or creed, or religious belief, religious association or religious activity—Age

(continued)

	Sex—Gender identity—Sexual orientation—Marital or family status—Source of income—Political belief, political association or political activity—Physical or mental disability—Social disadvantage
Protected areas	Service, accommodation, etc. (s.13)—Employment (s.14)—Contracts (s.15)—Rental of premises (s.16)—Purchase of real property (s.17)—Signs and statements (s.18)—Discriminatory Harassment (s.19)—Discriminatory reprisals (s.20)
Saskatchewan—*The Saskatchewan Human Rights Code*, SS 1979, c S-24.1	
Protected grounds	Sexual orientation—Ancestry—Colour—Race—Nationality—Place of origin—Receipt of public assistance—Disability—Age—Religion—Family status—Marital status—Sex—Gender identity
Protected areas	Occupation (s.9)—Purchase of property (s.10)—Occupancy of commercial unit or housing accommodation (s.11)—Places to which public admitted (s.12)—Education (s.13)—Publications (s.14)—Contracts (s.15)—Employment (s.16–19)
New Brunswick—*Human Rights Act*, RSNB 2011, c 171	
Protected grounds	Race—Colour—National origin—Place of origin—Ancestry—Religion—Age—Marital status Sex—Sexual orientation—Physical or mental disability—Social condition—Political belief or activity
Protected areas	Employment (s.4)—Housing and sale of property (s.5)—Accommodation and services (s.6)—Notices or signs (s.7)—Professional, business or trade association (s.8)—Sexual harassment (s.10)
Nova Scotia—*Human Rights Act*, RSNS 1989, c 214	
Protected grounds	Age—Race—Colour—Religion—Creed—Ethnic, national or aboriginal origin—Sex—Sexual orientation—Disability—Family status—Marital status—Source of income—Irrational fear of contracting an illness or disease—Association with protected groups or individuals—Political belief, affiliation or activity—Gender Identity/Gender Expression
Protected areas	(s.5(1)) Provision of or access to services or facilities—Accommodation—Purchase or sale of property—Employment—Volunteer public service—Publication, broadcast or advertisement—Membership in a professional association or organization—Harassment (s.5(2) and (3))—Publication (s.7)—Employment (s.8)
Prince Edward Island—*Human Rights Act*, RSPEI 1988, c H-12	
Protected grounds	Age—Colour, Race, Ethnic or National Origin—Criminal Conviction—Family or Marital Status—Gender Identity—Political Belief—Sexual Orientation—Association (with an individual or group of individuals who is protected under the Act)—Creed or Religion—Disability—Gender Expression—Sex or Gender—Source of Income
Protected areas	Accommodation (s.2)—Occupancy rights (s.3)—Property sales (s.4)—Employment (s.6, 7)—Association (s.8, 9)—Public functions and organizations (s.10)—Advertising (s.12)
Newfoundland—*Human Rights Act,* 2010, SNL 2010, c H-13.1	
Protected grounds	Race—Colour—Nationality—Ethnic origin—Social origin—Religious creed—Religion—Age—Disability—Disfigurement—Sex—Sexual orientation—Marital status—Family status—Source of income—Political opinion

(continued)

Protected areas	Goods, services, accommodation, and facilities (s.11)—Right to occupy commercial and dwelling units (s.12)—Harassment of occupant prohibited (s.13)—Employment (s.14, 15)—Harassment (s.17,18)—Publications (s. 19)—Contracts (s.21)
Northwest Territories—*Human Rights Act*, SNWT 2002, c 18	
Protected grounds	Race, Colour, Ancestry, Place of Origin, Ethnic Origin, Nationality—Religion or Creed—Age –Disability—Sex—Sexual orientation—Gender identity—Marital Status—Family Status—Family affiliation—Political belief, political association—Social condition—Pardoned criminal conviction or record suspension
Protected areas	Employment (s.7, 9)—Organizations (s.10)—Goods, services, accommodation and facilities (s.11)—Tenancy (s.12)—Publications (s.13)—Harassment (s.14)
Yukon—*Human Rights Act*, RSY 2002, c 116	
Protected grounds	Ancestry, including colour and race—National origin—Ethnic or linguistic background/origin—Religion or creed—Age—Sex—Sexual orientation—Disability—Criminal charges or criminal record Political belief, association, or activity—Marital or family status—Source of income—Actual or presumed association with any of the grounds listed above
Protected areas	Goods and services (s.9a)—Employment, and any aspect of employment (s.9b, c)—Housing, leasing or renting (s. 9d)—Public Contracts (s.9e)—Harassment (s.14)
Nunavut—*Human Rights Act,* Snu 2003, c 12	
Protected grounds	Race—Colour—Ancestry—Ethnic origin—Citizenship—Place of origin—Religion—Creed—Age—Disability—Sex—Sexual orientation—Marital and family status—Pregnancy—Lawful source of income—A conviction for which a pardon has been granted
Protected areas	Harassment (s.7(6))—Employment (s.9)—Organizations and associations (s.11)—Goods, services, facilities, contracts (s.12)—Tenancy (s.13)—Publications (s.14)

References

Agócs C (ed) (2014) Employment equity in Canada: the legacy of the Abella Report. University of Toronto Press, Toronto

Armstrong P (2007) Back to basics: seeking pay equity for women in Canada. Labour Ind 18(2):11 (A journal of the social and economic relations of work)

Bakan A, Kobayashi A (2000) Employment equity policy in Canada: an interprovincial comparison/Politique d'équité en matière d'emploi au Canada: une comparaison interprovinciale. Status of Women Canada, Ottawa

Bilge S, Roy O (2010) La discrimination intersectionnelle: la naissance et le développement d'un concept et les paradoxes de sa mise en application en droit antidiscriminatoire. Can J Law Soc 25:1

Brodsky G, Day S, Kelly F (2017) The authority of human rights tribunals to grant systemic remedies. Can J Human Rights 6(1):1

Brunelle C (2015) Chapitre VI - La mise en œuvre des droits et libertés en vertu de la Charte québécoise. In: Collection de droit 2015–2016. Y. Blais, Cowansville, p 11

Canada, Abella RS (1984) Report of the commission on equality in employment. Minister of Supply and Services Canada, Ottawa, p v

Canada (2002) Canada and the optional protocol to the convention to the convention on the elimination of all forms of discrimination against women: an overview. Status of Women, Canada. http://publications.gc.ca/collections/Collection/SW21-92-1-2002E.pdf

Canada, Canadian Human Rights Commission (2014) Special Report to Parliament on the Impact of Bill C-21. Minister of Public Works and Government Services, Ottawa

Canada, Employment and Social Development Canada (2014) Employment equity act Annual Report 2014. Employment and Social Development Canada, Ottawa

Clément D, Canadian Human Rights Commission (2012) The evolution of human rights in Canada. Canadian Human Rights Commission, Ottawa

Eliadis P (2014) Speaking out on human rights: debating Canada's human rights system. McGill-Queens University Press, Montreal, pp 26, 153

England K, Gad G (2002) Social policy at work? Equality and equity in women's paid employment in Canada. GeoJournal 56(4):281

Faraday F, Denike M, Kate Stephenson M (eds) (2006) Making equality rights real: securing substantive equality under the charter. Irwin Law, Toronto

Flaherty M (2013) Ontario and the direct access model to human rights. In: Day S, Lamarche L, Norman K (eds) Arguments for human rights institutions in Canada, vol 22. Irwin Law, Toronto, p 169

Fudge J (2007) Substantive equality, the Supreme Court of Canada, and the limits to redistribution. S Afr J Human Rights 23:235

Iyer N (1993) Categorical denials: equality rights and the shaping of social identity. Queen's Law J 19:179

Lepofsky D (1993) The duty to accommodate: a purposive approach. Can Lab Law J 1:1

Oreopoulos P, Dechief D (2011) Why do some employers prefer to interview Matthew, but not Samir? New evidence from Toronto, Montreal, and Vancouver. Metropolis British Columbia

Otobe N (2011) International Labour Office & Employment Sector, Global economic crisis, gender and employment: the impact and policy response. ILO, Geneva

Pinto A (2013) Ontario & Ministry of the Attorney General, Report of the Ontario Human Rights Review 2012. Ontario Ministry of the Attorney General, Toronto

Réaume DG (2002) Of pigeonholes and principles: a reconsideration of discrimination law. Osgoode Hall Law J 40:113

Roach K (2013) Enforcement of the charter: subsections 24(1) and 52(1). SCLR (2d) 62:473

Rodgers S, McIntyre S, Eberts M (eds) (2006) Strategizing systemic inequality claims: equality rights and the charter. LexisNexis, Toronto

Sharpe RJ, Roach K (2017) The Canadian charter of rights and freedoms, 6th edn. Irwin Law, Toronto, ch. 2

Sheppard C (1993) Study paper on litigating the relationship between equity and equality. Ontario Law Reform Commission, Toronto

Sheppard C (2001a) Grounds of discrimination: towards an inclusive and contextual approach. Can Bar Rev 80:893

Sheppard C (2001b) Of forest fires and systemic discrimination: a review of British Columbia (Public Service Employee Relations Commission) v. B.C.G.S.E.U. RD McGill 46:533

Sheppard C (2006a) Constitutional recognition of diversity. Vermont Law Rev 30:463

Sheppard C (2006b) Constitutional equality and shifting conceptions of the role of the state: obstacles and possibilities. In: Rodgers S, McIntyre S, Eberts M (eds) Strategizing systemic inequality claims: equality rights and the charter. LexisNexis, Toronto, p 251

Sheppard C (2010) Inclusive equality – the relational dimensions of systemic discrimination in Canada. McGill-Queen's University Press, Montreal

Sheppard C (2012) Mapping antidiscrimination onto inequality at work: expanding the meaning of equality in international labour law. Int Labour Rev 151:1–2

Sheppard C (2013) Institutional inequality and the dynamics of courage. Windsor YB Access Just 31:107–110
Sheppard C (2015) "Bread and Roses": economic justice and constitutional rights. Onati Socio-Legal Ser 5(1):225
Singh P, Peng P (2010) Canada's bold experiment with pay equity. Gender Manage Int J 25(7):570
Tanovich D (2008) The charter of whiteness: twenty-five years of maintaining racial injustice in the Canadian criminal justice system. SCLR (2d) 40:655
Tarnopolsky WS (1982) Discrimination and the law in Canada. R. De Boo, Toronto
Vizkelety B (2015) Les développements jurisprudentiels relatifs à l' "égalité réelle" en emploi: maintenant aux employeurs d'agir. In Barreau du Québec, Le tribunal des droits de la personne: 25 ans d'expérience en matière d'égalité. Éditions Yvon Blais, Montréal, p 43

Colleen Sheppard is a Professor of Law at the Faculty of Law, McGill University, Montreal and a member of the McGill Centre for Human Rights and Legal Pluralism. A graduate of University of Toronto and Harvard University, her teaching and research focus on equality rights, antidiscrimination and constitutional law. Selective publications include: Inclusive Equality: The Relational Dimensions of Systemic Discrimination in Canada (McGill-Queen's, 2010) and "Inclusive equality and new approaches to discrimination in transnational labour law" in A. Blackett & A. Trebilcock, eds., Research Handbook on Transnational Labour Law (Edward Elgar, 2015).

Canada

Stéphane Beaulac

1 Introduction

Dans le cadre du présent rapport, la terminologie employée n'est pas parfaitement uniforme avec la formule retenue pour le thème, soit le « droit à la non-discrimination ». Il faut en effet reconnaître que la problématique qui nous intéresse est parfois abordée en termes de « droit à l'égalité », d'autres fois eu égard à la dimension de « discrimination » (ou de « non-discrimination »), ou encore en combinant les deux facettes en parlant alors du « droit à l'égalité sans discrimination ». Ici, les trois expressions seront utilisées et il ne faudrait pas y voir une nuance quelconque quant au contenu normatif de la protection juridique accordée à ce droit fondamental.

Nous croyons ainsi pouvoir rejoindre, de la façon la plus transversale possible, les différentes manières que l'idée de base propre à ces enjeux a été exprimée dans l'histoire, et ce, tant dans les instruments nationaux qu'internationaux en matière de droits humains. En effet, si l'une des pionnières en droit constitutionnel interne appréhendait en termes d'égalité – « all men are created equal » : *Déclaration d'indépendance américaine*, 1776 – force est de constater que les conventions à l'international favorisent le concept de non-discrimination afin de traiter des impératifs égalitaires – une des premières, la *Convention n° 111 de l'OIT concernant la discrimination en matière d'emploi et de profession*, 1958. Marc Bossuyt résume ainsi : « En fait, tout comme les deux faces de Janus, l'égalité et la non-discrimination sont deux facettes d'une même réalité, mais qui est formulée tantôt de manière positive tantôt de façon négative ».[1]

---

[1]Bossuyt (1976), p. 37.

S. Beaulac (✉)
University of Montreal, Faculty of Law, Montreal, QC, Canada
e-mail: stephane.beaulac@umontreal.ca

2 Le droit de la non-discrimination est-il mis en œuvre?

Au Canada, qui est un pays dont la structure constitutionnelle est de type fédéral, la réponse est affirmative, absolument. Le droit de la non-discrimination est mis en œuvre, et ce, à la fois au niveau fédéral qu'au niveau des juridictions provinciales. En fait, il y a même une protection supra-législative des droits humains, comme nous le verrons. Cette question invite à un bref examen historique du droit à l'égalité sans discrimination.

Contrairement à nos voisins du sud, avec le « equal protection clause » prévu au XIVe Amendement de la Constitution des États-Unis d'Amérique, la tradition relative au droit à l'égalité sans discrimination est beaucoup plus récente au Canada. Cela dit, nous ne faisons pas exception quant à la contemporanéité de la protection juridique à cet égard puisque – faisant fi des documents à valeur plus symbolique que réelle, par exemple la *Magna Carte* de 1215 ou les *Traités de Westphalie* de 1648 – le mouvement mondial en faveur des droits humains, en général, tels que garantis dans des instruments normatifs écrits est relativement récent et, à vrai dire, était en réaction directe aux atrocités de la Deuxième Guerre Mondiale. Dans la foulée de la *Déclaration universelle des droits de l'homme*, adoptée à Paris en décembre 1948, la doctrine ici a longtemps réclamé, tant au Canada que dans la province de Québec,[2] de tels instruments de protection des droits fondamentaux, mais les législateurs ont fait la sourde oreille jusque dans les années 1960. Tout étant relatif par ailleurs, quand on regarde la mère-patrie en matière de droit public – c'est-à-dire la Grande-Bretagne, qui a mis en œuvre la *Convention européenne des droits de l'homme* en droit interne qu'au tournant des années 2000 – c'est le proverbial « quand on se compare, on se console » qui nous vient à l'esprit.

S'agissant plus précisément du droit à la non-discrimination, il est intéressant de noter une particularité canadienne : la plupart des initiatives législatives visant les droits humains, loin de constituer des instruments complets ou exhaustifs, ne s'attaquaient qu'à la problématique du droit à l'égalité. Ainsi, les premiers « bills of rights » adoptés par les provinces démontraient la volonté ferme de travailler à créer une société fondée sur des valeurs égalitaires. Une autre interprétation de l'évolution juridique à cet égard suggère plutôt que c'est l'absence de protection implicite au droit à l'égalité, par l'entremise de la jurisprudence, qui a emmené les autorités à intervenir par voie législative. En effet, l'on doit comprendre que plusieurs droits fondamentaux au Canada – par exemple, la liberté d'expression ou les droits des accusés – bénéficiaient depuis longtemps d'une protection grâce à un genre de « charte implicite des droits » découlant des décisions judiciaires; les tribunaux utilisaient les règles relatives au fédéralisme[3] ou les principes d'interprétation législative[4] pour déclarer inopérant ou réduire la portée de lois

---

[2]Voir Colas (1958), p. 317; Morin (1963), p. 273.
[3]Voir, par exemple, la décision de la Cour suprême du Canada dans le *Renvoi sur les lois de la presse en Alberta*, [1939] R.C.S. 100.
[4]Voir Beaulac and Bérard (2014), p. 343.

attentatoires aux droits et libertés. Ceci étant, l'égalité comme droit humain implicite était le parent pauvre de cette protection jurisprudentielle des droits humains, de telle sorte que les législateurs ont senti un besoin plus pressant d'intervenir afin de reconnaître le droit à la non-discrimination.

3   Comment le droit à la non-discrimination est-il mis en œuvre ?

Pour cette question, il est plus approprié de donner de l'importance à la hiérarchie des normes que de répertorier de façon complète les instruments de protection contre la discrimination. On notera néanmoins que ce sont les provinces qui ont pris les premières initiatives législatives en la matière, la Saskatchewan étant la pionnière en 1947.

L'article 15 de la *Charte canadienne des droits et libertés*, qui fait partie de la *Loi constitutionnelle de 1982* – l'un des deux principaux instruments de droit constitutionnel écrit – constitue la disposition phare, s'agissant du droit à l'égalité sans discrimination. Il jouit d'un statut supra-législatif, constitutionnellement supérieur à toute autre loi, et à ce titre, il influence aussi l'appréhension et imprègne des valeurs égalitaires l'ensemble du corpus législatif (fédéral, provinciaux). Formé de deux paragraphes, il se lit comme suit :

(1) La loi ne fait acception de personne et s'applique également à tous, et tous ont droit à la même protection et au même bénéfice de la loi, indépendamment de toute discrimination, notamment des discriminations fondées sur la race, l'origine nationale ou ethnique, la couleur, la religion, le sexe, l'âge ou les déficiences mentales ou physiques.

(2) Le paragraphe (1) n'a pas pour effet d'interdire les lois, programmes ou activités destinés à améliorer la situation d'individus ou de groupes défavorisés, notamment du fait de leur race, de leur origine nationale ou ethnique, de leur couleur, de leur religion, de leur sexe, de leur âge ou de leurs déficiences mentales ou physiques.

Cette disposition est entrée en vigueur trois ans après l'adoption de la *Charte canadienne*, donc en 1985, afin de permettre les ajustements nécessaires. Remarquons aussi que 15(2) permet expressément des mesures positives d'accès à l'égalité – en anglais, « affirmative action programs » – ce que la Cour suprême du Canada a expliqué ne constitue pas de la « discrimination positive » (expression souvent utilisée, malheureusement); l'objectif de ces mesures concerne les mêmes valeurs sous-jacentes au cœur du droit à l'égalité.[5]

---

[5]Voir *R. c. Kapp*, [2008] 2 R.C.S. 483.

La grille d'analyse sous l'article 15(1) *Charte canadienne* est en deux étapes : (a) une distinction prohibée, qui est par ailleurs (b) discriminatoire.[6] La première étape fait appel aux motifs de différenciation interdits qui sont énumérés à la disposition, mais la liste n'est pas exhaustive. Il y a donc des « motifs analogues » de distinction, comme par exemple l'orientation sexuelle[7] et l'état matrimonial.[8] S'il existe une telle distinction, la seconde étape est de savoir si son effet est discriminatoire, si elle entraîne un préjudice ou un désavantage.[9] La norme applicable est celle de « l'égalité réelle » (et non formelle uniquement) s'intéressant en outre aux attitudes empreintes de préjugés et de stéréotypes.

4 Qui met en œuvre le droit de la non-discrimination?

Cette question permettra d'élargir l'examen des moyens pour mettre en œuvre le droit à l'égalité sans discrimination, au-delà de la *Charte canadienne*. En effet, il existe au pays plusieurs autres instruments de protection juridique des droits humains, dont la *Déclaration canadienne des droits* et la *Loi canadienne sur les droits de la personne*, au niveau fédéral, ainsi que des « bills of rights » dans chacune des dix provinces, y compris au Québec avec la *Charte des droits et libertés de la personne*.[10] La jurisprudence a reconnu un statut spécial à cette législation, appelée « lois quasi-constitutionnelles » : quoiqu'elles ne font pas formellement partie des textes à valeur constitutionnelle, elles sont néanmoins hiérarchiquement supérieures aux simples lois (fédérales, provinciales).[11]

La plupart de ces instruments normatifs – dans le même texte de loi ou dans une législation afférente – ont mis sur pied un organe d'application, c'est-à-dire un organisme administratif responsable du schème de protection des droits humains. Plusieurs de ces régimes se sont par ailleurs dotés d'un tribunal des droits de la personne pour entendre et juger des plaintes formulées par les justiciables, et ce, tant dans leurs rapports privés que dans des litiges les opposants au gouvernement. Prenons la *Loi canadienne sur les droits de la personne*, concernant essentiellement le droit à l'égalité sans discrimination au plan juridique fédéral – dans l'emploi, mais aussi la fourniture de biens, services, hébergement et logement – elle crée tout d'abord la Commission canadienne des droits. Son mandat va bien au-delà des

---

[6]Voir l'arrêt de principe : *Andrews c. Law Society of British Columbia*, [1989] 1 R.C.S. 143.

[7]Voir *Egan c. Canada*, [1995] 2 R.C.S. 513; voir aussi le *Renvoi relatif au mariage entre personnes du même sexe*, [2004] 1 R.C.S. 698, qui a pavé la voie au mariage gay au Canada.

[8]Voir *Miron c. Trudel*, [1995] 2 R.C.S. 418; et encore récemment *Québec (P.G.) c. A.*, [2013] 1 R.C.S. 61.

[9]Voir aussi *Withler c. Canada (Procureur général)*, [2011] 1 R.C.S. 396.

[10]Voir, sur ces instruments, Beaulac (2015).

[11]Voir *Insurance Corporation of British Columbia c. Heerspink*, [1982], 2 R.C.S. 145; *Robichaud c. Canada (Conseil du Trésor)*, [1987] 2 R.C.S. 84; *Béliveau St-Jacques c. Fédération des employées et employés de services publics inc.*, [1996] 2 R.C.S. 345.

contentieux en matière de non-discrimination et incluent les fonctions et pouvoirs suivants : (a) élaborer des programmes de sensibilisation publique relatif à la non-discrimination; (b) entreprendre des programmes de recherche dans ce domaine; (c) collaborer avec les organismes provinciaux pour harmoniser les normes en la matière; (d) faire des études sur les droits et libertés de la personne que le ministre de la Justice lui demande; (e) participer au processus de rédaction et de révision de la conformité des lois fédérales eu égard à la non-discrimination; (f) sans affecter son rôle dans les contentieux, tenter d'empêcher la perpétration d'actes discriminatoires. En outre, le Tribunal canadien des droits de la personne a été instauré pour instruire les plaintes que la Commission lui aura soumises, le cas échéant, au nom des justiciables suite à son enquête.

Pour donner un autre exemple : la *Charte québécoise des droits et libertés de la personne*, dont la portée va plus loin que la non-discrimination et protège, à vrai dire, non seulement les droits de première génération (civils, politiques), mais également ceux de deuxième génération (économiques, sociaux, culturels).[12] Le mandat de la Commission des droits de la personne et des droits de la jeunesse du Québec inclut, outre le respect de la *Charte québécoise* – fonctions juridictionnelles et autres – de voir à la mise en œuvre de la loi sur la protection de la jeunesse et celle sur l'accès à l'égalité dans l'emploi. Le Tribunal des droits de la personne du Québec a compétence pour disposer des plaintes.

5 À qui profite la mise en œuvre du droit de la non-discrimination?

Il semble approprié pour discuter de la présente question – ainsi que la prochaine, concernant le négatif de la non-discrimination – de placer la problématique à l'intérieur de la structure analytique générale de la protection juridique des libertés fondamentales. S'agissant des droits, y compris les droits humains, il est en effet fort utile d'identifier les éléments suivants[13] : (i) le détenteur (« rightsholder »), (ii) le prestataire (« provider »), (iii) l'objet, et (iv) le contenu. S'agissant du droit à l'égalité sans discrimination, nous avons surtout parlé jusqu'à présent de leur objet et contenu; nous y reviendrons d'ailleurs un peu plus tard. Examinons les deux premiers points : les acteurs relatifs à ce droit.

S'agissant de la protection constitutionnelle, l'art. 15 de la *Charte canadienne* dit que toute « personne » en bénéficie; la version anglaise utilise « every individual », une terminologie qui se trouve aussi en français à 15(2) qui parle des « individus ou

---

[12]S'agissant de ces derniers, à l'instar de la situation à l'international, leur réalisation n'impose pas du tout les mêmes obligations : voir *Gosselin c. Québec (P.G.)*, [2002] 4 R.C.S. 429.

[13]Voir Joseph (2010), p. 150.

groupes défavorisés ». La jurisprudence nous enseigne que les détenteurs du droit constitutionnel à l'égalité sans discrimination se limitent aux personnes physiques[14]; en sont exclues, les sociétés[15] ou autres entités publiques ou privées. Plusieurs « bills of rights » provinciaux, pour leur part, étendent les bénéfices de ce droit aux personnes morales; c'est la situation au Québec, avec l'art. 10 de la *Charte québécoise des droits et libertés de la personne*.

Pour vraiment mesurer comment ces détenteurs profitent de la non-discrimination, il faut voir contre qui ces personnes peuvent la revendiquer. Qui sont les prestataires de ce droit? En matière constitutionnelle, cela soulève la question de la portée d'application des protections octroyées par la *Charte canadienne*. En effet, en vertu de son art. 32, tel qu'interprété en jurisprudence,[16] le droit à l'égalité de l'art. 15 ne peut être invoqué dans un litige purement privé, c'est-à-dire qui ne concerne pas une entité administrative ou un pouvoir exécutif, ni n'implique une source normative législative (loi ou règlement). Par exemple, une affaire de discrimination entre un salarié et son employeur, qui ne serait pas régie par un texte législatif, ne tomberait pas sous le coup de l'art. 15 *Charte canadienne*. En revanche, les régimes dits quasi-constitutionnels entreraient en jeu dans ces cas parce que les prestataires des droits sont à la fois les personnes privées et les entités publiques. La *Charte des droits et libertés de la personne* au Québec, par exemple, s'applique autant aux rapports privés entre individus qu'aux mesures associées à l'État (voir art. 54).

Dans l'évaluation de l'impact du droit à la non-discrimination au pays, il ne fait aucun doute que ce type de législation – au provincial comme au fédéral et, pour être complet, au niveau des territoires – permet à l'ensemble des justiciables de revendiquer leur droit à l'égalité, peu importe le prestataire (ou la nature de la source normative). Un domaine ayant connu une grande transformation depuis l'avènement de ces instruments – dont plusieurs se limitent, on le sait, à la non-discrimination – est celui du droit du travail et des normes d'emploi. Bref, les travailleurs et travailleuses en sont les grands gagnants.

6 Qui est lésé par la mise en œuvre du droit de la non-discrimination ?

Les éléments de la structure analytique relative à la problématique de la protection juridique des droits humains vus précédemment, en particulier (i) les détenteurs et (ii) les prestataires, nous serons d'une grande utilité de nouveau pour savoir, le cas échéant, qui est lésé quand il est question de non-discrimination.

---

[14] Voir, notamment, *Canada (P.G.) c. Hislop*, [2007] 1 R.C.S. 429.
[15] Voir *Edmonton Journal c. Alberta (P.G.)*, [1989] 2 R.C.S. 1326
[16] Voir *S.D.G.M.R. c. Dolphin Delivery*, [1986] 2 R.C.S. 573.

Concernant les détenteurs tout d'abord, seules les personnes morales eu égard à la *Charte canadienne* seraient laissées pour compte parce que, comme on a vu, elles sont exclues d'emblée de la portée de l'art. 15. En termes d'application juridictionnelle, il y a lieu de se rabattre sur les règles générales, la territorialité étant le principe de base. Ainsi, toute personne en territoire canadien – citoyen, étranger, visiteur – bénéficiera du droit à l'égalité sans discrimination; pour les lois provinciales, c'est la même logique territoriale (en plus d'être limité, *rationae materia*, aux domaines relevant des provinces; voir, par exemple, l'art. 55 de la *Charte québécoise*). Dans ce sens, on pourrait dire que les gens se trouvant à l'extérieur du territoire canadien se voient lésés parce qu'ils ne peuvent réclamer la protection de l'art. 15 *Charte canadienne*. Pour donner un exemple en lien direct avec l'actualité contemporaine, une politique de sélection à l'étranger des réfugiés syriens qui, de façon discriminatoire, distingue sur la base de d'état matrimonial ne serait pas soumise à l'application territoriale de la *Charte canadienne*. Ceci étant, il existe des cas d'exception où ces normes canadiennes s'appliqueraient de façon extraterritoriale, la Cour suprême du Canada ayant élaboré à ce sujet.[17] Il faudra voir si ces exceptions – consentement de l'État étranger, violation des obligations internationales du Canada – se présentent dans ces situations hypothétiques de violation du droit à l'égalité à l'étranger.

Pour ce qui est des prestataires de la non-discrimination maintenant, on peut dire qu'ils sont lésés, dans un certain sens, lorsque le droit à l'égalité mène à une obligation d'accommodement raisonnable. Cette notion – qui a eu mauvaise presse ici récemment[18] – est en lien avec le concept, développé en jurisprudence,[19] de discrimination par suite d'un effet préjudiciable (ou discrimination indirecte), c'est-à-dire une mesure *a priori* neutre mais qui crée une distinction interdite, par exemple sur la base de la religion.[20] La notion d'accommodement raisonnable, elle aussi entièrement jurisprudentielle,[21] impose une obligation au prestataire (par exemple, un employeur) de prendre des moyens qui, à moins de contrainte excessive, mettront fin ou atténueront l'effet discriminatoire indirect. La plus célèbre cause vient du Québec dans l'affaire du « kirpan »[22], du nom d'un petit couteau porté comme symbole religieux par les Sikhs. Le règlement scolaire interdisant la possession de couteaux à l'école causait une discrimination indirecte et les autorités ont eu l'obligation d'en permettre le port par l'élève sikh, à certaines conditions (de sécurité).

---

[17] Voir *R. c. Hape*, [2007] 2 R.C.S. 292; *Canada (Justice) c. Khadr*, [2008] 2 R.C.S. 125.

[18] Voir les travaux au Québec de la Commission Bouchard-Taylor, *Fonder l'avenir : Le temps de la conciliation*, Québec, La Commission, 2008.

[19] Voir *Commission ontarienne des droits de la personne et O'Malley c. Simpsons-Sears*, [1984] 2 R.C.S. 536.

[20] Voir Woehrling (1998), p. 325.

[21] Voir *Eldridge c. Colombie-Britannique (P.G.)*, [1997] 3 R.C.S. 624.

[22] *Multani c. Commission scolaire Marguerite-Bourgeoys*, [2006] 1 R.C.S. 256.

7 Quelles réparations sont prévues pour mettre en œuvre le droit de la non-discrimination?

Évidemment, la réparation (ou « remedies ») variera selon le type de litige, public ou purement privé, et suivant l'instrument juridique, la *Charte canadienne* ou une loi provinciale, comme la *Charte québécoise* par exemple. En vertu du premier régime, qui est supra-législatif parce qu'enchâssé dans la Constitution du Canada, la principale sorte de recours est en lien avec la déclaration d'inconstitutionnalité en vertu de l'art. 52(1) de la *Loi constitutionnelle de 1982*, qui se lit comme suit :

(1) La Constitution du Canada est la loi suprême du Canada; elle rend inopérantes les dispositions incompatibles de toutes autre règle de droit.

Un texte législatif qui viole le droit à l'égalité sans discrimination sous l'art. 15, si cette atteinte n'est pas justifiée en vertu de l'article premier de la *Charte canadienne*, pourra ainsi être déclaré inconstitutionnel par les tribunaux. D'autres recours ont été élaborés en jurisprudence,[23] sur la base de l'art. 52(1) : la dissociation (ou « severance ») de la partie inconstitutionnelle de la loi; la suspension de la déclaration d'inconstitutionnalité; ainsi que l'interprétation large (ou « reading in ») et l'interprétation atténuée (ou « reading down »).

L'autre disposition constitutionnelle pertinente pour ce qui est de la réparation en cas de discrimination est l'art. 24(1) de la *Charte canadienne* :

(1) Toute personne, victime de violation ou de négation des droits ou libertés qui lui sont garantis par la présente charte, peut s'adresser à un tribunal compétent pour obtenir la réparation que le tribunal estime convenable et juste eu égard aux circonstances.

Les tribunaux ont développé une panoplie de redressements en vertu de l'art. 24 (1), c'est-à-dire dans les situations où l'on reproche à un pouvoir public d'avoir porté atteinte à un droit garanti – sans nécessairement qu'il y ait inconstitutionnalité de la loi habilitante – comme celui de la non-discrimination dans l'exercice d'un pouvoir discrétionnaire, par exemple.[24] Ces réparations incluent : les dommages-intérêts, des ordonnances judiciaires comme des injonctions (prohibitives, mandatoires), voire même la supervision judiciaire subséquente du redressement prononcé par un tribunal dans une affaire.[25]

La loi du Québec sur les droits humains a une particularité en ce qu'elle ouvre la voie à un recours non-compensatoire, c'est-à-dire à des dommages-intérêts exemplaires (ou punitifs). En effet, l'art. 49, alinéa 2, de la *Charte québécoise* prévoit ceci : « En cas d'atteinte illicite et intentionnelle, le tribunal peut en outre

---

[23]Voir l'arrêt de principe : *Schachter c. Canada*, [1992] 2 R.C.S. 679.

[24]Voir Roach (2014), p. 1123.

[25]Ce dernier est exceptionnel. Voir *Doucet-Boudreau c. Nouvelle-Écosse (Éducation)*, [2003] 3 R.C.S. 3.

[en sus des dommages-intérêts compensatoires] condamner son auteur à des dommages-intérêts punitifs ».

8 Qui soutient la mise en œuvre du droit de la non-discrimination ?

Au plan juridique, nous l'avons mentionné, la plupart des régimes de protection des droits humains – au fédéral comme au provincial – en font également la promotion. Il s'agit en fait d'organes d'application (ou « treaty bodies » dirait-on en droit international), essentiellement des organismes administratifs, comme la Commission des droits de la personne et des droits de la jeunesse (ci-après « CDPDJ ») du Québec.

Prenons l'exemple québécois pour voir comment, concrètement, la mise en œuvre du droit à l'égalité sans discrimination est opérationnalisé à l'intérieur d'une juridiction au pays. Sur son site,[26] la CDPDJ se présente ainsi :

Sa mission inclut les responsabilités suivantes :

- **Informer** le public des droits reconnus par la Charte [québécoise], par la Loi sur la protection de la jeunesse (LPJ) et par la Loi sur le système de justice pénale pour les adolescents (LSJPA);
- **Faire enquête** sur des situations de discrimination et d'exploitation (en vertu de la Charte) et sur les atteintes aux droits des enfants et des jeunes (en vertu de la LPJ ou de la LSPJA);
- **Faire des recommandations** au gouvernement du Québec sur la conformité des lois à la Charte et sur toute matière relatives aux droits et libertés de la personne et à la protection de la jeunesse;
- **Produire et favoriser les recherches et les publications** sur les droits et libertés de la personne et sur les droits de la jeunesse;
- **Offrir un service-conseil en matière d'accommodement raisonnable** aux employeurs et aux décideurs;
- **Veiller au respect des programmes d'accès à l'égalité;**
- **Coopérer** avec toutes les organisations vouées à la promotion des droits et libertés de la personne, au Québec ou à l'extérieur.

Précisément, outre le volet juridictionnel – s'agissant de l'enquête et devant le Tribunal des droits de la personne – la CDPDJ joue un rôle important (i) quant à la médiation pour régler un conflit à l'amiable, (ii) afin d'accompagner un plaignant ou une plaignante et lui donner une représentation légale gratuite, et (iii) pour octroyer des services d'éducation-coopération visant la promotion des droits et libertés de la personne.

---

[26]Voir http://www.cdpdj.qc.ca/fr/commission/Pages/default.aspx.

Ajoutons que des organismes administratifs semblables existent à travers le pays, bien que leur mission puisse varier et, surtout, que la portée de leur mandat se limite dans plusieurs cas au droit à l'égalité sans discrimination. C'est la situation, par exemple, pour la Commission canadienne des droits de la personne.[27] À vrai dire, les autres organismes dans les provinces ont aussi des mandats axés exclusivement sur la non-discrimination, y compris sa promotion. Prenons la Commission ontarienne des droits de la personne, qui a tous les pouvoirs et fonctions au plan juridictionnel et autres, mais se concentre sur le droit à l'égalité, c'est-à-dire assurer à tous et à toutes « les mêmes droits et les mêmes chances sans discrimination dans des domaines sociaux spécifiques comme l'emploi, le logement, les services, les installations, les contrats et les ententes ».[28]

9 Qui s'oppose au droit de la non-discrimination ?

Ouvertement à tout le moins, il n'y a personne dans l'espace public ou au sein de la société civile qui s'oppose aux idéaux du droit à l'égalité sans discrimination. En fait, comment pourrait-on être contre la vertu, sérieusement, n'est-ce pas? Quand même, la présente question donne une belle occasion de relater un épisode à la fois récent et assez peu reluisant au pays, venant de la province de Québec, où se sont affrontées les valeurs sous-jacentes au droit à l'égalité et l'idéologie derrière le principe de la laïcité de l'État.

Baptisée malencontreusement la « crise des accommodements raisonnables », et malgré les efforts de discussion et d'éducation dans le cadre des travaux et du rapport de la Commission Bouchard-Taylor,[29] un certain malaise social – qui a été non seulement exagéré, mais surtout manipulé par le politique – a mené à une initiative législative de l'Assemblée nationale du Québec, à l'époque du gouvernement du Parti québécois dirigé par Pauline Marois, au pouvoir pendant quelque dix-huit mois en 2013-2014. Piloté par le ministre des institutions démocratiques, Bernard Drainville, le Projet de loi 60 prévoyait l'adoption d'une « Charte des valeurs québécoises ».[30] Plaidant devoir refléter la laïcité de l'État québécois, tous les membres du personnel des organismes publics – par exemple enseignants, éducateurs en garderie, médecins et infirmiers, juges provinciaux – seraient tenus de faire preuve de neutralité religieuse (art. 3), de réserve dans l'expression de leurs croyances (art. 4), et surtout de s'abstenir de porter des signes religieux dits ostentatoires au travail (art. 5), en plus de devoir exercer leurs fonctions à visage

---

[27]Voir http://www.chrc-ccdp.ca/fra.

[28]Voir http://www.ohrc.on.ca/fr.

[29]Voir *Fonder l'avenir : Le temps de la conciliation*, supra note 18.

[30]*Charte affirmant les valeurs de laïcité et de neutralité religieuse de l'État ainsi que d'égalité entre les femmes et les hommes et encadrant les demandes d'accommodement*, Projet de loi no. 60, 40e législature, 1e session.

découvert (art.6). En plus, indirectement, ces obligations pouvaient être étendues au secteur privé, afin d'avoir des contrats de service ou des ententes de subvention avec l'État. Le gouvernement avait le pouvoir d'établir par règlement ce qu'on entend par signes religieux ostentatoires (art. 36).

Ces limites flagrantes à l'exercice de la liberté de religion sans discrimination, à la fois directe et indirecte, n'avaient à peu près aucune chance de passer le test des chartes; la question est hypothétique maintenant puisque le Parti québécois a été chassé du pouvoir. Un des enjeux de cette élection fut cette proposition, qui a polarisé et divisé une partie de l'électorat. Beaucoup y ont vu l'expression d'une opposition à la non-discrimination.

10 Quelle est la portée du droit de la non-discrimination?

La présente question a déjà été abordée, par la bande (section 6), puisqu'on a parlé des volets relatifs à la discrimination par suite d'un effet préjudiciable (ou discrimination indirecte) – en lien avec le concept d'accommodement raisonnable – qui vient élargir considérablement la portée du droit à l'égalité en visant les mesures dites neutres, en ce qu'elles n'ont aucun objectif discriminatoire. Cela recoupe par ailleurs la position selon laquelle l'intention discriminatoire du prestataire n'est pas requise afin de donner droit à un recours au détenteur du droit à l'égalité.[31] On a également mentionné la distinction entre l'égalité formelle et l'égalité réelle (section 3), mais il y a lieu d'y revenir plus en détail ici. Un seul autre aspect sera discuté, soit le caractère autonome ou subordonné de la protection juridique du droit à l'égalité sans discrimination.

Dans l'arrêt de principe sur l'art. 15 de la *Charte canadienne*, soit *Andrews c. Law Society of British Columbia*,[32] notre Cour suprême dit clairement que c'est la conception non pas formelle, mais réelle (ou « substantive ») du droit à l'égalité qui sera retenue. Le critère stérile des distinctions fondées sur un modèle stricte de traitements analogues des situations semblables d'individus égaux (proche de l'idée du « separate but equal ») a été rejeté, et ce, au profit d'une compréhension plus large de l'égalité sans discrimination:

> Pour s'approcher de l'idéal d'une égalité complète et entière devant la loi et dans la loi [...] la principale considération doit être l'effet de la loi sur l'individu ou le groupe concerné. [...] [Bref], une loi destinée à s'appliquer à tous ne devrait pas, en raison de différences personnelles non pertinentes, avoir un effet plus contraignant ou moins favorable sur l'un que sur l'autre.[33]

L'analyse de l'égalité réelle articulée dans *Andrews* est en deux volets : « (1) La loi crée-t-elle une distinction fondée sur un motif énuméré ou analogue? (2) La

---

[31] Voir *Robichaud c. Canada (Conseil du Trésor), supra* note 11.
[32] *Supra* note 6.
[33] *Ibid.*, p. 165.

distinction crée-t-elle un désavantage par la perpétuation d'un préjugé ou l'application de stéréotypes? ».[34]

Maintenant, le droit à la non-discrimination est-il autonome ou subordonné?[35] Il est autonome si, à l'instar de l'art. 7 de la *Déclaration universelle des droits de l'homme*, la disposition énonce une norme d'application générale et protège le droit à l'égalité en tant que tel. L'article 15(1) *Charte canadienne*, ci-dessus (section 3) en est un exemple. En revanche, tous les instruments juridiques dits quasi-constitutionnels protègent ce droit de façon accessoire ou subordonné, c'est-à-dire que la non-discrimination se rattache à l'exercice d'une autre liberté fondamentale. L'article 10 *Charte québécoise*, qui à cet égard se compare à l'art. 2(1) du *Pacte international relatif aux droits civils et politiques*, l'illustre : « Toute personne a droit à la reconnaissance et à l'exercice, en pleine égalité, des droits et libertés de la personne, sans distinction, exclusion ou préférence [...] ».[36]

11 La mise en œuvre du droit de la non-discrimination varie-t-elle en fonction du critère discriminatoire ?

Ici, deux volets seront examinés : le premier a trait au seul tempérament explicite à un motif énuméré de distinction interdite; le second concerne le gabarit de protection minimale à la non-discrimination découlant de l'art. 15 *Charte canadienne*. Un petit mot tout d'abord sur la liste d'épicerie (comme on aime l'appeler) des motifs de distinction interdite, qui à vrai dire se ressemble beaucoup, qu'on soit à l'international, régional ou national. S'agissant de l'art. 15 *Charte canadienne*, on a vu que les motifs prévus sont considérés comme non-exhaustifs; on parle de motifs énumérés et de motifs analogues. En revanche, les lois sur les droits humains au provincial et au fédéral qui contiennent de telles listes ont été interprétées en jurisprudence comme étant exhaustives des motifs de distinction interdite pour lesquels il existe un recours pour discrimination.[37]

Il est maintenant utile de reproduire, à titre d'exemple, la liste de motifs énumérés à l'art. 10 de la *Charte québécoise* :

> 10. [...] sans distinction, exclusion ou préférence fondée sur la race, la couleur, le sexe, l'identité ou l'expression de genre, la grossesse, l'orientation sexuelle, l'état civil, l'âge sauf dans la mesure prévue par la loi, la religion, les convictions politiques, la langue, l'origine ethnique ou nationale, la condition sociale, le handicap ou l'utilisation d'un moyen pour pallier ce handicap [nos soulignements].

---

[34] *R. c. Kapp*, *supra* note 5, para. 17.
[35] Voir Moeckli (2010), p. 189.
[36] Suivent les motifs énumérés de distinction interdite par l'art. 10 *Charte québécoise*.
[37] Voir *Forget c. Québec (P.G.)*, [1988] 2 R.C.S. 90; et *Québec (Commission des droits de la personne et des droits de la jeunesse) c. Montréal (Ville)*, [2000] 1 R.C.S. 665.

Hormis l'âge, les motifs de distinction interdite ne varient pas en importance pour fins de mise en œuvre de la non-discrimination, au moins pas ouvertement. C'est évidemment différent pour l'âge, motif auquel on a ajouté « sauf dans la mesure prévue par la loi ». Il va sans dire que ce tempérament réduit considérément la protection juridique octroyée au droit à l'égalité dans ces situations. La jurisprudence au Québec confirme que les causes de discrimination fondée sur ce motif sont beaucoup plus rares puisque toute législation peut justifier – même indirectement, dans le cadre d'une convention collective de travail – un traitement différent sur la base de l'âge.[38]

Il est intéressant par ailleurs de souligner combien l'art. 15 *Charte canadienne* fait office de figure de proue, en ce qui a trait précisément à la liste les motifs de distinction interdite. En effet, la Cour suprême du Canada a statué que, loin de relever d'une marge d'appréciation souveraine des provinces, leur instrument quasi-constitutionnel devait, au minimum, garantir les mêmes bases de non-discrimination. C'est ainsi que dans l'affaire *Vriend*,[39] on est venu ajouter un motif de distinction interdite à la loi de l'Alberta,[40] en l'occurrence l'orientation sexuelle. En vertu de l'art. 52(1), vu plus haut (section 7), le recours approprié fut une interprétation libérale (ou « reading in ») pour ajouter ce motif.

12 Quel est le rapport entre la mise en œuvre de la non-discrimination et la recherche d'égalité au niveau individuel et systémique?

Sans l'ombre d'un doute, les lois quasi-constitutionnelles fédérale et provinciales, suivant le modèle de l'art. 15 *Charte canadienne*,[41] ont contribué de façon magistrale à modifier et à ajuster les pratiques et façons de gérer les relations entre sujets de droit, en matière de droit du travail et de normes d'emploi notamment. Comme exemple d'impact direct du droit à la non-discrimination, deux enjeux dans ce domaine : (1) le processus d'embauche, et (2) les programmes d'accès à l'égalité dans l'emploi.

Tous les régimes de protection juridique des droits humains au pays sont formels : dans le contexte d'embauche, aucune question touchant de près ou de loin les motifs de distinction interdite – dont on vient de discuter (section 11) – ne peut être abordée, que ce soit dans des formulaires d'embauche, des procédures (médicales, par exemple) de pré-embauche, et encore moins au moment de l'entrevue d'embauche. La Commission des droits de la personne et des droits de la jeunesse du Québec explique[42] : « un employeur n'a pas le droit de poser des questions sur l'âge, la

---

[38]Voir Brun et al. (2014), pp. 979 et ss.
[39]*Vriend c. Alberta*, [1998] 1 R.C.S. 493.
[40]*Individual's Rights Protection*, R.S.A. 1980, ch. I-2, loi depuis modifiée pour inclure explicitement l'orientation sexuelle comme motif de distinction interdite.
[41]Blache (2003), p. 151.
[42]Voir : http://www.cdpdj.qc.ca/fr/droits-de-la-personne/domaines/Pages/embauche.aspx.

religion, l'orientation sexuelle, l'état civil ou une autre caractéristique personne d'un candidat potentiel, sauf si ces questions traitent d'une qualité ou d'une aptitude requise par l'emploi ».[43] Le bémol, mentionne-t-on, ce sont les cas d'aptitudes requises qu'on répute non-discriminatoires, comme c'est prévu à l'art. 20 de la *Charte québécoise*, dont le fardeau de preuve incombe néanmoins à l'employeur. Un exemple nous vient de l'affaire *Québec (Commission des droits de la personne et des droits de la jeunesse) c. Montréal (Ville)*,[44] un cumul de trois dossiers où l'on a décidé que des candidats en contexte d'emploi (embauche, période probatoire) ont été victimes de discrimination fondée sur le « handicap », en violation de l'art. 10 *Charte québécoise*. Le refus découlait d'une perception préjudiciable d'anomalies physiques, affections que les candidats avaient été forcés de révéler, mais qui ne constituent pas des limitations fonctionnelles à leur capacité de faire leur travail dans les emplois postulés.

À l'instar de plusieurs de ses cousines provinciales, la *Charte québécoise* promeut expressément les programmes d'accès à l'égalité, notamment en matière d'emploi. Dans sa partie III, à l'article 86, on peut lire l'explication suivante :

> 86. Un programme d'accès à l'égalité a pour objet de corriger la situation de personnes faisant partie de groupes victimes de discrimination dans l'emploi, ainsi que dans les secteurs de l'éducation ou de la santé et dans tout autre service ordinairement offert au public.

Pour mémoire, l'art. 15(2) *Charte canadienne* traite nommément de cette problématique. Cela démontre combien la non-discrimination est intégrée aussi au plan systémique.

13 La mise en œuvre du droit de la non-discrimination est-elle perçue comme distincte de la mise en œuvre d'autres lois?

La présente question permet de souligner, tout d'abord, combien le mot d'ordre au Canada est d'harmoniser la protection (constitutionnelle et autre) des droits humains avec l'ensemble du droit écrit et non-écrit – tant au niveau fédéral que provincial – à la fois au sein des corpus législatifs et en droit jurisprudentiel (ou « judge-made-law »). S'agissant de l'influence de la *Charte canadienne* sur la normativité dans son ensemble, le signal a été envoyé tôt par la Cour suprême, en 1986 dans son arrêt *Dolphin Delivery* :

> Je dois toutefois dire clairement que c'est une question différente de celle de savoir si le judiciaire devrait expliquer et développer des principes de *common law* d'une façon

---

[43]Ces exigences découlent des articles 16 (non-discrimination dans l'embauche) et 18.1 (renseignements relatifs à un emploi) de la *Charte québécoise*.
[44]*Supra* note 37.

compatible avec les valeurs fondamentales enchâssées dans la Constitution. La réponse à cette question doit être affirmative.[45]

Évidemment, les valeurs fondamentales du droit à l'égalité à l'art. 15 *Charte canadienne* se sont imposées dans l'interprétation et l'application de tout le droit à travers le pays.[46]

La non-discrimination joue également un rôle interprétatif appréciable, s'agissant de la clause limitative de l'article premier de la *Charte canadienne*,[47] pour décider si des limites aux libertés fondamentales sont justifiables dans le cadre d'une « société juste et démocratique ».[48] Le juge en chef Dickson écrit ceci dans l'arrêt de principe *Oakes* :

> Les tribunaux doivent être guidés par des valeurs et des principes essentiels à une société libre et démocratique, lesquels comprennent, selon moi, le respect de la dignité inhérente de l'être humain, la promotion de la justice et de l'égalité sociales, l'acceptation d'une grande diversité de croyances, le respect de chaque culture et de chaque groupe et la foi dans les institutions sociales et politiques qui favorisent la participation des particuliers et des groupes dans la société.[49]

Pour être complet quant à l'application transversale des valeurs égalitaires, il faut mentionner deux clauses interprétatives de la *Charte canadienne*, une directement en lien avec la non-discrimination.[50] D'une part, l'art. 27 prévoit que la *Charte* doit s'interpréter de concert « avec l'objectif de promouvoir le maintien et la valorisation du patrimoine multiculturel des Canadiens ». D'autre part, l'art. 28 ajoute que « les droits et libertés qui y sont mentionnés sont garantis également aux personnes des deux sexes ».

14 Que révèle la mise en œuvre du droit de la non-discrimination sur la nature de votre système juridique et sur l'application des lois dans votre système juridique?

Comme on le sait, le Canada est un pays non seulement bilingue, mais également bi-juridique. La principale tradition juridique est celle anglo-saxonne de *common law*, à laquelle s'ajoute toutefois le droit civil en raison de la filiation française du

---

[45]*Supra* note 16, p. 603 [nos soulignements].

[46]Voir, en général, Côté et al. (2009), pp. 536 et ss.

[47]Voir *R. c. Keegstra*, [1990] 3 R.C.S. 697, p. 755.

[48]L'article premier de la *Charte canadienne*, qui est une clause limitative d'application générale, se lit ainsi : « La *Charte canadienne des droits et libertés* garantit les droits et libertés qui y sont énoncés. Ils ne peuvent être restreints que par une règle de droit, dans des limites qui soient raisonnables et dont la justification puisse se démontrer dans le cadre d'une société libre et démocratique ».

[49]*R. c. Oakes*, [1986] 1 R.C.S. 103, p. 136.

[50]Voir Schachar (2014), p. 147.

droit privé de la province de Québec. Le droit législatif fédéral également comporte une saveur civiliste puisqu'il doit s'harmoniser avec le droit privé de la province d'application, civiliste au Québec.[51] S'agissant du droit à l'égalité sans discrimination, eu égard à cette réalité bi-juridique au Canada, deux éléments distinctifs valent la peine d'être examinés brièvement ici : (1) l'accent mis sur les redressements en *common law*, et (2) le chevauchement entre les régimes de droit commun et celui de la *Charte québécoise*.

Aux yeux d'un juriste continental, la *common law* se distingue notamment quant à l'importance mise sur l'existence d'une réparation : « where there is a remedy, there is a right »,[52] diamétralement opposé au « *ubi jus, ibi remedium* » civiliste. Cela explique que la législation relative aux droits humains – fédérale et dans les neuf provinces de *common law* – a amené la jurisprudence à développer un recours (ou « cause of action ») donnant droit à des redressements judiciaires en cas de violation du droit à la non-discrimination. Un bon exemple nous vient de l'affaire *Robichaud c. Canada (Conseil du Trésor)*,[53] où se posait la question de savoir si, sous la *Loi canadienne sur les droits de la personne*, une employée victime de harcèlement sexuel au travail avait un recours non seulement contre le tortionnaire, mais également contre son employeur (qui n'était toutefois pas fautif). La Cour suprême s'est concentrée sur les dispositions de la loi portant sur les redressements, entre autres, pour justifier d'étendre le recours pour discrimination contre l'employeur.

La problématique s'est présentée de façon inverse au Québec, sous la *Charte des droits et libertés de la personne*, puisque suivant la tradition civiliste, on s'interrogeait sur le caractère autonome (comme en *common law*) ou complémentaire des recours en vertu de cet instrument quasi-constitutionnel. Pour régir le rapport entre le système de responsabilité civile de droit commun, d'une part, avec les droits subjectifs prévus par la *Charte québécoise*, d'autre part, la doctrine parlait de la théorie du chevauchement,[54] par opposition à la thèse dite de l'autonomie de principe de la loi.[55] Dans l'arrêt *Béliveau St-Jacques*,[56] la Cour suprême a favorisé la première : ainsi, un recours en vertu de l'art. 49 *Charte québécoise*, pour discrimination sous l'art. 10, s'imbrique dans le régime général en matière de responsabilité délictuelle aux art. 1457 et ss. du *Code civil du Québec*.

---

[51] Voir Gaudreault-DesBiens (2007).

[52] Voir *Ashby v. White*, (1703) Ld. Raym. 938 : « it is a vain thing to imagine a right without a remedy ».

[53] *Supra* note 11.

[54] Voir Perret (1981), p. 121; Caron (1985), p. 345.

[55] Otis (1991), p. 561; Drapeau (1994), p. 31.

[56] *Supra* note 11.

15 Conclusion

Pour récapituler, la réalité juridique dans le pays est complexe – avec son organisation constitutionnelle, sa structure fédérale de gouvernance, ses lois quasi-constitutionnelles, sa tradition juridique anglo-saxonne de *common law* et la filiation civiliste du droit privé au Québec. Cela signifie que la mise en œuvre du droit de la non-discrimination doit se comprendre eu égard à ces caractéristiques multidimensionnelles. Ceci étant, il est vrai que le Canada est résolument orienté et engagé, depuis plusieurs décennies, à l'égard de la défense et de la promotion des valeurs égalitaires.

Un point négatif, toutefois : le peu de considération des engagements internationaux dans l'interprétation et l'application des protections juridiques du droit à l'égalité par les tribunaux nationaux. Pour comprendre cette critique constructive, il faut rappeler que le Canada, au regard de l'inter-légalité et de la réception du droit international en droit interne,[57] est un pays à la fois dualiste et moniste. Selon la source de normativité internationale. Les traités doivent être transformés par une loi de mise en œuvre (fédérale, provinciale) pour produire ses effets juridiques en droit interne (dualisme); en revanche, le droit international coutumier est d'application automatique par nos tribunaux (monisme). En matière de *Charte canadienne* et autres lois relatives aux droits humains, il est établi que la normativitéla normativité internationale, sans être contraignante, constitue « une source pertinente et persuasive d'interprétation ».[58]

S'agissant du droit à l'égalité sans discrimination, – il importe de souligner qu'il y a peu, voire pas, d'influence du droit international sur ces enjeux dans notre droit interne. De fait, pour l'interprétation et l'application de l'art. 15 *Charte canadienne* (avec un potentiel rayonnement à l'égard de l'ensemble du droit du pays), la Cour suprême et autres tribunaux nationaux ont souvent eu l'occasion d'aller puiser dans la normativité et l'expérience internationale dans le domaine. Contrairement à ce que la Cour a régulièrement fait pour différentes libertés fondamentales, le traitement du droit à l'égalité sans discrimination est resté étanche à l'influence internationale, issue de traité ou découlant de la coutume. Un exemple parlant est le *Renvoi relatif au mariage entre personnes du même sexe*,[59] où le plus haut tribunal du pays a étudié en long et en large la problématique et ces enjeux sous l'angle de la non-discrimination, mais contrairement à ce qu'on aurait pu penser, on n'a aucunement tenu compte des réflexions et des réponses venant d'ailleurs (droit international, droit comparé).

D'aucuns diront du Canada qu'il est à l'avant-garde sur ces questions d'égalité et d'orientation sexuelle; l'expérience internationale, à la remorque, serait inutile. Un effort pour s'engager dans un dialogue global en la matière aurait néanmoins été souhaitable.[60]

---

[57] Voir, à cet égard, Beaulac (2011), c. 23 (mis à jour : 2015).
[58] *Renvoi relatif à la Public Service Employee Relations Act (Alta)*, [1987] 1 R.C.S. 313, p. 350.
[59] *Supra* note 7.
[60] Voir, sur l'importance des influences trans-judiciaires, Slaughter (1994), p. 99.

References

Beaulac S (2011) Interlégalité et réception du droit international en droit interne canadien et québécois. dans: Beaulac S, Gaudreault-DesBiens J-F (dir.) JurisClasseur Québec, collection « droit public » – Droit constitutionnel. LexisNexis, Montréal

Beaulac S (2015) Textes constitutionnels et document (nationaux, internationaux) relatifs aux droits humains. Éditions JFD, Montréal

Beaulac S, Bérard F (2014) Précis d'interprétation législative, 2e éd. LexisNexis, Montréal, p 343

Blache P (2003) Étude comparative de l'évolution des normes antidiscriminatoires ou égalitaires des articles 15 de la *Charte canadienne des droits et libertés* et 10 de la *Charte des droits et libertés de la personne*, convergences et divergences. R. du B. Québec (numéro spécial):151

Bossuyt M (1976) L'interdiction de la discrimination dans le droit international des droits de l'Homme. Bruylant, Bruxelles, p 37

Brun H et al (dir.) (2014) Alter Ego – Chartes des droits de la personne – Législation, jurisprudence, doctrine. Wilson & Lafleur, Montréal, pp 979 et ss

Caron M (1985) Le droit à l'égalité dans le Code civil et dans la Charte québécoise des droits et libertés. R. du B. Québec 45:345

Colas E (1958) Les droits de l'Homme et la constitution canadienne. R du B. Québec:317

Côté P-A, Beaulac S, Devinat M (2009) Interprétation des lois, 4e éd. Thémis, Montréal, pp 536 et ss

Drapeau M (1994) La responsabilité pour atteinte illicite aux droits et libertés de la personne. Revue juridique Thémis 28:31

Gaudreault-DesBiens J-F (2007) Les solitudes du bijuridisme au Canada – Essai sur les rapports de pouvoir entre les traditions juridiques et la résilience des atavismes identitaires. Thémis, Montréal

Joseph S (2010) Scope of application. dans: Moeckli D et al (dir.) International human rights law. Oxford University Press, Oxford, p 150

Moeckli D (2010) Equality and non-discrimination. dans: Moeckli D et al (dir.) International human rights law. Oxford University Press, Oxford, p 189

Morin J-Y (1963) Une Charte des droits de l'Homme pour le Québec. Revue de droit de McGill 9:273

Otis G (1991) Le spectre d'une marginalisation des voies de recours découlant de la Charte québécoise. R. du B. Québec 51:561

Perret L (1981) De l'impact de la Charte des droits et libertés de la personne sur le droit civil des contrats et de la responsabilité au Québec. Revue générale de droit 12:121

Roach K (2014) Enforcement of the Charter – Subsections 24(1) and 52(1). dans: Mendes E, Beaulac S (dir.) Charte canadienne des droits et libertés, 5e éd. LexisNexis, Toronto, p 1123

Schachar A (2014) Interpretation Sections (27 and 28) of the Canadian Charter. dans: Mendes E, Beaulac S (dir.) Charte canadienne des droits et libertés, 5e éd. LexisNexis, Toronto, p 147

Slaughter A-M (1994) A typology of transjudicial communication. Univ Richmond Law Rev 29:99

Woehrling J (1998) L'obligation d'accomodement raisonnable et l'adaptation de la société à la diversité religieuse. R.D. McGill 43:325

Stéphane Beaulac is a full professor at the University of Montreal. He graduated from the University of Cambridge with a Ph.D. in international law; he clerked at the Supreme Court of Canada. He was a Max Weber Fellow at the European University Institute in Florence, a Neil MacCormick Fellow at the University of Edinburgh, a Flaherty Fellow at the University College Cork, and a visiting professor in Amsterdam, Ulster and Trento. He is the author (co-author) or co-editor of some fifteen law books; his writings have won awards and, indeed, were cited by the International Court of Justice in The Hague.

Croatia

Emilia Mišćenić and Dijana Kesonja

1 Introduction

The development of a special antidiscrimination legal framework in Croatia began as a consequence of alignment of Croatian legislation with the *acquis communautaire* pursuant to duty set in Article 69 of the Stabilisation and Association Agreement[1] (SAA) between Croatia and the EU. Harmonization with key EU Antidiscrimination Directives (Racial Equality Directive 2000/43/EC; Framework Directive 2000/78/EC; Gender Goods and Services Directive 2004/113/EC; and Gender Equality Directive 2006/54/EC[2]) resulted in the adoption of the

---

[1] Act on Confirmation of the Stabilisation and Association Agreement between the Republic of Croatia and the European Communities and their Member States, OG IA Nos. 14/01, 15/01, 14/02, 1/05, 7/05, 9/05 and 11/06.

[2] Council Directive 2000/43/EC of 29 June 2000, implementing the principle of equal treatment between persons irrespective of racial or ethnic origin [2000] OJ L 180/22; Council Directive 2000/78/EC of 27 November 2000, establishing a general framework for equal treatment in employment and occupation [2000] OJ L 303/16; Council Directive 2004/113/EC of 13 December 2004, implementing the principle of equal treatment between women and men in the access to and supply of goods and services [2004] OJ L 373/37; Directive 2006/54/EC (recast) of the European Parliament and of the Council of 5 July 2006 on the implementation of the principle of equal opportunities and equal treatment between men and women in matters of employment and occupation [2006] OJ L 204/23.

E. Mišćenić (✉)
University of Rijeka, Faculty of Law, Rijeka, Croatia
e-mail: emiscenic@pravri.hr

D. Kesonja
Office of the Ombudswoman, Antidiscrimination Department, Zagreb, Croatia
e-mail: dijana.kesonja@ombudsman.hr

© Springer International Publishing AG, part of Springer Nature 2018
M. Mercat-Bruns et al. (eds.), *Comparative Perspectives on the Enforcement and Effectiveness of Antidiscrimination Law*, Ius Comparatum – Global Studies in Comparative Law 28, https://doi.org/10.1007/978-3-319-90068-1_8

Antidiscrimination Act[3] (ADA) in 2008, the Gender Equality Act (GEA) in 2003, and a new GEA in 2008.[4] Besides in the ADA as *lex generalis* and in the GEA as *lex specialis*, antidiscrimination provisions can be found scattered in numerous statutes of both public and private law, such as the Constitutional Act on the Rights of National Minorities, Same-Sex Communities Act, Same-Sex Persons Life Partnership Act, Labour Act, Act on Professional Rehabilitation and Employment of Persons with Disabilities, People's Ombudsman Act, Act on Protection from Domestic Violence, Criminal Code, etc.[5] Beyond that, protection against discrimination and guarantee of equal treatment is entrenched in the Croatian legal system and forms part of the Constitution of the Republic of Croatia[6] and of numerous international agreements ratified by it, such as the European Convention for the Protection of Human Rights and Fundamental Freedoms (ECHR) and its Protocols.[7] Being an EU *Member State,* Croatia adopts the Union's goals and values of combating discrimination and promoting equality.[8]

2 Is Antidiscrimination Law Enforced?

Although antidiscrimination law is enforced in the Republic of Croatia, its enforcement is not equal in all areas of social life and in all types of court proceedings initiated by victims of discrimination. The type and number of initiated court proceedings are the best indicators on the enforcement of antidiscrimination law. Since 2009, the number of validly completed civil and criminal court procedures have been in decline, while the number of validly completed misdemeanour procedures has

---

[3] OG Nos. 85/08 and 112/12.

[4] OG Nos. 82/08, 125/11, 20/12 and 138/12. The GEA from 2003 was published in OG No. 116/2003.

[5] Constitutional Act on the Rights of National Minorities, OG Nos. 155/02, 47/10, 80/10 and 93/11; Same-Sex Communities Act, OG Nos. 116/03 and 92/14; Same-Sex Persons Life Partnership Act, OG No. 92/14; Labour Act, OG No. 93/14; Act on Professional Rehabilitation and Employment of Persons with Disabilities, OG Nos. 157/13 and 152/14; People's Ombudsman Act, OG No. 76/12; Act on Protection from Domestic Violence, OG Nos. 137/09, 14/10 and 60/10; Criminal Code, OG Nos. 125/11, 144/12, 56/15 and 61/15.

[6] Articles 3 and 14(1) Constitution, OG Nos. 56/90, 135/97, 8/98 (consolidated text), 113/00, 124/00 (consolidated text), 28/01, 41/01 (consolidated text), 55/01 (correction), 76/10, 85/10 (consolidated text) and 5/14.

[7] The ECHR was ratified by the Republic of Croatia in 1997. See Act on Confirmation of the ECHR and Protocols Nos. 1, 4, 6, 7 and 11, OG IA Nos. 18/97, 6/99 and 8/99; Act on Confirmation of ECHR Protocol No. 13, OG IA Nos. 14/02 and 13/03; Act on Confirmation of ECHR Protocol No. 12, OG IA Nos. 14/02 and 9/05; Act on Confirmation of ECHR Protocol No. 14, OG IA Nos. 1/06 and 2/10.

[8] Act on Confirmation of Treaty between Member States of the European Union and the Republic of Croatia concerning the Accession of the Republic of Croatia to the European Union, OG IA Nos. 2/12 and 5/13. See also OJ L 112 of 24 April 2012.

been constantly on the rise. The reasons for this trend are the still existing ignorance about the legally provided judicial protection against discrimination, the lack of recognition of discrimination and criminal offences related to discrimination, the fear of victimization, the poor financial situation that prevents the victims from incurring the court proceedings' costs, and the durability of judicial procedures as well as the uncertainty of their outcomes.

In 2014, Croatia had 148 civil proceedings in connection with discrimination—31 initiated in that year and 117 transferred from the previous period. Only 15% of civil proceedings were validly resolved in 2014, none of which were in the victim's favour. The claim was denied in 13 cases, and 9 of them were resolved in another way. In 2014, there was not a single lawsuit for indirect discrimination or a collective lawsuit, which would require better knowledge of antidiscrimination law and which indicates a lack of interest of NGOs that had been initiating these types of procedures in previous years. For comparison, in 2013 Croatia had 152 civil discrimination suits, 100 of which were transferred from the previous year and 52 that started in 2013. In 2012, there were 116 civil proceedings. Thus, for the past three years, we have registered a continuous decline of civil law cases connected with discrimination. For criminal law cases connected with discrimination, Croatia had 19 proceedings in 2014, only 3 of which started that year, and 16 carried over from previous years. During the last year, only one criminal proceeding was validly resolved. For comparison, in 2013 Croatia had 17 criminal proceedings associated with discrimination, whereof 12 transferred from the previous period and 5 started in 2013. And in 2012 there were 16 criminal proceedings. Thus, apart from civil law cases, we also register a small, but continuous decline of criminal proceedings associated with discrimination. The new Criminal Code[9] has introduced the criminal offences of torture and other cruel, inhuman or degrading treatment or punishment, the infringement of the equality of citizens, infringement of the freedom of expression of national affiliation, and sexual harassment and public incitement to violence and hatred, but only one procedure[10] referred to these criminal offences in 2014.

The reason for this trend is not the absence of criminal offences related to discrimination, but the lack of knowledge as well as the lack of reporting and prosecuting the perpetrators. In 2014, Croatia had 207 misdemeanour procedures related to discrimination, 137 of which started in 2014, and 70 were retrieved from previous years. Ninety-four proceedings validly ended in 2014, 71 resulting in convictions. Out of 207 procedures, 113 remained unresolved. For comparison, in 2013 there were 114 and a year before 95 misdemeanour proceedings.[11] Thus, opposite to civil and criminal court proceedings, Croatia has been registering a

---

[9]Criminal Code, OG Nos. 125/11, 144/12, 56/15 and 61/15.

[10]Judgement of the Municipal Court in Koprivnica K-440/13 of 13 March 2014, relating to a criminal act of public incitement to violence and hatred.

[11]Information about the numbers and the type of judicial procedures is taken from the Ombudsman's Annual Reports, presented to the public and the Croatian Parliament on a yearly basis and available at: http://www.ombudsman.hr/index.php/en/.

continuous increase of misdemeanour procedures related to discrimination. However, one of the reasons for the constant rising trend of misdemeanour procedures is the incorrect identification of certain offences as misdemeanours instead of criminal offences. It is not uncommon for the amenable police administration to initiate the misdemeanour procedure for an act that contains the elements of a criminal offence, which calls for further education of the police officers dealing with these kinds of cases.

3 How Is Antidiscrimination Law Enforced?

The enforcement of antidiscrimination law in Croatia is guaranteed through various public and private law measures. Whatever the enforcement measures applicable, EU law, in particular EU Antidiscrimination Directives and the CJEU/ECJ case law[12] require them to be efficient, proportionate, as well as dissuasive. Generally, we can distinguish between pre-procedural protection, procedural protection (e.g. civil and criminal law court procedures), alternative dispute resolution (e.g. mediation), misdemeanour protection (e.g. monetary fines) and constitutional protection. Pre-procedural protection refers to different preventive, educational and informative protection measures, such as those of the Ombudsman on warning the public about discrimination occurrences, providing victims with necessary information on their rights and obligations and on the court and other forms of protection, conducting surveys concerning discrimination, etc. (Article 12(2) ADA).[13] According to Article 12(2) ADA, the Ombudsman is also in charge of conducting mediation between the parties.

Another efficient way of enforcing antidiscrimination law is the monetary sanctioning of misdemeanour liability, where fines can vary from 1.000,00 to 350.000,00 kuna according to Articles 25–29 ADA and Articles 31–38 GEA. Protection is also guaranteed through the prescription of certain special crimes, such as public incitement to violence and hatred in Article 325 of the Criminal Code.[14] On the other hand, special antidiscrimination law emphasises civil procedure protection, which even prior to the adoption of special legislation resulted in a considerable court practice on antidiscrimination, particularly

---

[12]See Case C-54/07, *Feryn* [2008] ECR I-05187; Case C-409/95, *Marshall* [1997] ECR I-06363; Case C-14/83, *von Colson* [1984] ECR I-01891; Case C-177/88, *Dekker* [1990] ECR I-03941, etc.

[13]About the lack of preventive enforcement methods such as education on antidiscrimination, see Vasiljević (2015), pp. 64 et seq.

[14]See also Special Part, Chapter IX on the crimes against humanity and human dignity, particularly Article 88 (genocide), Article 89 (crime of aggression), and Art. 90 (crime against humanity). E.g. Judgement of the Municipal (Criminal) Court in Zagreb II-KMp-209/2008 due to violation of Articles 331 (public order) and 89 CC during a public gathering of persons of homosexual orientation at the "Zagreb Pride 2008."

regarding employment relations.[15] ADA provisions on proceedings before the courts encompass incidental, i.e. prejudicial question and antidiscrimination actions that are divided into joint legal actions (i.e. action for injunctions) and special actions (action for determination of discrimination, action for prohibition or elimination of discrimination or of its consequences, and action for damage compensation and publication of the judgement in the media).[16] Apart from foreseeing the right to damage compensation in accordance with the obligations law—Civil Obligations Act[17] (COA)—indirect protection against discrimination is also offered by other COA provisions protecting the equality of private law parties through general principles of civil law, personality rights, or remedies such as nullity of contracts. Finally, constitutional protection is a very effective means against normative discrimination.[18] Constitutional protection in vertical relations is mainly guaranteed through the institute of constitutional complaint[19] and procedure on evaluation of constitutionality and legality.[20]

4 Who Enforces Antidiscrimination Law?

The predominant role in enforcing the special antidiscrimination legal framework in Croatia is assigned to municipal courts, county courts, and the Supreme Court, which in accordance with ADA and GEA provisions decide upon civil

---

[15] Bodiroga-Vukobrat and Martinović (2013), p. 11.

[16] Court protection is also regulated in Article 30 GEA. See *infra*, Answer to Question No. 6.

[17] OG Nos. 35/05, 41/08, 125/11 and 78/15.

[18] Protection of individuals against normative discrimination occurs through evaluation of statutory acts in accordance with the Constitution and of other regulations in accordance with the Constitution and statutory acts pursuant to Article 55 of the Constitutional Court Act of the Republic of Croatia (CCARC), OG Nos. 99/99, 29/02 and 49/02 (consolidated text).

[19] According to Articles 62–80 CCARC, everyone who deems that the individual act of a state body, a body of local and regional self-government, or of a legal person with a public authority, which decided about his/her rights and obligations, or about suspicion on or accusation of a criminal act, has violated his/her human rights or fundamental freedoms guaranteed by the Constitution, or his/her right to local and regional self-government guaranteed by the Constitution, may lodge such a complaint. See Decision of the Constitutional Court No. U-III/3192/2003 of 17 May 2006, para. 6: "Article 14(1) of the Constitution contains a constitutional guarantee of non-discrimination. Discrimination on the ground of Article 14(1) of the Constitution is not an independent legal basis for the constitutional complaint, but it has to be pleaded together with some other (material) constitutional right guaranteed by the Constitution."

[20] According to Article 55(3) CCARC, the Constitutional Court may annul a legal act or its separate provisions, taking into account all the circumstances important for the protection of constitutionality and legality, and especially bearing in mind how seriously it violates the Constitution or the law and the interest of legal security: if it violates human rights and fundamental freedoms guaranteed by the Constitution; if, ungrounded, it places some individuals, groups or associations in a more or a less favourable position.

antidiscrimination actions.[21] According to Article 18(1) ADA and Article 30 (1) GEA, municipal courts, as first instance courts, hold subject matter jurisdiction in civil procedures initiated on special antidiscrimination actions regulated in Article 17 ADA. County courts are, in the first instance, competent for procedures protecting the collective interests of groups claiming to be victims of discrimination under Article 24 ADA.[22] The Supreme Court, which rules on appeals in cases of collective redress or revision in cases of special antidiscrimination actions, has already played an important role in overruling imperfect antidiscrimination judgements of lower courts.[23] Due to the lack of knowledge and experience in applying and interpreting the relatively recent antidiscrimination framework of ADA, GEA, Same-Sex Communities Act (SSCA) etc. consistently with EU law, these courts tend to resort to the application of provisions on equality of other statutory acts, such as Labour Act (LA), COA or other relevant acts.

However, incidental protection of the special antidiscrimination framework is also enabled within other procedures by means of Article 16 ADA, according to which any person considering that his or her right has been violated because of discrimination may request the protection of that right in the proceedings deciding upon that right as the main issue.[24] Apart from the already mentioned Constitutional Court as one of the most important institutions combating normative discrimination,[25] one should emphasise the role of the Office of Ombudsman and offices of special ombudspersons. While the Ombudsman is an independent and central body for combating discrimination, special ombudspersons for gender equality, for children and for persons with disability are in charge of different ADA's and GEA's provisions falling under their competence.[26]

---

[21] Articles 17(2) and 24(4) of the ADA. The civil procedure in Croatia is regulated by Civil Procedure Act, OG Nos. 4/77, 36/77, 36/80, 69/82, 58/84, 74/87, 57/89, 20/90, 27/90, 35/91, 53/91, 91/92, 58/93, 112/99, 129/00, 88/01, 117/03, 88/05, 02/07, 96/08, 84/08, 123/08, 57/11, 25/13 and 89/14. Some provisions on judicial structure, subject matter and functional jurisdiction can be found in Act on Courts, OG Nos. 28/13, 33/15, 82/15.

[22] Articles 24(3) ADA and Article 30(3) GEA.

[23] See judgements of the Supreme Court of the Republic of Croatia Gž-25/11-2 and Gž-41/11-2 of 28 February 2012, analysed in Mišćenić (2015), p. 128.

[24] Besides the above-mentioned regular courts, specialized courts (such as commercial courts, the High Commercial Court, administrative courts, the High Administrative Court, misdemeanour courts, and the High Misdemeanour Court) also enforce provisions containing the prohibition of discrimination or guarantee of equality.

[25] See Decision of the Constitutional Court No. U-I-1152/2000 of 18 April 2007, OG No. 43/07 on the unconstitutionality of provisions of the Retirement Insurance Act, providing different conditions for the acquisition of certain rights for retirement insurance for women and men.

[26] Pursuant to Article 12(2) ADA, the Ombudsman also does the following: receives notifications on discrimination; offers independent assistance to victims by receiving their complaints and providing them with necessary information on their rights and obligations and forms of protection; examines complaints and takes actions for elimination of discrimination and for protection of victims; files criminal charges related to discrimination cases to the competent State attorney's office; and informs the Croatian Parliament on the occurrence of discrimination in annual reports, etc.

Finally, the Government's Offices for Human Rights and Rights for National Minorities or for Gender Equality and numerous non-governmental associations also play a role in preventing discrimination.

5 Who Benefits from the Enforcement of Antidiscrimination Law?

Provisions of both ADA and GEA, but also of SSCA, LA and other statutory acts offer broad protection to individuals by protecting them from various forms of discrimination, including direct and indirect discrimination, harassment and sexual harassment, enticement of another person to discriminate, segregation, etc.[27] In accordance with its definition, ADA protects any person who is placed in a less favourable position due to one or more discriminatory grounds defined in Article 1 (1), persons who are discriminated because of their family or other bonds with the victim of discrimination,[28] as well as persons who are discriminated against because of a misconception of the existence of grounds referred to in Article 1(1) ADA.[29] Moreover, ADA offers protection in Article 4(2) to persons with disabilities by defining a failure to make a reasonable adaptation to their specific needs as discrimination.[30]

Furthermore, provisions of ADA and GEA also protect persons who reported discrimination in good faith, who witnessed discrimination, who refused an instruction to discriminate, and who warned the public about discrimination or in any way

---

[27]For example, direct discrimination is prohibited by Article 2(1) ADA, Article 7(1) GEA, Article 21(3) SSCA and Article 7(4) LA. Prohibition of indirect discrimination is contained in Article 2 (2) ADA, Article 7(2) GEA, Article 21(4) SSCA and Article 7(4) LA. Harassment and sexual harassment are prohibited by Article 3 ADA and Article 8 GEA. In Article 4(1) ADA, Article 6 (5) GEA and Article 21(2) SSCA, enticement of another person to discriminate is considered to be discrimination. Forced and systematic separation of persons based on some grounds referred to in Article 1(1) ADA (segregation) is prohibited by Article 5 ADA. Article 6 ADA enumerates more serious forms of discrimination such as multiple discrimination, repeated discrimination, continued discrimination and discrimination with particularly harmful consequences for the victim.

[28]Article 1(2) ADA. This is in line with Case C-303/06, *Coleman* [2008] ECR I-05603, where the ECJ held that the prohibition of discrimination on the grounds of disability includes a mother taking care of a disabled child.

[29]Article 1(3) ADA. Article 1(1) ADA prohibits discrimination on 21 taxatively enumerated grounds: race, ethnic affiliation, colour, gender, language, religion, political or other belief, national or social origin, property, trade union membership, education, social status, marital status, family status, age, health condition, disability, genetic heritage, native identity, expression and sexual orientation.

[30]In accordance with their specific needs, persons with disabilities should be enabled when it would not unreasonably burden the person obliged to provide for it. This can be accomplished through providing access to the use of publicly available resources, participation in the public and social life, and giving access to workplace and appropriate working conditions through adaptation of infrastructure and premises and through use of equipment.

participated in proceedings pursued because of discrimination (victimization).[31] For example, there are a large number of reported cases of discrimination in the area of labour and employment. However, despite the already presented statutory protection, there is an even larger number of unreported cases of discrimination in this area because of victims' fears of the employers' revenge, the difficulties of proving discrimination in the working place, but also because of the victim's conciliatory approach to discrimination at work. Thus, although employees should benefit from the enforcement of antidiscrimination law, there is still a high percentage of those who are afraid to request judicial or other protection granted by ADA and other statutory acts.

Reporting discrimination is, however, no guarantee that the victim will actually benefit from the enforcement of antidiscrimination law. For example, the Krešić case dealt with special antidiscrimination legal action of the scientific assistant Dr. Krešić against his employer, the Faculty of Organization and Informatics in Varaždin. Dr. Krešić, who was denied promotion on the ground of his sexual orientation, successfully won the antidiscrimination proceedings.[32] However, he lost in another civil proceeding initiated by one of the professors accused of discriminating him, since the judge found that Dr. Krešić violated the professor's personality rights of dignity, honour and reputation by speaking about the event and the antidiscrimination court proceeding in public. The latter judgement of the first instance Municipal Court in Varaždin ordered Dr. Krešić to pay monetary compensation for non-proprietary damage to the professor.[33]

6 Who Is Harmed by the Enforcement of Antidiscrimination Law?

Pursuant to special antidiscrimination legislation discriminatory behaviour of any person is to be harmed by its enforcement. According to Article 8 ADA, it is applicable to the conduct of all state authorities, bodies of local and regional self-government units, legal persons vested with public authority, and to the conduct of all legal and natural persons. Moreover, there are additional provisions prohibiting discriminatory behaviour across other statutory acts, such as Article 7(4) LA in the areas of work and working conditions.[34] Despite the wide protection offered by the legislative

---

[31] Article 7 ADA and Article 2 GEA.

[32] Judgement of the Municipal Court in Varaždin P-3153/10-89 of 12 July 2012, confirmed by Judgement of the County Court in Varaždin Gž-5048/12-2 of 9 July 2013.

[33] Judgement of the Municipal Court in Varaždin P. 1802/11 from February 2013, not published. Available at: http://www.tportal.hr/vijesti/hrvatska/242279/Klicek-nije-diskriminirao-varazdinskog-gay-profesora.html.

[34] According to Article 7(4) LA, such behaviour concerns selection criteria, recruiting and promotion conditions, professional improvement, retraining, and vocational training pursuant to provisions of the LA and special laws.

framework, there were a few cases in which the enforcement of antidiscrimination law conclusively resulted in having an adverse effect, meaning harming the victim of discrimination instead of the discriminator. Apart from the Krešić case presented above,[35] this was reflected in one of the cases dealing with discrimination of persons of homosexual orientation through a public statement in the media. The statement—presenting a violation of personality rights under COA[36] and hate speech sanctioned by the Criminal Code[37]—came from the executive vice president of the football club "Dinamo" and active member of the Croatian Football Association.[38] Both first and second instance courts dismissed the claims raised in an antidiscrimination action for injunction in their entirety and justified the statement as the defendant's right to fundamental freedom of expression and thought.[39] Although the same happened in a similar case concerning two actions for injunction raised against the former president of the Croatian Football Association[40] at the first instance level,[41] the Supreme Court overruled both first instance judgements in favour of the victims of discrimination. The improvement of the court practice regarding discriminatory statements can be further noticed in two other antidiscrimination actions for injunction—one raised against a priest of the Catholic Church[42] and another against the governor of the prison in Osijek[43]—which both resulted in harm to the discriminators and ultimately successful enforcement of antidiscrimination law.

---

[35] See *supra*, Answer to Question No. 4.

[36] Under Article 19(1) COA any natural and legal person is entitled to the protection of its personality rights under the conditions provided by law. Article 19(2) COA enumerates in an exemplary manner the rights to life, physical and mental health, reputation, honour, dignity, name, privacy of personal and family life, freedom and others.

[37] Public incitement to violence and hatred in Article 325 Criminal Code.

[38] The following statement was published in the daily newspaper 'Jutarnji list' on 16 November 2010: *'In mine representation gays could also not play. I do not see the man of a gay representation going with head onto the football cleat, but I do see him as a ballet dancer, writer, journalist.'*

[39] Judgements of the County Court in Zagreb 15 Pnz-6/10-27 of 24 March 2011 and of the Supreme Court of the Republic of Croatia Gž-12/11-2 of 18 April 2012. Besides being in direct conflict with the conclusions of the ECJ/CJEU in cases C-54/07, *Feryn* [2008] ECR I-05187 and C-81/12, *Asociaţia Accept* [2013] EU:C:2013:275, these rulings violated the ADA's provision on the burden of proof.

[40] The statement published in the daily newspaper 'Večernji list' in November 2010: *"there is no room for a gay in the Fiery Ones [...] and luckily, only healthy people play football."*

[41] Judgements of the County Court in Zagreb Pnz-7/10 of 2 May 2011 and Pnz-8/10 of 28 July 2011.

[42] In 2010, the priest published several articles on his Internet blog and gave other public statements in the media that discriminated persons of same-sex orientation and encouraged violence against them. The County Court in Rijeka found discrimination and prohibited the further publication of discriminatory texts; it also ordered the removal of all discriminatory texts from the blog, as well as the publication of this judgement in two daily newspapers at the defendant's cost. See the Judgement of the County Court in Rijeka P-15/2010 of 3 October 2011 as confirmed by the Judgement of the Supreme Court of the Republic of Croatia Gž-38/2011-2 of 7 March 2012.

[43] The statement published in the daily newspaper 'Večernji list' from 27 November 2012 explained that minor prisoners are placed in the cells with adult prisoners *"only under the condition that these are people who will not have a negative impact on them. This means that we cannot accommodate them in a room with gays, addicts, or recidivists of criminal offences."* While the County Court in

7 What Remedies Are Provided by the Enforcement of Antidiscrimination Law?

The enforcement of Croatian antidiscrimination law is primarily pursued via civil procedure remedies. According to ADA provisions on proceedings before the courts (Articles 16–24), besides incidental protection through prejudicial question, victims of discrimination can request protection in special proceedings regulated by Article 17 ADA. The latter encompasses the possibility for the victim to (1) request adoption of a declaratory judgement by raising an action for determination of discrimination, (2) request adoption of a condemnatory judgement by raising an action for prohibition or elimination of discrimination or of its consequences, (3) raise an action for compensation of all proprietary and non-proprietary damage caused by violation of rights protected by ADA, or (4) request a publication of the ruling in the media at the defendant's cost.[44] Pursuant to Article 30 GEA, anyone who believes that some of his or her rights were violated based on discrimination regulated by Articles 6–8 GEA can bring an action to a municipal court.

Regarding damage compensation, as in Article 11 ADA, Article 30(2) GEA refers to the law provisions of the COA. But pursuant to Article 24 ADA, associations, bodies, institutions or other organisations constituted in accordance with the law and having a justified interest in the protection of collective interests of a certain group, or those which within their activities deal with the protection of the right to equal treatment, may bring a legal action against a person who has violated that right if they show it plausible that the defendant's conduct has violated a right to equal treatment of a larger number of persons who predominantly belong to the group whose rights they are defending.[45] Although this abstract legal protection, also foreseen by Article 30(3) GEA, does not encompass the possibility of damage compensation, judgements in collective redress proceedings can certainly contribute to successful individual proceedings before the courts. However, the scarce publicly available court practice demonstrates numerous shortcomings in the interpretation and application of antidiscrimination law, for example by interpreting the notion of the victim of discrimination inconsistently with the EU's *acquis* or by neglecting

---

Zagreb Pnz-2/13 of 5 June 2013 rejected the claim, the Supreme Court of the Republic of Croatia Gž-21/13-2 of 10 September 2013 overruled the first instance judgement and adopted the antidiscrimination claim.

[44]Article 17(1)(1)-(4) ADA. However, the fourth action can be raised only if a violation happened through the media or information on the conduct violating the right to equal treatment was published in the media, and if the publication of the ruling is necessary for the purpose of complete damage compensation or protection against unequal treatment in future cases.

[45]According to Article 24(2) ADA, a county court can be requested to (1) establish that the defendant's conduct has violated the right to equal treatment in relation to the members of the group, (2) prohibit activities that violate or may violate the right to equal treatment, or to carry out activities eliminating discrimination or its consequences in relation to members of the group, or (3) publish in the media the ruling establishing the violation of the right to equal treatment at the defendant's cost.

ADA's and GEA's provisions on the burden of proof[46] by shifting it completely to the claimants.[47]

Furthermore, bearing in mind the special provisions prohibiting discrimination in employment relations, housing, and access to and providing of goods and services, one should also mention private law remedies deriving from LA or COA provisions on pre-contractual, contractual and non-contractual liability in cases of violation of provisions guaranteeing equal treatment or equality.[48] Finally, there are other effective legal remedies such as the monetary fines for misdemeanour liability prescribed in Articles 25–29 ADA or Articles 31–38 GEA, mentioned above.

8 Who Supports the Enforcement of Antidiscrimination Law?

The enforcement of antidiscrimination law is supported by a whole series of governmental, non-governmental and private entities. One of the most supportive entities is the Ombudsman, who is the appointed representative of the Croatian Parliament for the protection of human rights and fundamental freedoms under Article 93 of the Constitution[49] and plays the role of a central body for combating discrimination under Article 12(1) ADA.[50] Within the Office of Ombudsman operates a special Antidiscrimination Department that works on various aspects of combating discrimination. For example, it addresses individual citizens' complaints

---

[46] According to Article 20 ADA, a party in court or other proceeding claiming violation of his or her right to equal treatment has a duty to show it is plausible that discrimination has taken place, and according to Article 30(4) GEA, to demonstrate facts to the court that justify the doubts on discrimination. Only then the burden of proof that there was no discrimination is shifted to the opposite party.

[47] See judgements in the collective redress proceedings of the County Court in Zagreb 15 Pnz-6/10-27 of 24 March 2011 and of the Supreme Court Gž 12/11-2 of 18 April 2012 analysed in Mišćenić (2015), p. 131.

[48] See Mišćenić (2014), pp. 100 et seq.

[49] According to Article 93 of the Constitution, the Ombudsman is an autonomous and independent body elected by the Croatian Parliament for a time period of eight years and is responsible for the protection and promotion of human rights and freedoms established by the Constitution, statutory acts, and international legal acts on human rights and freedoms ratified by the Republic of Croatia. Everyone considering that there has been a threat or violation of their human rights and fundamental freedom, because of illegal or irregular action of governmental bodies, bodies of local and regional self-government, and bodies vested with public authority, may lodge a complaint to the Ombudsman.

[50] Apart from being accredited at an "A" status by the International Coordinating Committee for Human Rights, the Ombudsman is also the National Equality Body—NEB in accordance with the ADA provision and the National Preventive Mechanism against Torture and other Cruel, Inhuman or Degrading Treatment or Punishment—NPM pursuant to the 9b Optional Protocol to the UN Convention Against Torture and Cruel Inhuman or Degrading Treatment or Punishment from 2002 and Act on National Preventive Mechanisms against Torture and Other Cruel, Inhuman or Degrading Treatment or Punishment, OG Nos. 18/11 and 33/15.

of discrimination, initiates *ex officio* procedures regarding discrimination cases introduced through the media, monitors the development of the relevant case law in Croatia and of the practice of the European Court of Human Rights, continuously raises the level of society's consciousness on discrimination and protection of human rights, informs the Croatian Parliament about current problems in the field of discrimination and recommends modalities for its successful combating and prevention. The latter include recommendations for individual discrimination cases with the aim of suspending the negative effects of discrimination and preventing further discrimination occurrences, including general recommendations concerning necessary amendments of legal regulations, and the education of judges, lawyers, and police officers.

Apart from the Ombudsman, there are three special ombudspersons, namely the Ombudswoman for Gender Equality, the Ombudswoman for Children and the Ombudswoman for Persons with Disability, which are in charge of different ADA provisions (Articles 12–13 ADA). Consequently, the Ombudswoman for Gender Equality is responsible for discrimination on the grounds of gender, sexual orientation and marital or family status, the Ombudswoman for Children is responsible for the protection of children's rights, and the Ombudswoman for Persons with Disability for the protection of disabled people's rights. All three special Ombudswomen fully support the enforcement of the antidiscrimination law in Croatia and are very active in combating discrimination.[51]

The enforcement of antidiscrimination law is also supported by numerous NGOs, which are very active in the protection of human rights and some of which initiated antidiscrimination collective redress court proceedings for the protection of discriminated groups of citizens.[52] These associations include, for example, the Centre for Peace Studies, Pride, Domino, LORI (Lesbian Organization Rijeka), Documenta, Centre for Civil Initiatives, Censorship Plus, Centre for Peace, Legal Advice and Psychosocial Assistance Vukovar, Civil Rights Project Sisak, and many others. Unfortunately, their activity concerning the enforcement of antidiscrimination law is very much dependent on their scarce financial resources evidenced by the decrease in the number of collective redress antidiscrimination proceedings they initiated.

---

[51]Provisions concerning non-discrimination can be found in the People's Ombudsman Act OG No. 76/12, Children's Ombudsman Act OG Nos. 96/03, 125/11 and 20/12, and Disability Ombudsman Act OG Nos. 107/07, 125/11 and 20/12.

[52]For more details on collective redress in Croatian antidiscrimination law, consult Miščenić (2014), p. 104.

9 Who Opposes the Enforcement of Antidiscrimination Law?

In the Republic of Croatia, there are no explicit official declarations that oppose the "enforcement" of antidiscrimination law.[53] However, this cannot be said with regard to the "observance" of antidiscrimination law. In practice, we are often witnessing discriminatory statements coming from the media or various social networks.[54] Their content is usually directed at incitement to violence and hatred towards certain categories of citizens, such as members of the LGBT community, and members of certain national minorities, especially Serbian and Roma national minorities and recently refugees from Syria, Iraq, Afghanistan and other countries whose citizens migrated to Europe. Apart from individual discriminatory acts, there were even cases of organized activities having discriminatory connotations, such as the one of the association "In the Name of the Family." In 2013, this association initiated a referendum resulting in amendments of the Constitution that, now in its Article 62,[55] defines marriage as a living community of woman and man.[56,57] Furthermore, the association "Headquarters for the Defence of Vukovar" publicly opposes the use of bilingual panels written in Latin and Cyrillic letters in Vukovar. In 2014, the association submitted a request for a referendum concerning amendment of Article 12(1) of the Constitutional Act on the Rights of National Minorities,[58] which was dismissed by the Constitutional Court for being

---

[53]For example, the adoption of the Medically Assisted Procreation Act in 2012, OG No. 86/12, that does not apply to same-sex communities, resulted in a strong disapproval of the LGBT community and initiated a debate in the Croatian media (as well as society) on whether same-sex couples should be allowed to adopt and raise children. The Croatian Prime Minister Milanović Z. reacted by publicly announcing a further extension of the rights for same-sex communities, which should enjoy rights and obligations equivalent to those in a heterosexual marriage, with the exception of the right to adopt children.

[54]See Miščenić (2018).

[55]Decision of the Constitutional Court regarding the finalization of the surveillance procedure on constitutionality and legality of pursuing a State referendum held on 1 December 2013, when Art. 62 of the Constitution of the Republic of Croatia was supplemented by the new para. 2, No. SuP-O-1/2014 of 14 January 2014, OG No. 5/2014.

[56]On their official webpage, the association promotes the prevention of a legal regulation that equalizes same-sex communities and marriage and a denial of rights deriving from it, as well as the protection of children from adoption by same-sex couples. Available at: http://referendumobraku.uimeobitelji.net/2014/07/16/name-family-new-life-partnership-act/#more-5671.

[57]Until the adoption of the Same-Sex Persons Life Partnership Act (SSPLPA), OG No. 92/14, partners of same-sex communities were deprived of the majority of rights granted to spouses or extramarital partners. In accordance with the ECJ/CJEU practice, the Croatian courts are now obliged to follow the outcome from cases C-267/06, *Maruko* [2008] ECR I-01757 and C-147/08, *Römer* [2011] ECR I-03591, according to which Articles 1-2 and 3(1)(c) of the Framework Directive 2000/78/EC preclude national legislation that differentiates life partners from spouses regarding their rights and obligations (i.e. benefits, when life partnership places persons of the same sex in a situation comparable to that of spouses).

[58]OG Nos. 155/02, 47/10, 80/10 and 93/11.

unconstitutional.[59] This resulted in various reactions, including physical destructions of panels, rejections of panels by the City of Vukovar,[60] and frequent hate speeches against the members of the Serbian national minority in Vukovar and Serbs in general.

10 How Broad Is the Coverage of Antidiscrimination Law?

The coverage of the special antidiscrimination framework is very broad: it covers conduct of all state authorities, bodies of local and regional self-government units, legal persons vested with public authority and of all legal and natural persons.[61] With regard to the material scope of application, Article 8 of the ADA applies to conduct of enumerated subjects *particularly* in these areas: (1) work and working conditions (access to self-employment and occupation, including selection criteria, recruiting and promotion conditions; access to all types of vocational guidance, vocational training, professional improvement and retraining); (2) education, science and sports; (3) social security, including social welfare, pension and health insurance and unemployment insurance; (4) health protection; (5) judiciary and administration; (6) housing; (7) public informing and the media; (8) access to goods and services and their provision; (9) membership and activities in trade unions, civil society organisations, political parties or any other organisations; and (10) access to participation in cultural and artistic creation. Due to the term "particularly," there is a generally accepted interpretation of Article 8 ADA as an open-end clause.[62]

The GEA prohibits discrimination in the acquisition and supplying of goods as well as regarding the provision of and access to services (Article 6(4)) and puts a special emphasis on protection against discrimination in the areas of employment and labour, education, and in matters of women's and men's representation in

---

[59] Decision of the Constitutional Court No. U-VIIR-4640/2014 of 12 August 2014, OG No. 104/14.

[60] By its Decision No. U-II-6110/2013 of 12 August 2014, OG No. 104/14, the Constitutional Court annulled Article 22 of the Statutory Decision on amendments of the Statute of the City of Vukovar, Classification: 012-03/09-01/01, No. 2196/01-01-13-31 of 4 November 2013 (OJ of the City of Vukovar No. 7/13), adopted by the City Council of the City of Vukovar, saying: "On the ground of provision of Art. 2 para. 2 and para. 4 of this Statute the City of Vukovar is completely exempted from application of provisions of the Act on the Use of the Language and Letter of National Minorities in the Republic of Croatia and of Art. 12 of the Constitutional Act on the Rights of National Minorities, until the fulfilment of conditions set in Art. 8 of the Constitutional Act on the Rights of National Minorities."

[61] Article 8 ADA. Article 3(1) GEA sets a duty for state authorities, bodies of local and regional self-government units, legal persons vested with public authority, legal persons predominantly owned by the state and units of local and regional self-government to estimate and evaluate the effects of their legal acts, decisions or actions on the position of women and men in every phase of their planning, adoption and implementation in order to achieve actual equality between women and men.

[62] Grgić et al. (2009), p. 62.

political parties, the media, and statistical data (Articles 13–17 and Chapters IV–VIII GEA). Within this wide scope of application, Article 1(1) ADA prohibits discrimination on 21 taxatively enumerated grounds: race, ethnic affiliation, colour, gender, language, religion, political or other belief, national or social origin, property, trade union membership, education, social status, marital status, family status, age, health condition, disability, genetic heritage, native identity, expression and sexual orientation.[63] The GEA covers gender, marital status, family status and sexual orientation, but also encompasses less favourable treatment of women on the grounds of pregnancy and maternity (Article 6(1)-(3)). Additionally, Article 21(1) SSCA prohibits discrimination on the grounds of same-sex community and of homosexual orientation, and Article 79 SSPLPA prohibits discrimination on the ground of life partnership of same-sex persons.

Despite the broad coverage and prohibition of discrimination in all appearances (direct, indirect, harassment and sexual harassment etc.),[64] there is a long list of exhaustive exceptions regarding certain areas and grounds of discrimination in Article 9(2) ADA (e.g. positive or affirmative measures, certain social or employment policy measures, exceptions relating to a particular job, an exception regarding insurance services, an exception regarding rights and obligations prescribed by the Family Act, etc.).[65] However, according to Article 9(3) ADA, all these exceptions must carry legitimate aim and must be appropriate and necessary for the realization of this aim.

11 Does Enforcement of Antidiscrimination Law Vary According to the Ground of Discrimination?

The fact that not all grounds of discrimination enjoy the same status is visible both from the Croatian special antidiscrimination legal framework and EU Antidiscrimination Directives to which it is approximated.[66] For example, there

---

[63] *Potočnjak* and *Grgić* say that the provision should nevertheless be considered as an open-ended one by interpreting antidiscrimination statutory law in accordance with the guarantee of non-discrimination in Art. 14(1) of the Constitution. See Potočnjak and Grgić (2011), p. 19.

[64] Article 9(1) ADA. With regard to definition and different forms of discrimination, see Mišćenić (2015), p. 114.

[65] Provisions on positive measures are also regulated in Chapter III, i.e. Articles 9–12 GEA. The last amendment of Article 9(2) ADA concerned the adjustment of insurance services exception to C-236/09, *Test Achats* [2011] ECR I-00773.

[66] This is also confirmed by the ECJ/CJEU practice, which raised the principle of non-discrimination particularly in cases of discrimination on the grounds of age and sex to the level of a general constitutional principle and recognized its fundamental rights value. See C-152/73, *Sotgiu* [1974] ECR I-00153, C-149/77; *Defrenne III* [1978] ECR I-01365; C-442/00, *Caballero* [2002] ECR I-11915; C-25/02, *Katharina Rinke v. Ärztekammer Hamburg* [2002] ECR I-08349; C-144/04, *Mangold* [2005] ECR I-09981; C-555/07, *Seda Kücükdeveci* [2010] ECR I-00365 etc.

are several ADA provisions that emphasize certain grounds of discrimination, such as Article 3(2) on sexual harassment, Article 4(2) on failure of reasonable adaptation to persons with disabilities, or Article 9 that taxatively enumerate exceptions to discrimination if it happens based on certain grounds.[67] The same conclusion can be reached in the enforcement practice of antidiscrimination law.

As it can be seen from the scarce Croatian antidiscrimination case law, some grounds of discrimination are more often used as a reason for unequal treatment than others. According to the Report of the Ombudsman from 2014, the most represented discrimination grounds were national origin, race, ethnic origin and skin colour.[68] In particular, members of Serbian and Roma national minorities have been very often affected by discrimination, which is also confirmed by many judgements of the European Court of Human Rights.[69] Besides already presented Croatian antidiscrimination case law concerning discrimination on the ground of sexual orientation,[70] the other most frequent grounds are gender, age and disability. Although these grounds of discrimination most commonly appear in the area of labour and employment relations, the special antidiscrimination court practice relating to them is still quite scarce.[71] The main reason for the lack of enforcement of special antidiscrimination law with regard to these grounds of discrimination lies in the inexperience of its application and interpretation in accordance with EU law as

---

[67]According to Article 9(2) ADA, placing in a less favourable position shall not be deemed to be discrimination in the following cases: "1. when such a conduct is set forth by law with the aim to preserve health, public security, maintain public order and peace, prevent criminal acts, and to protect rights and freedoms of other people and when the means used in democratic society are appropriate and necessary for achievement of the aimed goal, under condition that such conduct does not lead to direct or indirect discrimination *on the ground of race or ethnic origin, colour, religion, gender, national and social origin, sexual orientation and disability*; [...]. 3. pursuing measures of social politic that privilege persons or households in difficult property or social situation under condition that these measures do not lead to direct or indirect discrimination *on the ground of gender, sexual orientation, race, colour, ethnic origin, religion and disability.*[...]."

[68]Report of the Ombudsman from 2014. Available at: http://www.ombudsman.hr/index.php/en/documents-3/ombudsman-s-reports/finish/15-ombudsman-s-reports/648-summary-annual-report-for-2014.

[69]See cases on discrimination of Serbs regarding the takeover of property situated in occupied territories and belonging to persons who had left Croatia after 17 October 1990: *Saratlić v. Croatia*, App. No. 35670/03, ECHR (2006); *Radanović v. Croatia*, App. No. 9056/02, ECHR (2006); *Grlica v. Croatia*, App. No. 15579/04, ECHR (2006); *Vučak&Vučak v. Croatia,* App. No. 889/06, ECHR (2008); *Kunić v. Croatia*, App. No. 22344/02, ECHR (2007); Decision of the Constitutional Court U-III/1451/2004 of 9 December 2004. See also the Judgement in the case *Oršuš and Others v. Croatia* (2011) 52 ECHR 7 regarding racial discrimination and violation of the right to education of schoolchildren separated in Roma-only classes.

[70]See *supra*, Answer to Questions Nos. 4 and 5.

[71]For a detailed analysis of discrimination on the grounds of age, disability, sexual orientation, gender, race and ethnic origin, nationality, political and religious opinion and other grounds, consult Mišćenić (2014), pp. 93 *et seq*.

well as in resorting to the application of already familiar provisions on equality contained in numerous other statutory acts.[72]

12 What Is the Relationship Between the Enforcement of Antidiscrimination Law and the Quest for Equality on Both an Individual and Systemic Level?

The quest for equality on both an individual and systemic level is very strong in the Croatian legal system and still dominates over the enforcement of recent antidiscrimination law. Apart from being embodied in numerous provisions of the Constitution[73] and being integrated into international agreements forming part of the Croatian legal system (e.g. UN and ILO conventions, ECHR, CEDAW, ICCPR, ICESRC, etc.),[74] the right to equality is protected by numerous provisions scattered all over various statutory and other legal acts, whose origin is often not to be contributed to the approximation process with the EU *acquis*. These can be found in the COA, LA, Family Act, Inheritance Act, Act on Ownership and Other Real Rights, to name a few.[75] Their enforcement is guaranteed primarily through the constitutional duty of courts to rule based on the Constitution, international agreements and other valid sources of law, and through duty of the Supreme Court to

---

[72]The court practice prior to adoption of the ADA dealt with cases of discrimination based on the grounds mentioned above. For example: Judgements of the Supreme Court, Revr-459/07 of 25 September 2007 (age), Ur 4/07 of 17 May 2007 (age), Revr-90/06-2 of 4 July 2006 (age); County Court in Varaždin, Gž-473/2003 of 15 April 2003 (age and gender); Decision of the Constitutional Court U-III-611-I-1999 of 16 November 2000 (disability); and Decisions of the Constitutional Court U-I-402/2003 and U-I-2812/2007 of 30 April 2008 (national origin).

[73]According to Article 3 of the Constitution, "freedom, equal rights, national and gender equality, peace-making, social justice, respect for human rights, inviolability of ownership, conservation of nature and the environment, the rule of law and a democratic multiparty system are the highest values of the constitutional order of the Republic of Croatia and the ground for interpretation of the Constitution." Article 14(1) of the Constitution guarantees that "all persons in the Republic of Croatia (shall) enjoy rights and freedoms, regardless of race, colour, gender, language, religion, political or other conviction, national or social origin, property, birth, education, social status or other characteristics," and according to its para. 2, "all persons shall be equal before the law." References to the right to equality can be found in numerous other constitutional provisions (Articles 15, 26, 44, 49, 55 etc.).

[74]Article 141 Constitution.

[75]For example, the COA provisions on legal capacity (Article 17(1)), personality rights (Article 19), nullity of contracts (Article 322(1)), performance (Article 270–271), and condition (Article 298(1)), the Family Act provision on regulation of family relationships (Article 2); Inheritance Act provisions on inadmissible or unmoral conditions (Article 47(3)) or mandates (Article 48(2)); provisions of the Act on Ownership and Other Real Rights on acquiring ownership rights over real estate (Article 358a); or the LA provisions on direct and indirect discrimination (Article 7(4)); prohibition of unequal treatment of pregnant women (Article 67); equal pay to women and men for equal work or work of equal value (Article 83); and protection of workers dignity (Article 130).

ensure uniform application of laws and equality of all before the law.[76] A more comprehensive protection of the right to equality is also guaranteed by the constitutional duty of *everybody* to abide by the Constitution and the law and to respect the legal order of the Republic of Croatia.[77] Consequently, the judiciary is still applying provisions embodying the quest for equality than the more special antidiscrimination law, and the successful protection of the right to equality[78] resists developing antidiscrimination court practice.[79] The main reasons for this are the difficulties in determining the legal hierarchy between the statutory provisions protecting equality and the special antidiscrimination law, as well as the lack of knowledge on the uniform application and interpretation of harmonized Croatian antidiscrimination law with the transposed EU directives, ECJ/CJEU practice and EU law in general.

13 Is the Enforcement of Antidiscrimination Law Regarded as Different from the Enforcement of Other Laws?

The answer to this question arises from the particularities of the antidiscrimination law itself, especially certain procedural aspects of antidiscrimination law. For example, the reversal of the burden of proof in antidiscrimination proceedings is a serious issue for Croatian judges when enforcing antidiscrimination law. In accordance with Articles 20 ADA and 30(4) GEA, the claimant has to present the probability of discrimination, then the burden of proof switches over to the defendant, who then

---

[76] Articles 118(3) and 119(1) Constitution; Article 24(1) Courts Act.

[77] Article 5(2) Constitution. According to Article 20 of the Constitution, *anyone* violating the provisions of the Constitution on human rights and fundamental freedoms is personally responsible and may not be justified by a higher order.

[78] See the Decisions of the Constitutional Court: No. U-III/696/1996 of 11 October 2000, stating that "equality before the law within the meaning of that constitutional provision (Article 14 (2) Constitution) assumes, among others, the equal legal position of participants to legal relationship deriving from a certain legal transaction"; Nos. U-II-318/2003, U-II-643/2003 of 9 April 2003, according to which courts shall decide on conflicts of collective agreement with the Constitution, mandatory provisions and morals of society by applying the COA provisions on nullity of contracts; No. U-III-2029/01 of 28 March 2002, saying the "... constitutional guarantee of equality from Article 14 Constitution would be violated if it would be established that the party in the procedure preceding the challenged decision was not in equal position to other parties in the same legal situation [...]."

[79] See the Judgement of the County Court in Zagreb 15 Pnz-6/10-27 of 24 March 2011; the Judgement of the Supreme Court Gž-12/11-2 of 18 April 2012; the Judgement of the County Court in Zagreb Pnz-7/10 of 2 May 2011; the Judgement of the County Court in Zagreb Pnz-8/10 of 28 July 2011; the Judgement of the Supreme Court Gž-25/11-2 of 28 February 2012; the Judgement of the Supreme Court Gž-41/11-2 of 28 February 2012; the Judgement of the Municipal Court in Varaždin P-3153/10-89 of 12 July 2012; the Judgement of the County Court in Varaždin Gž-5048/12-2 of 9 July 2013 analysed in Mišćenić (2015), pp. 128 *et seq.*

needs to prove that there has been no discriminatory treatment with a level of certainty.[80] Since it represents a departure from the civil law procedure provisions on the burden of proof,[81] the lower court instances usually misapply the relevant provisions in antidiscrimination proceedings.

Similarly, procedural rules on imposing interim measures are significantly simplified in antidiscrimination proceedings and the court will order them if the claimant *inter alia* makes it "probable" that his or her right to equal treatment has been violated (Article 19 ADA).[82] In antidiscrimination proceedings, the court can shorten the deadline for the voluntary execution of judgements or even decide that an appeal shall not withhold the enforcement of the judgement (Article 22 ADA). And revision as an extraordinary remedy is always allowed in antidiscrimination proceedings (Articles 23 and 24(4) ADA). This is an effective means for the Supreme Court to guarantee the uniform application of antidiscrimination law. On more than one occasion, the Supreme Court corrected failures of lower courts in applying and interpreting harmonized Croatian antidiscrimination law in collective redress proceedings.[83]

All these novelties can have an adverse effect upon the judges and other applicants of law, who often resist novelties introduced by approximated national law,

---

[80] According to Dika (2011), p. 86, the concept of "probability" is not defined in the Croatian civil law procedure and it does not require that a claimant prove the facts with a level of certainty, which he or she would be required to do under the provisions of civil law procedure. By interpreting these provisions in accordance with Article 8 of the Directive 2000/43/EC and Article 10 of the Directive 2000/78/EC, *Dika* concludes that the concept of "probability" should be interpreted as *prima facie* evidence, a legal standard not applied in the Croatian law and practice.

[81] See examples of judgements in the area of labour and employment relations prior to ADA adoption: In Judgement Revr-617/2006-2 of 11 January 2007, the Supreme Court held that the burden of proof that there was no discrimination was, according to Article 6 LA, on the respondent. In another Judgement Revr-256/07 of 6 June 2007, the Supreme Court held that the worker must prove the discriminatory behaviour of the employer towards him. In Judgement Gž 286/2007-2 of 7 May 2007 the County Court in Varaždin said that the respondent (employer) does not need to prove that the worker's dismissal is not a consequence of discrimination if the claimant has not mentioned any facts that would sour doubt that discriminatory behaviour occurred.

[82] The provisions of the Execution Act (OG Nos. 112/12, 25/13 and 93/14) apply accordingly, while Article 19(2)(2) ADA requires for a measure to be necessary for the elimination of the danger of irreparable damage, of a particularly serious violation of the right to equal treatment, or because of the prevention of violence.

[83] For example, in case Gž-25/11-2 of 28 February 2012, the Supreme Court overruled the first instance judgment of County Court in Zagreb Pnz-7/10 of 2 May 2011 that dismissed the antidiscrimination claims because the respondent was not speaking in his own name, but in the name of Croatian Football Federation and is consequently not passively legitimated in the dispute, and because the claimants did not prove the harmful consequences of the respondent's behaviour. Besides establishing the discrimination and prohibiting the future discriminatory behaviour of the respondent (in line with cases C-54/07, *Feryn* [2008] ECR I-05187 and C-81/12, *Asociaţia Accept* [2013] EU: C:2013:275), the Supreme Court explained that public statements coming from the president of the Croatian Football Federation should also be looked at from the perspective of a person who is in the world of football, and on sports relations regarded as a person of competence and authority who unquestionably has an influence in the area of sport, in particular of football in Croatia.

which requires a deeper knowledge and understanding of national provisions in accordance with the EU *acquis*. Even when applying harmonized national provisions of antidiscrimination law, they often resort to their own interpretation of the norm instead of applying it consistently with the EU Antidiscrimination Directives and the established CJEU/ECJ case law.

14 What Does the Enforcement of Antidiscrimination Law Reveal About the Nature of Your Legal System or About the Enforcement of Laws in Your Legal System?

Despite the many issues with the enforcement of laws in the Croatian legal system,[84] prospects for the enforcement of the antidiscrimination law seem to be promising. The prohibition of discrimination emerges from and is an expression of the fundamental principle of equality, the protection of which is embodied in our legal framework. Numerous public and private law provisions existing prior to the legislative alignment with the EU *acquis* offered protection from the violation of the right to equality including unequal, discriminatory treatment.[85] Moreover, the Croatian legal system and its practitioners are affected by international law sources on human rights protection, particularly by the ECHR.[86] To a certain extent, this made enforcement of the "new" antidiscrimination law more complicated. For example, there were issues with the legal relationship and hierarchy between the ADA, GEA, SSCA as special antidiscrimination legislation, and other applicable statutory acts (e.g. LA, COA, CC, etc.).[87] In cases of collision between the right to equal treatment and non-discrimination and some other fundamental rights or freedoms, such as the freedom of opinion and thought expression, courts often ruled in favour of the latter.[88] Also, the success of the first Croatian case on "special"

---

[84]Pursuant to Article 36(1)(2) Accession Treaty, the Commission shall monitor, in particular, the commitments undertaken by Croatia in the area of the judiciary and fundamental rights (Annex VII), including the continued development of track records on judicial reform and efficiency.

[85]Judgement of the County Court in Varaždin Gž-3123/11-2 of 25 October 2011: "due to violation of *personality rights* on honour, dignity and reputation and *discriminatory behaviour* of defendant, and due to violation of claimant's fundamental human rights, which are protected to every person".

[86]Judgement of the County Court in Varaždin Gž-3123/11-2 of 25 October 2011: "defendants behaviour violated their dignity, reputation and honour, which are values protected also by *European Convention for the Protection of Human Rights* and to be equally valuated for every person".

[87]Judgement of the Supreme Court Kzz-11/11-3 of 6 September 2011 on the relation between LA, CC and ADA provisions in case of harassment and sexual harassment of an employee at their working place.

[88]Judgement in the collective antidiscrimination proceeding of the County Court in Zagreb 15 Pnz-6/10-27 of 24 March 2011, confirmed by the Judgement of the Supreme Court Gž-12/11-2 of 18 April 2012. The Judgement is based on the same arguments of the County Court in Zagreb Pnz-8/10 of 28 July 2011, which was dismissed and corrected by the Judgement of the Supreme Court Gž-41/11-2 of 28 February 2012.

antidiscrimination action was shadowed by the judgement in another dispute between the same parties, establishing a violation of the personality rights of the discriminator.[89] However, as mentioned, the main issues concerned misinterpretation and misapplication of relevant antidiscrimination statutory acts: lower court instances ignored their provisions on shifting of the burden of proof,[90] denied claims because of the non-existence of an identifiable victim of discrimination[91] and because discriminatory statements came from a person who could not make decisions in employment matters.[92] In doing so, they misapplied the harmonized antidiscrimination law and ignored the established CJEU/ECJ case law,[93] which they are obliged to observe by the *acquis* and by a constitutional guarantee on the protection of subjective rights based on the *acquis*.[94] Most of the enumerated issues were successfully dealt with by the Supreme Court,[95] thus demonstrating a strong potential for improvement of the enforcement of the Croatian antidiscrimination law.

15 Conclusion

The special antidiscrimination legal framework presented above is quite recent in the Croatian legal system. The ADA, as the main statutory act regulating the prohibition of discrimination entered into force on 1 January 2009. Nevertheless, protection from discrimination has always been guaranteed through numerous provisions on the protection of human rights incorporated in international agreements, the Croatian Constitution, and statutory provisions protecting the right to equality. Moreover, within the Croatian antidiscrimination law one can distinguish between special antidiscrimination legislation on the one hand (ADA and GEA) and numerous antidiscrimination provisions scattered all over various statutory acts on the other hand (e.g. LA, SSCA, SSPLPA, etc.).

Despite the broad protection from discrimination offered by the Croatian legal framework and relatively well-approximated special antidiscrimination legislation to

---

[89] See the Judgements of the Municipal Court in Varaždin P-3153/10-89 of 12 July 2012 and County Court in Varaždin Gž-5048/12-2 of 9 July 2013.

[90] Judgements of the County Court in Zagreb 15 Pnz-6/10-27 of 24 March 2011 and of the Supreme Court Gž-12/11-2 of 18 April 2012; Judgements of the County Court in Zagreb Pnz-7/10 of 2 May 2011 and Pnz-8/10 of 28 July 2011.

[91] Judgement of the County Court in Zagreb 15 Pnz-6/10-27 of 24 March 2011.

[92] Judgement of the County Court in Zagreb 15 Pnz-6/10-27 of 24 March 2011.

[93] In opposition to Articles 1–2 ADA and Arts. 6–7 GEA containing definitions of discrimination and CJEU/ECJ case law, e.g. in C-54/07, *Feryn* [2008] ECR I-05187 or in C-81/12, *Asociaţia Accept* [2013] EU:C:2013:275.

[94] Articles 145–146 Constitution.

[95] Judgements of the Supreme Court of the Republic of Croatia Gž-25/11-2 and Gž-41/11-2 of 28 February 2012.

EU Antidiscrimination Directives, the presented statistics and practice indicate difficulties in the enforcement of antidiscrimination law.[96] According to various reports of the Ombudsman and the special ombudsmen, as well as statements from NGOs protecting human rights, this can be ascribed mainly to the ignorance about existing legal and other remedies against discrimination, and also to strong doubts on their effectiveness in practice. The latter was confirmed by several antidiscrimination collective redress proceedings, where the lower court instances misapplied the provisions of special antidiscrimination statutory acts in different ways.[97] Due to insufficient background in EU law, they often apply national harmonized provisions on antidiscrimination together with their particularities in a manner comparable to the enforcement of national provisions in other areas of law. In addition, being used to more general protection of the right to equality, legal practitioners resort to the application of familiar provisions protecting equality in certain areas of law, such as labour law.[98]

Nonetheless, the scarce and still developing practice in Croatian antidiscrimination law also demonstrates a strong potential for improvement of the judicial enforcement. On more than one occasion, the Supreme Court successfully corrected the mistakes of lower courts' judgements in antidiscrimination proceedings, thus guaranteeing the uniform application and interpretation of the harmonized national provisions in accordance with the EU antidiscrimination *acquis*.[99] Apart from the improvement in judicial enforcement, one should also mention the strengthening of other enforcement methods in practice. These include, for example, the Ombudsman's activities on raising public awareness on discrimination as well as acting upon individual complaints of discrimination.[100] Through warnings and recommendations, the Ombudsman and special ombudsmen protect the rights of individual victims and seek to act preventively regarding all future potential victims of discrimination. In doing so, they contribute significantly to the strengthening of the enforcement of Croatian antidiscrimination law by *inter alia* affecting the general approach to and understanding of discriminatory behaviour in our society. The challenge of strengthening the enforcement of antidiscrimination law in Croatia can be managed successfully only by

---

[96] See *supra*, Answer to Question No. 1.

[97] See *supra*, Answer to Question No. 13.

[98] Bodiroga-Vukobrat and Martinović (2013), p. 11; Vasiljević (2015), p. 68.

[99] For example, Judgement of the County Court in Zagreb Pnz-7/10 of 2 May 2011, overruled by Judgement of the Supreme Court Gž-25/11-2; Judgement of the County Court in Zagreb Pnz-8/10 of 28 July 2011, overruled by Judgement of the Supreme Court Gž-41/11-2 of 28 February 2012; Judgement of the County Court in Zagreb Pnz-2/13 of 5 June 2013, overruled by Judgement of the Supreme Court Gž-21/13-2 of 10 September 2013.

[100] According to the Ombudsman's Annual Report of 2014, in 2014 the Ombudsman worked on 3892 cases, wherein the number of complaints was 40% higher compared to the two previous years. Available at: http://www.ombudsman.hr/index.php/en/.

both affecting certain discriminatory behaviours still accepted in society and by the common work of all institutions interested in deterring such a behaviour—namely courts, independent institutions for the protection of human rights, relevant governmental bodies, and NGOs.

References

Bodiroga-Vukobrat N, Martinović A (2013) Croatia's accession in the light of gender equality. EGELRev 1:11
Dika M (2011) Sudska zaštita u diskriminacijskim stvarima, in Crnić 2011, p 86
Grgić A, Potočnjak Ž, Rodin S, Selanec G, Šimonović Einwalter T, Uzelac A (2009) A guide to the anti-discrimination act. Government of the Republic of Croatia, Office for Human Rights, Zagreb, p 62
Mišćenić E (2014) Country report for Croatia. In: Reich N, Jessel-Holst Ch, Josipović T, Dollani N (eds) Autonomy and antidiscrimination in private law, South East European Law School Network, Civil Law Forum for South East Europe – collection for studies and analyses. Tirana, pp 100 et seq
Mišćenić E (2015) The impact of the Croatian anti-discrimination law on private law relations. In: Bodiroga-Vukobrat N, Rodin S, Sander GG (eds) New Europe – old values? Springer, p 128
Mišćenić E (2018) Slučajevi povrede prava osobnosti diskriminacijom u hrvatskim medijima [Cases of infringement of personality rights by discrimination in the Croatian media]. In: Slakoper Z, Bukovac Puvača M, Mihelčić G (eds) Liber Amicorum Aldo Radolović. Law Faculty of the University of Rijeka (forthcoming)
Potočnjak Ž, Grgić A (2011) Važnost prakse Europskog suda za ljudska prava i Europskog suda pravde za razvoj hrvatskog antidiskriminacijskog prava. In: Crnić I et al (eds) Primjena antidiskriminacijskog zakonodavstva u praksi. Centar za mirovne studije, Zagreb, p 19
Vasiljević S (2015) New law and values: anti-discrimination law in post-communist countries. In: Bodiroga-Vukobrat N, Rodin S, Sander GG (eds) New Europe - old values? Springer, pp 64 et seq

Emilia Mišćenić is an Assistant Professor of Law at the University of Rijeka. She holds a Ph.D from Karl-Franzens University of Graz, an LLM from Europa-Institut of Saarland University. She is the author and co-editor of the book 'Legal Risks in EU Law: Interdisciplinary Studies on Legal Risk Management and Better Regulation in Europe' (Springer, 2016). Ms. Mišćenić writes and teaches in the field of European Private Law.

Dijana Kesonja is a human rights lawyer working as a Legal Affairs and Strategic Litigation Advisor to the Ombudswoman for Croatia. She is working in the Antidiscrimination department in the Ombudswoman office, handling the discrimination cases and holding educations for diversity of stakeholders in the field of human rights and discrimination.

Czech Republic

Markéta Selucká, Martina Grochová, and Jana Komendová

1 Introduction

The Czech Constitutional Court in its decision from 6 June 2006, file no. Pl. ÚS 42/04, rules that the constitutional principle of equality in rights belongs to those fundamental human rights that constitute a system of values of modern democratic societies. The principle of equality is a legally philosophical postulate at the level of positive law guaranteed by prohibition of discrimination. Equality is not a changeless category as far as it goes through development especially in the area of political and social rights. Also, the international documents about human rights and numerous decisions of international control bodies emanate from the fact that not every unequal treatment with different subjects can be qualified as violation of the principle of equality, or accordingly, as illicit discrimination of ones in comparison with others. Violation of this principle requires several conditions be met: different subjects being in the same or comparable situation are treated in a different manner unless there are any objective and reasonable reasons for applying a different approach. Herein it can be added that the European Court of Human Rights similarly states that difference in treatment among persons being in analogical or comparable situations is discriminatory unless it has any objective and reasonable justification.

M. Selucká (✉)
Masaryk University, Department of Civil Law and Dean of Faculty of Law, Brno, Czech Republic
e-mail: marketa.selucka@law.muni.cz

M. Grochová
Constitutional Court of the Czech Republic, Brno, Czech Republic

J. Komendová
Masaryk University, Department of Labour Law and Social Security Law, Faculty of Law, Brno, Czech Republic
e-mail: jana.komendova@law.muni.cz

2 Constitutional and International Basis of the Czech Antidiscrimination Law

2.1 Constitutional Basis of the Prohibition of Discrimination

In the Czech Republic, the principle of prohibition of discrimination has its basis in the constitutional law. The Charter, part of Czech constitutional order, comprises the constitutional regulation of the prohibition of discrimination even though it does not explicitly mention the word *discrimination*. Article 1 of the Charter enshrines the concept of equality in rights. This article declares basic values being the core of the Charter, in addition to freedom and dignity, and the equality of human beings. Article 1 reflects Article 1 of the Universal Declaration of Human Rights.[1] It guarantees that neither application of law nor the legislation shall be inconsistent with the principle of equality.[2] The principle of equality permeates the whole Charter.[3] According to the case law of the Czech Constitutional Court, the provision shall not be interpreted as a requirement of the equality in all subjective rights but as enshrinement of the equality before the law.[4]

Article 3(1) of the Charter[5] is also considered the basis of the principle of the prohibition of discrimination in the Czech legal order.[6] The relation of the two provisions of the Charter proclaiming the equality of all beings (i.e. the prohibition of discrimination) remains unclear. Existing case law of the Czech Constitutional Court keeps making distinctions among them. Some of the decisions declare Article 1 as general prohibition of discrimination or general principle whereas Article 3(1) is seen as specific prohibition of discrimination or the concretization of a general principle. Like the European Court of Human Rights (hereinafter ECtHR) declares Article 14 of the European Convention on Human Rights (hereinafter ECHR) of accessorial nature, the Czech Constitutional Court also infers that the article (unlike Article 1) is of the accessorial nature.[7] But we identify ourselves with the view of Michal Bobek who does not find any ground for distinction of the two provisions on

---

[1] Article 1 of the Universal Declaration of Human Rights states: All human beings are born free and equal in dignity and rights.

[2] Baroš (2012), p. 49.

[3] Decision of the Czech Constitutional Court, 24 May 1995, ref. no. Pl. ÚS 31/94.

[4] Decision of the Czech Constitutional Court, 21 January 2013, ref. no. Pl. ÚS 15/02.

[5] Everyone is guaranteed the enjoyment of his or her fundamental rights and basic freedoms without regard to gender, race, colour of skin, language, faith and religion, political or other conviction, national or social origin, membership in a national or ethnic minority, property, birth, or other status.

[6] Bobek (2012), p. 99.

[7] Bobek (2012), pp. 99–100. On the matters of the accessorial nature of the provision enshrining the prohibition of discrimination see also decision of the Czech Constitutional Court, 26 June 2002, ref. no. Pl. ÚS 36/01.

the basis of their accessorial nature, as none of them reduces, explicitly or implicitly, the equality in rights to the rights enshrined in the Charter.[8]

The Charter further comprises provisions on discrimination in specific matters. Chapter III, dealing with rights of the national and ethnical minorities, is especially significant to antidiscrimination law. Article 24 states that "[a]ffiliation to any national or ethnical minority may not be to anyone's detriment."[9] Such provision is to be seen as a reaction to our historical experience and is not rare in international documents concerning human rights.[10] Apart from provisions stipulating the prohibition of discrimination the Charter also comprises provisions constituting positive discrimination.[11] Article 29 and Article 32 guarantee increased protection to specific vulnerable groups of people. Article 29 is considered *lex specialis* to the right to protection of health and to the right to appropriate working conditions. The special provision aims to eliminate direct discrimination toward vulnerable groups and encourages legislators to adopt positive measures.[12] Article 32(2) has to be understood as both the concretisation of the protection of parenthood and motherhood and as an antidiscriminatory provision reflecting the international obligations.[13]

2.2 *International Law Regarding Discrimination*

The prohibition of discrimination is a strong human rights imperative and is thus enshrined in a number of human rights international conventions of both general and specific nature.[14] The Czech Republic also acceded to a number of conventions providing provisions aiming to eliminate discrimination against specific groups of people.[15] Particularly important is the ECHR and its Article 14 proscribing

---

[8]Bobek (2012), pp. 100–101.

[9]Article 24 of the Charter of Fundamental Rights and Freedoms.

[10]Bobek (2012), p. 539.

[11]Positive discrimination is a deviation from the principle of equal treatment that permits preferential treatment of a protected group under certain circumstances in order to redress history of disadvantage. The scope of permitted positive discrimination remains unclear. See, among others, Collins (2003), p. 17.

[12]Wintr (2012), pp. 619–625.

[13]Convention came into effect for Czech Republic on 18 March 1982. See Decree of the Minister of Foreign Affairs, No. 62/1987 Coll., on the Convention on the Elimination of All Forms of Discrimination Against Women.

[14]See Article 14 of the European Convention on Human Rights, Art. 7 of the Universal Declaration of Human Rights, Articles 26 and 27 of the International Covenant on Civil and Political Rights, Article 2 section 2 of the International Covenant on Economic, Social and Cultural Rights.

[15]For instance, Convention on the Elimination of All Forms of Discrimination Against Women, Convention on the Elimination of All Forms of Racial Discrimination, Convention on the Rights of Persons with Disabilities, Convention relating to the Status of Refugees, Convention on the Rights of the Child, Revised European Social Charter, International Covenant on Civil and Political

discrimination in general. Article 14 of the ECHR has an accessorial nature. Current case-law of the ECtHR broadened the possible use of this article, as it stated that Article 14 may be invoked also when any of the guaranteed rights is not directly infringed but when the alleged infringement falls within the ambit of one of the rights guaranteed.[16] The prohibition of discrimination is also enshrined in the Twelfth Protocol to the ECHR, in which a self-standing prohibition of discrimination is included.[17] The rights enshrined in the ECHR and their interpretation adopted in the decisions of the ECtHR has an especially great impact on the national legal regulation. The ECHR is more than just ordinary reciprocal engagements between states; it has to be understood as a network of objective obligations that benefit from collective enforcement.[18]

Besides the ECHR, the European Union law is of utmost importance. The concept of the prohibition of discrimination may be found in both fundamental treaties of the European Union. The original Treaty founding the European Economic Community prohibited only gender discrimination in the field of equal pay and discrimination on grounds of nationality.[19] One aim of Article 3 of the Treaty on European Union (TEU) is to combat discrimination. The Treaty on the Functioning of the European Union (hereinafter TFEU) prohibits discrimination on grounds of nationality and also entitles the European Parliament and the Council to adopt rules designed to prohibit such discrimination in Article 18. In Article 19(1) TFEU also entitles Council to take, after obtaining the consent of the European Parliament, appropriate action to combat discrimination based on sex, racial or ethnic origin, religion or belief, disability, age or sexual orientation. The prohibition of discrimination is also stressed in several other articles thru both TEU and TFEU. Primary EU law still only directly prohibits discrimination on two grounds—gender and nationality—unlike other international law that states multiple discriminatory grounds (e.g. ECHR states 11 of them).[20]

Since 2000 the EU also has its human rights document, the Charter of Fundamental Rights of the European Union (hereinafter the EU Charter), proclaimed by the Council, Parliament and Commission on 7 December 2000.[21] The whole title III of the EU Charter is dedicated to equality. General prohibition of discrimination is enshrined in article 20. Following articles specifically deal with the equality between women and men,[22] the rights of the child,[23] the rights of the elderly,[24] and the rights

---

Rights, Framework Convention for Protection of National Minorities, International Convention on Economic, Social and Cultural Rights, ILO Convention No. 111 on Discrimination.

[16]Boučková et al. (2010), p. 28.
[17]Gerards (2005), p. 110.
[18]*Ireland v. United Kingdom*, ECtHR judgement, 18 January 1978, no. 5310/71, para 239.
[19]Schiek and Lawson (2011), p. 11.
[20]Schiek and Lawson (2011), pp. 13–14.
[21]Bell (2004), p. 23.
[22]Article 23 of the EU Charter.
[23]Article 24 of the EU Charter.
[24]Article 25 of the EU Charter.

of persons with disabilities.[25] The secondary EU law concerning the prohibition of discrimination consists of a number of different directives on that matter. The EU directives[26] were implemented into the Czech legal order by Act No. 198/2009 Coll., on Equal Treatment and on Legal Remedies of the Protection against Discrimination and the Change to Some Acts (Antidiscrimination Act).

3 National Legislation on the Matters of Discrimination

Apart from the constitution, the prohibition of discrimination is regulated by ordinary acts. The most important of them is the Antidiscrimination Act governing exclusively the matters of prohibition of discrimination, equality, and protection against discrimination. Beside the Antidiscrimination Act there are different provisions proscribing discrimination throughout the legal order.

3.1 Antidiscrimination Act

The Antidiscrimination Act consists only of 19 paragraphs and, as it states in Article 1, was adopted to implement the relevant EU directives and declare its continuity with the Charter and international treaties.[27] The act was drafted to fully implement all EU secondary antidiscrimination legislation and goes even beyond the requirements of the EU directives, which is the reason why it has such a broad scope covering work and employment relations, access to employment, self-employment and occupation, healthcare and education, social security and social protection, and social advantages and services.[28] The common ground for all areas regulated by the Antidiscrimination Act is their public overlap.[29] The main aim of the Antidiscriminatory Act is to regulate the prohibition of the discrimination in horizontal legal relations.[30] The Antidiscrimination Act is general legal regulation; any other legal regulation concerning equal treatment has to be regarded as *lex specialis* and is to be used preferably.[31]

---

[25] Article 26 of the EU Charter.

[26] For further information on EU directives on the matters of discrimination and their content see Boučková et al. (2010), pp. 32–36.

[27] Boučková et al. (2010), p. 31.

[28] Záhumenský (2014), pp. 5–6.

[29] Boučková et al. (2010), p. 117.

[30] Boučková et al. (2010), p. 31.

[31] Explanatory report to Act No. 198/2009 Coll., on Equal Treatment and on Legal Remedies of the Protection Against Discrimination and the Change to Some Acts (Antidiscrimination Act) or Čermák and Kvasnicová (2012), p. 20.

Antidiscrimination law enables individuals to invoke the right to equal treatment and protection against discrimination on suspicious grounds. Those grounds connect to stereotypes and prejudices towards certain groups that prevent members of such groups from being fully involved in the community. To attribute certain characteristics to an individual on the ground of his affiliation to certain group constitutes interference with dignity of the individual. The dignity of an individual is the basis of the right to equality, therefore the right to equality and the prohibition of discrimination have to be regarded as closely connected.[32]

3.2 Antidiscrimination Provisions in Private Law

From the conservatively civilian point of view within the private law, it is not quite usual to think about discrimination because the general private law is based on the thesis of autonomy of will, i.e. one can basically decide freely who to make a contract with, what the content of such a contract will be, etc. We could possibly say that by the very choice of being a party to a contract, other potential contract partners could have been discriminated. We can find freedom of contract—the highest principle of contractual law—in other civil codes across Europe, as well as the soft law principle of autonomy of will that can be found in 1:102 Principles of European Contract Law (PECL). Contractual freedom is characterized as an identified basic idea of the whole Draft Common Frame of Reference (DCFR)[33] (see II.—1:102 DCFR). Nevertheless, contractual freedom is not the sole principle of private law; there are other principles recognized by the Czech jurisprudence, such as protection of good faith, fair dealing or principle of equality. DCFR depicts the principle of legal peace, equity, and effectiveness of law as another fundamental principle, whereas justice is understood primarily in connection with general prohibition of discrimination. Other general principles of private law are correctives or limits of contractual freedom. It is not only DCFR that considers good faith or fair dealing a limit, but also Common European Sales Law (CESL) (Article 2), PECL (1:201 section 1) or United Nations Convention on Contracts for the International Sale of Goods (CISG) (Article 7).

3.3 Antidiscrimination Provisions in Civil Law

In respect to civil law—typically in cases of contracting process—it is unusual to think about discrimination. Moreover, the principle of prohibition of discrimination is not included in demonstrative enumeration of basic principles in the new Czech Civil Code (see Article 3 of Civil Code, hereinafter only CC) despite the fact this principle

---

[32]Kvasnicová (2011), p. 87.

[33]Von Bar et al. (2009), p. 62 et seq.

is expressly emphasized in other contemporary civil codes, and eventually in soft law (DCFR, ACQP etc.). However, this does not mean that the principle of prohibition of discrimination is not recognized by the Czech civil law or applied in legal relations. We see the general principle of equity, fairness, morality or equality in civil law relations or application of Article 1(1)(j) of the Antidiscrimination Act that prohibits discrimination in matters of access to goods and services, including accommodation in case they are offered or provided to the public. Furthermore, it is necessary to realize the Czech Republic is a member state of the EU so that it is obliged to respect the EU law, e.g. COUNCIL DIRECTIVE 2004/113/EC of 13 December 2004 implementing the principle of equal treatment between men and women in the access to and supply of goods and services. Basically, the Czech law prohibits discrimination in connection with providing services and goods not only by the Antidiscrimination Act, but also by the Act on Consumer Protection (Act No. 634/1992 Coll.). Moreover, one can use the general principle applicable in civil law requiring the rights to be treated fairly and morally. If the subject exercises his or her rights in abusive manner (see Article 8 CC), such an exercise does not enjoy legal protection.

The autonomy of will still applies in private law. In bargaining individual contracts, the choice of party to a contract depends on decision of a contractor. As soon as the services and goods are offered publicly, the general rule of prohibition of discrimination has to be applied. In the Czech Republic, we can meet illicit discrimination in cases of providing services and goods mostly in the form of refusal to provide them to specific ethnic or other minority group (e.g. refusing to serve the Roma people or Vietnamese in a restaurant because of their ethnicity, preventing access to the blind accompanied by guide dog, or prohibiting entrance with children to coffee or shop, etc.).We may also find dual pricing (higher prices for foreigners and lower prices for people speaking Czech in restaurants, taxi service, galleries, etc.). In spite of the fact that Antidiscrimination Act does not recognize discrimination on the basis of nationality, the District Court for Prague 6 in its judgment from 13 January 1999, file No. 6 C 209/1998 qualified such dual prices as immoral and awarded damages to plaintiff caused by a different admission fee to a gallery. Assignment of different prices for citizens of the Czech Republic and citizens of other member states of the EU is also a violation of the EU law (Article 18 and 56 TFEU). Discrimination on the basis of nationality is also prohibited by Article 12 of Act No. 222/2009 Coll.—free movement of services. Another relatively broad area, where we can possibly find discrimination, is the sphere of access to decent housing, especially for Roma people.

3.4 Antidiscrimination Provisions in Labour Law

The principle of equal treatment and prohibition of discrimination is considered one of the fundamental principles in Czech labour law.[34] Apart from the abovementioned

---

[34]See Galvas et al. (2015), p. 25.

international standards concerning the right to equal treatment and prohibition of discrimination in general, the Czech Republic has ratified conventions of the International Labour Organisation dealing with equality in employment and occupation, namely the Equal Remuneration Convention, 1951 (No. 100) and the Discrimination Employment and Occupation Convention, 1958 (No. 111).

The principle of equal treatment is explicitly expressed in section 1a of Act No. 262/2006 Coll. Labour Code (hereinafter the Labour Code), as amended, that enumerates the equal treatment of employees and prohibition of their discrimination among fundamental principles that are applied in labour relations governed by this act. The Labour Code contains provisions on equality of treatment and prohibition of discrimination in Articles 16 and 17. It is important to note that the obligation of employers does not consist only of the non-discrimination clause. The employer is responsible for compliance with the principle of equal treatment and non-discrimination with his/her employees. According to Article 16 of the Labour Code, employers are obliged to ensure equal treatment for all employees regarding working conditions, remuneration for work and other emoluments in cash and in kind (of monetary value), vocational training, and opportunities for career promotion. Besides conditions of work guaranteed by legal regulation, an employer is obliged to comply with the principle of equal treatment with all employees with respect to care of employees and advantages provided by the employer on a voluntary basis.[35]

The Labour Code explicitly prohibits any form of discrimination. However, it makes reference to the Antidiscrimination Act as to particular forms of discrimination. The Labour Code does not consider as discrimination different treatment arising from the nature of occupational activities where this different treatment is a substantial requirement necessary for work performance. The purpose followed by this derogation must be legitimate and the requirement must be adequate. In addition, measures that are justified and aimed at preventing or levelling out disadvantages arising from an individual's belonging to a certain group shall not be deemed as discrimination. Moreover, the Labour Code makes reference to the Antidiscrimination Act regarding remedial measures relating to protection against discrimination in labour relations.

As mentioned, particular prohibited forms of discrimination in labour relations are defined in the Antidiscrimination Act. It should be noted that Article 3(2) of this Act recognizes as a form of indirect discrimination on grounds of disability a refusal or failure to take appropriate measures to enable to a person with a disability to have access to a certain employment, working activities, career promotion or other promotion to use employment advice, or participate in other vocational training, unless such a measure represents an unreasonable burden. It is noteworthy that international standards relating to protection of persons with disabilities use the term "reasonable accommodation."[36] The reasonable accommodation is provided with the purpose to

---

[35]See Stránský (2013), pp. 208–219.
[36]See The International Convention on Rights of Persons with Disabilities.

ensure the compliance with the principle of equal treatment in relation to persons with disabilities.[37] According to Article 3(3) of the Antidiscrimination Act, in determining whether any specific measure represents an unreasonable burden, regard shall be given to the degree of benefit which the person with a disability has from the implementation of a measure, the financial tenability of the measure for the natural or legal person intended to implement the measure, the availability of financial and other assistance for the implementation of the measure, and the capacity of substitute measures to satisfy the needs of the person with a disability.

3.5 Antidiscrimination Provisions in Criminal Law

Exceptionally severe acts of discrimination constitute a criminal offense and are prosecuted under Act No. 40/2009 Coll., the Criminal Code (hereinafter Criminal Code).[38] A number of provisions proscribing acts of discrimination may be found in Criminal Code. Most of the relevant provisions proscribe acts of discrimination on racial, ethnic, national, religious, and class grounds. Affiliation to a race, ethnic origin and nationality may not be strictly distinguished and are therefore closely connected. Those are also the strongest discrimination grounds.[39]

The Criminal Code prohibits restriction of the freedom of religion (Article 176), defamation of nation, race, ethnic or other groups of people (Article 355), encouragement of hatred against a group of people or restricting their rights and freedoms (Article 356), genocide—the intention to completely or partially eradicate a racial, ethnic, national, religious, class, or other similar group of people (Article 400), apartheid and discrimination against groups of people (Article 402), establishment, support and promotion of movements seeking to suppress human rights and freedoms (Article 403), expressions of sympathy for movements seeking to suppress human rights and freedoms (Article 404) and denial, questioning, approval and justification of genocide (Article 405). Also other provisions of the Criminal Code proscribing different criminal acts contain a qualified clause aggravating the sanction for such crime if it was motivated by discriminatory pretext.[40] Currently, a proposal for an amendment to Criminal Code was submitted, aiming to broaden the catalogue of groups of people whose defamation or encouragement of hatred against them is

---

[37]See Komendová (2009), p. 766.
[38]Záhumenský (2014), p. 19.
[39]Šamánek (2015), pp. 118–119.
[40]See Article 140 (murder) section 3 g) Criminal Code; Article 149 (torture and other cruel and inhumane treatment) section 2 c) Criminal Code; Article 401 (attacks against humanity) section 1 e) and f); Article 352 (violence against a group of people or an individual) section 2.

considered a crime.[41] Such regulation is to be adopted to meet the commitments of the Czech Republic towards the European Union.[42]

3.6 Antidiscrimination Provisions in Administrative Law

Also some of the provisions of the administrative law proscribe discrimination. Discriminatory conduct may amount into either misdemeanour or other administrative offense. The legal regulation in the area of administrative law is broad and consists of a large number of laws. Misdemeanours are named and codified administrative offenses. The merits of misdemeanours are enshrined primarily in Act No. 200/1990 Coll., on Misdemeanours (hereinafter Misdemeanours Act) but in specific cases the merits may also be enshrined in other acts. So it is in case of about 100 misdemeanours.[43] The merits of misdemeanours are contained in a special section of the Misdemeanours Act. The other administrative offenses are enshrined in different legal regulations on legal regime of different sections of the public administration.

In Article 49(1)(d) the Misdemeanours Act labels as misdemeanour any conduct leading to restrict or to prevent the national minorities from the enjoyment of the rights of national minorities. According to Article 49(1)(e) it is also a misdemeanour to harm another person due to his affiliation to a national minority or due to his ethnical origin, his race, skin colour, gender, sexual orientation, language, belief of religion, his political or other views, membership and activity in political party or political movement, trade unions or other organizations or associations, his social origin, property, ancestry, health condition or his marital or family status.

The antidiscrimination provisions may also be found in a number of other legal regulations, especially in the area of labour law. Article 16 of the Labour Act enshrines the obligation of the employers to ensure equal treatment of all employees and also the prohibition of discrimination. This provision is reflected in Act No. 251/2005 Coll., on the Trade Inspection (hereinafter Act on the Trade Inspection) that regulates (in Article 11) the misdemeanours in the section of equal treatment and in Article 24 the administrative offenses of legal entities in the section of equal treatment. Act No. 435/2004 Coll., on Employment (hereinafter Act on Employment) also in Articles 139 and 140 regulate administrative offenses consisting of the breach of the prohibition of discrimination and the obligation to equal treatment. It is difficult to decide which of the above-mentioned legal

---

[41] *ČR zavádí trestný čin hanobení životního stylu třídy i podněcování nenávisti khomo, trans a asexuálům.* Česká justice, 2016. Dostupné z: http://www.ceska-justice.cz/2016/04/cr-zavadi-trestny-cin-hanobeni-zivotniho-stylu-tridy-i-podnecovani-nenavisti-k-homo-trans-a-asexualum/.

[42] Framework decision of the Council No. 2008/913/SVV of the 28 November 2008, on combating certain forms and expressions of racism and xenophobia by means of criminal law.

[43] Hendrych et al. (2009), p. 319.

regulations is applied in a particular case. If the discriminatory conduct happens within basic labour relations, the Labour Act is to be used. If the discriminatory conduct happens before such relation is concluded, the Act on Employment is to be used.[44]

The antidiscriminatory clause may also be found in other acts: Act No. 221/1999 Coll., on Professional Soldiers,[45] Act No. 361/2003 Coll., on Service Relationship of Members of Security Forces,[46] Act No. 198/2002 Coll., on Voluntary Service,[47] Act No. 634/1992 Coll., on the Protection of the Consumer,[48] Act No. 257/2001 Coll., on Libraries and Conditions of Providing Public Library and Information Services,[49] Act No. 40/1995 Coll., on Regulation of Publicity,[50] Act No. 137/2006, on Public Procurements,[51] or Act No. 561/2004 Coll., on Preschool, Elementary, Higher Professional and other Education (Education Act).[52]

4 Sanctions for Discriminatory Conduct

Different sanctions for discrimination may be imposed thru civil, criminal and administrative procedure as described above. This section discusses different forms of sanctions that may be imposed.

4.1 Civil Sanctions

Thru specific civil procedure,[53] a plaintiff may claim both pecuniary and non-pecuniary compensation for damages suffered. Victims may demand discrimination be stopped and redress and satisfaction be given. Victims also have right to claim monetary compensation but only in exceptional cases. Exceptional character of monetary compensation corresponds to the traditional concept of protection of

---

[44] Stádník and Kieler (2012).

[45] Article 2 section 3 Act No. 221/1999 Coll, on Professional Soldiers.

[46] Article 77 Act No. 361/2003 Coll., on Service Relationship of Members of Security Forces.

[47] Article 7 section 6 Act No. 198/2002 Coll., on Voluntary Service.

[48] Article 6 Act No. 634/1992 Coll., on the Protection of the Consumer.

[49] Article 2 a) Act No. 257/2001 Coll., on Libraries and Conditions of Providing Public Library and Information Services.

[50] Article 2 section 3 Act No. 40/1995 Coll., on Regulation of Publicity.

[51] Article 6 Act No. 137/2006, on Public Procurements.

[52] Article 2 section 1 a) the Act No. 561/2004 Coll., on Preschool, Elementary, Higher Professional and other Education (Education Act).

[53] Article 10 Antidiscrimination Act.

personal rights.[54] Sanctions imposed in antidiscrimination disputes can hardly be effective if they are not linked to monetary compensation. Even though the formulation of the law is such, in court practice, monetary compensation is the rule. But the amount is often very low and thus may not be considered effective.[55] The court may award non-pecuniary damages of up to the amount demanded by the plaintiff but may also lower the amount, which is often the case.[56]

4.2 Criminal Sanctions

In criminal procedure courts may impose a wide range of penalties.[57] In cases of criminal acts related to discriminatory conduct, mainly imprisonment or community service may be imposed.[58] In practice, criminal prosecution of discriminatory conduct is quite rare and only the most serious crimes (such as racially motivated murder) are prosecuted under criminal law. In cases of less dangerous crimes, the investigative bodies usually conclude that the act committed is not harmful enough to constitute a crime and refer them to misdemeanour commissions.[59]

4.3 Administrative Sanctions

Sanctions imposed in administrative procedure may be inflicted by employment offices, the Labour Inspectorate, the Czech Trade Inspectorate, and by misdemeanour commissions. In the area of employment and labour law, the natural and legal persons may be fined up to 1 million CZK.[60,61] Also the Czech Trade Inspectorate may impose sanctions up to 1 million CZK. However, the sanctions effectively imposed are usually much lower. The number of discrimination cases punished thru administrative procedure is very limited. Therefore, administrative sanctions may not be considered effective.[62] Acts of discrimination may also be sanctioned according to Misdemeanours Act.[63] But only natural (and not legal) persons may

---

[54] Article 11 Civil Code.
[55] Záhumenský (2013), p. 81.
[56] Záhumenský (2013), p. 91.
[57] Article 27 Criminal Code.
[58] See relevant provisions regulating such crimes as listed above that always regulate the punishment that may be imposed.
[59] Záhumenský (2013), p. 90.
[60] 1 million CZK is about 50,000 USD.
[61] Articles 139–140 Act on Employment.
[62] Záhumenský (2013), pp. 82, 89.
[63] Article 159 Misdemeanors Act.

be imposed sanctions by misdemeanour commissions. Also, the law requires completion of the procedure within 1 year and the administrative investigation of misdemeanours is hence extremely ineffective.[64]

5 Judicial Review of Discrimination Cases

Courts ensure protection of the right to equal treatment and the right to protection against discrimination in the first place.[65] The Constitution states that all fundamental rights and freedoms are under the protection of the judicial power.[66] This section discusses the enforcement of antidiscrimination law through civil, administrative, and criminal actions, and the specifics of these proceedings.

5.1 Civil Procedure

As the Antidiscrimination Act may be regarded the key legal regulation in the area of antidiscrimination law, the general antidiscrimination civil action introduced by Article 10 of the Antidiscrimination Act[67] would be the most common mean used when claiming discrimination. Provision Article 10 of the Antidiscrimination Act states that "if the breach of rights and obligations arising from the right to equal treatment or discrimination occurs, the person affected by such conduct may claim in court the waiver of discrimination, the elimination of all consequences and the reasonable satisfaction." In cases of particularly serious harm, the person affected may also claim non-pecuniary damages.[68]

Before the enactment of the Antidiscrimination Act, all claims of discrimination were dealt with within the actions on personality protection.[69] Since the Antidiscrimination Act became effective, Article 10 has to be regarded as *lex specialis* to general provisions on personality protection.[70] Thus, if the contested conduct falls within the scope of Article 10 of the Antidiscrimination Act, civil action under the Act is appropriate. If the contested unequal treatment does not fall within the ambit of the Antidiscrimination Act, a general civil action on protection of

---

[64]Záhumenský (2013), p. 89.
[65]Explanatory report to Act No. 198/2009 Coll., on Equal Treatment and on Legal Remedies of the Protection Against Discrimination and the Change to Some Acts (Antidiscrimination Act).
[66]Articles 4 and 36 of the Constitution.
[67]Záhumenský (2014), p. 97.
[68]Article 10 of the Antidiscrimination Act.
[69]Čermák and Kvasnicová (2012), p. 20.
[70]Articles 81–117 of the Act No. 89/2012 Coll., Civil Code.

personality should be brought.[71] Ordinary procedure according to Civil Procedure Code[72] applies with the exception of the provision regarding the burden of proof[73] (to be discussed hereafter). Nevertheless, the explanatory report claiming the competence of the regional courts to deal with antidiscrimination civil actions in the first instance,[74] the antidiscrimination civil actions have to be brought before district courts, as the general rule regarding the substantive jurisdiction applies.[75]

5.1.1 Burden of Proof

As mentioned above, general procedural rules according to Civil Procedure Code apply when the antidiscrimination action is brought, with the exception of the regulation of burden of proof. In general civil proceedings it is the plaintiff who has to proof its allegations.[76] The burden of proof in the antidiscrimination civil actions is shifted. The Antidiscrimination Act (Article 14) added to the Civil Procedure Code a provision stating that if the plaintiff presents facts to court that indicate that the defendant committed direct or indirect discrimination, it is up to the defendant to prove that he has not breached the principle of equal treatment (Article 133a). Such regulation has its origin in the EU law that initially reflected such model in the case law of the Court of Justice of the European Union and later in the EU antidiscrimination legislation.[77] The ECtHR also assumed the principle. It commented in detail on the principle in its judgment *D. H. and other v. The Czech Republic*.[78] Some claim that such legal regulation does not reflect the actual position of the parties and constitutes a flat disadvantage to a certain group according to its status in business life. Such legislation may therefore lead to breach of the right to a fair trial guaranteed by the Constitution.[79] But the Czech Constitutional Court rejected such objection and found the provisions on burden of proof compatible with the constitutional order.[80]

---

[71]Čermák and Kvasnicová (2012), p. 20.
[72]Act No. 99/1963 Coll., Civil Procedure Code.
[73]Article 133a of the Civil Procedure Code.
[74]Explanatory report to Act No. 198/2009 Coll., on Equal Treatment and on Legal Remedies of the Protection Against Discrimination and the Change to Some Acts (Antidiscrimination Act).
[75]Article 9 section 1 Civil Procedure Code.
[76]Article 120 Civil Procedure Code.
[77]Scheu (2013), p. 18.
[78]*D.H.and others v. Czech Republic*, Grand Chamber judgement, 13 November 2007, no. 57325/00.
[79]Scheu (2013), p. 21, also Benda (2006), pp. 36–37, 46.
[80]Záhumenský (2014), p. 89.

5.1.2 Actio Popularis

Actio popularis is an institution encouraged by the EU law that permits an organisation to bring the case before court in case of the absence of an individual victim to stop discriminatory practice.[81] Such procedure is not permitted in discrimination cases in the Czech Republic.[82] It was suggested by the Public Defender of Rights already in 2003 that legislation should be amended in a way to permit non-governmental organisations to bring actio popularis actions before court.[83] Neither is a *class action* that would allow an association to act in the interest of more than one individual victim for claims arising from the same event permitted.[84] Nevertheless, it is possible for such NGOs to represent the victims of discrimination in the court if such activity is enshrined in their statutes.[85] The role of NGOs in discrimination cases will be further discussed hereafter.

5.2 Criminal Procedure

The criminal procedure in cases of the commission of the above-mentioned crimes is regulated by the Criminal Procedure Code.[86] No specific procedural rules apply in cases of the crimes related to discrimination conduct.

5.3 Administrative Procedure

The administrative judicial procedure is regulated by the Code on Administrative Court Procedure,[87] which regulates the judicial review of administrative decisions. The revision of the administrative decisions may be the result of discriminatory practice and the courts also review the decisions of administrative bodies that have identified as discriminatory certain conduct of petitioners.[88] Unlike the Civil

---

[81] Legal Standing—The Practical Experience of a Hungarian Organization. *European Antidiscrimination Law Review*, 5/2007, p. 25. http://ec.europa.eu/justice/discrimination/files/lawrev5_en.pdf.

[82] Záhumenský (2014), p. 88.

[83] Annual report of the Public Defender of Rights, 2013, p. 18.

[84] Záhumenský (2014), p. 88.

[85] Explanatory report to Act No. 198/2009 Coll., on Equal Treatment and on Legal Remedies of the Protection Against Discrimination and the Change to Some Acts (Antidiscrimination Act).

[86] Act No. 141/1961 Coll., on Judicial Criminal Procedure (Criminal Procedure Code), in the wording of later amendments.

[87] Act No. 150/2002 Coll., The Code on Administrative Court Procedure, in the wording of later amendments.

[88] Záhumenský (2014), p. 82.

Procedure Code, the Code on Administrative Court Procedure does not contain any provision on the shift of the burden of proof. No obligation to incorporate such institute to national legal order arises from the EU law as long as the administrative procedure is governed by the principle of investigation.[89] Courts also share such view.[90]

6 Other State Authorities Entitled to Enforcement of the Antidiscrimination Law

6.1 The Public Defender of Rights

Besides courts, the most important state authority entitled to protection against discrimination is certainly the Public Defender of Rights. The Public Defender of Rights contributes to combating racism and xenophobia and to the promotion of the equal treatment of all persons.[91] He may provide methodical aid to victims of discrimination and strictly follows the principle *audiatur et altera pars*, which means he may only provide a legal analysis of client's situation and advice him or her on possible further procedure in the case, but may not represent him or her in court.[92] He may also conduct research, publish reports and recommendations on questions regarding discrimination, and exchange information with other equality bodies in Europe.[93] However, due to his limited financial and personal capacities, the Public Defender of Rights is not able to fully fulfil his role.[94]

The Public Defender of Rights is not a quasi-judicial institution. It does not have authority to issue decisions and therefore no appeals are possible.[95] The Public Defender of Rights is elected by the Chamber of Deputies of the Czech Parliament for period of 6 years and is responsible to this Chamber. The Czech President and the Senate propose candidates. The body is funded from the state budget. The office is incompatible with the office of President of the Republic, Members of the Parliament, senators or judges, and the Public Defender of Rights may not be a member of any political party or a political movement.[96]

---

[89]Čermák and Kvasnicová (2012), p. 23.
[90]See judgement of the Municipal court in Prague, 9. 4. 2014, ref. no. 7 A 156/2010.
[91]Záhumenský (2013), p. 7.
[92]Čermák and Kvasnicová (2012), p. 22.
[93]Olexa (2009), p. 14.
[94]Záhumenský (2013), p. 94.
[95]Záhumenský (2013), p. 95.
[96]Záhumenský (2013), p. 93.

6.2 Other State Authorities

Administrative bodies and inspectorates called to protect victims of discrimination are established within the scope of specific laws. These bodies are empowered to impose sanctions, mainly financial penalties.[97] Monitoring of discrimination with regard to access to goods and services is governed by Act No. 634/1992 Coll., on the Protection of the Consumer, which delegates competences to the Czech Trade Inspectorate. This body is authorised to inspect legal entities and individuals that sell or deliver goods and provide services. The sanctions always have to be linked to findings by the Czech Trade Inspectorate and do not allow administrative proceedings to be launched in response to petitions filed and evidence produced by other legal entities and individuals. Evidence provided by consumers may only serve as a reason to carry out an inspection.[98]

Also, Labour Inspectorates are entitled to protection of victims of discrimination, and its activities are governed by Act No. 251/2005 Coll. on the Inspection of Labour. This act regulates the position of the bodies of inspection of labour as control organs in the area of labour relations and working conditions.[99] Employment offices also have powers in the area of employment and labour relations. Their competences are defined by the Act No. 435/2004 Coll. on Employment, and their conduct is governed by the Administrative Procedure Code. A procedure may be initiated by a complaint or on an employment office's own initiative.[100] Also, the Czech School Inspectorate[101] and misdemeanour commissions[102] have competences in this area.

7 The Role of the NGOs

Non-governmental organizations have a special position in the mechanism of enforcement of antidiscrimination law. According to the Civil Procedure Code[103] and Antidiscrimination Act,[104] legal entities established in order to provide legal aid

---

[97]Záhumenský (2013), p. 7.
[98]Záhumenský (2013), p. 83.
[99]Olexa (2009), p. 14.
[100]Záhumenský (2013), pp. 82–83.
[101]Diskriminace v ČR: oběť diskriminace a její překážky v přístupu ke spravedlnosti. Shrnutí. *Veřejný ochránce práv*, 2015. Accessible: http://www.ochrance.cz/fileadmin/user_upload/DISKRIMINACE/Vyzkum/CZ_Diskriminace_v_CR_shrnuti.pdf.
[102]Záhumenský (2013), p. 80.
[103]See Article 26 section 3.
[104]See Article 11.

to victims of discrimination may represent those victims in court.[105] NGOs may also submit motions to administrative bodies.[106] They may also provide information on possible legal procedures and provide aid in drafting lawsuits and other legal filings.[107] Such services are provided by a number of NGOs such as the Czech Helsinki Committee (Český helsinský výbor),[108] Frank Bold,[109] League of Human Rights (Liga lidských práv),[110] Pro Bono Alliance (Pro bono aliance)[111] and others. However, NGOs do not have any other special rights in this area. The NGO may only represent a victim as chosen representative. This type of engagement of NGOs is reserved to civil proceedings only. *Actio popularis* is not permitted.[112]

8 Deficiencies of the Enforcement Mechanisms of the Antidiscrimination Law

We perceive as the most pressing problem the ineffectiveness of current mechanisms of protection of victims of discrimination. The origin of problematic enforcement of the antidiscrimination law may be seen in historical context and in its perception by the society. Hardly any other act aroused so many emotions as the Antidiscrimination Act. Due to fierce debate and rather cold reception of the antidiscriminatory legislation by the Czech society, it took almost 10 years to pass the law.[113] The Czech Republic was the last of 27 EU members to adopt antidiscrimination legislation and was at risk to face a number of lawsuits from the European Commission.[114]

The situation of victims of discrimination is often uneasy. They face procedural risk, long duration of legal disputes, psychological stress and prospect of negligible amount of compensation awarded,[115] unpredictability of court decision-making, lack of case law concerning discrimination, high court fees and difficulties finding legal aid.[116] The stakeholders in equal rights indicate that a low number of lawsuits result from lack of information of the victims, discouragement from the possibility

---

[105]Explanatory report to Act No. 198/2009 Coll., on Equal Treatment and on Legal Remedies of the Protection Against Discrimination and the Change to Some Acts (Antidiscrimination Act).

[106]Záhumenský (2014), pp. 87–88.

[107]Olexa (2009), p. 14.

[108]Czech Helsinki Committee. Accessible: http://www.helcom.cz/cs/en.

[109]Frank Bold. Accessible: http://en.frankbold.org.

[110]Liga lidských práv. Accessible: http://llp.cz/en/.

[111]Pro bono aliance. Accessible: http://www.probonoaliance.cz/en/.

[112]Záhumenský (2014), pp. 87–88.

[113]Boučková et al. (2010), p. 12.

[114]Olexa (2009), p. 13.

[115]Scheu (2013), p. 22.

[116]Záhumenský (2013), p. 5.

that their case might be made public, and the fear of authorities, courts, trials and judgments.[117] Even though about 11% of the Czech citizens claim to have experienced discrimination or harassment on any ground, most of them refrain from complaining.[118] Even in the cases where the Public Defender of Rights recommends filing an action with court, the victims most often do not use this possibility.[119] That is because almost 75% of the Czech population believe that the victims have little chance of getting justice.[120]

One of the deficiencies of the system is also legal representation of victims before courts. Legal entities established according to special law in order to provide legal help to victims of discrimination may represent them in court. However, they have no special status in such disputes and may not challenge systematic discrimination. The Public Defender of Rights has no financial capacity to secure representation before courts either.[121] People are therefore more likely to file their complaints with authorities other than the courts, such as filing a complaint with the State Labour Inspection Office, the Czech Trade Inspection Authority, or the Czech School Inspectorate.[122] Criminal prosecutions for crimes related to discrimination are quite rare and it is usually concluded that the act committed is not so harmful as to be regarded as a crime. These cases are consequently referred to misdemeanours commission. The administrative investigation of misdemeanours is, however, extremely ineffective, as it has to be completed within 1 year.[123]

9 Overall Assessment of the Situation Regarding Discrimination in the Czech Republic

We may conclude that the Czech Republic does have a system of antidiscrimination legal regulation. On 1 September 2009 the Antidiscrimination Act finally became effective and the Czech Republic, being the last of all member states of the European Union to implement the antidiscrimination directives, thus avoided lawsuits by the European Commission. It has to be noted though, that the transposition was called

---

[117]Záhumenský (2013), p. 51.

[118]Diskriminace v ČR: oběť diskriminace a její překážky v přístupu ke spravedlnosti. Shrnutí. *Veřejný ochránce práv*, 2015. Accessible: http://www.ochrance.cz/fileadmin/user_upload/DISKRIMINACE/Vyzkum/CZ_Diskriminace_v_CR_shrnuti.pdf.

[119]Záhumenský (2013), p. 7.

[120]Diskriminace v ČR: oběť diskriminace a její překážky v přístupu ke spravedlnosti. Shrnutí. *Veřejný ochránce práv*, 2015. Accessible: http://www.ochrance.cz/fileadmin/user_upload/DISKRIMINACE/Vyzkum/CZ_Diskriminace_v_CR_shrnuti.pdf.

[121]Záhumenský (2013), p. 86.

[122]Diskriminace v ČR: oběť diskriminace a její překážky v přístupu ke spravedlnosti. Shrnutí. *Veřejný ochránce práv*, 2015. Accessible: http://www.ochrance.cz/fileadmin/user_upload/DISKRIMINACE/Vyzkum/CZ_Diskriminace_v_CR_shrnuti.pdf.

[123]Záhumenský (2013), p. 7.

minimalistic and therefore did not have the desired effect, at least not in all areas of law. Besides the Antidiscrimination Act, other antidiscrimination provisions may be found in other legal documents. Such regulation provides detailed regulation and effective remedies in some areas (such as labour law) but remains rather incomplete and ineffective in other areas (such as protection of sexual minorities in the area of family law).

The current state is not tragic but it is not ideal either. The Czech legal order does not contain any openly discriminatory provisions (such as for example criminalisation of homosexual orientation that persists in some foreign legal orders), but on the other hand, a number of legal provisions and practices of some state authorities remain problematic. The most problematic is though an access to effective remedies in cases of discrimination. As follows from above-mentioned numbers, even though the Czech Republic formally established measures to provide protection against discrimination and to press sanctions for discriminatory conduct, those measures remain rather ineffective and are often not used by victims.

References

Baroš J (2012) Komentář k článku 1. In: Wagnerová E et al (eds) Listina základních práv a svobod. Komentář. Wolters Kluwer, Praha, p 49
Bell M (2004) Anti-discrimination law and the European Union. Oxford University Press, Oxford, p 23
Benda M (2006) In: Čurdová A et al (eds) Antidiskriminační zákon, pomoc slabší, nebo převrácení právo? Centrum pro ekonomiku a politiku, pp 36–37, 46
Bobek M (2012) Komentář k článku 3. In: Wagnerová E et al (eds) Listina základních práv a svobod. Komentář. Wolters Kluwer, Praha, p 99
Boučková P et al (2010) Antidiskriminační zákon. Komentář. C.H. Beck, Praha
Čermák M, Kvasnicová J (2012) Několik poznámek k českému antidiskriminačnímu právu. Bulletin advokacie, roč. 3/2012
Collins H (2003) Discrimination, equality and social inclusion [cited 16-04-2016]. Mod Law Rev 66(1):17. http://www.jstor.org/stable/1097547
Galvas M et al (2015) Pracovní právo. Masarykova univerzita v Brně, Brno, p 25
Gerards JH (2005) Judicial review in equal treatment cases. Martinus Nijnhoff Publishers, Leiden – Boston, p 110
Hendrych D et al (2009) Správní právo. Obecná část. 7. vyd. C.H. Beck, Praha, p 319
Komendová J (2009) Zákaz diskriminace na základě zdravotního postižení v pracovněprávních vztazích. In: Europeanization of the national law, the Lisbon Treaty and some other legal issues, COFOLA 2008, the conference proceedings. Masarykova univerzita, Brno, p 766
Kvasnicová J (2011) (Ne)diskriminace, rovnost nebo rovné zacházení? Právní rozhledy, 3/2011, p 87
Olexa L (2009) Česko má konečně antidiskriminační zákon. Bezpečnost a hygiena práce, 10/2009
Šamánek J (2015) Komentář k § 2. In: Kvasnicová J et al (eds) Antidiskriminační zákon. Komentář. Wolters Kluwer, Praha, pp 118–119
Scheu HC (2013) Problematika důkazního břemene v evropském antidiskriminačním právu. Jurisprudence, 4/2013
Schiek D, Lawson A (2011) European Union non-discrimination law and intersectionality: investigating the triangle of racial, gender and disability discrimination. Ashgate Publishing Limited, Farnham, p 11

Stádník J, Kieler P (2012) Diskriminace v oblasti zaměstnanosti jako správní delikt. Práce a mzda, 6/2012
Stránský J (2013) Diskriminace a nerovné zacházení v oblasti péče o zaměstnance. In: Dny práva 2012 – Days of Law 2012, the conference proceedings. Masarykova univerzita, Brno, pp 208–219
Von Bar Ch et al [Study Group on a European Civil Code/Research Group on EC Private Law (Acquis Group)] (2009) Principles, definitions and model rules of European private law. Draft Common Frame of Reference (DCFR). Outline Edition. Sellier. European Law Publishers GmbH, Munich, p 62 et seq
Wintr J (2012) Komentář k článku 29. In: Wagnerová E et al (eds) Listina základních práv a svobod. Komentář. Wolters Kluwer, Praha, pp 619–625
Záhumenský D (2013) Country Report Czech Republic 2013 on measures to combat discrimination. European network of legal experts in the non-discrimination field, p 81. http://www.equalitylaw.eu/downloads/767-2013-cz-country-report-In-final
Záhumenský D (2014) Report on Measures to Combat Discrimination. Directives 2000/43/EC and 2000/78/EC. Country Report 2013. Czech Republic. European Network of Legal Experts in the Non-Discrimination Field

Markéta Selucká is the Expert in Civil Law at Masaryk University specializing in consumer protection in EU and Czech law and national contributor to the EC Consumer Law Compendium and since 2011 responsible for the most recent Czech up-dates. She was an assistant to the President of the Czech Constitutional Court, a head of committee of Ministry of Justice for tenancy law in the new Czech Civil Code. Now she is the dean of the Faculty of Law at Masaryk University.

Martina Grochová is a doctoral student of the programme "Constitutional Law and Theory of State" at Masaryk University, Faculty of Law. She specializes in human rights law. She is a former assistant to a judge at the Supreme Court of the Czech Republic and now works as an assistant to a judge at the Constitutional Court of the Czech Republic.

Jana Komendová is the expert in labour law and social security law at Masaryk University specialising in EU social law and Czech national labour law. She is focusing on equality and non-discrimination law in employment and social security law.

Denmark

Pia Justesen

1 Introduction

Antidiscrimination law in Denmark does not consist of one single piece of legislation. It is rather a combination of many acts that have been introduced or amended when EU-legislation, public debate, or the ratification of international obligations have focused on a specific field of application or a specific group. Hence, protection against discrimination is ensured by a web of civil and criminal legislation ranging from the Constitution to specific acts covering areas inside and outside the labor market. The fact that there are different antidiscrimination laws in various areas with different levels of protection makes it a challenge to explain the legal situation. The public and the ordinary citizen therefore also have difficulties understanding the legal situation when it comes to antidiscrimination and equality.

There is no general principle of equality and protection against discrimination in the Danish Constitution.[1] There are, however, a number of equality-related provisions in the Constitution from 1953. These provisions include that no Danish subject shall be deprived of liberty because of her political or religious convictions or because of her descent. Also, that no person shall be denied the right to full enjoyment of civil and political rights by reason of his creed or descent, nor shall

---

Information in this report is largely but not exclusively taken from the Danish 2015 country report to the European Equality Law Network by Pia Justesen. See: http://www.equalitylaw.eu/country/denmark.

[1] Act No. 169 of 5 June 1953.

P. Justesen (✉)
Justadvice, Evanston, IL, USA

Department of Disability and Human Development, University of Illinois at Chicago, Chicago, IL, USA
e-mail: pj@justadvice.dk

he for such reasons evade any common civil duty. The Constitution further provides that no one shall be liable to make personal contributions to any denomination other than the one to which he adheres, and that citizens shall be entitled to form congregations for the worship of God.

The Act on the Prohibition of Discrimination Due to Race makes it a criminal offence to refuse services or access to public places to a person on the basis of his or her race, color, national or ethnic origin, religious belief or sexual orientation.[2] Criminal law does not cover indirect discrimination, harassment or victimization.

The Act on Ethnic Equal Treatment ensures protection against direct and indirect discrimination based on race or ethnic origin within the areas of: (1) access to social protection, including social security and health care, social benefits, education, (2) access to and supply of goods and services, including housing, and (3) membership of and access to services from organizations whose members carry on a particular profession.[3] The Act also includes a prohibition against harassment on the grounds of race and ethnic origin.

The Act on the Prohibition of Discrimination in the Labor Market prohibits direct and indirect discrimination based on race, skin color, religion or faith, political conviction, sexual orientation, age, disability, and national, social or ethnic origin.[4] The Act covers recruitment, dismissal, transfer and promotion as well as discrimination with regard to pay and working conditions. The Act provides protection against harassment. Employers are also not allowed to discriminate among employees by restricting access to vocational education and training. The same prohibition applies to people providing guidance and training, to those involved in work placement activities, to those in making rules and decisions about the right to perform professional activities, and those facilitating membership to trade unions and employers' organizations.

The discrimination grounds of age, sexual orientation, disability and religion or belief do not enjoy protection outside the labor market in Danish civil law.

With regard to the protection against discrimination based on gender, the Equal Treatment Act[5] applies to access to employment and working conditions, including dismissal. The Equal Pay Act[6] applies to equal pay. The Gender Equality Act[7] applies to the promotion of gender equality and the prohibition of gender discrimination in areas other than the labor market.

---

[2]Consolidated Act No. 626 of 29 September 1987 with later amendments.
[3]Consolidated Act No. 438 of 16 May 2012 with later amendments.
[4]Consolidated Act No. 1349 of 16 December 2008.
[5]Consolidated Act No. 645 of 8 June 2011 with later amendments.
[6]Consolidated Act No. 899 of 5 September 2008 with later amendments.
[7]Consolidated Act No. 1678 of 19 December 2013.

2 Is Antidiscrimination Law Enforced?

It is not possible to describe the extent of actual discrimination in Denmark. However, a number of studies establish that discrimination is a serious problem.

A 2015 survey from the Danish Institute for Human Rights establishes that having children is associated with a number of negative work and career consequences, especially for women.[8] Also, Denmark has an education system that is very much segregated by gender, which is reflected in the labor market.[9] The labor market in Denmark is currently one of the most gender-segregated in Europe, yet Denmark has one of the highest proportions of women in the labor market. Gender segregation in the labor market is one of the reasons why unequal pay is still an issue in Denmark.

In 2014, the Danish Integration Barometer documented that 43% of responding immigrants and descendants of non-Western origin had experienced discrimination due to their ethnic origin within the past year.[10] In 2013, a study documented that 92% of responding persons with a mental illness had experienced discrimination because of their disability.[11]

There are no special rules regarding enforcement and access to the Danish courts when it comes to cases on equality issues. Alleged victims of discrimination will have court access according to the Administration of Justice Act.[12] Alleged victims of discrimination may also issue a complaint to the administrative Board of Equal Treatment.[13] Legal standing for interest groups depends on how concrete an interest they have in the case.

The police and public prosecutors enforce the criminal antidiscrimination law dealing with access to public places and services like nightclubs and discotheques (Act on the Prohibition of Discrimination Due to Race). There is criticism that this law is not sufficiently enforced, especially in the nightlife arena. Almost one out of three young people have experienced or witnessed abuse, pushes and condescending jokes because of ethnic origin, disability or sexual orientation in the Copenhagen nightlife.[14] Only a few number of cases are brought to the courts. And in the cases where the courts hold that discrimination has taken place, restaurants and discotheques only pay a very low compensation to the individuals who experienced discrimination.

---

[8]Warming (2015).
[9]Institut for Menneskerettigheder, Køn – Status 2014–2015, p. 23 ff.
[10]The National Integration Barometer: http://integrationsbarometer.dk/integrationsbarometer_maal?goal=5&kommunenr=0.
[11]Rasmussen og Johansen (2013).
[12]Consolidated Act No. 1255 of 16 November 2015 with later amendments.
[13]Consolidated Act No. 905 of 3 September 2012 with later amendments.
[14]Rådgivende sociologer, Unges syn på diskrimination i det københavnske natteliv – en kvalitativ og kvantitativ afdækning (2014). See http://www.dkr.dk/kamp-mod-diskrimination-nattelivet.

In Denmark, there are no official statistics on the number of cases concerning discrimination brought before the national courts. Furthermore, there is a lack of research on case law dealing with the principle of equality and protection against discrimination, which makes it impossible to provide a clear answer as to whether antidiscrimination law is sufficiently enforced by the Danish courts. Quick research indicates[15] that, in 2015, the Supreme Court issued 3 rulings on antidiscrimination.[16] There was only one ruling selected for publication on the Court Administration website from the High Courts, and there were no published rulings on discrimination from city courts.[17]

All rulings from the Board of Equal Treatment are available on the website of the Board.[18] From January 2009 until the end of 2015, the Board of Equal Treatment issued 1355 discrimination rulings.[19] Divided by discrimination grounds during that period, 603 rulings dealt with gender, 203 rulings dealt with ethnic origin, 472 rulings dealt with age and disability, and 86 rulings dealt with other or multiple discrimination grounds.

The few number of court rulings about discrimination and the relatively few number of rulings from the Board of Equal Treatment contrast with the levels of discrimination experienced in Denmark. This discrepancy makes it questionable whether the current antidiscrimination legislation is sufficiently enforced.

3 How Is Antidiscrimination Law Enforced?

Most enforcement depends on individual victims of discrimination taking action.

If the alleged case of discrimination is a criminal matter, like a discriminatory job advertisement or a discriminatory denial of access to a public place, the victim must report the case to the police. The police will then assess whether to start investigations and whether to charge the alleged discriminator.

If the case is a civil matter regarding discrimination on the labor market, in housing, education, etc., the victim can choose from various routes:

- Civil courts, directly;
- His or her trade union if it is a case within the labor market;
- The Board of Equal Treatment;

---

[15]Search terms: "diskrimination" (in English: discrimination) and "forskelsbehandling" (in English: differential treatment).

[16]Supreme Court database on rulings: http://domstol.fe1.tangora.com/New-Søgeside.31488.aspx.

[17]Database on selected rulings from all national courts: http://www.domstol.dk/om/Nyheder/domsresumeer/Pages/default.aspx.

[18]Board of Equal Treatment database on rulings: http://www.ligebehandlingsnaevnet.dk/naevnsdatabase/default.aspx.

[19]Statistics are found on the website of the Board of Equal Treatment: https://ast.dk/naevn/ligebehandlingsnaevnet/tal-og-statistik-fra-ligebehandlingsnaevnet.

- The Institute for Human Rights—The National Human Rights Institute of Denmark (DIHR) (advice or assistance);
- The public Citizens Advice Service, which exists in some municipalities (advice or assistance);
- NGOs;
- The Parliamentary Ombudsman [Folketingets Ombudsmand] (for cases dealing with public authorities);
- The Danish Press Council [Pressenævnet] or the Radio and Television Board on Commercials [Radio- og TV-Nævnet];
- The Consumer Ombudsman [Forbrugerombudsmanden].

There is no official surveillance of the enforcement of Danish antidiscrimination law. However, the Institute for Human Rights—The National Human Rights Institute of Denmark (DIHR) has been designated as a body for the promotion of equal treatment and effective protection against discrimination on grounds of racial or ethnic origin, gender and disability.[20] DIHR has been given the authority to assist victims of discrimination, to conduct surveys concerning discrimination, and to publish reports and make recommendations on discrimination. Also, DIHR issues a yearly report to the Parliament on the human rights situation in Denmark. Finally, DIHR has recently been given the authority to bring discrimination complaints directly to the Board of Equal Treatment in cases that are a matter of principle or of general public interest.[21]

4 Who Enforces Antidiscrimination Law?

The police and the national court system enforce antidiscrimination law according to the general rules on civil and criminal law enforcement in the Administration of Justice Act. The lower city courts, the high courts, the Maritime and Commercial Court and the Supreme Court hear cases on discrimination. Court rulings are legally binding.

The Board of Equal Treatment started functioning on 1 January 2009. In practice, the Board deals with most complaints of discrimination and issues administrative rulings in discrimination cases.[22] The Board of Equal Treatment is competent to hear individual complaints related to discrimination in employment based on gender, race, skin color, religion or belief, political opinion, sexual orientation, age, disability or national, social or ethnic origin. Outside employment, the Board only deals with complaints related to discrimination based on race, ethnic origin or gender.[23]

---

[20]Consolidated Act No. 553 of 18 June 2012 with later amendments.
[21]Act No. 1570 of 15 December 2015.
[22]Consolidated Act No. 905 of 3 September 2012.
[23]Consolidated Act No. 905 of 3 September 2012.

There is no requirement of legal representation when filing a complaint to the Board of Equal Treatment and there are no costs involved in submitting a complaint. The Board's case handling is on a written basis only—it is not possible to present a complaint to the Board in person, and the Board is not empowered to hear oral testimonies. The Board also cannot force the parties to produce documents, give their opinion, or reveal the factual circumstances of a case.

Victims of discrimination can be awarded compensation for non-pecuniary damages directly by the Board. Rulings from the Board are legally binding and the Board is entitled to take a case to the civil courts if a discriminating party is not willing to pay compensation. Both parties to a case can also bring a ruling from the Board to the civil courts. The courts follow the Board's rulings in most cases.

As mentioned in #3 (above), the Danish Institute for Human Rights (DIHR) is the designated national body for the promotion of equal treatment and for the effective protection against discrimination, and has the authority to bring discrimination complaints to the Board.[24]

Trade unions and employers' associations (the social partners) play a predominant role on the Danish labor market. If a discrimination claim is based on a collective agreement, the social partners are the only ones who can enforce it in the Labor Court and in the labor arbitration bodies.

Associations, organizations, and trade unions are entitled to act in court cases on behalf of individual victims of discrimination under certain conditions, and they can act in the interest of more than one individual victim (class action) for discrimination claims arising from the same event. For example, most employment law cases brought before the ordinary courts are brought by a trade union on behalf of a member. There is no law or tradition allowing associations, organizations, or trade unions to act in the public interest on their own behalf, without a specific victim to support or represent (actio popularis).

NGOs are also entitled to represent individuals in complaints to the Board of Equal Treatment. But there are only few NGOs specializing in assisting victims of discrimination in filing complaints to the Board of Equal Treatment. The fact that these organizations are typically located in Copenhagen makes it difficult for victims of discrimination outside the Copenhagen area to get free legal help with their cases.

5 Who Benefits from the Enforcement of Antidiscrimination Law?

All individuals within Danish jurisdiction regardless of their status, whether they have a permanent or time-limited residence permit or have status as undocumented migrants, and irrespective of citizenship and nationality, are protected from discrimination under Danish law. All victims of discrimination based on gender, race, skin

---

[24]Consolidated Act No. 553 of 18 June 2012 with later amendments.

color, religion or belief, political opinion, sexual orientation, age, disability or national, social or ethnic origin could benefit from the enforcement of antidiscrimination law. Legal persons, however, are not encompassed by the protection against discrimination.

Most of the discrimination grounds in the law must be understood as social constructs in contrast to objective categories.

Discrimination by association is protected in Danish law. This means, for example, that if an employee has been discriminated against because of her daughter's disability, the employee has been discriminated against because of disability and the non-discrimination law has been violated.

Finally, Danish law features legal measures of protection against victimization. This means that the law prohibits subjecting a person to any adverse treatment or adverse consequence as a reaction to a complaint or to any type of proceedings aimed at enforcing compliance with the principle of equal treatment.

6 Who Is Harmed by the Enforcement of Antidiscrimination Law?

In Denmark, antidiscrimination law covers natural and legal persons for the purpose of liability for discrimination. And there is no distinction between the two when it comes to liability for discrimination outside of employment.

On the labor market, there is no distinction between different kinds of employers when it comes to liability for discrimination. The prohibition of discrimination also applies to anybody who runs vocational training and assigns employment, anyone who issues decisions on access to self-employment, and anyone who issues decisions on membership and benefits provided by trade unions or employers' associations. Furthermore, employers can be penalized for discriminatory job advertisements, including being sentenced to a fine.

There is no Danish research or study documenting the kind of discrimination cases or the kind of discriminator that typically get the most negative press coverage and thus is potentially harmed the most by the enforcement of antidiscrimination laws.

7 What Remedies Are Provided by the Enforcement of Antidiscrimination Law?

By way of introduction, the typical sanction for a breach of the duty not to discriminate is compensation, which may cover economic and noneconomic loss. Some violations of the non-discrimination principles can also be sanctioned by way of fines. This typically happens in cases of discriminatory job advertisements and in cases regarding denial of access to public places like restaurants and discotheques.

But discrimination in access to public places and services is covered by criminal law and may also result in up to 6 months imprisonment.

Discrimination in the private and public labor market may result in pecuniary compensation. Re-instatement in a job that a person has been dismissed from is not a possible remedy. Also, it is not possible to commit employers to implementing equality measures or attend antidiscrimination training.

Discriminatory job advertisements are covered by criminal law and may result in a fine. In public and private employment as well as in fields outside of employment, persons who have been subject to discrimination can be awarded compensation for non-economic damages.

Furthermore, civil courts can award damages for an established economic loss, according to the general Danish rules concerning damages. The Danish law of torts is developed through case law. Damages can be awarded if negligent behavior has resulted in an economic loss and there is a causal link between the behavior and the loss. Furthermore, the loss has to be foreseeable to the person acting negligently.

Finally, a person who is responsible for an unlawful violation of another person's freedom, honor, or integrity must pay compensation according to section 26 of the Damage Liability Act.[25] Compensation claims must be brought to the courts within 3 years of the unlawful violation.[26]

There is no ceiling on the maximum amount of compensation that can be awarded. Typically, the following amounts of compensation will be awarded to victims of discrimination:

- In cases of denial of access to public places like discotheques: from DKK 5000 (€ 675) to DKK 10,000 (€ 1350);
- In cases of discriminatory job advertisements: DKK 25,000 (€ 3360);
- In cases of discriminatory denials of employment/new job: DKK 25,000 (€ 3360);
- In cases of discriminatory dismissals: 3–9 months of salary.[27]

The level of compensation for discrimination on the labor market seems proportionate and dissuasive. Outside the labor market, the level of compensation for discrimination is very low and it can be questioned whether it is sufficiently fair and dissuasive. This is, for example, the situation in cases where discotheques have denied access to young men with ethnic minority background for which sanctions typically have been very mild.

---

[25]Consolidated Act No. 266 of 21 March 2014 with later amendments.

[26]Section 3 of Act on Limitations (Forældelseslov), Consolidated Act No. 1063 of 28 August 2003 with later amendments.

[27]Board of Equal Treatment, Annual Report 2015 (November 2016), p. 19 ff.

8 Who Supports the Enforcement of Antidiscrimination Law?

It is not possible to generalize the individuals and organizations that typically either support or oppose the enforcement of antidiscrimination laws. However, more rightwing Danish national and local political parties tend to argue that there is no need for a strict enforcement of antidiscrimination laws. They will typically favor voluntary mechanisms and financial incentives. On the other hand, more leftwing political parties will argue that movement towards an equal society is not going to happen by itself. In their point of view, stronger laws and stronger enforcement of existing antidiscrimination laws is a necessary precondition.

One recent illustrative example was a suggestion from the integration mayor in Copenhagen to use "undercover agents" to detect and document when nightclubs or discotheques exclude individuals from entering because of their ethnic origin. The more rightwing political parties in the Copenhagen city council vetoed the initiative in January 2016 and suggested that the city instead intensifies its cooperation with the police and the nightlife business.[28]

9 Who Opposes the Enforcement of Antidiscrimination Law?

See #8.

10 How Broad Is the Coverage of Antidiscrimination Law?

Danish civil law contains a broad societal protection against direct and indirect discrimination including harassment because of gender, race and ethnic origin. More specifically, the following areas are covered: employment and labor market; vocational training; access to social protection, including social security and health care; social benefits; education; access to and supply of goods and services, including housing; and membership of and access to services from organizations whose members carry on a particular profession.

Within employment and the labor market, harassment and discrimination (direct or indirect) because of religion or belief, political conviction, sexual orientation, age, disability, national and social origin is also prohibited.

---

[28] Politiken, Borgerlige blokerer for undercoveragenter i Københavns natteliv, 9 February 2016: http://politiken.dk/indland/ECE3057539/borgerlige-blokerer-for-undercoveragenter-i-koebenhavns-natteliv/.

The discrimination grounds of religion or belief, political conviction, sexual orientation, age, disability, national and social origin do not enjoy protection outside the labor market in Danish civil law.

Criminal law makes it a criminal offense to refuse access to public places and services on the basis of a person's race, color, national or ethnic origin, religious belief or sexual orientation. The law only criminalizes direct discrimination.

11 Does the Enforcement of Antidiscrimination Law Vary According to the Ground of Discrimination?

Danish legislation prohibiting discrimination consists of several acts offering different levels of protection depending on the discrimination ground in question. The result is a varying enforcement of the protection against discrimination when it comes to different groups in society. It is, for example, illegal as well as criminalized for restaurants to refuse admittance based of the ethnic origin of a person, meaning that both the police and the Board of Equal Treatment can handle such a case. On the other hand, it is not a violation of Danish law for a restaurant to refuse admittance because of a person's disability or age. Another example is that discrimination because of sexual orientation within commercial or non-profit services is criminalized and can be dealt with by police and public prosecutors. However, individuals who have experienced discrimination because of their sexual orientation in other arenas are unable to bring a complaint to the Board of Equal Treatment because such discrimination is not illegal according to civil law.

The Board of Equal Treatment's rulings in favor of the complainant vary depending on the ground of discrimination.[29] In 2014, the Board issued rulings in 225 cases. One hundred seven of them dealt with discrimination based on gender, approximately half of which were decided in favor of the complainant. There were 45 rulings about age, in which more than a third of the cases (19) turned out in favor of the complainant. There were 26 rulings about disability and the complainant only succeeded in 4 cases. There were 37 rulings about ethnic origin, with less than a third of the cases (11) ending in favor of the complainant.

With regard to the level of compensation, there has been a tendency to award lower amounts of compensation in cases dealing with discrimination on account of ethnic origin and disability than in cases on gender discrimination. The Supreme Court issued a ruling in October 2014 making a clear statement that the level of compensation in discrimination cases regarding ethnic origin, disability, age, etc., should be the same as in gender discrimination cases.[30]

---

[29]Board of Equal Treatment, Annual Report 2014 (August 2015), Introduction in English, p. 48.

[30]Supreme Court Ruling of 1 October 2014 in Case No. 322/2012. Printed in U2015.1H.

12 What Is the Relationship Between the Enforcement of Antidiscrimination Law and the Quest for Equality on Both an Individual and Systemic Level?

There is a continuing reluctance in Denmark to approach discrimination as a structural and systemic societal problem. One example is that statistical evidence has only been used in a few cases on age and gender discrimination and would not be accepted as the only proof in a concrete case of discrimination. Furthermore, the experimental method of situation testing aiming to establish discrimination is not regulated in Danish legislation and there is no tradition for using the results of situation testing in discrimination cases before the courts or the Board of Equal Treatment. It is primarily journalists and NGOs who have used situation testing as a method to confirm a presumption of widespread discrimination in a specific sector.

Individuals making complaints to the Board of Equal Treatment must have an individual and current interest in the case in question. An individual cannot complain about a discriminatory job advertisement unless the complainant has applied for the job himself. A person who has submitted a complaint from a general interest in combatting discrimination will have her case dismissed. Also, the Board of Equal Treatment does not have the mandate to take up cases on its own initiative.

However, the law has recently changed and now allows for a more structural combatting of discrimination by the Institute for Human Rights—The National Human Rights Institute of Denmark. The Institute is authorized to bring complaints to the Board of Equal Treatment on its own behalf in discrimination cases that are of a matter of principle or of general public interest, even absent an identifiable individual complainant.[31]

There is a general unwillingness in Denmark to use positive or special measures as strategic means to counteract systemic discrimination and discriminatory structures. On the labor market, for example, employers have no obligation to actively promote real equality by positive or special measures. Furthermore, employers who voluntarily establish programs to promote diversity and employment of marginalized groups are very limited by the law in doing so. The Act on Prohibition of Discrimination in the Labor Market, for example, contains a strict rule prohibiting employers to ask for, obtain, receive, or use information about the race, skin color, religion or belief, political opinion, sexual orientation or national, social or ethnic origin of a job applicant or an employee. This prohibition makes it difficult for employers to establish positive measures and to monitor whether diversity management programs or recruitment programs aiming at achieving diversity among staff members are succeeding.

The limit on employers regarding the improvement of equality for marginalized groups is illustrative of the lack of a genuine societal quest for equality on a systemic level in Denmark.

---

[31] Act no. 1570 of 15 December 2015 amending the Act on the Board of Equal Treatment.

13 Is the Enforcement of Antidiscrimination Law Regarded as Different from the Enforcement of Other Laws?

The scheme of a shared burden of proof in antidiscrimination cases recognizes that it is difficult to enforce antidiscrimination laws by using the traditional rules on burden of proof. In civil law, the Act on Ethnic Equal Treatment and the Act on the Prohibition of Discrimination in the Labor Market include provisions on the shared burden of proof, aiming to ensure that the principle of equal treatment is applied effectively. The shared burden of proof implies that when there is a prima facie case of discrimination, the burden of proof shifts back to the alleged discriminator. In other words, if a person who considers herself to be discriminated against is able to establish facts of possible discrimination, then the employer, the shop owner, the landlord, etc., has to prove that no discrimination has taken place.

The shared burden of proof is to be applied in cases of direct and indirect discrimination, harassment and instruction of discrimination, but not in cases regarding victimisation.

The scheme only exists in the enforcement of civil antidiscrimination law and not in criminal law cases.

14 What Does the Enforcement of Antidiscrimination Law Reveal About the Nature of Your Legal System or About the Enforcement of Laws in Your Legal System?

There is a general lack of statistics and research about antidiscrimination and the enforcement of antidiscrimination laws in Denmark.

The general population often regards discrimination as a very serious and intentional violation of an individual person's rights. But the content of direct and indirect discrimination in a legal sense is not generally understood and appreciated. Discrimination on account of ethnic origin, for example, is often understood as something that can only be committed by a racist person with a racist intent. This may explain why there is such a profound lack of recognition that indirect and systemic discrimination takes place in the current Danish society. This may also be at least part of the reason why existing antidiscrimination laws are not enforced more vigorously.

There are no official statistics on the number of cases concerning discrimination brought before the Danish courts. Summaries of all rulings from the Supreme Court as well as select rulings from the High Courts and City Courts are posted on the national court administration's website. Rulings not posted can be obtained from the individual court by paying a fee and by knowing the exact reference of the ruling in question. Case law in the court systems is sorted without reference to the legislation applied and is therefore not available through public registers. It is possible to subscribe to an expensive private database (the Weekly Law Journal), which contains all Supreme Court rulings and selected High Court rulings. But City Court rulings are only rarely published, which makes the monitoring of discrimination cases problematic since these cases are rarely appealed and therefore often remain unknown.

Thus, monitoring Danish case law is severely hindered by the lack of free public access to court rulings, which poses a huge challenge to the monitoring of antidiscrimination law enforcement.

15 Conclusion

Denmark faces challenges and barriers for minorities and women to take part in all aspects of society on an equal footing. More research should be undertaken to examine institutional and systemic barriers preventing genuine equality.

Danish legislation prohibiting discrimination consists of several acts offering different degrees and scopes of protection depending on the discrimination ground in question. The result is insufficient protection against discrimination for certain groups and an unequal approach to the combating of discrimination. Another issue is that this complex legal system is difficult for ordinary citizens and practitioners of law to apply, which results in lack of enforcement and predictability. Enacting a general prohibition of discrimination covering all relevant aspects of society would make the legal system more transparent and enforcement more obtainable. A general prohibition would also promote equality amongst different protected groups.

For individuals who have experienced discrimination, there are barriers to seeking enforcement and redress. To initiate a civil court case requires the appointment of a lawyer, which is a huge financial cost for many victims of discrimination, as free legal aid is scarce. In theory, it is not necessary to obtain the assistance from a lawyer to file a complaint with the Board of Equal Treatment. In practice, however, many victims of discrimination cannot manage to file the complaint by themselves without legal aid.

In recent years there has been an increase in the number of employment related discrimination cases for the courts and the Board of Equal Treatment. There is no doubt that the knowledge among employers on the prohibition of discrimination has increased. The level of compensation in discrimination cases is higher than in traditional cases of unfair dismissals. The higher sanctions, combined with the increased knowledge among employers, are factors likely to have a dissuasive effect when it comes to discrimination in the labor market.

Outside of employment, within the realm of the civil Act on Ethnic Equal Treatment and the criminal Act on the Prohibition of Discrimination Due to Race, sanctions are so mild and compensations so small that it must be questioned whether they are sufficiently effective and dissuasive.

The Board of Equal Treatment is the most accessible agency for the enforcement of antidiscrimination laws. However, a major challenge for the Board is often the lack of evidence. As described above, there is a low success rate for complainants in cases related to ethnic origin and disability, raising a number of issues with regard to the mandate and functioning of the Board. The recommendations below constitute areas for future improvement when it comes to enforcement of antidiscrimination laws:

- Although there has been a general rise in the number of complaints to the Board of Equal Treatment, the visibility of the Board among possible victims is relatively low. Information about the Board should to be much more widespread.
- The Board should be given the authority to accept complaints in person and to hear oral testimonies.[32]
- The Board should be given the authority to demand that the parties disclose material, produce documents, give their opinion, and reveal factual circumstances of a case in order to elucidate a case.
- The Board should be given the mandate to take up cases on its own initiative.

References

Rasmussen P, Johansen K (2013) Oplevet diskrimination og stigmatisering, blandt mennesker med psykisk sygdom (Experienced discrimination and stigma among individuals with mental illnesses). KORA

Warming K (2015) Oplevet diskrimination i forbindelse med graviditet og barselsorlov – En kortlægning (Experienced discrimination based on pregnancy and maternity leave—A survey). Institute for Human Rights – The National Human Rights Institution of Denmark

Pia Justesen, Ph.D. is an independent human rights lawyer and consultant at Justadvice. She holds a Ph.D. from the University of Copenhagen. She serves as the Expert Legal Advisor on Denmark in the European Union Network of legal experts in gender equality and non-discrimination and teaches disability rights at the University of Illinois at Chicago. Ms. Justesen writes and teaches in the field of international human rights law with a special focus on the protection against discrimination based on race and/or disability.

---

[32]Danish Institute for Human Rights, Parallel Report on Denmark—May 2015—CERD, p. 26.

France: le jeu des acteurs

Sophie Latraverse

1 Introduction

Avant les années 2000 en France, les quelques affaires invoquant une discrimination portées devant les tribunaux échouaient. Elles étaient paralysées par les difficultés liées au régime de preuve du droit civil français, par la charge de la preuve et la difficulté de l'approche juridique française à avoir recours à une approche empirique de la faute, fondée sur l'analyse comparée de la situation d'un groupe de personnes pour en tirer des conclusions en droit pour une seule et en déduire la responsabilité d'un auteur pour un constat de faits, dont l'action elle-même n'a pas à être discutée.

Le cadre juridique des discriminations imposé par l'Union européenne a dû s'insérer dans un panorama peu favorable.

Le droit français est structuré autour de sa propre théorie de l'égalité, formelle et universaliste, qui reste l'un des piliers du droit public français, et propose une rhétorique de raisonnement reposant sur "l'égale application de la règle", l'égalité devant l'État et le service public, qui exige que les exceptions soient fondées sur la nécessité de poursuivre un objectif d'intérêt général.

Les traditions politiques et juridiques françaises sont systématiquement réservées face aux approches qui questionnent l'application uniforme de la règle afin de répondre aux besoins d'intérêts particuliers.

Quant au droit civil, il est fondé sur le principe de liberté contractuelle et porte une philosophie selon laquelle les restrictions à ce principe doivent être prévues par la loi, l'ordre public ou répondre à l'intérêt général.

Dans ce contexte, le droit de la non-discrimination est toujours perçu par les acteurs juridiques et politiques comme le vecteur de l'importation dans le système français

---

S. Latraverse (✉)
Defender of Rights, General Secretariat, Paris, France
e-mail: sophie.latraverse@defenseurdesdroits.fr

d'une approche anglo-saxonne qui remet en cause l'équilibre au cœur de la conception française du bien public. De surcroit, dans le contexte de l'introduction du droit des discriminations dans le système juridique français, l'action contentieuse est perçue comme un moyen détourné et illégitime de soutenir l'évolution sociale et un agenda politique imposé de l'étranger, remettant en cause les valeurs universalistes fondamentales de la société française. La plupart des ONG préfèrent soutenir l'action pénale contre le racisme, et les syndicats ne sont pas favorables à une mobilisation qui soutient les intérêts particuliers de groupes minoritaires.

Or, aujourd'hui la France dispose en droit de la non - discrimination d'un régime juridique étoffé qui a pu se développer sous l'impulsion du droit communautaire, en dépit des réserves qu'entretiennent à son égard les juristes, les acteurs politiques, les associations et les syndicats.

En effet, la transposition du droit communautaire a été portée par l'ambition de quelques-uns de surmonter les barrières existantes et assurer l'effectivité du droit des discriminations, qui s'est particulièrement incarnée dans l'action des organismes de lutte contre les discriminations d'état qu'a été la Haute autorité de lutte contre les discriminations et le Défenseur des droits, son successeur.

2 Le droit de la non-discrimination est-il mis en œuvre?

Avant 2005, le cadre juridique était en place mais les recours étaient inopérants en raison, d'une part, de la méconnaissance de ce droit, matière de spécialiste difficilement accessible au praticien français et, d'autre part, des difficultés d'accès à la preuve. Ce contexte posait un réel problème d'accès au droit pour le justiciable.

En outre, le droit français ayant développé sa propre théorie de l'égalité, formelle et universaliste (cf. Question 11), le cadre juridique applicable était perçu comme l'importation superflue d'une approche anglo-saxonne, donc illégitime et ne devant pas trouver application car entrant en conflit avec les repères conceptuels relatifs à l'application de la théorie de l'égalité, toujours en place, tels que « nul ne peut se plaindre de l'uniforme application de la règle ».

Depuis 2005, le droit de non-discrimination est mis en œuvre et la qualité de cette mise en œuvre a significativement progressé sous l'impulsion de la transposition des directives européennes dans la législation nationale et des exigences de la commission européenne à l'égard des institutions françaises.

Paradoxalement, la liste des critères visés par la loi en matière civile, sociale et pénale compte aujourd'hui plus de 30 critères. Elle évolue chaque année au point de possiblement dénaturer le concept même de discrimination. Aux critères traditionnels du droit international et européen que sont l'origine, le sexe, la grossesse, l'état de santé, le handicap, les caractéristiques génétiques, l'orientation sexuelle, l'âge, les opinions politiques et philosophiques, l'appartenance ou la non-appartenance, vraie ou supposée, à une ethnie, une nation, une race ou une religion déterminée, la législation française a ajouté des critères qui illustrent les critères traditionnel et les complètent : le refus d'accès aux soins, la situation de famille, l'apparence physique, le patronyme, le lieu de résidence, les mœurs, les activités syndicales. Or depuis quelques années, le législateur français en allonge sans cesse la liste, le nouveau critère répondant à une pure opportunité politique. Il a créé un critère fondé sur la perte d'autonomie en 2015 et, en 2016, 3 nouveaux critères, soit la particulière vulnérabilité résultant de sa situation économique, l'identité de genre et la capacité à s'exprimer dans une langue autre que le français. Finalement en 2017, le législateur a encore créé avec la loi Egalité citoyenneté du 27 janvier 2017, trois nouveaux critères, soit le refus d'inscription à la cantine, le refus de subir de subir des faits de bizutage et la domiciliation bancaire (article 225-1 du Code pénal, article L1132-1 du Code du travail, Article 1 de la loi no 2008-496 du 27 mai 2008).

Le droit français vise le refus d'accès intentionnel de nature pénale, en matière d'embauche, de sanction et de licenciement, et d'accès aux biens et services, d'entrave à l'activité économique (article 225-2 du Code pénal) et d'entrave à l'exercice d'un droit par une personne dépositaire de l'autorité publique (article 432-7 CP).

Par ailleurs, il sanctionne la discrimination directe, indirecte, la provocation à la discrimination, le harcèlement sexuel et moral et les représailles dans l'emploi, l'accès aux biens et services, privés et publics (article 1 de la loi no 2008-496 du 27 mai 2008). Sa portée a été étendue par la loi de modernisation de la justice du 21e siècle du 18 novembre 2016, pour créer un régime juridique uniforme sur l'ensemble des critères de discrimination interdits par la loi.

Un colloque sur l'évolution du droit en France depuis 10 ans organisé conjointement avec le Conseil d'Etat, la Cour de cassation et le Conseil national des Barreaux, s'est tenu en Grand'Chambre de la Cour de cassation avec la participation des juges européens et des présidents de chambres et de juridictions, consacrant la place qu'a pris le sujet dans le droit national[1].

3 COMMENT est-il mis en œuvre?

En France le droit des discriminations est mis en œuvre par la loi, les institutions d'application de la loi et, sporadiquement, par les politiques publiques.

Le droit des discriminations a été transposé législativement par plusieurs textes successifs qui ont créé un délit pénal de discrimination, d'une part, une interdiction des discriminations en droit de l'emploi privé, de l'emploi public et des professions indépendantes, d'autre part, et enfin, dans l'accès aux biens et services, privés et publics:

– La loi Pleven du 1972 qui a créé les dispositions du code pénal interdisant les discriminations fondées sur l'origine en matière d'embauche, de sanction et de licenciement, et d'accès aux biens et services (articles 225-1 et 225-2 du Code

---

[1]Actes du colloque: http://www.defenseurdesdroits.fr/fr/outils/actes-de-rencontres/actes-du-colloque-dix-ans-de-droit-de-la-non-discrimination

pénal), d'entrave à l'exercice d'un droit par une personne dépositaire de l'autorité publique (article 432-7 CP), qui ont ensuite été amendées pour s'étendre à tous les critères de discrimination interdits par le droit français.
- La loi no. 1006-2001 du 16 novembre, 2001, transposant les directives 2000/43 du Conseil du 29 juin 2000 relative à la mise en œuvre du principe de l'égalité de traitement entre les personnes sans distinction de race ou d'origine ethnique et 2000/78 du Conseil du 27 novembre 2000 portant création d'un cadre général en faveur de l'égalité de traitement en matière d'emploi et de travail, et amendant le code du travail, le code pénal, la loi 83-634 du 13 juillet, 1983 sur la fonction publique.
- L'article 158 de la loi de modernisation sociale no 2002-73 du 17 janvier, 2002, en matière d'accès au logement privé et public.
- La loi no 2005-102 du 11 février 2005 pour l'égalité des droits et des chances, la participation et la citoyenneté des personnes handicapées (Loi handicap) qui a revu la définition du Handicap de l'article L114 du Code de l'action sociale et l'accompagnement du handicap en amendant tous les textes afférents à la prise en charge du handicap et déployant un programme d'intégration des personnes handicapées dans toutes les sphères de la société, l'éducation à l'emploi et l'accessibilité des biens et services.
- La loi no 2008-496 du 27 mai 2008 amendée par la loi de modernisation de la justice du 21e siècle du 18 novembre 2016, complétant la transposition du droit communautaire et couvrant les protections suivantes:

  - La protection civile sur tous les critères de discrimination contre toutes les discriminations directes et indirectes en matière d'emploi et d'accès aux biens et services;
  - La protection des travailleurs indépendants pour les critères visés par la directive 2000/78 et la directive 2006/54 relative à la mise en œuvre du principe de l'égalité des chances et de l'égalité de traitement entre hommes et femmes en matière d'emploi et de travail (refonte).

Les jurisprudences judiciaire et administrative ont construit dans les dossiers relatifs aux discriminations dans le déroulement de carrière, une approche de l'analyse des faits se fondant sur la méthode élaborée par la CGT dans le cadre des dossiers de discrimination syndicale, consistant à élaborer des panels de comparaison permettant de comparer la situation des personnes visées par un critère avec celle des autres personnes pour fonder la présomption de discrimination (Méthode Clerc : Cass.soc. 28 mars 2000, Fluchère no 97-45258 et45259 ; CE 20/11/2013, n°362879).

L'article 71-1 de la Constitution de 1958 et la loi organique no. 2011-333 du 29 mars 2011 créent le Défenseur des droits, autorité constitutionnelle, qui a notamment pour mission d'assurer les fonctions d'autorité nationale de lutte contre les discriminations prévue par les directives européennes. Il succède à la Haute autorité de lutte contre les discriminations (Halde), et couvre toutes les discriminations interdites par la loi française et les conventions internationales ratifiées par la France.

Par ailleurs, la Convention européenne de sauvegarde des droits de l'homme est appliquée directement par les juges français et fonde la plupart des recours en discrimination contre l'Etat, les collectivités territoriales et les services publics en général. Les principes qu'elle pose sont complétés par le principe général de droit public relatif à l'égalité devant le service public, qui fonde également bon nombre de recours administratifs.

4 QUI met en œuvre le droit de la non-discrimination?

Les politiques publiques sont mises en œuvre par l'Etat et les lois sont mises en œuvre par les juridictions nationales, avec le concours de l'autorité nationale de lutte contre les discriminations, des associations et des syndicats.

La Halde puis le Défenseur des droits ont mené depuis 2005 une stratégie d'enquête et d'accès à la preuve ayant pour objet d'alimenter le dossier juridictionnel et la construction d'une jurisprudence sur l'accès à la preuve, et permettre par ailleurs de présenter des observations dans le cadre du procès et contribuer au développement de la jurisprudence sur les discriminations.

Cette stratégie fut complétée par un travail sur le développement des compétences des professionnels qui a accompagné la multiplication des recours. La Halde puis le Défenseur des droits ont appuyé le développement d'une offre de formation accrue au niveau des organismes professionnels comme le Conseil National des Barreaux, le Barreau de chaque ville ou l'Ecole nationale de la magistrature, mais aussi au sein de l'Université.

Cette mobilisation des institutions, des universitaires et des juristes a permis la construction d'une jurisprudence sur l'accès à la preuve et la charge de la preuve au niveau des cours suprêmes des deux registres de juridictions français, à savoir la Cour de cassation et le Conseil d'Etat. C'est leur autorité qui a permis de légitimer le cadre juridique des discriminations. Cette jurisprudence a été particulièrement intégrée au cadre juridique par la chambre sociale de la Cour de cassation en matière de droit du travail et par le Conseil d'Etat en matière de droit de l'emploi public et d'accès à l'éducation.

Cependant, en matière d'accès aux biens et services l'on peut déplorer un très faible taux de contentieux civil, celui-ci se concentrant plutôt sur les recours pénaux soumis aux exigences de la preuve pénale et aux arbitrages du parquet et du ministère public quant à l'opportunité des poursuites.

Certaines associations antiracistes (SOS Racisme, le MRAP, la Ligue des droits de l'homme, Open Society) sont mobilisées en matière de discrimination fondée sur l'origine dans l'accès aux biens et services, privés et publics, et notamment sur le contrôle de police au faciès. L'association ADDH-CCIF (Association de défense des droits de l'homme - Collectif contre l'islamophobie en France) est très impliquée en matière de contentieux relatif au port de signes religieux et sur les discriminations à l'encontre des personnes de religion musulmane.

Les associations de droits des migrants comme le GISTI, ou de droits des Roms, comme Romeurope ou la voix des Roms, agissent en matière d'accès au service public.

Les associations restent cependant peu mobilisées sur l'emploi, sauf quelques associations spécialisées comme l'AVFT en matière de harcèlement sexuel. D'autres associations spécialisées dans l'emploi, comme HOMO boulot, ou l'Autre cercle, sont impliquées sur le critère de l'orientation sexuelle, mais elles s'intéressent à la représentation et l'évolution des pratiques et agissent très peu au contentieux.

Les syndicats commencent à s'intéresser aux négociations sur les droits afférents au principe de non-discrimination dans le cadre du dialogue social, en matière d'évaluation des emplois à prédominance féminine ou de discriminations fondées sur l'âge, mais, en dehors des discriminations fondées sur les activités syndicales, elles agissent très peu au contentieux et ne sont pas l'élément porteur de l'action judiciaire en emploi.

Les directives européennes imposent aux acteurs sociaux d'intégrer les questions liées aux discriminations dans le dialogue social et le législateur français a intégré des obligations de négocier au sujet de l'égalité de rémunération homme femme (article 13 de l'ANI de 2004, article 2242-8 du code du travail) et de la prise en compte de l'âge dans l'entreprise (Loi n° 2008-1330 du 17 décembre 2008 de financement de la sécurité sociale pour 2009, articles 87 à 93). Par ailleurs, en matière d'égalité femmes hommes, des indicateurs non financiers sont imposés aux entreprises par la loi, et la transposition de la Directive 2014/95 du 22 octobre 2014 modifiant la directive 2013/34/UE en ce qui concerne la publication d'informations non financières et d'informations relatives à la diversité par certaines grandes entreprises et certains groupes devrait amener le législateur à imposer la mise en place d'indicateurs sur d'autres attributs de la diversité qui devraient viser d'autres critères de discrimination comme l'âge, le handicap et peut-être l'origine.

Enfin, l'Etat met régulièrement en place de nouvelles politiques publiques pour lutter contre les discriminations, qui sont fondées sur le financement des associations et de leurs actions, la formation des acteurs au repérage des discriminations afin de les mobiliser sur l'accès aux droits, l'expérimentation de dispositifs en matière d'emploi, comme le CV anonyme, ou la politique d'accompagnement de l'habitat ou de scolarisation des gens du voyage.

Par ailleurs, depuis 15 ans la politique publique de l'Etat a largement mobilisé la recherche publique, pour documenter les situations de discrimination, pour susciter et évaluer la mobilisation du droit, et alimenter les données. Elle a également suscité un travail de bonnes pratiques et de labellisation en matière d'emploi, la mise en place de divers dispositifs d'accès au droit, notamment dans le cadre de la politique de la ville. Les administrations concernées sont:

- Le ministère de l'Intérieur, le ministère de l'Education, le ministère de la Justice, le ministère des affaires sociales, le ministère de l'habitat et du développement urbain.
- Le service des droits des femmes, la direction de l'accueil, de l'accompagnement des étrangers et de la nationalité, la direction des relations de travail, la direction

de la cohésion sociale, la délégation générale à l'emploi et la formation professionnelle, la direction des libertés publiques et affaires judiciaires du ministère de l'Intérieur, la direction générale de l'administration et de la fonction publique, le commissariat général à l'égalité des territoires (CGET).
- La délégation interministérielle à la lutte contre le racisme et l'antisémitisme, la délégation interministérielle à l'hébergement et à l'accès au logement, la délégation interministérielle aux personnes handicapées, la délégation interministérielle à l'égalité républicaine et à l'intégration.
- Le Comité national consultatif des droits de l'homme, le Comité interministériel du handicap, la Commission nationale consultative des gens du voyage, le Haut conseil à l'égalité, le Conseil supérieur de l'Egalité Professionnelle, le Conseil national consultatif des personnes handicapées, la Commission dépendance et autonomie des personnes âgées.

De leur côté, les syndicats et associations d'employeurs, mobilisés par le mouvement de la responsabilité sociale des entreprises ont pu accepter de se concerter et de s'engager pour revoir certaines de leurs pratiques. Cependant, cet engagement est resté non contraignant et s'est plutôt orienté vers la promotion de normes infra législatives qui ne traduisent par toute la portée des exigences de la loi. C'est ainsi que de nouveaux concepts comme ceux de diversité ont été promus pour se substituer aux exigences substantielles du principe de non-discrimination.

Aujourd'hui en France, les entreprises ne sont soumises à l'obligation de tenir que des indicateurs globaux sur l'âge, le handicap et le sexe. Le handicap impose un quota de 6 % de présence des personnes handicapées qui peut être compensé par le paiement d'une taxe. La loi française ne pose aucune exigence d'audit ou de respect d'autre norme de performance qualité.

Seuls les labels diversité et égalité proposent des normes, mais leur cahier des charges ont été élaborés par consensus des employeurs, sous l'égide d'un organisme non étatique, l'AFNOR, et la norme à laquelle ils se réfèrent pose des standards inférieurs aux exigences de la loi. Ces labels ne sont que des outils de communication, n'étant pas exigés pour les appels d'offres publics.

5 A QUI PROFITE la mise en œuvre du droit de la non-discrimination?

La loi prohibe les critères de discrimination suivants : l'origine, le sexe, la situation de famille, la grossesse, l'apparence physique, le patronyme, le lieu de résidence, l'état de santé, le handicap, la perte d'autonomie, les caractéristiques génétiques, les mœurs, l'orientation sexuelle, l'identité de genre, l'âge, les opinions politiques et philosophies, les activités syndicales, l'appartenance ou la non-appartenance, vraie ou supposée, à une ethnie, une nation, une race ou une religion déterminée, la particulière vulnérabilité résultant de sa situation économique, la capacité à s'exprimer dans une langue autre que le français, le refus d'inscription à la cantine, le refus de subir des faits de bizutage et la domiciliation bancaire.

La loi Handicap est l'outil de protection des personnes handicapées au-delà du strict droit des discriminations.

Le premier critère sur lequel le droit des discriminations a été opérationnel, et dont la mise en œuvre a fondé l'élaboration du régime juridique des discriminations en France, est le critère des activités syndicales, qui fut mobilisé par les organisations syndicales dans un contexte de discrimination à l'encontre des syndicalistes d'une telle ampleur, qu'il menaçait l'avenir du syndicalisme en France.

Aujourd'hui le droit des discriminations est opérationnel en faveur des salariés du secteur privé et des agents du service public et ce, particulièrement en faveur des personnes malades, des personnes handicapées, des syndicalistes, des femmes, en ce qui concerne les discriminations fondées sur le sexe dans la rémunération, les retours de congés de maternité et la discrimination dans la carrière en lien avec la maternité.

Des évolutions législatives apportées par la loi no 2014-873 du 4 août 2014, ont également consolidé la protection offerte par la loi du 27 mai 2008 aux professions libérales, particulièrement visées par les discriminations en lien avec la grossesse.

En matière d'embauche, le cadre juridique a permis de faire évoluer les textes et les pratiques relatives aux discriminations fondées sur l'âge en amenant peu à peu les opérateurs publics et l'Etat à supprimer les limites d'âge dans l'accès à l'emploi public. Par ailleurs, en France, il n'y a pas d'âge de la retraite obligatoire, mais les salariés subissent d'importantes discriminations fondées sur l'âge dans la carrière à partir du milieu de la quarantaine.

La discrimination fondée sur l'origine en embauche, très répandue, est très difficile à réprimer en raison du principe de liberté de l'embauche, de la difficulté à en rapporter la preuve et du fait que les réclamations ne sont pas à la mesure du phénomène. Une approche de ces dossiers a cependant pu être développée dans les dossiers relatifs à des entreprises qui recrutent les personnes en contrat durée indéterminée au sein d'un vivier interne de personnes recrutées en contrat durée à déterminée. Le nombre de personnes en CDD et en CDI et l'historique d'emploi permettent de documenter la proportion de salariés recrutés et d'embauches par rapport à une disponibilité de main d'œuvre, ce qui a permis à plusieurs reprises d'établir la discrimination fondée sur l'origine (Cass.soc. no 10-15873, 15/12/2011).

Par ailleurs, les vieux migrants (Chibanis), arrivés dans les années 60 et 70, soumis à des conditions d'emploi défavorables en raison de statuts d'emploi les excluant des conditions générales d'embauche en raison de conditions de nationalité française, invoquent la discrimination indirecte fondée sur l'origine pour réclamer en groupe (830 réclamants pour la SNCF) des dommages sur l'cnsemble de leur carrière. Ils ont presque tous eu gain de cause devant le Conseil de prud'hommes de Paris le 21 septembre 2015 (CPH Paris, 21/09/2015, RG N°F 05/12309 et suivants), avec des dommages moyens de 190 000 €. La décision a été confirmée en appel (C.A. Paris, 31/01/2018, n° 15-11389). La valeur du contentieux est estimée à plus de 35 000 millions d'euros. Des dossiers similaires ont été portés contre Renault ou les Compagnies minières publiques.

Sur les contrôles d'identité, le cadre juridique français sur les contrôles d'identité se heurte à un cadre juridique autorisant les contrôles sans motifs (article 78-2 du code de procédure pénale) et qui ne prévoit aucune voie de recours. La Cour de cassation a donc retenu l'application de l'aménagement de la charge de la preuve prévu par la directive 2000/43 pour faciliter l'accès au recours effectif. Elle a de surcroit conclu à l'obligation positive de l'État de prendre des mesures effectives pour prévenir les discriminations fondées sur la race et l'origine et à la responsabilité de l'Etat pour le contrôle relevant du profilage racial (Cass. Civ. 1ere, 9 novembre 2016, 15- 24210[2]). Plus généralement, les situations de discriminations fondées sur l'origine et sur l'orientation sexuelle qui trouvent une réponse judiciaire sont bien souvent des discriminations avérées prenant même la forme de harcèlement.

Les décisions aujourd'hui soulèvent quelques fois des discriminations indirectes fondées sur l'état de santé (Cass. soc. Sportfabrics, n° 05-43962, 09/01/2007), sur le sexe (Cass.soc., AGIRC, n°10-21489, 06/06/2012), ou sur l'origine (Cass.soc., Airbus, N° 10-15873, 15/12/2011 et Dos Santos, n° 10-20765, 03/11/2011), mais la stratégie judiciaire est peu mobilisée par les acteurs sur ces questions, et notamment sur l'évaluation des emplois à prédominance féminine.

Cependant en France, le droit des discriminations comporte aussi un recours contre l'Etat. Les droits que doit garantir l'Etat sans discrimination aux termes de la CEDH et de la loi du 27 mai 2008 sont régulièrement invoqués à l'appui des recours des femmes voilées, des enfants handicapés, des personnes âgées, des migrants précaires, des Roms et des gens du voyage au soutien du droit au respect de la vie privée, de l'accès à l'éducation ou l'accès à l'hébergement d'urgence.

A l'exception du recours aux principes de droits fondamentaux, le contentieux des discriminations reste cependant un contentieux principalement mobilisé par les personnes qui demeurent des acteurs de l'espace économique. Considérant les matières visées par le droit des discriminations – l'emploi, l'accès aux biens et services- les personnes sont employables, ont les ressources pour payer le logement qui leur a été refusé. Surtout, elles ont accès aux ressources sociales et culturelles nécessaires pour mobiliser le droit des discriminations.

Au sein des publics dont est saisi le Défenseur des droits, le public de la lutte contre les discriminations est le plus privilégié. On constate très peu de recours des femmes précaires, des femmes migrantes, des migrants précaires, des Roms, des gens du voyage, et très peu de recours contre l'éducation nationale, sauf en matière d'intégration des enfants handicapés. Cette situation rejoint celle des difficultés d'accès au droit des publics défavorisés en général.

Par ailleurs, en France, où de nombreuses politiques sont axées sur l'accompagnement des publics précaires, le critère du territoire et de la domiciliation sont au cœur des dispositifs d'action positive mis en place en faveur des populations les plus précarisées, qui recoupent les migrants.

---

[2]https://www.legifrance.gouv.fr/affichJuriJudi.do?oldAction=rechJuriJudi&
idTexte=JURITEXT000033374748&astReqId=844390297&fastPos=17

Il est intéressant de souligner que l'intégration de critères fondés sur des critères non essentialistes (liés à une caractéristique de la personne) pour rejoindre des catégories de l'action publique française comme le lieu de résidence (loi n° 2014-173 du 21 février 2014), entre en résonnance avec la place du territoire dans les politiques publiques. Ces critères entendent mobiliser de nouvelles catégories pouvant croiser des discriminations systémiques à l'encontre des personnes immigrées, qui sont également pauvres et résidantes dans des espaces confrontés à la discrimination et la pénurie de services publics.

C'est dans ce contexte que le Défenseur des droits a été saisi à l'automne 2014 de réclamations mettant en cause la disparité de la couverture territoriale par les services publics, par des parents d'élèves et le maire d'une commune de la Seine Saint-Denis, au sujet des conditions dans lesquelles s'est effectuée la rentrée scolaire 2014, marquée par de nombreuses vacances de postes d'enseignants et le recours massif à des contractuels, souvent peu ou pas expérimentés. Les requérants estimaient que ces éléments constituaient une discrimination en raison du lieu de résidence des familles qui obérait la qualité des enseignements prodigués et donc les chances de réussite de leurs enfants. Il a également été saisi sur l'impact financier et fonctionnel de la situation du seul établissement hospitalier métropolitain accueillant une population ayant un taux de précarité supérieur à 30%, au-delà duquel il est admis que les surcoûts organisationnels se multiplient et influencent significativement les durées de séjour, la mobilisation de moyens humains et la qualité du service. Ces saisines soulignent l'importance pour l'effectivité des droit de l'existence de dispositifs alternatifs aux juridictions traditionnelles qui aient la capacité d'intervenir sur le respect des droits lorsqu'il s'agit d'enjeux systémiques et structurels que la voie judiciaire traite avec lenteur et difficulté.

Par ailleurs, le nouveau critère de perte d'autonomie introduit par la loi no 2015-1776 du 28 décembre 2015, devrait permettre de situer sur le terrain de la discrimination les maltraitances institutionnelles, en emploi et dans les lieux de vie, fondées sur la fragilisation de l'Etat de santé des enfants, personnes âgées et personnes malades.

En France, il existe une polémique à savoir si le droit des discriminations doit traiter les désavantages liés à la condition sociale et économique. Une proposition de loi pour introduire un critère fondé sur la précarité sociale a été adoptée en à l'unanimité le 14 juin 2016[3]. Le simple ajout de ce critère à la liste des critères interdits pose le problème de l'opérationnalité du traitement juridique et procédural d'un tel critère de discrimination. Par ailleurs, dans le contexte d'un pays où les politiques publiques d'action sociale sont très développées, le droit des discriminations avait initialement vocation à occuper le registre des facteurs d'inégalité non pris en compte par l'action publique classique. Or, le danger de réintroduire les critères sociaux dans l'analyse des processus discriminatoires est justement de

---

[3] Loi du 24 juin 2016 visant à lutter contre la discrimination à raison de la précarité sociale, https://www.legifrance.gouv.fr/affichTexte.do?cidTexte=JORFTEXT000032769440&fastPos=1&fastReqId=220687561&categorieLien=id&oldAction=rechTexte

réintroduire un a priori de prééminence des facteurs sociaux au détriment de l'analyse de l'impact de la spécificité des autres critères de discrimination comme explication de la situation défavorable des personnes.

6   QUI EST LESE par la mise en œuvre du droit de la non-discrimination?

Dans la mesure où la personne poursuivie ou tenue de mettre en œuvre la norme de non-discrimination agissait au paravent dans l'illégalité et où le droit français intervient sur les discriminations en ajustant à la hausse les droits des salariés discriminés, nous ne pouvons pas dire que d'autres salariés ou que l'employeur seraient lésés.

Par ailleurs, le droit européen, qui irrigue le droit français, ne permet pas la discrimination positive ou l'inégalité de traitement à rebours, en défaveur de quelqu'un en raison de son sexe ou de son origine, etc... Il autorise à prendre des mesures pour favoriser l'accès à l'égalité en prenant les moyens pour favoriser les candidatures de personnes de groupes cibles ou la remise à niveau des personnes de certains groupes afin d'assurer l'égalité des chances, mais ne permet pas un traitement défavorable à l'égard de quelqu'un appartenant au groupe dominant (homme, blanc, etc...) (CJCE, Abrahamsson, C-407/98, REC [2000] I-05539).

Cependant, la mise en œuvre de la règle peut emporter des conséquences financières, l'obligation d'entreprendre des réformes et/ou des réorganisations de la part des employeurs, ou encore contraindre les syndicats à prendre en compte des problématiques qu'ils n'estiment pas prioritaires.

Enfin, de facto, les personnes anciennement privilégiées par les politiques discriminatoires ont vocation à perdre leurs avantages au profit de l'égalité de traitement.

7   QUELLES REPARATIONS sont prévues pour mettre en œuvre le droit de la non-discrimination ?

En matière de discrimination directe liée à l'embauche, la sanction, le licenciement, l'accès à la formation professionnelle, l'entrave à l'activité économique et l'accès aux biens et services, l'action pénale permet d'obtenir des dommages mais surtout la condamnation pénale du discriminant à l'initiative du procureur de la République (article 225-2 Code pénal), ainsi que la condamnation de la personne dépositaire de l'autorité publique (article 432-7 Code pénal), soumettant les représentants de l'Etat, qu'ils soient politiques ou non, à la sanction du juge. Cependant les condamnations prennent rarement la forme de condamnation à la prison, quelques fois avec sursis et surtout d'amendes, somme toute peu élevées.

Par ailleurs, le droit français permet d'obtenir réparation face à toute discrimination directe ou indirecte interdite par la loi contre les personnes privées et les personnes publiques, et ce devant les tribunaux civils et administratifs. Les recours juridictionnels permettent également de faire déclarer par les tribunaux l'illégalité d'une convention collective, d'une décision d'une personne privée, d'une politique publique ou d'un texte législatif ou réglementaire. Si les dommages moraux restent faible, principalement parce qu'ils ne font l'objet d'aucune preuve, le droit n'impose aucune limite au montant des dommages.

En matière civile, la réparation sera indemnitaire et ne permettre pas l'octroi de dommages punitifs. Très peu d'actions sont initiées en matière civile devant les tribunaux de droit commun, seuls compétents en matière d'accès aux biens et services.

Par ailleurs, la majorité du contentieux civil porte sur le droit du travail, toujours soumis au principe indemnitaire (article L1133-3 CT). Cependant, on peut également obtenir l'annulation d'une décision, qui peut emporter la réintégration du salarié (L1132-4 CT), ou d'une convention collective (art L.2262-9 CT).

En droit administratif, les recours tendront à obtenir l'annulation de la décision illégale, permettant de remettre la personne dans la situation antérieure à la prise de décision, et dans certains cas, des indemnités. En matière d'emploi public, le principe indemnitaire est également applicable (Article 6 et. s. de la loi no. 83-634 sur la fonction publique), mais la loi prévoit aussi la sanction disciplinaire de l'agent fautif ayant commis une discrimination (Article 6 quinquies de la loi no. 83-634).

Au-delà de l'action en justice, la victime peut s'adresser au Défenseur des droits afin qu'il enquête sur sa situation et intervienne pour procéder à une médiation ou présenter des observations en justice comme tiers intervenant, afin de produire son dossier d'enquête et éclairer le tribunal sur son analyse du dossier et du droit.

8 QUI SOUTIENT la mise en œuvre du droit de la non-discrimination?

Le Défenseur des droits est l'autorité nationale qui soutient la mise en œuvre du droit de la non-discrimination. Il a pour mission d'enquêter sur les réclamations de discrimination et peut interroger toute personne privée ou publique qui est tenue de lui répondre. A l'issue de son enquête, il peut faire des recommandations, transmettre au parquet pénal ou présenter des observations devant le tribunal pénal, civil ou administratif. Par ailleurs, il favorise la recherche sur les processus discriminatoires, les groupes discriminés et le droit des discriminations, mène également des actions pour la promotion des processus de gestion et de décision non-discriminatoires, et organise des campagnes pour l'accès aux droits et la promotion des droits.

L'Etat français soutient aussi la mise en œuvre du droit de la non-discrimination par le financement qu'il donne aux associations de lutte contre les discriminations, d'une part, et les politiques publiques qu'il met en œuvre, d'autre part. De surcroit, les tribunaux judiciaires et administratifs sont au cœur du dispositif de mise en œuvre du droit de la non-discrimination.

La Commission européenne, quant à elle, porte une politique publique très active de promotion de la lutte contre les discriminations et particulièrement à l'endroit de certains publics comme les femmes, les personnes handicapées ou les Roms. Elle finance de nombreux projets de soutien, allant de la formation des acteurs, aux actions de mobilisation sur le terrain et à la commande d'études. Elle finance également l'Agence des droits fondamentaux (FRA) et l'Institut européen pour l'égalité entre les hommes et les femmes (EIGE) qui recensent les actions de terrain et commandent des études.

Quelques fondations privées et quelques fondations américaines, comme Open Society Foundation, financent quelques actions. Cependant, la mobilisation en France ne se caractérise pas par la contribution des mécènes privés. Les actions des associations sont principalement financées par l'Etat français, et leurs capacités d'action sont par conséquent tributaires de la générosité de la politique du gouvernent à cet égard.

Les personnes agissant au sein d'associations issues des groupes visés par les critères de discriminations - comme les personnes handicapées, les personnes LGBTI, les personnes engagées au soutien des droits des migrants (l'association GISTI), les femmes, les personnes engagées au soutien des libertés publiques - sont soutenues par le bénévolat de leurs militants.

Très peu d'associations ont pour mission de soutenir le contentieux, sauf pour l'AVFT (harcèlement sexuel) et le GISTI (droits des migrants). Cependant, leur mission n'a pas vocation à assurer le financement de ces contentieux, mais plutôt l'expertise des avocats mobilisés, presque toujours bénévolement.

Les autres associations font sporadiquement de l'aide au recours, mais leur engagement est très aléatoire et leurs moyens sont limités. L'organisation du soutien aux recours juridictionnels liés à l'égalité homme femme est presqu'inexistante. En matière de discrimination raciale, la LICRA (Ligue internationale contre le racisme et l'antisémitisme), le MRAP (Mouvement contre le racisme et pour l'amitié entre les peuples) et SOS racisme sont actifs principalement sur le terrain de l'action pénale contre les gestes de racisme et d'antisémitisme et de violence raciste. Elles sont peu présentes sur le terrain de l'action civile ou administrative en matière de lutte contre les discriminations.

Les syndicats agissent par l'action judicaire ou le dialogue social, quoique leur implication dans le sujet ne soit pas le moteur des avancées des dernières années.

Les syndicats se sont particulièrement impliqués en matière de discriminations syndicales, implication qui a permis de construire les fondements de la jurisprudence sociale et de la rhétorique qu'elle propose en matière de discrimination en France (méthode Clerc). Ils ont également porté plusieurs contentieux relatifs aux limites d'âges dans les emplois statutaires des établissements publics tels que la SNCF ou

EDF, et sur les limites d'âge dans la fonction publique. Par ailleurs, ils sont peu impliqués dans le contentieux de l'égalité homme femme, de la discrimination fondée sur l'origine ou l'orientation sexuelle.

Les syndicats se sont récemment impliqués dans le dialogue social relatif aux dispositifs de maintien en emploi et de valorisation des salariés âgés, et, suite à plusieurs pressions législatives issues de la loi (loi 2001-397 du 9 mai 2001, la loi n°2006-340 du 23 mars 2006, loi n° 2010-1330 du 9 novembre 2010 et loi n°2014-873 du 4 août 2014), dans les instances de négociation relatives à l'égalité professionnelle entre les femmes et les hommes.

9 QUI S'OPPOSE au droit de la non-discrimination?

L'extrême droite s'oppose à la répression des discriminations relatives à l'origine.

La droite conservatrice, dans ses composantes universitaires, judicaires et parlementaires, s'y oppose également en ce que la rhétorique du droit des discriminations importe un concept étranger à la tradition française dans les outils de construction du raisonnement juridique : atteintes à la liberté contractuelle, limites au déploiement du principe de laïcité, remise en cause de l'universalité du principe d'égalité au profit d'un raisonnement catégoriel créateur de droit en raison de l'appartenance à un autre ensemble que le fait d'être un citoyen membre de la nation.

A cet égard, il est intéressant de souligner l'action législative invoquant la valeur de la neutralité religieuse de la laïcité et s'affirmant contre l'aménagement raisonnable en faveur de la religion, par voie de résolution de l'Assemblée nationale (Proposition de résolution no 3397 du 5 Mai 2011 sur l'attachement au respect des principes *de* laïcité, fondement du pacte républicain, *et de* liberté religieuse) ou la résolution n° E 3918 de la commission des Affaires sociales du Sénat du 17 novembre 2008, à l'occasion de la discussion de la proposition de directive du Conseil relative à la mise en œuvre de l'égalité de traitement entre les personnes sans distinction de religion ou de convictions, de handicap, d'âge ou d'orientation sexuelle. Dans cette résolution les parlementaires soulignent les dangers de dérives communautaristes découlant de la prolifération du concept de discrimination indirecte et la menace du droit communautaire à l'endroit de l'universalité du principe d'égalité : « derrière cette question juridique se profile une interrogation de fond : dans le combat contre les discriminations, veut-on inciter au repli sur soi, à l'excitation des identités particulières, ou veut-on faire valoir des valeurs et des principes communs ? La proposition de résolution considère que la future directive relève d'une inspiration communautariste qui transparaîtrait au moins sur deux points : l'absence d'un principe général d'égalité de traitement et la définition de la discrimination indirecte. »

Sur un plan plus économique, l'essor de la protection offerte par le droit des discriminations soulève systématiquement l'opposition de certains syndicats d'employeurs, qui estiment que la protection des employés non productifs (femmes enceintes, salariés malades ou handicapés), et le coût de la correction des inégalités représentent des charges démesurées pour les entreprises altérant leur compétitivité. Cette tendance s'est traduite au cours des dernières années par une pression forte du patronat sur le gouvernement pour limiter la portée des obligations liées à la correction des inégalités salariales entre les femmes et le shommes, de l'évolution des droits liés à la protection de la parentalité et à l'accès au recours collectif en matière de discrimination.

En outre, de nombreux patrons, sans s'exprimer officiellement, ne sont pas prêts à mettre en place les mesures de nature à corriger ou lutter contre les discriminations dans l'entreprise. Certains grands groupes opèrent systématiquement un calcul stratégique qui s'accorde à obliger les salariés à obtenir un jugement avant d'intervenir, ou même, plaident le coût exorbitant de la correction de l'inégalité pour justifier la situation. C'est ce que l'on observe dans le contentieux de la SNCF contre les vieux migrants magrébins, qui ont été maintenus tout au long de leur carrière au plus bas de l'échelle salariale ou de la BNP contre les femmes au sein de la banque. Ces entreprises attendent systématiquement que les salariés instituent des actions et refusent de corriger collectivement des discriminations systémiques documentées et judiciairement établies de longue date.

Mais, le droit français couvre plus de 30 critères prohibés et des situations qui visent directement ou indirectement toutes les personnes. Ainsi, tous les groupes dénoncent celles des discriminations qu'ils acceptent de protéger. Tout repose sur l'analyse de la liste des critères qu'ils dénoncent ou estiment illégitimes.

10 QUELLE EST LA PORTEE du droit de la non-discrimination?

Le droit de la non-discrimination couvre l'emploi, de la formation professionnelle à la retraite, incluant le stage, l'embauche, la sanction, le licenciement, l'évolution professionnelle, la mutation, la rémunération, l'évolution de carrière, les avantages sociaux et la retraite.

Il couvre l'accès aux biens et services, privés et publics, l'éducation, le logement, la protection sociale, les droits protégés par la Constitution et les politiques publiques visées par la CEDH (voir réponse 2).

Son impact reste judicaire et se limite aux personnes qui ont les moyens d'accéder aux droits.

En matière d'embauche par exemple, la répression judiciaire s'avère un outil totalement inefficace en raison des difficultés de preuve et de la faible mobilisation des recours par les personnes en recherche d'emploi.

Le droit des discriminations a pu susciter des bonnes pratiques dans les entreprises et des efforts de citoyenneté économique par le biais de la promotion des labels. Quoique ces outils n'aient pas fait l'objet d'évaluation, ils ont certainement contribué à faire évoluer certaines pratiques dans les grandes entreprises et le service public. Cependant, aujourd'hui, la loi française n'impose l'obligation de publier des indicateurs que sur l'égalité homme femme (Article. L. 2323-57 et suivants du code du travail) ou sur l'action en faveur des personnes handicapées dans l'entreprise (article L2323-61 code du travail).

D'autre part, l'embauche de personnes handicapées dans le secteur public et le secteur privé est soumise à un quota de 6 % pour tout employeur occupant au moins 20 salariés depuis plus de 3 ans (articles 2323-2 du code du travail), sinon il doit verser une contribution à l'Association de gestion du fonds pour l'insertion des personnes handicapées (AGEFIPH).

Par ailleurs, la Halde, puis le Défenseur des droits, ont toujours eu recours à la promotion de recommandations générales pour corriger des pratiques observées dans les dossiers sur lesquels ils ont pu enquêter, ces recommandations générales pouvant dépasser les limites de la casuistique et avoir, au-delà de la situation individuelle, un impact sur les pratiques qui pourraient être qualifiées de systémiques.

Cependant, alors qu'au début des années 2000 et particulièrement à la création de la Halde en 2005, l'enjeu était de rendre le droit des discriminations opérationnel et effectif, aujourd'hui on constate que la portée du droit des discriminations face à l'ampleur du phénomène reste casuistique.

Quelques affaires soulevant des discriminations indirectes (en matière de retraite des femmes : AGIRC : Cass. Soc. N° 10-23013, 03/07/2012; ou de régulation du temps de travail eu égard aux discriminations liées aux absences pour raison de santé : Sportfabrics Cass. Soc. N0 05-43962, 09/01/2007), ont pu avoir un impact systémique, mais ces contentieux restent marginaux.

Enfin, la loi de modernisation de la justice du XXIe siècle du 16 novembre 2016 a créé un régime de recours collectif en matière de discrimination pour répondre à la réalité collective des discriminations qui ne trouve pas de réponse dans le litige individuel. Or, l'objectif d'efficacité de cette réforme a été bridé suite aux demandes insistantes des syndicats pour leur donner le monopole du recours collectif en matière d'emploi, en dépit de leur faible mobilisation sur les discriminations autre que syndicales. Les associations ne peuvent intervenir qu'en matière d'accès aux biens et services. Cette importante réforme procédurale qui portait des enjeux forts pour l'effectivité du droit des discriminations aura cédé le pas aux équilibres politiques du moment.

L'Etat français n'a pas encore fait le choix de mettre en œuvre des obligations de diagnostiques et de suivis systémiques au niveau des entreprises. Par ailleurs, aucun dispositif d'élaboration systémique d'études d'impact en matière législative et réglementaire sur les critères de discrimination autre que le sexe et le handicap n'est aujourd'hui en place pour assurer le *mainstreaming* des questions de discrimination (loi organique n°2009-403 du 15 avril 2009 ; circulaire (n° 5598/SG) a été prise le 23 août 2012, circulaire (n° 5602/SG) prise le 4 septembre 2012).

11 LA MISE EN OEUVRE DU DROIT DE LA NON DISCRIMINATION VARIE-T-ELLE en fonction du critère discriminatoire?

En droit non, mais comme nous l'avons mentionné plus haut, le fondement discriminatoire de toutes les mesures liées à la prise en compte de critères interdits ne sont pas toutes aussi faciles à établir en fonction de la disponibilité de traceurs objectifs de ces critères (comme l'âge, la nationalité, le sexe), et chaque critère intervient dans des circonstances de lieu, de temps et d'activités différents.

Il faut d'une part distinguer entre les critères qui font l'objet de recensement quantitatif, comme le sexe, l'âge ou la nationalité, et qui peuvent par conséquent fonder des calculs statistiques et une qualification quantitative des résultats en termes de preuves indirectes, et les critères qui relèvent de données sensibles qui ne sont pas comptabilisées en France, comme l'origine, la religion ou l'orientation sexuelle. Ceci aura un impact direct sur le type de situation pouvant faire l'objet d'une judiciarisation et d'une preuve de discrimination.

Le syndicalisme est une activité revendiquée qui déclenche une perception hostile et emporte des conséquences sur la carrière. C'est la méthode de preuve de ses conséquences en utilisant un panel de comparaison entre la progression de carrière de personnes en situations différentes par rapport à un critère de discrimination, désignée sous le terme méthode Clerc (du nom de son auteur), qui a fondé tout le développement du droit des discriminations en France (supra: Cass.soc. 28 mars 2000, Fluchère no 97-45258 et 45259 ; CE 20/11/2013, n°362879).

L'approche stratégique du contentieux de la discrimination fondée sur la grossesse s'est directement inspirée de la méthode d'analyse des faits de la méthode Clerc, s'appuyant sur la rupture qui intervenait après la connaissance de l'activité syndicale. La grossesse correspond aussi à l'impact d'une annonce sur la subjectivité de l'employeur, celle d'une indisponibilité momentanée, qui déclenche des réactions dans un contexte de temps à proximité de cette annonce ou de l'absence liée à la maternité. Elle aura un impact qui pourra se situer dans le temps par rapport à l'annonce de la grossesse et fonder une présomption fondée sur la chronologie des faits.

L'origine et ses indices sont des invariants, des caractéristiques de la personne entrant dans la catégorie des données sensibles qui ne sont pas comptabilisée en France. En matière d'embauche, sa prise en compte ne laisse aucune trace sauf dans certains contextes spécifiques : (1) liés à l'incompétence du recruteur, qui restent anecdotiques par rapport à l'ampleur du phénomène, ou (2) du recrutement au sein d'un vivier qui permet d'établir une inégalité de traitement à partir d'une approche quantitative (Airbus Cass. Soc. N° 10-15873, 15/12/2011). Mais c'est principalement dans le contexte d'un comportement avéré, lié au harcèlement que l'origine suscite chez le raciste, que la discrimination fondée sur l'origine dans la carrière pourra être établie.

L'âge est un critère qui surgit. Il emporte une non-prise en compte d'une candidature, ou l'exclusion d'un processus de promotion, dans un contexte où cette décision serait autrement inexplicable ; sinon, un plafonnement qui se concrétisera par une interruption de la progression de carrière. C'est cette interrogation qui déclenchera une présomption et pourra susciter une demande d'explication.

L'orientation sexuelle est un invariant. Elle est souvent inconnue, ou la preuve de sa connaissance par le défendeur peut poser difficulté. Lorsqu'elle est connue, elle donnera lieu à des discriminations directes, elle déclenchera des réactions de harcèlement chez les homophobes (Cass. Soc. N° 11-15204, 24/04/2013).

En termes de discriminations indirectes, jusqu'à l'adoption du droit au mariage, plusieurs situations conditionnant l'accès à certains droits ou avantages liés à l'emploi, fondés sur la qualité d'époux, ont été traitées sous l'angle de la discrimination indirecte fondée sur l'orientation sexuelle (CJUE, Crédit Agricole c. Hay, C-267/12, 12/12/2013). Mais puisqu'en France la situation de famille est un critère de discrimination interdit par la loi, ces situations ont aussi pu être traitées sous l'angle de la discrimination directe fondée sur la situation de famille.

Le handicap fait l'objet d'une politique publique qui emporte des obligations positives, qui si elles ne sont pas mises en œuvre, donnent lieu à une conclusion de discrimination. C'est la réalisation ou non des obligations positives afférentes au respect des droits des personnes handicapées qui emportera la discussion, avec une obligation de l'employeur de se justifier.

La religion en France, fonde des prises de position avérées, dont la légitimité même devient l'objet du débat. Ses signes extérieurs provoquent des réactions de principe ou du harcèlement qui pourront être attaqués. Sinon, il s'agit d'une donnée sensible qui n'a pas vocation à être connue, ce qui, en dehors de la question des signes religieux, rend la preuve de la discrimination indirecte difficile.

Par ailleurs, les normes applicables au port de signes religieux à l'école et en emploi ont donné lieu à d'importantes polémiques judiciaires. Alors qu'elles ont été résolues par l'adoption de la loi du 15 mars 2004 en ce qui concerne l'école, que le service public est soumis à une stricte obligation de neutralité des agents publics, les restrictions qui peuvent être apportées à la liberté religieuse restent en débat en ce qui concerne l'emploi privé.

La Cour de cassation a précisé que toute personne travaillant pour un employeur public ou privé concourant au service public est tenu de respecter l'obligation de neutralité des agents publics (Cass.soc., CPAM, 19 mars 2013, n°12-11.690), mais qu'au-delà des restrictions aux droits et libertés admissibles en raison des particularités de l'emploi, la laïcité de l'employeur ne pouvait pas fonder un projet fondé sur l'orientation d'une entreprise de tendance et soumettre le salarié à une obligation de neutralité (Ass. Plén., Baby Lou, 25/06/2014, n° 13-28.369). La Cour de cassation a adressé une question préjudicielle à la Cour de Justice de l'Union européenne la question de savoir si un employeur pouvait imposer à une consultante intervenant auprès d'un client prônant un environnement laïque, d'enlever son voile et de la licencier en cas de refus. La Cour de justice a décidé que l'employeur ne pouvait s'appuyer sur les demandes de son client pour interdire le port de signes religieux dans l'exécution de la prestation de travail (CJUE, 14 mars 2017, C-188/15 Bougnaoui).

L'article 15 de la loi n° 2014-173 du 21 février 2014 de programmation pour la ville et la cohésion urbaine a introduit le critère du lieu de résidence dans la législation prohibant les discriminations dans l'emploi et l'accès aux biens et services. Il a été adopté afin de permettre aux personnes résidant dans des lieux ou quartiers défavorisés, déjà fortement touchés par les discriminations fondées sur l'origine, de contrer les discriminations dans l'accès à l'emploi ou aux biens et services.

Le droit des discriminations a eu historiquement pour objectif de mettre en lumière les facteurs d'inégalité fondés sur les spécificités de la personne, qui interviennent pour mettre en échec les politiques sociales, pour exclure et miner les fruits du mérite et des talents reconnus comme source de distinctions objectives et légitimes.

La législation consacrée à la lutte contre les discriminations est censée symboliser le refus d'autoriser l'Etat, les services publics et les personnes privées à prendre en compte ces caractéristiques fondamentales et durables de leur identité pour pénaliser les individus (le sexe, la couleur de peau, l'origine, le handicap ...).

A l'inverse, on peut soutenir que le lieu de résidence, comme la condition sociale ou la pauvreté, ne constituent pas des invariants mais des contextes susceptibles d'évoluer. Le critère du lieu de résidence est le premier critère de discrimination interdite fondé sur une situation et un stéréotype qui ne soient pas un attribut de la personne.

A l'instar du critère de l'apparence physique, ce vingtième critère légal de discrimination est porteur de significations multiples. Il fait référence aux stéréotypes qui sont accessoirement liés aux critères de discrimination classiques, comme l'origine, mais permettrait, au-delà d'un critère indirect visant les caractéristiques de populations vivant dans certains espaces géographiques identifiés, telles que l'origine, de corriger les refus d'accès aux droits de certaines autres catégories de populations.

Il pose enfin plus largement, une nouvelle question à la théorie de l'égalité française (cf. question 10) en termes d'égalité des territoires et des effets d'arbitrages défavorables des pouvoirs publics en fonction du lieu de résidence. Ainsi, comme pour le critère de discrimination fondée sur l'apparence physique, on crée un critère de discrimination directe pour contourner les difficultés à traiter la discrimination indirecte fondée sur l'origine.

12 QUEL EST LE RAPPORT entre la mise en œuvre de la non-discrimination et la recherche d'égalité au niveau individuel et systémique?

La tradition française apporte une définition spécifique au principe d'égalité, dont la mise en œuvre s'insère dans un régime juridique autonome structurant l'ensemble du droit administratif français sur le fondement de l'égale application de la loi, l'égalité face à l'état et au service public.

La lutte contre le racisme et la xénophobe bénéficie en France d'une mobilisation associative ancrée dans la société française depuis la fin du 19e siècle et d'un arsenal législatif pénal important de plus de quarante ans. Sa conception de l'égalité et de l'être humain récuse toute distinction fondée sur les catégories comme l'origine, sa conception du peuple français étant fondée sur la reconnaissance de ses nationaux comme êtres humains adhérant aux valeurs de la République.

Cette tradition antiraciste a construit un régime juridique de l'égalité fondé sur une grille d'analyse se référant à d'autres concepts que ceux présidant au déploiement de celui de discrimination. C'est sous l'impulsion du droit communautaire que la France à la fin des années 90 abordera ce champ nouveau qui bouleverse et transforme son approche juridique de l'égalité.

Son défi est celui d'intégrer à sa culture juridique forte et fondatrice de l'identité française égalitaire, les éléments nouveaux de la grille d'analyse des discriminations.

12.1 L'égalité formelle: un fondement opératoire du droit français

La tradition *juridique* française est construite autour de la vision encyclopédiste de l'égalité consacrée par la Déclaration universelle des droits de l'homme et du citoyen de 1789. Le principe d'égalité en est un pilier « qui exprime avec la défense des libertés, l'essentiel du contenu juridique de la devise républicaine »[4]. Il s'est forgé dans un cadre institutionnel universaliste fondé sur les principes abstraits d'Etat, de Nation et de Citoyenneté.

Il faudra attendre la fin de la deuxième guerre mondiale pour que les droits et libertés fondamentaux soient le fondement de l'interdiction du racisme et de la discrimination, sur la base des textes constitutionnels de 1946 et de 1958 et des grands traités internationaux des droits de l'Homme régulièrement ratifiés et publiés. Ces textes affichent toujours une volonté de lutter contre le racisme fondée sur une conception absolue et abstraite de l'être humain, indissociable du respect de sa dignité, des droits de l'homme et de l'universalité du principe d'égalité.

Ces droits inaliénables et sacrés confèrent à chaque être humain la liberté, la dignité, l'égalité des droits et devoirs en dehors notamment de tout critère discriminatoire et de toute notion de « race ». C'est dans cet esprit que le concept de « race » a été banni du droit français. Il est important de souligner d'ailleurs que la question de l'utilisation même du mot « race » dans les textes juridiques antiracistes fait constamment débat en France (la loi n° 2017-256 du 28 février 2017 a remplacé le terme race par "prétendue race" dans les textes interdisant les discriminations). La conception française de l'égalité rejette en outre toute différenciation ou même prise en compte de l'origine. Le droit conçoit l'être humain comme une essence affranchie des stigmates subjectifs et culturels de l'origine, d'où l'impossibilité d'établir des statistiques liées à l'origine et de comparer la situation des groupes en relation avec

---

[4]Rapport du Conseil d'Etat 1996, Sur le principe d'égalité. La documentation Française, 1998, p. 15.

leur origine même s'il s'agit bel et bien d'un paramètre de contrainte construit par la société.

Le droit français substitue à l'origine d'autres types de catégories qui n'atteignent pas sa conception de l'universalité (les femmes, les jeunes, le lieu de résidence, les conditions socio-économique). Ainsi, il ne peut intervenir sur les stigmates du racisme et leurs effets que par les dispositifs qu'il construit en fonction d'autres critères tels que l'âge, pour les programmes d'accès à l'emploi des jeunes, ou la condition socio-économique, pour l'accès au logement.

C'est l'égale application de la loi qui garantit qu'aucune fraction du peuple ne puisse dominer l'autre. La règle satisfait aux contraintes du principe d'égalité si elle est la même pour tous. La rupture de la généralité de la loi est donc nécessairement illégale et l'égalité devant la loi épuise le principe d'égalité. Cette voie égalitaire s'accorde avec la volonté générale et permet d'affirmer l'unité de la République, mais elle ignore toute construction pluraliste de l'égalité.

Les juges administratifs et constitutionnels français considèrent que le principe d'égalité réside essentiellement dans la généralité de la règle. Ils n'admettent pas qu'un traitement uniforme de situations différentes puisse donner lieu à une inégalité protégée par l'ordre juridique (CE, Ass., 28 mars 1997, Sté Baxter).

La conception du principe d'égalité développée par la Cour de justice de l'Union européenne (CJUE) apparaît plus large, plus concrète et, contrairement à la conception classique française, tient compte des différences de situations. Elle exige qu'à situation comparable des règles similaires soient appliquées mais considère de surcroît qu'un traitement uniforme de situations différentes (notamment en raison de l'origine) n'est pas conforme aux exigences du principe d'égalité. Ainsi, le droit communautaire exige de dépasser l'uniformité de la règle et requiert qu'à des situations différentes soient appliquées des règles différentes.

Le droit français reconnaît cependant que certaines différences de situation puissent justifier la mise en place de dispositifs spécifiques et que soient donc appliquées des règles différentes (CE, Ass., 28 juin 2002, *Villemain*, Rec. 586). C'est en ce sens qu'il reconnaît la construction de certaines catégories en matière de pondération ou d'aide, mais ce en fonction de critères non identitaires et neutres tels les critères socio-économiques.

Par ailleurs, doivent être interdites en toutes circonstances les différences de traitement fondées sur la « race » ou l'origine. Le Conseil constitutionnel affirme ne reconnaître que le peuple français sans distinction d'origine, de « race » ou de religion, et le droit refuse toute forme de reconnaissance de ces critères comme catégorie (CC 15 novembre 2007). Les concepts de peuple français et de citoyenneté n'admettent donc aucune définition identitaire fondée sur l'origine, la « race » ou la religion qui exprimerait la culture d'une fraction du peuple, autorisant celle-ci à revendiquer à ce titre des droits spécifiques. Par conséquent, le droit français n'admet pas l'existence de minorités identifiées par des particularismes ethniques, linguistiques ou religieux. Il apporte à chaque individu la même protection de la loi, laquelle permet à tous d'affirmer leurs convictions, mais cette garantie est offerte à l'individu, et non à un groupe qui voudrait être officiellement défini et reconnu par référence auxdits particularismes.

C'est ainsi que la France s'oppose systématiquement aux clauses des conventions ou déclarations internationales qui tendent à reconnaître aux individus des droits spécifiques à raison de leur appartenance à une minorité. La Convention-cadre pour la protection des minorités nationales élaborée par le Conseil de l'Europe engage les Etats signataires à reconnaître l'existence de minorités nationales. Le Conseil d'Etat a estimé dans son avis du 6 juillet 1995 que cette convention était incompatible avec la Constitution française qui ne reconnaît pas l'appartenance des individus à des communautés différentes (Conseil d'Etat, avis relatif à la « Convention-cadre pour la protection des minorités nationales », 6 juillet 1995).

Le juge administratif fait vivre le principe d'égalité en construisant un régime juridique jurisprudentiel de l'égalité en droit administratif, fondé sur l'atteinte à l'égalité formelle qui prohibe toute distinction fondée sur l'origine. Il se décline en égalité fiscale, égalité des usagers devant le service public et égalité devant les charges publiques, pour être consacré principe général du droit et intégré aux textes constitutionnels à compter de 1946[5].

Il annulera un acte prenant en compte l'origine pour accorder ou refuser un droit : par exemple, un acte refusant le bénéfice d'un congé à une catégorie d'agents publics en raison de leur origine ethnique, un acte qui interdit l'accès à l'école aux enfants étrangers ou un acte favorisant une population en raison de son origine (CE, 21 novembre 1962, République Malgache c/ Mme Rasafindranaly, recueil Lebon page 618).

Il est cependant important de souligner que certains auteurs considèrent que les dispositifs récents d'accompagnement vers l'égalité de chances font apparaître des « fissures différentialistes » qui tendent à mettre en place de façon détournée des systèmes de quotas ou d'aide ciblée, construits sciemment sur la base de critères apparemment neutres mais de manière à prendre en compte la réalité de l'origine[6].

12.2 L'impact du principe de discrimination indirecte

C'est dans la mise en œuvre de la discrimination indirecte que le principe de non-discrimination dépasse le principe d'égalité et prend une dimension collective. Aujourd'hui elle est reconnue par la loi et mise en œuvre par les juridictions, mais elle ne repose que sur l'initiative des acteurs judicaires et la casuistique.

Or, on observe que même en cas de preuve de discrimination indirecte ayant un impact collectif, en l'absence de recours collectifs et de mobilisation syndicale d'ampleur, les décisions n'ont pas d'impact au-delà de la situation individuelle du demandeur.

Or, l'on constate une très faible mobilisation syndicale sur les questions d'égalité homme femme à l'étape des négociations collectives, qui ne prenne que très peu la

---

[5]Premier alinéa du préambule de la Constitution de la IVe République (1946)
[6]Maisonneuve (2002), p. 561.

forme d'une mobilisation autour d'un dossier judiciaire démontrant la discrimination collective. Par ailleurs, l'historique du dossier des 830 Chibanis de la SNCF (cf. Question 4), qui ont dû attendre la retraite pour se mobiliser, et ce sans l'aide des syndicats et des associations, dont la décision favorable a été portée en appel par la compagnie de chemin de fer nationale (SNCF) en raison de son impact financier, révèle l'absence totale de mobilisation syndicale autour des discriminations fondées sur l'origine.

Par ailleurs, la France n'a pas encore adopté de dispositif contraignant de correction des discriminations systémiques. Les entreprises ne doivent pas discriminer et doivent publier des indicateurs sur l'âge, le handicap et le sexe (cf. question 3) mais aucune obligation légale de diagnostic et de mise en place d'une programmation de rattrapage. La mise en œuvre de l'obligation d'égalité repose entièrement sur la capacité des personnes à initier des recours.

Il est important cependant de souligner que la loi handicap du 11 février 2005, a insufflé un changement de paradigme dans la prise en compte des personnes handicapées qui porte des enjeux programmatiques systémiques d'évolution de l'accessibilité de la société aux personnes handicapées à tous les niveaux : l'accessibilité matérielle de la cité, l'accessibilité du poste de travail, de l'accès à l'école et à la formation, de l'accès aux loisirs et aux droits

13 LA MISE EN OEUVRE DU DROIT DE LA NON DISCRIMINATION EST-ELLE PERCUE COMME DISTINCTE de la mise en œuvre d'autres lois?

Le régime juridique français étant dominé par le principe d'égalité, le principe de non-discrimination emporte une dérogation aux modes de raisonnements traditionnels qui a pu se justifier politiquement par la reconnaissance de la gravité des discriminations, la sensibilisation aux modes opératoires des stéréotypes, qui agissent à l'insu des personnes, et à l'impact de l'effet systémique des discriminations sur l'égalité des chances.

Le droit des discriminations est par ailleurs perçu comme une importation étrangère imposée par l'Union européenne, qui non seulement impose au législateur français l'adoption d'une norme, mais l'importation dans le raisonnement juridique de modes d'analyse et de preuve étrangers à la culture juridique française.

Il suscite à cet égard une défiance certaine.

En outre, le potentiel d'impact collectif du droit de la non –discrimination tarde à se réaliser parce qu'en France, le droit est le domaine de la demande individuelle et non de la mobilisation collective. C'est l'atteinte à la dignité individuelle et la faute de l'auteur de la mesure qui sont sanctionnées par le tribunal, la juridiction n'ayant pas vocation à être un acteur de la réforme systémique, qui elle est syndicale ou politique.

En outre, le réflexe selon lequel la discrimination est intentionnelle et du registre de la sanction pénale, perdure, et de ce fait induit sinon un réflexe de contentieux pénal, certainement une difficulté conceptuelle à penser la discrimination comme un levier systémique.

14 QUE REVELE LA MISE EN OEUVRE DU DROIT DE LA NON DISCRIMINATION sur la nature de votre système juridique et sur la mise en œuvre des lois dans votre système juridique?

Au début des années 2000, le bilan de la mise en œuvre de l'interdiction des discriminations fondées sur le sexe mettait en lumière les difficultés centrales liées au décalage des règles de procédure civile et de preuve en France, où le demandeur a la charge de la preuve, où il n'y a pas de processus d'accès à la preuve préalable au procès, et où le demandeur ne peut pas faire sa preuve avec les éléments de la partie adverse. A l'inverse, le régime juridique anglo-saxon qui a conçu le droit des discriminations s'articulait autour de principes d'accès à la preuve du demandeur qui étaient étrangers au droit français.

L'évolution de la mise en œuvre des règles de preuve était l'un des défis posés par le droit des discriminations aux régimes juridiques de droit civil. Les acteurs judiciaires de régimes civilistes ne perçoivent pas les règles de preuve comme une dimension cruciales du processus judiciaire et n'ont aucune expérience des techniques de preuves et de la manipulation des règles comme enjeux du procès.

Ainsi, pour rendre le droit des discriminations opérationnel en France, non seulement fallait-il construire une adhésion à l'évolution des modes de raisonnement, mais faire reconnaître le droit du demandeur à avoir accès à la preuve en possession de la partie adverse, ainsi que les conséquences que cette évolution induit en termes de capacité professionnelle à construire des stratégies probatoires et d'accès à la preuve.

La mise en œuvre du droit des discriminations exige donc que soit investie une matière nouvelle, dont le fond dépend exclusivement de la maîtrise d'une nouvelle rhétorique de la preuve, à trois niveaux:

- une analyse juridique essentiellement fondée sur l'analyse des indices mis en preuve pour en tirer des présomptions,
- l'affirmation du droit d'accès à la preuve du demandeur, et
- certaines évolutions quant au déroulement du processus judiciaire pour permettre la réalisation de l'étape de l'accès à la preuve.

La preuve quitte la sphère procédurale du droit pour devenir une question de fond, et c'est cette reconnaissance par la Cour de cassation qui jettera les bases de l'émergence d'un nouveau droit de l'accès à la preuve du demandeur. La Cour de cassation, s'appuyant sur la jurisprudence communautaire, a peu à peu accepté l'analyse comparative de la situation du demandeur avec celle d'autres personnes pour induire une présomption de discrimination. Ensuite, la Cour a éventuellement reconnu qu'à moins que le demandeur ait accès à la preuve de la partie qui détient les clefs de la comparaison, soit la partie adverse, son droit d'action ne pourrait être exercé (Cass. Soc. 9/04/1996, no. 1727 P, *RJS* 5/96 no. 550; Cass. Soc. 23/11/1999 no. 4290, RJS 5/00 no. 498 ; Fluchère Supra).

Dans un contexte où le fait de demander des éléments de preuve à la partie adverse est une révolution, la Cour est allée aussi loin que de décider qu'en dérogation à la règle, c'est le devoir du juge d'unilatéralement demander au défendeur de produire les éléments afin de vérifier l'allégation d'inégalité de traitement du demandeur (Fluchère, Supra), et que le refus de communiquer pouvait fonder une présomption de discrimination (IBM c. Buscail, CA Montpelier, 25/03/2003 N° 0200504).

Cette jurisprudence ouvrant l'accès à la preuve en matière de discrimination pourrait fonder plus largement des évolutions substantielles en termes de procédure judiciaire et de principe d'accès à la preuve en matière civile.

15 Conclusion

La conjugaison de la pression européenne, de l'action de la Halde et du Défenseur des droits, et de la construction jurisprudentielle des Cour suprêmes ont permis l'émergence d'évolutions significatives concernant l'impact et l'effectivité du droit des discriminations et la création d'un véritable droit des discriminations en France.

Il aura aussi introduit une institution d'un genre nouveau, qui agit au soutien des droits de manière indépendante au sein même de l'État, et qui a trouvé sa légitimité et porté des modes de raisonnement originaux qui ont finalement été acceptés par les cours suprêmes.

Le contentieux stratégique a commencé à émerger et produire des évolutions significatives de l'approche contentieuses elle-même ou la construction de recours nouveaux en matière de profilage racial et de discriminations indirectes. Sa mise en œuvre aura incidemment amené une révolution de la pratique judicaire, reconnaissant un droit d'accès à la preuve du demandeur et imposant au défendeur de s'exprimer pour se justifier. Cependant, ces actions restent encore le propre de quelques universitaires et avocats qui font levier et portent la plupart des évolutions.

Le droit des discriminations n'a certes pas atteint son potentiel, mais la gravité des enjeux qu'il porte peuvent laisser croire qu'il saura proposer à l'avenir d'autres évolutions.

La France est un pays multiculturel moderne, qui fait face à des défis considérables. Le droit des discriminations occupe déjà une place qui permet de croire qu'il a vocation à offrir un outil conceptuel susceptible de protéger les personnes, produire des mobilisations nouvelles et porter certaines des solutions pertinentes aux problèmes actuels.

Reference

Maisonneuve M (2002) les discriminations positives ethniques ou raciales en droit public interne : vers la fin de la discrimination positive à la française, AFDA, mai-juin 2002, p 561

Sophie Latraverse is Director of the General Secretariat of the Défenseur des droits. She is member of the Bar of Quebec in Canada, has a B.C.L. from Mc Gill University and a D.E.A. From the University of Paris Ouest- Nanterre. Since 2000, she has contributed to the creation and legal direction of the French antidiscrimination body, HALDE, which has been integrated in the Défenseur des droits in 2011. Ms Latraverse is also the French expert in the European Network of Legal Experts in the non-discrimination field since 2004.

Discrimination Et Matiere Penale En France

Dominique Viriot-Barrial

1 Le droit de la non-discrimination, un droit amplement consacré dans la matière pénale

Le droit de la non-discrimination revêt paradoxalement en droit pénal français une symbolique très forte mettant au cœur de son combat le concept de dignité mais pour autant il ne revêt en termes d'efficacité qu'une efficacité réduite. La voie pénale n'apparaît pas comme la voie idoine, chemin parsemé d'embûches et de doutes, d'incertitudes trop fortes quant à son issue. Elle apparaît comme une voie secondaire face à la voie civile ou à celle qui conduit au défenseur des Droits. Même si l'on sent une timide évolution sur le plan du contentieux, elle mérite que l'on s'attache à lui redonner sa valeur qui passera automatiquement par une réelle harmonisation entre toutes les branches du droit.

En théorie, le droit de la non-discrimination se traduit dans la matière pénale par des incriminations qui luttent contre des comportements à caractère discriminatoire. Si l'on examine ces comportements, on s'aperçoit que le législateur va dans deux sens soit le sens d'une répression et donc d'un droit réactif, soit dans le sens d'un droit préventif et donc un droit proactif. Quelque soit la direction, on peut faire une remarque générale selon laquelle le droit de la non-discrimination est assez éclaté.

D. Viriot-Barrial (✉)
Aix-Marseille University, CDS, School of Law, Aix-en-Provence, France
e-mail: d.viriot-barrial@univ-amu.fr

1.1 Une mise en œuvre dans un sens répressif

Dans le Code Pénal, le droit de la non-discrimination se traduit, en premier lieu, par la répression aggravée de certains comportements en érigeant certains critères discriminatoires en **circonstances aggravantes**. Ainsi, le motif « raciste » qui a été l'un des critères fondamentaux[1] et le motif lié à « l'orientation ou l'identité sexuelle » ont été érigés en circonstances aggravantes spéciales (il faut que le texte de l'incrimination le prévoie) dans le cadre de ses dispositions générales[2]. A l'origine, l'article 132-76 visait l'appartenance ou de la non-appartenance, vraie ou supposée, de la victime à une ethnie, une nation, une race ou une religion déterminée et l'article 132-77, depuis la loi du 6 août 2012[3], l'orientation ou l'identité sexuelle. Pour chacun de ces critères discriminatoires, le législateur impose l'existence d'une matérialisation résidant dans l'exigence que l'infraction soit précédée, accompagnée ou suivie de propos, écrits, images, objets ou actes de toute nature portant atteinte à l'honneur ou à la considération de la victime ou d'un groupe de personnes dont fait partie la victime à raison de ces critères. Ainsi plusieurs infractions, notamment depuis la loi du 9 mars 2004[4] voient leur peine aggravée eu égard à ces deux critères que ce soit traditionnellement le meurtre, le viol mais encore la profanation de sépulture (C. pén., art. 225-18), menaces (C. pén., article 225-18-1), vol (C. pén., article 311-4, 9°), extorsion (C. pén., article 312-2, 3°). Depuis la loi égalité et citoyenneté du 27 janvier 2017[5], les circonstances aggravantes liées au « racisme et à l'homophobie », (même si les termes ne sont pas véritablement adéquats), actuellement prévues pour certaines infractions limitativement énumérées apparaissent comme des circonstances générales applicables à l'ensemble des crimes et des délits. La loi réécrit à cette fin les articles 132-76 et 132-77. L'article 132-76 ne fait par ailleurs plus référence aux infractions commises à raison de l'appartenance ou de la non-appartenance, vraie ou supposée, de la victime à une « race », mais à une prétendue race. Il faut que les infractions soit portent atteinte à l'honneur ou à la considération de la victime ou d'un groupe de personnes dont fait partie la victime à raison des critères évoqués plus haut soit établissent que les faits ont été commis contre la victime pour l'une de ces raisons, De même sont visés dans l'article 132-77, les critères

---

[1] C'est initialement un décret-loi du 21 avril 1939 (DP 1939. 4. 351), plus connu sous le nom de « loi Marchandeau qui marqua la première initiative du législateur dans la lutte contre le racisme. Ce n'est qu'avec la loi n° 72-546 du 1er juillet 1972 relative à la lutte contre le racisme (JO 2 juill., D. 1972. 328) que l'on peut situer le point de départ du mouvement législatif actuel qui consiste à incriminer de plus en plus de comportements discriminatoires pour une présentation de l'historique des législations sur les discriminations V. Danti-Juan, Discriminations, rép. Dalloz, 2014, spéc. n°3 et s.

[2] Elles sont définies dans la Section 3 (De la définition de certaines circonstances entraînant l'aggravation, la diminution ou l'exemption des peines du chapitre 2 (régime des peines) du Titre 3 des peines du Livre Ier des dispositions générales

[3] Loi n° 2012-954 du 6 août 2012 relative au harcèlement sexuel.

[4] Loi n° 2004-204 du 9 mars 2004 portant adaptation de la justice aux évolutions de la criminalité.

[5] Loi n° 2017-86 du 27 janvier 2017 relative à l'égalité et à la citoyenneté.

traditionnels du sexe ou de l'orientation sexuelle mais plus actualisés comme celui de l'identité de genre vraie ou supposée. Dans ces deux cas, le législateur prévoit un relèvement des maxima des peines prévues spécifiquement pour les infractions. Seuls ces deux critères font l'objet d'une définition dans le cadre des dispositions générales.

Le droit de la non-discrimination se traduit également en législation pénale par **des infractions autonomes** dont le but est la lutte contre la discrimination qui trouvent leur source soit dans le code pénal soit dans les législations pénales techniques. Dans le cadre du code pénal, on peut citer la traditionnelle et autonome infraction de discrimination[6] dans le chapitre relatif à la dignité, valeur très symbolique, visée aux articles 225-1 (énumération des critères discriminatoires) et 225-2 du code pénal (description des éléments constitutifs précis[7]). Cette incrimination est reprise dans le livre IV lorsqu'elle est commise par une personne dépositaire de l'autorité publique ou chargée d'une mission de service public (article 432-7 du Code pénal)[8].

D'autres qualifications s'avèrent **être très proches des discriminations** et peuvent servir le droit de la non-discrimination On peut citer le *harcèlement sexuel* qui est, en lui-même, une forme de discrimination à raison du sexe (C. pén., article 222-33[9]) ou encore le *harcèlement moral* défini à l'article 222-33-2 comme le fait de harceler autrui par des propos ou comportements répétés ayant pour objet ou pour effet une dégradation des conditions de travail susceptible de porter atteinte à ses droits et à sa dignité, d'altérer sa santé physique ou mentale ou de compromettre son avenir professionnel. La sanction de ces deux délits est de deux ans d'emprisonnement et de 30 000 € d'amende. Très souvent d'ailleurs les poursuites peuvent être fondées sur les deux incriminations ou sur une autre qualification telle celle de discrimination syndicale souvent couplée avec le harcèlement moral dont on reconnaît qu'elles défendent deux valeurs distinctes[10]. Le législateur, par la technique législative de l'assimilation, tend à définir comme discrimination des comportements qui résident dans une distinction opérée entre deux personnes dès lors qu'elles ont subi , refusé de subir ou témoigné de faits infractionnels particuliers . L'article 225-1-1 créé par la loi

---

[6]V. Danti-Juan, Discriminations, rép. Dalloz, 2014, F. Desporte, discrimination, juriscl. Pénal,

[7]1° A refuser la fourniture d'un bien ou d'un service ; 2° A entraver l'exercice normal d'une activité économique quelconque ; 3° A refuser d'embaucher, à sanctionner ou à licencier une personne ; 4° A subordonner la fourniture d'un bien ou d'un service à une condition fondée sur l'un des éléments visés à l'article 225-1 ou prévue à l'article 225-1-1 ; 5° A subordonner une offre d'emploi, une demande de stage ou une période de formation en entreprise à une condition fondée sur l'un des éléments visés à l'article 225-1 ou prévue à l'article 225-1-1 ; 6° A refuser d'accepter une personne à l'un des stages visés par le 2° de l'article L.412-8 du code de la sécurité sociale.

[8].-Cl. Pénal Code, Art. 432-7, fasc. 20 ou J.-Cl. Public-Contentieux pénal, V° Discrimination, fasc. 20

[9]v. Harcèlement sexuel: la loi et la circulaire, E. Alain, AJ pénal 2012. 438.

[10]crim. 28 mai 2013 — AJ pénal 2013. 544, Cour de cassation, crim. 11 juillet 2012 — AJ pénal 2012. 655, Cour de cassation, crim. 21 juin 2005, AJ pénal 2005. 329 v. aussi Harcèlement moral au travail: le positionnement pragmatique du parquet, F. Le Sueur, AJ pénal 2010. 529.

n°2012-954 du 6 août 2012 précise que « constitue une discrimination toute distinction opérée entre les personnes parce qu'elles ont subi ou refusé de subir des faits de harcèlement sexuel tels que définis à l'article 222-33 ou témoigné de tels faits, y compris, dans le cas mentionné au I du même article, si les propos ou comportements n'ont pas été répétés ». De même l'article 225-1-2 créé par la loi n°2017-86 du 27 janvier 2017 précise que « constitue une discrimination toute distinction opérée entre les personnes parce qu'elles ont subi ou refusé de subir des faits de bizutage définis à l'article 225-16-1 ou témoigné de tels faits ».

Enfin, les articles 211-1 et 212-1 du Code pénal incriminent, sous la qualification de *génocides et crimes contre l'humanité*, les agissements les plus gravement réprimés (perpétuité) qui puissent être commis pour des motifs discriminatoires créés dans le code pénal issu des lois du 22 juillet 1992.

Dans le cadre des législations pénales techniques, le Code du travail comporte un certain nombre de textes dont le champ d'application recoupe pour partie celui des articles 225-1 et suivants du Code pénal. Ainsi, le Code du travail prévoit (C. trav., article L. 1142-1) et réprime (C. trav., article L. 1146-1) les discriminations dans le travail à raison du sexe, de la situation de famille ou de la grossesse. Les sanctions qui s'attachent à la violation de l'article 1142-1 ont été étendues par l'article L.3222-1 aux infractions prévues par les articles L3221-2 et s. relatives à l'égalité de rémunération entre les hommes et les femmes. De même, les articles L. 2141-5 et L.2141-7 du Code du travail prévoient et répriment la discrimination syndicale individuelle et collective de manière plus large que le Code pénal. Dans des domaines différents, l'entrave à l'exercice du droit syndical (C. trav., article L. 2146-2, L.2141-5) se confond parfois avec la discrimination syndicale[11]. En l'état, il paraît en tout cas artificiel d'étudier les articles 225-1 et suivants du Code pénal sans évoquer les textes du Code du travail qui n'en sont, en dépit de différences rédactionnelles, que le prolongement ou la répétition. Une partie de la doctrine souhaite que le législateur harmonise ces divers textes, au moins en supprimant du Code du travail les incriminations reprises dans le Code pénal.[12] De même en matière de harcèlement moral et sexuel, le code du travail, qui prévoit respectivement l'interdiction de ces comportements respectivement par les articles L. 1152-1 et L.1153-1, incrimine spécifiquement non les comportements en eux-mêmes mais les mesures de rétorsion suite à ces harcèlements. On remarquera que depuis la loi Travail du 8 août 2016, aux termes de l'article L. 4121-2 du code du travail, l'employeur a une nouvelle obligation de prévention des risques professionnels vis-à-vis de ses salariés : il doit mettre en place des actions pour lutter contre les agissements sexistes sur le lieu de travail. Dans la même optique, aucun fonctionnaire ou assimilé ne doit subir d'agissement sexiste selon l'article 7 de la loi travail qu'il s'agisse de recrutement, de titularisation, de rémunération, de formation, d'évaluation, de notation, de discipline, de promotion, d'affectation ou de mutation.

---

[11] V. pour un cumul de qualifications: Cass. crim., 25 janv. 2000: Juris-Data n° 2000-000723 ; Bull. crim. 2000, n° 38.

[12] Fortis (1994), spécialement p. 626. – Guerder (1995), p. 447.

1.2 Une mise en œuvre effective du droit de la non-discrimination dans une optique préventive.

Dans le cadre du code pénal, l'article 226-19 du Code pénal modifié par la loi n°2012-954 du 6 août 2012 incrimine le fait, hors les cas prévus par la loi, de mettre ou de conserver en mémoire informatisée, sans le consentement exprès de l'intéressé, des données à caractère personnel qui, directement ou indirectement, font apparaître les origines raciales ou ethniques, les opinions politiques, philosophiques ou religieuses, ou les appartenances syndicales des personnes, ou qui sont relatives à la santé ou à l'orientation ou identité sexuelle de celles-ci. Ces informations constituent autant de possibles critères discriminatoires. La sanction consiste en cinq ans d'emprisonnement et de 300 000 euros d'amende. Cette disposition a été utilisée dans le cadre du problème très spécifique du don de sang dans le cas des personnes homosexuelles[13].

Enfin on peut relever que les diffamations et injures non publiques présentant un caractère discriminatoire sont aussi incriminées dans le code pénal sous la qualification de contravention de 4ème classe (article R. 624-3 et R. 624-4 du CP). Les critères discriminatoires visés sont l'origine, l'appartenance ou la non-appartenance, vraie ou supposée, à une ethnie, une nation, une race ou une religion déterminée mais aussi le sexe, l'orientation sexuelle ou le handicap. On peut aussi citer dans l'optique préventive la provocation non publique à la discrimination publique (article R. 625-7 du CP) qui est une contravention de 5ème classe. L'article R. 625-7 du Code pénal punit, quant à lui, de peines contraventionnelles cette même provocation lorsqu'elle est non publique. Cette incrimination contraventionnelle a été créée lors de la réforme du Code pénal, puis complétée par le décret n° 2005-284 du 25 mars 2005 (art. 4, 1°).

S'agissant de la législation sur la presse, l'injure et la diffamation raciales ou motivées par le sexe, l'orientation sexuelle, l'identité de genre ou encore le handicap de la victime (L. 29 juill. 1881, article 32, al. 2 et 3 et article 33, al. 3 et 4. – C. pén., article R. 624-3) sont des délits, le premier sanctionné par six mois d'emprisonnement et de 22 500 euros d'amende et le second sanctionné d'un an d'emprisonnement et de 45 000 euros d'amende ou de l'une de ces deux peines seulement. De même l'article 24 de la loi du 29 juillet 1881 sur la liberté de la presse incrimine, en son alinéa 6 issu de la loi du 1er juillet 1972, les provocations publiques à la discrimination lorsqu'elles sont commises à l'égard d'une personne ou d'un groupement de personnes à raison de leur origine, ou de leur appartenance ou

---

[13]Cass. crim., 8 janvier 2015, n° 13-86.267: l'exception à l'exigence d'un consentement de la personne à l'enregistrement et à la conservation de données personnelles relatives à la santé ou à l'orientation sexuelle, qui découle des dispositions combinées des articles 226-19 du Code pénal et 8 de la loi du 6 janvier 1978, constitue une mesure légitime nécessaire à la protection de la santé, définie par la loi avec suffisamment de précision pour éviter l'arbitraire, et de nature à assurer, en l'état, entre le respect de la vie privée et la sauvegarde de la santé publique, une conciliation qui n'est pas déséquilibrée.

non-appartenance à une ethnie, une nation, une race ou une religion déterminée. En son alinéa 7, issu de la loi n° 2004-1486 du 30 décembre 2004 dernièrment modifié par la loi n° 2017 86 du 27 janvier 2017 relative à l'égalité et à la citoyenne, ce même article incrimine également ces provocations lorsqu'elles sont commises à raison du sexe, de l'orientation sexuelle, de l'identité de genre ou du handicap des personnes concernées, mais à condition qu'elles portent sur des agissements entrant dans les prévisions des articles 225-2 et 432-7 du Code pénal. On peut aussi citer dans l'optique préventive l'incrimination de la provocation à la haine ou à la violence raciale (L. 29 juill. 1881, article 24),

La répression est accrue dans le cadre de la loi n°2017-86 du 27 janvier 2017 dite loi égalité et citoyenneté. En effet les dispositions du chapitre IV prennent en compte les préconisations du plan de lutte contre le racisme annoncé en avril 2015 par le Gouvernement, en modifiant en particulier la loi du 29 juillet 1881 sur la liberté de la presse. L'article 170 de la loi améliore tout d'abord la répression des délits de provocations, de diffamations et d'injures racistes ou discriminatoires (fondées sur le sexe, l'orientation ou l'identité sexuelle, ou sur le handicap) figurant dans la loi de 1881, notamment en : remplaçant le critère de l'identité sexuelle par l'identité de genre ; ajoutant pour ces délits la peine complémentaire de stage de citoyenneté visant désormais « l'apprentissage des valeurs de la République et des devoirs du citoyen » ; élevant la peine des injures racistes ou discriminatoires (6 mois d'emprisonnement et 22 500 euros d'amende) au même niveau que celle des provocations et des diffamations racistes ou discriminatoires (1 an et 45 000 euros) ; excluant l'excuse de provocation en matière d'injures racistes ou discriminatoires ; prévoyant que la requalification est toujours possible entre les délits de provocations, de diffamations et d'injures racistes ou discriminatoires, par dérogation à l'interdiction de principe posée par la loi de 1881 et enfin en supprimant pour ces délits l'exigence d'articulation et de qualification des faits dans les réquisitions du parquet interruptives de prescription.

D'autres législations techniques comme celles touchant l'ordre économique peuvent aussi reposer sur des critères discriminatoires. On peut ainsi citer le refus de vente, réprimé en lui-même à l'article L121-11 créé par l'ordonnance n°2016-301 du 14 mars 2016 selon les termes suivants « est interdit le fait de refuser à un consommateur la vente d'un produit ou la prestation d'un service, sauf motif légitime », motif pouvant aussi mettre en exergue des critères discriminatoires.

2 Une mise en œuvre effective du droit de la non-discrimination dans la matière pénale?

D'un point de vue théorique c'est-à-dire s'appuyant sur la définition pénale des comportements, on peut s'apercevoir que le législateur pénal, est assez frileux de s'engager dans la voie de la non-discrimination par la référence exclusive au concept d'égalité, contrairement à certains textes nationaux, internationaux ou encore européens[14] même si pour ces derniers une référence à la discrimination est faite directement dans les derniers textes[15]. Les lois successives ont étendu le champ de l'incrimination en prévoyant de nouveaux motifs discriminatoires et en complétant la liste des agissements punissables. Mais le législateur pénal n'est pas allé aussi loin que certaines lois françaises qui, sous l'impulsion européenne, reconnaissaient deux types de discrimination directe et indirecte[16]. La jurisprudence en la matière est assez divisée. Quelques arrêts [17] ont pu faire apparaître une potentielle prise en compte de la discrimination indirecte à l'embauche fondée sur la nationalité[18] mais il y a une véritable hostilité de la part de certaines cours d'appel qui précisent que « les dispositions de l'article 1er, alinéa 2, de la loi du 27 mai 2008 permettant de sanctionner comme discrimination indirecte, un critère ou une pratique neutre en apparence mais susceptible d'entraîner, notamment pour un motif tiré de l'appartenance à une nation déterminée, un désavantage pour des personnes par-rapport à d'autres personnes, n'est pas transposable dans le domaine du droit pénal et reste circonscrit au domaine civil »[19] . Assez adroitement la cour de cassation réfute cette notion [20] coupant court à toute velléité d'y faire référence. On peut aussi mettre en exergue une sorte d'extension de la définition de la discrimination dans certains agissements qui mêlent discrimination et harcèlement comme l'article 225-1-1 créé par la loi n°2012-954 du 6 août 2012 qui précise que « Constitue une discrimination toute distinction opérée entre les personnes parce

---

[14]Pour les textes nationaux v. entre autres l'article 1er de la loi n° 2008-496 du 27 mai 2008 portant diverses dispositions d'adaptation au droit communautaire dans le domaine de la lutte contre les discriminations qui définit la discrimination comme le fait pour une personne d'être traitée de manière moins favorable qu'une autre ne l'est, ne l'a été ou ne l'aura été dans une situation comparable) ou encore la Déclaration des droits de l'Homme et du citoyen de 1789 et l' art. 1er et 6 ; Const. du 4 oct. 1958, art. 2. Pour les textes internationaux V. aussi Charte des Nations unies, art. 76 ; Déclaration universelle des droits de l'Homme, art. 1er, 7 et 10.

[15]par ex. art. 2-1 du Pacte international relatif aux droits civils et politiques ; art. 14 de la Convention européenne de sauvegarde des droits de l'homme et des libertés fondamentales

[16]Une discrimination directe se produit lorsqu'une personne est traitée de manière moins favorable qu'une autre ne l'est, ne l'a été ou ne le serait dans une situation comparable. La discrimination indirecte se produit lorsqu'une pratique apparemment neutre est susceptible d'entraîner un désavantage particulier pour des personnes par rapport à d'autres personnes, à moins que cette disposition, ce critère ou cette pratique ne soit objectivement justifié par un objectif légitime et que les moyens de réaliser cet objectif ne soient appropriés et nécessaires.

[17]crim. 20-01-2009 n° 08-83.710, Recueil Dalloz 2009 p. 997, obs . S. Detraz Discrimination indirecte à l'embauche

[18]La société qui procède à la diffusion d'une offre d'emploi pour laquelle est exigée la présentation de la carte d'électeur du candidat, alors que le droit de vote n'est accordé qu'aux nationaux et, dans une certaine mesure, aux ressortissants de l'Union européenne, subordonne l'offre à une condition de nationalité, constitutive d'une discrimination prohibée.

[19]Cour d'appel d'Amiens, du 11 mars 2015

[20]procédant de son appréciation souveraine des faits et circonstances de la cause contradictoirement débattus, dont il résulte que le refus d'embaucher la partie civile, au motif de la nature de sa carte de séjour, ne dissimulait pas, en réalité, un refus d'embauche fondé sur la non-appartenance à la nation française, la cour d'appel a justifié sa décision au regard des articles 225-1 et 225-2 du code pénal ;

qu'elles ont subi ou refusé de subir des faits de harcèlement sexuel tels que définis à l'article 222-33 ou témoigné de tels faits, y compris, dans le cas mentionné au I du même article, si les propos ou comportements n'ont pas été répétés. » comme on l'a déjà mis en évidence.

D'un point de vue pratique c'est-à-dire dans le cadre du contentieux, la voie pénale est plutôt symbolique même si elle n'est pas totalement inexistante. Si l'on fait l'étude de la jurisprudence, le contentieux est très réduit en comparaison de la politique très offensive menée par les gouvernements successifs. Si l'on fait la recherche dans la seule matière pénale c'est-à-dire la référence au code pénal, on doit trouver sur les dix dernières années une cinquantaine de décisions de la cour de cassation, tous critères confondus[21] mais il convient de remarquer, que si chaque année on oscillait entre 3 ou 5 décisions, les dernières années de 2015 à 2018 ont été particulièrement riches en contentieux de la discrimination. En 2017, les récents contentieux ont porté soit sur la définition des éléments constitutifs comme celui de la discrimination directe ou indirecte comme précité ou encore les critères de l'état de santé dans le cadre des tests aux concours d'entrée dans la gendarmerie [22] ou encore la nationalité dans le cadre d'un refus d'embauche lié à une carte séjour « vie privée et familiale ». Par contre le contentieux en matière de presse est assez abondant dans l'optique de l'appréhension préventive à travers les infractions de presse d'injures et diffamation publiques ou provocation à la discrimination sur deux types de critères essentiellement la connotation raciste et religieuse[23] et l'orientation sexuelle[24]. On peut remarquer qu'en cette matière les conditions de mise en œuvre des actions étaient assez restreintes que ce soit pour l'action civile [25] ou la

---

[21]L'étude de la non-discrimination par critère se fera dans la question 10.

[22]Cass. Crim. 7 juin 2016, 15-80827: Attendu que, pour confirmer l'ordonnance de non-lieu du chef de discrimination, l'arrêt retient notamment que l'objectif du test incriminé était de déterminer les aptitudes physiques, morales et psychiques d'un candidat, à intégrer le corps de la gendarmerie nationale dans la perspective des missions pouvant être lui confiées sur le terrain ou dans le cadre d'une enquête, tout comportement inadéquat pouvant se révéler dangereux pour un aspirant ou ses futurs collègues, ou pour le succès des opérations requises, cette appréciation de la part de la gendarmerie apparaissant nécessaire, légitime et appropriée pour procéder à un recrutement efficace et pertinent.

[23]crim. 10 mai 2006 — AJ pénal 2006. 372, Provocation à la discrimination religieuse ou critique politique d'un culte ? crim. 30 mai 2007 — AJ pénal 2007. 383, Délit de provocation à la discrimination, éléments constitutifs, crim. 29 janvier 2008 — AJ pénal 2008. 141, L'appel au boycott entre dans le cadre normal de la liberté d'expression, TGI Pontoise 20 décembre 2013 — AJ pénal 2014. 78 ; Provocation à la haine raciale et complicité, crim. 10 novembre 2009 — AJ pénal 2010. 36 Déontologie journalistique: état des lieux et perspectives, Philippe Piot — AJ pénal 2013. 24.

[24]Injures à raison de l'orientation sexuelle, crim. 12 novembre 2008 — AJ pénal 2009. 228.

[25]crim. 30 octobre 2012, Refus d'informer justifié par le caractère insuffisamment précis de la plainte dénonçant des infractions en matière de presse, AJ pénal 2013. 103, Recevabilité de l'action civile par voie d'intervention d'une association sur le fondement de la loi du 29 juillet 1881, crim. 12 octobre 2010 — AJ pénal 2011. 133)

prescription de l'action publique[26] mais la loi égalité et citoyenneté de janvier 2017 a fortement assoupli les conditions. Ce mouvement est fortement relayé par le CEDH.[27]

3 Les acteurs du droit de la non-discrimination en matière pénale

La mise en œuvre du droit de la non-discrimination en matière pénale revêt ce particularisme d'une compétence concurrente ou complémentaire de multiples institutions pour appréhender ce phénomène. Ces institutions sont soit judiciaires, soit administratives.

La lutte contre les discriminations n'est pas l'apanage du juge pénal[28]. D'une part, de nombreux comportements discriminatoires n'entrent dans les prévisions d'aucun texte répressif et ne peuvent donc donner lieu qu'à une action civile. Ainsi en est-il, dans le cadre du Code du travail de comportements qui rentreraient dans la définition donnée par l'article L. 1132-1 [29] comme par exemple une discrimination indirecte visée en droit du travail mais non en droit pénal ou encore des agissements en matière d'intéressement non visé par l'article 225-2 du code pénal. D'autre part et en tout état de cause, la sanction pénale n'exclut pas l'intervention du juge civil ou administratif qui pourra prononcer, le cas échéant, l'annulation de l'acte

---

[26] Dreyer (2006), p. 294 ; Loi de 1881 sur la liberté de la presse: constitutionnalité de l'allongement de la prescription, inconstitutionnalité des exceptions à l'exceptio veritatis, Conseil constitutionnel 12 avril 2013, AJ pénal 2013. 410 ; Racisme: le nouveau délai d'un an ne s'applique pas aux contraventions, crim. 23 mai 2006, AJ pénal 2006. 366 ; Conseil constitutionnel 7 juin 2013, AJ pénal 2013. 410.

[27] Balance entre exercice du droit à la liberté d'expression et respect de la réputation d'autrui, Cour européenne des droits de l'homme 22 décembre 2005, AJ pénal 2006. 169.

[28] Masse-Dessen (1995), p. 442

[29] Aucune personne ne peut être écartée d'une procédure de recrutement ou de l'accès à un stage ou à une période de formation en entreprise, aucun salarié ne peut être sanctionné, licencié ou faire l'objet d'une mesure discriminatoire, directe ou indirecte, telle que définie à l'article 1er de la loi n° 2008-496 du 27 mai 2008 portant diverses dispositions d'adaptation au droit communautaire dans le domaine de la lutte contre les discriminations, notamment en matière de rémunération, au sens de l'article L. 3221-3, de mesures d'intéressement ou de distribution d'actions, de formation, de reclassement, d'affectation, de qualification, de classification, de promotion professionnelle, de mutation ou de renouvellement de contrat en raison de son origine, de son sexe, de ses mœurs, de son orientation sexuelle, de son identité de genre, de son âge, de sa situation de famille ou de sa grossesse, de ses caractéristiques génétiques, de la particulière vulnérabilité résultant de sa situation économique, apparente ou connue de son auteur, de son appartenance ou de sa non-appartenance, vraie ou supposée, à une ethnie, une nation ou une prétendue race, de ses opinions politiques, de ses activités syndicales ou mutualistes, de ses convictions religieuses, de son apparence physique, de son nom de famille, de son lieu de résidence ou de sa domiciliation bancaire, ou en raison de son état de santé, de sa perte d'autonomie ou de son handicap, de sa capacité à s'exprimer dans une langue autre que le français.

discriminatoire et accorder une réparation à la victime de la discrimination en se fondant le cas échéant sur une disposition légale.

Deux autres institutions sont marquantes dans le cadre de mise en œuvre. La première vise les autorités en charge de la législation du travail comme les inspecteurs du travail. La deuxième vise les associations qui selon l'article 2-1 du code de procédure pénale leur permet d'exercer les droits reconnus à la partie civile dés lors que leur statut propose de combattre le racisme ou les victimes de discriminations raciales ou d'incriminations contre la vie ou l'intégrité commises à raison de ces critères ou qui selon l'article 2-6 du cpp leur permet de lutter contre les discriminations à raison du sexe, de la situation de famille ou des mœurs[30]. On regrettera un article général du Code de procédure pénale qui vise les associations qui luttent de manière générale contre les discriminations quel qu'en soient les critères. On retiendra que la loi n° 2016-1547 du 18 novembre 2016 de modernisation de la justice du XXIe siècle étend notamment l'action de groupe sur le fondement de la loi n° 2008-496 du 27 mai 2008 portant diverses dispositions d'adaptation au droit communautaire dans le domaine de la lutte contre les discriminations mais aussi sur le fondement des articles L. 1134-6 à L. 1134-10 du code du travail ; c'est-à-dire aux discriminations, directes et indirectes, discrimination dans les relations relevant du code du travail ou encore en matière de discrimination imputable à un employeur et portée devant la juridiction administrative. Les associations régulièrement déclarées depuis cinq ans et les syndicats représentatifs pourront agir dans ce domaine. La loi égalité et citoyenneté ayant précisé dans l'article L. 1134-7 que les associations pourront aider les syndicats dans leur action liée un emploi, à un stage ou à une période de formation en entreprise. Pour autant ces nouveautés n'ont pas spécifiquement d'impact sur le plan purement pénal et la question de l'articulation se pose.

En théorie, le juge pénal semblerait être l'institution idoine pour traiter du contentieux de la non discrimination pour autant sa compétence en cette matière est fortement liée à une Autorité Administrative Indépendante marquante le Défenseur des droits[31]. Il existe un certain nombre de conventions de coopération entre le Défenseur des droits et les parquets pour favoriser l'échange d'informations et la coordination des actions afin de mieux lutter contre toutes formes de discriminations. Pour ce faire des référents au sein des parquets sont désignés. Quand on se réfère à la définition des comportements discriminatoires, le domaine de compétence du défenseur des droits apparaît comme beaucoup plus large que les discriminations qui sont définies dans la législation pénale (article 225-2) dans laquelle les comportements discriminatoires sont limitativement énumérés et ne reposent pas spécialement sur le non-respect de l'égalité[32]. Le Défenseur des droits est compétent pour toutes les discriminations directes ou indirectes prohibées par la loi ou par un engagement international auquel la France est partie. Si elle s'éloigne de la définition

---

[30]Saas (2008), p. 83; Jakubowicz (2006), p. 111.

[31]V. pour une étude exhaustive: Sereno (2017).

[32]Pour cette analyse en matière de discrimination liée à la santé Viriot-Barrial (2011).

pénale, elle se rapproche de la définition qui est donnée dans la législation sociale c'est-à-dire non d'une infraction de discrimination, mais d'un véritable principe de non discrimination (article L. L1132-1 du Code du travail).

4 A qui profite la mise en œuvre du droit de la non-discrimination en matière pénale?

Pour déterminer les personnes qui profitent le plus de la mise en œuvre de ce droit de la non discrimination, le renvoi aux critères de la discrimination est nécessaire.

On en retire que ce sont surtout **les salariés** qui en bénéficient. Cette protection s'explique par une volonté réelle de protéger la dignité du salarié fortement influencée par le droit européen et international[33]. Cette protection évolue même d'une protection individuelle vers une protection collective que certains rapports mettaient en évidence visant à rechercher les améliorations susceptibles d'être apportées dans la détection et le traitement des discriminations collectives dans le monde du travail[34]. Il convient de préciser que le constat d'une augmentation des discriminations en période de crise, montre que sont principalement touchés les femmes, les seniors, les salariés titulaires de mandats représentatifs, et les salariés d'origine étrangère.

5 Qui est lésé par la mise en œuvre du droit de la non-discrimination en matière pénale?

Pour sa défense, l'employeur a donc intérêt à prendre en compte l'ensemble des procédures objectives (CV anonyme) et conserver des notes écrites des entretiens de recrutement. Ces garanties sont lourdes et coûteuses, elles impliquent une charge financière pour l'employeur mais, pour se préserver du risque pénal, il lui faut en assumer le coût.

On peut remarquer qu'un nombre conséquent de discriminations sont réalisées dans le cadre des activités publiques soit dans le cadre d'opérations classiques comme celles de préemption[35] soit dans le cadre de la gestion quotidienne des collectivités[36].

---

[33] Viriot-Barrial (2014), p. 9.

[34] Droit social 2014 p. 106, Publication du rapport Pécaut-Rivolier sur les discriminations collectives en entreprise, Synthèse générale du rapport, Christophe Radé.

[35] Interprétation stricte de l'article 432-7 du code pénal, crim. 17 juin 2008, AJ pénal 2008. 418: abus dans l'exercice du droit de préemption.

[36] Discrimination à raison de l'appartenance religieuse d'un conseiller municipal: crim. 1 septembre 2010, AJ pénal 2010. 506.

6 Quelles réparations et sanctions sont prévues pour mettre en œuvre le droit de la non-discrimination en matière pénale?

En théorie, les sanctions strictement pénales encourues sont virtuellement particulièrement lourdes avec une tendance à l'aggravation du fait de l'évolution de la législation[37] (note ?). L'aggravation de la répression s'est également manifestée par la suppression de la possibilité d'invoquer à titre de fait justificatif un "motif légitime" en matière d'embauche et de licenciement (L. n° 83-635, 13 juill. 1983, dite "loi Roudy") et, en toute matière, en cas de discrimination raciale (L. n° 87-588, 30 juill. 1987) et désormais pour l'incrimination de discrimination quelque soit les critères. Mais aussi par la création de plusieurs peines complémentaires en particulier par la loi n° 90-615 du 13 juillet 1990[38]. Les sanctions complémentaires sont très diversifiées[39]. On peut se pencher sur la peine de stage de citoyenneté créée par la loi 2004-204 du 9 mars 2004, et prévue par l'article 131-35-1 du C. pén[40]. Elle constitue aux termes de cet article, une peine alternative à l'emprisonnement, mais elle est également instituée comme peine complémentaire en matière délictuelle et contraventionnelle, comme obligation du sursis avec mise à l'épreuve, comme mesure alternative aux poursuites et enfin comme mesure de la composition pénale. Définie à l'origine comme l'obligation pour le condamné d'accomplir « *un stage qui a pour objet de lui rappeler les valeurs républicaines de tolérance et de respect de la dignité humaine sur lesquelles est fondée la société.* » et désormais depuis la loi égalité et citoyenneté « tendant à l'apprentissage des valeurs de la République et des devoirs du citoyen », les modalités, la durée et le contenu de cette peine, qui est applicable aux mineurs, sont fixés par les articles R. 131-35 à R. 131-44 du C. pén., issus du décret n° 2004-1021 du 27 septembre 2004. Cette mesure sous-estimée, initialement destinée à lutter aussi contre les actes de discrimination, tend à être de plus en plus prononcée.

En pratique, les peines prononcées sont clémentes quand il ne s'agit pas de simples amendes assorties d'un sursis. Les parquets explorent de plus en plus les voies pénales alternatives : rappel à la loi, classement sous condition de réparation,

---

[37]Initialement dans le code pénal, la répression était de deux ans d'emprisonnement et de 30 000 euros d'amende mais la loi n° 2004-204 du 9 mars 2004 portant adaptation de la justice aux évolutions de la criminalité a aggravé la répression en prévoyant une peine de trois ans d'emprisonnement et 45 000 euros d'amende.

[38]Véron (1990), p. 1.

[39]Elles résident dans 1° L'interdiction des droits prévus aux 2° et 3° de l'article 131-26 pour une durée de cinq ans au plus ; 2° L'affichage ou la diffusion de la décision prononcée, dans les conditions prévues par l'article 131-35 ; 3° La fermeture, pour une durée de cinq ans au plus ou à titre définitif, de l'un, de plusieurs ou de l'ensemble des établissements de l'entreprise appartenant à la personne condamnée ; 4° L'exclusion des marchés publics à titre définitif ou pour une durée de cinq ans au plus ; 6° L'obligation d'accomplir un stage de citoyenneté, selon les modalités prévues par l'article 131-5-1.

[40]Germain and Lassalle (2014), p. 467.

comparution sur reconnaissance de culpabilité. Les amendes civiles peuvent aussi être la sanction de ces comportements. [41]

En marge de cette voie pénale, le Défenseur des droits a reçu, depuis 2006, la faculté légale de proposer **des transactions**, dans certaines matières strictement délimitées, en fixant des amendes plafonnées à 3 000 euro pour une personne physique et 15 000 euro pour une personne morale. Il ne s'agit certes pas d'une sanction pénale mais le mis en cause qui doit s'acquitter d'une amende, qu'elle soit transactionnelle ou ordonnée par un juge pénal, en ressent bien le caractère punitif, ce d'autant que l'amende infligée par le défenseur des droits ne peut être assortie d'un sursis, à la différence de l'individualisation des peines par le juge pénal. A terme, outre ces amendes, une éventuelle diffusion de la sanction par voie de presse, assimilable à la publication des décisions de justice, est possible.

7 Qui soutient la mise en œuvre du droit de la non-discrimination en matière pénale?

D'un point de vue politique, la mise en œuvre du droit de la non discrimination est soutenue de manière très claire par les gouvernements qui se sont succédés au pouvoir dans la mesure où la lutte contre les discriminations apparaît comme un élément fort des politiques criminelles depuis ces dernières années sans distinctions de couleur politique. La création de la Halde et désormais du défenseur des droits dont les avis fortement médiatisés revêtent en la matière une importance particulière en est la meilleure preuve[42].

D'un point de vue pragmatique les praticiens du droit sont engagés fortement dans cette lutte. D'importantes actions de formation initiale et continue sont créées depuis trois ans sous l'égide du conseil national des barreaux et en partenariat avec le défenseur des droits. Mais, au-delà, le traitement de ces dossiers suppose un investissement énorme en temps. Le syndicat des avocats de France, fortement engagé depuis longtemps dans ce combat, souligne la nécessité de constituer un réseau d'avocats structuré afin de partager l'information entre les confrères et agir de façon rapide et efficace dans le souci de relayer utilement l'action des associations de terrain.

Les inspecteurs du travail et le directeur régional des entreprises, de la concurrence, de la consommation, du travail et de l'emploi (Direccte) ont d'importantes missions en matière de lutte contre la discrimination. Ils sont en outre habilités à constater les infractions commises en matière de discriminations prévues à l'article

---

[41]Invitation faite par la chambre de l'instruction au ministère public de prendre des réquisitions aux fins de prononcé d'une amende civile, crim. 1 mars 2011, AJ pénal 2011. 423.

[42]Amegadjie (2008), p. 307, L'avis de la Halde en matière de discrimination: une règle de procédure directement applicable, crim. 24 janvier 2007, AJ pénal 2007. 130.

225-2 (3° et 6°) du code pénal. En ce cas, ils dressent un procès-verbal qui est transmis au procureur de la République.

On peut rappeler que les associations de lutte contre le racisme revêtent un rôle désormais primordial depuis les récentes évolutions législatives et en particulier depuis la consécration de l'action de groupe.

8 Quelle est la portée effective du droit de la non-discrimination dans la matière pénale?

Réputé plus menaçant que le droit du travail ou le droit civil et leurs sanctions à caractère privé, le droit pénal est souvent considéré, en apparence, comme plus efficace car plus intimidant. Rien n'est moins sûr. Les signalements sont statistiquement rares, les poursuites et les condamnations pénales sont faibles. Les causes de cet échec relatif sont multiples et variées: désintérêt des services de police plus rompus à l'enregistrement d'une plainte pour vol qu'une plainte pour discrimination, mauvaise qualité de certains dossiers soumis au défenseurs des droits, insuffisance des preuves, les juridictions pénales malgré la création dans certaines d'un parquet entièrement voué aux discriminations sont suspectées par ailleurs de refuser de s'investir dans ce domaine. A l'exception de quelques associations particulièrement actives, peu de justiciables envisagent les moyens juridiques leur permettant d'engager une action judiciaire. La voie pénale a fondamentalement une vocation exemplaire sinon pédagogique. Même si l'on a favorisé la création de nouveaux modes de preuves tels le testing, elle apparaît comme une « voie hasardeuse sur le terrain de la preuve, coûteuse sur le plan des moyens, et aléatoire quant à son issue, l'encombrement séculaire des juridictions correctionnelles par les matières traditionnelles reléguant sans doute au second plan l'intérêt de ces matières nouvelles ».

La problématique de la preuve est bien évidemment prégnante en particulier dans le domaine du droit du travail[43]. Le testing est désormais validé comme mode de preuve depuis la loi n° 2006-396 du 31 mars 2006 qui a consacré la possibilité de solliciter des biens ou services dans le but de démontrer l'existence de comportements discriminatoires (art. 225-3-1)[44]. Ainsi, le délit de discrimination peut être constitué quand bien même la victime (candidat acquéreur ou à une location, candidat à une embauche...) s'est présentée dans le seul dessein de démontrer l'existence d'une discrimination. Le juge pénal ne peut plus dorénavant refuser d'examiner les éléments de preuve obtenus par ce moyen au seul prétexte qu'ils auraient été obtenus de façon déloyale. La jurisprudence récente est

---

[43]De la charge de la preuve en matière de discrimination syndicale, crim. 11 avril 2012, AJ pénal 2012. 418

[44]Lasserre Capdeville (2015), p. 139; Verges (2006), p. 354; Lasserre Capdeville (2008), p. 310; Vouland (2005), p. 275.

d'ailleurs vigilante sur ce point[45]. Mais il y aura la nécessité d'une adaptation de notre droit à l'évolution de la technique en particulier touchant la problématique particulière des discriminations, provocation à la haine raciale sur internet. Les réseaux sociaux par leur large diffusion présentent un champ de répercussion particulièrement étendu de certaines atteintes à la dignité dont notamment les discriminations. On s'interroge sur l'adaptation de l'arsenal juridique pour lutter contre ces atteintes [46]

9 La mise en œuvre du droit de la non-discrimination en matière pénale varie-t-elle en fonction du critère discriminatoire?

En matière législative, la volonté de lutter contre le racisme a déterminé le mouvement de lutte contre les discriminations. Longtemps, la législation pénale française est restée en la matière très lacunaire. L'incrimination de l'injure et de la diffamation raciale par le décret-loi du 21 avril 1939, dit "loi Marchandeau", qui modifia à cet effet la loi du 29 juillet 1881 sur la liberté de la presse, constitua un premier pas dans la répression. Mais les dispositions issues de ce texte étaient d'une mise en oeuvre difficile et laissaient en tout état de cause hors de leur champ d'application les comportements discriminatoires qui n'étaient pas accompagnés de considérations injurieuses ou diffamatoires. Ce n'est que par la loi n° 72-546 du 1er juillet 1972 que, pour la première fois, la discrimination raciale a été incriminée en tant que telle. Cette loi, qui modifiait par ailleurs la loi sur la presse, a introduit dans le Code pénal un article 416 sanctionnant certains comportements (refus ou offre conditionnelle d'un bien ou d'un service, refus d'embauche et licenciement) lorsqu'ils étaient déterminés par l'appartenance ou la non-appartenance de la victime à une ethnie, une nation, une race ou une religion déterminée[47]. On peut remarquer que désormais au vu des controverses sur le concept de race, la loi n° 2016-1547 du 18 novembre 2016 de modernisation de la justice du XXIe siècle a substitué au mot « race » la notion de « prétendue race ».

Mais, dès la loi n° 75-625 du 11 juillet 1975, la lutte contre les discriminations a cessé de se confondre avec la lutte contre le racisme. Ce texte a en effet étendu la répression aux discriminations fondées sur le sexe et la situation de famille. Dix ans plus tard, la loi n° 85-772 du 25 juillet 1985 a incriminé celles fondées sur les mœurs.

---

[45]Cass. Crim. 28 février 2017, 15-87378: Attendu qu'en se déterminant ainsi et, dès lors que l'autorité publique peut, sans provoquer à la commission d'une infraction ni manquer au principe de la loyauté des preuves et au droit à un procès équitable, prendre l'initiative de la mise en œuvre des dispositions de l'article 225-3-1 du code pénal, la cour d'appel a justifié sa décision au regard des dispositions législatives et conventionnelles invoquées ; D'où il suit que le moyen n'est pas fondé
[46]Peronne and Daoud (2014).
[47]Foulon-Piganiol (1972), p. 261 ; La lutte contre le racisme, esquisse d'un bilan de trois années de jurisprudence: D. 1975, chron. p. 159

Elle fut suivie des lois n° 89-18 du 13 janvier 1989 et n° 90-602 du 12 juillet 1990 qui ajoutèrent le handicap et l'état de santé au nombre des motifs discriminatoires.

Sur le fond, la réforme du Code pénal a marqué une nouvelle avancée de la répression. D'une part, les discriminations à raison des opinions politiques et des activités syndicales ont fait leur apparition dans la liste des discriminations punissables. Dans le cadre de l'évolution postérieure à la réforme du Code pénal, les dispositions des articles 225-1 à 225-4 du Code pénal ont été modifiées successivement par la loi n° 2001-1066 du 16 novembre 2001 relative à la lutte contre les discriminations[48] qui a rajouté apparence physique, le patronyme, l'orientation sexuelle ou encore l'âge puis, plus ponctuellement, par la loi n° 2002-303 du 4 mars 2002 relative aux droits des malades et à la qualité du système de santé (art. 4) visant les caractéristiques génétiques, la loi n° 2006-340 du 23 mars 2006 relative à l'égalité salariale entre les femmes et les hommes (art. 13, II) rajoutant la grossesse et enfin la loi n°2014-173 du 21 février 2014 de programmation pour la ville et la cohésion urbaine sur le critère de la résidence..

Mais il n'y avait toujours pas d'harmonisation totale entre les critères de discrimination visés le code pénal et ceux de la loi du 27 mai 2008. Ainsi le critère de la perte d'autonomie a été inséré par la loi du 28 décembre 2015 relative à l'adaptation de la société au vieillissement[49] dans l'art. 1er de la loi n° 2008-496 du 27 mai 2008 portant diverses dispositions d'adaptation au droit communautaire dans le domaine de la lutte contre les discriminations et non dans le code pénal. Mais c'est la loi n° 2016-1547 du 18 novembre 2016 de modernisation de la justice du XXIe siècle qui a intégré le critère lié à la perte d'autonomie dans l'article 225-1du code pénal. De même dans l'optique de l'élargissement au critère général discriminatoire de la condition sociale souvent utilisé dans les droits étrangers, notamment canadien[50], la loi n° 2016-1547 du 18 novembre 2016 de modernisation de la justice du XXIe siècle a intégré plusieurs critères liés directement ou indirectement à la condition sociale tels que la particulière vulnérabilité résultant de leur situation économique, apparente ou connue de son auteur mais aussi la capacité à s'exprimer dans une langue autre que le français.

On peut remarquer que la non-harmonisation entre les critères visés par le code pénal et ceux visés par le code du travail posait problème. L'article 87 de la loi n°2016-1547 du 18 novembre 2016 de modernisation de la justice du XXIème siècle a modifié la rédaction de l'article L.1132-1 du Code du Travail. En effet, dans sa nouvelle version, l'article L.1132-1 du code du travail, qui pose, en droit du travail, le principe de non-discrimination, ne cite plus les critères de discrimination. L'article 41 du projet de loi égalité et citoyenneté, dont est issu le texte finalement repris à

---

[48]Keller (2002), p. 1355. – Seuvic (2002), p. 367

[49]Dans le cadre du Chapitre IV – Droits, protection et engagements des personnes âgées, et plus précisément dans la section 1: Droits individuels des personnes âgées hébergées ou accompagnées.

[50]D.Roman, Recueil Dalloz 2013 p. 1911 La discrimination fondée sur la condition sociale, une catégorie manquante du droit français: les droits étrangers prouvent que la sanction des discriminations fondées sur la condition sociale est un outil pertinent pour lutter contre certains phénomènes d'exclusion sociale

l'article 87 de la loi du 18 novembre 2016, visait, selon les travaux parlementaires, à « *offrir la même protection en matière civile qu'en matière pénale* », en alignant « *la liste des motifs discriminatoires prévue dans la loi du 27 mai 2008 sur celle prévue à l'article 225-1 du code pénal* ». Mais suite à une récente loi de février 2017[51], cette harmonisation est remise en cause introduisant des critères tels que la domiciliation bancaire ou revenant sur la définition du critère lié à la religion dans l'article L.1132-1 du code du travail.

La liste de ces critères n'étant pas close on pourrait s'interroger sur de nouveaux critères de discrimination liée aux évolutions médicales. Dans certains projets de loi, on vise à interdire toute discrimination fondée sur **les résultats des techniques d'imagerie cérébrale**. Mais cette proposition n'a pas été retenue car des textes relatifs à la protection contre les discriminations existent par ailleurs[52].

En pratique, dans un contentieux assez limité en matière de discriminations, certains critères reviennent de manière récurrente. Parmi eux, ceux liés à la race désormais "prétendue race" ou encore à l'origine mais aussi particulièrement ceux relatifs à la religion sont souvent mis en exergue et ont fait grande presse. En matière de discriminations raciales et religieuses, le problème du voile et des signes ostensibles de la religion a été prégnant[53]. Cette discrimination « raciale » se retrouve aussi en matière de discrimination liée à une entrave économique en particulier dans les conflits politiques[54] ou simplement dans la gestion des mairies[55]. Le contexte est aussi marquant comme dans le cadre des manifestations sportives[56]. Mais ce sont surtout les discriminations syndicales qui tiennent le haut du pavé[57] et qui représentent de véritables risques psycho-sociaux[58] et une potentielle atteinte à la

---

[51] Loi n° 2017-256 du 28 février 2017 de programmation relative à l'égalité réelle outre-mer et portant autres dispositions en matière sociale et économique

[52] Sordino (2014), p. 58, v. aussi Bénéjat (2012), p. 392.

[53] L'interdiction du port du voile dans l'enseignement supérieur peut être le signe d'une discrimination, Cour d'appel de Paris 8 juin 2010, AJ pénal 2011. 79 ; de Nayves (2013), p. 400 ; Discrimination à raison de l'appartenance religieuse d'un conseiller municipal, crim. 1 septembre 2010 — AJ pénal 2010. 506),

[54] Poissonnier and Dubuisson (2012), p. 592.

[55] Un maire peut dissuader un propriétaire de vendre son terrain à « des gens du voyage », crim. 24 mai 2005, AJ pénal 2005. 415.

[56] Lagarde (2013), p. 311.

[57] La pression exercée pour tenter de réduire l'influence d'un syndicat constitue le délit de discrimination syndicale, crim. 2 septembre 2008, AJ pénal 2008. 466 ; Pas de discrimination à l'égard du salarié syndiqué refusant d'appliquer les règles de son contrat de travail, crim. 3 avril 2007, AJ pénal 2007. 282 ; Les délits de discrimination syndicale et de harcèlement moral violent des valeurs sociales distinctes, crim. 6 février 2007, AJ pénal 2007. 179, Atteinte à l'exercice régulier des fonctions de conseiller prud'homme et discrimination syndicale, crim. 6 mai 2008, AJ pénal 2008. 375 ; La proposition de résiliation amiable de son contrat de travail à une déléguée syndicale constitue un délit d'entrave à l'exercice du droit syndical, crim. 6 janvier 2004, AJ pénal 2004. 158 ; la responsabilité pénale des personnes morales et le cumul de qualifications redondantes, crim. 28 avril 2009, AJ pénal 2009. 357,

[58] Roussel (2010), p. 526.

vie privée du salarié[59]. On peut aussi citer deux critères importants tels que le sexe et la santé.

D'autre part, toute référence à la possibilité d'invoquer un "motif légitime" à titre de fait justificatif a été supprimée.

Aux côtés du symbole et de l'exemplarité inhérents à la voie pénale, l'importance quantitative - le chiffre noir – des situations réelles de discrimination justifie l'émergence de modes alternatifs de traitement de ces contentieux, qu'ils soient civils ou administratifs.

10 Quel est le rapport entre la mise en œuvre de la non-discrimination en matière pénale et la recherche d'égalité au niveau individuel et systémique?

La lutte contre les discriminations en matière pénale apparaît au moins en théorie moins marquée par la recherche de l'égalité en particulier au niveau individuel. On veut éviter une situation apparemment préjudiciable pour l'individu mais la recherche absolue de l'égalité n'est pas marquante. Cela se déduit en premier lieu par la définition même de la discrimination en matière pénale. Elle ne vise que des comportements discriminatoires très précis et ne reprend pas les définitions générales que l'on trouve dans les textes de l'Union européenne et inscrits dans certaines lois françaises comme la loi n° 2008-496 du 27 mai 2008 portant diverses dispositions d'adaptation au droit communautaire dans le domaine de la lutte contre les discriminations qui définit la discrimination comme le fait pour une personne d'être traitée de manière moins favorable qu'une autre ne l'est, ne l'a été ou ne l'aura été dans une situation comparable. De même en est-il pour les discriminations indirectes même si certaines jurisprudences pénales s'y réfèrent comme on l'a montré précédemment[60].

Pour autant la recherche de l'égalité au niveau systémique pourrait se traduire par le biais de l'action collective. La loi sur la « justice du XXIème siècle » permet désormais à une association ou un syndicat de porter en justice des situations de discrimination concernant plusieurs salariés. La loi sur la « justice du XXIème siècle », prévoit la possibilité d'actions collectives en justice, inspirées des « class actions » à l'américaine, notamment pour les discriminations au travail. Si le dispositif existe déjà en matière de consommation, depuis une loi de mars 2014, la loi l'a élargi à d'autres contentieux. Le texte prévoit ainsi un dispositif « socle » d'action de groupe, qui permettra en diverses matières à une association de saisir le juge (judiciaire ou administratif) pour un groupe de personnes qui *« placées dans une même situation, subissent un dommage causé par une même personne, ayant pur cause commune un manquement légal ou contractuel de même nature »*. La procédure prévoit une mise

---

[59]Lepage (2005), p. 9.
[60]Recueil Dalloz 2009 p. 997 Discrimination indirecte à l'embauche fondée sur la nationalité, 20-01-2009, n° 08-83.710.

en demeure obligatoire de la personne mise en cause, avant l'action en justice elle-même, où le juge pourra reconnaître sa responsabilité, prononcer une amende civile, et déterminer le groupe de personnes susceptibles de réclamer une indemnisation. Le dispositif est ensuite adapté aux cas de discrimination au travail, qui se réglaient jusqu'à maintenant de manière individuelle, devant les prud'hommes. Avec cette nouvelle loi, tout syndicat représentatif pourra lancer une action devant le tribunal de grande instance ou le juge administratif, en apportant des éléments pour établir que plusieurs salariés font l'objet d'une discrimination (syndicale, liée au sexe, à l'âge, etc). De même, des associations constituées depuis au moins cinq ans, pourront agir mais seulement pour les discriminations à l'embauche ou sur l'accès à un stage. La procédure prévoit que le syndicat demande d'abord à l'employeur de faire cesser le trouble. Celui-ci a six mois pour entamer une discussion et agir, faute de quoi le syndicat peut porter l'affaire en justice. Le circuit rejoint alors le dispositif « socle » : injonction à l'employeur par le juge de faire cesser le trouble, amende possible, détermination du groupe de salariés susceptibles d'être indemnisés. Mais si l'employeur n'obtempère pas, c'est vers les prud'hommes que les salariés devront se tourner pour obtenir une indemnisation. Mais on attend la coloration pénale de ce type de procédure.

11 La mise en œuvre du droit de la non-discrimination en matière pénale est-elle perçue comme distincte de la mise en œuvre d'autres lois?

Trois points pourraient mettre en exergue une différenciation dans le traitement des discriminations.

Le premier est lié à une volonté d'un traitement efficace préconisant des solutions spécifiques en matière procédurale comme par exemple le fait de l'intervention d'institutions administratives indépendantes comme le défenseur des droits avec des pouvoirs assez étendus et quelquefois concurrents à la voie pénale , mais aussi par le fait de favoriser non le contentieux classique mais les modes alternatifs de règlement des conflits, le développement de la transaction en matière pénale étant caractéristique de ces types de délinquances [61]. On peut encore citer la prolifération incontrôlée des fichiers de police [62] liée à la commission de certaines contraventions de cinquième classe comme la provocation à la discrimination, à la haine ou à la violence raciale. On peut enfin citer l'importance des pouvoirs d'enquête de l'inspection du travail[63].

Le deuxième point réside dans le fait de favoriser la prévention dans le traitement de ce type de contentieux. Ainsi a été créée par la loi n° 73-1195 du 27 décembre

---

[61]Cimamonti (2015), p. 460; Perrier (2015), p. 474; Crocq (2015), p. 465.
[62]V. Gautron, AJ pénal 2007. 57.
[63]F. Chopin, AJ pénal 2015. 116.

1973, l'Agence nationale d'amélioration des conditions de travail (ANACT) et ses antennes régionales, les ARACT, ont une administration tripartite : État (ou collectivité), représentants des organisations patronales, représentants des organisations salariées dont l'une des missions est de veiller à la lutte contre les discriminations et le harcèlement.

Le troisième point est la permanente nécessité d'une harmonisation entre les dispositions internationales et européennes relatives aux discriminations d'une part et les dispositions françaises d'autre part.

12 Que révèle la mise en œuvre du droit de la non-discrimination en matière pénale sur la nature de votre système juridique et sur la mise en œuvre des lois dans votre système juridique?

La lutte contre les discriminations s'inscrit dans un mouvement unanimement soutenu et mettant en avant une diversité de réponses et de moyens. Mais en matière pénale cette lutte contre les discriminations s'inscrit aussi dans un environnement compliqué liant aussi terrorisme et immigration clandestine. Il convient de ce fait de toujours faire la part entre respect des droits de l'homme et préservation de la sécurité publique. Ainsi les discriminations sont aussi liées à des problématiques taboues, à toute une réflexion sur la politique d'intégration des communautés d'origines ethnique, raciale et religieuse différentes. Et dans un contexte politique difficile liant terrorisme et immigration, écho d'une politique idéologique toujours liée à la balance difficile et dangereuse entre sécurité et respect des droits de l'homme, les discriminations dans la matière pénale touchent un certain nombre de situations difficiles.

La lutte contre les discriminations prend une dimension particulière dans un contexte de lutte contre le terrorisme et l'immigration clandestine. On peut citer pour exemple toute la problématique du « contrôle au faciès ». Ainsi dans une série d'arrêts du 9 novembre 2016, la première chambre civile de la cour de cassation a pris position sur la délicate question du contrôle d'identité au faciès[64]. Le 24 juin 2015, la cour d'appel de Paris avait condamné l'État dans cinq dossiers[65]. La première chambre civile indique qu'un contrôle d'identité présente un caractère discriminatoire lorsqu'il est « réalisé selon des critères tirés de caractéristiques physiques associées à une origine, réelle ou supposée, sans aucune justification objective préalable ». Dans une telle situation, « la faute lourde résultant d'une déficience caractérisée par un fait ou une série de faits traduisant l'inaptitude du service public de la justice à remplir la mission dont il est investi » doit être regardée

---

[64]Fleuriot (2016).
[65]Portmann (2015), p. 1813.

comme constituée. Selon la première chambre civile, « il appartient à celui qui s'en prétend victime d'apporter des éléments de fait de nature à traduire une différence de traitement laissant présumer l'existence d'une discrimination ». L'administration, quant à elle, doit « démontrer, soit l'absence de différence de traitement, soit que celle-ci est justifiée par des éléments objectifs étrangers à toute discrimination ».

Parmi les diverses illustrations apportées, la première chambre civile signale que l'invocation d'études et informations statistiques attestant de la fréquence de contrôles d'identité effectués, selon des motifs discriminatoires, sur une même catégorie de population appartenant aux « minorités visibles » est, à elle seule, insuffisante à laisser présumer une discrimination (nos 15-24.213 ; 15-24.209 et 15-24.208). L'optique du contrôle des contrôles d'identité [66] enjoint les différents acteurs dont le Défenseur des Droits et la commission nationale consultative à réclamer une réforme législative reposant sur un système de traçabilité des contrôles d'identité et la modification de l'article 78-2 du code de procédure pénale en insérant le critère d'objectivité et le principe de non-discrimination. On peut citer un autre exemple en matière d'extradition comme en matière de déchéance de nationalité. En ces matières, la distinction entre français d'origine et français d'acquisition a entraîné la question de la constitutionnalité de ces mesures au regard du principe d'égalité. À l'instar de la non-extradition des nationaux, seuls les Français d'origine bénéficient, en effet, d'une protection absolue contre la déchéance de nationalité. Dans deux décisions du 16 juillet 1996 en matière de déchéance de nationalité et du 14 novembre 2014 en matière d'extradition, le Conseil constitutionnel a, concernant le grief tiré de la violation du principe d'égalité, rappelé que ce principe « ne s'oppose ni à ce que le législateur règle de façon différente des situations différentes ni à ce qu'il déroge à l'égalité pour des raisons d'intérêt général pourvu que dans l'un et l'autre cas la différence de traitement qui en résulte soit en rapport avec l'objet de la loi qui l'établit ». La distinction opérée entre Français d'origine et Français d'acquisition au regard de la non-extradition des nationaux n'est donc pas contraire au principe d'égalité[67].

On ne peut aussi passer sous silence ce statut « d'étranger » en droit pénal qui dans le contexte d'une immigration clandestine, favorise tant une délinquance par et contre les migrants poussant à réfléchir sur les politiques criminelles en matière d'immigration irrégulière dans le contexte de l'Union européenne[68].

Ce principe de non discrimination se voit étendu dans le cadre d'une réflexion générale sur le droit de la sanction pénale avec toutes les interrogations sur la fameuse double peine de l'interdiction du territoire français[69]. Mais elle est aussi prégnante dans le cadre du milieu pénitentiaire. On peut même citer l'émergence du concept de discrimination au sens large du sens dans le cadre du milieu pénitentiaire dans lequel toute atteinte aux droits fondamentaux est très souvent

---

[66]v. aussi Propositions pour un contrôle des contrôles, AJ pénal 2012. 567.

[67]Chassang (2015), p. 86.

[68]d'Ambrosio (2011), p. 502.

[69]Fourment (2008), p. 12; Liger (2004), p. 102.

liée à un problème de discrimination[70]. Dans le cadre de la loi n° 2009-1436 du 24 novembre 2009 pénitentiaire, l'article 22 précise que « L'administration pénitentiaire garantit à toute personne détenue le respect de sa dignité et de ses droits. L'exercice de ceux-ci ne peut faire l'objet d'autres restrictions que celles résultant des contraintes inhérentes à la détention, du maintien de la sécurité et du bon ordre des établissements, de la prévention de la récidive et de la protection de l'intérêt des victimes. Ces restrictions tiennent compte de l'âge, de l'état de santé, du handicap et de la personnalité de la personne détenue. » Ce qui consacre de manière implicite l'absence de toute discrimination dans le traitement pénitentiaire des détenus ce qu'ont toujours souligné les Règles pénitentiaires européennes[71] dont l'application est suivie de très près par le contrôleur général des lieux privatifs de liberté[72].

Le droit de la non discrimination en matière pénale ne pourra véritablement prendre sa place dans l'arsenal de lutte en cette matière que lorsque la voie pénale apparaîtra comme une voie à part entière, reposant sur la défense de la valeur universelle de dignité mais avec un impact pratique en termes de contentieux qui ne fera plus douter le justiciable de la véritable volonté de la justice pénale d'en faire une priorité. Cela doit se concrétiser dans une optique de complémentarité par rapport aux autres voies même si elle doit intervenir lorsque tous les préalables non contentieux et les mesures de prévention ont été voués à l'échec. C'est une véritable prise de conscience à laquelle doivent participer tous les acteurs judiciaires pour faire de la non discrimination un objectif de la justice "pénale" du XXI ème siècle afin qu'elle ne reste pas dans la seule symbolique.

References

Amegadjie F (2008) La compétence pénale de la HALDE, contours et enjeux. AJ pénal, p 307
Bénéjat M (2012) Les relations du droit pénal et de la bioéthique. AJ pénal, p 392
Beziz-Ayache A (2006) Les nouvelles règles pénitentiaires. AJ pénal, p 400
Céré J-P (2007) l'institution d'un contrôleur général des lieux de privation de liberté par la loi du 30 octobre 2007: remarques sur un accouchement difficile. AJ pénal, p 525

---

[70]L'encadrement de la liberté d'expression politique dans les établissements pénitentiaires: le numéro d'équilibriste de la CEDH, Cour européenne des droits de l'homme 25 janvier 2011, AJ pénal 2011. 201: la règlementation pénitentiaire et la sanction disciplinaire qui en découlait violaient le droit à la liberté d'expression (art. 10) et constituaient une discrimination fondée sur les opinions politiques (art. 14) ou encore Collège de la HALDE 22 février 2010, AJ pénal 2010. 455, rejet à la demande d'agrément en tant qu'aumônier par des témoins de Jehova et discrimination par rapport à d'autres cultes.
[71]Beziz-Ayache (2006), p. 400.
[72]Senna (2011), p. 404, Céré (2007), p. 525.

Chassang C (2015) Français d'origine et français d'acquisition face à l'extradition: la distinction validée par le Conseil constitutionnel. AJ pénal, p 86
Cimamonti S (2015) Le développement de la transaction en matière pénale. AJ pénal, p 460
Crocq J-C (2015) Du droit de la transaction au droit à la transaction en matière pénale: pour une recomposition des procédures alternatives et simplifiées. AJ pénal, p 465
d'Ambrosio L (2011) Quelques réflexions sur l'après El Dridi au regard des expériences italienne et française. AJ pénal, p 502
de Nayves PdC (2013) La Chambre criminelle jette le voile sur la Convention européenne. AJ pénal, p 400
Dreyer E (2006) La prescription des infractions commises par les médias. AJ pénal, p 294
Fleuriot C (2016) Contrôles d'identité au faciès: confirmation de la condamnation de l'État, Dalloz actualité, 10 novembre 2016
Fortis E (1994) Les infractions du nouveau Code pénal créées ou remaniées: Dr. soc. 1994, spécialement p 626
Foulon-Piganiol VF (1972) La lutte contre le racisme, Commentaire de la loi du 1er juillet 1972: D., chron, p 261
Fourment F (2008) Peines perdues. AJ pénal, p 12
Germain G, Lassalle S (2014) Stage de citoyenneté: une mesure inégale? AJ pénal, p 467
Guerder P (1995) La poursuite et la répression des discriminations en droit du travail: Dr. soc. 1995, p 447
Jakubowicz A (2006) La défense et le rôle des parties civiles dans les "grands" procès. AJ pénal, p 111
Keller M (2002) La loi du 16 novembre 2001 relative à la lutte contre les discriminations: D., p 1355
Lagarde F (2013) La répression de la violence des supporters. AJ pénal, p. 311
Lasserre Capdeville J (2008) Le testing. AJ pénal, p 310
Lasserre Capdeville J (2015) L'article 225-3-1 du code pénal, régissant le testing, est conforme aux droits de la défense et au droit à un procès équitable. AJ pénal, p 139
Lepage A (2005) Vie privée du salarié et droit pénal, AJ pénal, p 9
Liger D (2004) La réforme de la double peine. AJ pénal, p 102
Masse-Dessen VH (1995) La résolution contentieuse des discriminations en droit du travail – Une approche civile: Dr. soc., p 442
Peronne G, Daoud E (2014) Discriminations et réseaux sociaux. AJ pénal
Perrier J-B (2015) Réflexions et perspectives sur la transaction en matière pénale. AJ pénal, p 474
Poissonnier G, Dubuisson F (2012) L'appel citoyen au boycott des produits de l'État d'Israël constitue-t-il une infraction ? crim. 22 mai 2012. AJ pénal, p 592
Portmann VA (2015) Dalloz actualité, B. Camguilhem, AJDA, 25 juin 2015, p 1813
Roussel S (2010) Prévenir les risques psycho-sociaux en entreprise. AJ pénal, p 526
Saas C (2008) L'action civile paralysée par le consentement impossible. AJ pénal, p 83
Senna E (2011) État des lieux à mi-mandat du Contrôle général des lieux privatifs de liberté. AJ pénal, p 404
Sereno S (2017) Le Défenseur des droits et les discriminations dans l'emploi. Thèse AMU, PUAM
Seuvic J-F (2002) Discriminations: Rev. sc. crim., p 367
Sordino M-C (2014) Le procès pénal confronté aux neurosciences: science sans conscience...? AJ pénal, p 58
Verges E (2006) Provocation policière, loyauté de la preuve et étendue de la nullité procédurale. AJ pénal, p 354
Véron VM (1990) Le renforcement du dispositif répressif contre la discrimination et le racisme. Présentation des lois des 12 et 13 juillet 1990: Dr. pén., chron. p 1
Viriot-Barrial D (2014) La protection pénale de la dignité du travailleur au sein du code pénal sous influence et pression européennes, rev. pénitentiaire et de droit pénal, n°1, p 9

Viriot-Barrial VD (2011) Les discriminations liées à la santé: confrontation de la vision pénaliste et de la vision "haldiste". Dernier état des lieux avant l' "entrée en scène" du défenseur des droits". In: Rev. générale de droit médical, n°40, les études hospitalières 2011

Vouland P (2005) l'exercice quotidien de la fonction de défense et la loyauté de la preuve. AJ pénal, p 275

Dominique Viriot-barrial is a Professor of Law at Aix-Marseille University. She is the publication director of various books concerning social policy responses to ageing or sanitary problems. She is the scientific coordinator of a an ANR project about family careers from comparative law perspective. Mrs Viriot-barrial writes and teaches in the field of social and sanitary policies as well as criminal law.

France and the Netherlands: Toward Convergence?

Réjane Sénac, Janie Pélabay, and Lisa Ammon

1 Introduction

In a twenty-first century characterized by distrust,[1] questioning resistance to implementation of non-discrimination law involves analyzing contemporary expressions of one of the main conceptual principles of liberal democracy: political and legal equality.

How does implementation of non-discrimination law derive meaning given the borders between the political "us" and the building of otherness? While most social groups mainly owe their cohesion to their power of exclusion,[2] drawing as they do on the differentiation of those who are not "us," internal classifications and the political mechanisms of exclusion and inclusion are numerous. In her work on

---

This chapter is the result of a research project entitled "Les juridictions et les instances publiques dans la mise en œuvre du principe de non-discrimination: perspectives pluridisciplinaires et comparées", funded by the Défenseur des droits et la Mission de recherche Droit et Justice du Ministère de la justice (June 2014–June 2016). Special thanks to the Défenseur des droits and to the Ministère de la Justice for financing this research and to all the researchers who took part in it, in particular the Professor of Law, Marie Mercat-Bruns, who coordinated.

[1]Cf. Norris (1999, 2011).
[2]Elias (1994), pp. 15–18.

R. Sénac (✉) · J. Pélabay
Sciences Po, Centre for Political Research, Paris, France
e-mail: rejane.senac@sciencespo.fr; janie.pelabay@sciencespo.fr

L. Ammon
University of Paris VIII Vincennes Saint-Denis, Department of Political Sciences, Saint-Denis, France

pluralism and national identity in Canada, Elke Winter uses the expression "processes of conditional inclusion" to analyze the construction of "others" alongside "us" and "them" in a triangular relations model.[3] This process is central to an understanding of the distinctions that determine differentiated implementations of the principle of equality.

Using this approach, the present chapter will explore resistance to non-discrimination law by analyzing the political issues raised by tracking the borders of the political "us." Through the prism of a comparative analysis of France and the Netherlands[4] we explore convergence and divergence surrounding the content and implementation of non-discrimination law. We will thus explore the issues involved in the struggle against discrimination in two "integration models,"[5] which are currently undergoing profound change, giving rise to ambivalence if not tensions, in the relationship to otherness and to "us": France, which is associated with a culture of so-called "republican" integration but which has recently complemented it by "diversity" policies,[6] and the Netherlands, which until recently adopted a "multicultural" approach but which has moved toward integration and indeed assimilation.

For each country, we will examine three issues through the prism of this comparative analysis: the relationship to the principle of equality, the role played by the actors, and controversies surrounding implementation non-discrimination law.

2 Non-discrimination and the Principle of Equality

From the outset, non-discrimination seems to be closely linked to the principle of equality from both a conceptual and a normative point of view. What needs to be determined is the meaning attributed to this principle and the relationship it entertains with non-discrimination law.

---

[3]Winter (2011).

[4]For France, the analysis is based on a qualitative survey carried out in 2014–2015 among some 30 political, institutional, civil association and union leaders and completed by an analysis of public discourse, reports and statements on implementation of the principle of non-discrimination. For the Netherlands, some 15 interviews were carried out in 2014–2015 among political and institutional actors in synergy with analysis of public reports and statements of position.

[5]While remaining heuristic in our analysis in that it explores tensions between so-called "republican," "multicultural," and "liberal" approaches, the notion of "models" is itself an object of controversy. With regard to the France/Netherlands comparison, see the special issue edited by Bertossi et al. (2012), pp. 237–376. More generally, see: Brubaker (1992) and Joppke (2007), pp. 1–22.

[6]Sénac (2012).

2.1 Equality in the French Republic: Interpreting the Legal and Political Principle

The "*Liberté, égalité, fraternité*" triptych has been the motto of the French Republic since its founding constitution in 1848. Although this motto continues to attain broad consensus it is also the object of continuous questioning surrounding the definition of each of its terms and the relationship between them. The qualitative survey reveals the central role played by the principle of equality in the meaning of non-discrimination. Its role must be placed in the context of a "crisis" which is not only economic but also political, social, and moral.[7] As the survey shows, references to both the 2005 French suburban riots and the 2008 economic crisis and their aftermath inform the diverging but recurrent views held by political, union, and civil association actors of the struggle against discrimination.

The economic crisis has led to a refocusing on employment, particularly access to employment, salary progression, and career advancement. In parallel, what is currently preventing the execution of non-discrimination law is frequently linked to a series of phenomena such as the loss of trust in political institutions and in collective action and also loss of "values" at the very foundation of the "republican pact." However, civil association leaders note that distrust is not the sole preserve of society at large and ordinary citizens, but that public institutions in general and political decision-makers in particular also display a lack of trust in younger generations. Following the January and November 2015 terrorist attacks in Paris, a "Charlie effect"[8] which has had consequences for the conceptualisation and implementation of non-discrimination can be discerned in France. The impact of these consequences has led to a shift toward policy designed to re-establish the political bond through the public promotion of the "Values of the Republic." One example of this shift is the "*Grande mobilisation de l'École pour les valeurs de la République*"[9] initiated as early as January 2015.[10]

Moreover, some of these conceptions of equality differ greatly and are at times in competition with each other, thus giving palpably different practical orientations to the struggle against discrimination. Significantly, persistent debate on the pertinence of recourse to positive action measures reveals some tension between equality of opportunity and equality of results.[11] In this respect, three conceptions of equality stand out.

---

[7] d'Allonnes (2012).

[8] This refers to the shooting dead of 12 people at the offices of the satirical weekly newspaper *Charlie Hebdo* in Paris on January 7, 2015, by Saïd and Chérif Kouachi, who identified themselves as belonging to Al-Qaeda's branch in Yemen, which took responsibility for the attack.

[9] http://www.education.gouv.fr/cid85644/onze-mesures-pour-un-grande-mobilisation-de-l-ecole-pour-les-valeurs-de-la-republique.html.

[10] Pélabay (2013), pp. 39–59; Pélabay (2015), pp. 93–99.

[11] Dahlerup (2007), pp. 73–92.

In France, the so-called "country of human rights", equal rights (*égalité de droit*), which include equality in law and equality in rights, mark the concept of non-discrimination. What is at stake with non-discrimination, considered as a fundamental right, is nothing less than the status of citizen. Discrimination can then be interpreted as an attack on the "dignity" due to the person as a human being. This notion of a moral-cum-political nature is used, for example, by associations such as ATD Quart Monde (All Together in Dignity to Overcome Poverty—Fourth World). Equality of treatment (*égalité de traitement*) follows and raises the attendant problem of how to execute such a principle. The gaps between *de jure* equality and *de facto* inequality continue to nourish the fundamental question of how to concretely satisfy the demands of equality and the persistent question of whether treating equally means treating in the same way. In this respect, the questions raised by the *Comité de Réflexion sur le Préambule de la Constitution*, presided by Simone Veil, who in 2008 declared her attachment to the "colour-blindness" of French positive discrimination policies, are still relevant today.[12] The same is true for the position expressed in a public report by the *Conseil d'Etat* in 1996 explaining that the principle of equality allows for different treatment in unequal situations. For its part, equality of opportunity (*égalité des chances*) reveals the ambiguities inherent to a republican meritocracy centered on individual responsibility. A number of the leaders interviewed, and in particular leaders of civil associations, underlined the danger of focusing on equality of opportunity alone, which can place responsibility for failure on the shoulders of the individual who "was not able or did not know how to seize the opportunity offered to him or her."[13]

Neither is translating the principle of equality into legal norms an easy task. A variety of questions surrounding the legal qualification of non-discrimination arise. Many of the interviewees were critical of the lack of semantical clarity surrounding non-discrimination. They partly attributed this to the scope of the legal category as such, together with its successive extensions that they saw as leading to the danger of "diluting" non-discrimination in a sort of legal "new-speak." Although the idea of racial harassment was mentioned, for example, by the MRAP (Movement Against Racism and For Friendship Among Peoples) in connection with ethno-cultural based discrimination, rapprochements likely to be made with the legal category of moral harassment were seen to be part of this same adverse extension of non-discrimination. This explains why a number of civil association and institutional leaders deplore the fact that the principle of non-discrimination seems at times to have become a holdall category, whose legal frontiers are either ill-defined or ill-perceived by the victims themselves.

The link between equality and non-discrimination has been unanimously established from a conceptual and normative perspective. However, and somewhat paradoxically, this link does not serve as a concrete driver for the implementation of non-discrimination law. With the exception of associations such as the MRAP and *SOS Racisme*, who consider the law to be an essential weapon in the denunciation

---

[12]*Comité de réflexion sur le Préambule de la Constitution* presided over by Veil (2009), p. 62.
[13]Poirmeur (2000), p. 111.

and response to inequality, the link between equality and non-discrimination is not strong enough in practice for the law to function as a legitimate and necessary means to implement the principle of equality. Furthermore, the expressed attachment to the ideal of equality can contribute to delegitimising non-discrimination law, as it can be perceived to weaken social and national cohesion (segmenting society according to discrimination criteria), the balance between different types of actors (opposition between employees and employers in legal procedures), and belief in republican axiology. For this latter element, recourse to litigation is seen as an admission of political failure and as an unconstructive step that is both expensive and ineffective.

2.2 The Netherlands: An Exemplary Model of Equality?

Article 1 of the Dutch Constitution enshrines the principle of equality of treatment. The law adopted in 1983[14] also refers to equality of treatment and not to the prohibition of discrimination. The term "discrimination" is essentially reserved to the domain of criminal law. In spite of its limited presence in the texts, the concept of non-discrimination plays an important role in the Netherlands with respect to both activist work in civil associations and public policy. There is thus neither incompatibility nor competition between equality and non-discrimination as can be the case in France, but rather a perception of complementarity between the two notions. Both are equally present and both discourses exist in parallel. However, the registers of equality and non-discrimination—and also the instruments of hard and soft law linked to these different notions—seem to be differently applied depending on the type of discrimination concerned and the criteria defining it.

The genealogy of the notion of non-discrimination in the Netherlands partly explains this intricate intertwining of the two notions. From the end of the 1970s and the beginning of the 1980s and long before the adoption of European directives[15] in 2000, feminists and anti-racism activists took ownership of the notion of discrimination, together with the notions of emancipation and equality of treatment, partly as a result of proximity with the English-speaking world and notably the United Kingdom. At national level, such lobbying by the civil association sector rapidly led to the creation of the *Commissie gelijke beloning* (Equal Pay Commission) in 1975. The Commission was transformed into the *Commissie gelijke behandeling van mannen en vrouwen* (Equal Treatment Commission on Men and Women) in 1980 and incorporated into the *Commissie Gelijke Behandeling* (Equal Treatment Commission) which was established in 1994 along the lines of the Commission for Racial Equality in the United Kingdom. In 2012, it became the

---

[14]Algemene wet gelijke behandeling or General Equal Treatment Act, in English, can be consulted on the website of *College voor de Rechten van de Mens*: https://mensenrechten.nl/sites/default/files/2013-05-08.Legislation%20Equal%20Treatment.pdf, consulted on the 17.10.2016.

[15]The history of non-discrimination in the Netherlands is not about the national development of a communitarian notion, but rather the recognition of a demand nurtured among activists and subsequently exported to the European Union.

College voor de Rechten van de Mens, in English the Netherlands Institute for Human Rights (hereafter *'the College').*[16]

Among those who worked on these advances, the *Clara Wichmann Institut*[17] and the National Bureau against Racial Discrimination (LBR: *Landelijk Bureau ter bestrijding van Rassendiscriminatie*)[18] should be noted. For these two organisations, the notion of discrimination and access to legal recourse have played a central role in activist strategies since the 1980s. Thus in the Netherlands, non-discrimination was perceived as an essential legal instrument from very early on. Indeed, although equality seems to have maintained the status of a meta-principle that guided the work of the actors concerned, non-discrimination became the instrument perceived to be the most effective in the attainment of equality of treatment.

Today, the focus of the antidiscrimination struggle has shifted with the development of an approach based on human rights. This shift became institutionalised with the creation of the *College voor de Rechten van de Mens* in October 2012, which replaced the *Commissie Gelijke Behandeling.* The effects of this change were judged to be both positive and negative for the *College*'s work specifically on non-discrimination. Although its mission focusing on Human Rights enabled the *College* to play a more political role, as it did in the *"Zwarte Piet*"[19] affair and in the court case against Geert Wilders,[20] the survey also revealed fears of a "dilution of discrimination" within a broader approach similar to those expressed in France

---

[16]Goldschmidt (2012), p. 33.

[17]The *Clara Wichmann Instituut* was founded in 1983 driven by feminist movements. Its aim was to improve the situation of women through legal action by supporting complainants and providing financial aid when the litigation undertaken had a potentially broader impact at national or European level. The Foundation focused essentially on strategic litigation and legal aid (social security and equal wages issues, for example). The network continues to exist today through the association known as *Vrouw en Recht* (Women and Law/rights), even though the Foundation itself ended its legal support activity in 2004 due to lack of financial support.

[18]The *National Bureau against Racial Discrimination (NBRD)* was also founded in the 1980s by activist jurists who had very close links with similar movements in Brussels and London. Beyond the lobbying carried out in the Netherlands aimed at recognition of discrimination against immigrants, the *NBRD* was one of the founders of the *Starting Line Group*, an organisation which actively worked on inclusion of the notion of non-discrimination in the Amsterdam Treaty and, later on, the adoption of the European directive known as "Racial Equality Directive." On the role of the *Starting Line Group* see: Iyiola (2009) and Andrew (2006), pp. 334–353.

[19]The figure of *"Zwarte Piet*" ("Black Piet"), which is omnipresent in November and December, is a servant to Saint Nicolas. He wears black make-up, red lipstick and an afro wig. At Christmas time, he features on a variety of products and many people dress up in *Zwarte Piet* costumes. For some it incarnates a beloved Christmas figure and for others a symbol of the racism inherent to a postcolonial society. This affair is symptomatic of the tensions surrounding questions of racism in Dutch society and led to much debate far beyond the Netherlands. In a difficult context, the *College* declared "Black Piet" to be discriminatory in 2014. The judgement was reiterated in 2015.

[20]The *College* declared itself to be in favour of condemning Geert Wilders, a politician and founder of the nationalist PVV (Freedom Party), during his court case for incitation to hatred against Muslim residents in the Netherlands. The position of the *College* can be consulted at the following address: http://www.mensenrechten.nl/toegelicht/uitlatingen-geert-wilders-over-%E2%80%98marokkanen%E2%80%99. Page consulted on November 23, 2015.

subsequent to the integration of the HALDE[21] (The Equal Opportunities and Antidiscrimination Commission) which was created in 2004 and became the *Défenseur des droits* (Defender of rights) office in 2011.

3 The Actors Involved in Non-discrimination

Because the struggle against discrimination takes place at so many different levels (European, national, local) that are at times in competition with each other, there is a need to focus on the multiple actors involved. Analysis of the role played by the different actors will then show the plurality of registers (political, economic, social, legal) and of spheres of action (institutional, unions, civil associations), undoubtedly revealing some level of tension between them. Finally, practices adopted by the actors will provide insight into advances in and resistance to implementation of non-discrimination law.

3.1 France: A Multiplicity of Actors and a Need for Coordination

In spite of the lead role played by the EU and European bodies, and particularly the European Commission in the struggle against discrimination, the qualitative survey shows that with very few exceptions, current perceptions of the European scale of involvement and the role played by the EU are very limited. This is why a conception centered on the national framework predominates in France. Furthermore, the idea that there exists a "French model" for this issue as well as for others is prevalent among a large number of actors. Such an idea leads to calls for a "French exception" in how discrimination is dealt with. These calls are reaffirmed by the perceived value of the "French-style republican model" whose difference is then marked in comparison to multiculturalist and/or "anglo-saxon" models. This primacy of the national is also present at the local level that stresses the need for a decentralised handling of complaints (local *Défenseur des droits* agents and the existence or not of antidiscrimination sections in the Public Prosecutor's office, for example) and for the struggle against discrimination to be taken into account in urban policies. When the local level is taken into account, tensions become visible (notably with respect to the allocation and sharing of resources) between policy centered on particular areas in towns and cities on the one hand, and policies on rural and peri-urban areas on the other hand. Beyond institutional and civil association actors directly involved in non-discrimination, schools play a central role as instruments of socialisation in the

---

[21] In French: *Haute autorité de lutte contre les discriminations et pour l'égalité*.

struggle against prejudice and as training grounds for citizens who are well adapted to the political community and to the labour market.

Under the combined weight of the economic crisis and political distrust in France, non-discrimination policies are largely centered on the economic level, as evidenced by the refocusing on employment among a large number of actors. The inter-partner working group *Lutte contre les discriminations en entreprise* (Struggle Against Discrimination in Private Companies) illustrates the primacy of the economic. It was set up on 29 October 2014 by the *Ministère du Travail, de l'Emploi, de la Formation professionnelle et du Dialogue social,* and the *Ministère de la Ville, de la Jeunesse et des Sports,* subsequent to litigation undertaken by the *Fédération de la Maison des potes* (an anti-racist association) to protest the absence of a decree for the implementation of the anonymous Curriculum Vitae enshrined in the 2006 law on equality of opportunity. The actors underline that beyond this particular objective, the working group was one of the rare platforms where different points of view on non-discrimination were exchanged. Strong divergence was expressed about the division of competences between unions and associations and the parameters of their respective domains of action. Debate surrounding implementation of class actions provides a good example of these tensions. One of the main points of contention was to decide who should be appointed as the plaintiff and in what domain. The *Modernisation de la Justice du 21ème siècle* law adopted by the *Assemblée Nationale* on 12 October 2016 settled the question by empowering the representative unions (at the national, branch or company level) to initiate a class action on discrimination at work (work relations throughout the career), while associations are authorised to act only on discrimination in hiring or outside the workplace such as access to housing or to goods and services. With respect to the fundamental issue of employment, the benefits, but also the limits of social dialogue were underlined, with the role of employers being strongly questioned by the unions. The importance of this issue for the unions should be noted at a time when several agreements on diversity and gender equality are on the point of being renegotiated.

The vast majority of interviewees stressed how important it was for coordinating bodies and platforms to be permanently available to them. Association and union leaders in particular deplored the loss of such platforms allowing different actors to network, following the annexing of the *HALDE* by the *Défenseur des droits.*[22] The "equality and racism"[23] platform established at the initiative of the *Défenseur des droits* and in partnership with the *Délégation Interministérielle à la Lutte contre le Racisme et l'Antisémitisme (DILCRA)*[24] gave rise to strong expectations in this

---

[22]Concerning debate on the consequences of the HALDE's merger with the *Défenseur des droits,* see in particular written question n° 13046 by Roland Courteau, a Socialist Party Deputy for Aude published in the Senate's *JOURNAL OFFICIEL* on April 15, 2010 and the answer from the Minister of Justice published in the same Journal on December 9, 2010. "*Éric Molinié défend l'autonomie de la Halde*", *Libération,* 13 December 2010; Allal et al. (2010), and also Martinel and Boulos (2011).

[23]http://www.egalitecontreracisme.fr/.

[24]Instituted by decree n°2012-221 of February 16, 2012 and placed under the Prime Minister since December 15, 2014.

respect. Indeed, eyes have turned towards the State to stimulate and achieve the ambition of creating a network of actors and a concerted inter-connecting of practices supporting their work. This attitude also reflects expectations in terms of normative orientation as it is considered to be the State's duty to "make the rules" and to keep the political focus on equality. This explains why some actors—associations in particular—are critical. They believe that since 2008, the State has pulled back on the ideological and financial front. They regret the disintegration of the "associative chain," following a decrease in subsidies and therefore a loss in levels of intervention among citizens, both in supporting victims of discrimination and in engaging in preventative work. Similarly, an absence of dialogue with the legal professions is frequently regretted. Both judges and the *Ministère de la justice* are sometimes considered to have too few links with other actors involved in the struggle against discrimination.

3.2 The Netherlands: Decentralization and Coordination

From as early as the 1980s, the commitment of civil society to non-discrimination has been a determining factor in understanding the current institutional structure in the Netherlands. Because this notion has long been in existence and because it was introduced through a bottom-up process, it has produced a network of multiple actors operating at different levels between whom strong coordination exists.

The core of the network is made up of regional agencies that, in a certain sense, are the prolongation of the organizations described above. The *National Bureau against Racial Discrimination*, now known as "*Artikel 1*"[25] was set up in 1985, and, along with other regional organizations such as RADAR in Rotterdam and the MDRA in Amsterdam, represents an important innovative force in the struggle against discrimination. These organizations were established a long time ago and victims of discrimination, the general population, and public authorities recognize them as political actors.

A 2009 government reform considerably reinforced the decentralized system of antidiscrimination centers. In order to extend such services throughout the country and to increase their effectiveness, all citizens henceforth have access to an "Antidiscrimination Service" at municipal level. The municipalities themselves receive financial support from the government according to number of inhabitants. In the same year, the establishment of these services was accompanied by a national campaign to publicize the local centers and encourage victims of discrimination to make their experiences known ("*Do you have to leave yourself at home when you go out?*"). For this reason, the number of discrimination alerts has greatly increased:

---

[25] In reference to Article 1 of the Constitution on equality of treatment.

according to a Council of Europe report it tripled during the year of the campaign.[26] Today, the overall conclusion on the reform is varied as many local Antidiscrimination Service centers continue to suffer from a lack of financial means and qualified personnel. Only a few reported cases can therefore be dealt with by the *College voor de Rechten van de Mens*[27] or by a judge. The survey shows that the local network favors a more general approach in dealing with victims of discrimination and focuses on legal empowerment and listening to the victims and their experience.

Victims of discrimination can also make a complaint to the police who run a national expertise center on discrimination. The center is in charge of cooperation with local offices and internal reflection on discrimination.[28] Since 1998, the police in Amsterdam run a service, called *"Pink in Blue,"* specifically dedicated to combatting discrimination on the basis of sexual orientation. It is staffed by specially trained police officers that are sensitive to this particular question. A national expertise center on discrimination (*Landelijk expertise centrum discriminatie*) was established in 1998 within the Public Prosecutor's office. All data mandatorily recorded by the police are transferred to this service which decides if discrimination took place or not and if the complaint can be followed up. Furthermore, a specialized "discrimination" prosecutor in each regional service deals with all complaints made in the region. The regional prosecutors are coordinated by the National Expertise Center. Ultimately, victims of discrimination have a choice between several interlocutors (local centers, the *College*, the police), depending on the type of discrimination or the individual's particular situation.

At the political level, the struggle against discrimination is dealt with by different ministries, according to discrimination criteria, while the Ministry of Internal Affairs took on the role of coordinator in 2013. The ministry's role has increased in importance by means of regular action plans and major awareness campaigns. Furthermore, unlike in other countries, in the Netherlands the existence of an infrastructure that ensures close coordination between actors and is present throughout the country already existed before public authorities began coordinating. The effectiveness of these exchanges is ensured by quarterly meetings between regional and local centers and the police. In Rotterdam, for example, the regional agency "RADAR" has created a partnership with the local police; the two entities set up a filtering system for police to which RADAR employees have direct access allowing

---

[26]Report by the Council of Europe: Examples of good practice in the field of protection and promotion of Human Rights. In response to the invitation by the Commissioner for Human Rights. Example from the Netherlands Municipal Antidiscrimination Services: http://www.coe.int/t/commissioner/Activities/GoodPractices/Netherlands_antidiscriminationservices.pdf.

[27]According to the Ministry for Internal Affairs in the Netherlands, the *Collège* has taken on all the tasks dealt with by its predecessor, the Commission for Equality of Treatment, but its potential scope has been broadened. The *Collège* has the power to investigate and can be addressed, free of charge, by victims of discriminations or by organizations. The *Collège*'s opinions are followed in roughly 75% of cases.

[28]For example, on ethnic profiling.

them to identify cases of discrimination among other complaints made at regional level.

4 The Law and Non-discrimination Policies: A Paradoxical Relationship

The application of non-discrimination law can be seen as a test to determine whether the law functions as an instrument for transformative politics toward truly egalitarian societies, or whether its essential function is "the objective support of the dominant social system."[29] In keeping with *critical legal studies*[30] and *feminist legal studies*,[31] analysis of the current struggle against discrimination raises the question of whether the law contributes to fostering the perpetuation of power relations or, on the contrary, to deconstructing them. Beyond this alternative, non-discrimination law merits being questioned given the function of medium and translator that Jürgen Habermas assigns to it: to ensure that claims made by individuals who experience discrimination can be dealt with by means of public policy.[32]

4.1 France: The Law on the Sidelines

The majority of interviewees underlined that the issue is no longer of concern for the legal corpus, which is seen as satisfactory overall in its current state, but rather in the efforts that need to be made to render the law both effective and efficient. One of the few questions raised concerns the relevance of bundling discrimination criteria together or adding new criteria to facilitate a demonstration of proof. The addition to the criteria of 'place of residence' in February 2014 was not universally agreed on. Whereas those who were most favourable expected that it would contribute to the shift toward a multi-criteria approach, the meaning attributed to it was questioned as to its possible application not only in areas covered by urban policy, but also to rural areas. Furthermore, the proposal made by ATD Quart Monde and relayed by the CNCDH, the French National Consultative Commission on Human Rights, to add 'social precarity' to the criteria was integrated into the June 2016 Equality and Citizenship law. Its supporters saw it as a dissuasive mechanism to denounce the impunity with which the poorest sections of the population could be excluded. However, although they agreed in principle, many of the actors interviewed

---

[29]Miaille (1976), p. 342.
[30]Michaut and Michelman (2010).
[31]Cf. in particular Cardi and Devreux (coord.) (2014).
[32]Habermas (1996).

underlined the difficulties of putting it into practice (too many situations concerned, lack of clarity in the legal categorisation).

Beyond the specific question of criteria, a diagnosis was more generally made of the existence of persistent and indeed worsening difficulties particularly with respect to providing proof in the case of a criminal complaint and the recognition of indirect, systemic, and multi-criterial or intersectional discrimination. Moreover, civil association leaders stressed the obstacles encountered in the making of a complaint and legal admissibility (state officials lacking in knowledge or not taking antidiscriminatory law into account which excludes an act from being considered discriminatory). Civil association leaders also deplored that in most cases the complaints were not followed up, that they were dismissed, or indeed that they resulted in a minimum sentence. For these actors, the normative and limited dimension of non-discrimination law is thus an issue whose consequence is that victims feel discouraged, if not despised, by such a state of play. The sidelining of the law is visible through two controversies: the relationship between hard and soft law, and the respective importance of sanctions, compensation, and prevention within non-discrimination law.

The creation of soft law instruments (the "Diversity Charter" and the "Gender Equality Label" in 2004, and the "Diversity Label" in 2008) by the business community and also their re-appropriation by the State and by some of the unions and associations raises the question of how these instruments connect with implementation of non-discrimination by means of hard law.[33] Even though the unions and associations (particularly *ANI diversité*) are somewhat sceptical of a number of these instruments, they consider that the adoption of the law is not enough and that there is therefore a need to resort to the language of soft law which they judge to be more positive and more acceptable to the private sector than the language of sanction. A number of institutional and political actors believe that private companies need to be protected from risks (legal, financial, image, etc.) posed by litigation and legal sanctions for non-compliance of non-discrimination law. These kinds of penalties are defended only by the associations who stress that the involvement of private companies in the RSE, corporate social and environmental responsibility, and the promotion of diversity would not have happened without the dissuasive dimension of legal decisions that created a precedent, such as the 2007 condemnation of *L'Oréal* and *Adecco* for racial discrimination in hiring practices. However, the unions favour maintaining people in employment and therefore mediation. The enthusiasm for mediation is broader and is presented as a solution to ensure that "the struggle against discrimination does not rely solely on criminal law" as affirmed by Christine Lazerges, president of the CNCDH.

Does this mean that mediation and prevention should be substituted for the law's power of sanction? The survey reveals the emergence of a framework for the prevention of discrimination by means of an approach adopted in the name of

---

[33] Junter and Sénac-Slawinski (2010), pp. 167–195.

economic, social, or political performance,[34] to the detriment of litigation and compensation for victims. A corollary to the importance attributed to the educational power of the law is the quasi-unanimous call for a reform in mentalities among all actors involved. Improvement in access to the law, the development of a *"savoir-être"* among potential victims, and the struggle against prejudice and stereotyping constitute three elements of this framework which is supported by union, association, political, and institutional leaders. The framework is part of a tendency to depoliticize the political issues and choices. From a critical theory perspective, it can be analyzed as the expression of "changes resulting from neo-liberalism: the transformation of political norms into technical norms, of social problems into moral problems, and the reduction of moral problems to problems of individual responsibility.[35]" The framework corresponds to a preventive and individualized management model for social risk[36] by means of which the struggle against discrimination is taken in hand by a system that is limited to "equipping individuals with the basic capital to survive in an uncertain and competitive world.[37]" With this in mind, stress is placed on the development of training modules designed to prevent discrimination aimed at private sector personnel (HR and managers), civil servants (police officers, *gendarmes*, prosecutors and magistrates), and to personnel working in the other sections of the public sector (employment offices, family services, schools, etc.).

On the question of whether all training in non-discrimination calls for an objectification of discrimination, debate on the gathering of ethnic statistics continues to polarize non-discrimination actors as it does the general public. By way of example, the statements made by Robert Ménard in May 2015[38] on the proportion of Muslim children in public schools in Béziers where he is Mayor, reactivated the fear that the ethno-racial and religious framework would be used politically for the purposes of stigmatization. A consensus seems to exist on the dangers of generalizing data collection likely to be useful for research but that can also be used for ethnic record-keeping/profiling. At the same time, the debate is nourished by studies that show the existence of religious discrimination in hiring practices such as the study made by the *Institut Montaigne* in October 2015 on the basis of over 6000 Curriculum Vitae they sent out.[39]

---

[34]Sénac (2012).
[35]Genel (2007), p. 92.
[36]Beck (1999) and Vielle et al. (dir.) (2005).
[37]Dupriez et al. (eds) (2005), p. 6.
[38]"*Robert Ménard entendu par la police sur le "fichage" des écoliers de* Béziers", *LeMonde.fr*, 6 mai 2015: http://www.lemonde.fr/politique/article/2015/05/05/quand-robert-menard-fiche-les-enfants-des-ecoles-de-beziers_4627511_823448.html.
[39]Valfort (2015).

4.2 The Netherlands: A Mixed Relationship with the Law

Even though non-discrimination law as a principle is very well esteemed in the Netherlands, it is also in competition with other means of action. As in France, hard law, whose usefulness is recognized in theory, is significantly restricted in application. The aim of soft law is to present the issues involved in the struggle against discrimination from a more "positive" angle in order to encourage social dialogue. The *Charter Diversiteit*, which was launched in July 2015,[40] is part of this approach.

Many of those interviewed in the Netherlands who have been involved in the associative network and the Equal Treatment Commission stress that hard law is henceforth reserved for specific cases and types of discrimination.[41] As in France, but in this case with a shift toward a strategy implemented in the name of human rights rather than performance, it is usually soft law instruments—charters, social dialogue, negotiation, and mediation that are promoted. After many years of experience and mobilization of the right to non-discrimination, such a right is often perceived to generate too much tension within a society on subjects that "require a real social dialogue over time." Thus, with regard to discrimination against women, people with disabilities, and to a lesser extent the LGBTI community, a number of interviewees spoke of an emancipation or equality issue rather than discrimination.

The situation is different with respect to racial questions, as these questions divide society as much as they divide the actors of non-discrimination. As in France, taking racial and ethnic discrimination into account constitutes one of the main challenges for Dutch society and in this area hard law is often seen as the legitimate and best-adapted instrument to deal with the question. However, the police and more especially the *Landelijk expertise centrum discriminatie* (National Expertise Center of the Public Prosecutor's Office) have frequently been criticized for the small number of effective prosecutions made. Although a very large number of complaints have been made to the police, very few cases are investigated by the prosecutor: only those where there is direct discrimination and whose intention is clear. For example, in cases of insults on social networks, very few get extensive media coverage, so hard law is perceived as a powerful tool to use. Although there exists a very favourable policy position toward hard law with respect to the necessary repression of racial discrimination throughout society, in practice, indirect and systemic discrimination is not dealt with but rather cases of overt racism only. The selfie affair involving the national football team led to much debate in 2014/2015. A group photo posted by team member Leroy Fer on his twitter account led to racist remarks where the players were called "monkeys," "slaves," or *Zwarte Piet*. The UNHCHR published a report on August 28, 2015, encouraging the Dutch government to promote the elimination of racist representations of *Zwarte Piet* that reflect negative stereotypes of people of colour in the Netherlands.

---

[40]See: http://diversiteitinbedrijf.nl/.

[41]A number of individuals interviewed in the Netherlands, who have been active for many years in the associative network and in the Commission for Equality of Treatment, share this perception.

As underlined in interviews with an officer from the *College voor de Rechten van der Mens*, representatives from a local antidiscrimination service, and a lawyer specialised in labour law in The Hague, the small number of court decisions on indirect discrimination and civil litigation can be explained by the fact that this type of discrimination is more frequently dealt with by the *College*, i.e. outside of the legal system (even if its opinions are made public).

When recommendations made by the *College* are not implemented, an appeal is made to a civil law judge as a last resort—even though compensation remains negligible. Criminal law is mostly used to sanction cases where the aim is to remind society that discrimination is prohibited by law. From this perspective, the educational dimension of the law is what counts. Although class action suits exist in the Netherlands, they are rarely used even by the regional agencies.

In the Netherlands, perception of the role played by the law depends on the actors involved and on the type of discrimination concerned. A representative of the Ministry for Social Affairs and Employment specified that, generally speaking, government actors and the different ministries in charge of combatting discrimination are primarily interested in prevention and in eliminating stereotypes by means of widespread public campaigns, for example. Local centers involved in the fight against discrimination have adopted a more ambivalent position. They use legislation as a basis for their work, without which their mission to support and empower victims would be compromised or in vain. According to a representative from RADAR (an important regional agency), the use of law and strategic litigation remains one of their main missions, even if strategic work with different actors to deal with more systematic problems is ever-increasing. The educational potential of the law as a symbolic and compensatory arm is present, but resources and expertise in legal issues are very insufficient for this instrument to be much used. According to officials who receive victims of discrimination at *Artikel 1* Utrecht, services in small municipalities focus on listening to victims and, if needed, transferring their complaints to the *College* or other relevant organisations.

Civil associations are calling for more frequent use of the law in the struggle against indirect and systemic discrimination, and for structural problems in the areas of housing and the labour market to be made more visible. In reality, this type of issue is dealt with by the *College* and, more generally by use of soft law. In parallel to this, there is very little thinking on multiple types of discrimination. This question was not raised very often during the survey apart from mention of veiled or migrant women, but the difficulties in providing proof, of access to the law, or the visibility of these victims was not formulated as problematic for discussion. The regional agencies take the multi-criteria dimension of certain parts of their work with victims into account, but neither ministry officials, nor the police, nor the *College*, nor the prosecutors seem to take these specific situations into consideration. For many of them, the notion of intersectionality carries the risk of diluting the issue contained in the various criteria.

Thus, the question arises as to whether the division of criteria and the different problems among a number of ministries and departments, together with such a decentralised infrastructure as is in place in the Netherlands, does not finally prevent reflection on multiple and systemic discrimination.

5 Conclusion

In both the French and Dutch contexts, the same paradox arises between promoting prevention of discrimination and promoting alternative responses to the law. The crucial role of law is recognized only for the types of discrimination considered the most serious, i.e. racism and anti-Semitism. This paradox is also expressed through the setting of both a political and a legal agenda for the priority given to simplifying the law, which contrasts with expanding recognition of the complexity of prohibited discriminatory acts (which can be indirect, multiple, intersectional, coupled with harassment, offensive to basic liberties, etc.) and with the multiplication of discrimination criteria, without any real appropriation of these criteria by those involved. Does such a paradox illustrate the absence of a veritable antidiscrimination policy that "takes the law seriously"?[42]

This is the question that the above cross-case analysis ultimately raises. It reveals the existence of two models of equality both of which are undergoing profound change. Beyond the specific national context in France and the Netherlands, the emergence of a paradoxical response poses the question of convergence toward a common model based on the promotion of soft law instruments (announcements, charters, labels, etc.). More than a complement to improving the implementation of hard law, the development of soft law is in effect presented by institutional, political, and economic actors as a response that reconciles the principle of equality with the imperative of effectiveness. In both countries, this is manifested by a citizenship regime[43] that tends to include individuals in the political community along the lines of individual responsibility and mutual benefit. Such a development does not, however, preclude divergence. In the Netherlands, the importance granted to soft law is presented as a mark of general progress made against discrimination and as the beginnings of a new stage. On the other hand, in France, this development is presented as being imposed by the economic crisis and the need to deal with it pragmatically at the risk of distending the link between non-discrimination and fundamental rights.

References

Allal MT, Amellal K, Elkaïm D, El Haïte N (2010) La Halde en halte forcée, Libération, "Rebonds", December 13, 2010
Andrew G (2006) Britain, France, and EU anti-discrimination policy: the emergence of an EU policy paradigm. West Eur Polit 27(2):334–353
Beck U (1999) World risk society. Polity, Cambridge
Bertossi C, Duyvendak JW, Schain M (2012) The problems of national models of integration: a Franco-Dutch comparison. Comp Eur Polit 10(5):237–376

---

[42] According to Ronald Dworkin's expression.
[43] Cf. Jenson (2007), pp. 53–69.

Brubaker R (1992) Citizenship and nationhood in France and Germany. Harvard University Press, Cambridge
Cardi C, Devreux A-M (coord.) (2014) Cahiers du genre. "L'engendrement du droit", n° 57
d'Allonnes MR (2012) La Crise sans fin. Essai sur l'expérience moderne du temps. Seuil, Paris
Dahlerup D (2007) Electoral gender quotas: between equality of opportunity and equality of result. Representation 43(2):73–92
Dupriez V, Orianne J-F, Verhoeven M (eds) (2005) De l'école au marché du travail, l'égalité des chances en question. Peter Lang, Bruxelles
Elias N (1994) Introduction: a theoretical essay on established and outsider relations. In: Elias N, Scotson JL (eds) The established and the outsiders. A sociological enquiry into community problems. Sage Publications, London, pp 15–18
Genel K (2007) "Responsabilité morale et théorie sociale dans l'École de Francfort", Raisons politiques, n° 28, 2007/4, pp 91–109
Goldschmidt J (2012) Protecting equality as a human right in the Netherlands: from specialized equality body to human rights institute. Equal Rights Rev 8(1):32–49
Habermas J (1996) Between facts and norms, contributions to a discourse theory of law and democracy (trans: Rehg W). MIT Press, Cambridge
Iyiola S (2009) Making anti-racial discrimination law: a comparative history of social action and anti-racial discrimination law. Routledge, London
Jenson J (2007) The European Union's citizenship regime: creating norms and building practices. Comp Eur Polit 5(1):53–69
Joppke C (2007) Beyond national models: civic integration policies for immigrants in Western Europe. West Eur Polit 30(1):1–22
Junter A, Sénac-Slawinski R (2010) La diversité: sans droit ni obligation. Revue de l'OFCE 114:167–195
Martinel A, Boulos M (2011) Le défenseur des droits: un ombudsman en trompe-l'œil. Note by the Terra Nova Foundation, January 7, 2011
Miaille M (1976) Une introduction critique au droit. Maspero, Paris
Michaut F, Michelman F (2010) Le mouvement des "critical legal studies" entre républicanisme et libéralisme: préface à la session 1985 de la Cour suprême. Presses Universitaires de Laval, Québec
Norris P (1999) Critical citizens. Oxford University Press, Oxford
Norris P (2011) Democratic deficit: critical citizens revisited. Cambridge University Press, New York
Pélabay J (2013) Privatiser les valeurs publiques: La citoyenneté comme intime conviction? In: Muxel A (ed) La Vie privée des convictions: Politique, affectivité, intime. Presses de Sciences Po, Paris, pp 39–59
Pélabay J (2015) Inculquer les "valeurs de la République". L'école face aux défis d'une intégration pluraliste. Diversité, n° 182, 4 trismestre, pp 93–99
Poirmeur Y (2000) Le double jeu de l'égalité des chances. In: Koubi G, Guglielmi GJ (eds) L'égalité des chances. Analyzes, évolutions, perspectives. La Découverte, Paris
Sénac R (2012) L'invention de la diversité. Presses Universitaires de France, Paris
Valfort M-A (2015) Discriminations religieuses à l'embauche: une réalité. Institut Montaigne, Paris October 2015: http://www.institutmontaigne.org/fr/publications/discriminations-religieuses-lembauche-une-realite
Veil S (2009) Report *Redécouvrir le préambule de la Constitution* delivered to the French president in December 2008, Paris, La Documentation française
Vielle P, Pochet P, Cassiers I (dir.) (2005) L'État social actif. Vers un changement de paradigme? Bruxelles, Peter Lang.
Winter E (2011) Us, them, and others: pluralism and national identity in diverse societies. University of Toronto Press, Toronto

Réjane Sénac is a CNRS tenured researcher/lecturer at the Centre for Political Research at Sciences Po (CEVIPOF). Her publications include "The Contemporary Conversation about the French Connection 'Liberté, Egalité, Fraternité': Neoliberal Equality and 'Non-brothers'" (Revue Française de Civilisation Britannique, 2016), "Tracking Change in the French-Style Gender Gap: Through the 2012 Presidential Election" (Revue française de science politique, 2013) and Les non-frères au pays de l'égalité (Presses de Sciences Po, 2017). She focuses on public justifications of equality policies (parity, diversity, same-sex marriage, etc.).

Janie Pélabay is a FNSP Research Fellow at the Centre for Political Research (CEVIPOF) at Sciences Po Paris, with a specialization in political philosophy. Previously she was a researcher at the University of Montreal, at the University of Oxford, at the Université libre de Bruxelles and at the University of Luxembourg. She holds a PhD from the University of Paris-Sorbonne. Her publications and lectures focus on issues of value pluralism, political community and liberal integration, notably regarding the EU as well as education and immigration policies.

Lisa Ammon is a PhD candidate in political sciences at the University of Paris VIII Vincennes Saint-Denis where she teaches political sciences to undergraduate students. She holds an M.A. in Gender Studies from the University of Paris VIII and a B.A. in political sciences from the University of Freiburg (Germany).

Germany

Malte Kramme

1 Introduction and Overview of Antidiscrimination Legislation

German antidiscrimination law is not a sealed system: provisions prohibiting discrimination as well as legislative measures aiming at prevention of discrimination can be found all over the legal system.[1]

1.1 Constitutional Principle of Equal Treatment

The most basic rule of antidiscrimination law is Article 3 of the Basic Law (*Grundgesetz—GG*), the German Constitution. Its para. 1 GG provides for a general principle of equal treatment "before the law." According to this principle, a public entity must not treat two natural or legal persons in a different manner without a good reason to do so. This principle of equal treatment has a broad *personal* scope of application. Like all other fundamental rights, it is binding to all holders of public authority. The *material* scope is also very broad: it notably is not limited to certain grounds of discrimination, such as race, sex or age. The downside of this broad scope

---

Court decisions and further references were generally taken into account until 2016. Subsequent legal changes were taken into account until April 2018.

[1] For an overview of the legal grounds of antidiscrimination law, see Handbuch "Rechtlicher Diskriminierungsschutz," of the Antidiskriminierungsstelle des Bundes (2014), p. 32.

M. Kramme (✉)
University of Bayreuth, Research Centre for Consumer Law, Bayreuth, Germany
e-mail: malte.kramme@uni-bayreuth.de

© Springer International Publishing AG, part of Springer Nature 2018
M. Mercat-Bruns et al. (eds.), *Comparative Perspectives on the Enforcement and Effectiveness of Antidiscrimination Law*, Ius Comparatum – Global Studies in Comparative Law 28, https://doi.org/10.1007/978-3-319-90068-1_14

of application is that it can be restricted for any good reason justifying an unequal treatment.[2]

Para. 2 states that men and women shall have equal rights. It further obliges the state to promote the actual implementation of equal rights for women and men, and to take steps to eliminate disadvantages that now exist.

Para. 3 provides that no person shall be favoured or disfavoured because of sex, parentage, race, language, homeland and origin, faith, or religious or political opinions.[3] The requirements for the justification of unequal treatment for one of these grounds are higher than the requirements for the justification of other kinds of unequal treatment. Unequal treatment because of one of these grounds is only permissible if there are particularly serious reasons behind the justification.[4]

Legal scholars derive the impermissibility of discrimination also from Article 1 para. 1 GG, the guarantee of human dignity.[5]

Such constitutional sources of antidiscrimination law do not only prohibit discrimination. To a certain extent, they also give rise to an obligation of the state to provide for protection against discrimination.[6] Moreover, these constitutional sources of antidiscrimination law have a significant impact on legal relationships between subjects of private law when courts interpret private law stipulations, notably general clauses, under the Constitution.[7]

1.2 General Equal Treatment Act

The most elaborate source of antidiscrimination law in the German legal system is the General Equal Treatment Act (*Allgemeines Gleichbehandlungsgesetz—AGG*) of

---

[2]For a wealth of details developed in decades of vivid jurisdiction, see *P. Kirchhof* in: Maunz and Dürig (2015), Article 3, para. 72 et seq.; *Kischel* in: Beck'scher Online-Kommentar GG, 26th edn (2015), Article 3, para. 64 et seq.

[3]Disability is referred to in Article 3 para. 3 sentence 2 stating that it is prohibited to disfavor a person because of his disability. Accordingly, it is permissible that a disabled person is favored.

[4]*Kischel* in: Beck'scher Online-Kommentar GG, (2015), Article 3, para. 214. See also *Krieger* in: Schmidt-Bleibtreu et al. (2014), Art. 3, para. 62.

[5]*Höfling* in: Sachs (2011), Article 1, para. 33; *Mahlmann* (2013), p. 8.

[6]*Krieger* in: Schmidt-Bleibtreu et al. (2014), Article 3, para. 62; *Mahlmann* (2013), p. 28.

[7]See, for the impact of Article 3 para. 2 GG, the decision of the Federal Constitutional Court, official collection (BVerfGE), volume 89, p. 285; for further details, see *Grünberger* (2013), p. 298; see also *Mahlmann* (2013), p. 6.

14 August 2006.[8] It implements four Directives of the European Union into German law.[9] According to its Section 1, the purpose of the Act is to prevent or to stop discrimination on the grounds of race or ethnic origin, gender, religion or belief, disability, age, or sexual orientation.

1.2.1 Application in Labour Law

Its material scope encompasses labour law, notably conditions for access to dependent employment and self-employment, employment and working conditions, irrespective of whether the employer is a private or public entity.[10] It does not only prohibit discrimination of employees, but it also obliges the employer to take measures necessary to ensure protection against discrimination, including preventive measures.[11]

If an employee feels discriminated against by her or his employer or superior, by another employee or a third party, she or he is permitted to file a complaint with the employer.[12] If the employer knows about a case of harassment or sexual harassment and takes no or obviously unsuitable measures to stop the harassment, the affected employees can refuse performance without loss of pay insofar as this is necessary for their protection.[13] The employer can be held liable for damages even if an employee or a third party has committed the discriminatory conduct, provided that the conduct can be attributed to the employer.[14]

---

[8] English translations of provisions of the AGG in this text are based on the translation of the Federal Antidiskrimination Agency, see http://www.antidiskriminierungsstelle.de/SharedDocs/Downloads/DE/publikationen/AGG/agg_in_englischer_Sprache.pdf; jsessionid=45944B11C2A7836C9B7295CCC40C286C.2_cid322?__blob=publicationFile&v=2, date of last access: 30 January 2016.

[9] Directive 2000/43/EC of 29 June 2000, implementing the principle of equal treatment between persons irrespective of racial or ethnic origin (OJ L 180, 19.7.2000, p. 22); Directive 2000/78/EC of 27 November 2000, establishing a general framework for equal treatment in employment and occupation (OJ L 303, 2.12.2000, p. 16); Directive 2002/73/EC (OJ L 269, 5.10.2002, p. 15 (recasted by: Directive 2006/54/EC of 5 July 2006), on the implementation of the principle of equal opportunities and equal treatment of men and women in matters of employment and occupation (OJ L 204 of 26 July 2006, p. 23); and Council Directive 2004/113/EC of 13 December 2004, implementing the principle of equal treatment between men and women in the access to and supply of goods and services (OJ L 373, 21.12.2004, p. 37).

[10] For the application on public-law employers, see Section 24 AGG.

[11] See Section 12 para. 1 AGG.

[12] See Section 13 AGG.

[13] See Section 14 AGG.

[14] See Section 15 para. 1 AGG.

1.2.2 Application in Private Law

Moreover, the General Equal Treatment Act applies to the access to and supply of goods and services that are available to the public, including housing.[15] However, the regulation of legal relations in this field of law is less intense—it is focused on the prohibition of discrimination for the formation and execution of private insurance contracts and (other) mass contracts.[16]

1.3 Further Sources of Antidiscrimination Law in the German Legal System

Further sources of antidiscrimination law can be found in public law especially. They appear predominantly in the form of stipulations concretising the aforementioned constitutional provisions, notably aiming to enhance the situation of disabled persons[17] or the situation of women in public employment relationships.[18]

The German states (*Bundesländer*) also enact antidiscrimination laws.[19] For example, the Bavarian Equality Act for Disabled Persons (*Bayerisches Behindertengleichstellungsgesetz*) aims at providing accessible State buildings, transportation and internet services (*Barrierefreiheit*).

2 Is Antidiscrimination Law Enforced?

As shown above, in the German legal system, various stipulations can be found dealing with antidiscrimination law.[20] Nearly all of these stipulations are enforceable legal positions.[21] The extent to which affected persons make use of these possibilities in practice is difficult to assess. There are only few statistic recordings of discrimination cases. According to a study carried out between summer 2006 and December 2009, 147 courts reported 1113 discrimination cases, 90% of which fell

---

[15] For the scope of application in detail, see Section 2 AGG.

[16] For further details, see Section 19 AGG and below in question no. 9.

[17] See, for example, the Federal Equal Opportunities for People with Disabilities Act (*Behindertengleichstellungsgesetz*, BGG).

[18] See, for example, the Federal Equality Act (*Bundesgleichstellungsgesetz*) or the Federal Equality Act for Soldiers (*Soldatengleichstellungsgesetz*, SGleiG).

[19] This includes the prohibition of discrimination in the State Constitutions. For an overview of the provisions in States' constitutions and their differences from the Federal constitution, see Mahlmann (2013), p. 27.

[20] For an overview of these stipulations, see question no. 9.

[21] For details, see questions no. 2 and no. 6.

under the jurisdiction of labour courts. However, only 0.2% of all cases at labour courts relate to the AGG.[22]

The Federal Antidiscrimination Agency publishes an overview of court decisions regarding antidiscrimination law. It confirms the statement of the study that the vast majority of court decisions deal with cases in the field of labour law, while there are only a few cases in other civil law fields.[23] However, this overview does not claim to be comprehensive.[24]

3 How Is Antidiscrimination Law Enforced?

How antidiscrimination law is enforced depends on whether a private person or a public authority is responsible for the discriminatory conduct.

3.1 Enforcement in the Private Sector

If a private person is responsible for the discrimination, the enforcement of the applicable antidiscrimination laws is predominantly organised under civil law. Notably, a violation of the AGG is not treated as a criminal or administrative offense and is not fined.

Persons suffering from discrimination are granted claims for abatement, injunction and compensation of material and immaterial losses. Such rights are provided for by the AGG. However, there is no specific regime for the judicial enforcement of the rights granted under the AGG.[25] Thus, in principle, the general rules regarding judicial enforcement apply as a default: In civil law, affected persons may bring an action before the courts of general jurisdiction (*ordentliche Gerichte*). If the court upholds the plaintiff's claim in a final or provisionally enforceable decision, the plaintiff may request their enforcement according to the general rules of enforcement law which are set out in the 8th book of the Code of Civil Procedure (*Zivilprozessordnung—ZPO*). In the field of labour law, specialised labour courts (*Arbeitsgerichte*) have jurisdiction. However, a comparable procedure applies.

The AGG provides only for certain modifications concerning the enforcement:

---

[22]*Mahlmann* (2013), p. 103.

[23]For the overview, see http://www.antidiskriminierungsstelle.de/SharedDocs/Downloads/DE/publikationen/Rechtsprechungsübersicht/rechtsprechungsuebersicht_zum_antidiskriminierungsrecht.pdf?__blob=publicationFile, date of last access: 30 January 2016.

[24]See overview, p. 4 ("ausgewählte Entscheidungen").

[25]*Mahlmann* (2013), p. 103.

- Section 22 AGG provides for an easement of the burden of proof: If the party who claims to be discriminated against demonstrates facts from which it can be presumed that said discrimination has taken place, the defendant then has to prove that he has not committed any discrimination.[26]
- Section 23 para. 2 AGG allows disadvantaged persons to seek assistance from antidiscrimination organisations in court proceedings.

Besides enforcement by means of individual actions, organisations can be entitled to initiate court proceedings in certain cases laid down by law.[27]

3.2 Enforcement in Public Employment Law and Other Fields of Public Law

With regard to discrimination in employment relationships, the public sector is also bound by the AGG.[28] Additionally, Article 33 para. 2 GG guarantees equal chances for access to public offices; every German shall be equally eligible for any public office according to his aptitude, qualifications and professional achievements. The candidate who meets these three criteria the most in a recruitment procedure may derive a right to be appointed from Article 33 para. 2 GG.[29]

In other fields of public law, authorities are bound by Article 3 GG: the general principle of equal treatment.[30] According this principle, public authorities must not treat two natural or legal persons in a different manner without a good reason.[31] This principle applies to all state activities.

If an individual is discriminated against by a decision or administrative action, the affected person may initiate judicial review of the discriminatory activity before administrative courts (*Verwaltungsgerichte*), according to administrative procedural law.

---

[26]However, Section 22 is interpreted relatively strictly. The reversal of the burden of proof is limited to the question of if a case of unequal treatment is based on one of the discriminatory grounds outlawed by the AGG. See Kocher in: Schiek (2007), § 22, para. 10. See also *Mahlmann* (2013), p. 108/109 emphasising that Section 22 AGG does not apply in (public law) proceedings before administrative courts, as these proceedings are inquisitorial. See also *Schnabel*, p. 173; *Gaier* in: Gaier/Wendtland (2006), AGG, p. 66 et seq.

[27]For details, see question no. 3.

[28]Depending on the nature of the claim, either administrative courts (*Verwaltungsgerichte*) or ordinary courts have jurisdiction. If administrative courts have jurisdiction, the enforcement of their judgments is stipulated in Section 167 et seq. of the Code for Administrative Court Procedure (*Verwaltungsgerichtsordnung—VwGO*).

[29]This applies equally to citizens of other EU Member States. See *Hense* in: Beck'scher Online-Kommentar (2015), Article 33, para. 21.

[30]For more details regarding Article 3 para. 3, see "Introduction."

[31]See "Introduction."

Germany   263

3.3 Alternative Dispute Resolution

Discrimination cases can also be settled by means of alternative dispute resolution (ADR). ADR bodies exist for this purpose in many sectors and branches. For disputes regarding obligations stemming from sales contracts or service contracts between a trader established in the EU and a consumer resident in the EU, the Directive 2013/11/EU on alternative dispute resolution (and its implementation Act)[32] allow every consumer to submit their case to an ADR body. Settlements facilitated by such bodies are usually not directly enforceable, but if they become binding according to the procedural rules of the respective ADR body, they lead to a justiciable right.[33] However, ADR does not play a major role in the enforcement of antidiscrimination law.

4 Who Enforces Antidiscrimination Law?

4.1 Affected Person

As a general principle of German civil procedural law, a person who is entitled to a certain claim under material law may bring an action before the courts in order to enforce this claim.[34] The most common tools of private enforcement of antidiscrimination law are claims for abatement and, if the discriminatory conduct is likely to be repeated, injunction. An affected person may also be entitled to damages for material and immaterial losses.[35]

4.2 Antidiscrimination Organisations

Further actors in the field of enforcing antidiscrimination law are antidiscrimination organisations.[36] According to Section 23 para. 2 AGG, such organisations are

---

[32] The Implementation Act came into force on 1 April 2016.

[33] For details about the enforceability of ADR settlements in German law, see *Prütting* (2015), p. 157 et seq.

[34] This applies *mutatis mutandis* in the field of administrative procedural law, notably if an individual is discriminated against by an administrative decision or activity.

[35] For details see question no. 6.

[36] Section 23 AGG implements Article 7 para. 2 Directive 2000/43/EC, Article 9 para. 2 Directive 2000/78/EC, Article 8 para. 3 Directive 2004/113/EC and Article 17 para. 2 Directive 2006/54/EC into German law. See *Benecke* in: Beck-Online Großkommentar (2015), § 23 AGG, para. 1. Such rights to assist are limited to organisations with the statutory purpose to safeguard the interests of persons or groups facing discrimination for one of the grounds to which the AGG is applicable. The organisation must have at least 75 members or must be an association comprising seven or more organisations.

authorised to act as legal advisors to affected persons in court hearings (*Beistände in der Verhandlung*). This includes accompanying the affected person to court hearings and speaking in her or his name, provided that the affected person gives her or his consent to do so. The statements made by an advising organisation are deemed to be submissions by the party unless the latter immediately recasts or corrects such statements.[37] However, the organisation is neither entitled to litigate in its own name on the affected person's behalf (*Prozessstandschaft*)[38] nor to act as a representative for the affected person (*Prozessvertretung*).[39]

Antidiscrimination organisations are generally not entitled to initiate legal proceedings in their own name on their behalf (*Verbandsklagerecht*), either. This principle is subject to the following exemptions:

- According to Section 85 (formerly: Section 63) of the 9th Book of the Social Code (*Sozialgesetzbuch IX*), dealing with the social benefits for disabled persons, in case of a violation of a person's right listed therein, organisations with the statutory purpose to represent disabled persons may file a suit with the consent of the affected person.[40]
- According to Section 15 (formerly: Section 13) Federal Equal Opportunities for People with Disabilities Act (*Behindertengleichstellungsgesetz—BGG*), an organisation may file a suit if a public authority violates certain provisions of the BGG. In such actions, it is irrelevant if individual rights of a disabled person have been violated. Since its coming into force on 1 May 2002, there has been only one lawsuit reported that is based on Section 15 BGG.[41] It concerned the accessibility of a rebuilt train station.[42]
- If the employer commits a gross violation of a provision set out in Section 6 to 18 AGG, the works council (*Betriebsrat*) or a trade union (*Gewerkschaft*) in the enterprise may apply to the labour court for an order requiring the employer to cease and desist from an act, allowing an act to be performed, or performing an act (Section 17 para. 2 AGG).[43]
- Registered consumer protection organisations[44] may, according to the Act on Injunctive Relief (*Unterlassungsklagengesetz*), initiate court actions for injunctions if standard terms and conditions violate the AGG or other mandatory

---

[37]This follows from Section 90 para. 2 ZPO and from Section 67 para. 7 VwGO.

[38]*Benecke* in: Beck-Online Großkommentar (2015), § 23 AGG, para. 12.

[39]For details, see *Schnabel* (2014), p. 141.

[40]For details, see *Majerski-Pahlen* in: Neumann et al. (2010), § 63 SGB IX, para. 1 et seq.; *Kossens* in: Kossens et al. (2015), § 63 SGB IX, para. 1 et seq.

[41]See *Dopatka* in: Kossens et al. (2015), § 13 BGG, para. 12.

[42]Federal Administrative Court (*Bundesverwaltungsgericht—BVerwG*), decision of 5 April 2006—9 C 1/05, NVwZ 2006, p. 817.

[43]This only applies to enterprises in which the conditions pursuant to Section 1 para. 1 sentence 1 Works Constitution Act are present. Thus, it does not apply to small businesses.

[44]See Section 4 Act on Injunctive Relief.

provisions.[45] They may also initiate court proceedings if consumer protection provisions are violated in other ways than through general terms and conditions.[46] It is argued that Sections 19 and 20 AGG prohibiting certain discriminatory conduct in civil law relations are properly classified as such consumer protection provisions.[47]
- A violation of the AGG may conceivably be deemed a case of unfair competition.[48] If so, besides consumer protection associations, associations promoting commercial or independent professional interests (*Verbände zur Förderung gewerblicher oder selbständiger beruflicher Interesse*) as well as Chambers of Industry and Commerce or Craft (*Industrie- und Handelskammern*) could initiate court proceedings.[49]
- Finally, there is a legal debate whether antidiscrimination organisations may initiate legal proceedings if an affected person has transferred his claims to that organisation.[50]

4.3 Federal Antidiscrimination Agency

The Federal Antidiscrimination Agency arose after the AGG came into force in 2006. Beside its work in public relations and with measures to prevent discrimination, it is the Agency's task to assist persons who have suffered discrimination in enforcing their rights. For details about the Agency's tasks, see question 7.

4.4 Trade Offices (Gewerbeämter)

If a commercial enterprise violates antidiscrimination laws in a consistent manner, this gives rise to doubts as to its reliability and could entitle the trade office to shut down the business.[51] However, there is no data available on if trade offices have

---

[45] OLG Schleswig, Decision of 11 December 2015, BeckRS 2016, 02570; BGH, Decision vom 26 Januray 1983—VIII ZR 342/81, NJW 1983, p. 1320 (p. 1322); *Micklitz* in: Krüger et al. (2013), § 1 UKlaG, para. 14.
[46] See Section 4 Act on Injunctive Relief.
[47] *Köhler* in: Köhler and Bornkamm (2016), § 2 UKlaG, para. 2; OLG Schleswig, decision of 11 December 2015, BeckRS 2016, 02570, para. 27 has left this question unanswered; for the contrary view see *Bassenge* in Palandt (2015), § 2 UKlaG, para. 4.
[48] See Ohly in: Ohly and Sosnitza (2014), § 4 para. 11/80. However, there are no apparent court decisions on this question.
[49] See Section 8 Unfair Competition Act (*Gesetz gegen den unlauteren Wettbewerb—UWG*).
[50] *Benecke* in: Beck-Online Großkommentar (2015), § 23 AGG, para. 21; Monen (2008), p. 214.
[51] See Section 35 Trade Law (*Gewerbeordnung*); for details, see Kühn and Klose (2012), p. 1443 (1447); but see *Lindner* (2008), p. 436.

actually ever prohibited the operation of businesses due to violations of antidiscrimination law.

5 Who Benefits from the Enforcement of Antidiscrimination Law?

5.1 Employees

In light of the court decisions dealing foremost with labour law, employees suffering from discrimination are benefitted the most from the enforcement of antidiscrimination law. By contrast, there are relatively few decisions regarding antidiscrimination law in other fields of private law.[52]

Upon closer inspection, most cases deal with discrimination on the grounds of gender, age and disability; there are few cases regarding ethnic or religious discrimination. This finding does not offer a clear answer to the question of if the benefit varies depending on the ground of discrimination. It has to be taken into consideration that a small number of court proceedings could indicate either a rather high degree of compliance with the legal standards or the inadequacy of the existing enforcement regime to deal with specific grounds of discrimination.

Effects of the introduction of the AGG are noticeable also outside of court activities. Recruitment advertisements use more and more non-discriminatory wording, notably by addressing both men and women. These changes could be interpreted to conclude that enforcement of antidiscrimination leads to a benefit not only of the plaintiffs but also of all employees who could potentially be disadvantaged by discrimination. Ultimately, it remains unclear how often discrimination appears under the guise of formal equality.[53]

5.2 Particularly: Female Employees in the Public Sector

Equal Opportunity Officers (*Gleichstellungsbeauftragte*) participate in recruitment processes of public authorities with more than 100 employees in order to make the decision-making process regarding staffing choices more transparent and

---

[52]See Overview of selected Court Decisions, published by the Federal Antidiscrimination Agency, http://www.antidiskriminierungsstelle.de/SharedDocs/Downloads/DE/publikationen/Rechtsprechungs%C3%BCbersicht/rechtsprechungsuebersicht_zum_antidiskriminierungsrecht.pdf?__blob=publicationFile, last accessed: 20 February 2016.

[53]See *Pfeiffer*, p. 15 et seq.

objective.⁵⁴ Section 8 Federal Equality Act (*Bundesgleichstellungsgesetz—BGleiG*, BGleiG) may also enhance the career opportunities for women in the public sector, prescribing that women must be given priority over equally qualified men in staffing choices if they are underrepresented in the specific sector.⁵⁵

6 Who Is Harmed by the Enforcement of Antidiscrimination Law?

6.1 Persons Bound by Antidiscrimination Laws

The enforcement of antidiscrimination law may harm the persons obliged by the relevant antidiscrimination laws. As the main field of application of antidiscrimination law is employment relations, employers could be regarded as the most affected group. Notably, there are three burdening factors:

In order to comply with the obligations of antidiscrimination law, it is not sufficient that the employer refrains from discriminatory conduct. In fact, pursuant to Section 12 para. 1 AGG, the employer is obliged to take measures to ensure protection against discrimination, including preventive measures. If the employer does not take such measures, she or he can be held liable for organisational faults if a discrimination case arises.⁵⁶

Employers are not only held liable for their own discriminatory conduct, but also for the discriminatory conduct of their employees and other third parties whom the employer makes use of in the course of business.⁵⁷

The enforcement of antidiscrimination law is said to lead to a rise of bureaucratic costs for the employers, caused by increased documentation.⁵⁸ Such documentation efforts are triggered by the easement of the burden of proof according to Section 22 AGG: If the party who claims to be discriminated against provides indications of discrimination, the employer (as the defendant) has to prove that he has not breached antidiscrimination laws. Being able to provide such evidence requires detailed documentation of work processes in HR departments. These documentation duties also affect insurance companies and companies concentrating on bulk business, which are also bound by the AGG when making such contracts.

---

[54] See Section 25 Federal Equalitiy Act (*Bundesgleichstellungsgesetz*, BGleiG).
[55] This applies *mutatis mutandis* to men if they are under-represented (Section 8 para. 1 sentence 5 Federal Equality Act).
[56] Kocher (2007), § 15 AGG, para. 22; *Benecke* in: Beck-Online Großkommentar (2017), § 15 AGG, para. 20.
[57] For details, see Kocher (2007), § 15 AGG, para. 21 et seq.; *Benecke* in: Beck-Online Großkommentar (2017), § 15 AGG, para. 21 et seq.
[58] *Monen* (2008), p. 233 et seq. For thoughts on an economic analysis of civil-law-governed antidiscrimination law, see *Kirchner* (2008), p. 37.

6.2 Discrimination by Positive Measures?

According to Section 5 AGG, unequal treatment shall be permissible where suitable and appropriate measures are adopted to prevent or to compensate for existing disadvantages in one of the discriminatory grounds outlawed by the AGG.[59] Such positive measures may affect others who do not have the attribute of the group that is intended to be protected by the positive measure. Therefore, such positive measures are subject to strict requirements of proportionality.[60]

One of the most common positive measures is to give priority to a female candidate for a job offer over an equally suitable male candidate, when females are under-represented in the specific sector. For the public (federal) sector, Section 8 Federal Equality Act prescribes such a preference for the candidate of the under-represented sex.[61] The European Court of Justice declared such measures (and thus, naturally, their enforcement) to be admissible. The Court argued, "[T]he mere fact that a male candidate and a female candidate are equally qualified does not mean that they have the same chances"[62]: "Prejudices and stereotypes concerning the role and capacities of women in working life" could decrease women's chances on the job market.[63] As, in the view of the ECJ, such measures involve discrimination on grounds of sex,[64] specific criteria in the individual case must be examined to see if they tilt "the balance in favour of the male candidate ('saving clause')."[65]

---

[59]The Federal Antidiscrimination Agency lists the following examples of positive measures.
In the field of labour:

- Purposeful recruiting methods and scholarships for disadvantaged groups of persons,
- Implementation of diversity training programmes at companies,
- In-plant agreements to promote diversity within the workforce,
- Preferential employment of disadvantaged groups of persons and management by objectives,
- Flexible quota arrangements.

In the field of goods and services:

- Special conditions of soft loans to disadvantaged groups of persons,
- Quotas of allocation of housing preferably to disadvantaged persons,
- Special opening hours in public baths.

See www.antidiskriminierungsstelle.de/SharedDocs/Downloads/DE/publikationen/Factsheets/factsheet_engl_positive_massnahmen.pdf?__blob=publicationFile, last accessed: 28 February 2016.

[60]*Roloff* in: Beck'scher Online-Kommentar Arbeitsrecht (2015), 38. edition, § 5 AGG, para. 3.

[61]This applies *mutatis mutandis* to men, if they are under-represented (Section 8 para. 1 sentence 5 Federal Equality Act).

[62]ECJ, Decision of 11 November 1997, C-409/95, para. 30.

[63]ECJ, Decision of 11 November 1997, C-409/95, para. 29.

[64]ECJ, Decision of 11 November 1997, C-409/95, para. 23.

[65]ECJ, Decision of 11 November 1997, C-409/95, para. 33.

Since 1 May 2015, Section 96 para. 2 Stock Corporation Act (*Aktiengesetz*) provides for a quota for women (or men) of at least 30% in the supervisory boards of listed stock corporations, without providing for a saving clause.[66] Measured against the above standards of the ECJ, legal scholars doubt the legitimacy of such a strict quota.[67]

7 What Remedies Are Provided by the Enforcement of Antidiscrimination Law?

While the material rules of German antidiscrimination law are based largely on the European Directives, such Directives leave the member states wide discretion on how to enforce these rules. Article 15 Directive 2000/43/EC, Article 17 Directive 2000/78/EC, Article 14 2004/113/EC and Article 25 Directive 2006/54/EC only set forth that the member states shall lay down rules on penalties for infringements of the national provisions in order to implement the Directives. Such penalties shall be "effective, proportionate and dissuasive."[68]

While some member states decided to establish an administrative enforcement regime allowing public authorities to impose fines for infringements of antidiscrimination law,[69] in Germany the enforcement of antidiscrimination law, and thus the provided remedies, falls under the purview of civil law.[70]

7.1 Remedies in Private Labour Law

In private labour law, a person affected by discriminatory conduct has the following remedies:

- Section 13 para. 1 AGG sets forth an out-of-court right of complaint. Employees shall have the right to file a complaint with the relevant department in the firm when they feel discriminated against by their employer, superior, another employee, or a third party in connection with their employment. In such a case, the employer shall investigate and inform the employee of the outcome.

---

[66]Provided that the stock corporation falls under the scope of the Co-Determination Act.

[67]*Grünberger/Block* in: Beck-Online Großkommentar (2015), § 5 AGG, para. 63.

[68]By contrast, precise specifications regarding the remedies are rare, but do exist. According to Article 6 para. 2 Directive 2002/73/EC Member States shall "ensure real and effective compensation or reparation as the Member States so determine for the loss and damage sustained by a person injured as a result of discrimination." See *Stoffels* (2009), p. 204 (205); see also *Busche* (2008), p. 159 (163).

[69]See question no. 13.

[70]*Stoffels* (2009), p. 204 (205). See also question no. 2.

- If the employer becomes aware of a case of harassment or sexual harassment in the workplace and does not take sufficient action to stop it, Section 14 AGG entitles the affected employee to refuse to perform his or her obligations under the contract without loss of pay insofar as it is necessary for her or his protection.
- An employee may request damages from her or his employer for material and immaterial losses. This requires that the employer has committed discriminatory conduct or that the discriminatory conduct of a third person that he uses to perform his obligations (notably other employees) is attributed to her or him.[71] However, according to Section 15 para. 1 Sentence 2 AGG, the employer can ward off the compensation of material losses if she or he proves that the discriminatory act has not been committed in a faulty manner (*Vertretenmüssen*). Such a fault would usually require negligence in the meaning of Section 276 German Civil Code.[72]

If a person suffered discrimination during a recruitment process, the compensation for immaterial losses shall not exceed three monthly salaries if the affected person would not have been hired through an equal recruitment process.

- Section 15 para. 6 AGG expressly stresses that an employer's violation of AGG will not justify a claim to the establishment of an employment or apprenticeship relationship, or to a promotion.
- According to Section 16 para. 1 AGG, an employee may refuse to carry out instructions violating the antidiscriminatory provisions of the AGG.

7.2 Remedies in Public Labour Law

The provisions of the AGG apply *mutatis mutandis* to employment relationships in the public sector.[73] However, an applicant for a position as a civil servant (*Beamter*)

---

[71] *Stoffels* (2009), p. 204 (207).

[72] This possibility of exculpation is regarded to be contrary to the European Directives, see *Roloff* in: Beck'scher Online-Kommentar, § 15 AGG, para. 2; *Stoffels* (2009), p. 204 (207). Thus, some authors are of the opinion that national courts shall disapply Section 15 para. 1 sentence 2 AGG, see *Schlachter* in: Müller-Glöge et al. (2016), § 15 AGG, para. 6. For immaterial losses, Section 15 para. 3 sets forth a liability privilege if the discrimination arises out of the application of collective bargaining agreements. In such cases, the employer shall be held liable if she or he acted with intent or with gross negligence. For details, see *Benecke* in: Beck-Online Großkommentar (2015), § 15 AGG, para. 68 et seq.

[73] See Section 24 AGG.

who is discriminated against in the recruitment process may under certain circumstances file a claim before the administrative courts to be appointed to the said position.[74]

7.3 Remedies in Private Law (Other Than Employment Law)

If discrimination occurs in other fields of private law, the AGG provides for the following remedies:

- A disadvantaged person may, according to Section 21 para. 1 AGG, demand that the discriminatory conduct be stopped. If a person bound by Section 21 AGG has refused to enter into a contract with another person on discriminatory grounds, it is highly debatable if this includes the obligation to conclude said contract (*Kontrahierungszwang*).[75]
- If there is a risk that the discriminatory conduct will be continued, the affected person may sue for an injunction.[76]
- The disadvantaged person may further claim damages for material losses, unless the person committing the discrimination is not responsible for the breach of duty, i.e. the discriminatory act has not been committed with intention or negligence. But the person committing the discrimination is obliged to compensate immaterial losses without the possibility of exculpation.[77]

In cases where the AGG is not applicable, the general tortious liability regime of Section 823 para. 1 BGB may give rise to claims for injunctions and damages. This requires that the discrimination has led to a violation of one's general right of personality (*allgemeines Persönlichkeitsrecht*). If there is contractual nexus between the parties, discriminatory conduct might violate the contractual duties of protection and care, giving rise to compensation claims pursuant to Section 280 para. 1 and Section 241 para. 2 BGB.[78]

---

[74] According to Article 33 para. 2 GG, every German shall be equally eligible for any public office according to his aptitude, qualifications and professional achievements. See also question no. 2.

[75] In favor of an obligation to close a contract: *Grünberger/Block* in: Beck-Online Großkommentar (2015), § 21 AGG, para. 38 et seq.; *Grünberger* (2013), S. 729 (with further references). See also *Gaier* in: Gaier/Wendtland (2006), p. 104 et seq.; see also *Schmidt-Kessel* (2006), p. 53 (p. 64 et seq.) giving an overview on European legal systems.

[76] Section 21 para. 1 Sentence 2 AGG.

[77] *Lingemann* in Prütting et al. (2015), § 21 AGG, para. 4.

[78] *Grünberger/Block* in: Beck-Online Großkommentar, § 21 AGG, para. 98 et seq.

8 Who Supports the Enforcement of Antidiscrimination Law?

8.1 Federal Antidiscrimination Agency

The Federal Antidiscrimination Agency (*Antidiskriminierungsstelle des Bundes*) shall assist affected persons suffering from discrimination in enforcing their rights.[79] Such assistance may involve providing information concerning claims and possible legal action, arranging for advice to be provided by others, and endeavouring to achieve out-of-court settlements between the parties.[80]

In order to settle a dispute, the Agency may request that the parties make submissions (if the person who has turned to the Agency has consented thereto).[81] If the other party is a Federal authority (*Bundesbehörde*) or another Federal public office (*sonstige öffentliche Stelle im Bereich des Bundes*), such authority is obliged to assist and to supply the requested information insofar as data protection law is not affected.[82]

8.2 Commissioners for Matters Relating to Disabled Persons

According to Section 17 Act on Equal Opportunities of Disabled People (*Behindertengleichstellungsgesetz, BGG*), the Federal cabinet appoints a Federal Government Commissioner for Matters relating to Disabled Persons (*Bundesbeauftragter für die Belange behinderter Menschen*) each legislative term.[83] The Commissioner has to work towards equal living conditions for people with and without disabilities, within all areas of social life.[84] In doing so, "the Commissioner is consulted by the federal ministries on all legislative, regulatory and other major projects bearing on the integration of disabled persons. Where the applicable legislation has negative consequences for disabled people, the

---

[79] See Section 27 para. 2 AGG. Between August 2006 and December 2010, the Agency had 7875 "contacts concerning the AGG." See *Mahlmann*, p. 114.
[80] See Section 27 AGG.
[81] See Section 28 para. 1 AGG.
[82] See Section 28 para. 2 AGG.
[83] The Commissioner is assisted by fulltime co-workers at his disposal who support him in fulfilling his tasks. See http://www.behindertenbeauftragte.de/EN/Englisch.html?nn=2950120#doc2967342bodyText2, date of last access: 18 February 2016.
[84] See Section 15 BGG.

Commissioner shall strive for amendments in their interest and shall ensure that their interests are duly taken into account in any new project."[85]

However, the Commissioner has no power to directly influence the enforcement of antidiscrimination law case by case. Notably, he or she does not provide legal advice and has no power to interfere in lawsuits or administrative procedures.[86] Moreover, the jurisdiction of the Federal Commissioner is limited to the Federal level. If state issues are concerned, Commissioners of the states are responsible, such as the Bavarian Commissioner for Disabled Persons (Article 17 Bavarian Act on Equal Opportunities for Disabled Peoples).

8.3 Equal Opportunity Commissioners (Gleichstellungsbeauftragte)

In Federal public authorities with 100 employees or more, female employees elect an Equal Opportunity Commissioner. She is mandated to promote and supervise the enforcement of the Federal Equality Act (*Bundesgleichstellungsgesetz—BGleiG*) and of the AGG. In the performance of her tasks, she shall be involved in all measures of the public authority concerning gender equality. This includes participation in recruitment procedures.

There are comparable provisions for the appointment of Equal Opportunity Commissioners in public authorities on the state level.[87]

8.4 Private Antidiscrimination Organisations

Pursuant to Section 23 para. 3 AGG, disadvantaged persons can entrust antidiscrimination organisations with managing their legal affairs (*Besorgung von Rechtsangelegenheiten*). They can advise the affected person and represent her or him in out-of-court matters (*außergerichtliche Vertretung*).[88] According to Section 23 para. 2 they can also act as legal advisors to disadvantaged persons in court hearings.

---

[85] http://www.behindertenbeauftragte.de/EN/Englisch.html?nn=2950120#doc2967342bodyText2, date of last access: 18 February 2016.

[86] http://www.behindertenbeauftragte.de/EN/Englisch.html?nn=2950120#doc2967342bodyText2, date of last access: 18 February 2016.

[87] See for example Bavarian Act on the Equality of Women and Men (*Bayerisches Gleichstellungsgesetz, BayGlG*).

[88] *Benecke* in: Beck-Online Großkommentar (2015), § 23 AGG, para. 20; Section 23 para. 2 AGG; for details, see question no. 3.

8.5 Worker's Councils and Trade Unions

According to Section 17 para. 2 AGG, worker's councils and trade unions represented in the company have a right to initiate court action in order to stop a gross violation of antidiscrimination laws.[89]

9 Who Opposes the Enforcement of Antidiscrimination Law?

In the course of the implementation of the European Directives into German law by introduction of the AGG, business associations representing companies bound by the new regulation argued to restrict the implementation to the absolute minimum prescribed by the Directives (one-to-one implementation).[90] They were particularly opposed to the possibility of compensation for immaterial losses, the fact that such compensation does not require that the breach of law is conducted in a faulty manner (*Vertretenmüssen*), the rights of the antidiscrimination organisations to assist disadvantaged persons in the enforcement procedure, and the right of work councils and trade unions to initiate court proceedings.[91] Legal scholars also criticized the introduction of the AGG, mainly for its interference with the principle of private autonomy (*Privatautonomie*).[92]

---

[89]For further details, see question no. 3.

[90]See, for example, the statements of the German Employers Association: http://webarchiv.bundestag.de/archive/2005/0825/parlament/gremien15/a12/Oeffentliche_Sitzungen/20050307/18.pdf, last access to website: 21 February 2016; the statements of the Federal Association of German Associations for Commercial Agencies and Distribution (CDH) of 22 May 2006, http://www.bundesgerichtshof.de/SharedDocs/Downloads/DE/Bibliothek/Gesetzesmaterialien/16_wp/antidiskrg/stellung_cdh_24_mai_06.pdf?__blob=publicationFile, last access to website: 21 February 2016; the statements of the German Chamber of Commerce (DIHK), see http://webarchiv.bundestag.de/archive/2005/0825/parlament/gremien15/a12/Oeffentliche_Sitzungen/20050307/5.pdf, last access to website: 22 February 2016.

[91]Statement of the German Employers Association (BDA), see http://webarchiv.bundestag.de/archive/2005/0825/parlament/gremien15/a12/Oeffentliche_Sitzungen/20050307/18.pdf, last access to website: 21 February 2016; see also Statement of the German Chamber of Commerce (DIHK), http://webarchiv.bundestag.de/archive/2005/0825/parlament/gremien15/a12/Oeffentliche_Sitzungen/20050307/5.pdf, last access to website: 22 February 2016.

[92]See, for example, Säcker (2004), pp. 16 and 19; *Pfeiffer*, p. 15 et seq., *Monen* (2008), p. 228; *Adomeit* (2002), p. 1622. But see *Schmidt-Kessel* (2006), pp. 53 and 71 emphasising as the result of a comparative law overview that the relevance of general discrimination prohibitions in civil law is rather low.

10 How Broad Is the Coverage of Antidiscrimination Law?

The coverage of antidiscrimination law is rather broad. Provisions aiming to protect individuals from discrimination can be found throughout the whole legal system, *inter alia:*

10.1 Public Law

- According to Article 3 German Constitution (*Grundgesetz*, *GG*), public authorities must not treat two natural or legal persons in a different manner without a good reason.[93]
- Article 33 para. 2 GG provides for a right of for equal chances for access to public offices.
- Disability Law: The Federal Equal Opportunities for People with Disabilities Act (*Behindertengleichstellungsgesetz*) aims not only at prohibiting discrimination, but also provides for mechanisms to enhance the situation of disabled people. In so doing, it introduces the principle of accessibility (*Barrierefreiheit*) as a target definition. According to its Section 8, new buildings shall conform to the technical standards of accessibility. Further, people with disabilities are entitled to various social benefits according to the 9th Book of the Social Code (*Sozialgesetzbuch IX*), aiming to enhance their self-determination and their equal participation in society.

As Germany has a federal structure, the federal states (*Bundesländer*) have also introduced Equal Opportunity Acts with comparable regulations.

- Public Employment Law: The Federal Equality Act (*Bundesgleichstellungsgesetz*, BGleiG) aims at achieving gender equality in public offices. The States have passed comparable acts binding the State's public offices. The Federal Equality Act for Soldiers (*Soldatengleichstellungsgesetz*, SGleiG) aims to achieve gender equality in the Armed Forces (*Bundeswehr*). The AGG is also binding for public offices.

10.2 Private Employment Law

- Employers are bound by the AGG. Its main regulatory content is the prohibition of discrimination on the grounds of race or ethnic origin, gender, religion or belief, disability, age, or sexual orientation.[94]

---

[93]For details, see "Introduction."
[94]For further details, see "Introduction" and questions nos. 2, 3, 4, and 6.

- Section 75 of the Work Constitution Act (*Betriebsverfassungsgesetz*) stipulates that the employer and the Works Council shall ensure that all employees in a firm are treated in accordance with the principles of law and equity, and in particular that no one is subject to discrimination on the grounds of race, ethnic origin, descent or other origin, nationality, religion or belief, disability, age, political or trade union activities or convictions, or on the grounds of gender or sexual identity.
- Section 164 of the 9th Book of Social Code (*Sozialgesetzbuch IX*) outlines the obligations of employers towards severely disabled persons.

10.3 Other Fields of Civil Law

- According to Section 19 AGG, discrimination is prohibited when founding, executing or terminating private insurance contracts or civil law obligations relating thereto. The same applies to mass contracts and related obligations. Mass contracts are contracts that are typically concluded without regard of person in a large number of cases under comparable conditions.

An exception to the strict prohibition of discrimination applies for housing rentals. A different treatment shall not be deemed as discrimination where such differentiation serves to create or maintain stable social structures and balanced settlement structures, as well as balanced economic, social and cultural conditions.

The prohibition of discrimination shall not apply to obligations resulting from family law and the law of succession as well as to obligations where the parties or their relatives are closely related or a relationship of trust exists.

For the remedies in case of a violation, see question 6.

- The principle of "good faith" (expressly stipulated in Section 242 Civil Code, but applicable in the whole legal system) precludes certain cases of arbitrary discrimination.[95]
- A discriminatory act may constitute a violation of one's general right of personality, protected by Section 823 para. 1 Civil Code.[96] In case of a serious violation of the right of personality, the victim is entitled to compensation for intangible losses.[97]

---

[95] *Schmidt-Kessel and Kramme* in: Prütting et al. (2015), § 242, para. 16.
[96] Federal Labour Court (*Bundesarbeitsgericht—BAG*), decision of 14 March 1989, BAG, AP § 611a BGB Nr. 5.
[97] Federal Labour Court, decision of 24 September 2009, NJW 2010, p. 554.

11 Does Enforcement of Antidiscrimination Law Vary According to the Ground of Discrimination?

There are differences in the enforcement of antidiscrimination law according to the ground of discrimination. The main reason for such differences is the fact that the scope of application of the AGG is limited to certain grounds. Section 1 AGG lists the following grounds: race or ethnic origin, gender, religion or belief, disability, age, and sexual orientation. To other possible grounds of discrimination, such as illness or social status,[98] the AGG, and thus its remedies, are not applicable.[99] Consequently, due to private autonomy, (natural and legal) private persons may treat others unequally on such grounds, unless such treatment violates the principle of good faith or the right of personality of the discriminated person.[100] But even in such a case, the procedural aids in enforcing possible claims, notably the change of the burden of proof (Section 22 AGG) and the assistance rights of antidiscrimination organisations (Section 23 AGG), would not apply.[101]

Even within the scope of the AGG, differences according to the ground of discrimination apply. According to Section 19 AGG, discrimination on the grounds of sex, religion, disability, age or sexual orientation are only prohibited when founding, executing or terminating private law insurance contracts or mass contracts (i.e. contracts which are typically concluded without regard of person in a large number of cases under comparable conditions) or obligations related to such contracts. By contrast, discriminations on grounds of *race* or *ethnic origin* are illegal also in the field of labour law and when founding, executing or terminating civil-law obligations regarding social protection, including social security and health care, social advantages, education, access to and supply of goods and services which are available to the public, including housing.

In the field of public law, the protection of antidiscrimination law varies according to the ground of discrimination, too. Article 3 para. 1 GG provides for a general principle of equal treatment "before the law" without a limitation to certain grounds of discrimination. The downside of this broad scope of application is that it can be restricted for any good reason justifying an unequal treatment. Article 3 para. 3 GG privileges certain grounds (sex, parentage, race, language, homeland and origin, faith, or religious or political opinions)[102]: An unequal treatment because

---

[98] In favor of social status as a ground of discrimination: *Klose*, p. 16, http://www.berlin.de/imperia/md/content/lb_ads/materialien/diskriminierung/ladg.pdf?start&ts=1310721827&file=ladg.pdf, date of last access: 17 January 2016.

[99] See *Schnabel* (2014), p. 141.

[100] See question no. 8.

[101] See *Schnabel* (2014), p. 141 emphasising that the scope of Section 22 is limited to cases falling under the AGG.

[102] Disability is referred to in Article 3 para. 3 sentence 2, stating that it is prohibited to disfavor a person because of his disability. Accordingly, it is permissible that a disabled person is favored.

of one of these grounds is only permissible if there are particularly serious reasons.[103] Further, no person shall be disfavoured because of disability. Consequently, granting advantages to disabled people is permissible.[104] Creating gender equality is also a privileged constitutional aim according to Section 3 para. 2 GG, which obliges the state to eliminate actual inequalities.

Differences can also be observed on a less than constitutional level[105]:

- The Equal Treatment of Soldiers Act (Gesetz über die Gleichbehandlung der Soldatinnen und Soldaten, SoldGG) does not cover age. Further, an unequal treatment because of a severe disability may be permissible for good reasons described in Section 18 of the Act.
- Section 9 of the Federal Law on Civil Service (*Bundesbeamtengesetz*) prohibits discrimination for certain grounds listed. Age is not explicitly mentioned. However, it is covered by Section 24 AGG, which is applicable to civil service.

12 What Is the Relationship Between the Enforcement of Antidiscrimination Law and the Quest for Equality on Both an Individual and Systemic Level?

The relationship between the enforcement of antidiscrimination law and the quest for equality on an individual level is very immediate. This is due to the enforcement regime of German antidiscrimination law granting claimable rights to individuals facing discrimination. Consequently, on this individual level, the quest for equality depends on the enforceability of these rights in practice. As the German legal system does not provide a specific enforcement regime for antidiscrimination law,[106] individuals are exposed to nearly all advantages and disadvantages of judicial proceedings in general. Two decisive factors in this regard are the length of proceedings and court costs—both of which can be described as moderate.[107] However, one of the biggest challenges for a plaintiff is to bring evidence, as discrimination typically does not come to light clearly. The easing of the burden of proof compensates for the related procedural detriment (Section 22 AGG).

However, this should not hide the fact that the quest for equality on the individual level depends very much on the initiative of individuals facing discrimination. If she or he does not take action, equality might not be achieved. Organisations have only

---

[103] *Kischel* in: Beck'scher Online-Kommentar GG, 26th edn (2015), Art. 3, para. 214.

[104] In this context, see the legislation in the field of disability law (question no. 9).

[105] See *Mahlmann*, p. 29.

[106] See question no. 2.

[107] See, *Roth* (2013), p. 637 (p. 641). Furthermore, financially weak plaintiffs are entitled to assistance with court costs in Section 114 et seq. Civil Procedural Code.

limited rights to initiate court proceedings, and the administrative enforcement of antidiscrimination law plays only a minor role in practice.[108]

As the focus of enforcement of antidiscrimination law is on the individual case, the relationship between enforcement and quest for equality on a systemic level can be described as indirect. Nonetheless, the enforcement of antidiscrimination law on the case level is not without influence on the systematic level: the effective enforcement might trigger a higher compliance with antidiscrimination law. If, as a consequence, fewer cases of discrimination occur, there will be less need for systemic (legislative) measures providing for factual equality or for equal outcomes.[109] In this context, the 30% quota for the under-represented sex in supervisory boards of stock corporations could be explained as the result of a lack of enforcement of antidiscrimination law.[110]

13 Is the Enforcement of Antidiscrimination Law Regarded as Different from the Enforcement of Other Laws?

Specific elements of the enforcement of antidiscrimination law are regarded as different from the enforcement of (most) other laws. One of the main differences legal scholars detect is the claim for compensation granted under Sections 15 and 21 AGG. This is remarkable because, first, it includes the compensation of immaterial losses. Although this is not unique in the German legal system, it is nevertheless an exception from the general principle to restrict compensation to material losses.[111] Second, the compensation for immaterial losses does not require a fault (*Vertretenmüssen*) for the breach of the AGG, which is usually given in case of negligence. It is sufficient that the defendant, a representative of the defendant or another person whose conduct can be attributed to the defendant has breached the AGG through action or omission.

Moreover, if a company has refused to conclude a contract with a potential customer for a discriminatory reason, it is very controversial whether the obligation to remedy such impairment according to Section 21 AGG includes the obligation to close a contract (*Kontrahierungszwang*). Critics argue that such an obligation is contrary to the core principle of German civil law—private autonomy (*Privatautonomie*).

---

[108]See question no. 3.
[109]For the possible discriminatory effect of such measures, see question no. 5.
[110]Such understanding is based on the statement regarding the draft legislation introducing the 30% quota: The Federal Government argues that there is no good reason, such as a shortage of suitable female candidates, which could explain the under-representation of women in top positions in the German economy (BR-Drs. 636/14, p. 1 et seq.). Thus, the under-representation might be explained with discriminatory staffing choices for positions that would qualify for a mandate in a supervisory body, enabled by a weak enforcement of antidiscrimination law.
[111]See Section 253 Civil Code.

Finally, the easement of the burden of proof and the role of organisations in the enforcement procedure are regarded as atypical. However, they are familiar in other fields of law, such as consumer protection law.

14 What Does the Enforcement of Antidiscrimination Law Reveal About the Nature of Your Legal System or About the Enforcement of Laws in Your Legal System?

The enforcement of antidiscrimination law is predominantly organised under civil law. While the European Union's Directives prescribe the material standards, the enforcement regime is mainly based on decisions of the German legislature. It would have been equally possible to introduce an administrative (*ex officio*) enforcement regime.[112] However, the choice for a civil law governed enforcement regime based on the initiative of the individual and granting certain procedural rights for organisations is regarded as fairly typical to the German legislature when implementing European standards. Especially, it can also be found in the field of consumer law.

References

Adomeit K (2002) Diskriminierung - Inflation eines Begriffs. Neue Juristische Wochenschrift (NJW) 2002:1622–1623
Bamberger HG, Roth H, Hau W, Poseck R (eds) (2015) Beck'scher Online-Kommentar, 38th edn
Bojarski Ł (2016) Country report Non-discrimination Poland, European network of legal experts in gender equality and non-discrimination. http://www.equalitylaw.eu/
Busche J (2008) Effektive Rechtsdurchsetzung und Sanktionen bei Verletzung richtliniendeterminierter Diskriminierungsverbote. In: Leible S, Schlachter M (eds) Diskriminierungsschutz durch Privatrecht
Epping V, Hillgruber C (2015) Beck'scher Online-Kommentar Grundgesetz, 26th edn
Gaier R, Wendtland H (2006) Allgemeines Gleichbehandlungsgesetz: AGG – Eine Einführung in das Zivilrecht
Grünberger M (2013) Personale Gleichheit
Gsell B, Krüger W, Lorenz S, Reymann C, Looschelders D (2016) Beck-Online Großkommentar. AGG
Kirchner C (2008) Zivilrechtlicher Diskriminierungsschutz: ein ökonomischer Ansatz. In: Leible S, Schlachter M (eds) Diskriminierungsschutz durch Privatrecht
Klose A (2012) Entwurf für ein Berliner Landesantidiskriminierungsgesetz (LADG) www.diss.fu-berlin.de/docs/servlets/MCRFileNodeServlet/FUDOCS_derivate_000000002116/ladg.pdf, date of last access: 17 January 2016 [date of publication unknown]
Köhler H, Bornkamm J (eds) (2016) UWG Kommentar, 34th edn

---

[112] As examples of administrative enforcement regimes, see *Zahumenský*, p. 82, describing the purviews of the Employment offices, Labour Inspectorates and the Trade Inspectorate; *Bojarski*, Country Report Poland, p. 110, describing the Polish National Labour Inspectorate Act. Both Reports were drafted for the European Network of Legal Experts in the Non-discrimination Field and can be downloaded at http://www.equalitylaw.eu/.

Kossens M, von der Heide D, Maaß M (eds) (2015) SGB IX Kommentar, 4th edn
Krüger W, Rauscher T (eds) (2013) Münchener Kommentar zur Zivilprozessordnung, 4th edn
Kühn K, Klose A (2012) Maßnahmen der Gewerbeaufsicht bei Verstößen gegen das Allgemeine Gleichbehandlungsgesetz. Neue Zeitschrift für Verwaltungsrecht (NVwZ) 2012:1443–1447
Lindner JF (2008) Gewerbeuntersagung wegen Verletzung des Allgemeinen Gleichbehandlungsgesetzes? Gewerbearchiv (GewA) 2008, p 436 et seq
Mahlmann M (2014) Country report 2013 for Germany on measures to combat discrimination. http://www.migpolgroup.com/portfolio/country-reports-on-measures-to-combat-discrimination-2013/
Maunz T, Dürig G (eds) (2015) Grundgesetz Kommentar, 75th supplement (September 2015)
Monen K (2008) Das Verbot der Diskriminierung, Eine Untersuchung aufgrund der Rasse, des Geschlechts und der sexuellen Identität im deutschen und U.S.-amerikanischen Privatrecht
Müller-Glöge R, Preis U, Schmidt I (eds) (2016) Erfurter Kommentar zum Arbeitsrecht, 16th edn
Neumann D, Pahlen R, Majerski-Pahlen M (2010) Sozialgesetzbuch IX – Rehabilitation und Teilhabe behinderter Menschen
Ohly A, Sosnitza O (eds) (2014) UWG Kommentar, 6th edn
Palandt O (2015) Bürgerliches Gesetzbuch Kommentar, 74th edn
Pfeiffer T (2005) Stellungnahme zum Entwurf eines Gesetzes zur Umsetzung europäischer Antidiskriminierungsrichtlinien. http://webarchiv.bundestag.de/archive/2005/0825/parlament/gremien15/a12/Oeffentliche_Sitzungen/20050307/pfeiffer.pdf; last access to website, 22 Feb 2016
Prütting H (2015) Alternative Streitbeilegung in Verbraucherangelegenheiten -Bindungswirkungen und Vollstreckbarkeit. In: Schmidt-Kessel M (ed) Alternative Streitschlichtung - Die Umsetzung der ADR-Richtlinie in Deutschland
Prütting H, Wegen G, Weinreich G (2015) Bürgerliches Gesetzbuch Kommentar, 10th edn
Roth H (2013) Bedeutungsverluste der Zivilgerichtsbarkeit durch Verbrauchermediation. Juristenzeitung (JZ) 2013:637 et seq
Sachs M (ed) (2011) Grundgesetz Kommentar, 6th edn
Säcker FJ (2004) Europäische Diskriminierungsverbote und deutsches Zivilrecht, Betriebs-Berater (BB). Beilage zu Heft 51:16 et seq
Schiek D (ed) (2007) Allgemeines Gleichbehandlungsgesetz (AGG): Ein Kommentar aus europäischer Perspektive
Schmidt-Bleibtreu B, Hofmann H, Henneke H-G (eds) (2014) Grundgesetz Kommentar, 13th edn
Schmidt-Kessel M (2006) Fremde Erfahrungen mit zivilrechtlichen Diskriminierungsverboten. In: Leible S, Schlachter M (eds) Diskriminierungsschutz durch Privatrecht
Schnabel A (2014) Diskriminierungsschutz ohne Grenzen?
Stoffels M (2009) Grundprobleme der Schadensersatzverpflichtung nach § 15 Abs. 1 AGG. Recht der Arbeit (RdA) 2009:204–215
Zahumenský D (2016) Country report Non-discrimination Czech Republic. http://www.equalitylaw.eu/

Malte Kramme studied law at the universities of Osnabrück and Lausanne, first state exam in 2006. After his legal clerkship (Rechtsreferendariat) and second state exam (2010) in Hamburg, Malte Kramme worked as an attorney-at-law (Rechtsanwalt) at Linklaters LLP, Berlin, specializing in regulatory and European law. Since October 2013 he is research fellow at the University of Bayreuth's Research Centre for Consumer Law (Forschungsstelle für Verbraucherrecht). He has various publications in the field of civil law, civil procedural law, consumer law and European law. Malte Kramme is co-editor of European Union Private Law Review" (Zeitschrift für das Privatrecht der Europäischen Union—GPR).

Greece

Antonia Papadelli

1 Introduction

The financial crisis in Greece has dramatic consequences on citizens' lives as well as the state's function. Delayed pension payments, abrogation of social benefits, and unbearable tax burdens constitute examples of the acute problems that citizens face. Under these extraordinary conditions, the life of vulnerable social groups worsens while citizens' rights are violated. The increased risk of women's dismissals (particularly during the period of maternity), the acute tension at schools between students of different race or origin, the deterioration in the conditions of life of the disabled, are some of the examples that show that mediation on various levels is sought by the Greek society in order to cast off its strong feeling of insecurity.

The lack of funding resources does not only influence life on a horizontal basis but also on a vertical scale. The state's difficulty in meeting its obligations and the inability of the administration to support a society that is sorely tried creates an extremely demanding environment. In this legal and structural environment characterized by fluidity, public administration is called to function effectively with less staff. The inability of the administration to handle the intense problems of these difficult times leads to a significant lack of trust in institutions, a fact that induces polarization and puts social cohesion at risk.

Under this pressure, parts of the Greek population tend to adopt extreme positions, views and actions, leading to simplistic and often dangerous solutions. In such a socially and politically charged climate where the protection of human rights is endangered and the states as well as citizens are running out of options, all bodies are called upon to find realistic solutions and mediate between public administration and citizens in order to help the latter in exercising their rights effectively.

A. Papadelli (✉)
Greek Independent Authority for Public Revenue, Directorate of Legal Services, Athens, Greece

© Springer International Publishing AG, part of Springer Nature 2018
M. Mercat-Bruns et al. (eds.), *Comparative Perspectives on the Enforcement and Effectiveness of Antidiscrimination Law*, Ius Comparatum – Global Studies in Comparative Law 28, https://doi.org/10.1007/978-3-319-90068-1_15

2 Is Antidiscrimination Law Enforced?

Antidiscrimination law is not always enforced. Here are some of the most notable cases, where the antidiscrimination legislation is not literally enforced.

With regard to education, Roma (see cases of schools refusing to register Roma children for attendance or cases of Roma children being separated from other children within the same school) and disabled (deprived of their right to parade or excluded from a university department), remain at a great disadvantage.

With regard to employment, women are often discriminated against due to "social prejudice," leading to only nominal gender equality. More and more enterprises invoke vague financial reasons when exercising illegal and improper job rotation on employees returning to work from maternity leave. Although job rotation is an institution to be implemented in case of financial shrinking of a business which wishes to avoid job loss and therefore may not refer exclusively to one employee (male/female), various enterprises impose job rotation on working mothers, thus infringing upon the regulations pertaining to gender discrimination in the workplace as well as the regulations related to maternity protection.

Alien minors are still victims of discriminative behavior in Greece. Being a minor is not taken into account when violating the immigration law. This leads to a further violation of the rights of the minor. In this respect the greatest problem lies in the complete inadequacy of the infrastructure on the one hand, which results in particularly harsh and unsuitable conditions of detainment considering the age of the detainees, and of the legislation governing issues of administrative detention and deportation on the other.

Racist attacks—not only against minors—are unfortunately a striking example of existent discrimination. Although most of these cases are never reported or recorded, the bodies dealing with discrimination refer often to the inaction and reluctance exhibited by the administration to arrest perpetrators or record incidents, and to the victims' very own fear that they may be arrested or stigmatized, together with their conviction that they will not be vindicated. It is characteristic that in areas where, by evidence and by various report's data, the phenomenon is particularly heightened is in a large part of downtown Athens.

3 How Is Antidiscrimination Law Enforced?

A victim of discrimination in the private sector can raise a complaint before the Greek civil courts (Articles 13–14 Law 3304/2005, hereafter antidiscrimination Law[1]) and penal courts (Article 16 antidiscrimination Law), whereas a victim in the public sector, including the field of employment, may appear not only before the Greek civil and penal courts but also before the administrative courts.

---

[1] About antidiscrimination legislation, see below Question 7.

Associations are entitled to act on behalf of victims (Article 13(3) - antidiscrimination Law) or in support of victims by joining already existing proceedings (Article 82 Code of Civil Procedure), providing the possibility of "additional intervention" in a court process.

The enforcement of antidiscrimination law differs depending on the authority[2] it is addressed to. For example, when some illegal action or lack of action by the public administration has infringed a right or a legal interest of individuals or legal entities, a complaint may be submitted to the Greek Ombudsman. Complaints are submitted by anyone (legal entities or associations of individuals), regardless of nationality, after having first come unsuccessfully into contact with the public service involved in the infringement case. The Greek Ombudsman, in his function as a mediator, makes recommendations and proposals to the public administration but does not impose sanctions or annul illegal acts of the public administration.

The Economic and Social Council of Greece (ESC[3]), as described below in Question 3, issues opinions either on its own initiative or after receiving draft bills from the competent Minister or from Members of Parliament. In cases relating to extremely serious matters, opinions are drawn up by ad hoc working committees, which have the right to request from the competent Ministry and from every competent public service useful information and data. In cases relating to matters of more general interest and lasting importance, the ESC organizes events to stimulate public dialogue over the issues it has dealt with in its opinions.

The Greek Labour Inspectorate (SEPE) instigates an investigation in case of a violation of the principle of equal treatment or discrimination. In such cases, the burden of proof is placed on the employee, who is not in a position to access the financial data of the enterprise while employers invoke general financial difficulties without providing evidence on the downsizing of their enterprise. Within its limited resources, the Labour Inspectorate performs inspection and control at workplaces and targets the effective implementation of the relevant legislation.

4 Who Enforces Antidiscrimination Law?

Under the Greek Constitution, the courts enforce the law (Article 87) and nobody can be deprived against his will of the judge assigned to him by law (Article 8). Therefore, as a matter of principle, law enforcement bodies other than courts may not

---

[2] About the authorities charged with the enforcement of antidiscrimination legislation, see below Question 4.

[3] The ESCs as an institution began to develop in the 1950s on a national level and were adopted by the Treaty of Rome for the European Economic Community. Since then, they have rapidly grown in most countries of the Community. More recently ESCs were also established in the countries of Eastern Europe as part of the enlargement process, as well as in third Mediterranean countries, for which they have been an important mechanism for direct cooperation with the European Union.

be established. However, various public authorities play a considerable part in the law enforcement environment.

The antidiscrimination legislation in Greece is mainly enforced through the following four official bodies:

(a) The Greek Ombudsman is an independent authority operating since 1998 under Article 103 of the Constitution and Law 2477/1997 for the promotion of children's rights, as well as the implementation of the principle of equal treatment, regardless of racial or ethnic origin, religious or other beliefs, age, disability or sexual orientation, in the public sector, drafting reports and investigating complaints on violations of this principle.[4]

(b) The Equal Treatment Committee established in 2006 under the provisions of Article 21 antidiscrimination Law and supervised by the Minister of Justice aims at ensuring the principle of equal treatment in various fields (with the exception of the occupation and employment field). Therefore, it examines complaints of violations of the principle of equal treatment within its field of competence, and tries to conciliate between the conflicting parties. It can also conduct independent surveys concerning discrimination and publish independent reports or make recommendations concerning discrimination. The Committee has no authority to impose sanctions. However, it has the right to hear witnesses and to demand the supply of information by public authorities or individuals.

(c) SEPE, the central service of the Ministry of Labour and Social security established in 1999 under the title "Corps of Labour Inspectors," is structured through one central and various local offices and aims at the (1) supervision and

---

[4]This body, in order to meet the requirements of its role is divided in various departments: The Department of Human Rights is concerned with the defence of individual, political and social rights protected by the Constitution, by international agreements, or by national law. In particular, it deals with cases regarding: violations of personal freedom; freedom of religious belief and worship; discrimination on grounds of nationality or ethnic origin; violations of the rights of immigrants; equal access to public education; recognition of foreign academic titles; protection of professional rights; infringements of the right to appeal to the administrative authorities and access to judicial protection; as well as the right to political asylum and aliens' rights to entry and residence. The Department of social protection health and welfare focuses on the protection of the rights of vulnerable groups such as the elderly, people with disabilities, and the physically and mentally ill, in the fields of social policy, social security and welfare. The Department of Quality of Life is concerned with violations of environmental and urban planning legislation affecting the natural and cultural environment and public health, whereas the State-Citizen Relation Department is concerned with a wide range of issues such as transport and communications, agriculture, employment, trade and industry, energy, taxation and customs, public procurement and public contracts, etc. Particular focus is laid upon the quality of public services, organization and procedures, as well as citizens' access to information. The Department of Children's Rights is concerned with the protection and promotion of children's rights, while the Department of Gender Equality is concerned with the implementation of the principle of equal opportunities and equal treatment of men and women in access to employment, vocational training and promotion, as well as working conditions both in the public and the private sector, including employment, self employment, work and pay. It also deals with discrimination based on gender in the area of access to and supply of goods and services in the public sector.

control of the labour legislation, (2) investigation and prosecution in cases of infringement of the labour legislation and illegal activity as well as the insurance coverage of the employees and (3) suggestion for the effective application of the labour legislation. The Labour Inspectorate performs inspection and control at public or private workplaces 24 h a day to ensure the proper implementation of legislation, with powers to institute criminal proceedings or in some cases impose fines against employers. In concreto, the Labour Inspectorate (1) controls the application of labour legislation in enterprises of private and public sectors, (2) searches for the grounds of deadly or serious industrial accidents, (3) investigates the complaints submitted by employees, (4) imposes administrative sanctions or seek the imposition of criminal sanctions before courts, (5) intervenes in a conciliatory manner for the resolution of labour disputes.

(d) The Economic and Social Council of Greece, based on the model of the ESC of the European Union, is a constitutionally recognized institution of the Greek state (Article 82) since 2001. Its mission is to conduct the social dialogue on the country's general policy and in particular on economic and social policy guidelines, as well as to formulate opinions on government bills or law proposals referred to it. The objective of the ESC is to promote the social dialogue and through it to formulate (if possible) mutually acceptable positions on issues of concern to society as a whole or specific social groups. The scope of the ESC is not to curb different ideological and political views, but to reach consensus on social and economic issues by launching various arguments and proposals. Through its proposals and opinions, it also seeks to maximize the social benefit or minimize any possible negative effects of decisions taken by executive and legislative powers.

In addition to the above mentioned bodies, there are various organizations which fight for the implementation of antidiscrimination legislation in special fields such as (1) Employers and Employees Unions (Civil Servants Union (ADEDY), General Federation of Greek Workers (GSEE), Greek Manufacturers Association (SEB)), (2) religious communities, (3) NGOs (ANTIGONE—Information and Documentation Center on Racism, Ecology, Peace and Non Violence, National Confederation of Disabled People, Greek Council for Refugees, OLKE for the protection of human rights of LGBT people in Greece, 50plus Greece for people over 50 years old, HIP-positive Greek Club, etc.).

5 Who Benefits from the Enforcement of Antidiscrimination Law?

The victims of discriminative behavior (children, disabled, women, aliens, homosexuals, etc.) are those who most benefit from the enforcement of antidiscrimination law. Moreover, those more seriously affected by the financial crisis in Greece and unable to meet their financial obligations may benefit from the actions of bodies acting in the field of enforcement of antidiscrimination laws. As mentioned above, the relevant bodies help them by providing basic information on their rights, by mediating exhaustively on potential settlements or by seeking leniency in certain cases. Consequently, the society as a whole profits from efficient enforcement of the antidiscrimination legislation.

6 Who Is Harmed by the Enforcement of Antidiscrimination Law?

Every modern society aims at the enforcement of antidiscrimination law as all its members may only profit from such enforcement. Nevertheless, some groups oppose the enforcement as they wrongly regard such enforcement as harming their rights. (More on this in Question 8.)

7 What Remedies Are Provided by the Enforcement of Antidiscrimination Law?

Equality for all Greeks was always constitutionally protected. Nevertheless, the Constitution came up with more provisions strengthening the human rights in 1975.

First of all, a gender equality provision was introduced into the Constitution stating that Greek men and women have equal rights and obligations (Article 4(2)). Furthermore, the Greek Constitution in its first part assigns to the State the primary obligation to respect and protect the value of the human being (Article 2(1)). The Greek Constitution also contains a specific and general non-discrimination provision that explicitly protects all people, national citizens and aliens, men and women, old and young when developing freely their personality and participating in the social, economic and political life of the country, insofar as they do not infringe the rights of others or violate the Constitution and the principles of morality (Article 5(1)). Accordingly, all persons living within the Greek territory shall enjoy full protection of their life, honor and liberty irrespective of nationality, race or language and of religious or political beliefs. Exceptions shall be permitted only in cases provided by international law (Article 5(2)).

In this framework, the Greek Constitution introduces the following principles: human dignity (Article 2(1)); free development of personality (Article 5(1)); general equality (Article 4(1)); protection of health (Article 5(5)); freedom of religion (Article 13(1)); freedom of opinion and of the press (Article 14); freedom of art, science, research and teaching (Article 16); judicial protection (Article 20); protection against misuse of personal data (Article 9A); free education on all levels at state educational institutions (Article 16(4)); the right to a family, marriage, motherhood, childhood, families with many children (Article 21); the right to work and to receive equal pay for work of equal value (Article 22); the right for respect of human and social rights (Article 25(1)); and the right to enjoy affirmative measures to counterbalance real inequality (Article 116(2)).

All these rights and principles conceptually cover all antidiscrimination grounds and material fields mentioned in Directives 2000/43/EC and 2000/78/EC. Theoretically, therefore, victims of discrimination, regardless of their racial or national origin, religious or other beliefs, disability, age or sexual orientation, may invoke these provisions while attempting to initiate a discussion towards promoting social integration and inclusion and combating discrimination. Although constitutional provisions cover every aspect of human life and personal development, and as such they offer a resource for people, it would be extremely difficult to derive specific enforceable rights from these general clauses.

The need for specific legislation, which brings clarity and enforceability to people rights, spurred the introduction of various national laws. In this context, Law 3304/2005 (antidiscrimination law) transposes Directives 2000/43/EC and 2000/78/EC into Greek national law and fills the conspicuous gap in the Greek legal system. According to Article 1 the purpose of this Law is to lay down a general regulatory framework for combating discrimination on the grounds of racial or ethnic origin, as well as combating discrimination on the grounds of religion or belief, disability, age or sexual orientation as regards employment and occupation, in accordance with the Commission Directives, with a view to putting into effect the principle of equal treatment. This new statute protects all persons in both the public and private sectors, and covers the fields of access to employment and occupation (but not to self-employment), vocational training and education, social protection, including social security and healthcare, education, and access to goods and services, including housing.

According to Article 26 antidiscrimination law, this Law repeals any legislation or rule and abrogates any clause included in personal or collective contracts, general dealing terms, internal enterprise regulations, charters of profit or non-profit organizations, independent professional associations, and employee or employer trade unions opposed to the equal treatment principle as defined in this Law.

Other Laws serving the antidiscriminative behavior are the following: Law 2472/1997 (data protection law, Law 4074 /2012 ratified the U.N. Convention on the Rights of Persons with Disabilities, Law 2817/2000, relating to education for children with disabilities, mandating the free education of children with special needs in kindergartens, and elementary and secondary level schools and educational institutions in different curriculum models, Law 1414/1984 on the implementation of the principle of sex equality in employment relations and other provisions, and Law 927/1979 on punishing acts or activities aiming at racial discrimination (antiracist penal Law).

Some aspects of discrimination may come under the scope of certain provisions of the Penal Code, as for example sexual harassment, which may fall under the scope of Article 337 Penal Code (insult to a person's sexual dignity).

8 Who Supports the Enforcement of Antidiscrimination Law?

See Question 4.

9 Who Opposes the Enforcement of Antidiscrimination Law?

Unfortunately some groups of people aim at profiting to the detriment of vulnerable social groups. These people who oppose the enforcement of antidiscrimination law belong mostly to politically extreme parties or religion fanatics. The democratic Greek society has always succeeded in isolating such groups. Nevertheless, the financial crisis increased their powers as they take advantage of the general disappointment in order to exercise their power by sharpening the social inequalities. In this regard associations of employers oft oppose the enforcement of employees' rights in order to safeguard more profits for their members.

10 How Broad Is the Coverage of Antidiscrimination Law?

The antidiscrimination Law in Article 1 explicitly introduces as its purpose a general regulatory antidiscrimination framework and does not provide specific regulations with regard to the implementation of the principle of equal treatment. The introduction of a general framework through national law is not within the spirit of the Directive, the latter establishing the general framework for the member states to make specific regulations and take concrete implementation measures.

Although the number of complaints brought before the Greek Ombudsman remains limited, this does not mean a real absence of discrimination in Greece, as this body in its reports points out the limited coverage of antidiscrimination law and the general lack of awareness of discrimination within Greek society and public administration. Most of the complaints for racial discrimination in housing that the Ombudsman usually examines concern Roma cases, whereas complaints for discrimination in the field of employment and education/vocational training concern mostly the grounds of age, disability and sexual orientation. The Reports conclude, among others, that every year the general number of complaints of discrimination is slightly higher than the previous year, but it is still low. Another interesting point resulting from the special reports is that the number of complaints of discrimination on the grounds of disability has risen, mainly due to the submission of complaints to the Ombudsman by disability organizations.

It is not only people that have to activate themselves to enforce their rights. It is also the state that has to amend the relevant legislation in order to extend the field of protection of antidiscrimination Law so as to cover all grounds of discrimination (as for example the prohibition of direct discrimination and harassment by association as required by the CJEU judgment in Coleman (case C-303/06).

11 Does Enforcement of Antidiscrimination Law Vary According to the Ground of Discrimination?

See Questions 4 and 6.

12 What Is the Relationship Between the Enforcement of Antidiscrimination Law and the Quest for Equality on Both an Individual and Systemic Level?

The enforcement of antidiscrimination law is intensely related to the quest for equality on both an individual and systemic level. The apparent regression of Greek society and the State in terms of their readiness to combat discrimination influences the level of equality among citizens of different race, religion, sex or education. In a society where racist violence, both in the number of incidents reported and their intensity is raising continuously, and the protection of vulnerable social groups is being disputed, ensuring equality on an individual as well as systemic level seems impossible. Nevertheless, the Greek Ombudsman's activity as a national equality body promoting the principle of equal treatment, irrespective of racial or ethnic origin, religion or faith, disability, age or sexual orientation, aims at activating the antidiscrimination legislation and succeeds in applying equality standards in various fields.

13 Is the Enforcement of Antidiscrimination Law Regarded As Different from the Enforcement of Other Laws?

The antidiscrimination law differs from other laws in the way it is enforced. In particular, the way the qualified bodies are informed of the infringements of antidiscrimination law is immediate and varies from the way such information takes place in other legal fields. For example, the possibility to submit complaints before the Greek Ombudsman not only in person and in writing but also by post, by fax or even by e-mail, had a positive response by citizens who used it immediately. Complaints received by the Ombudsman are entered in the electronic protocol, so that the progress of each case may be followed easily while the essential control and transparency in the operation of the institution is ensured. The familiarization of this body with the modern techniques is deemed to be necessary in order for the Greek Ombudsman to be able to function in favor of the Greek society.

Another main difference in the way antidiscrimination law is enforced is that enforcement does not mainly mean the imposition of sanctions when the antidiscriminative legislation is infringed. In times of financial restrictions, enforcement is inextricably linked with the demand for social justice, which mainly means proportionality in spreading burdens and participation in these burdens, and observation of regulations and transparency in handling public cases.

14 What Does the Enforcement of Antidiscrimination Law Reveal About the Nature of Your Legal System or About the Enforcement of Laws in Your Legal System?

The enforcement of antidiscrimination law reveals the fact that the Greek administration must change its modus operandi and culture. Although the qualified bodies intervene at all levels in order to reform and efficiently apply the antidiscrimination legislation, the procedures, standards and work practices remain mostly untouched. Administration changes at such a slow pace that difficulties for civil servants and citizens in general remain present.

As long as the methods of the administration's operation do not adapt accordingly, the state fails to effectively fulfill its role in supporting its citizens. Under these findings, upgrading the administration is the only way to improve the Greek community as well as the functioning of the legal system.

15 Conclusion

Inextricably linked to the economic crisis in Greece are the signs of social fatigue, which leads parts of the population to extreme positions, views, and actions. The young, the unemployed and the financially vulnerable deprived of courage and hope slide down a dangerous path, where the respect and protection of the freedom and personality of others is questioned. The adoption of simplistic solutions on offer in the market place of public debate seems more probable than ever. The black and white logic carried forward by special groups supports confrontation and self-interested behavior endangering the protection of human rights in the Greek society.

In such a socially and politically charged climate sobriety in assessing the situation and responding to its demands is even more essential. Otherwise there is a very real danger that this economic crisis will evolve into a crisis of shared democratic values and social cohesion for the country.

The strengthening of the confidence in institutions and public authorities and the intensification of trust in the values of the European civilization, such as solidarity, tolerance, mutual respect, becomes even more urgent in order to reconstruct a better tomorrow and to restore the democratic character of this country. Let's hope that people extract the best out of the crisis, which may act as a catalyst for rapid changes towards the enforcement of antidiscrimination law, and the Greek administration practices proportionality in allocating burdens, respect of rights in a non discriminatory manner, observance of rules in a transparent manner indispensable conditions for the Greek State to identify viable solutions and provide support for people suffering from the social consequences of the prolonged economic crisis.

Antonia Papadelli is working for the Directorate of Legal Services of the Greek Independent Authority for Public Revenue. She holds a PhD in the field of antitrust law and an LLM in the field of company law both from Hamburg University. From 2010 till 2016 she served as a scientific associate of the Hellenic Institute of International and Foreign Law. The present paper reflects the legal framework in force until October 2016.

India

Maithili Pai and Nupur Raut

1 Introduction

The right to equality and non-discrimination is being spoken about increasingly at a global level. At the same time, social stratification in one form or the other has existed in all societies.[1] In this paper, the researchers seek to examine the Indian framework on antidiscrimination laws.

India's caste system is perhaps the world's longest surviving social hierarchy.[2] Caste is a form of complex social grouping that divides all Hindus into rigid hierarchical groups. A Hindu is considered a member of the caste of the family into which he or she is born and remains within that caste until death.[3] Differences in caste are justified by the religious doctrine of *karma*, a belief that one's place in life is determined by one's deeds in previous lifetimes.[4] People at the lowest level of the caste hierarchy as well as those outside the caste system known as 'Dalits' or 'untouchables' have been subject to widespread discrimination for centuries.

When India gained independence from British rule in 1947, the question of caste rose to the forefront of national political discourse. One of the key architects of the country's new constitution, B.R. Ambedkar, was a Dalit himself who argued against caste-based discrimination and the practice of untouchability. Independent India's

---

We would like to thank Danish Sheikh and Tarunabh Khaitan for their input.

[1]Nayyar (2011).
[2]Human Rights Watch (2016).
[3]Human Rights Watch (2016).
[4]Human Rights Watch (2001).

M. Pai (✉) · N. Raut
Supreme Court of India, New Delhi, India
e-mail: maithilipai@nujs.edu

constitution banned discrimination on the basis of caste, and with a view to correct historical injustices and provide a level playing field to those discriminated against, quotas were provided in government jobs and educational institutions for scheduled castes and tribes, the lowest in the caste hierarchy, in 1950. Thus, India was one of the first countries in the world to provide for affirmative action in its constitution.[5]

Articles 14, 15 and 16 of the Indian constitution form the cornerstone of the constitutional protection of the rights to equality and non-discrimination in India.[6] There is limited legislation prohibiting discrimination.[7] And, at present, India lacks a comprehensive antidiscrimination law that can tackle all forms of discrimination.

This report primarily focuses on caste-discrimination in India. This is due to caste as a social status being unique to Indian society, and also as caste remains one of most prevalent forms of discrimination in India. However, other forms of discrimination are referred to in various parts of the report.

2 Is Antidiscrimination Law Enforced?

Yes. India has a diverse historical background, with a population that is highly segregated. As the second most populated country in the world, India also has an extremely diverse population in terms of cultures, religions and languages. At the same time, and unlike several developed countries, India lacks a comprehensive antidiscrimination law that can tackle all forms of discrimination.

Differences arise amongst the people of the country on various grounds: sex, religion, class, caste, and physical and mental disability. In the Indian subcontinent, as in most places, women are not seen as equal to men in all spheres of life. On account of a significant majority of the population being Hindu, communities from other religions find themselves relegated to the lower echelons of society. Class differences based on the socio-economic status of individuals operate insidiously within society. The country is most deeply ensnared in the hierarchies of caste—a term unique to Indian society, which means a complex hierarchical societal structure that categorizes persons on the basis of which family she is born in and, more often than not, the type of occupation her family has been carrying on for generations.[8]

Those at the top of the hierarchy, in their attempt to maintain their position, practise various forms of discrimination against the marginalized. Discrimination is rampant in the workplace, in places of religious worship, and in other public spaces. Acts of discrimination range from denying promotions to openly treating others as untouchable.[9] Despite the presence of prohibitions and safeguards in the Indian

---

[5]Nayyar (2011).
[6]The Equal Rights Trust (2016).
[7]The Equal Rights Trust (2016).
[8]*See* Deshpande (2011), pp. 19–20.
[9]Untouchability is a phenomenon wherein members of the Dalit community are forbidden from touching other persons or objects; the Protection of Civil Rights Act, 1955 seeks to counter this.

Constitution, political parties have played various sections of the population against each other, thereby deepening the fault lines that divide them. Consequently, antidiscrimination law and its enforcement is a necessity in India.

Successive governments have made policies and enacted legislation in order to attempt to undo years of discrimination against the marginalized. Each of these laws sets a variety of enforcement mechanisms to ensure that the victims of discrimination are granted redress, and attempt to deter such instances of discrimination from occurring in the future.

3 How Is Antidiscrimination Law Enforced?

The method of enforcement of antidiscrimination laws varies for each law, with courts being the primary mechanism of enforcement in each case. Compensatory damages are generally awarded. Most of the time, the statutory remedies are individualistic in nature, with litigants being required to approach courts of law themselves.[10] With the Public Interest Litigation (PIL) mechanism, however, litigants have the opportunity of fighting against widespread discrimination against a class of persons directly before the High Courts and the Supreme Court of India.[11] A recent instance of this is the petition against the age-old practice of disallowing women between the ages of 10 and 50 into the Sabarimala temple in Kerala, South India, as it is believed that their ability to menstruate makes their surroundings "impure". Filed by the Indian Young Lawyers' Association on behalf of all Indian women in the age group between 10 and 50, the petition contends that disallowing women entry is in violation of the right to equality, the prohibition of discrimination on grounds of sex and the right to profess, practise and propagate a religion of one's choice under the Constitution of India.[12] It has been referred to a Constitutional Bench of the Supreme Court of India.[13]

In accordance with its constitutional mandate,[14] the Indian government has reserved seats in government educational institutions and workplaces for Scheduled Castes, Scheduled Tribes and Other Backward Classes.[15] Unfortunately, there is no

---

[10]Unlike the UK, which has the Equal Opportunities Commission and the Commission for Racial Equality specifically empowered to enforce antidiscrimination law: See Townshend-Smith (1998), pp. 497–538.

[11]Under Articles 32 and 226 of the Constitution of India, 1950.

[12]Article 51A(e) of the Constitution of India, 1950 also imposes a duty to renounce practices derogatory to women.

[13]The Supreme Court (2016).

[14]Under Article 16(4) of the Constitution of India, 1950.

[15]In accordance with Article 16(4) of the Constitution of India, 1950.

specific mechanism to enforce affirmative action other than individual writ petitions and Public Interest Litigations, which are most often inaccessible. Members of the lower castes cannot carry on protracted litigation on account of their socioeconomic condition, and Indian courts are alleged to have an upper caste bias amongst them.[16] In addition to this, the reservation policy is not perfect: Indian Christians and Muslims have been left out despite the fact that the caste system is just as much a part of their religious setup.[17]

4 Who Enforces Antidiscrimination Law?

The enforcement mechanisms for each type of antidiscrimination law change from law to law. For this reason, the powers and functions of the enforcement authorities, if any, are not uniform. This leads to disparity in the nature of remedies available to different categories of persons, and the extent to which they are able to enforce their rights under the law.

For instance, under the Sexual Harassment of Women at Workplace (Prevention, Prohibition and Redressal) Act, 2013, enforcement takes place through an Internal Complaints Committee or a Local Committee. After receiving a complaint, it conducts an internal inquiry, and provides recommendations to the employer to take action against the offender and pay compensation to the aggrieved woman. The Committee also submits a report to the investigating authority, after which criminal proceedings may be initiated against the offender in a criminal court. Criminal courts are also empowered to give compensation to the aggrieved woman.[18] This Committee, therefore, acts as the enforcing authority for complaints of sexual harassment by women.

The Persons with Disabilities (Equal Opportunities, Protection of Rights and Full Participation) Act, 1995, on the other hand, provides for enforcing authorities, but grants no remedies. While it deals mostly with affirmative action for disabled persons, it also includes a chapter on non-discrimination against disabled persons in the workplace or in the non-availability of suitable infrastructure in public places. A Chief Commissioner appointed by the Central Government,[19] and Commissioners for every State,[20] are the authorities to hear complaints and "take up the matter with the appropriate authorities" in certain instances. However, there is no provision in

---

[16]Deshpande (2011), p. 221.

[17]Harlieb (2016).

[18]Section 11(2), Sexual Harassment of Women at Workplace (Prevention, Prohibition and Redressal) Act, 2013.

[19]Section 59, Persons with Disabilities (Equal Opportunities, Protection of Rights and Full Participation) Act, 1995.

[20]Section 60, Persons with Disabilities (Equal Opportunities, Protection of Rights and Full Participation) Act, 1995.

the law for disabled persons to seek *remedies* for being discriminated against. The structure of this enforcing authority leaves much to be desired.

Finally, under the Scheduled Castes and Scheduled Tribes (Prevention of Atrocities) Act, 1989, there is no body to enforce the rights of victims of caste discrimination. The victims have the option of approaching a court of law individually to seek criminal remedies. A Sessions Court in each district is designated as a Special Court to try offences under this Act.[21] Anyone who discriminates against members of Scheduled Castes or Scheduled Tribes by insulting or intimidating them, or coercing or convincing them to commit certain acts is liable to be punished with imprisonment along with a fine.[22] In addition to compensation, the Act and the Rules[23] provide for economic and social rehabilitation,[24] which makes it the most comprehensive antidiscrimination legislation in terms of remedies available to victims.

In addition to statute-specific remedies, the National Human Rights Commission, the National Commission for Backward Classes and the National Commission for Minorities are empowered to take up any perceived violations with the appropriate authorities.[25]

5 Who Benefits from the Enforcement of Antidiscrimination Law?

The direct beneficiaries of antidiscrimination law, most obviously, are the marginalized sections of Indian society. These include members of the Scheduled Castes and Scheduled Tribes, members of the Dalit community women, religious minorities and disabled persons who fall within the statutory definition. Typically, these are the most oppressed sections of society and are discriminated against on a daily basis. The enforcement of antidiscrimination law provides a degree of respite to victims, allowing them access to their rights in several instances. The Supreme Court of India has, on one significant occasion, safeguarded the constitutional right to religion for the members of the Dalit community among Hindus by upholding a law mandating that they be allowed entry into temples.[26]

The enforcement of antidiscrimination law also creates a deterrent effect that benefits the rest of the marginalized community in the long run, gradually contributing to a better status for them in society. The social standing of, and the respect

---

[21] Section 14, Scheduled Castes and Scheduled Tribes (Prevention of Atrocities) Act, 1989.
[22] Section 3, Scheduled Castes and Scheduled Tribes (Prevention of Atrocities) Act, 1989.
[23] Scheduled Castes and Scheduled Tribes (Prevention of Atrocities) Rules, 1995.
[24] Section 21(2)(iii), Scheduled Castes and Scheduled Tribes (Prevention of Atrocities) Act, 1989.
[25] Section 12, Protection of Human Rights Act, 1993; Section 9, National Commission for Backward Classes Act, 1993; Section 9, National Commission for Minorities Act, 1992.
[26] Singh (2016).

accorded to an oppressed person increases greatly within her community for initiating a legal battle against the oppressors of that community. The enforcement of antidiscrimination law also benefits the dependents and legal heirs of the victims of discrimination in some instances, as they also stand to gain from receiving compensation. It is important to note that in Indian antidiscrimination laws, oppressors and the oppressed are defined concretely, with no room for variation. Therefore, among the class of oppressed persons, the beneficiaries can only be of a certain type—women and not men; Scheduled Castes, Scheduled Tribes, and Dalits, and not Other Backward Classes; defined categories of disabled persons.

Organs of the State also stand to benefit from the enforcement of antidiscrimination laws, as it improves their perception in the eyes of the public. The proper enforcement of antidiscrimination laws gives political mileage to the ruling government, and provides testament to the efficacy of law enforcement authorities and the judiciary. Therefore, society at large stands to benefit from the enforcement of antidiscrimination law.

6 Who Is Harmed by the Enforcement of Antidiscrimination Law?

Antidiscrimination law in India causes the most harm to the privileged. The Prevention of Atrocities Act categorizes perpetrators only as persons who are not part of the Scheduled Castes and Scheduled Tribes, and victims only as persons belonging to Scheduled Castes/Scheduled Tribes.[27] Enforcement can only be in one direction—for the lower castes, and against the upper castes. Consequently, members of upper caste communities perceive harm to themselves and to their community through the enforcement of the Prevention of Atrocities Act.

Similarly, the binary nature of the oppressor-oppressed dynamic causes harm to those persons who have been mistreated because of systemic oppression, but cannot be categorized as a victim owing to the language of the law. The Sexual Harassment Act in India is a gendered legislation—victims can only be women.[28] Consequently, only a certain demographic can enforce this law. Unfortunately, men have also suffered harassment at the hands of their male or female employers, as sexual harassment at the workplace is often a function of power relations.[29] The law does not, however, envision men as victims of discrimination at the workplace. The enforcement mechanism given in the Act may prove actively harmful to men in that false complaints may be made against them for completely consensual sexual

---

[27]Section 3, Scheduled Castes and Scheduled Tribes (Prevention of Atrocities) Act, 1989.

[28]Much like the Indian law on rape: Section 375 of the Indian Penal Code, 1860. Men who have been raped or sexually harassed may take recourse to the controversial Section 377 of the Indian Penal Code, 1860.

[29]*See* MacKinnon (1979).

acts, or sexual acts performed upon them by women without their consent. However, given that power structures at workplaces traditionally put women in the position of the oppressed by equipping them with less bargaining powers, the enforcement of the Act will not give rise to a significant amount of collateral damage.

The enforcement of antidiscrimination law also causes harm to individual litigants. They are burdened economically and socially. There exists a higher burden upon them to prove that they were mistreated *specifically* because of their identity and status in society.[30] Further, as these laws do not account for intersectional discrimination, litigants who have been discriminated against for a variety of reasons can claim redressal only for one of them.

7 Who Supports the Enforcement of Antidiscrimination Law?

Several groups of persons and entities—marginalized communities, civil society activists, and organs of the State, support the enforcement of antidiscrimination law in India. Enforcement is accorded widespread support by marginalized communities, for the present unwieldy set of laws is the only means for them to enforce their rights at present. In addition to marginalized groups, civil society activists have tried their best to rally for the enforcement of existing antidiscrimination laws. Human rights organizations and other non-governmental organizations have rallied for the better enforcement of the existing laws against discrimination.[31] Better enforcement is advocated through improvement of the existing mechanism, including setting up of Internal Complaints Committees in workplaces and other institutions that are not equipped with them, and amending legislation adequately to ensure that individual litigants can access justice at all times. In addition to the reformation of existing laws, one section of campaigners seeks to advocate a new, unified antidiscrimination law that tackles intersectional discrimination and provides civil remedies to all aggrieved individuals for both direct and indirect discrimination.[32] The movement does not, however, preclude support for the enforcement of existing laws against discrimination.

As stated earlier, the government, law enforcement officials and the judiciary stand to benefit from the enforcement of antidiscrimination laws and therefore offer broad support for the same. In addition to the government and the judiciary, statutory bodies such as the National Human Rights Commission, the National Commission for Backward Classes and the National Commission for Minorities also support the enforcement of antidiscrimination laws in the country. Their functions include

---

[30]Sheikh and Bhatia (2016).
[31]Alternative Law Forum (2014).
[32]Centre for Policy Research (2015).

receiving complaints and taking them up with the appropriate authorities on behalf of minorities within the country.

8 Who Opposes the Enforcement of Antidiscrimination Law?

In most cases, those disadvantaged by the enforcement of antidiscrimination law are the most opposed to its enforcement. This includes, most obviously, members of privileged communities such as those belonging to the upper castes, men, people without disabilities, and people not from the Dalit community.

Protests against the enforcement of antidiscrimination law have been ongoing since India's Independence. A rather unpleasant example of widespread opposition to the enforcement of antidiscrimination law is the protest against the Mandal Commission Report, which advocated the grant of affirmative action to Other Backward Classes. This was greatly contested, as what constitutes other backward classes was not distinctively delineated in society (and continues to remain amorphous even today). The release of the Report was followed by widespread protests.[33] One of the main grounds of opposition that was not directly related to the deprivation of privilege of the upper classes, was that determining beneficiaries and ensuring affirmative action to them is a matter of great difficulty. However, the more disadvantaged Other Backward Classes are most definitely in need of affirmative aid[34] and with the exclusion of the "creamy layer" of individuals who constitute Other Backward Classes, targeting the true beneficiaries of the policy is somewhat easier. Even today, large sections of the population continue to oppose affirmative action as a whole on the ground that admissions to educational institutions and workplaces ought to be merit-based.[35]

This, and several other such instances, indicates how those at the top of the hierarchy react when there exists a threat to their privilege, and is partly why the enforcement rate of antidiscrimination laws does not see any appreciable change.

---

[33] *Sunday Story: Mandal Commission report, 25 years later*, The Indian Express (September 1, 2015), *available at* http://indianexpress.com/article/india/india-others/sunday-story-mandal-commission-report-25-years-later/ (last visited on July 30, 2016).
[34] Deshpande (2011), p. 221.
[35] Gandhi (2016).

9 What Remedies Are Provided by the Enforcement of Antidiscrimination Law?

Under Article 32 and Article 226 of the Indian Constitution, the Supreme Court and High Courts have the power to enforce fundamental rights guaranteed in the Constitution including the right to equality and non-discrimination as provided in Article 14, 15, 16 and 17. The right to seek constitutional remedy for violation of fundamental rights is itself considered a fundamental right.[36] For the enforcement of fundamental rights, the Supreme Court has expanded the scope of *locus standi*, which has resulted in "public interest litigation" on behalf of socially and economically marginalized communities.[37]

Since there is no single antidiscrimination law in India, the remedies provided under various statutes differ significantly. Certain legislation like the Prevention of Atrocities Act offer criminal remedies, while the more recent Sexual Harassment of Women at the Workplace (Prevention, Prohibition and Redressal) Act, offers civil remedies.[38] Legislations such as the Persons with Disability (Equal Opportunities, Protection of Rights and Full Participation) Act, 1995 adopts a "welfare approach."[39] Even though some legislation provides for various internal mechanisms, the last remedy under most of this legislation is approaching the courts. It has been argued that in criminal law for the deterrent effect to operate it is necessary that both the criminal and public are can link the crime with the subsequent punishment that follows.[40] However, in India due to lengthy trials, often the punishment follows so many years after the crime that it dilutes the memory of the public regarding the crime, thus weakening the deterrent effect.[41]

The Draft Equality Bill that was drafted in 2015, and subsequently revised in 2016 with the inputs of civil society members and lawyers, has provided for civil remedies instead of criminal remedies. This is one of the most crucial aspects of this bill. The civil remedies provided by the bill include abandonment and amendment of the discriminatory conduct by the perpetrator, providing compensation, written apology, and mechanisms such as providing diversification measures and training. The goal is to move from the retributive aspect of punishment to an effective remedy having elements of restoration that are more likely to lead to lasting change.[42]

---

[36]Rakshit (1999), pp. 2379–2381.
[37]Lawyers Collective (2016).
[38]Centre for Law and Policy Research (2016).
[39]Centre for Law and Policy Research (2016).
[40]Weisser (2016).
[41]Weisser (2016).
[42]Frontline (2016).

10 How Broad Is the Coverage of Antidiscrimination Law?

Presently, antidiscrimination laws in India may be grouped into the following categories—caste, sex and disability. There is no uniformity in terms of which remedies are available, whether they are civil or criminal in nature, or how they are enforced.

There are also several lacunae in their extent of coverage. There are no provisions in India against indirect discrimination[43] and, consequently, no means to enforce the same. There is also no law on religious discrimination in the private sector,[44] on the treatment of HIV positive/AIDS patients, on discrimination in housing, or differential treatment based on class. Furthermore, personal laws remain untouched by Indian antidiscrimination laws. A Muslim woman is still viewed as one half of a man, and the *triple talaaq*[45] practice is still prevalent.[46]

The laws presently in place cover only obvious forms of discrimination. The Sexual Harassment of Women at the Workplace (Prevention, Prohibition and Redressal) Act, 2013 provides penal sanctions for harassing women in the workplace. It does not provide any remedy for the inequality of opportunity that women face at work merely by virtue of being women. The Equal Remuneration Act, 1976 only rights the economic disadvantages faced by women in relation to payment of wages. There exists other legislation directed towards the protection or provision of benefits to women, such as the Maternity Benefits Act, 1961 and the Indecent Representation of Women (Prohibition) Act, 1986. Though these are not technically against discrimination, they may be included in the legal framework on antidiscrimination as their purpose is to uplift an oft discriminated-against section of society.

The current legal framework is too unwieldy and complex, often missing out on nuanced forms of discrimination. As stated earlier, these laws do not account for intersectionality—a Dalit woman finds it more difficult to seek employment or education opportunities on account of her class, caste *and* gender.[47] A unified law is a step towards recognizing that most times, multiple causes for one single act of discrimination are interlinked, and will provide a wider range of victims with an appropriate remedy.

---

[43] *See* Townshend-Smith (1998), p. 511.

[44] Sudhir (2015).

[45] A form of divorce recognized by Muslim law where the husband pronounces the word "talaaq", meaning divorce, thrice in one sitting. A divorce is irrevocably effected upon this pronouncement. The wife has no option to assent to or object to the divorce; *see* Agnihotri (2017).

[46] The practice of *triple talaaq* has recently been declared unconstitutional by the Supreme Court.

[47] Deshpande (2011), pp. 106–146.

11 Does the Enforcement of Antidiscrimination Law Vary According to the Ground of Discrimination?

Yes, the enforcement of Antidiscrimination law varies according to the ground of discrimination. At the very outset, the enforcement depends on whether the ground is recognized as a ground for discrimination under the Indian Constitution or specific statutes dealing with different forms of discrimination.

Article 15(1) of the Indian Constitution states "the State shall not discriminate against any citizen on grounds only of religion, race, caste, sex, place of birth or any of them." The term 'only' has been interpreted restrictively to mean that this indicates an exhaustive list of grounds for claiming discrimination. Thus, discrimination on the grounds of sex would not include discrimination on the basis of gender identity and sexual orientation, both of which form the basis of widespread discrimination in India. Further, the term 'only' can also be interpreted to mean that discrimination must be only based on one of the enumerated grounds and cannot be a combination of one enumerated ground with another enumerated or non-enumerated ground.[48]

In India, there is no cohesive antidiscrimination law. A variety of legislation has been enacted to tackle discrimination in in the workplace and in other public spaces. Each of these legislation is based on different grounds—caste, sex, religion, and physical and mental disabilities. Further, each law provides for a different framework to combat the specific type of discrimination for which it was enacted. The Prevention of Atrocities Act for instance, has special courts to enforce the provisions of the Act. The Prevention of Disability Act on the other hand, gives power to appointed Commissioners to enforce the Act at the national and state level. Therefore, the enforcement of these laws varies to a great extent according to the ground of discrimination, the relevant statutes, and the structure and the efficacy of the authorities empowered to enforce them.

12 What Is the Relationship Between the Enforcement of Antidiscrimination Law and the Quest for Equality on Both an Individual and Systemic Level?

It is difficult to map precisely the relationship between the enforcement of antidiscrimination law and the quest for equality, given the varied meaning of equality itself.

As discussed earlier, antidiscrimination law in India has mainly been focused on affirmative action for lower castes or 'Reservation' as it is known in India. One of the greatest drawbacks of the system is that it covers only caste, which a status that is

---

[48]Oxford Pro Bono Publico (2012).

unique to the Hindu religion. This leads to exclusion of members of all other religions from the protection of affirmative action. Muslims in India have been known to suffer various historical disadvantages, but there have been no such reservations for them. Apart from excluding members of other religions, similar quotas are not granted to all other members of discriminated groups.

The original goal of temporary affirmative action was the abolition of social inequalities due to caste in Indian society. However, the usage of caste as an identity-marker in censuses as well as in the current reservation system that necessitates the usage of caste for all quotas in education and employment, perpetuates and legitimizes 'caste.'[49] Many argue that affirmative action, due to its reliance on labels, reinforces notions of exclusion.[50] Issues such as these complicate the quest for equality and struggle for social justice.

In many ways the purpose of the reservation system, which was to promote a more egalitarian society, has been defeated because of caste politics, where politicians promise caste-based incentives as a political bargaining chip to garner votes.[51] This rhetoric has deepened social divisions and led to recent incidents such as the Jat Protests.[52]

Whatever we do must unite rather than divide people in the quest for social justice. Therefore, policies that seek to address embedded discrimination must integrate rather than separate people in society. After all, we are a society plagued by so many divides that our quest for inclusion or social justice should not accentuate those divides.[53] For measures to be successful in reducing or eliminating discrimination, the discourse on discrimination and equality should not be limited to certain castes, but take into account the concerns of all. As the debate for extending reservation into the private sector continues, a solution needs to be found that does not completely do away with meritocratic principles.

13 Is the Enforcement of Antidiscrimination Law Regarded as Different from the Enforcement of Other Laws?

The enforcement of discrimination law is different from the enforcement of other laws because of the unique nature of discrimination law. Some of the questions that are not always easy to answer include what constitutes discrimination, who is protected under antidiscrimination laws, and who are the 'duty-bearers.'[54]

---

[49]Mitra (2016).
[50]Nayyar (2011).
[51]Mitra (2016).
[52]Jaffelot (2017).
[53]Nayyar (2011).
[54]Khaitan (2015).

The Indian legal system is plagued with an acute problem of pendency of litigation and lengthy trials, which are significant impediments in access to justice. The lengthy trials in India particularly affect marginalized communities, as they are often economically or socially disadvantaged. Due to the delay in cases, victims and witnesses are pressured by dominant groups and are either threatened or bribed to withdraw their cases or retract their testimonies.[55] Long trials also make it more difficult for witnesses to accurately remember the details of events about which they are testifying, which is used by the defense to weaken evidence against the perpetrators. Protracted litigation is also very expensive. Victims often have less financial ability to support the costs of litigation than their usually wealthier perpetrators. Perpetrators exploit this by intentionally causing delays, leading to victims inability to support the costs of almost never ending litigation.[56]

This is particularly evident in data related to the implementation of the Prevention of Atrocities Act. According to the most recent government statics available, the conviction rates under the Prevention of Atrocities Act are much lower than general conviction rates. Whereas the general conviction rate was 45%, the conviction rate for cases filed under the Prevention of Atrocities Act was as low as 15.6%.[57] The low rate of convictions compared to the high number of atrocities reported against Dalits speaks to the caste bias of prosecutors as well as other organs of justice, including the judiciary.[58] Presumably, since enforcement officials are members of the same society, victims of other grounds of discrimination who approach courts or other institutions for the enforcement of their constitutional rights or rights under other well intentioned legislations are often confronted with the bias and discrimination that they face in society while seeking redressal.

14 What Does the Enforcement of Antidiscrimination Law Reveal About the Nature of Your Legal System or About the Enforcement of Laws in Your Legal System?

India is the second most populated country in the world and is characterized by great diversity in terms of languages, religions and cultures. Taking into account this diversity and the clash that exists between different groups of society, independent India's constitution made a commitment to equality and non-discrimination among its citizens. Having started with few recognized grounds of discrimination under the constitution, this list has been expanded through legislation as well as judicial interpretations.

---

[55] Khaitan (2015).
[56] Weisser (2016).
[57] Weisser (2016).
[58] Center for Human Rights and Global Justice & Human Rights Watch (2007).

The first affirmative action measures were taken to protect members of lower castes in an effort to undo the historical disadvantages and oppression suffered by this group. In addition to constitutional protection, there were also specific statutes to protect this group from discrimination. At present, most of the data related to enforcement of discrimination laws is based on laws prohibiting caste discrimination. In addition to the general problems plaguing the Indian legal system, protected groups under antidiscrimination law suffer additional hurdles in accessing justice due to their identity and the face bias that institutions and law enforcement officials have towards members of traditionally discriminated groups.

This is not to say that there have been no benefits arising from affirmative action. Affirmative action has succeeded even if this success has been modest. There is representation of the scheduled castes and schedules tribes due to the quotas in terms of education and jobs in the public sector. However, there is inclusion for only very few while many others still continue to suffer discrimination. Several antidiscrimination statutes that provide for strong enforcement mechanisms have not had the intended result. Antidiscrimination statutes are rendered futile if the individuals entrusted with the implementation of law and justice dispensation consciously or unconsciously discriminate and defeat the purpose of the law. There are instances of hostility even in the judiciary, which often throws out cases on technical grounds. Discrimination is often embedded in beliefs and ideologies, which is difficult to change through the instrument of law. However, the law does provide a signal of what is considered right and wrong in a society at a given point of time.

15 Conclusion

The importance of the non-discrimination principle was recognized as early as the 1950s in independent India's constitution. Additionally, India was one of the first countries to provide affirmative action to historically oppressed and traditionally disadvantaged communities. Since independence, various legislation has been passed to deal with the discrimination of other groups such as schedules castes and scheduled tribes, women, children, persons with disability, etc. One of the most recent additions to this group is transgender persons through both judicial decisions and legislation. Similarly, even though discrimination on the basis of sexual orientation is neither a ground recognised under the constitution nor under legislation, the judiciary has passed decisions acknowledging the discrimination against sexual minorities.

While there is a dearth of research and empirical data analyzing the implementation and enforcement of all discrimination laws in India, existing data on the implementation of some caste-based discrimination law reveals that even well intentioned legislation fails to fulfil their purpose due to poor enforcement. Thus, there needs to be a systematic review of the efficacy of existing discrimination laws to see what changes can be made to ensure that the intentions of legislation are realized.

India is amongst the few countries in the world with a constitutional commitment to a liberal democracy that lacks comprehensive antidiscrimination legislation that also extends to the private sector. The discussion regarding this has been ongoing for almost a decade. These discussions have finally taken the form of a draft Equality Bill, which seeks to be a comprehensive antidiscrimination law covering various forms of discrimination that were not covered under previous legislation and providing for different forms of remedies and enforcement mechanisms. The bill is also constantly being discussed, debated and enriched with inputs from lawyers, activists and members of civil society. Whether the bill is eventually passed as law and how it is implemented and enforced will be a question of political will and other factors that go beyond the law.

References

Agnihotri S (2017) Triple talaq: how it affects lives of India's 90 million Muslim women. India Today, 30 Mar 2017. http://indiatoday.intoday.in/story/triple-talaq-muslim-women-supreme-court-sharia-law-islam/1/916882.html. Accessed 4 May 2017

Alternative Law Forum (2014) Consultation on antidiscrimination laws, 22 Dec 2014. http://altlawforum.org/campaigns/consultation-on-antidiscrimination-laws/. Accessed 30 July 2016

Center for Human Rights and Global Justice & Human Rights Watch (2007) Caste discrimination against dalits or so-called untouchables in India, February 2007. http://tbinternet.ohchr.org/Treaties/CERD/Shared%20Documents/Ind/INT_CERD_NGO_Ind_70_9036_E.pdf. Accessed 30 July 2016

Centre for Law and Policy Research (2016) Soft judicial review, conflicts with other rights, and other problems in the draft equality bill. http://blog.mylaw.net/. Accessed 30 July 2016

Centre for Policy Research (2015) CPR workshop on a draft anti-discrimination bill, 18 Dec 2015. http://www.cprindia.org/events/4871. Accessed 30 July 2016

Deshpande A (2011) The grammar of caste: economic discrimination in contemporary India. Oxford University Press, pp 19–20

Frontline (2016) Systemic barriers, 19 Feb 2016. http://www.frontline.in/cover-story/systemic-barriers/article8183612.ece#test

Gandhi M (2016) Stand up India and the belittling of reservations under the Garb of Merit. The Wire, 12 Apr 2016. http://thewire.in/29134/stand-up-india-and-the-belittling-of-reservations-under-the-garb-of-merit/. Accessed 30 July 2016

Harlieb GD (2016) Status update: research for an Indian comprehensive anti-discrimination statute. Altern Law Forum. http://altlawforum.org/campaigns/status-update-research-for-an-indian-comprehensive-anti-discrimination-statute/. Accessed 30 July 2016

Human Rights Watch (2001) Caste discrimination: a global concern, August 2001. https://www.hrw.org/reports/2001/globalcaste/caste0801-03.htm. Accessed 30 July 2016

Human Rights Watch (2016) Broken people: caste violence against India's "Untouchables". https://www.hrw.org/reports/1999/india/. Accessed 30 July 2016

Jaffelot C (2017) Why Jats want a quota. http://indianexpress.com/article/opinion/columns/jats-reservation-stir-obc-quota-rohtak-haryana-protests/. Accessed 8 May 2017

Khaitan T (2015) A theory of discrimination law. Oxford Scholarship Online, August 2015. http://www.oxfordscholarship.com/view/10.1093/acprof:oso/9780199656967.001.0001/acprof-9780199656967-chapter-3

Lawyers Collective (2016) Anti-discrimination/sex equality. http://www.lawyerscollective.org/womens-rights-initiative/anti-discriminationsex-equality.html. Accessed 30 July 2016

MacKinnon C (1979) Sexual harassment of working women. Yale University Press

Mitra M (2016) Caste in crisis: the limits of positive discrimination in India. Brown Polit Rev, 30 Mar 2016. http://www.brownpoliticalreview.org/2016/03/caste-crisis-limits-positive-discrimination-india/. Accessed 30 July 2016

Nayyar D (2011) Discrimination and justice: beyond affirmative action. Econ Polit Wkly, 15 Oct 2011. http://www.epw.in/journal/2011/42/special-articles/discrimination-and-justice-beyond-affirmative-action.html. Accessed 30 July 2016

Oxford Pro Bono Publico (2012) Submission to the Attorney General's Department: Reponses to question 5 and 10 on the consolidation of commonwealth anti-discrimination laws, January 2012. https://issuu.com/opbp/docs/2012_australian_equality_submission/1. Accessed 30 July 2016

Rakshit NB (1999) Right to constitutional remedy: significance of Article 32. Econ Polit Wkly 34 (34/35):2379–2381 (August 21–September 3)

Sheikh D, Bhatia G (2016) Systemic barriers. Frontline, 19 Feb 2016. http://www.frontline.in/cover-story/systemic-barriers/article8183612.ece. Accessed 30 July 2016

Singh G (2016) Temples of injustice. Governance Now, 20 Feb 2016. http://www.governancenow.com/views/columns/temples-injustice#sthash.NGVxhFnx.dpuf. Accessed 30 July 2016

Sudhir A (2015) Religious apartheid: India has no law to stop private sector from discriminating on grounds of faith. Scroll.in, 4 June 2015. http://scroll.in/article/731392/religious-apartheid-india-has-no-law-to-stop-private-sector-from-discriminating-on-grounds-of-faith. Accessed 30 July 2016

The Equal Rights Trust (2016) Universal periodic review of the Republic of India 2011. http://www.equalrightstrust.org/ertdocumentbank/ERT_UPR_India_2011.pdf. Accessed 30 July 2016

The Supreme Court (2016) Entry ban in Sabarimala, matter referred to Constitutional Bench. NDTV, 11 July 2016. http://www.ndtv.com/india-news/sabrimala-matter-may-be-referred-to-constitution-bench-supreme-court-1430244. Last visited on July 30, 2016

Townshend-Smith RJ (1998) Discrimination law: text, cases and materials. Cavendish Publishing Ltd. pp 497–538

Weisser E (2016) Despite A 2015 amendment to the prevention of atrocities act, justice remains out of reach to scheduled castes, 16 May 2016. http://www.caravanmagazine.in/vantage/despite-2015-amendment-prevention-atrocities-act-justice-remains-reach-scheduled-castes. Accessed 30 July 2016

Maithili Pai holds a B.A., LL.B. (Hons.) degree from the National University of Juridical Sciences, Kolkata. She has a keen interest in human rights law, constitutional law and dispute resolution. She is currently working as a judicial clerk in the Supreme Court of India.

Nupur Raut holds a B.A., LL.B. (Hons.) degree from the National Law School of India University, Bangalore. She has worked extensively at various human rights litigation offices in India, and served as an editor of the NLS Socio-Legal Review. She is currently working as a judicial clerk at the Supreme Court of India.

Israel

Tamar Kricheli Katz and Donna Zamir

1 Introduction

1.1 Recognized Disadvantaged and Discriminated-Against Groups in Israel

As in many other countries, in Israel there are disadvantaged groups that are discriminated against in various walks of life, both public and private. Similarly to many other countries, in Israel the law seeks to protect, to varying degrees, the interests of disadvantaged groups, which are defined based on gender, religion, race, nationality, ethnicity, sexual orientation, age, health status, and more.

With the establishment of the State Israel, in 1948, it was stated in the Declaration of Independence (the document declaring the establishment of the State of Israel and expressing "the vision of the people and its credo")[1] that the state "will ensure the complete equality of social and political rights to all its inhabitants irrespective of religion, race or sex." Over the years, the judiciary, headed by the Supreme Court, recognized the right to equality as a fundamental right in Israel.[2] Nevertheless, the State of Israel never enacted a comprehensive constitution that includes all the basic principles upon which the Israeli regime is founded. Over the years, the Knesset (the legislative authority in Israel) enacted several separate basic laws, which from a normative point of view are considered superior to other legislation in the country. In 1992, after extensive parliamentary discussions, the Knesset enacted the Basic Law: Human Dignity and Liberty. This law explicitly includes several basic human

---

[1] HCJ 73/53, Kol Ha'am Ltd. vs. Minister of Interior, PD 7 871 (1953).
[2] HCJ 98/69, Bergman vs. Minister of Finance, PD 23(1) 693, 698 (1969).

T. Kricheli Katz (✉) · D. Zamir
Tel Aviv University, Faculty of Law and the Department of Sociology, Tel Aviv, Israel
e-mail: tamarkk@post.tau.ac.il

rights,[3] but for various reasons, mainly political,[4] it does not include explicitly the right to equality and the prohibition against discrimination.

The Supreme Court interpreted the Basic Law: Human Dignity and Liberty broadly, as having produced a constitutional revolution,[5] and as such, as one that incorporates—at least to some degree—the right to equality.[6] According to the way in which the Supreme Court understands this right, "equal treatment must be given to equals and differential treatment to those who are different, in proportion to the extent of their differences,"[7] and different needs require different conceptions of equality.[8]

As described in detail below, in addition to this legislation and to case law since the establishment of the state to date, the legislature has passed several other laws with lower normative status than that of the basic laws. These laws have regulated and enshrined the principle of equality for a range of disadvantaged groups in several areas, particularly in the field of employment and in the management of public places.

1.2 Public and Private Law

In general, in Israel the principle of equality and non-discrimination applies foremost to the state, mainly within the framework of public law, whether the state operates in the public or the private sector. In addition, when organizations have a dual nature (incorporated under private law, but in their essence contain public attributes), they are obliged to behave equitably and not to discriminate. Moreover, there is extensive legislation regulating the field of labor in both the public and private sectors that imposes a duty on many employers to deal equitably under various circumstances with their current and prospective employees. A special judicial system operates in Israel that specializes exclusively in labor law and operates specialized courts separate from the general judicial system. Finally, in the year 2000 a law was enacted prohibiting discrimination in the provision of goods and services and in entry to public places, even by privately owned businesses.

---

[3]The law explicitly includes the right to property, the right to leave the country, the right to privacy and intimacy, and the protection against imprisonment, arrest, and extradition.

[4]For a history of the enactment of the basic law, see Yehudit Karp, "Basic Law: Human Dignity and Liberty – A biography of power struggles."

[5]Mizrachi Bank ruling.

[6]HCJ 4541/94, Miller vs. Minister of Defense, PD 49(4) 94, 135 (henceforth the Miller case); HCJ 6427/02, The Movement for Quality Government in Israel vs. The Knesset (published in Nevo 11.05.06).

[7]HCJ 6924/98, Association for Civil Rights in Israel vs. Government of Israel, PD 55(5) 15.

[8]Miller case.

2 Are Antidiscrimination Laws Enforced?

There are statutory bodies whose task, among others, is to ensure the enforcement of the prohibition against discrimination. Because the activities of these bodies are transparent and public, it appears that measures are being taken for the enforcement of this legislation.

Every year hundreds of requests are filed with the commissions responsible for enforcing the prohibition against discrimination, and these exercise their various authorities to address the requests, including their authorities in the areas of civil, administrative, and criminal law. As it is true also of other legislative areas, however, enforcement is only partial, and in practice there is a great deal of discrimination that for various reasons is not reported and against which no enforcement measures are taken. These claims are borne out in the reports of the State Comptroller, a statutory body established by a special basic law, whose function is to perform an external audit of a range of activities of government ministries, local and municipal authorities, and various public organizations. For example, the State Comptroller's Report for 2015 reveals that although there are enforcement agencies with special budgets within the government, there is no effective enforcement of workers' rights in Israel. Complaints filed with the various commissions are scarce (only a few hundred per year), whereas in the field the number of violations appears to be far greater.

3 How Is Antidiscrimination Law Enforced?

As stipulated by various antidiscrimination laws in Israel, unlawful discrimination is a civil tort. A person who believes to have been discriminated against unlawfully can file a civil suit against the discriminating entity. Several items of legislation decree legal presumptions in favor of the plaintiffs and lighten the burden of proof for them. In addition to the injured party, the law often allows representative workers' unions as well as organizations active in the field of the victims' violated rights to initiate legal action with their consent.

Consistent with several laws, the court has the authority to grant the right of intervention to an organization dealing with the rights of those against whom it is prohibited to discriminate, and of voicing an opinion in the matter. As described in detail in the next section, it is the function of several organizations, established by law, to advance the enforcement of antidiscrimination legislation in Israel and to help victims realize their rights under the law.

4 Who Enforces the Antidiscrimination Laws?

In Israel, several institutions established by law are responsible for enforcing the antidiscrimination legislation. These are:

Labor Court As noted above, the labor court is the main legal instance for enforcing this legislation.

Ministry of Economy and Industry In general, the Ministry of Economy and Industry, and the minister heading it, are responsible for driving the enforcement of existing labor laws and for maintaining adequate working conditions.

Administration Regulation and Enforcement Unit Within the Ministry of Economy and Industry One of the functions of this unit is to drive the implementation of labor laws and increase awareness on the part of employers and employees of the various provisions of the law. The unit has the authority to investigate violations of the provisions of labor laws, to initiate administrative action against violators, and to impose financial sanctions.

Commission for Equal Opportunity at Work The Commission is an independent unit within the Ministry of Economy and Industry, established by the Equal Employment Opportunities Law. Its function is to promote recognition of the rights pursuant to the legislation prohibiting discrimination at work and to exercise these rights. The Commission is responsible for enforcing the prohibition against discrimination in the workplace at the civil level. The Commission is responsible for enforcing the Equal Employment Opportunities Law, the Male and Female Workers (Equal Pay) Law, the Employment of Women Law, the Women's Equal Rights Law, the Prevention of Sexual Harassment Law, and other laws aimed at ensuring the proper representation of disadvantaged groups.

The legal activity of the Commission includes addressing complaints from the public, investigating complaints of discrimination, providing legal advice to employees, employers, and the general public, writing legal opinions, filing civil suits and submitting expert opinions to the labor courts and to the general courts, obtaining general court orders instructing employers to take action in order to meet their obligations under the equal employment opportunities legislation, and issuing orders for obtaining data and documents from employers. The Commission also has the authority to carry out publicity and training activities to raise public awareness about equality and discrimination in the labor market.

Commissioner for the Employment of Women Law The Commissioner responsible for this law operates within the Ministry of Economy. A woman usually fills the position. Her role includes implementation and enforcement of the Employment of Women Law (see Sect. 10 for details). She is also responsible for examining requests from employers for dismissing women who are protected by the Employment of Women Law, and for granting permits to dismiss such women if the requests are justified.

Ministry of Justice The Ministry of Justice and the minister at its head are responsible for the enforcement and implementation of several laws prohibiting discrimination, including the Women's Equal Rights Law, the Prevention of Sexual Harassment Law, as well as the law prohibiting discrimination at activities conducted in public places. In 2014, an Information Center for Victims of Discrimination and Racism opened at the Ministry of Justice, with the mission to raise awareness of the legal prohibition as well as the moral ban against racism and discrimination in Israel. The Center provides legal assistance for people who believe that they were harmed and unlawfully discriminated against. A website was also established to provide information about laws and regulations that deal with discrimination and its prevention.

Commission for Equal Rights of Persons with Disabilities The Commission operates within the Ministry of Justice. It was established pursuant to the Equal Rights for People with Disabilities Law. Its function is to work for the prevention of discrimination and to promote the integration of people with disabilities in Israeli society in a variety of areas including employment, housing, education, legal capacity and guardianship, social security, culture, and leisure. To achieve these goals, the Commission cooperates with relevant entities in all sectors: government, local authorities, the private sector, and third sector organizations. The Commission is also responsible for the implementation of the International Convention on the Rights of Persons with Disabilities.

In the employment area, the Commission has the authority to initiate civil actions. It also advises the Minister of the Economy with regard to appropriate representation for persons with disabilities and with regard to the enactment of regulations in the field of employment. In the area of accessibility, the Commission has authority to take enforcement measures, conduct monitoring, file claims, and discharge other administrative functions. The Commission can issue accessibility orders for those who are obligated to make their facilities accessible for disabled people; conduct inquiries regarding violation or suspected violation of accessibility orders or regarding the discrimination of people with disabilities in a public place or in the provision of a public service; file civil claims in these matters; and publish information to the public concerning obligations and rights, and concerning discrimination in public areas and services.

The Commission also works to promote policy concerning the rights of people with disabilities, and provides solutions to individuals through professional counseling, legal solutions for claimants, and supervision. It files indictments and civil actions, promotes and initiates legislation, organizes conferences and seminars, distributes and edits educational materials and books, collects data, and more.

5 Who Benefits from the Enforcement of Antidiscrimination Laws?

Israeli antidiscrimination legislation protects a wide range of disadvantaged groups, as noted in the Introduction, and as detailed in Sect. 10. Israeli antidiscrimination law prohibits some forms of discrimination based on religion or religious group, race, nationality, country of origin, ethnic origin, gender, sexual orientation, marital status, pregnancy, fertility treatments, IVF, parenthood, age, residence, socio-economic background, health limitations (including mental and cognitive disabilities), visual impairment and the need for a guide dog, worldview, political party affiliation, and army reserve service. Most of the legal protection is granted to these groups with respect to the labor market for both state and private employers. The Equal Employment Opportunities Commission is responsible for enforcing antidiscrimination legislation in the field of labor.

Special protection is provided for women. First, there are laws that provide special protection for women's rights, including the Women's Equal Rights Law and the Employment of Women Law, applicable to a variety of fields, both in the public and the private spheres. It is prohibited to discriminate against women in the employment area as far as wages are concerned, and broad protection is granted for pregnant women, women undergoing various fertility treatments, and women after childbirth. A Commissioner at the Ministry of Economy is responsible for implementing and enforcing the Employment of Women Law.

Another group that benefits from the enforcement of non-discrimination is people with disabilities. Although the prohibition against discrimination on grounds of disability is not included in most labor laws, a separate special law protects the rights of the physically, emotionally, and mentally disabled in the public and private domains, including in the employment field. The Commission for Equal Rights of Persons with Disabilities is responsible for promoting the principles of the law and its enforcement.

6 What Remedies Are Provided by the Enforcement of Antidiscrimination Laws?

Most antidiscrimination laws allow the filing of civil actions for violations, usually with the labor court. These laws authorize the court to grant several remedies, some at the discretion of the court, according to circumstances.

As part of a civil action, the court may award monetary damages to the plaintiff in compensation for any discriminatory act. The court may award compensation without proof of damage, up to a certain amount, which varies for the different laws. Furthermore, if the granting of compensation alone does not appear to be adequate, the court has jurisdiction to issue an injunction or a *mandamus* order in the matter. As part of an action in the employment field, the law generally requires that the court take into account the effect of the order on labor relations in the workplace and the possibility of another employee being harmed by it. Several laws prohibiting discrimination allow the filing of class action suits in response to violations.

The violation of most prohibitions against discrimination is also a criminal offense. The penalty is usually a fine that can reach NIS 150,000. Several laws, such as the Women's Employment Law and the Prevention of Sexual Harassment Law, also impose prison sentences ranging from several months to four years. Note further that with regard to the law prohibiting discrimination related to activities in public places, in addition to punitive fines, the court has the authority to order the business that committed the prohibited discriminatory act to cease activities.

7 Who Supports the Enforcement of Antidiscrimination Laws?

In Israel, several entities in various sectors support the enforcement of legislation prohibiting discrimination. First, the function of several state entities is to support antidiscrimination legislation and its enforcement. As noted in Sect. 4 above, one of the main roles of the Ministry of Economy and Industry is to protect employee rights and to enforce the extensive legislation in the matter. Several units operate within the ministry—for example the Administration Regulation and Enforcement unit, which is responsible for the enforcement of the Women's Employment Act, and the Equal Employment Opportunities Commission, whose function is enforcement of the legislation prohibiting discrimination in employment, and raising public awareness of the matter.

The Commission for Equal Rights of People with Disabilities reports to the Minister of Justice who is responsible for the implementation and enforcement of several laws prohibiting discrimination. Within the framework of various projects and campaigns, the ministry attempts to promote anti-racism and antidiscrimination, as well as promote an awareness of the prohibition against discrimination that is enshrined in a variety of laws.

Several third-sector organizations in Israel act on behalf of antidiscrimination legislation and its enforcement in a wide range of areas. Among these are human rights groups, women's rights organizations, human rights organizations for people with disabilities, Arab minority rights organizations, and other human rights organizations.

8 Who Opposes the Enforcement of Antidiscrimination Laws?

Given that most of the antidiscrimination legislation in Israel applies to the field of employment, the employers are those who oppose the burden imposed on them in the management of their business. Indeed, such attitudes are apparent in employer surveys conducted by the research arm of the Ministry of Economy and Industry. In a survey about the attitudes of employers regarding diversity in the work force in 2011, employers declared that they believed that a policy of equal opportunities contributes to the business and that business owners should be generally encouraged to integrate many populations in their organizations, such as mothers of small children, older workers, and Arabs. On the other hand, contrary to legislation prohibiting discrimination, most of the managers surveyed believed that employers should have the right to employ whomever they want, without government interference. They also believed that businesses must recruit people based on personal acquaintance rather than through advertising open to all potential candidates, that in their business there was no advantage of employing workers of different origins and backgrounds, and that managers and senior professionals must work in the business beyond the normal working hours (a requirement that can harm the equal opportunity of mothers of young children).

A survey concerning employers' awareness and attitudes about labor laws conducted in 2015 found that most employers believe that workers' rights in the workplace in Israel are sufficiently enforced. This clearly indicates that they do not believe that enforcement of workers' rights should be increased, contrary to the opinions of employees, as reported in surveys conducted in this area. It was found that most employers agree in particular with the statement that state authorities tend to overly protect the rights of workers, ignoring and damaging employers.

9 How Broad Is the Coverage of Antidiscrimination Laws?

The obligation to act equitably applies to the state in all its activities, in both the public and the private sectors.[9] At the same time, most of antidiscrimination legislation in Israel regulates employment, which also includes private employers. Antidiscrimination legislation also applies to other areas, as detailed below.

As a preliminary comment, we note that in the Israeli Penal Code there is a special and extensive part prohibiting incitement to racism and many hate crimes, and imposing significant prison sentences for violating these provisions.

---

[9]HCJ 6698/95, Kaadan vs The Israel Lands Administration, PD 54(1) 258, 272.

9.1 Existing Legislation in Israel

Equal Employment Opportunities Law, 1988 This is one of the main and most comprehensive laws within the framework of equality legislation. The law prohibits discrimination in the workplace at the recruiting stage, as well as in working conditions, training or professional development, promotion, retirement, and dismissal. The prohibition against discrimination is sweeping and includes discrimination based on gender, sexual orientation, marital status, pregnancy, fertility treatment, IVF, parenting, age, race, religion, nationality, country of origin, place of residence, worldview, membership in a political party, and army reserve service. The prohibition against discrimination applies also to contract workers who work for the employer, and to the publication of advertisements related to the workplace. The above list has been expanded and updated over the years by a large number of amendments. Recently, the National Labor Court interpreted the prohibition against discrimination based on sexual orientation to include also the prohibition against discrimination based on gender identity.

The law also includes a prohibition against employers requesting from employees or applicant for employment genetic information or demanding that they undergo genetic testing. Another prohibition added recently concerns the request from employees or applicants for employment to provide their military profile (a numeric value assigned by the IDF to all recruits and soldiers denoting their medical suitability for various service units and functions). The law also stipulates that a particular action is not considered to be discrimination if it is required by the character or nature of the assignment or of the position.

Those harmed by discrimination for any one of the above reasons are entitled to file a civil suit with the labor court. If employees or applicants for employment deem that they have the right skills for the position, the burden of proof is transferred to employers to show that they did not act in violation of the law.

Employers who have been found to have violated the provisions of the law must compensate those discriminated against, including for non-pecuniary harm, and may be ordered to pay compensation without the need to prove harm. The amount of compensation is at the discretion of the court. The court may issue an injunction or a *mandamus* order if it deems that the awarded compensation alone is not adequate. Employees who file complaints or claims under this law or on the grounds of sexual harassment benefit from legal protection. The protection applies also to other employees who assist in filing such complaints and lawsuits. In 2008, the law was amended, establishing the Equal Employment Opportunities Commission, which is responsible for enforcement of the law.

The Male and Female Workers (Equal Pay) Law, 1996 This law was designed to promote equality and eliminate gender discrimination in salary and other remuneration for work. The law grants workers total rights that cannot be made conditional or waived. The law states that male and female employees employed by the same employer at the same workplace are entitled to equal pay not only for the same work (under its formal definition) but also for work that is essentially equal or of equal value. The law stipulates that one work is considered to be of equal value with another even if the two are not the same work or essentially equal if they are of equal importance among others from the point of view of the qualifications, effort, skills and responsibility required to perform them, and from the point of view of the environmental conditions in which they are performed. The labor court may appoint a job evaluation expert to provide an opinion whether the jobs at issue are the same, essentially equal, or equal in value. The law applies also to any other remuneration that an employer gives to (or for) employees in connection with their work.

The law qualifies its applicability and states that its provisions do not rule out a difference in wages or other remuneration that is made necessary by the nature or essence of the work in question as long as it does not constitute gender discrimination. The burden of proof is on the employer once the court has determined that, as defined by law, the two works are the same. The law also allows employees to request and receive information from employers regarding the salary levels of their employees, taking into consideration the privacy of the employees who are the objects of the information.

Employment of Women Law, 1954 This is one of the first laws of equality enacted in Israel. The law contains provisions for the protection of working women, including those working in private households, in order to ensure the health, safety, and rights of women at work, in particular the rights of women during pregnancy, after giving birth or aborting, and during fertility treatments, as well as the rights of women residing in shelters for abused women. The law has been recently amended to permit paternity as well as maternity leaves.

The labor court has exclusive jurisdiction to litigate civil proceedings concerning violations of this law and it is entitled to award compensation, even without proof of financial loss, at its discretion. The court is also authorized to issue an injunction or a *mandamus* order if it deems that the awarded compensation alone is not adequate.

Discharged Soldiers Law (Return to Work), 1949 This law prohibits employment discrimination based on compulsory or reserve military service, for example, when it comes to accruing seniority at the workplace, and prevents dismissal due to military service. To enforce non-discrimination, an Employment Committee was established whose function is to hear and decide claims of reservists against their employers in case they were dismissed because of reserve service. The Equal Employment Opportunities Commission is responsible for enforcing this law.

Prevention of Sexual Harassment Law, 1998 The purpose of this law is to prohibit sexual harassment in the name of the protection of human dignity, freedom, and privacy, and to promote equality between the genders. The law defines various types of behavior that constitute sexual harassment or persecution, including the framework of labor relations, and determines which behaviors represent a criminal offense, in addition to being a civil offense that allows the court to award compensation without proof of damage. In a labor relations action against an employer the burden of proof is on employers to show that they did not break the law. The law also imposes an obligation on employers to take reasonable steps to prevent sexual harassment or persecution within the framework of employee relations.

The labor court has exclusive jurisdiction to litigate civil suits for violations of this law and it is authorized to award compensation even without proof of financial loss. The court is also authorized to issue injunctions and *mandamus* orders if it deems that the awarded compensation alone is not adequate.

In addition to these laws, there are several statutory provisions that enshrine the obligation of ensuring fair representation; the Equal Employment Opportunity Commission is responsible for their enforcement. These provisions are:

- **Women's Equal Rights Law, 1951**. This law was one of the first laws of equality in Israel. The purpose of the law is to establish guidelines to ensure full equality between women and men, "to prevent and eradicate all legal discrimination against women" in a variety of areas, including the workplace. The law requires proper representation of women in public bodies, in the various types of positions and levels of employees, managers, directors, and members of executive councils. The Equal Employment Opportunities Commission is responsible for enforcement of the law.
- **Civil Service Law (Appointments), 1959**. The law decrees a broad obligation for proper representation of employees in the civil service at all levels and at all ministries, for men and women, people with disabilities, members of the Arab community including Druze and Circassians, and of members of the Ethiopian community.
- **Government Companies Law, 1957**. The law establishes an obligation for proper representation of citizens of both genders, members of the Arab community, members of the Ethiopian community, and members of the Druze community, among employees of government companies in all positions and at all levels.
- **Municipalities Ordinance (New Version)**. This law also establishes the obligation of fair representation among municipal employees in all positions and at all levels, of members of the Ethiopian and of the Druze communities.

Intensification of Labor Law Enforcement Law, 2011 The purpose of this law is to intensify and streamline the enforcement of labor laws in Israel. The law seeks to enhance the enforcement of the Employment of Women Law, which prohibits dismissing or reducing the amount of work of pregnant women (and of women in the process of fertility treatments) and of employees on maternity leave. The law seeks to enhance the enforcement of the prohibition against discrimination in job advertisements, both on the grounds of gender and of disability.

Equal Rights for People with Disabilities Law, 1998 The purpose of this law is to protect the dignity and freedom of persons with disabilities; to enshrine their right to equal and active participation in all spheres of life; to provide an appropriate solution to their special needs in a manner that enables them to live their lives with maximum independence, privacy, and dignity; and to fully achieve their potential. The law defines a person with a disability broadly as one with physical, emotional, or mental disabilities, including cognitive ones, permanent or temporary, as a result of which his functioning is substantially limited in one or more main spheres of life.

In general the law seeks to make the public and private space accessible to people with disabilities. This applies to disabled people receiving services provided to the public at large, including services provided by public organizations and services in the field of employment. The law establishes broad prohibitions against discrimination in this area and imposes an obligation for proper representation of persons with disabilities in a variety of businesses and workplaces. It also prohibits discrimination in public transportation and public spaces.

Law Prohibiting Discrimination Against Blind People Assisted by Guide Dogs, 1993 The law seeks to protect blind people in the field of employment and in public spaces. The law states that being accompanied by a guide dog shall not constitute, in itself, grounds for not employing a blind person in any position. It also states that it is prohibited to restrict the right of a blind person to enter a public place and use any facility therein, including public transportation, because the person is accompanied by a guide dog. The law prohibits collecting any fee from a blind person for entering a public place, using the facilities therein, or using public transportation because of being accompanied by a guide dog.

The law imposes a fine on violators. The Minister of Labor and Social Affairs is responsible for the implementation of this law.

Prohibition of Discrimination in Products, Services and Entry to Places of Entertainment and Public Places, 2000 This law is designed to promote equality and prevent discrimination in entering public venues, in supplying products, and providing services. The law imposes an obligation on businesses, both private and non-profit, not to discriminate in the provision of products or public services, in allowing entry to public places, or in providing services in public places. The law also prohibits a business that provides a public service to publicize an announcement that contains prohibited discrimination under this law. In this sense, the law is somewhat of an exception in that it regulates the private business sector and imposes a duty of equality not only on the state.

The law protects a range of disadvantaged groups and prohibits discrimination based on race, religion or religious group, nationality, country of origin, gender, sexual orientation, worldview, political affiliation, age, marital status, or parenthood. At the same time, the law stipulates that an action is not considered discrimination if it is required by the nature or essence of the product, service, or public place. Similarly, the action is not considered discrimination if it is carried out by an organization or non-profit club, and it is conducted for the purpose of advancing a special need of a particular group associated with that organization (as long as these needs are not against the law). The law also allows, in given circumstances, the operation of certain facilities in which there is a separation between men and women.

The law establishes a civil tort and creates several presumptions that make it easier for claimants to prove their claim. As part of such a claim, the court may award compensation even without proof of damage. The Minister of Justice is responsible for the implementation of this law. Unlike other antidiscrimination laws, no special enforcement body has been established for it and the police are exclusively responsible for enforcing it.

9.2 Legislation That Does Not Exist in Israel

Over the years, alongside the legislation described above, the Knesset rejected several bills that sought to expand the prohibition against discrimination under Israeli law. Below is a list of such proposed bills (that were proposed and rejected).

Bill: Prohibition Against Discrimination Because of Sexual Orientation or Gender Identity, 2015 The proposed bill sought to add to all legislation and regulations prohibiting discrimination an interpretation stating that discrimination based on sexual orientation or gender identity is also prohibited. Note that there is no law in Israel that explicitly protects against discrimination based on gender identity, but there are Supreme Court rulings that provide such protection.

Bill: Prohibition Against Discrimination in Housing, 2012 The proposed bill sought to impose an obligation not to discriminate against individuals in housing when renting or selling apartments in Israel for any of a variety of reasons.

Bill: Patients' Rights Act (Prohibition Against Discrimination), 2013 The proposed bill sought to extend the grounds on the basis of which it is prohibited to discriminate when receiving or requesting medical care.

9.3 Bills Pending

Bill: Prohibition Against Discrimination on Grounds of Weight, 2016 The proposed bill seeks to ban discrimination based on weight in obtaining employment or being promoted at work, in receiving services, in being admitted to public places, and to ban contemptuous attitudes based on a person's weight.

10 Does the Enforcement of Antidiscrimination Laws Vary According to the Ground of Discrimination?

Antidiscrimination legislation in Israel provides protection to a large number of disadvantaged groups in society in several areas of life. Within each individual item of legislation there is no legally mandated hierarchy between the various grounds for discrimination, and where several such grounds are included, the degree of enforcement appears to be completely equal among them.

There are, however, several disadvantaged groups with regard to which the legislation prohibiting discrimination is more extensive and grants more tools for implementing and enforcing the law in their case. As discussed in detail in Sect. 5 above, there are several bodies, established by law, whose function is to promote the enforcement of antidiscrimination in certain areas.

One of these bodies is the Commission for Equal Rights of People with Disabilities, which was established pursuant to the Equal Rights for People with Disabilities Law. Its function is to protect specifically the rights of people with physical and mental disabilities, and to ensure that public places are made accessible for these people. The activity summary report of the Commission for the years 2013–2014 shows that the Commission carries out hundreds of audits every year at public institutions and assesses the degree of accessibility and the implementation of the law in the matter. The Commission also issues hundreds of warning letters and dozens of orders instructing these institutions to improve accessibility for people with disabilities. The report noted that based on the experience accumulated by the Commission over the years, most violations of the law are corrected quickly by the institutions.

Another organization that acts to enforce antidiscrimination legislation is the Equal Employment Opportunity Commission. The Commission was established by the Equal Employment Opportunities Law, and it is responsible for enforcing the prohibition against discrimination at work at the civil level. This authority is a key element in the work of the Commission, and it includes handling complaints from the public, investigating complaints of discrimination, providing legal advice to many entities, writing legal opinions, filing civil suits, and providing expert opinions to the labor and other courts, and more.

A report summarizing the activities of the Commission in 2014 (which includes similar data for previous years as well), notes that the Commission receives about 900 inquiries per year. In 2014, the most prominent complaints concerned discrimination on grounds of pregnancy (34%), age (10%), reserve duty (7%), religion (6%), nationality (6%), and parenting (5%). Each complaint receives an initial legal response but does not necessarily result in a legal action that requires the involvement of the Commission. As the report states, when selecting the cases and procedures in which it becomes involved, the Commission applies its discretion based on the goals and objectives set in its strategic plan, on its areas of responsibility, and on the authority vested in it, as well as on the jurisprudential value and the implications of the legal issue at hand—all for the purpose of preventing discrimination and promoting equality of opportunity in the labor market.

Out of 900 referrals received in the course of the year, the Commission dealt with 19 cases and legal proceedings including 8 gender discrimination cases, 4 cases concerning discrimination based on pregnancy and parenting, cases of discrimination based on nationality and origin, age, and worldview (2 cases in each category), and one case of discrimination because of gender identity. It transpires from the above that the Commission focuses most of its activity on discrimination based on gender, pregnancy, and parenting, which also constitute a large part of the complaints it receives.

11 What Is the Relationship Between the Enforcement of Antidiscrimination Law and the Quest for Equality on Both an Individual and Systemic Levels?

Many studies have been conducted in Israel seeking to measure the effect of antidiscrimination laws on the situation on the ground. But because of problems that arise in the course of empirical research and in light of the challenge of establishing a causal link between the existing legislation and case law on one hand and the situation on the ground on the other, it is difficult to determine accurately the precise effect of this legislation.[10] In this section we also try to examine the situation of various disadvantaged groups, in different areas of life, based on current research and on various surveys and studies on this subject.

11.1 The Labor Market: Introduction

Over the years 1980–2007, there has been a significant increase in litigation in labor courts regarding discrimination. A study conducted on this topic[11] reveals that between 1980 and 2007 there has been an increase in the use of the Equal Employment Opportunity Law, the Employment of Women Law, and the use of the term "discrimination." Naturally, reference to the concept does not necessarily indicate enforcement, but it is indicative of greater willingness of victims of discrimination to sue, which can also indicate greater willingness of the courts to address the matter. Nevertheless, a general assessment of the labor market in Israel reveals that the market structure, and the changes that it has undergone over the years, preserve and even deepen the existing inequalities between different groups in society.[12]

For example, over the years, there has been a continuous increase in the number of workers joining the labor market. But this phenomenon went hand in hand with an increase in part-time jobs and in the rates of part-time employment, especially among women and contrary to their wishes (women work part-time because they were not able to find full-time work). Women's employment in Israel, more than that of men, is also characterized by contract and temporary employment arrangements that provide fewer rights. These data suggest increasing employment difficulties in the labor market in Israel and are yet another expression of gender inequality.[13]

Studies and research further indicate that over the years a clear hierarchy has been institutionalized in Israeli society in general and the labor market in particular, with Ashkenazi Jews at the top of the socioeconomic ladder, Jews of Eastern origin in the

---

[10]Mundlak, Antidiscrimination laws in employment.
[11]*Ibid.*
[12]Shtier (2006) (henceforth, Shtier).
[13]*Ibid.*

middle, and the Arab citizens at the bottom. Within each group, not surprisingly, men are above women, at least as far as income from work is concerned. Many studies conducted over the years show that this hierarchy has not changed in 50 years, and has been replicated in the second generation (Israel-born children of immigrants).[14] Yet another problematic fact is that while wage disparities between different groups have been preserved or increased over the years, the educational disparities between them have narrowed.[15]

The ethnic and national composition of the Israeli workforce reveals the connection between deprivation and discrimination processes that occur before one joins the labor market, especially in the educational system and in the employment opportunities available to individuals. Disparities in education, particularly in higher education, between the Sephardic and Ashkenazi Jews and between Jews and Arabs, are manifest in the types of skills acquired by the various groups. Furthermore, processes of discrimination and the differences in opportunities in the labor market that members of the various groups (particularly Jews and Arabs) face, create a *de facto* distinction on ethnic and national grounds in one's position in the labor market. The data show that employees of Arab and Eastern Jewish origin, as opposed to those of Ashkenazi Jewish origin, are over-represented in fields that provide lower wages and working conditions such as blue-collar occupations and non-professional areas.[16]

Changes in the labor market in Israel, as in the rest of the world, have resulted in the expansion of advanced, knowledge-intensive industries which affect economic indicators and growth, improve Israeli competitiveness in the global market, but also deepen the inequality between social groups.[17] In an interview granted in 2015 by outgoing Equal Employment Opportunities Commissioner, Atty. Tziona Koenig-Yair, on the occasion of her leaving the Commission, said that in the eight years of her tenure the Commission received 5300 complaints of which only 68 cases resulted in the filing of a claim, a rate of only 1.5%. "They all need consultation, but it is necessary to decide which cases reach court for the purpose of setting precedents," she explained. "We try to choose strategic cases, with broad consequences."

Regarding society as a whole and the changes required to reach equality, particularly gender equality, Koenig-Yair stated, "We need a deep social change. As long as women in Israel are seen as the primary caregivers even when they do not happen to be, and as long as men do not realize their paternity, women cannot assume their positions. It is necessary to change this perception among employers and employees, including the fathers. What is needed is a somewhat different distribution of parental responsibility, and the inculcation among employers that not every woman is a walking womb."

Koenig-Yair also called for increased enforcement with emphasis on disadvantaged groups in the population. "There is still a long way to go," she added.

---

[14]Cohen (2006) (henceforth, Cohen).
[15]*Ibid.*
[16]Shtier.
[17]Shtier.

"Nevertheless, public discourse is different now, and there is greater awareness on the part of workers and employers. Many people call to consult with us these days, which did not happen eight years ago. It is true that this is not enough, but we must remember that the processes of achieving equality take years, and that the process has a beginning."

11.2 Women

In the twenty-first century, women in Israel make up approximately 46% of the civilian workforce but earn on average one-third less than men do. The wage disparities between men and women have hardly changed since the 1970s despite an increase in women's education and the accumulated experience of women at work.[18] In Israel, gender explains wage differences between people with similar human capital more than ethnicity or nationality do. Women employed in the public service in identical ranks with men earn less than the men do, advance more slowly, and are less likely to reach positions of authority and power. 60% of those earning up to minimum wage are women, and so are approximately 65% of recipients of income support. More than 60% of the unemployed are women, and in situations of unemployment they are the first to be expelled from the labor market.[19]

Another mechanism that works to women's detriment is occupational segregation. Ostensibly, the job market is open to women and men alike. But in practice, women's opportunities are subject to the gendered structure of the market, which separates occupations into "feminine" and "masculine," and creates a hierarchy between and within these occupations. The segregation of occupations by gender makes it possible for women to join the labor market without threatening the binary, gender-based division of labor.[20]

11.3 Mizrachi Jews

Jews of Eastern origin, together with other disadvantaged groups, are over-represented in unskilled jobs that pay low wages. Studies on the subject indicate that although in the first decades following the establishment of the State of Israel social mobility was high, especially among the Mizrachi Jews, this did not contribute significantly to a reduction of inter-ethnic disparities.[21]

---

[18] Herzog (2006) (henceforth, Herzog).
[19] Izraeli (1999), pp. 167–215 (henceforth, Izraeli).
[20] *Ibid.*
[21] Lewin-Epstein (2006).

Studies have shown that the differences between Ashkenazi and Mizrachi Jews in education and employment have increased in the second generation compared to the generation of their parents. Analysis of the disparities between Ashkenazi and Mizrachi Jews in the second and third generations (all native born) shows one out of every four recipients of a BA degree is Mizrachi and three are Ashkenazi. The findings concerning the differences in income between Ashkenazi and Mizrachi Jews are even harsher, and the differences appear not only in labor market but also in the ownership of property. Although various data on the subject show clearly that there is discrimination against this group in a variety of areas, because this group is part of the Jewish collective in Israel, unlike the Arab Muslim and Christian minorities, the protest of this group has often been marginalized and was even denied by the authorities in Israel over the years.

11.4 Arabs

Ostensibly, Israel's Arab citizens enjoy equal civil and political rights. But given that various legislative arrangements define the State of Israel as a Jewish state, its non-Jewish citizens, primarily its Arab citizens, experience inherent discrimination in a variety of fields. For example, Israel's Law of Return grants every Jew the right to immigrate to Israel and receive citizenship. As a result, all non-Jews must follow another, much more complicated path to citizenship. Furthermore, because most Jewish citizens in Israel are obligated to serve in the military, whereas for security reasons, most Israeli Arab citizens are not, the latter are excluded from many goods and benefits provided to veterans, such as preference in the labor market, housing benefits, and more.

In addition to inherent discrimination under the Israeli regime, Arab citizens are excluded from the centers of power in society—courts, universities, government offices, and business elites. Most of the discrimination stems from unequal admission to universities, hiring at work, and acceptance to institutions.[22]

A similar picture emerges from a survey concerning the sense of discrimination of job seekers and employees (Survey Conducted by the Minestry of Economy and Industry in 2010a). Among Arab job seekers, 29% reported that they had encountered rejection that they interpreted as discrimination on the basis of sectorial affiliation. Additionally, 17% of Arabs whose workplaces are located in the Jewish sector reported sectorial discrimination. Regarding perceptions of the general population, 39% of the general public believes that there is discrimination against Arabs in the area of employment, the second largest category after that of the elder working population.

Interviews conducted with employers as part of yet another qualitative study revealed that employers' considerations not to hire or promote Arabs in their

---

[22]Shenhav.

businesses clearly belong to the category of unconscious bias (Survey Conducted by the Ministry of Economy and Industry in 2010b). The study suggested that these findings could be explained partly by the absence of legislation prohibiting discrimination against Arabs until the mid-1990s, and by flaws in the legal process (difficulties of proof and inadequate remedies).[23]

In the last decade, there has been a trend of worsening relations between Arabs and Jews in Israel, with discrimination and exclusion of the Arab minority on the rise. After serious violent incidents that took place in October 2000 between the Arab and Jewish civilians, a special commission was established (the Or Commission). This was the first expression of an official recognition by a national body of the depth of institutionalized discrimination and exclusion that have been the lot of Arab citizens of the state since its inception.[24] Many hoped that such a seminal event would mark a positive turning point in relations with the Arabs and open the door to a change in government policy toward them. In practice, most of the recommendations of the Commission have not been implemented, and over time no real improvement has been felt in the attitude of the state and of its institutions toward Arab citizens. This was despite the fact that the Commission specifically noted that the feelings of frustration and alienation among Arabs are nourished, among others, by neglect in addressing the disparities between the two populations, and by the "no policy" policy.[25]

11.5 The Elderly

In the State of Israel, characterized by a culture of youth and male militarism, the elderly are excluded together with women and national and ethnic minorities.[26]

Recent writing on the subject suggests that there is widespread age discrimination in Israel, especially at the hiring stages, both in the private and public sectors. The source of discrimination appears to be customer preference or the desire to use the criterion of age as an inexpensive predictor of physical condition, two considerations that are not considered legitimate.

There are very few comprehensive or representative empirical studies or surveys that would make it possible to obtain an accurate picture of the extent of the phenomenon of age discrimination. But a review of general statistical data on employment and unemployment rates and a review of literary and journalistic writing on the subject show that the Israeli labor market and society are deeply affected by ageism—a negative attitude toward older workers and discrimination against them in practice.

---

[23]Wolkinson (1999).
[24]Arab society in Israel: Information portfolio, The Abraham Fund Initiatives, 2009.
[25]*Ibid.*
[26]Hazan (2006).

A recent empirical-qualitative study examining the case law in this area in district labor courts came to the conclusion that formal legislation in Israel that prohibits discrimination on grounds of age was not enough to bring about a substantial change in employers' patterns of conduct. This study showed that from the perspective of the plaintiffs, reality is characterized by ageism, discrimination, humiliation, and personal injury of older workers, who feel that they are rejected and harmed without substantive justification in an abusive and humiliating process. A key difficulty claimants (employees) must contend with is the attempt by defendants (employers) to tarnish them personally during the long legal process.

From the perspective of the defendants, naturally, a completely different picture emerges, according to which there is no age discrimination. From their vantage point, there is no discrepancy between the law and reality, because in practice there is no age discrimination, but substantive decisions, at the personal level, based on the particular circumstances of each case that justify the specific treatment of the individual employees. The conclusion is, therefore, that additional strategies must be adopted to achieve social change, such as public education and information, targeting not only the public at large but also, and especially, the employers and the key personnel responsible for hiring.

Another source of information on the subject is a survey regarding a sense of discrimination among job seekers and employees. The survey found that among job seekers, the sense of discrimination was highest in those over the age of 45. Approximately 48% of the older job seekers reported that they were turned down for reasons that, in their impression, were age-related. These findings are reinforced by impressions prevalent in the general population. Of the survey respondents, 45% thought that older workers were greatly discriminated against at work.

11.6 Sexual Orientation

Organizations representing the LGBT community and other sexual minorities in Israel have been working for years to promote the legal status and rights of sexual minorities. It is possible to point to several areas that have been addressed successfully[27]: abolition of the prohibition against sexual intercourse that has been defined as "unnatural" (1988); the right to social benefits of same-sex couples (amendment of the Equal Employment Opportunities Law, 1992; Danilovich ruling); recognition of same-sex relationships for purposes of taxation, health insurance, pensions, and the like; openness to gay and lesbian portrayals in popular culture and art; and a prohibition against hate crimes aimed at individuals because of their sexual orientation.

But these achievements are partial.[28] They protect primarily gay men and lesbian women, not other sexual minorities. Not all branches of government recognize same-

---

[27]Yonai (2006).
[28]*Ibid.*

sex couples, and it is conditional on the adoption of the common marital pattern, demanding proof of coupledom that is not required of married couples. The right to adopt children is not yet recognized, and even the rights of non-biological parents to raise the child of a same-sex partner remains legally unclear. After a struggle, the right of transgender people to funding for sex change therapy has been recognized in principle, but the medical establishment still makes it difficult to exercise this right.

A survey that examined the feelings and experiences of discrimination of LGBT employees in the Israeli labor market conducted by the Equal Employment Opportunities Commission (2014) shows that feelings of discrimination are quite high. For example, the overwhelming majority of respondents believed that members of the LGBT community were discriminated against in the labor market to a moderate-to-very great extent, particularly at the following stages: hiring (79.8%), general treatment (70.7%), events in the workplace (70.1%), promotions (69.1%), and job search (68.3%). Much higher rates of people who identified themselves as transgender felt that their community was discriminated against in the labor market than did other survey participants. When asked about their personal experiences, lesbian and bi-sexual women noted that a significant rate suffered from derision at the workplace, as well as harassment, name-calling, and verbal threats. The survey found that 40% of transgender people were required to dress in accordance with the original gender—at times, often, or all the time. Other frequent harmful behaviors reported by transgender people were harassment in the bathrooms (33.4%), derision on the part of their supervisor (32.1%), sexual harassment by colleagues (28.6%), and harassment, name-calling, or verbal threats on the part of their supervisor (21.5%). The survey also found that among respondents, and especially among transgender respondents, about 10% reported absenteeism of varying frequency for fear of discrimination in the workplace.

12 What Does the Enforcement of Antidiscrimination Law Reveal About the Nature of Your Legal System or About the Enforcement of Laws in Your Legal System?

Despite a broad body of antidiscrimination legislation, the enforcement of this legislation is only partial, and various groups still experience extensive inequality in many areas (as outlined in detail in Sect. 2 above). One possible reason for the existing discrimination and for the partial enforcement of the antidiscrimination legislation is the erosion of the support for the welfare policy in Israel since the 1980s and 1990s.

In addition, there are practical reasons for the problems that the enforcement of antidiscrimination laws faces within the existing legal system in Israel, especially in the field of employment.[29] First, some difficulties are built into the legal process,

---

[29] As described in the article by Mundlak (2006), (henceforth: Mundlak, Legal aspects).

particularly the difficulties of proof. Few are the cases in which the plaintiff, the alleged victim of discrimination, succeeds in bringing to court clear, unequivocal, and incontrovertible evidence proving discrimination.

This is especially true when it comes to discrimination in the hiring process, as the allegedly discriminatory employer can always argue that the particular claimant was not hired because she was not professionally suited for the job. Note that most antidiscrimination laws stipulate that an action does not constitute discrimination when it is made necessary by the character or nature of the job. Therefore, the more narrowly the employer chooses to define the job, especially if the job requirements are formulated in such a way as to contain features or characteristics that exist only among certain groups in society and not in others ("pre-market discrimination"), failure to hire a person who belongs to a disadvantaged group does not appear to be illegal discrimination on the face of it.

Another practical difficulty encountered by employees who are discriminated against is the economic cost of legal proceedings against the discriminating employer, particularly in view of the fact that such cases involve low-wage workers who earn very little. Furthermore, during a lawsuit against the employer, the employee-plaintiff must most likely deal with counter-claims and allegations against him on the part of employers about the quality of his professional work, which is not easy to cope with mentally, and it lowers the likelihood of victims choosing to pursue this enforcement process. A review of case law on the subject shows that even after the employee-plaintiff decides to initiate a legal process, often with the support and guidance of human rights groups, and a "pro-worker" precedent is created in labor court, later claimants are left on their own in the arena, without proper support in the management of the expensive and difficult litigation.

Furthermore, as shown in Sect. 2 concerning the positions of Israeli employers on the integration of workers belonging to different groups in their businesses, it transpires that there is no sweeping consensus about the impropriety of discrimination and about the need for an external state agency to intervene in the matter. At the same time, it is possible to see that even the workers themselves often do not perceive their workplace as part of the public domain, but as a place belonging to the employer who can act as he pleases. In this sense, the discrimination that occurs may not be perceived as such in the consciousness of the workers, and therefore the courts do not enforce it.

The combination of problems presented above suggests that at times the attempt to ensure observance of the rights granted by the antidiscrimination laws and to establish a broad social concept of equality faces a social reality that is not suitable for receiving the legal message. A possible conclusion is, therefore, that as long as there is no change in the common perceptions of the general public about the rights of various groups in society and about the obligations of employers toward them, and as long as their daily lives are characterized by continuous, built-in obstacles that make it difficult for various populations to exercise their rights (e.g., existing norms of division of labor in the family unit, discrimination in the educational system, and lack of proper public transportation for people with disabilities), we ought not to blame only the employers and criticize them for considering what Israeli law tells them in other contexts, which is to act to maximize their profits.[30]

13 Conclusion

The above survey shows that the state of enforcement of antidiscrimination laws in Israel is most complex and problematic. On one hand, there is a broad system regulating antidiscrimination based on legislation, institutional measures, and case law. The regulation concerns primarily the area of employment, but not only. Antidiscrimination obligations apply to all actions of the state, and there is legislation regulating the prohibition against discrimination in the public domain as well, which is often privately owned. This regulation has been in place since the establishment of the State and continues uninterruptedly to this day.

On the other hand, the findings of various studies, the current data, and the spirit of the public atmosphere (as reflected, for example, in newspaper reports) indicate that the phenomenon of discrimination in Israel is fairly widespread. Israeli society is particularly complex and contains a large number of sub-groups divided by religion, ethnicity, and more. Thus, Israeli society is characterized by a relatively large number of "types" of disadvantaged populations, some quite unique for this society. Therefore, despite extensive and institutionalized efforts to enforce existing antidiscrimination laws, these efforts do not appear to make significant headway. Nevertheless, available data on the number of cases in which law enforcement agencies (various commissions and courts) have been approached show an increase over the years, and the situation can be expected to change.

References

Cohen Y (2006) National, gender, and ethnic wage disparities. In: Ram U, Berkowitz N (eds) In/equality. Ben Gurion University
Hazan H (2006) Age. In: Ram U, Berkowitz N (eds) In/equality. Ben Gurion University
Herzog H (2006) Gender. In: Ram U, Berkowitz N (eds) In/equality. Ben Gurion University
Izraeli D (1999) Gender in the labor market. In: Sex, gender, politics, red line, pp 167–215
Lewin-Epstein N (2006) Mobility. In: Ram U, Berkowitz N (eds) In/equality. Ben Gurion University
Mundlak G (2006) Discrimination in employment: legal aspects. In: Ram U, Berkowitz N (eds) In/equality. Ben Gurion University
Shtier H (2006) The labor market. In: Ram U, Berkowitz N (eds) In/equality. Ben Gurion University
Survey Conducted by the Minestry of Economy and Industry (2010a) http://economy.gov.il/Research/Pages/default.aspx

---

[30]Mundlak, Legal aspects.

Survey Conducted by the Ministry of Economy and Industry (2010b) http://employment.molsa.gov.il/Employment/Shivyon/Pages/ResearchandSurveys.aspx?WPID=WPQ6&PN=2

Wolkinson BW (1999) Arab employment in Israel: the quest for equal employment opportunity. Greenwood Press, Westport

Yonai Y (2006) Sexuality. In: Ram U, Berkowitz N (eds) In/equality. Ben Gurion University

Tamar Kricheli Katz holds a joint appointment in the faculty of law and the department of sociology at Tel Aviv University. She received her PhD and JSM from Stanford University and her LL.B from the Hebrew University. Prior to her graduate studies, Tamar served as a law clerk and a legal advisor to Justice T. Or of the Israeli Supreme Court. She studies inequality, antidiscrimination law, empirical legal studies, sociology of law and employment law.

Donna Zamir holds a LL.B and a B.A in Psychology from Tel-Aviv University.

Italy

Marzia Barbera and Alberto Guariso

1 Is Antidiscrimination Law Enforced?

International and European Antidiscrimination Law have essentially been implemented in the Italian legal system by the following pieces of legislation:

1.1 Article 43 of Legislative Decree no. 286 of 25 July 98 (Testo Unico Immigrazione, Consolidated Immigration Act)

Article 43 provides the same definition of discrimination as in Article 1 of the International Convention on the Elimination of All Forms of Racial Discrimination of 1965, and therefore has the same scope of application. Paragraph 2, however, also contains a list of conduct that, in different areas (public officials' activity, goods and services offered to the public, access to housing, access to employment, etc.) constitute "in any case" discrimination, with no reference to the protection of already established "human rights and fundamental freedom," which effectively sets a limit to the enforceability of the first paragraph.

The types of prohibited discrimination referred to in paragraph 2 are actually not entirely clear, because while in some areas the prohibition only refers to

---

This report is the result of work jointly carried out by the two authors. However, paragraphs 1–7 have been written by Alberto Guariso, paragraphs 8–13 and the conclusions by Marzia Barbera.

M. Barbera (✉) · A. Guariso
University of Brescia, Department of Law, Brescia, Italy
e-mail: marzia.barbera@unibs.it; guariso@studiodirittielavoro.it

discrimination grounded on "race, religion, ethnicity, nationality", in the area concerning the employer's conduct it also refers to language and citizenship. Furthermore, Article 43 does not contain a definition of indirect discrimination and only even mentions the concept with reference to the realm of employment. "Language" and "geographical origin" were added to the grounds of prohibited discrimination with Legislative Decree no. 150 of 1 September 2011, but to date the latter has not been enforced in courts.

1.2 Legislative Decree no. 215 of 9 July 2003

It tracks Directive 2000/43 almost literally and, in doing so, also excludes differential treatments grounded on nationality from the decree's scope of application. Article 2(2), however, establishes that "the provisions of Article 43 of the Consolidated Immigration Act shall remain valid," which allows judges to refer to discrimination by nationality also under Legislative Decree no. 215/03.

1.3 Legislative Decree no. 216 of 9 July 2003

It tracks Directive 2000/78 almost literally. It changes, inter alia, Article 15 of the *Statuto dei lavoratori* (Workers' Statute) of 1970, which already prohibited anti-union conduct, and prohibited the employer from carrying out any action "aimed at political, religious, racial, linguistic or sexual discrimination." Consequently, the list of prohibited discrimination in relation to employment is wider than that provided by the European law.

The original text of the decree omitted the provisions of Article 5 of Directive 200/78, concerning reasonable solutions for disabled persons. In 2013, following an infringement procedure by the European Commission, it was amended to add the duty for employers to adopt "reasonable accommodation," which also complies with the UN Convention on the Rights of Persons with Disabilities.

1.4 Legislative Decree no. 198 of 11 April 2006 (Gender Equal Opportunities Code)

It concerns the prohibition of discrimination on grounds of gender (including maternity, pregnancy and family status), in the areas referred to in Directive 2006/54 (access to employment, including promotion, and vocational training; working conditions, including pay; occupational pensions schemes). The Code also covers self-employment, social security, flexible pensionable age and victimization, as well as access to goods and services under Directive 2004/113.

1.5 Law no. 67 of 1 March 2006

It extends the prohibition of discrimination on grounds of disability to all areas of social life, in order to ensure the disabled "the full enjoyment of their civil, political, economic and social rights," leaving in effect, for the employment field, Legislative Decree no. 216/03. It adopts the EU definitions of direct and indirect discrimination and harassment; the notion of disability, however, does not mirror the huge definition provided by the UN Convention, but rather the narrower definition of Article 3 of Law no. 104 of 5 February 1992, according to which "the handicapped person is one who has a physical, mental or sensory impairment, stable or progressive, which is the cause of difficulty in learning, relationships or integration."

2 How Is Antidiscrimination Law Enforced?

2.1 Various Grounds of Discrimination

In Italian law the prohibitions of discrimination are formulated differently with regard to the various grounds of discrimination and various fields of application.[1]

The most relevant differences are the following:

- Under Legislative Decree no. 216/03 (implementing Directive 2000/78), the religion ground is only considered in relation to employment; for all other areas of social life, it is taken into account by Article 43 of Legislative Decree no. 286/98 (Consolidated Immigration Act) that, however, as we have seen, does not contain the definitions of discrimination developed by EU law over time (direct and indirect discrimination, collective discrimination, harassment, etc.).
- The geographic origin and nationality grounds are only considered under Article 43 and Article 44 of the Consolidated Immigration Act (as modified by Legislative Decree no. 150 of 1 September 2011), but not by other laws;
- The special civil proceeding designed to enforce the right not to be discriminated against on the ground of gender in the field of employment (Article 27, Gender Equal Opportunities Code) is different from the one provided for all other forms of discrimination (Article 28 of Legislative Decree no. 150/11).

---

[1] For an overall picture of the Italian antidiscrimination law, see Barbera (2007).

This normative inequality jeopardizes the capacity to enforce antidiscrimination rights. For this reason, many legal experts and social activists have suggested a reorganization of the subject matter as to make it more coherent and effective.

2.2 Fast-Track Proceedings

The various discrimination prohibitions contained in the aforementioned laws are implemented in Italian law through two special fast-track legal proceedings and through specialised equality bodies. As mentioned above, it is necessary to distinguish the general antidiscrimination proceeding from the proceeding especially provided for gender discrimination in employment. The general antidiscrimination proceeding was radically changed in 2011 under Article 28 of Legislative Decree no. 150/2011.[2]

The new fast-track procedure follows these rules:

– The alleged victim of discrimination (even without a lawyer's assistance), an association acting on the victim's behalf, or an association acting on its own behalf (see below, paragraph 3), can file a claim in the court with jurisdiction over the place of his or her residence—an exception to the general principle of suing in the court with jurisdiction over the place of residence of the defendant. The alleged victim can also bring an action after the employment relationship has ended, subject to the ordinary statute of limitations applicable in labour law (10 years for non-economic rights and 5 years for economic rights).
– The court, which must "omit any formality not essential to decide the case," can order the discriminatory conduct to end and the remedy for its effects and award compensation for pecuniary and non-pecuniary losses. In case of collective discrimination, the judge can also order a discrimination removal plan. Moreover, the judge may order the publication of the decision in a national newspaper at the defendant's expense.
– In determining the amount of compensation, the judge shall take into account whether the unlawful conduct constitutes victimization (i.e. a reaction to a complaint or to proceedings aimed at enforcing compliance with the principle of equal treatment).
– In employment discrimination cases, the judge notifies the public administration that grants public benefits or funding to the employer (losing party) of his or her

---

[2]The special antidiscrimination action, provided for by Article 44, paragraph 3.8 of the Consolidated Immigration Act, expressly maintained by the legislation implementing the Race Directive and the Framework Directive, has been replaced by Article 28 of Legislative Decree no. 150/2011 to include a general fast-track procedure. According to human rights lawyers and activists, the two proceedings are substantially equivalent in terms of effectiveness. However, as a consequence of the reform, a large number of cases concerning immigration and asylum will be handled under the new procedure, and this may produce a negative impact on the speediness of the lawsuits. Unfortunately updated data on this issue are not available.

Italy 339

decision. The administration may withdraw the funding, and in severe cases may bar the losing party from receiving any further benefit for 2 years. In practice, however, this procedure has never been applied.
- Failure to comply with the judge's order may incur a penalty or up to 6 months imprisonment and a fine for each day of delay.
- The judge's decision can be appealed to the Court of Appeal (second instance) within 30 days; the decision on appeal can be challenged before the Court of Cassation (third instance).
- A lightened burden of proof is on the claimant, who only has to provide facts from which the existence of discrimination can be presumed; the burden of proof then shifts to the defendant, who has to prove that there has been no breach of the principle of equal treatment.
- For civil servants who still come under the jurisdiction of the Administrative Court (military, university professors, judges, etc.), a special antidiscrimination proceeding is conducted before that court.

The proceeding for gender discrimination in employment, on the other hand, follows different rules:

- The alleged victim, or the local Equality Advisor on her behalf or, in case of collective discrimination, the Equality Advisor on her/his own behalf (see below paragraph (c)) can start the proceeding by filing a claim to the Labour Court of the place where the discrimination took place.
- Within a very short time period, parties are summoned by the judge to attend a hearing for a summary examination of the case.
- There, the claimant must produce facts "able to establish in precise and consistent terms the presumption of discrimination"; the burden of proof on the claimant is therefore more difficult to satisfy than in other discrimination cases.
- The decree by which the Court decides the case can be appealed to the same Court, this time following the ordinary rules of labour proceedings; the appeal decision can be challenged before the Court of Cassation.

As for remedies, the types of remedies applicable under the general fast track procedure also apply to gender discrimination proceedings. Both procedures involve quite reduced times for the first instance decision (from 2 to 6 months, depending on the court). It has been argued that it would be prudent to unify the two procedures, both for the sake of clarity and consistency, and to allow a single appeal in cases of multiple discrimination (for example, one based on grounds of gender and religion).

2.3 Enforcing Equality Bodies

The equality bodies with enforcement competences are the following:

2.3.1 Ufficio Nazionale contro le discriminazioni razziali (UNAR), (National Bureau Against Race Discrimination)

It is part of the Department for Equal Opportunities of the Presidency of the Council of Ministers and therefore is not an independent authority. It is in charge of monitoring, reporting, and advocacy. This means that UNAR can give advice and opinions in the face of reported discrimination, but it is not empowered to act directly before the courts. It has exclusive authority in ethnic and nationality discrimination, but in recent years, despite the absence of a rule that explicitly authorizes it, it has extended its operations to the field of sexual orientation.

Recently UNAR and the National Lawyers' Association (Consiglio Nazionale Forense) agreed on a Protocol of cooperation aimed at strengthening the legal defense of victims of discrimination. The two bodies will manage a solidarity fund for access to justice by victims of discrimination, financed by the Department for Equal Opportunities of the Presidency of the Council of Ministers. The financial support is a counterpart to the legal aid provided by the State for those who are eligible on the basis of their incomes.

2.3.2 Consigliera di Parità (Gender Equality Advisor)

This gender equality body was introduced by Article 8 of Law no. 125/1991, later amended by Legislative Decree no. 196/2000, which strengthened its functions.

The Equality Advisors are set up at national, regional, and provincial levels and jointly appointed by the Ministry of Labour and the Ministry for Equal Opportunities upon the advice of the regions and provinces. This enforcement body also does not constitute an autonomous authority.

The advisors' terms of office last 4 years and are renewable only once. They monitor the implementation of the principles of equality and non-discrimination for women and men in employment and promote equal opportunities in the labour market and at the workplace. They may take legal action on behalf of the discriminated person and act on their own behalf in cases of collective discrimination.

In sum, neither equality body is autonomous from governmental power, despite the fact that EU directives require such. In particular, the European Commission against Racism and Intolerance (ECRI) of the Council of Europe underlined that UNAR is still not entitled to bring legal proceedings and it still comes under the Department for Equal Opportunities of the Presidency of the Council of Ministers. The conclusion was that "this direct institutional link runs counter to the type of independence that is necessary for the effective operation of such a body."[3] ECRI recommends that the Italian authorities "take steps to enhance the role of UNAR, in particular by formally extending its powers so that the relevant legislation clearly covers discrimination based not only on ethnic origin and race but also on colour,

---

[3] See ECRI, Third report on Italy, 2005.

language, religion, nationality and national origin; by granting it the right to bring legal proceedings; and by ensuring that its full independence is secured both in law and in fact." Finally, ECRI stressed that UNAR must also be provided with all the necessary human and financial resources, in light of its workload. This lack of autonomy has been the focus of criticisms also by EU institutions. So far, nothing has resulted from these criticisms.

As for the gender equality bodies, a recent reform (Decree no. 151/2015, Articles 27–42) established that the "spoil system"—the possibility of having one's position revoked following the appointment of a new government (a rule that the Council of State surprisingly upheld in judgment no. 5031 of 2010)[4]—is not applicable to the equality advisors. However, the lack of human and financial resources also adversely impacts the effectiveness of the action of gender equality bodies, which even the recent reform has not remedied.

3 Who Enforces Antidiscrimination Law?

In the Italian systems, not only the individual who has been discriminated against but also institutional and collective actors can enforce antidiscrimination law. As already mentioned, Gender Equality Advisors, associations and legal persons which have a legitimate interest in ensuring that the provisions of the antidiscrimination legislation are complied with, are entitled to bring a legal action in support of or on behalf of the victim, with his or her approval. (See Article 44 of Legislative decree no. 286/98; Article 5 of Legislative decree no. 215/2003; Article 5 of Legislative decree no. 216/2003; Article 37(2) and Article 55 of the Gender Equal Opportunities Code).

The same is provided for by Article 4 of Disability Act no. 67/2006, which grants legal standing to associations and legal persons.

In cases of collective discrimination, the same associations are entitled to act on their own behalf. This distinctive feature of the Italian enforcement mechanism goes beyond the prescriptions of the European Directives, which only provide the association with an auxiliary *locus standi*, and it likely ensures a higher level of effectiveness. However, the concept of collective discrimination is not exactly defined by the law. In some cases (discrimination by nationality and gender), legal standing is granted to associations when the individuals discriminated against are not identifiable; in other cases, associations are granted legal standing "only if" the victim(s) are not identifiable (for example, as happens with public administration's regulations or employer's general measures).

---

[4]Council judgment no. 5031 of 29 July 2010 (confirming the Administrative Tribunal decision of 19 July 2009). This stated that the National Equality Adviser can be removed under the spoil system if she or he is not 'tuned in' with the Government's policies, as the National Equality Adviser is not an independent body (despite her/his wide autonomy over internal organisation).

There are specific requirements for these associations to act:

1. For discrimination on grounds of race and ethnicity, only registered associations are granted legal standing, based on their statutory purposes and continuity of action (Article 5 of Legislative Decree no. 215/03);
2. For the grounds envisaged by Directive 2000/78, standing is granted on an *ad hoc* basis to trade unions and all "bodies representing the injured interest." This particularly broad formulation is a result of an infringement procedure by the European Commission, which had considered the previous wording restrictive and unlawful.
3. With regard to action based on the Disability Act no. 67/2006, a 2007 decree established a register jointly managed by the Ministries of Labour and Equal Opportunities, along roughly the same model as established for race and ethnicity under Legislative Decree 215/03;
4. For discrimination based on nationality, legal standing is granted to the local sections of trade unions (Article 44 of Consolidated Immigration Act). Many judges, however, have recognized legal standing also to various associations by categorizing discrimination by nationality as indirect discrimination by ethnicity.

Regardless of the recognition of a right to engage in proceedings, many organizations and associations operating in the fight against discrimination support individuals by providing specialized lawyers in order to ensure, even in individual cases, adequate assistance.

4 Who Benefits from the Enforcement of Antidiscrimination Law?

There are no available statistics on cases related to discrimination brought to justice. UNAR has among its tasks the drafting of an annual report to the Parliament, which includes data on its activity on racial discrimination cases. According to the report released in 2011, 95 cases related to racial discrimination were brought to justice.[5] However, UNAR does not conduct surveys or collect more detailed data on case law.

A more in-depth analysis is supplied by a book, edited by one of this report's authors, which reports and classifies 52 cases related to nationality discrimination decided between 2008 and 2009 by courts sitting in Northern Italy and 7 decisions by the Constitutional Court.[6]

The vast majority of antidiscrimination actions coming before the courts concern acts of discrimination against non-citizens, often enabled by public administration (so-called institutional discrimination). It concerns violations of the equal treatment

---

[5]http://2.228.163.148/unar/_image.aspx?id=fddf67ab-5f6d-449c-bc551fdbb702b360&sNome=RelazioneattivitàUNAR2011.pdf.

[6]Guariso (2012).

guaranteed to non-nationals by EU Directive 2003/109 (concerning the status of third-country nationals who are long-term residents) and Directive 2011/98 (concerning the rights of third-country workers legally residing), in fields like welfare benefits (financial support for poor families or the disabled, or access to housing, etc.), health services, and public employment.

A fairly high number of cases involved discrimination against Roma people, as well as discrimination of non-citizens by the public registry, resulting in an obstacle to regular residence in a given municipality, and harassment due to ethnicity consisting of racist or xenophobic statements often uttered in the context of political speeches. Much rarer were the cases relating to discrimination on grounds of ethnicity or nationality in private relationships between individuals. Those reported primarily concern the activities of real estate agencies, insurance companies with higher premiums for foreigners, and finance companies that charge higher interest rates or impose more severe conditions based on the claimant's nationality.

Case law in respect to disability has focused primarily on the issue of support teachers for disabled pupils in compulsory education. Many judges have recognized the discriminatory nature of the reduction of support teachers because it prevents disabled people from enjoying their fundamental right to education.

Case law relating to age discrimination was very marginal and only significant in challenging certain types of contracts reserved for certain age groups or as criterion for selecting the workers to be made redundant due to enterprise crises. On the other hand, the antidiscrimination law has not been used to raise questions, even though much debated, regarding retirement age.

Gender discrimination has taken a back seat when, previously, it was the front runner in case law, based mainly on maternity discrimination or victimization due to the request of parental leaves or special working arrangements.

On whole, in the last decade, the biggest beneficiaries of the antidiscriminatory laws have been non-nationals, with large differences between the north of the country (where litigation is quite frequent) and the south (where antidiscrimination case law is very limited, although it sees some significant issues, like the exploitation of foreigner workers and the *refoulement* of refugees).

Virtually no benefit from judicial enforcement of antidiscrimination law has been felt by those belonging to certain religions, and there is a dearth of case law on point. Discrimination on grounds of personal beliefs came to light in a very important lawsuit, successfully brought to challenge anti-union conduct by Fiat Company. In choosing staff to be rehired into a new company created to put their business back on an even keel, Fiat excluded members of the FIOM CGIL union, leaving them in charge of the company destined for closure.

Finally, it must be underlined that most cases have concerned discriminatory public law and regulations, and formal or institutional policies. Discriminatory actions and practices by individuals had rarely been tried before the courts (although a number of housing and employment cases had considerable public resonance). This reflects the difficulties encountered in claiming protection against discriminatory actions and practices by individuals in the private sector.

5 Who Is Harmed by the Enforcement of Antidiscrimination Law?

The most significant effects of the application of antidiscrimination law have been borne by the public administration, which, as a result of judicial decisions extending benefits or rights initially granted to Italian citizens only, had to revoke discriminatory administrative measures and reformulate them in accordance with the new, more egalitarian rules dictated by the judges.

The most significant case of this kind concerns the national call for applications for admission to civil service, which was originally intended for Italian citizens only and was then reformulated without citizenship restrictions as a result of a Court of Milan order. The judgment was appealed to the Court of Cassation, which brought the issue in front of to the Constitutional Court, which then decided that the rule which reserved civil service just for Italians was unconstitutional.

A similar procedure was necessary in other cases concerning calls for access to public employment or services provided by regional or local authorities. In all these cases, the group that initially benefited from the discriminatory rule is then disadvantaged by the enforcement of the antidiscrimination law. In fact, the goods, benefits, or opportunities in question are often limited in number (e.g. the number of jobs to be applied for, or the maximum amount payable for services), and extending the number of beneficiaries produces a redistributive effect.

In one case, a municipality (municipality of Brescia) initially withdrew the benefit in question after the judge had ordered its extension to foreigners, thus exposing the association that had started the legal action (ASGI) to the risk of being singled out as guilty for the benefit loss. The judge to whom the association turned for a second decision on the case ordered instead an inclusive solution, applying the prohibition of acts of victimization established by Article 4 of Legislative Decree 215/03. In another similar case (municipality of Adro), the administration had even started an action for recovering money from Italian citizens in order to redistribute it to the foreigners who benefited from a judge's ruling; however, the judges considered this initiative to be a form of retaliation and hence unlawful.

6 What Remedies Are Provided by the Enforcement of Antidiscrimination Law?

The judicial remedies provided for by antidiscrimination laws are those described in paragraphs 2.1 and 2.2. The non-judicial remedies consist of informal interventions by the equality bodies mentioned above (UNAR—National Bureau Against Race Discrimination and the Gender Equality Advisors) towards the alleged discriminator in order to conciliate the case. However, it is more common that informal interventions are put in place by the NGOs that receive the application from the interested party.

7 Who Supports the Enforcement of Antidiscrimination Law?

The greatest support in applying antidiscrimination laws is from NGOs and trade unions or associations that collect applications through help desks or public campaigns and carry out both advocacy and legal interventions according to the rules of legal standing seen above.

There is not much support from political forces, which is another reason for the lack of attention to equality issues in the political discourse.

8 Who Opposes the Enforcement of Antidiscrimination Law?

Reports from international and local organizations and academics suggest an ever-growing climate of racism and xenophobia in Italy. Several NGOs, like ERRC (European Roma Rights Association) NAGA and Article 21, have documented increasing instances of discrimination and hate crimes against Roma by State and non-State actors. For example, from January 2013 to March 2015 ERRC have documented more than 100 cases of hate speech by public figures and by citizens, including demonstrations, flyers, and protests to ban Roma.

As mentioned above, the reactions by institutions and political actors to such conducts are generally weak. Some parties, like Lega, have even built their political success on a spreading xenophobic attitude. Acting as political entrepreneurs, some groups are taking advantage of feelings of hostility, racism and xenophobia hugely widespread in the public opinion, especially in matters such as the inclusion of non citizens in the distribution of welfare benefits or the entry of refugees and asylum seekers who have arrived during the most severe migration crisis ever experienced by European countries.

In the Italian legal system, specific criminal laws prohibit any manifestation of thoughts aimed at disseminating racial or ethnic superiority or hatred or at inciting others to commit acts of discrimination or violence for racial, ethnic or religious reasons (Law no. 654/1975, which ratifies and implements the International Convention on the Elimination of All Forms of Racial Discrimination, as amended by Decree no. 122/1993). But many cases of violence against foreigners and Roma remain unreported because individuals fear retaliation against themselves and their families, especially due to the lack of identity documents. Alternatively, when these cases are reported, they are not prosecuted.

There are, however, some examples of effective legal challenges of instances of racism and hate speech; NGOs active in this field have successfully brought criminal and civil suits against politicians and private individuals.

It must also be recalled the fierce opposition of some catholic associations against a draft bill on homophobia (which has been pending in Parliament for some time now), and to the recent law recognizing same-sex civil unions that provides same sex couples with most of the legal protections enjoyed by married couples.

Finally, it is worth mentioning another, more subtle form of opposition. Judicial decisions often face a strategy of "contained compliance" by political actors who neglect the wider policy implications of judicial decisions while simultaneously respecting individual judgments. The term "justice contained" has been coined by political scientist Lisa Conant when analysing the European Court of Justice's influence over the substantive policies of member states and the interaction between law and politics.[7] Conant argues that member states often seek to "contain justice" by limiting the application of innovative ECJ decisions. The Italian experience shows that the same also happens at the national level towards innovative domestic courts' decisions.

9 How Broad Is the Coverage of Antidiscrimination Law?

Antidiscrimination law covers the grounds of discrimination and fields of application specified under Sect. 1 of this report. Therefore, it covers the same grounds and fields as the EU law and the most relevant international human rights conventions.

10 Does the Enforcement of Antidiscrimination Law Vary According to the Ground of Discrimination?

Gender equality has been, together with anti-union discrimination, the first field of enforcement of antidiscrimination law in the Italian system. Comments on the gender equality legislation adopted to mirror the European Gender Equality Directives of the Seventies—law n. 903/77 and law n.125/91, now merged in the Gender Equal Opportunities Code, law n. 198/2006—were almost unanimous in lamenting a very low level of litigation under the two laws. This is somewhat surprising if one considers the high number of claims filed under Article 28 of the Workers' Statute, which gives trade unions standing before the courts for defending their collective interest in cases of anti-trade union discriminatory behaviour.

The explanation of such difference, given by Dagmar Schieck, is that while trade unions defend their own rights under Article 28 as collective organizations, equality rights are seen and conceptualized by the equality directives as individual rights. This explains the low level of litigation based on these different grounds.[8]

This conclusion, however, is contradicted by the traditionally huge volume of labour law disputes concerning individual rights brought before the courts each year.

---

[7]Conant (2002).
[8]Schieck (2012), p. 489 ff.

Claire Kilpatrick gave a different account of the same issue in a well-known essay on multilevel gender equality litigation.[9] She argued that, while the percentage of litigation on gender equality rights was a small percentage of the overall litigation of labour law disputes, there were still a significant amount of gender equality cases going on. They went unnoticed by scholars for specific, path-dependent reasons: legal doctrine did not pay much attention to antidiscrimination litigation, nor support its strategic use because academics channelled their expertise and experience toward legislative reform, as a way to incorporate EC law within the Italian system. This attitude can be better understood by considering that, in Italy, there has traditionally been a huge crossover between academic and governmental spheres.[10] In her analysis, the author stressed the importance of taking into account a number of factors in order to get an adequate account of the enforcement of antidiscrimination law, such as the mobilization by actors around equality legislation and the institutional build-up of doctrinal and interpretative practices.

While the author was specifically referring to the role played by the judicial dialogue in European legal integration, these factors are relevant in any legal mobilization strategy. If we compare the enforcement of gender equality law with the most recent cases on the subjects of race, ethnic origin and nationality, the impression we get is that the enforcement mechanisms are more effective when used in a targeted, appropriate, tenacious way by actors determined to employ the law as an instrument of social change and re-establishment of justice.

Also, the analyses of the first cases brought in the fields covered by the Directives 43/2000 and 78/200, as well as by the Consolidated Act of 1998 (race, ethnic origin, nationality) reported that litigation was not frequent. In its first reports on Italy (2001), ECRI noted that the 1998 antidiscrimination provisions on racial discrimination had been very rarely applied. However, the figures regarding the most recent implementation of this legislation shows a different picture, with a substantial rise in litigation (still mainly aimed at challenging institutional discrimination).

This is the result of a purposive, strategic action on the part of a group of human rights lawyers belonging to NGOs active in these fields (such as ASGI; APN; NAGA; Rete Lenford), often undertaken in the absence of alternative forms of social or political mobilization. These actors, who have a sophisticated expertise in antidiscrimination law, quite unusual in the professional environment, select the cases, file the claims (on behalf of the victims or in the organization's name), defend the victims in court, and provide effective arguments to judges for legally founded decisions.

---

[9]Kilpatrick (2001), p. 31 ff.

[10]Nor has the situation substantially changed, in the wake of the creation of the network of Gender Equality Advisors in 1991, partly because of the already mentioned scarcity of resources allocate to them, and partly because they tend to favour alternative means of dispute resolution, although they have not proved to be particularly effective.

At least until now, it can be said that the bet of the European legislator to entrust the antidiscrimination protection not only to individual victims but also, in a broad sense, to civil society, has been a winning one. This confirms that the courts' policy-making capability depends heavily on the mobilization of social actors and public institutions in response to its decisions. However, the effects of this strategy in the long run have to be verified, given the absence of stable links between the above-mentioned NGOs and grassroots' organizations and movements representing the disadvantaged groups whose rights are litigated. This could prevent those organizations and movements from channelling victories in courts in the political discourse. Relying on litigation to overcome situations of social and political weaknesses, instead of being an auxiliary weapon of social mobilization and collective action, might become their substitute.

11 What Is the Relationship Between the Enforcement of Antidiscrimination Law and the Quest for Equality on Both an Individual and Systemic Level?

Some years ago, in the already mentioned comparative analysis of the British and Italian enforcement mechanisms of antidiscrimination law, Diegmar Schieck described the differences between the two systems as two different conceptions of equality. She argued that, while the readiness of countries like Britain to embrace this field of law is tied to a tradition of individualism and multiculturalism, in countries like Italy the policies aimed at reducing inequalities have developed more along the dividing lines of class. This has lead to a limited perception of specific diversities based on ascribed characteristics.

The assessment reflects the cultural and political divide existing between the two countries, but these differences have reduced over time. On the one hand, while the protection of workers' collective interests through trade unions is still a distinctive feature of the Italian system, a process of individualisation of labour conditions has given a new priority to the judicial enforcement of individual rights. On the other hand, traditional forms of social conflict and mobilization tend to take on new forms in Italy, too. Individuals are not defined any more mainly by virtue of their position within the productive structure and their class memberships, but also in relation to personal characteristics such as gender, race, age, or religion and beliefs. Strategic antidiscrimination litigation reflects such changes and, in turn, reshapes the identity of the actors and the nature of the interests at stake, in terms of a quest for recognition of such identities and their value.[11]

---

[11] See Barbera and Protopapa (2015), p. 36 ff.

12 Is the Enforcement of Antidiscrimination Law Regarded as Different from the Enforcement of Other Laws?

Antidiscrimination law constitutes a distinctive form of protection of individual and group rights, different from traditional forms of control of the exercise of public or private powers. This difference is mirrored by its enforcement. Indeed, antidiscrimination protection entitles people to rights, which are additional to the rights they already hold. As the Tribunal of Brescia said in a decision regarding a local municipality's refusal of a family allowance to foreign residents (the so called "baby bonus"), "antidiscrimination enforcement is functional for the removal not so much of the injury caused by the infringement of an individual right to which the person is already entitled to [...] but rather of the injury suffered in the allocation of an additional right or benefit or service because of the discriminatory conduct or measure adopted by a private or the public administration in the exercise of their own prerogatives."[12]

This autonomous and not derivative nature of antidiscrimination protection and its capacity to limit an otherwise discretionary power have a number of important implications. First, it is clear that the remedial and redistributive nature of the protection afforded by the antidiscrimination law aims to restore equality or to remove unfair obstacles in the acquisition or enjoyment of social goods. Thus, the prohibitions on discrimination are not only past-oriented so as to compensate the damage suffered, but they are also future-oriented so as to ensure redistribution of a given good or chance.

Second, the antidiscrimination protection has political significance, in the sense that its enforcement affects the distributive choices adopted by political actors. For example, in the case mentioned above, the enforcement of antidiscrimination measures changed the choices made by public powers on how to allocate a social benefit between citizens and non-citizens. This does not alter the discretionary nature of political power "but rather delimits its space of action,"[13] as clarified by the Italian Constitutional Court when deciding a case where the President of a regional Council had appointed the commissioners of a public body without respecting the constitutional principle of a balanced participation of men and women in the decision-making process (Article 51 Cost.).

---

[12]Tribunal of Brescia, Ordinance 12 March 2009.

[13]Constitutional Court, Judgement n. 81/2012.

13 What Does the Enforcement of Antidiscrimination Law Reveal About the Nature of Your Legal System or About the Enforcement of Laws in Your Legal System?

Any given enforcement mechanism can make rights effective or weak. Acting on the enforcement mechanisms is therefore an indirect way of acting on the substantive rights they are designed to protect. This is the reasoning underlying the transplant of typical techniques of the labour law rights enforcement that have proved to be particularly effective over time, into the antidiscriminatory law enforcement field. For example, the discipline of legal standing in cases of gender discrimination and of discrimination based on race, ethnic origin and nationality is partly modelled on Article 28 of the Workers' Statute: collective actors, such as equalities bodies, trade unions and associations, are entitled to act not only on behalf of or in support of victims of discrimination, but also in their own name (in the case of race discrimination, under the condition that a specific victim is not identified or identifiable).

Other legacies of the labour law enforcement mechanisms are: the provision of an effective (temporary or permanent) relief, such as an injunction requiring termination of the discriminatory conduct along with the elimination of any effects; the adoption of fast-track mechanisms and procedures and the possibility of conferring the jurisdiction to the same labour judge who has jurisdiction (and has developed a specific expertise) on the welfare or labour issues involved in the discrimination case; and the rule according to which the judge can order the plaintiff to pay only his or her own legal costs, even when he or she loses the case, as an exception to the general rule under which the losing party pays the prevailing party's costs.

On whole, these rules aim to not discourage the plaintiff (often the more socially vulnerable party) from seeking redress in court and, at the same time, to overcome the weakness of a redress mechanism relying only on the individual initiative. In 2014 a reform changed the legal costs discipline, making it more difficult for the judge to apply the rule favourable to the plaintiff. According to the Government, the reform was intended to decrease the rate of the civil law cases brought in courts and hence to speed the whole civil law litigation system. In fact, the first effect of the reform has been to dramatically decrease the number of labour and welfare disputes, threatening also the effectiveness of antidiscrimination enforcement. This reform has been said not only to violate the constitutional right to be heard by a tribunal and to a fair trial, but it has also been described as a way of redistributing social power in favour of the stronger party. The Constitutional Court, however, recently repealed the reform.

14 Conclusion

Antidiscrimination law can be seen as a theory and a practice of transformation—a form of a "realistic utopia" that can be reasonably pursued even if it does not reflect existing social arrangements. However, a theory and a practice that entrust the solution of problems of justice mainly to public institutions and the state (in particular, to courts and enforcement agencies) may conflict with a pluralist conception of society, which assigns great value to intermediate social bodies.

For example, combating wage discrimination between men and women in the courtroom may mean ignoring the role of social partners and collective bargaining in wage setting and in rebalancing the social powers in employment relationships. As research conducted by Simon Deakin shows, there can be "a potential conflict between individuals' legal rights and collective attempts to agree on viable, affordable guarantees of long-term pay equality for all employees." But, on the other side, "litigation strategies can deliver tangible gains for some of the most disadvantaged groups in society."[14] In this sense, the author argues, legal and social mobilization are best regarded as complements: litigation is unlikely to be effective in the absence of well-functioning collective bargaining. Conversely, collective bargaining conducted under a non-discrimination scrutiny is likely to lead to more egalitarian and equitable outcomes than would be obtained from a purely voluntarist approach based on the autonomy of collective agreements. By the same token, comprehensive efforts to reassess the impact of antidiscrimination litigation should link courtroom battles to political mobilization and community organizing.

References

Barbera M (2007) Il nuovo diritto antidiscriminatorio. Il quadro comunitario e nazionale. Giuffrè ed., Milan
Barbera M, Protopapa V (2015) The Fiat case: reframing an industrial dispute in antidiscrimination language. Eur J Hum Rights, p 36 ff
Conant L (2002) Justice contained. Law and politics in the European Union. Cornell University Press, Ithaca
Deakin S et al (2015) Are litigation and collective bargaining complements or substitutes for achieving gender equality? A study of the British Equal Pay Act. Camb J Econ, p 381 ff
Guariso A (ed) (2012) Quattro anni alle discriminazioni istituzionali nel Nord Italia. Terre di Mezzo, Milan
Kilpatrick C (2001) Gender equality: a fundamental dialogue. In: Sciarra S (ed) Labour law in the courts: national judges and the ECJ. Hart Publishing, Oxford, p 31 ff
Schieck D (2012) Enforcing (EU) non-discrimination law: mutual learning between British and Italian labour law? Int J Comp Labour Law Ind Relat 4, p 489 ff

Marzia Barbera is a Professor of Law at the Department of Law of the University of Brescia, where she teaches Labour Law, Antidiscrimination Law, Legal Clinic. From 2003 to 2006 Head of the Department of Legal Studies of Brescia and member of the University Senate and of the Equal Opportunities Committee. She has served as member of FRANET, a network of legal experts assisting the Fundamental Rights Agency of the European Union, and as National Equality Advisory to the Ministry of Labour. She is the author of several books and articles on labour law, antidiscrimination and civil rights issues and member of the editorial board of several legal reviews.

---

[14]Cfr. Deakin et al. (2015), p. 381 ff.

Alberto Guariso is an attorney at law in Milan. He specialized in labor law, immigration law and antidiscrimination law and has handled important civil rights cases in front of national and international high courts. He teaches antidiscrimination law at the University of Brescia, is the author of several articles and editor of a casebook on antidiscrimination law and has been general editor of the "Critical Journal of Labor Law". He is member of the board of directors of Asgi (Association of Legal Studies on Immigration).

Japan

Akiko Ejima

1 Introduction

This article aims to show how issues of discrimination have been dealt with in Japan and to explore the problems and prospects of Japanese antidiscrimination law by focusing particularly on the aspect of enforcement of antidiscrimination law.

In Japan, there is no general antidiscrimination law that covers essential problems related to discrimination. Absence of a comprehensive antidiscrimination law does not mean the Japanese law does not cope with the issues of discrimination. Major issues of discrimination are covered by a specific law, which has to be compatible with and realize the Constitution of Japan prescribing equality under the law. Therefore, it is necessary to look at the Constitution, international human rights treaties Japan ratifies and relevant domestic law. In other words, it is essential to examine whether discrimination issues typically covered by antidiscrimination law elsewhere are protected and dealt with by any agency in Japan.[1] The article selects the following issues most of the antidiscrimination laws cover: race, gender, ethnicity, nationality, religion and belief, sexual orientation, gender reassignment, disability, age and social status.[2] It examines whether those issues are covered by law and

---

[1] For example, the Equality Act 2010 (UK) defines age, disability, gender reassignment, marriage and civil partnership, pregnancy and maternity, race, religion or belief, sex, sexual orientation as protected characters.

[2] Social status is one of the grounds of discrimination. According to the case law of the Supreme Court of Japan (judgment of 27 May 1964) it is a status a person holds in society for a permanent period.

A. Ejima (✉)
Meiji University, School of Law, Tokyo, Japan
e-mail: ejima@meiji.ac.jp

enforced by any agency. In other words, it is a process to discover antidiscrimination law in the existing law.

Another important characteristics of the Japanese situation concerning the prevention and abolishment of discrimination are that there is no comprehensive machinery that can promote and ensure implementation of antidiscrimination law. Particularly it should be noted that a national human rights institution has not been established yet despite several attempts in vain. Instead each problem has been individually dealt with long-time legal and political battles of the people or the group of the people who suffered from certain discrimination. In many cases they first have to discover that their problems can be seen as discrimination. In order to define their problems as discrimination international human rights treaties are helpful. Particularly, the Convention on the Elimination of All Forms of Discrimination against Women (CEDAW), the International Convention on the Elimination of All Forms of Racial Discrimination (ICERD), and the Convention on the Rights of Persons with Disabilities (CRPD) provides more concrete content of discrimination and specific obligations of the government while the Constitution of Japan stipulates only 'equality under the law' and prohibition of 'discrimination in political, economic or social relations because of race, creed, sex, social status or family origin'. It is necessary to embody the meaning of the constitutional protection but its realization remains passive as the legislature has been slow to realize it and the judiciary has been deferential to the legislature in general.

2 Is Antidiscrimination Law Enforced?

In order to answer this question, it is necessary to ask if there exists antidiscrimination law in Japan. The Constitution of Japan (promulgated in 1946 and taken into effect in 1947) has several articles concerning equality and discrimination:

> **Article 14.** All of the people are equal under the law and there shall be no discrimination in political, economic or social relations because of race, creed, sex, social status or family origin. Peers and peerage shall not be recognized. No privilege shall accompany any award of honor, decoration or any distinction, nor shall any such award be valid beyond the lifetime of the individual who now holds or hereafter may receive it.
>
> **Article 24.** Marriage shall be based only on the mutual consent of both sexes and it shall be maintained through mutual cooperation with the equal rights of husband and wife as a basis. With regard to choice of spouse, property rights, inheritance, choice of domicile, divorce and other matters pertaining to marriage and the family, laws shall be enacted from the standpoint of individual dignity and the essential equality of the sexes.
>
> **Article 26.** All people shall have the right to receive an equal education correspondent to their ability, as provided by law.
>
> **Article 44.** The qualifications of members of both Houses and their electors shall be fixed by law. However, there shall be no discrimination because of race, creed, sex, social status, family origin, education, property or income.

It is possible to say that the first enforcement of the Constitution took place just after World War II by a thorough legal reform to abolish and/or amend an existing legislation that discriminated some groups of people in Japan. A striking example is women. Because of Articles 14 and 24 of the Constitution previous family law and inheritance law based on the feudal system where the status of women had been inferior was completely abolished in order to give an equal legal status to women. Women obtained right to vote even before the establishment of the Constitution that guaranteed a right to vote a posteriori (Article 44). Moreover, aristocracy was abolished. However, social discrimination remains after legal discrimination was abolished.[3] For example, as far as gender equality is concerned, Japan is ranked 111th among 144 countries according to the current gender gap index (World Economic Forum).[4] Other than the Constitution, several laws prohibit discrimination against race, gender, ethnicity, nationality, belief (creed), disability and age in certain area such as employment. However, it is a serious problem that there are many gaps in aforesaid laws and a holistic and structural approach towards discrimination is lacking.

Each issue has been covered by several laws and bylaws as below:

- Race and ethnicity: Osaka City (local government) for the first time in Japan passed the Osaka City Bylaw concerning Measures against Hate Speech (BMHS, 大阪市ヘイトスピーチへの対処に関する条例) to prohibit hate speech (promulgated on 28 January 2016).[5] In contrast, the first national anti-hate speech law passed the Diet (Japanese legislature) on 24 May 2016 and took effect on 3 June 2016. The title of the Act is the Act Concerning Promotion of Endeavor to Abolish Unjust Discriminatory Speech and Activity Against Peoples Whose Birthplace is Outside Japan (AUDSA, 本邦出身者に対する不当な差別的言動の解消に向けた取組の推進に関する法律).[6]
- Sex/Gender: The Labor Standards Act (LSA, 労働基準法) stipulates the principle of equal wages for men and women[7]; the Act on Securing of Equal Opportunity and Treatment between Men and Women in Employment (EQA, 男女雇用機会均等法) prohibits discrimination based on sex in employment.[8]

---

[3]There are some exceptions such as a gap in marriageable age between women and men (Civil Code Article 731), a period (6 month) of prohibition of remarriage for women (Civil Code Article 733) that the SCJ finally held unconstitutional last year (judgment of 16 December 2015, Grand Bench) and a choice of surname of husband and wife (Civil Code Article 750). The latter is controversial because the Article itself does not discriminate women and men ('A husband and wife shall adopt the surname of the husband or wife in accordance with that which is decided at the time of marriage.') but 97% of women presently choose husband's surname as a couple's surname.

[4]http://reports.weforum.org/global-gender-gap-report-2016/rankings/ (visited 16 June 2017).

[5]http://www.city.osaka.lg.jp/shimin/page/0000339043.html (visited 16 June 2017).

[6]Act No. 68 of 3 June 2016.

[7]Act No. 47 of 7 April 1947.

[8]The realization of the Act took the form of an amendment of the existing Act (Act No. 113 of 1 July 1972) in 1985.

- Nationality: The LSA prohibits employers to engage in discriminatory treatment based on nationality with respect to wages, working hours or other working conditions.
- Religion and belief: The LSA prohibits employers to engage in discriminatory treatment based on creed (belief) with respect to wages, working hours or other working conditions. There is no specific legislation.
- Sexual orientation: There is no specific parliamentary legislation. Shibuya Ward (one of the special local municipalities in Tokyo) passed the Shibuya Ward Bylaw to Respect for Equality between Men and Women and Diversity (BREMWD渋谷区男女平等及び多様性を尊重する社会を推進する条例) in 2015.[9] Several local governments are following the Shibuya's initiative.
- Gender reassignment: There is no specific parliamentary legislation to prohibit discrimination against the person whose gender is reassigned. The above bylaws cover this area too.[10]
- Disability: The Act concerning the Promotion of Disappearance of Discrimination based on Disability (APDDD, 障害者差別解消法) prohibits discrimination based on disability.[11]
- Age: The Employment Measures Act (EMA, 雇用対策法) prohibits discrimination based on age in recruitment and hiring.[12]
- Social status: The LSA prohibits employers to engage in discriminatory treatment based on social status with respect to wages, working hours or other working conditions. There is no specific legislation.

3 How Is Antidiscrimination Law Enforced?

Major discrimination issues in certain areas (particularly employment) are covered by several laws, but insufficiently and inadequately.

Among them labor law is the most effective one against some forms of discrimination in a sphere of employment. The LSA prohibits employers to use the nationality, creed (belief) or social status of any workers as a basis for engaging in discriminatory treatment with respect to wages, working hours or other working conditions (Article 3). Furthermore, the Act stipulates the principle of equal wages for men and women. Employers shall not use the fact that a worker is a woman as a basis for engaging in differential treatment in comparison to men with respect to

---

[9]https://www.city.shibuya.tokyo.jp/reiki_int/reiki_honbun/g114RG00000779.html#e000000276 (visited 15 December 2015).

[10]In 2003 certain people who changed their gender by operation obtained a new legal status based on reassigned gender by the Act on Special Cases in Handling Gender Status for Persons with Gender Identity Disorder. Act No. 111 of 16 July 2003(性同一性障害者の性別の取扱いの特例に関する法律).

[11]Act No. 65 of 26 June 2013.

[12]Amendment in 2007 to the existing Act (Act No. 132 of 21 July 1966).

wages (Article 4). The EMA ensures equal opportunities regardless of age in recruitment and hiring by ordinance of the Ministry of Health, Labor and Welfare (MHLW) when it is considered necessary (Article 10).

Further development in the sphere of employment has been achieved by the EQA, which was passed in order to ratify the CEDAW. The purposes of the Act are to promote securing equal opportunity and treatment between men and women in employment, in accordance with the principle in the Constitution of Japan of ensuring equality under law, and to promote measures, among others, to ensure the health of women workers with regard to employment during pregnancy and after childbirth (Article 1). Section II of the Act prohibits discrimination on the basis of sex (gender). With regard to the recruitment and employment of workers, employers shall provide equal opportunities for all persons regardless of sex (Article 5). Employers shall not discriminate against workers on the basis of sex with regard to the following matters: (1) assignment (including allocation of duties and grant of authority), promotion, demotion, and training of workers; (2) loans for housing and other similar fringe benefits as provided by ordinance of the MHLW; (3) change in job type and employment status of workers; and (4) encouragement of retirement, mandatory retirement age, dismissal, and renewal of the labor contract. The Act prohibits disadvantageous treatment by reason of marriage, pregnancy, childbirth (Article 9). In the event that an employer is in violation of EQA, the Minister of Health, Labor and Welfare gave recommendations but the employer has not complied with it, the Minister may make a public announcement of such violation. There is only one case of public announcement in 2015 since the EQA was legislated.[13] Taken into account the unsatisfactory situation, effectiveness of this measure is doubtful.

The most recent addition to the sporadic assemblage of Japanese antidiscrimination law is the APDDD. It is for the first time that the Japanese Act includes the word 'discrimination' in the title of the Act. Moreover, the Act was introduced in 2013 in order to ratify the CRPD. It is proven again that the international human rights treaty is influential to let Japan adopt new ideas. The Act took into effect on 1 April 2016. Therefore, the effect of the Act remains to be seen.

4   Who Enforces Antidiscrimination Law?

Labor Standards Inspectors (LSI) play a principal role enforcing labor law. The LSA is supervised by the supervised bodies such as the Labor Standards Management Bureau (i.e., the department established within the MHLW with administrative responsibility for matters relating to labor conditions and the protection of Workers), Prefectural Labor Offices, and Labor Standards Inspection Offices where, LSI may be appointed (Article 97). LSI are authorized to inspect

---

[13] See http://www.mhlw.go.jp/stf/houdou/0000096409.html (visited 16 June 2017).

workplaces, dormitories, and other associated buildings; to demand the production of books and records; and to conduct the examination of Employers and Workers. With respect to a violation of the Act, LSI shall exercise the duties of judicial police officers under the Code of Criminal Procedure (Article 99). In the event that a violation of this Act or of an ordinance issued pursuant to the Act exists at a workplace, a worker may report such fact to the relevant government agency or to a LSI. In the event that a LSI deems it necessary to enforce the Act, the LSI may have an employer or a worker submit a report on the necessary matters or order an employer or a worker to appear. In the case of the EMA, the Minister of Health, Labor and Welfare may request that an employer submit necessary materials and give explanations if the Minister considers this to be necessary for the enforcement of this Act (Article 34).

The Minister of Health, Labor and Welfare enforces the EQA (gender) by formulating a basic policy concerning measures in connection with the securing of equal opportunity and treatment between men and women in employment (Article 4 of EQA). When a complaint is submitted by workers concerning discrimination based on sex at work place (except the recruitment and employment of workers), employers shall endeavor to achieve voluntary resolutions by such means as referring a complaint to grievances bodies (which are bodies for resolving complaints from the workers of the workplace, composed of representatives of the employer and representatives of the workers of the said workplace) (Article 15). The director of each Prefectural Labor Office shall refer to the competent Disputes Adjustment Commission provided for in Article 6, paragraph 1 of the Act on Promoting the Resolution of Individual Labor Disputes (hereinafter referred to as the "Commission") for the conciliation of disputes provided for in Article 16 (except a dispute on the recruitment and employment of workers) when either party or both parties to said dispute (hereinafter referred to as the "parties concerned") apply for conciliation and the Director finds conciliation necessary to resolve said dispute (Article 18). The Commission may prepare a conciliation proposal and recommend its acceptance to the parties concerned (Article 22). There is no penalty other than a public announcement of violations by the Minister of Health, Labor and Welfare as it is explained before.

The APDDD has several new characteristics as antidiscrimination law. The administrative organs shall not violate rights and interests of the person with disability by giving him/her unfair discriminatory treatment based on disability. Furthermore, the administrative organs shall provide necessary and reasonable accommodations in order to remove social barriers when a person with disability expresses necessity of removal of social barriers and the burden of realization of removal is not overloading (Article 7). Private sectors are also under the similar obligation (Article 8) although providing necessary and reasonable accommodation is no more than an endeavor for them. There is no penalty for private sectors that fail to provide reasonable accommodations. The ministers can require private sectors to submit a report (Article 12) while they can provide advice, guidance and recommendation. In other words, the APPDDD is based on a model where the prevention and abolishment of discrimination is realized through the dialogue and consultation between the parties concerned, community and private and public sectors. For those purposes the Local Council for Promotion of Disappearance of Discrimination against the Person with Disability may be established including public sectors that are engaged in works of medical service, care service and education to promote independence and social participation of the person with disability, NGOs and academics (Article 17).

In the case of bylaws such as BMHS and BREMWD a city mayor or a head of a ward is responsible for enforcement with the support of councils usually consisting of experts.

5 Who Benefits from the Enforcement of Antidiscrimination Law?

The first and most direct beneficiary is a person who are discriminated by pubic and/or private sectors. It is the case when the person who brings his or her case to the court and wins. However, softer enforcement measures (public announcement of violations and consultations with parties concerned and a third party) do not offer direct remedy to a victim and therefore the direct effect is limited.

The employers may obtain benefits by achieving fair and comfortable environment for everyone, which might contribute in improving productivity and creativity of the activities of the companies themselves. Diversity of employees can also enhance the strength of companies. Moreover, employees and future candidates of employees can appreciate those conditions, which works advantageously for companies who want to employ talented applicants as many as possible. Even for consumers those characteristics of companies are appealing. After all a policy of diversity is highly appreciated from a perspective of corporate social responsibility.[14]

It is not only the parties concerned such as employees and employers but also the society who can enjoy discrimination-free environment. For example, before the EQA was introduced a comment that women are like Christmas cakes could be freely given as a joke in public. It suggested that women over 25 years old cannot marry as Christmas cakes cannot be sold after Christmas. This was a reflection of the reality that women were only hired as supporting staff (lower wage than men) and they were supposed to quit their job when they marry. Therefore, companies thought that it was waste of money and time to train female workers and to promote them. From a perspective of female workers, they did not expect companies to consider them as candidates of managerial or professional work. Therefore, they were less motivated to fulfill their ambition as an employee of the company. It was a vicious circle on both sides of the female workers and companies. The EQA changed mindset of female and male graduates of career building as well as companies'

---

[14]Mizumachi (2008), p. 246.

mindset as the companies obliged to recruit the people regardless of sex.[15] 96.9% of male graduates successfully obtained jobs when 98.4% of female graduates did in 2016.[16] The number of double-income household overtook the number of single-income household in the 1997. It should be kept in mind that those results came from not only the EQA but also from the economic situation.

6 Who Is Harmed by the Enforcement of Antidiscrimination Law?

It is difficult to think of the person or public or private institutions who are directly harmed by the enforcement of antidiscrimination law as the enforcement mechanism heavily relies on recommendations and weak penalty such as a public announcement of a name of the violators. On the other hand companies always find a loophole in law or a way to escape the legal requirement. For example, after the EQA took into effect and required companies to equally recruit and employ women and men, they incorporated a new system. They abolished the previous course based on gender but established two courses not associated to gender. One course is for general support work (ippanshoku) and the other course for career track (sogoshoku), in which a person can be promoted to a manager and above. Most of female workers have been hired in the ippanshoku course in which the treatment is similar to the previous course for women. Most of male workers, particularly most male university graduates are hired in the course for sogoshoku. Even female workers themselves often prefer to be hired as ippanshoku as their duty of household is heavier than their husbands once they marry. The result is the aforesaid low gender ranking (a wage gap between women and men and very few female COE in the companies). On the other hand it is difficult to call the two-course system discriminatory system as women have a choice to choose courses. The real problem is long-hour working (notorious overtime work) style of Japanese labor custom. Government currently introduces several policies such as promotion of 'Work and Life' balance and 'Emphasized Guideline on Promotion of an Active Role of Women'. Their effect remains to be seen.[17]

The APDDD stipulates for the first time an obligation of providing necessary and reasonable accommodation of administrative organs and employers when a person with disability expresses necessity of removal of social barriers and the burden of realization of removal is not overloading. There are several questions to be answered. First, to what extent of burden do they have to accept? In other words,

---

[15]Many Japanese companies still keep a custom of recruitment to hire a fixed number of fresh graduates at one time. Therefore, job hunting for would-be graduates is as important as recruitment of fresh graduates for companies.

[16]See http://www.mhlw.go.jp/stf/houdou/0000164865.html (visited 16 June 2017).

[17]See http://www.gender.go.jp/english_contents/index.html (visited 16 June 2017).

when can they refuse to offer necessary and reasonable accommodation because their burden is too heavy? Secondly, what are necessary and reasonable accommodations? Thirdly, when they neglect to offer the accommodation or they only offer unsatisfactory accommodation, can the person with disability bring the case to the court? If the burden on public sectors will turn out to be quite substantial, it would harm their business. Moreover, if the obligation on private sectors will be taken seriously, it would harm their business too although private sector's obligation is mitigated (they are required to endeavor to offer necessary and reasonable accommodation). What does it mean in reality? It remains to be seen as the APDDD came into force on 1 April 2016. The Cabinet Office already provides the information concerning reasonable accommodation by setting up a database on the website where people can search what is required as reasonable accommodation according to the specific situation.[18]

In the case of speech based on racial discrimination (hate speech), according to the Osaka City Bylaw (BMHS) enables a city mayor to publicize the name of the person who used hate speech after receiving opinion of the council consisting of experts. Therefore, the harm upon freedom of speech will be in question although it remains to be seen yet.

7   What Remedies Are Provided by the Enforcement of Antidiscrimination Law?

Because there is no general antidiscrimination law, there are no remedies which general antidiscrimination can offer.

If the public authorities or the legislation itself treat the person differently without reasonable reason, it can be unconstitutional. In general, the SCJ admits a wider discretion on the legislature and it is rare for the SCJ to admit unconstitutionality of legislation (there is only ten cases where unconstitutionality of legislation was admitted since the SCJ was established in 1949). It is, however, interesting to note that the SCJ admitted unconstitutionality of legislation based on Article 14 (equality) in six cases out of the above ten cases. Afterwards parliamentary statutes were amended.[19]

In labor law there is an established case law concerning the interpretation of antidiscrimination clauses in the LSA. When the employee (plaintiff) wins the case, the remedies available for them are compensations, payment of unpaid salaries, return to the previous post etc. Furthermore, the EQA stipulates that employers shall

---

[18] Cabinet Office provides a search system of cases concerning reasonable accommodation. See, http://www8.cao.go.jp/shougai/suishin/jirei/index.html (visited 16 June 2017).

[19] In the last example of the Judgment of 16 December 2015 the Ministry of Justice advised the administrative agency to work in a way which is compatible with the 2015 judgment before the legislation was amended in 2016.

establish necessary measures in terms of employment management to give advice to workers and cope with problems of workers, and take other necessary measures so that workers they employ do not suffer any disadvantage in their working conditions by reason of said workers' responses to sexual harassment in the workplace, or in their working environments do not suffer any harm due to said sexual harassment (Article 11). Therefore, when employers ignore a complaint of sexual harassment from employees, employers themselves are liable for damages.

Weaker forms of remedies are a public announcement of name of the person or the company who violated the law (EQA and BMHS). Its effectiveness remains to be seen.

There are interesting developments of case law. The SCJ supported the high court ruling, which ordered a group of anti-Korean activists that expressed hate speech against a Korean School in Kyoto to pay 12 million yen in damages to the school and ban it from demonstrating around the school.[20] In the field of sexual reassignment a lower court awarded a plaintiff compensation for damages when a golf club refused the plaintiff's membership because of gender reassignment.[21] The national legislation against hate speech (AUDSA) also promoted the judiciary and executive to change to tackle with hate speech more actively despite the AUDSA has is a soft law without penalty. A district court ordered an activist using hate speech not to do a march a certain area where an office the activist had targeted and a city refused to give a permission to an organization who had been involved in hate speech.

8 Who Supports the Enforcement of Antidiscrimination Law?

The people or the group of the people who have been discriminated against support the enforcement of antidiscrimination law. Moreover, NGOs who campaigns against discrimination gradually began to play an important role in finding problems, looking for solutions and oversighting the implementation of antidiscrimination law.

The most recent enactment of the APDDD (and ratification of CRPD) is a good example. The NGOs, which have been working on the issue of discrimination of persons with disabilities, are the major driving force for the passage of the APDDD by establishing a network between the parties concerned, public or/and private sectors and even politicians. It is noteworthy that some MPs, who have family members with disability, worked passionately for passage of the APDDD beyond

---

[20]Decision of the SCJ (petty bench), 9 December 2014.

[21]Judgment of Shizuoka District Court, 8 September 2014 (the judgment was supported by Tokyo High Court on 1 July 2015). Presently a transgender business manager in the city of Kyoto sued major fitness club operator because she was forced to use its facility in Kyoto Prefecture as a man before undergoing sex reassignment surgery. Japan Times (25 December 2015).

party affiliation.[22] It shows that the people who do not have disability or who do not have family and/or friends who have disability tend to take the issue less seriously because of lacking imagination. Therefore, drafters of the APDDD carefully chose the word 'disappearance' of discrimination instead of 'prohibition' of discrimination in order to avoid any possibility to give an impression that the Act is going to establish a strong legal mechanism based on punishment and penalties which would cause oppositions from companies and even general public.

9 Who Opposes the Enforcement of Antidiscrimination Law?

Since there is no general antidiscrimination law as such, there is no general opposition against the enforcement of antidiscrimination law.

A general characteristic of the Japanese legal system to prevent and prohibit discrimination is a soft approach based on awareness and education program and consultation. Therefore it is also difficult to find any specific opposition against this approach.

The drafting process of the APDDD shows that they deliberately avoid the confrontational measures and choose the softer scheme (see 7). Recently, a rise of hate speech as racial discrimination against ethnic minorities increasingly challenges the conventional approach (soft approach). Other than the Korean School Case (see 6) a group of anti-Korean activists visited areas where many Korean residents live and marched a public street while using hate speech. The people who are against such speech expressed their disagreement by counter speech. Occasionally it resulted in physical confrontation and several people of both sides got arrested. Therefore, if a stronger enforcement including criminal and financial punishment is going to incorporate to handle with the present situation, a question of freedom of expression should be raised. As previously described (see 5), the implementation measures adopted by the BMHA and AUDSA were so weak that opposition to the legislation was also week. The AUDSA passed the upper house by 221 to 7 votes and passed in the lower house by a majority (a standing vote).

10 How Broad Is the Coverage of Antidiscrimination Law?

As there is no general antidiscrimination law, the coverage of each piece of legislation that regulates certain aspects of discrimination is limited (see 1, 2 & 3).

---

[22] Shougaisha Sabetsu Kaisho Ho Kaisetsu Henshu Iinkai [Commentary and Editing Commission on the APPDB], *Gaisetsu Shougaisha Sabetsu Kaisho Ho* [Outline of the APDDD] (Horitsu Bunkasha, 2014), p. 27.

The list below explains how each item is covered and by what law:

- Race and ethnicity: There is no specific parliamentary legislation. The recent national legislation (AUDSA) and local bylaw (BMHS) cover this area in term of hate speech but it does not have criminal or financial penalties. The exceptional cases like the Kyoto School Case (see 6) have a chance to be dealt with by the general principles of Civil Code (Damages).
- Sex/Gender: This sphere of employment has been covered by labor law (such as the LSA) and the EQA.
- Nationality: Other than the LSA there is no specific law to prohibit discrimination based on nationality.
- Religion and belief: Other than the LSA there is no specific law to prohibit discrimination based on religion and belief.
- Sexual orientation: Shibuya ward (MREMWD) and a few local governments started to take measure to protect sexual minority. No national legislation exists.
- Gender reassignment: Shibuya ward (MREMWD) and a few local governments started to take measure to protect sexual minority. No national legislation exists.
- Disability: The APDDD prohibits discrimination based on Disability.
- Age: Other than the EMA there is no specific law to prohibit discrimination based on age.

11 Does Enforcement of Antidiscrimination Law Vary According to the Ground of Discrimination?

Enforcement of antidiscrimination law does not vary according to the ground of discrimination.

Enforcement can be classified into three approaches. The first one is the civil law approach where the parties concerned bring a case to the court and they can get remedies when they win. Secondly, the criminal law approach where criminal punishment is given to the person or corporate and the existence of punishment can prevent discrimination in advance. The third and last one is the administrative law approach. The administrative bodies are in charge of establishing policy, offering education and awareness program and overseeing the conduct of private persons and corporates. They receive complaints from victims, giving them advice, holding consultation process and giving recommendation to the accused.

In Japan it is possible to use the civil law approach but it is difficult for the ordinary people to go to the court because of money, time and accessibility of the court. Therefore it is the last recourse for them unless discrimination in question is really severe and unbearable. Japanese mainstream approach is the third one. Particularly the APDDD put emphasis on consultation of all the parties and experts. Taken into account the nature of discrimination on disability, it is effective to highlight the importance of consultation. However, it is a question whether the similar approach is also effective for other recent issues, such as hate speech based on race and ethnicity.

12 What Is the Relationship Between the Enforcement of Antidiscrimination Law and the Quest for Equality on Both an Individual and Systemic Level?

Each law that deals with the question of discrimination has to be in accordance with the guarantee of equality under law in the Constitution of Japan. The EQA clearly stipulates that 'the purposes of this Act are to promote securing equal opportunity and treatment between men and women in employment in accordance with the principle in the Constitution of Japan of ensuring equality under law'. The LSA does not mention the equality under law or the Constitution but it is supposed that the LSA is embodiment of the Article 27 of the Constitution (rights to work). It can be safely said that each law covers certain aspect of discrimination exists for securing equality.

Then, what kind of discrimination does the equality principle under the Constitution prohibit? The case law of the SCJ says that reasonable discrimination is not unconstitutional.[23] Then, what is reasonable discrimination? If reasonableness varies according to the change of society and public consciousness, it is difficult to define discrimination in advance (actually many law avoids to define discrimination). Once the 'Christmas case' joke was a safe joke even in front of women of mid-twenties. Now it is not a joke anymore. It can be considered as sexual harassment in certain circumstances. On the other hand even if the content of discrimination is changeable and therefore flexible, it is not an easy situation for certain groups of the people who are discriminated based on some features such as race and ethnicity, gender, sexual orientation because they have been and still are democratically under-represented. However, the SCJ is likely to consider that it is the legislature who decides how society and people's consciousness changed. Only few exceptional cases the SCJ decides by itself.[24]

---

[23] Judgments of the SCJ (grand bench), 4 April 1973.

[24] As recent examples, see, Judgments of the SCJ (grand bench), 4 September 2013 and 16 December 2015.

13 Is the Enforcement of Antidiscrimination Law Regarded as Different from the Enforcement of Other Laws?

As there is no general antidiscrimination law with the strong enforcement measures, the enforcement of law that covers some discrimination is not different from the enforcement of other laws.

14 What Does the Enforcement of Antidiscrimination Law Reveal About the Nature of Your Legal System or About the Enforcement of Laws in Your Legal System?

The fact that there is no antidiscrimination law with the strong enforcement measures reflects some characteristics of Japanese legal system in general. First, it is frequent to legislate a statute stipulates only general principles and polices and delegates to administrative organs to realize them. Its flexibility is convenient for adjustment with changes but there is a danger that no substantial measures are taken in some environments where there is no consensus on what should be done or no political will to realize it. This is very true with discrimination issues. For example, Basic Act for Persons with Disabilities was legislated in 1970 but it took 43 years to obtain an Act for prohibition of discrimination based on disability (APDDD).[25]

Secondly, the conventional perception on the roles of the judiciary and legislature in Japan is also problematic in terms of implementing antidiscrimination law. If the judiciary sticks with the conventional role and pay deference to the legislature, victims suffers from discrimination have to wait long until they obtain decent remedies. On the other hand, bringing the case to the court is not necessarily an ideal solution for every case. Conversations among the parties concerned, with the help of experts, is more productive and effective for some cases. There should be mixed approaches according to the different nature of discrimination.

Thirdly, there is a general tendency of Japanese law to adopt the moderate enforcement measures in order to avoid conflicts and smoothen the passage of the Act. Some cases (such as the Kyoto School Case), however, clearly show necessity of a stronger measure to cope with a severe and serious case.

---

[25] Act No. 84 of 21 May 1970.

15 Conclusion

Since the drastic and thorough legal reform during the occupation era, the efforts to update the legal system in order to cope with new challenges has been paid at minimum level. Therefore, international human rights treaties have played a role to some degree in re-examining the effectiveness of the present sporadic assemblage of weak antidiscrimination legal scheme in Japan. The EQA, ICERD and APDDD are good examples to see the impact and input of the international human rights treaties.

The problematic aspect of Japanese implementation is a tendency to choose the least effective measures for implementation in order to avoid conflicts and smoothen the passage of the Act. The original EQA is a good example. It was heavily criticized that it had many loopholes and was lacking the effective enforcement measures, particularly penalties. The present EQA has been reinforced by several amendments adding an obligation of employers to protect employees from sexual harassment and a penalty as a public announcement of names of violators.

On the other hand the APDDD shows a new aspect in enforcement. It is true that the APDDD itself is also lacking a strong enforcement such as criminal and financial penalties. However, the drafting process of the APDDD reveals that they considered the disadvantages of strong enforcement mechanisms and chose a soft approach emphasizing on dialogue and consultation among the people with disability and all the concerned parties, private and public sectors and NGOs.[26] Although it is too early to evaluate effectiveness of its soft approach, it seems persuasive to take this course, taking into account the difficulty of defining discrimination based on disability.

Lastly, a surge of hate speech which shocked general public in Japan and international community reveals insufficiency of the Japanese legal system against hate speech and racial discrimination in general. The necessity of anti-racial discrimination law is presently discussed among politicians and NGOs. It is a new challenge for the Japanese bricolage of antidiscrimination law.

Reference

Mizumachi Y (2008) Jinjikanri karano Approach [Approach from personnel management]. In: Morito H, Mizumachi Y (eds) Sabetsukinshiho no Shintenkai [A new development of anti-discrimination law]. Nihon-Hyoron-sha, p 246

---

[26] See, Shougaisha note 22, at p. 41.

Akiko Ejima is a Professor of Law at School of Law, Meiji University (Tokyo). She holds a Ph.D from Meiji University. She was a visiting scholar at King's College London, a visiting scholar at Harvard Law School, a visiting scholar at Faculty of Law and Hughes Hall, University of Cambridge and a visiting scholar at Wolfson College, University of Oxford. Professor Ejima writes and teaches in the field of Constitutional Law, Comparative Constitutional Law and International Human Rights Law.

Republic of Korea

Jean Ahn

1 Introduction

With the exception of the Equal Employment Act of 1987, antidiscrimination laws did not begin appearing in South Korea until the start of the new millennium. The Equal Employment Act was enacted following the 1987 June Struggle, driven by Korea's working class, and which would become a milestone in Korea's democratization process. Korea's Constitution, which restricts presidency to single 5-year terms and establishes the Constitutional Court system, was amended as a result of this historic event.

Years later, in 2001, a key antidiscriminatory measure emerged. The establishment of a national human rights commission, which Korean human rights organizations had been advocating since the Vienna International Human Rights Conference of 1993, became a key policy proposal of Kim Dae-jung's 1998 presidential campaign. Following Kim's victory, legislation for the commission's creation was accelerated and, on 24 May 2001, the National Human Rights Commission Act (NHRCA) was enacted into law. This was one of the remarkable achievements of the Kim Dae-jung administration (1998–2002). Although its name basically refers to Korea's national human rights institution, the NHRCA covers non-judicial or quasi-judicial remedies for addressing violations of equality rights. Since coming into force on 25 November 2001, NHRCA has significantly impacted discriminatory customs and practices in the public sphere, albeit by relying on voluntary compliance. Crucially, however, there is still no comprehensive (or general) antidiscrimination law in Korea that is legally binding.

J. Ahn (✉)
Chonnam National University, School of Law, Gwangju, South Korea

Following the consolidation of Korea's civilian government in 1993, the legislative movement working to pass equality law has become much more active. The Equal Employment Act of 1999 (EEA) was amended to regulate sexual harassment[1] largely as a result of the Supreme Court's decision in the case of Professor Shin Jung-hyu.[2] The EEA has since developed and its name has been changed (now, the Act on Equal Employment and Support for Work-Family Reconciliation, AEESWFR) so that it more substantively promotes gender equality through family support services. The Act on the Prohibition of Sexual Discrimination, another gender equality law from 1999, was abolished in 2005.

Laws addressing other kinds of discrimination—against the disabled, irregular workers (discrimination based on the form of employment), and the aged—were also enacted during the first decade of the 2000s. However, since the 1990s, it is surely human rights advocates for the disabled who have produced the most active antidiscrimination campaign and movement in Korea. Since 2000, they have made great efforts and strides to enact antidiscrimination laws benefiting persons with disabilities; and, in 2007, a Korean-styled human rights act for the disabled—the Act on the Prohibition of Discrimination against the Disabled (APDAD), the most powerful individual antidiscrimination law yet in Korea, came into force.

Labor movement have also begun raising the issue of discrimination against irregular workers, whose numbers have risen in conjunction with the remarkable growth and change in the Korean economy since the 1990s; the Act on the Protection of Fixed-term and Part-time Workers, enacted in 2007, has begun to address these changes. Further, in February of 2008, a Korean version of America's ADEA law silently moved through the regular legislative channels and passed the National Assembly.[3]

But a comprehensive, general antidiscrimination law has yet to be enacted in Korea, though both the Roh Moo-hyun administration (2003–2007) and the National Human Rights Commission of Korea (NHRCK) made unprecedented efforts in this direction.[4] A group of human rights activists is currently mobilizing (organizing)

---

[1]The first law addressing sexual harassment was the Basic Act on Women's Development, enacted in 1995. It was amended into the Basic Act on Gender Equality in 2015.

[2]Professor Shin Jung-hyu's case ignited, for the first in Korean society, a deep and sustained argument over sexual harassment, which lasted from the beginning of the suit against him until final judgment by Korea's Supreme Court (1993–1997). The Supreme Court overturned the high court's decision and ultimately acknowledged that Professor Shin had engaged in sexual harassment, finding that Shin's employer, Seoul National University, was not legally responsible for his actions.

[3]The Act on the Prohibition of Age Discrimination in Employment and Elderly Employment Promotion (APADE) was enacted on 21 March in 2008 by just adding some provisions in chapter one of the Act on the Elderly Employment Promotion and renaming it.

[4]The Roh Moo-hyun administration included inequality reduction among its "Ten Great National Tasks," establishing the Poverty Disparity and Discrimination Rectification Committee as a presidential agency. This Committee quickly pointed to what it saw as the five leading types of discrimination in Korea: that based on sex, disability, academic clique, immigration status (i.e., foreign workers), and form of employment (irregular workers). Age discrimination was added

people through a signature-collection campaign in support of legislation that would introduce comprehensive antidiscrimination law.

2 Is Antidiscrimination Law Enforced?

Korean antidiscrimination laws have just been legislated and enforced since the 2000s. The Equal Employment Act (EEA) prohibiting sexual discrimination in employment was the only antidiscrimination law introduced before the 2000s. In 1999, the EEA was amended to include sexual harassment. In 2007, it was renamed the Act on Equal Employment and Support for Work-Family Reconciliation and further amended to create Chapter *III*-2—Support for Work-Family Reconciliation—to provide family care, striving for de facto gender equality. A separate measure, The Act on the Prohibition of Sexual Discrimination, was also created in 1999 but repealed in 2005 when remedies for discrimination were integrated under the National Human Rights Commission of Korea.

In 2007, the Act on the Prohibition of Discrimination against the Disabled (APDAD)—the most stringent antidiscrimination law in Korea—was enacted. In 2008, the National Assembly passed the Act on the Prohibition of Age Discrimination in Employment and Elderly Employment Promotion (APADE). Although not antidiscrimination laws per se, measures addressing irregular workers such as the Act on the Protection of Fixed Term and Part-time Workers and the Act on the Protection of Temporary Agency Workers have also been introduced in order to prohibit discrimination based on type of employment. The former was enacted in 2007 as a result of strong labor movement support, while the latter, amended in 2008, protects irregular employees from disparate treatment and provides remedies through the Labor Relations Committee.

3 How Is Antidiscrimination Law Enforced?

The National Human Rights Commission Act (NHRCA), enacted in 2001, provides quasi-legal remedies for discriminatory acts. NHRCA is enforced by the National Human Rights Commission of Korea (NHRCK). There are two primary subcommittees that function under the Commission. One is the Subcommittee for Relief from Infringement, whose oversight involves the liberty rights guaranteed by Articles 10 through 22 of the Constitution. The other is the Subcommittee for Correction

---

subsequently. Two bills to establish an Antidiscrimination law were submitted during President Roh's term, yet never fully addressed due to the termination of the National Assembly session. One of the bills was proposed by the Labor Party lawmaker Roh Hoe-chan. The other was submitted by the government, which based its bill on recommendations from NHRCK.

of Discrimination (SCD), which provides remedies when the equal rights guaranteed by Article 11 of the Constitution are violated. Mainly through these two committees, the Commission provides non-judicial or quasi-judicial remedies for infringements of fundamental rights. More importantly, the remedies for discrimination apply to violations occurring in both the private and public spheres, whereas relief from infringement applies only to violations occurring in the public sphere, such as within state agencies, local governments, schools, public service-related organizations, or detention or caring facilities.

SCD receives petitions from those who have allegedly been discriminated against, decides whether a discriminatory act has in fact occurred, and then recommends corrective measures. The SCD's decisions are not legally binding but provide quick and cost-efficient decisions in controversial cases. In the process, discriminatory acts based on disability, gender, age, and other criteria have become more visible in Korean society, leading to major changes in social perception. But if a perpetrator does not accept SCD's recommendations, then the victim, in order to obtain redress, will have to resort to a separate litigation process that may result in a legally binding remedy.

For example, through voluntary compliance, universities have repealed hiring policies that limited applicants for professional positions to those under age forty. But because the Commission's decisions are not legally binding, NHRCA remedies are not available when those who discriminate refuse to adopt the Commission's recommendations. However, as seen through a case brought by KTX train female attendants,[5] even when the respondent does not accept the recommendation made by the SCD, the process of bringing a case to the Commission and having it render a decision can have a major social impact.

4 Who Enforces Antidiscrimination Law?

As alluded to earlier, NHRCA is the most comprehensive antidiscrimination law in Korea, but its remedies are not legally binding and only advisory in nature. However, NHRCK can mediate conciliatory processes in all types of discrimination cases, covering a wide variety of grounds for discrimination. The remedy under APDAD and APADE is legally binding since they enforce the corrective order when the case is regarded as malicious discrimination, whereas the remedy under NHRCA is limited to the right to recommend. Separate governmental agencies, presiding over different types of discrimination, enforce the corrective orders guaranteed under the individual antidiscrimination statutes. For instance, APDAD enforcement is undertaken by the Ministry of Justice, APADE enforcement by the Ministry of

---

[5]NHRCK resolution on the case of KTX employment discrimination against female attendants, 2006.9.11 Ja 06 Jin-Cha 116, 06 Jin-Cha 136 (the joinder) resolution.

Employment and Labor, and the Act on the Protection of Temporary Agency Workers (APTAW) enforcement by the National Labor Relation Committee.

5 Who Benefits from the Enforcement of Antidiscrimination Law?

In short, the groups and individuals that benefit most from the enforcement of antidiscrimination law are social minorities. With respect to NHRCA, although its remedies are not legally binding, it does frequently provide relief to a wide range of social minorities who have been discriminated against and subjected to unequal treatment due to various factors relating to social status. Yet particular groups of minorities have benefited the most from more specific and targeted antidiscrimination laws. For instance, female workers facing various hurdles and inequalities in the workplace have benefited to some degree from the EEA, while disabled workers facing discrimination have gained from enactment of the Act on the Prohibition of Discrimination against the Disabled. Similarly, workers over the age of 55 (and even some over age 50) have benefited significantly from APDAE. Finally, various laws relating to irregular workers, such as the Act on the Protection of Fixed Term and Part-time Workers, have helped protect the basic rights of various irregular workers.

6 Who Is Harmed by the Enforcement of Antidiscrimination Law?

If the notion of "harm" can be used to describe instances where the privilege or power of certain parties is diminished, then it may be said that elite individuals and groups, who are in charge of society's key decision-making processes (managing corporations, hiring work forces, etc.) are sometimes "harmed" by the enforcement of antidiscrimination laws. Because of the EEA, APDAD, and APDAE, employers who are in privileged positions within the labor market may be constrained in the extent to which they can engage in discriminatory, if profitable, employment-related actions.

7 What Remedies May Be Provided Through Enforcement of Antidiscrimination Law?

As noted previously, NHRCK remedies are recommendations and thus not legally binding. When a case is a valid instance of discrimination, NHRCK may recommend the revision, correction, or amelioration of policies or conventions, and may also proffer further opinions on specific discriminatory cases (NHRCA Article 25). Also, if needed, it may recommend a conciliatory process (Article 40). In addition to setting forth recommendations, NHRCK may also convene a committee to respond to an instance of discrimination. However, very rarely has damage inflicted through discriminatory acts been remedied by the conciliatory process (Article 41).

With respect to more specific antidiscrimination laws, diverse councils and agencies enforce remedies, which are mostly penal punishments such as issuance of a corrective order (by the Ministry of Law, Ministry of Employment and Labor, National Labor Relations Committee), penalties, surcharges, imprisonment, or fines. For instance, although violation of the EEA, APDAD, or APDAE may result in criminal punishment, the discriminatory contracts or policies themselves will not be annulled. In comparison, violation of the antidiscrimination clause (Article 6) of the Basic Labor Act does annul employment contracts based on discrimination, as well as treaties and employment policies that go against equality rights. However, as prescribed by the Basic Labor Act, the grounds for discrimination that may result in the annulment of discriminatory contracts are limited to sex, nationality, religion, and social status; thus, the scope of application is somewhat limited.

The EEA encourages above all else the autonomous resolutions of disputes involving discriminatory conduct. Article 25 of the EEA prescribes that a joint labor-management committee be established in order to resolve instances of workplace discrimination. In cases judged as valid instances of discrimination the EEA usually imposes fines; However, in cases involving gender discrimination with respect to the retirement and dismissal of workers and employment contracts that mention pregnancy and child birth as reasons for discharge (Article 37:1), the EEA may enforce fairly heavy penal punishment of up to 5 years imprisonment or fines as high as 30,000,000 won (roughly equivalent to $30,000 USD). Similarly, for cases involving violation of equal pay for equal work policies (Article 37:2:1), or sexual harassment (Article 37:2:2), the EEA may enforce fairly heavy punishment of up to 3 years imprisonment or fines up to 20,000,000 won (roughly equivalent to $20,000 USD). Such penal punishments are enforced fairly rigorously by APDAE (Article 4:9, Article 23:3:1) and APDAD, which may prescribe strong penal punishment in cases involving disadvantageous treatment for claim of discrimination.

8 Who Supports the Enforcement of Antidiscrimination Law?

The main groups of people who support the enforcement of antidiscrimination law are women, the disabled, aged workers, irregular workers, and other social minorities. Most of these groups have been demanding broad, legally binding antidiscrimination laws. Some groups have developed into organized forces that have actively shaped the legislative processes leading to some of Korea's currently existing antidiscrimination statutes. For example, feminist and labor movements have been continually and actively involved with amending the EEA and with laws relating to irregular workers. Similarly, disability rights organizations fought actively for passage of APDAD.

One minor exception to this correlation between minority movements and legislation would be APDAE, which, under the direction of the government, came into existence almost silently, without much prior public discussion. South Korea discriminates heavily against the aged, so attention toward, and organized support for, APDAE may partly be lacking because of the social context in which it was first established.

Indeed, the process of enacting laws is often strongly shaped by the social context in which it occurs. This might explain why APDAD is the most strongly and widely supported statute among the Korean people, and why it is also the most effectively enforced. The NGOs fighting for the basic rights of the disabled have continued to closely monitor APDAD enforcement, and have already demanded amendments to some of its insufficient clauses. In a similar vein, the major amendment to the EEA in 2007 that added a clause on caring for the family (Clause 3:2), was heavily influenced by the women's rights and feminist movements. The broader coverage of childcare leave (in the late 1990s it covered only the care of infants under the age of 1, whereas now it covers children up until age 8), as well as other legislative actions taken to move towards gender equality in the workforce, have been most strongly supported by Korean women.

9 Who Opposes the Enforcement of Antidiscrimination Law?

In the employment sector, it is mostly employers who are against—or not in favor of—the enforcement of antidiscrimination laws. However, regular workers may also oppose the enforcement of laws relating to the protection of irregular workers because there is a limited amount of pay and work opportunities to be divided amongst them.

Korea's Christian fundamentalist groups are those most against the legislation or enforcement of antidiscrimination law relating to sexual orientation. Conservative Christian organizations have actively fought against not only individual antidiscrimination laws specifically designed to protect sexual minorities, but also more general antidiscrimination law that ensure equal rights for other minorities. Intense pressure from conservative Christian organizations was the main reason that National Assembly did not address an antidiscrimination bill covering sexual orientation, immigration, and some other serious types of discrimination in 2007. At the time, the Christian Council of Korea—convinced that their own religious beliefs were morally superior to the basic equality rights set forth in the Constitution—aggressively fought against any legislation to establish general antidiscrimination law that included sexual orientation. Consequently, the Ministry of Law erased some grounds for discrimination in the final bill submitted to National Assembly.

Most married couples generally support the EEA, which is intended to promote balance between work and family life. However, there has been opposition from male workers with respect to the ruling in the Constitutional Court that policies favoring former soldiers are unconstitutional.[6] Some employment practices have favored those with experience of military service and they are often supported by male workers. Further, some male workers are, in general, against policies and antidiscrimination laws that promote realistic (de facto) gender equality.

10 How Broad Is the Coverage of South Korea's Antidiscrimination Laws?

NHRCA describes 19 types of discrimination.[7] It is also very broad in scope, covering not only employment but also use of goods and services, education, and sexual harassment. The EEA targets five grounds of sexual discrimination in employment: sex, marriage, family status, pregnancy, and childbirth (Article 2:1). In particular, the EEA has played a key role in regulating sexual harassment in Korea by creating a new provision (through amendment in 1999) following the conclusion of the Professor Shin Jung-hyu case.

APDAD is the broadest individual antidiscrimination law in terms of scope of application; it applies not only to employment area like EEA and APDAE, but also to education, use of goods and supplies, political rights, sexuality, family, and the

---

[6]Constitutional Court 1999.12.23. pronouncement, 98 HunMa 363. (The decision on the extra-point policy for discharged soldiers in the recruitment examination of public officials).

[7]Article 2, Section 3 of NHRCA refers to the definition of discrimination as follows: The term "discriminatory act violating the equal right" means any of the following acts, without reasonable grounds, on the grounds of sex, religion, disability, age, social status, region of origin (referring to a place of birth, permanent domicile, principal area of residence before the full adult age, etc.), state of origin, ethnic origin, physical condition such as features, marital status such as single, separated, divorced, widowed, remarried, married de facto, or whether pregnant or having given birth, types or forms of family, race, skin color, ideology or political opinion, record of crime whose effect of punishment has been extinguished, sexual orientation, academic career, medical history, etc.

Republic of Korea 377

right to health. No individual antidiscrimination law incorporates "hate speech" into its definition of discrimination; APDAD merely has a provision to prescribe punishment for harassment. The regulation of hate speech and harassment is one of the issues to be addressed in the drafting of comprehensive antidiscrimination legislation in Korea.

11 Does the Enforcement of Antidiscrimination Law Vary According to the Grounds of Discrimination?

In Korea, the degree of enforcement of antidiscrimination law varies depending on the reason for discrimination. NHRCA has quasi-judicial effects in terms of its remedies, and can, in principle, be applied to all grounds for discrimination. NHRCA was enacted via the recommendations by NHRCK, is linked to the executive branch even though it is an independent public agency. NHRCK is first to decide whether a given case relating to APDAD or APADE involves a valid instance of discrimination. If the parties involved in APDAD or APADE violation do not follow NHRCK's recommendations, then the relevant administrative agency may step in to enforce corrective orders, thus strengthening the power of remedy that would have been deployed by NHRCK alone. Such corrective orders from an administrative agency are also enforced in cases where the damage inflicted by the discriminatory act is severe. The Ministry of Justice holds corrective power for APDAD, and the Ministry of Employment and Labor holds corrective power for APADE. In cases where such corrective orders are not followed, penalties are prescribed. APDAD prescribes a right to file for compensation or indemnification for damages, but does not prescribe criminal punishments for discriminatory acts perpetrated against another party. In contrast, APADE prescribes criminal punishments for discriminatory acts, but does not prescribe compensation for damages.

NHRCK has become the sole, unified branch undertaking corrective orders relating to gender discrimination. For the EEA, which applies to gender discrimination in employment, separate branches that can undertake the conciliatory process have not existed since the dissolution of the Employment Equality Committee in 2005. Consequently, the only way for victims of sexual harassment or other forms of gender-related discrimination in the workplace (as determined by the EEA) to receive redress is by filing a complaint or a petition with NHRCK, or by filing a lawsuit. In short, responsibility for enforcing corrective orders, originally taken on by the EEA now lies with NHRCK. Further, the Act on Prohibition of Sexual Discrimination passed in 1999, and the Committee on Improvement of Sexual Discrimination was formed (within the Ministry of Gender Equality and Family), which assumed responsibility for issuing corrective orders. Yet this function was again transferred to NHRCK. In the history of Korean antidiscrimination law, the decisions to abolish the Act on Prohibition of Sexual Discrimination and dissolve the

Committee on Improvement of Sexual Discrimination have come to be regarded as careless and anachronistic.

Finally, the Discrimination Correction Committee (within the Labor Relations Committee)—a kind of quasi-labor court—enforces laws relating to the protection of irregular workers. It is noteworthy that, regardless of the consolidation of agencies previously undertaking corrective measures into NHRCK, the Labor Relations Committee still addresses remedies for irregular workers.

12 What Is the Relationship Between the Enforcement of Antidiscrimination Law and the Quest for Equality on Both an Individual and Systemic Level?

Although in Korea the enforcement of antidiscrimination law is closely tied to the quest for equality at both the individual and organizational level, the enacted legislation appears insufficient for changing certain discriminatory acts and prejudices of individuals and organizations.

We can see the close connection between the law, individuals (private), and organizational sectors by observing how experiences of discrimination, as well as the desire for equality, can grow into movements demanding requisite legal protections, sometimes culminating in the legislation of meaningful antidiscriminatory statutes. One can see traces of minority movement demands in specific law clauses. For instance, the demand for realistic equality was incorporated into the EEA and NHRCA as clauses defining affirmative action, which resulted in greater participation by women and other minorities in the workplace.

However, as previously noted, the effects of antidiscriminatory law in the private sector level seem weak and mostly ineffective. For instance, large corporations such as Samsung often do not follow the mandatory employment rate for hiring disabled people (3%, as prescribed by the Act for the Advancement of the Employment of the Disabled). Similarly, corrective orders prescribed by APDAD, APADE, and laws related the protection of irregular workers, usually do not have enough enforcement power; even when one does not follow the prescribed corrective orders, the punishment is weak.

13 Is the Enforcement of Antidiscrimination Law Regarded as Different from the Enforcement of Other Laws?

Lay citizens have come to regard antidiscrimination law as a kind of "soft law" that is only implemented through voluntary compliance. This is because remedy through NHRCA, which is currently regarded as substantive, comprehensive antidiscrimination law, is not legally binding. The enforcement of individual antidiscrimination law also tends to be regarded as very different from enforcement of other laws because many Koreans don't perceive that the former involves a kind of tort. That is, there is no direct remedy for those whose equality rights have been violated. There are only a few cases in which legally binding remedies—such as "corrective orders" (correction by administrative agencies) or penal sanctions—have been implemented.

14 What Does the Enforcement of Antidiscrimination Law Reveal About the Nature of Your Legal System or About the Enforcement of Laws in Your Legal System?

As we have seen, the remedies provided for by Korean antidiscrimination laws are supplementary measures designed to protect equality rights, operating mainly in public law such as Constitutional, administrative, and labor law. If the principle of prohibiting discrimination is able to concretize through litigation in the ordinary (primary) legal system, supplementary remedies can establish their own roles to protect the equality rights of individuals. The Constitutional Court has played a critical role in ensuring the equality rights guaranteed by the Constitution.[8] In contrast, the principle of prohibition of discrimination has just begun to be applied to areas covered by the Civil Law. Enforcement of antidiscrimination laws shows there is surely a gap between an ideal legal system and the current reality. Ideally, the Constitutional value of equality should be pervasive in everyday life, while discriminatory acts are torts to be covered by Article 750 of the Civil Act. In reality, however, discrimination in Korea is still treated more like unethical behavior than a possibly illegal act. This is why there have been only a few cases of discrimination brought before the courts. Consequently, enforcement of antidiscrimination laws tends to be regarded as peripheral and supplementary—an area apart from ordinary legal enforcement—that typically occurs through the administrative remedy of corrective, binding orders.

---

[8]The jurisdictions of constitutional court addresses not only adjudication on constitutionality of statutes, impeachment, competence dispute, and dissolution of political party, but also constitutional complaint. Every Korean citizen can bring a constitutional complaint to the Constitutional Court when he/she finds his/her equality right under Article 11 of the Constitution is violated.

15 Conclusion

NHRCA, which is currently regarded as comprehensive antidiscrimination law, has undoubtedly enhanced equal treatment under the law throughout Korea. But it is also deeply flawed because, even though its scope of application is broad, it provides only for the right to a recommendation for correction. In contrast, remedies provided for under the EEA, APDAD, and APDAE, as well as laws relating to the protection of irregular workers, have administrative remedies that include corrective orders establish penal sanctions (though neither is often used).

In Korea, the enforcement of antidiscrimination law tends to be considered fundamentally different from the enforcement of more traditional law because many people do not fully grasp that the former involves torts. Thus, legal remedy for claims of compensation for damages under Civil Law, Article 750, and similar provisions, is not pervasive, though it is possible to file a suit in civil court apart from filing petition under individual antidiscrimination laws such as the EEA, APDAD, and APDAE. For legal professionals to help change the perception of lay citizens, litigation strategies utilizing tort law need to develop more fully—even if there are limited opportunities to do so before the lower courts. The other way to improve direct remedies for those who have been discriminated against is to establish individual antidiscrimination law, with specific provisions allowing for claims of compensation for damages, as occurs under APDAD.

The greatest effort so far to legislate a comprehensive antidiscrimination law was during the Roh Moo-hyun administration, when two antidiscrimination bills were submitted to the National Assembly. The government emphasized five major types of discriminations—based on sex, disability, academic clique, immigration, and forms of employment (irregular workers)—and was able to establish the Presidential Committee on Poverty and Discrimination Rectification. However, both bills were repealed due to termination of the legislative session.

Public discussion over comprehensive antidiscrimination law seems to have disappeared after the Roh administration. But there is still hope that public debate can be resumed and better bills moved forward through the legislature, as the ruling conservative party does not enjoy a majority in the current National Assembly. Also, a significant number of human rights activists are organizing people to support legislation for comprehensive antidiscrimination law in South Korea. Such legislation would help overcome the limits of NHRCA by establishing a path for filing damage claims and by containing *legally binding* provisions. Launching the progressive government of President Moon Jae-in in 2017 can widen the space of public discussion on the human rights for the social minorities. There is much more possibility to make a comprehensive discrimination law.

Jean Ahn is a professor of Law School at Chonnam National University in South Korea. She holds a Ph.D from Seoul National University. She teaches and does researches in the field of Human Rights Law, Sociology of Law, and Gender Studies.

Liban (Lebanon)

Maan S. Bou Saber

1 Introduction

La règle juridique est une règle sociologique. Ubis Jus, Ubis societatis. Pour comprendre le droit libanais, il faut comprendre la société libanaise. Le Liban est une société multiconfessionnelle. Dix-neuf communautés religieuses sont reconnues par la Constitution.

Au niveau de la législation, il y a une dichotomie. Certaines lois sont laïques, tel le Code Civil, le Code de commerce, le Code pénal, le Code de travail.... D'autres lois sont confessionnelles, notamment les lois du statut personnel, tel le mariage, le divorce, l'adoption... Chaque communauté a ses propres lois de statut personnel et ses propres juridictions. Il y a une discrimination religieuse. Le régime politique libanais est confessionnel. Selon le Pacte National Coutumier, le Président de la République est Chrétien maronite, le Premier ministre est musulman sunnite, le Président de la Chambre est musulman chiite. Les hauts-fonctionnaires sont nommés selon un critère confessionnel. C'est le confessionnalisme politique. Une autre discrimination religieuse. Le Liban étant un pays arabe du Moyen-Orient, la société est plus ou moins patriarcale. Une certaine discrimination sexuelle persiste. Le Liban se situe géographiquement dans une région perturbée. Les conflits militaires en Syrie, en Iraq, ainsi que le conflit israélo-arabe, ont causé le déplacement d'une population étrangère vers le Liban. On compte au Liban 1.500.000 déplacés syriens et 500.000 réfugiés palestiniens. À ce niveau, il y a certes une discrimination entre les libanais et les non libanais.

M. S. Bou Saber (✉)
Notre Dame University – Lebanon, Faculty of Law and Political Science, Zouk Mosbeh, Lebanon
e-mail: mbousaber@ndu.edu.lb

2 Première Partie : La description du droit libanais de la non-discrimination

Le droit libanais de la non-discrimination est mis en œuvre. Le Préambule de la Constitution[1] affirme l'égalité des citoyens devant la loi, sans discrimination. L'article 95 de la Constitution prévoit une période transitoire pour abolir le confessionnalisme politique. Le Code civil garantit l'égalité des citoyens dans leurs droits et obligations. À titre d'exemple, les règles juridiques sur la capacité s'appliquent à tous les citoyens sans discrimination sexuelle. Le Code de commerce garantit l'égalité entre l'homme commerçant et la femme commerçante. La femme mariée n'a plus besoin de l'autorisation de son mari pour exercer le commerce. Le Code de travail garantit l'égalité de sexe ainsi que l'égalité entre les salariés libanais et les salariés étrangers. La législation pénale a aboli le crime d'honneur. Quant au crime d'adultère, une certaine discrimination légale persiste ; l'adultère du mari n'est pénalisé que s'il est commis dans le domicile conjugal ; quant à l'épouse, tout adultère est pénalisé ; les forces de la Société Civile poussent le législateur à unifier le régime juridique de l'adultère. D'autre part, une nouvelle loi de 2013 a défini et sanctionné la violence familiale.

Mais la discrimination persiste dans notre législation. La loi sur la nationalité[2] interdit à la mère libanaise d'octroyer la nationalité libanaise à ses enfants. D'autre part, les lois du statut personnel défient toute évolution. Le Liban ne connaît pas le mariage civil, voire facultatif. Mais les libanais peuvent conclure un mariage civil à l'étranger et l'inscrire au Liban sur le registre du statut personnel. Situation paradoxale. Ces lois varient d'une communauté à une autre. À titre d'exemple, la loi successorale est laïque pour les Chrétiens et les Juifs[3], confessionnelle pour les musulmans ; c'est la shari'a qui s'applique. Les lois sur le mariage, le divorce, les fiançailles, l'adoption, la pension alimentaire... sont confessionnelles.[4]

Le droit de la non-discrimination est mis en œuvre par les réformes législatives. Le Liban connaît la séparation de pouvoirs : le pouvoir législatif, le pouvoir exécutif, le pouvoir judiciaire. Le régime politique libanais s'est profondément inspiré de la Constitution de la Troisième République Française.[5]

Le droit de la non-discrimination est essentiellement l'œuvre du pouvoir législatif. C'est surtout un droit écrit, étant donné que le système juridique libanais appartient à la famille Romano-Germanique et non pas à la famille du Common Law.

Le législateur constitutionnel a posé des règles constitutionnelles de non-discrimination qui ont la portée de principes généraux garantissant l'égalité des citoyens dans leurs

---

[1] V. La Constitution libanaise de 1990, et la loi constitutionnelle du 21/9/1991.
[2] Le Code libanais de la nationalité, modifié par la nouvelle loi portant le numéro 40 et ratifié par le Parlement libanais en date du 24 novembre 2015.
[3] La loi successorale du 23 juin 1959.
[4] *ibid.*
[5] Op.cit., n°1.

droits et obligations, et notamment l'égalité devant les charges publiques, sans aucune discrimination. Le législateur constitutionnel a aussi pris soin de garantir les droits fondamentaux du citoyen, qui constituent ce que la doctrine appelle « le bloc de constitutionnalité ».[6]

Une autre technique de mise en œuvre du droit de la non- discrimination est la ratification par le Liban de plusieurs Conventions Internationales relatives aux droits de l'homme et à la lutte contre la discrimination sous tous ses aspects. Selon un principe classique de droit constitutionnel, les conventions ratifiées font partie intégrante du droit interne.

Respectant la hiérarchie des normes, le Parlement légifère conformément au droit conventionnel et aux principes constitutionnels. D'où, par exemple, la consécration législative des principes généraux de non-discrimination, tel, le procès équitable, les droits de la défense, le principe du contradictoire, la présomption d'innocence, l'égalité de sexe,...

Le droit de la non-discrimination est mis en œuvre théoriquement par le législateur, mais pratiquement par le pouvoir exécutif, le pouvoir judiciaire, et les forces actives de la Société Civile incluant les partis politiques et les organisations non gouvernementales.[7]

Dans le domaine de l'emploi par exemple, le droit de la non-discrimination est mis en œuvre par le Ministère du Travail et le Conseil de Prud'hommes. Dans le domaine pénal, par le Ministère de l'Intérieur, le Parquet, et les Tribunaux Répressifs. Dans le domaine de l'enseignement, par le Ministère de l'Education Nationale et de l'Enseignement Supérieur.

Le droit de la non-discrimination est aussi mis en œuvre par le pouvoir judiciaire et à sa tête le Conseil Constitutionnel, le Conseil d'Etat, et la Cour de Cassation ; mais aussi par certains juges inférieurs éclairés. Un cas de jurisprudence mérite d'être mentionné. La loi sur la nationalité interdit formellement à la mère libanaise mariée à un étranger de donner la nationalité libanaise à ses enfants. En revanche, les enfants issus d'un père libanais sont libanais. Un juge libanais, le Président John Azzi, a rendu un jugement par lequel il a attribué la nationalité libanaise aux enfants d'une mère libanaise mariée à un syrien, considérant qu'une interprétation textuelle et restrictive de la loi crée une discrimination entre les citoyens et, par voie de conséquence, une violation de la Constitution. Mais le jugement a été réformé par la juridiction supérieure.[8]

Un autre cas mérite d'être mentionné. Un notaire libanais, maître Joseph Béchara, a permis à un couple libanais de communautés différentes de conclure un mariage civil dans son cabinet. On peut imaginer la réaction des autorités religieuses.

Quant à certaines lois non-discriminatoires, elles sont mises en œuvre par la lutte poursuivie et sans lassitude des forces de la Société Civile. Nous citons à titre d'exemple « the National Commission for Lebanese Women » qui a lutté pour la

---

[6]*ibid.*

[7]V. notamment, The Legal Agenda (NGO), info@legal-agenda.com.

[8]John AZZI, la nationalité, en arabe, Beyrouth, 2012, p.p. 110 s.

mise en œuvre de la « United Nations Convention on the Elimination of All Forms of Discrimination Against Women ».

La mise en œuvre du droit de la non-discrimination est soutenue par:

- Le milieu académique et notamment les Facultés de Droit,[9] de Science Politique, de Sciences Sociales. Dans nos programmes, certains cours, direct ou indirect, ont pour objet, directement ou indirectement, le droit de la non-discrimination.
- Les forces de la Société Civile, et notamment des organisations non gouvernementales nationales et internationales.
- Certains partis politiques laïcs qui luttent ouvertement contre la discrimination et qui encouragent concrètement la femme à être très active dans la vie politique à toute échelle.
- Certains intellectuels luttent pour l'abolition de toute forme de discrimination et le respect du droit de la non-discrimination.
- Certains juges libanais sont très favorables au droit de la non-discrimination.
- Certains parlementaires ont cette idéologie et cette culture de lutte contre les lois discriminatoires, et notamment les lois confessionnelles dans l'action politique et la fonction publique.
- Les Ordres des professions libérales, notamment l'Ordre des avocats.

La mise en œuvre du droit de la non-discrimination révèle deux phénomènes contradictoires, deux réalités différentes:

- Un Liban archaïque, figé dans l'histoire, qui appartient à un autre siècle. Le droit de la non-discrimination n'a pas influencé la nature du système juridique, ni la mise en œuvre des lois dans notre système juridique. La discrimination du système est toujours en place.
- Un Liban dynamique, évolutif, civilisé, ou, du moins, en voie de civilisation et de développement. Le droit de la non-discrimination a influencé la nature du système juridique ainsi que la mise en œuvre de certaines lois dans notre système juridique.

3 Deuxième Partie : La portée du droit libanais de la non-discrimination

La mise en œuvre du droit de la non-discrimination profite aux destinataires directs de la règle de droit qui a aboli la discrimination, aux citoyens, aux étrangers vivant au Liban, au pays dans son ensemble promu au développement.

Dans le domaine des droits politiques, le droit de la non-discrimination profite aux femmes citoyennes qui ont le droit de voter et d'être élues, le droit de se

---

[9]Le programme des études de droit à la Faculté de Droit et de Science Politique à Notre Dame University adopte de multiples cours sur le droit de la non-discrimination. V. www.ndu.edu.lb.

présenter à toute fonction politique et administrative, à être députée, ministre, juge, Procureur de la République, chef de municipalité, préfet...

Dans le domaine de l'emploi, le droit de la non-discrimination profite aux femmes libanaises qui ont les mêmes droits et les mêmes avantages que les hommes, quant au salaire, au nombre d'heures de travail, aux congés, aux stages professionnels, à la promotion... Le droit de la non-discrimination a aussi profité à la main d'œuvre étrangère qui a les mêmes droits et bénéfices que la main d'œuvre libanaise.[10]

Dans le domaine de l'éducation, le droit de la non-discrimination profite aux femmes libanaises qui ont les mêmes droits que les hommes quant au statut d'étudiant ou de professeur. Ce droit profite aussi aux étudiants étrangers qui bénéficient des mêmes conditions d'étude que les étudiants libanais.[11]

Dans le domaine du commerce, le droit de la non-discrimination profite à la femme libanaise commerçante qui jouit des mêmes droits et est soumise aux mêmes obligations que l'homme libanais commerçant.[12]

Dans le domaine pénal, le droit de la non-discrimination profite à la femme libanaise suite à l'abolition du crime d'honneur et à la possibilité très accrue de modifier le régime juridique du crime d'adultère.

Les personnes lésées par le droit de la non-discrimination sont :

- Les autorités religieuses qui craignent de perdre leurs privilèges. Comme nous l'avons souligné au préalable, chaque communauté libanaise a ses propres lois de statut personnel ainsi que ses propres juridictions. Ces lois sont, par définition, discriminatoires et n'assurent pas l'égalité des citoyens. Le mariage maronite est différent du mariage grec orthodoxe, du mariage sunnite,... La loi successorale de 1959 qui s'applique au chrétiens est différente de la Shari'a islamique qui s'applique aux musulmans...

Ces lois confessionnelles confèrent aux autorités religieuses un grand pouvoir. Il va sans dire qu'un droit de la non-discrimination ira à l'encontre des intérêts des autorités religieuses.

- Certains chefs politiques, les féodaux, sont lésés par le droit de la non-discrimination. Toute loi non-discriminatoire est de nature à accentuer le rôle des forces de la Société Civile au détriment des autorités religieuses et de la classe féodale.
- Les hommes à mentalité et à psychologie patriarcales sont lésés par le droit de la non-discrimination.
- Certains pays étrangers sont lésés pour le droit de la non-discrimination. Un cas est révélateur. L'ancien Président de la République, Elias Hraoui, a proposé au

---

[10]V. le Code libanais du travail- Dr. Charbel Aoun, Labor Law course, FLPS, Notre Dame University, Lebanon, 2017.

[11]La loi de l'Enseignement Supérieur Privé, du 26 Décembre 1961, modifiée par la loi n°. 63/36, du 25 Novembre 1963.

[12]V. Charles Fabia et Pierre Safa, Le Code de commerce libanais annoté, dernière édition, Beyrouth, Liban.

Conseil des Ministres un projet de loi sur le mariage civil facultatif. L'Arabie Séoudite s'y est opposée et elle a avorté le projet. Les autorités religieuses libanaises n'étaient pas très mécontentes.

Les remèdes prévus pour mettre en œuvre le droit de la non-discrimination sont :

- Au niveau de l'enseignement :
  a) introduire dans le programme du droit un cours intitulé « le droit de la non-discrimination » qui englobe l'enseignement des cours fondamentaux, tel les droits de la personne, le droit pénal international....[13]
  b) organiser dans les écoles et les facultés des ateliers de travail ainsi que des stages professionnels sur le droit de la non-discrimination.[14]
  c) organiser des Moot Court à l'échelle nationale et internationale sur le droit de la non-discrimination.[15]
  d) aider financièrement et logistiquement les chercheurs dans le domaine du droit de la non-discrimination.
- A l'échelle nationale, organiser des colloques sur tous les aspects du droit de la non-discrimination.
- Au niveau de l'action politique, créer un Ministère du droit de la non-discrimination, et une Commission Parlementaire du droit de la non-discrimination. D'autre part, les Chartes de tous les partis politiques doivent mentionner la lutte contre la discrimination sous toutes ses formes.
- Au niveau de l'action de la Société Civile, encourager par des moyens appropriés les organisations non gouvernementales qui luttent pour le rayonnement et l'efficacité du droit de la non-discrimination.
- Au niveau du pouvoir judiciaire, former des juges avec une culture assez approfondie de tous les aspects du droit de la non-discrimination. Une revue libanaise, « The Legal Agenda », a publié un ouvrage de grande importance, qui contient les jugements les plus marquants rendus par les tribunaux libanais sur la discrimination.
- Au niveau du pouvoir exécutif, assurer une meilleure éducation des forces de l'ordre.
- Au niveau législatif, modifier certains textes de loi. À titre d'exemple, nous citons les articles 14, 24 al. 5, 625, 626, 627, 628, 629, 642, du Code de commerce qui font une discrimination entre la faillite de la femme commerçante et la faillite de l'homme commerçant.

---

[13]La Faculté de Droit et de Science Politique à Notre Dame University organise chaque année une compétition nationale interscolaire sur les droits de la personne.

[14]La Faculté de Droit et de Science Politique à Notre Dame University organise des séminaires et des colloques sur les divers aspects du droit de la non-discrimination. Nous citons, à titre d'exemple, le colloque sur « le mariage, réalité et perspectives d'avenir », « les libertés fondamentales et le droit constitutionnel », ...

[15]Nos étudiants ont participé à la compétition internationale organisée, par Oxford University- Law School, intitulée « Price Media Law Moot Court Competition ».

La portée du droit de la non-discrimination est variable. Elle est à la fois importante et limitée. Elle varie en fonction de la loi discriminatoire et de la loi non-discriminatoire.

- Une portée importante : un certain droit de la non-discrimination a une portée importante. Nous citons le droit civil non-discriminatoire qui reconnaît aux hommes et aux femmes les mêmes droits et obligations. La femme a la même capacité civile que l'homme. Le droit commercial est un droit non-discriminatoire ; l'homme et la femme ont la même capacité commerciale. Le Code de procédure civile, le Code de procédure pénale, sont des codes non-discriminatoires ; les garanties du procès sont assurées à tous les justiciables sans discrimination aucune. Le Code du travail est non-discriminatoire dans ses principes généraux. La portée importante du droit de la non-discrimination est aussi due à la jurisprudence de certains juges qui appliquent, sur les cas litigieux, les principes fondamentaux de la Constitution, et qui ne sont pas otages du texte de la loi mais cherchent son esprit.
- Une portée limitée :
    a) L'article 95 de la Constitution, qui a prévu une période transitoire pour abolir le confessionnalisme politique, est resté lettre morte.[16]
    b) Le Préambule de la Constitution qui garantit l'égalité des citoyens n'est pas toujours respecté : la loi sur les élections législatives est discriminatoire. Dans le domaine de l'emploi, dans la pratique, il y a une discrimination sexuelle et religieuse. Une municipalité a interdit à des ressortissants de vendre des terrains à des citoyens d'une autre appartenance religieuse. Dans l'administration publique, « the Committee to oversee and regulate the oil and gaz sector » est composé de six personnes appartenant aux six communautés suivantes : Maronite, Sunnite, Shiite, Druze, Grecque Catholique, et Grecque Orthodoxe.

La mise en œuvre du droit de la non-discrimination varie en fonction du critère discriminatoire.

- Si le critère discriminatoire est religieux, la mise en œuvre du droit de la non-discrimination s'avère difficile. Aux lois confessionnelles discriminatoires, s'ajoute une pratique discriminatoire.
- Si le critère discriminatoire est sexuel, la mise en œuvre du droit de la non-discrimination est plus facile. Nous rappelons les exemples du Code civil, du Code de commerce, du Code de travail, du Code de procédure, du Code pénal… La pratique révèle une bonne mise en œuvre du droit de la non-discrimination. En revanche, quant à la loi de 2013 sur la violence familiale, sa mise en œuvre par les tribunaux s'est avérée inefficace.

---

[16]Op.cit., n°.1.

- Si le critère de la discrimination est la nationalité, la mise en œuvre du droit de la non-discrimination varie d'un cas à un autre. Dans la pratique, il n'y a pas une discrimination à l'égard de la main d'œuvre étrangère. Mais, rappelons- le, la loi sur la nationalité est une loi discriminatoire à l'égard de la mère libanaise.
- Si le critère est politique, la pratique révèle une double discrimination sexuelle et confessionnelle.

Le rapport entre la mise en œuvre de la non-discrimination et la recherche d'égalité au niveau individuel est acceptable. En effet, la mise en œuvre de la non-discrimination au niveau individuel s'avère efficace.

A l'échelle individuelle, tous les citoyens jouissent des droits les plus fondamentaux : les droits politiques d'élire et d'être élu, le droit d'accès à la fonction publique, à la magistrature, les droits sociaux, les droits économiques, le droit à l'éducation.....

Le rapport entre la mise en œuvre de la non-discrimination et la recherche d'égalité au niveau systémique est moins acceptable. Illustrons avec des exemples : il n'y a pas au Liban une loi sur le mariage civil facultatif ; les lois de statut personnel sont impérativement des lois confessionnelles ; les fonctions publiques du haut rang sont réparties selon un critère confessionnel ; le régime politique est basé sur des critères confessionnels ; les lois électorales sont confessionnelles...

La mise en œuvre du droit de la non-discrimination est perçue comme différente de la mise en œuvre d'autres lois, elle est plus difficile et plus compliquée :

- Parce que certaines lois discriminatoires sont d'origine confessionnelle dans un Liban où il y a dix-neuf communautés reconnues par la Constitution.
- Parce que certaines communautés sont plus nombreuses et plus puissantes que d'autres.
- Parce que certaines communautés sont soutenues par des États étrangers.
- Parce que les autorités religieuses sont assez puissantes. Elles génèrent la majorité des forces politiques.
- Parce que la psychologie des gens est discriminatoire et leur mentalité est sectaire.

4 Conclusion

Une bonne application du droit de la non-discrimination nécessite :

a) Une application plus efficace du Préambule et de l'esprit de la Constitution, par les différentes autorités compétentes : législative, exécutive, judiciaire.
b) Un rôle plus efficace du Conseil Constitutionnel libanais, gardien des droits de l'homme et des droits fondamentaux.
c) Une meilleure formation des administrateurs et des juges, notamment dans le domaine des droits de la personne.
d) Un enseignement à tout niveau des droits fondamentaux.

e) Des partis politiques et des organisations non gouvernementales plus dynamiques dans le domaine du droit de la non-discrimination.

Bibliographie

La Constitution libanaise de 1990, et la loi constitutionnelle du 21/9/1991
Le Code libanais de la Nationalité
La loi successorale libanaise du 23 juin 1959
Président John AZZI, la nationalité, en arabe, Beyrouth, 2012
Les Recueils des décisions du Conseil Constitutionnel libanais
Le Code libanais du travail
Dr. Charbel Aoun, Labor Law Course, Notre Dame University, Lebanon, 2017
Charles Fabia et Pierre Safa, le Code de commerce libanais annoté, dernière édition, Beyrouth, Liban
Président John AZZI, Le mariage civil, en arabe, Beyrouth, 2011
Président John AZZI, Les statuts personnels entre le texte et la jurisprudence, en arabe, Beyrouth, 2013

Maan Bou Saber is the Dean of the Faculty of Law and Political Science at Notre Dame University (Lebanon). He is Founding Dean of the department of Droit. Il is admitted to the Bars of Beirut and Paris. He founded the Center for Banking Studies at the University Saint-Joseph. Il has founded the Faculty of Droir of USJ has Dubai. Il is Peofesseur Civil Law, Civil Procedure, the Arbitration Law, Law of Commercial Societies. He is the author of several articles. He has four books under publication: Introduction to Law, Law of Obligations and Contracts, Banking Law, the Arbitration Law.

Portugal

Ana Maria Guerra Martins

1 Introduction

Portugal has a long tradition of contact with other cultures and peoples. Due to sixteenth century maritime discoveries and the experience of Portuguese emigration to Brazil and Latin America in general, as well as to other countries in Europe, such as France and Germany in the 1960s, the Portuguese are used to tolerating difference, at least in terms of ethnic origin, race and religion.[1]

In Portugal, racist or fascist political parties are forbidden (Article 8 of the Organic Law No. 2/2008 of 14 May 2008).[2] Therefore, in contrast to other countries, such parties do not exist in Portugal.[3]

In recent years, open conflicts between religious groups have not been reported. However, as the majority of the population is Catholic, other religions face greater problems in practice, for example, in ministering to people in hospitals and prisons. In addition, meals in state schools are still not adapted to meet the needs of other religions, particularly to those of Islam. Notwithstanding those facts, religious diversity remains a fairly neutral topic in Portuguese society.

With regard to non-discrimination on grounds of sex or gender, it should be mentioned that remarkable progress has been registered over the past years in the field of employment with maternity, paternity and parental leave as well as in the occupational social security schemes and statutory social security schemes. Non-discrimination in self-employment and gender equality in the access to and providing of goods and services are also issues that have recently evolved.

---

[1] Guerra Martins (1999), pp. 901–917.
[2] Available at: https://dre.pt/application/file/249115.
[3] Compare: Guerra Martins (2012), pp. 185–214.

A. M. Guerra Martins (✉)
University of Lisbon, School of Law, Lisbon, Portugal

Furthermore, public policies have been implemented to promote gender equality and to combat discrimination on grounds of gender, sexual orientation and gender identity. Moreover, Portugal is one of few countries in Europe that allows civil marriage for same-sex partners (Law 9/2010 of 31 May 2010)[4] as well as adoption of children (Law 143/2015 of 8 September 2015).

Concerning age discrimination, Portuguese society is not yet fully aware of the issues involved in this relatively new field, and is only slowly becoming conscious of their implications.

Finally, it must be emphasized that the Portuguese financial and economic crisis, which led to the austerity measures that have been in place between 2010 and 2015,[5] has not helped the implementation of positive or support measures for the groups who need them. The current Governemnt and Parliament have been making a significant effort in order to improve the antidiscrimination law.

2 Is Antidiscrimination Law Enforced?

In Portugal, antidiscrimination law is enforceable and enforced. The Constitution of the Portuguese Republic of 1976[6] (hereafter CPR) enshrines the right to legal protection against any form of discrimination in Article 26(1), guaranteeing thereby legal remedies to violations of antidiscrimination provisions.[7] The law provides for legal remedies, including judicial, administrative and alternative dispute resolution. However, there are no statistics available concerning the enforcement of antidiscrimination law in Portugal.

3 How Is Antidiscrimination Law Enforced?

According to Article 20(1) of the CPR, "everyone is guaranteed access to the law and the courts in order to defend those of his rights and interests that are protected by law (...)".[8] That means everyone has free access to justice. Consequently, judicial and administrative courts are empowered to control violations against antidiscrimination law.

---

[4]Available at: http://dre.pt/pdf1s/2010/05/10500/0185301853.pdf.
[5]On these measures compare: Guerra Martins (2015), pp. 678–705.
[6]An English version of the Constitution can be consulted on the website: www.parlamento.pt.
[7]On the legal protection against any form of discrimination, see, above all, Miranda (2014), p. 371 ff. Gomes Canotilho (2003), p. 433 ff. Gomes Canotilho and Moreira (2006), pp. 470–471.
[8]On the right to free access to justice, compare, above all, Miranda (2014), p. 352 ff. Gomes Canotilho (2003), p. 433 ff. Miranda and Medeiros (2010), p. 423 ff. Gomes Canotilho and Moreira (2006), p. 408 ff.

However, antidiscrimination law is, first and foremost, enforced by administrative bodies such as the High Commissioner for Migrations (ACM), Commission for Equality and Against Racial Discrimination (CEARD), Gender Equality Agency in the Field of Employment (CITE), and the Commission for Citizenship and Gender Equality (CIG), all of which will be studied in the next section.

Finally, alternative means of dispute resolution are also available.

The enforcement of antidiscrimination law operates in the legal system covering all fields: labour law, administrative law, criminal law, civil law, etc.

4 Who Enforces Antidiscrimination Law?

Antidiscrimination law is, firstly, enforced by general governmental and administrative bodies. When the enforcement by those bodies fails, the individuals have access to justice in general and specially to courts.

In fact, there are specialized bodies for the promotion of enforcement of antidiscrimination treatment and the promotion of equality with regard to several grounds of discrimination.

Starting with racial and ethnic discrimination, the High Commissioner for Migrations (ACM)[9] was created by Decree-law 31/2014 of 27 February 2014[10] and it is assisted by the Commission for Equality and Against Racial Discrimination (CEARD) *(Comissão para a Igualdade e Contra a Discriminação Racial)*. The ACM is a public institution integrated in the indirect administration of the State, with administrative and financial autonomy.

Concerning gender discrimination, there are two official bodies—the Gender Equality Agency in the Field of Employment *(Comissão para a Igualdade no Trabalho e no Emprego—CITE)*,[11] and the Agency for Gender Equality and Citizenship *(Comissão para a Cidadania e Igualdade de Género—CIG)*.[12]

The CITE is a public body, which is directly dependent on the Government and is financed by a public institution (Institute for Employment and Professional Training—*Instituto do Emprego e Formação Profissional*).

The CIG is a governmental body, within the ambit of the Presidency of the Council of Ministers, so it is not an independent body. Nevertheless, the CIG has

---

[9]It was formerly governed by Decree-law 167/2007 of 3 May 2007.

[10]This decree-law repealed the Decree-law 167/2007 of 3 May 2007, which created the High Commissioner for Immigration and Intercultural Dialogue. Available at: https://dre.pt/application/file/572214.

[11]The CITE (www.cite.gov.pt) is currently established in Decree-Law No. 76/2012 of 26 March 2012. Available at https://dre.pt/application/file/553863.

[12]The CIG (www.cig.gov.pt) was instated by Decree-Law No. 202/2006 of 7 October 2006.

a scientific counseling body where private experts in gender equality are represented and works closely with private associations and NGOs in this area.

Besides these bodies, there is also the Labour Inspection Services (*Autoridade para as Condições de Trabalho—ACT*), which has inspection powers over the employers' activities and organizations and it is empowered to apply administrative fines in issues related to employment.

Finally, associations, with specific aims listed in their by-laws, which include the protection of people against discrimination or the protection of fundamental rights in general, as well as organizations and trade unions are entitled to participate in the enforcement of antidiscrimination law.

For instance, associations with the objective of combating discrimination based on racial or ethnic origin have the right to engage in 1 admnistrative procedures on behalf of the interested persons, with their approval (Article 12(1) (2) of Law 93/2017 of 23 August)[13] and associations for people with disabilities and other similar organizations defending the rights and interests of people with disabilities have the right to intervene in support or on behalf of a complainant in his/her respective legal proceedings (Article 15(1) of Law 46/2006 of 28 August 2006).[14] Such associations and organizations also have the right to monitor administrative procedures that may culminate in a fine for any discriminatory act referred to in Law 46/2006. In addition, Decree-law 163/2006 of 8 August 2006[15] on accessibility for people with disabilities provides that legal entities (NGOs and associations) representing people with disabilities have legal standing in court to assist or act on behalf of individuals with disabilities in court cases in which they are involved. Where a crime has been committed against a disabled person, these associations and organizations have the right to assist in subsequent criminal proceedings as well. In cases of minor offences (*contra-ordenações*), the associations and organizations have the right to denounce the discriminator.

Trade unions are entitled under national law (Article 5 of the Labour Procedure Code, Decree-law 480/99 of 9 November 1999, and Articles 5 and 8 of Law 3/2011 of 15 February 2011)[16] to participate in the enforcement of antidiscrimination law. They may act on behalf of victims of discrimination. It is also possible for trade unions to engage in some cases on behalf of victims of discrimination in judicial or administrative procedures under the Labour Code and the Labour Procedure Code.

Furthermore, Article 443(1)(d) of the Labour Code grants legal standing to trade unions in administrative proceedings, imposing fines in cases of violation of the antidiscrimination rules of the code, with the right to file an appeal or to answer an

---

[13] Available at: http://dre.pt/application/conteudo/108038372/.
[14] Available at: https://dre.pt/application/dir/pdf1sdip/2006/08/16500/62106213.pdf.
[15] Available at: https://dre.pt/application/dir/pdf1sdip/2006/08/15200/56705689.pdf.
[16] Available at: https://dre.pt/application/dir/pdf1s/2011/02/03200/0080900811.pdf.

appeal by the person found guilty. Article 5 of the Labour Procedure Code (*Código de Processo do Trabalho*) allows the intervention of trade unions in employment cases.

NGOs working in the antidiscrimination field focus on areas of discrimination in which they have expertise at national, regional or local level, such as gender, race, religion, sexual orientation or age. These NGOs are also entitled to participate in the enforcement of antidiscrimination law, as they may act on behalf of the victims of discrimination (Article 7 of Law 3/2011). Some immigrants' NGOs focus on their own communities.

NGOs for people with disabilities (*organizações não governamentais das pessoas com deficiência*—ONGPD) are entitled to act on behalf of victims of discrimination according to Article 5(2) of Decree-law 106/2013 of 30 July 2013 defining the statute of ONGPD.[17] The ONGPD is entitled to assist and support victims in criminal procedures including where crimes have been committed against people with disabilities, perpetrated on grounds of disability.

Immigrant and anti-racism NGOs have legal standing only in cases concerning racist crimes.

In general the NGOs can engage in support of the victims in criminal judicial procedures, and under Law 3/2011 they can engage on behalf of victims in administrative procedures. Legal entities (NGOs and associations) representing the interests of people with disabilities have legal standing in court to bring cases on behalf of disabled individuals.

5 Who Benefits from the Enforcement of Antidiscrimination Law?

Everyone benefits from the protection and enforcement of antidiscrimination law. In fact, there are no residence or citizenship/nationality requirements for protection under the relevant national antidiscrimination law, since Article 15 CPR establishes a principle of equivalence of rights and duties between foreigners and stateless persons and Portuguese citizens.[18]

According to that provision, foreigners and stateless persons temporarily or habitually resident in Portugal enjoy the same rights and are subject to the same duties as Portuguese citizens. There are exceptions to this general rule: political rights, the exercise of public functions (which are not predominantly technical), and the rights and duties (which according to CPR or the law are restricted to Portuguese citizens).

---

[17] Available at: https://dre.pt/application/file/498646.

[18] On this constitutional provision, see, above all, Gomes Canotilho (2003), p. 417 ff. Miranda and Medeiros (2010), p. 263 ff. Gomes Canotilho and Moreira (2006), p. 356 ff.

Discrimination based on nationality is specifically prohibited in labour law (Article 24(1) of the Labour Code) and, in general, in Article 4(1) of Law 93/2017.

Both natural and legal persons benefit from the enforcement of antidiscrimination law, as according to Article 12(2) of the Constitution, legal persons have the rights and duties compatible with their nature, including personal rights.[19]

Article 24(1) of the Labour Code prohibits 'employers' from discriminating and this applies to natural and legal persons (Article 551(1) and (3) of the Labour Code)[20] and fines are higher for legal persons than for natural persons (Article 554 of the Labour Code).

The prohibition of discrimination on the ground of race and ethnic origin provided by Law 93/2017 binds all natural and legal persons (Article 2). Similar reasoning applies to the prohibition of discrimination on the ground of disability contained in Law 46/2006 (Article 2(1)) and the sanctions may be different for natural persons and for legal ones (Article 9 of Law 46/2006 and Article 12 of Law 14/2008).

By contrast, only natural persons are subject to criminal liability, except in cases specified by law (Article 11(1) of the Criminal Code). One such case is specifically the crime of discrimination on grounds of race, religion or sexual orientation set out in Article 240 (2) of the Criminal Code.

Furthermore, private and public sectors, including public bodies such as public undertakings, benefit from the protection and enforcement against discrimination. Furthermore, most provisions that forbid discrimination bind all public or private persons (see Article 2(1) of Law 93/2017, Article 11(3) of the Criminal Code, and Article 2(1) of Law 46/2006).

The personal scope of antidiscrimination law covers both private and public sector including public bodies for the purpose of liability for discrimination.

The public sector is liable for equality and non-discrimination in the same terms as the private sector (Article 4(1), (c) and (e) of Law 35/2014 of 20 June 2014, which approves the General Regime of the Contract Work for Public Sector)[21] and the private sector is liable according to Articles 23–32 of the Labour Code.

---

[19]On this constitutional provision, see, above all, Miranda (2014), p. 261 ff. Gomes Canotilho (2003), p. 416; Miranda and Medeiros (2010), p. 207 ff. Gomes Canotilho and Moreira (2006), p. 328 ff.

[20]Articles 351(2)(b)(c) and (i) specifically stipulate that a worker may be dismissed if he or she breaches co-workers' rights, repeatedly enters into conflict with co-workers, or commits any crime in the workplace against co-workers.

[21]Law 35/2014 of 20 June establishes the regime for employment relations in public services. Available at: http://www.sippeb.pt/sippeb/2014/06/LGTFP_Lei-n°-35-201420junho1.pdf. The law entered into force on 1 August 2014, amended by Law 82-B/2014 of 31 December 2014 (State Budget for 2015). Available at: https://dre.pt/application/conteudo/66016527.

6 Who Is Harmed by the Enforcement of Antidiscrimination Law?

In Portugal, the culture of acting judicially against antidiscrimination practices is almost nonexistent. For all judicial procedures, the victims have to instruct a lawyer and advance some funds. They are, however, entitled to legal assistance (*apoio judiciário*) if they do not have sufficient financial means to cover a lawyer's fees and litigation costs. This is also valid for foreigners. However, the length, the complexity and the difficulty in obtaining evidence in the judicial procedure may act as deterrents to those seeking redress. Therefore, there are few judicial decisions on these issues, which diminishes the enforcement of antidiscrimination law.

However, administrative complaints are more frequent and as they usually achieve the objective of the victims—cessation of discrimination and/or compensation for damages—they are very often considered as a sufficient remedy. Mediation—when it is admissible—can be used as a means to overcome the barriers of judicial and administrative procedures.

Naturally, potential discriminators—employers, providers of goods and services—try to avoid the consequences of antidiscrimination practices, such as negative publicity, expensive fines, and costs of litigation.

7 What Remedies Are Provided by the Enforcement of Antidiscrimination Law?

The following procedures exist for enforcing antidiscrimination law: judicial procedures, administrative procedures, and alternative dispute resolution, such as mediation.

7.1 Judicial Procedures

Every common jurisdiction (either judicial or administrative) is empowered to apply antidiscrimination law. Moreover, every court shall not apply norms that contravene the principle of equality and the principle of non-discrimination (Article 204 CPR). The refusal of the application of any norm on the grounds of its unconstitutionality or the application of a norm whose unconstitutionality has been raised during the proceedings may be the subject of an appeal to the Constitutional Court against court decisions (Article 280(1) of the Constitution).[22]

---

[22] On the Portuguese judicial control of constitutionality see, among many others: Correia (2016), p. 163 ff. Otero (2010), p. 409 ff. JJ Gomes Canotilho (2003), p. 657 ff. Miranda (2013), p. 189 ff.

Secondly, specialized labour courts (*Tribunais do Trabalho*) deal with discrimination in employment in the private sector. They are part of the general judicial system but deal only with labour law cases concerning employment relationships, work-related accidents and illness, appeals against fines, and disputes concerning social security rights. They deal with all questions arising from the drafting, execution and termination of employment contracts. These courts also deal with appeals regarding sanctions imposed by administrative agencies for non-compliance with employment laws.

A specific sanction has been recently established concerning the breach of maternity rights. Under Law No. 133/2015 of 7 September 2015,[23] companies condemned by the Court for having illegally dismissed pregnant workers, recent mothers or workers who were breastfeeding, cannot benefit from public allowances or public financial benefits of any kind for a period of 2 years after the court's judgment.

7.2 Alternative Disputes Resolution for Private Sector in Labour Law

No specific procedures for mediation in relation to discrimination are provided for in the Labour Code. However, the rules for the labour courts make it mandatory for the judge presiding over a case to hold at least one conciliation conference between the parties before trial, and require them to try to mediate in any labour dispute coming under their jurisdiction (Articles 32(2), 36(2), 51(1), 51(2), 55(2) and 70(1) of the Labour Procedure Code.[24] Mediation by labour courts is binding.

Article 492(2)(f) of the Labour Code also states that collective agreements should include mechanisms for conciliation (Articles 523 *et seq.*), mediation (Articles 526 *et seq.*) and arbitration (Articles 529 and 506–511) in labour disputes.

Racial discrimination is subject to disciplinary measures and the sanctions may go as far as dismissal. However, victims have no right to intervene in the disciplinary procedure. They have the right to file a complaint to the labour courts and to give evidence or to present witnesses.

---

[23] Available at: https://dre.pt/application/file/70202875.
[24] Labour Procedure Code, available at: http://www.verbojuridico.com/download/codigoprocessotrabalho.pdf.

7.3 Administrative Procedures and Administrative Courts for Public Sector

For public employees, the law provides a system of internal (hierarchical) administrative appeals that, once exhausted, allows public employees to challenge final decisions taken by public bodies before the administrative courts (Article 4(3) (d) of Law 13/2002 of 19 February 2002, latest amended by Law 20/2012 of 14 of May 2012, entered into force on 15 May 2012).

Mediation is not an option for dispute resolution for public employees. They are required to file an action in the administrative courts.

7.4 Criminal Law Procedures

If the discrimination is considered a crime under the Criminal Code, the victim may lodge a complaint with the police or the Public Prosecution Service (*Ministério Público*), or bring a civil case to a court.

Procedures for mediation in criminal law are currently implemented by the Ministry of Justice. In the biggest Portuguese towns, there are Justices of the Peace (*Julgados de Paz*), who can also work in mediation.

7.5 Civil Law Procedures

Civil damages can be awarded for all types of discrimination under the general principles of Articles 483, 484 and 496 of the Civil Code. In labour law, it should be noted that Article 28 of the Labour Code expressly states that the occurrence of any discriminatory act gives the worker or job applicant concerned the right to be compensated for pecuniary or non-pecuniary damages in accordance with the general provisions of civil law (i.e. Articles 483, 496, 799 and 800(1) of the Civil Code).

7.6 Administrative Procedures for Private Sector

The Authority for Working Conditions (*Autoridade para as Condições de Trabalho*)[25] is responsible for monitoring enforcement of Labour Code provisions

---

[25] See Decree-law 167-E/2013 of 31 December 2013, available at: http://www.act.gov.pt/(pt-PT)/SobreACT/QuemSomos/Missao/Documents/Decreto-Lei_167_c_2013.pdf and Regulamentar Decree 47/2012 of 31 July 2012, available at: https://dre.pt/application/dir/pdf1sdip/2012/07/14700/0395903962.pdf.

on equality and non-discrimination, investigating any complaints arising from infringement of these provisions, and imposing administrative sanctions for such violations as set out in the code.

It should be stressed that the Authority for Working Conditions has played a useful role in combating discrimination on the grounds of nationality and, in some cases, disability.

7.7 Ombudsman

According to Article 23(1) CPR, citizens may submit complaints against actions or omissions by the public authorities to the Ombudsman (*Provedor de Justiça*),[26] who will assess them without the power to make decisions and will send the appropriate entities and organs the recommendations needed to prevent or make good any injustices. The Ombudsman's work is independent of any non-judicial or judicial remedies provided for in the Constitution or the law. The entities, organs and agents of the Public Administration must cooperate with the Ombudsman in the fulfilment of his mission.

The Ombudsman pays special attention to discrimination cases.

7.8 Actions by Public Bodies

7.8.1 The High Commissioner for Migrations

The High Commissioner for Migrations acts in many cases as a (*de facto*) mediator to try to solve conflicts and avoid formal legal procedures. Mediation by the High Commissioner is not binding.

7.8.2 The Gender Equality Agency in the Field of Employment (CITE)

CITE works with Labour Inspection Services in actions regarding discrimination at the company level (such as visits, denouncing discriminatory practices, etc.), namely after receiving a complaint of a victim of discrimination. The CITE is also empowered to give assistance to victims of discrimination in the form of provision of advice. It also analyses collective agreements after their publication to check whether they have discriminatory clauses. If that is the case, the Agency can present

---

[26]On Article 23 CPR see, above all, Miranda (2014), p. 379 ff. Gomes Canotilho (2003), p. 513; Miranda and Medeiros (2010), p. 486 ff. Gomes Canotilho and Moreira (2006), p. 440 ff.

the case before the public attorney, who can take it to court in order to have these clauses declared null and void.

In practice, the role of the CITE has been very important over the years.

7.8.3 The Commission for Citizenship and Gender Equality (CIG)

In pursuit of its goals the CIG has wide powers in relation to gender equality, including the areas of gender violence and domestic violence, reconciliation of family and professional life, women's studies, education, and self-employment. In these areas, the Commission develops studies and researches, provides for legal information and counseling, edits publications and disseminates information, and works with NGOs in the several areas related to gender equality.

In practice, the main role of this body has been developed in the area of legal counseling (especially as regards domestic violence, gender violence and maternity/paternity issues) and in the publication of gender studies.

8 Who Supports the Enforcement of Antidiscrimination Law?

The support of the political power concerning the enforcement of antidiscrimination law has been undergoing a positive evolution in the last decades. The need to implement the Constitution, which contains many provisions on equality and non-discrimination, and to enact in conformity with the international and the European Union commitments of the Portuguese state, can be envisaged as the main reasons for this trend.

Furthermore, associations (see Article 12(1) of Law 93/2017), organizations (Article 15(1) of Law 46/2006, which allows ONGPD and all organizations defending and promoting the interests of people with disabilities) and trade unions (see Articles 5 of the Labour Procedure Code, 5 and 8 of Law 3/2011 and Article 23 of Law 107/2009) are entitled to act in support of victims of discrimination. That means they indirectly support the enforcement of antidiscrimination law.

Employees may benefit without cost from the support of the Public Prosecutor and the Authority for Working Conditions and they may also benefit from legal aid.

9 Who Opposes the Enforcement of Antidiscrimination Law?

Portugal is a democratic state based on the rule of law and the protection of fundamental rights. Therefore, the antidiscrimination principle and the promotion of equality are part of the Portuguese legal system's core. In principle, there should be no opposition to the enforcement of antidiscrimination law. Once entered into force, the legislation should be fulfilled.

However, prior to the adoption of some laws combating antidiscrimination, particularly the ones founded on the ground of sexual orientation, some sectors of society had opposed. For instance, in the case of the marriage of same-sex partners and the adoption of children by same-sex partners, the majority of members of parliament belonging to the right-wing parties were against. The Catholic Church, which has much influence in the Portuguese society, also constituted a blockade force.

Nevertheless, the legislation was approved with the votes of the left-wing parties. By contrast, there is a wide consensus, at least in theory, concerning the adoption of legislation combating discrimination and promoting equality between men and women and the legislation on non-discrimination on the ground of race and ethnic origin.

However, the difference between the reduced number of actions brought before the courts and the intense work of some administrative bodies, like the CITE, gives ground for the conclusion that the practical implementation of equality and non-discrimination provisions is still difficult and the most effective action is in fact done outside the courts.

10 How Broad Is the Coverage of Antidiscrimination Law?

The coverage of antidiscrimination law is rather broad.

10.1 European Union Law

As a member of the European Union,[27] Portugal is bound by EU law concerning antidiscrimination, whether primary law[28] or secondary legislation, such as antidiscrimination directives.[29]

---

[27] Portugal became a full member of the European Communities on 1st January 1986.

[28] See, mainly, Articles 2 *in fine*; 3 (3); 9 TEU; 18 and 19 TFEU, and 20; 21 and 23 CFREU.

[29] Above many others, Directive 2000/43/EC [of 29 June 2000] implementing the principle of equal treatment between persons irrespective of racial and ethnic origin (known as "racial equality" directive) [2000] OJ L 180/22; Directive 2000/78/EC [of 27 November 2000] establishing a general framework for equal treatment in employment and occupation (known as "employment equality" directive) [2000] OJ L 303/16; and Directive 2004/113/EC [of 13 December 2004] implementing the principle of equal treatment between men and women in the access to and supply of goods and services [2004] OJ L 373/37.

On these Directives, among many others, see Guerra Martins (2011), pp. 327–352; Guerra Martins (2010), p. 477 f. and all references quoted therein.

According to Article 8(4) of the Constitution "The provisions of the treaties that govern the European Union and the norms issued by its institutions in the exercise of their respective competences are applicable in Portuguese internal law in accordance with Union law and with respect for the fundamental principles of a democratic state based on the rule of law." The meaning of this provision is rather disputable by the Portuguese scholarship.[30] In our view, that means European Union law prevails over Portuguese domestic law, including constitutional law, except when it does not respect the fundamental principles of a democratic state based on the rule of law.[31]

10.2 International Law

As a member of several international organizations, such as the United Nations and the Council of Europe, Portugal is not only bound by some general international human rights instruments but also by specific international conventions on the elimination of discrimination.

Portugal has indeed ratified main international (regional and universal) conventions on equality and non-discrimination, like the European Convention on Human Rights (ECHR),[32] the Convention on the Elimination of All Forms of Racial Discrimination,[33] the Revised European Social Charter,[34] the Convention on the Elimination of Discrimination against Women,[35] the International Covenant on Civil and Political Rights,[36] the International Covenant on Economic, Social and Cultural Rights[37] and ILO Convention 111[38] on Discrimination in the field of employment and profession. In addition it has ratified the Convention on the Rights of Persons with Disabilities[39] and it was the first EU member state to ratify the Istanbul Convention on preventing and combating violence against women and domestic violence.

---

[30]For a strong criticism compare, above all, Miranda and Medeiros (2010), p. 172 ff. Supporting this solution see Guerra Martins (2017), p. 540 ff. Otero (2010), p. 133; Gomes Canotilho and Moreira (2006), p. 265.

[31]For further developments on the supremacy/primacy of EU law over Portuguese law see Guerra Martins (2017), p. 540 f. and all references quoted therein.

[32]Approved by Law No 65/78, *Diário da República,* I Série-A, No. 236/78 of 13 October 1978.

[33]Approved by Law No. 7/82, *Diário da República,* I Série-A, No. 99/82, of 29 April 1982.

[34]Approved by Resolution No 64-A/2001, *Diário da República,* I Série-A, No 241/2001 of 17 October 2001.

[35]Approved by Law No. 23/80, *Diário da República*, I Série-A, No. 171/80, of 26 July 1980.

[36]Approved by Law No. 29/78, *Diário da República*, I Série-A, No. 133/78, of 12 June 1978.

[37]Approved by Law No. 45/78, *Diário da República*, I Série-A, No. 157/78, of 11 July 1978.

[38]Approved by Decree-law No. 42520 of 23 September 1959, *Diário do Governo*, I Série, No 219 of of 23 September 1959.

[39]Approved by Resolution No 56/2009, published in *"Diário da República"*, I Série-A, No 146/2009 of 30 July 2009.

With accordance to Article 8(1) CPR, 'the norms and principles of general or common international law form an integral part of Portuguese law', and as regards Article 8(2) CPR, 'the norms contained in duly ratified or approved international conventions come into force in Portuguese internal law once they have been officially published, and remain so for as long as they are internationally binding on the Portuguese state.'[40] That is to say that as regards international law, the Portuguese Constitution includes a fundamental principle of "friendship" to international law.[41]

10.3 Domestic Law

10.3.1 Constitutional Law

The Portuguese Constitution itself includes many provisions dealing with the protection against discrimination and the promotion of equality.

The guarantee of fundamental rights and freedoms and the respect for the principles of a democratic state based on the rule of law (Article 9(b) CPR) are one of the fundamental tasks and objectives of the Portuguese state as well as the active promotion of equality between men and women (Article 9(h) CPR).

Furthermore, the Portuguese Constitution enshrines the principle of equal treatment before the law (Article 13(1) CPR) and it prohibits discrimination (Article 13(2) CPR) founded on a large and non-exhaustive list of protected grounds ('ancestry, gender, race, language, territory of origin, religion, political or ideological beliefs, education, economic situation, social circumstances or sexual orientation').[42]

The Constitution develops the general prohibition of discrimination established in Article 13(2) in several areas.

In the chapter on workers' rights, freedoms and guarantees, the Constitution includes the prohibition of dismissal without fair cause or for political or ideological reasons (Article 53).

In Title III on economic, social and cultural rights and duties, Article 59(1) of the Constitution foresees equal opportunities in access to employment (Article 58(2)(b)), equal pay (Article 59(1)(a)), reconciliation of work and family life (Article 59(2)(b)) and it forbids discrimination at work against any worker on grounds such as age, gender, race, citizenship, place of origin, religion, or political or ideological convictions. Article 59(2)(c) refers to the special protection of the work done by minors, the disabled and those whose occupations are particularly strenuous or are

---

[40]For a commentary on these provisions see Gomes Canotilho and Moreira (2006), p. 253 ff. Miranda and Medeiros (2010), p. 162 ff.

[41]Medeiros (2015), p. 291 ff. Guerra Martins and Roque (2015), p. 314 ff. Guerra Martins and Roque (2013), p. 307 ff. Guerra Martins (2013), p. 205 ff.

[42]Miranda (2014), p. 263 ff. Gomes Canotilho (2003), p. 426; Miranda and Medeiros (2010), p. 219 ff. Gomes Canotilho and Moreira (2006), p. 336 ff.

undertaken in unhealthy, toxic or dangerous conditions. Although it does not expressly refer to sexual orientation, it must be interpreted in connection with Article 13, which forbids discrimination on the ground of sexual orientation.

The Constitution also includes in Title III the right to protection of health (Article 64(2)(a) and (b)), which is a universal right, the protection of pregnancy, maternity and paternity (Article 68), the protection of childhood (Article 69(1) and the protection of youth (Article 70).

The prohibition of discrimination on the ground of disability is provided for in Article 71(1).

In addition, Article 72(1) and (2) CPR state that 'the elderly have the right to economic security and to conditions in terms of housing and family and community life that respect their personal autonomy and avoid and overcome isolation or social marginalization' and 'the policy for the elderly shall include measures of an economic, social and cultural nature that tend to provide elderly persons with opportunities for personal fulfillment by means of an active participation in community life.'

The right to education and culture is provided for Article 73(1) (2) CPR and with regard to access to education, Article 74 CPR states that 'everyone has the right to education with a guarantee of the right to equal opportunities for access to and success in schooling'. In education policies, the state must promote and support the access of people with disabilities to education and, where necessary, support special education (Article 74(2)(g) CPR). This constitutional provision aims to compensate for the inherent disadvantages that may be suffered by people with disabilities in order to guarantee real equality of opportunity.

All provisions on specific rights should be read together with Article 13 of the Constitution.

According to Portuguese constitutional case law, differences in treatment are considered acceptable when they are based on an objective distinction of situations, have legitimate objectives in accordance with the principles of the Constitution and can be considered necessary, adequate and proportionate (see, among many others, Constitutional Court judgment No. 232/2003 of 13 May 2003).[43]

10.3.2 Domestic Legislation

The national legislation develops and transposes EU law, implements the international treaties' provisions and embodies the Portuguese Constitution.

The main national legislation on equality and non-discrimination can be divided in two sections: (1) general legislation and (2) specific legislation.

---

[43] The Portuguese version of this decision is Available at: http://www.tribunalconstitucional.pt/tc/acordaos/.

General Legislation

- Labour Code approved by Law 7/2009 of 12 February 2009,[44] transposing, among many others, Directive 2000/43/EC (the Racial Equality Directive) and Directive 2000/78/EC (the Employment Equality Directive) contains many provisions on non-discrimination and equality.
- Criminal Code approved by the Decree-Law 48/95, last amended in 2017 by the Law 94/2017[45] of 23 of August 2017: Article 132 (2) (f)—homicide motivated by hatred based on race, religious or political beliefs, colour, ethnic origin or nationality, religion, gender or sexual orientation; Article 145 (1) and (2)—physical injuries; Article 239—genocide, abrogated by Law 31/2004 of 22 July 2004 and now covered by Article 8; Article 240—discrimination on grounds of race, religion or sexual orientation; Articles 251 and 252—insults on grounds of religion; Article 253—violence or threats against funeral processions or ceremonies; and Article 254—profanation of a corpse or a cemetery.
- Law No. 35/2014, of 20 June 2014, which approves the General Regime of the Contract Work for Public Sector also includes many provisions on non-discrimination and equality.

Specific Legislation

- Decree-Law 307/1997 of 11 November 1997 transposes Directive 86/378/EEC, including the changes introduced by Directive 96/97/EC, into domestic legislation.
- Law 93/2017 of 23 of August establishing the legal regime of prevention, prohibition and fight against discrimination on the ground of race/ethnic origin, nationality, ancestry and territory of origin.[46,47]
- Law 38/2004 of 18 August 2004 defines the general legal basis for the prevention of the causes of disability, and the training, rehabilitation and participation of people with disabilities.[48]
- Law 46/2006 of 28 August 2006 prohibits and punishes discrimination based on disability and on a pre-existing risk to health (*risco agravado para a saúde*).[49]
- Decree-law 163/2006 of 8 August 2006[50] approves the standards and rules governing physical access to buildings and public spaces.

---

[44]Available at: http://www.dgaep.gov.pt/upload/Legis/2009_l_07_12_02.pdf.

[45]Available at: http://www.pgdlisboa.pt/leis/lei_mostra_articulado.php?nid=109&tabela=leis.

[46]Available at: https://dre.pt/application/dir/pdf1sdip/1999/08/201A00/59455947.pdf.

[47]Available at: http://dre.pt/pdf1sdip/2004/05/110A00/29712974.pdf.

[48]Available at: http://dre.pt/pdf1s/2004/08/194A00/52325236.pdf.

[49]Available at: https://dre.pt/application/dir/pdf1sdip/2006/08/16500/62106213.pdf.

[50]Available at: https://dre.pt/application/dir/pdf1sdip/2006/08/15200/56705689.pdf.

- Decree-Law 12/2006 of 20 January 2006[51] on trust funds deals with professional social security schemes.
- Law 4/2007 of 16 January 2007[52] (Social Security General Law—*Lei de Bases da Segurança Social*) deals with gender equality in statutory social security schemes.
- Law 110/2009 of 16 September 2009[53] on Social Security Contribution System Code ("*Código dos Regimes Contributivos de Segurança Social*"—*CRCSS*).
- Law 14/2008 of 12 March 2008 on gender equality in the access to and providing of goods and services transposes Directive 2004/113; this law was changed by Law 9/2015 of 11 February 2015, in view of the *Test-Achats Judgment*.
- Law 3/2011 of 15 February 2011, which transposes into national law Directives 2000/43/EC, 2000/78/EC and 2006/54/EC and establishes the general framework for the protection of self-employed as regards the prohibition of discrimination in the access to and in the development of independent work in the private sector, in the public sector, and in the cooperative sector.[54]
- Decree-Law 133/2013 of 3 October 2013[55] (General Features of Public Companies—*Estatuto das Empresas Públicas*) establishes that the governance boards of public companies (administration board and surveillance board) must aim to have both men and women as members, and establishes the obligation of public companies to put in place equality plans.
- Law No. 67/2013 of 28 August 2013[56] (General Features of Administrative Independent Agencies for the Monitoring of Economic Activity in the Private and in the Public Sector—*Lei-Quadro das Entidades Reguladoras*) establishes that the board of these agencies must integrate at least 33% of the members of each sex, and that the presidency of this board must be alternatively occupied by persons from both sexes.[57]
- Organic Law 3/2006[58] of 21 August 2006 (known as the Parity Law—*Lei da Paridade*) imposes gender quotas for elections for the National Parliament, for the European Parliament and for local political representatives. This Law

---

[51] Available at: https://dre.pt/web/guest/pesquisa-avancada/-/asearch/advanced/maximized?types=SERIEI&anoDoc=2006&tipo=Decreto-Lei&numero=12&search=Pesquisar&p_auth=STIfcz3c&fpb=dHJ1ZQ%3D%3D.

[52] Available at: https://dre.pt/application/file/522716.

[53] Available at: https://dre.pt/application/file/490287.

[54] Available at: https://dre.pt/application/dir/pdf1s/2011/02/03200/0080900811.pdf.

[55] Available at: https://dre.pt/application/file/500153.

[56] Available at: https://dre.pt/application/file/499437.

[57] On the contrary, there is no specific legislation concerning the members of the boards of the private sector companies, from the perspective of gender.

[58] Available at: https://dre.pt/application/file/540504.

establishes the lists presented by the political parties for these elections must include at least 33.3% women, in eligible positions.[59]

11 Does the Enforcement of Antidiscrimination Law Vary According to the Ground of Discrimination?

As a rule, the enforcement of antidiscrimination law does not vary according to the ground of discrimination.

Giving an example, the penal sanctions provided for by the Criminal Code cover discrimination based on almost every ground.

Article 240(1) imposes a punishment of imprisonment from 1 to 8 years on anyone who establishes organizations or engages in organized propaganda activities that incite or encourage discrimination on grounds of race, colour, ethnic origin or nationality, religion, gender or sexual orientation.

Article 240(2) imposes a penal sanction of imprisonment from 6 months to 5 years on anyone who in a public meeting, in writing intended for dissemination, or by any other means of social communication, provokes acts of violence against an individual or a group of individuals on grounds of their race, colour, ethnic origin or nationality, religion, gender or sexual orientation with the intention of inciting to or encouraging discrimination.

Under Article 132(2)(4) of the Criminal Code on homicide, motives based on hatred on grounds of race, religious or political convictions, colour, ethnic origin or nationality, religion, gender or sexual orientation are regarded as aggravating circumstances, resulting in a more severe penalty. Such aggravating circumstances may also apply in cases of assault causing bodily harm under Article 146 of the Criminal Code.

The fact that victims are especially vulnerable due to age and disability is also considered to be an aggravating circumstance in such crimes.

Besides the Criminal Code, the Portuguese legal order is particularly concerned with violation of antidiscrimination provisions on grounds of race and disability. Therefore, it establishes special administrative sanctions without prejudice of civil liability. For instance, the Labour Code states in Article 85(3) that the violation of Article 85(1), which forbids discrimination against people with disabilities, is a 'very serious offence'.

---

[59]These rules are slightly binding, since if the list of candidates does not comply with the proportion requirements, the party responsible is officially notified and asked to correct the list. If such correction is not made, the list is accepted with reservations and the party responsible suffers a serious reduction of the public subsidies for campaign expenses (Article 7 of Organic Law 3/2006).

12 What Is the Relationship Between the Enforcement of Antidiscrimination Law and the Quest for Equality on Both an Individual and Systemic Level?

The enforcement of antidiscrimination law is particularly linked to the quest for equality on an individual and systematic level, since the Constitution directly or indirectly accepts and promotes both. As we have already mentioned, the Constitution does not only provide for non-discrimination, above all, in Article 13(2), but it also requires equality in several provisions.

Thus, according to Article 9, one of the fundamental tasks of the state is to "promote the people's well-being and quality of life and real equality between the Portuguese" and under the terms of Article 13(1) on the principle of equality, "all citizens possess the same social dignity and are equal before the law".

Furthermore, the Constitution refers several times to equal opportunities (Articles 58 (right to work), 73(1) (right to education and culture), 74(1) (in access to and success in schooling) and 76(1) (access to university and higher education)). Furthermore, one of the priority duties of the state is to promote social justice, to ensure equal opportunities and carry out the necessary corrections to inequalities in the distribution of wealth and income, particularly by means of the fiscal policy (Article 81(b)).

Consequently, on the one hand, the Portuguese constitution confers solid legal basis to the legislature and to the administration to condemn all forms of discrimination and to enforce antidiscrimination measures and, on the other hand, the Constitution imposes to the legislature and the administration a duty to promote either formal equality or substantive equality and to adopt measures of positive action.

13 Is the Enforcement of Antidiscrimination Law Regarded As Different from the Enforcement of Other Laws?

No.

14 What Does the Enforcement of Antidiscrimination Law Reveal About the Nature of Your Legal System or About the Enforcement of Laws in Your Legal System

The enforcement of antidiscrimination law reveals a very well equipped legal system, which has some difficulties regarding the implementation and practical application. This problem is spread throughout the Portuguese legal system. That means the written law on a certain field easily accompanies the last legal trends but, in practical terms, it is not always efficient and effective enough. In Portugal it is rather common to approve legislation that would be completely appropriate to achieve the right goals, but which, due to several factors, like our financial and economic weakness but also our mentality, does not function properly. This particularly applies to the implementation of social rights and to the enforcement of antidiscrimination law.

This problem could be overcome if there were appropriate judicial and administrative means to react to this status quo. However, the length of the judicial procedures and the costs involved constitute two disincentives to accessing justice. In the last years some progress has been made in the public services in order to compensate the judicial obstacles, but they were clearly insufficient.

15 Conclusion

Equality and non-discrimination are two key concepts intrinsically linked in every constitutional order.

In Portugal, like in other European countries, the debate on antidiscrimination and equality law is anchored in the values of the modern constitutionalism, which are mainly the respect for human dignity, the respect for democracy, the rule of law and the protection of fundamental rights.

After the Revolution of April 1974, the prohibition of discrimination and the search for equality have become two major concerns of the politicians and the civil society in general. This is evidenced not only by the text of the Constitution, but also by antidiscrimination and equality legislation passed at the parliament and at the government and the commitment by the Portuguese state to the international human rights treaties. The accession to the EU also contributed to the development of antidiscrimination and equality law.

In fact, in Portugal, discrimination is prohibited on several grounds. Ancestry, gender, race, language, place of origin, religion, political or ideological convictions, education, economic situation, social condition or sexual orientation are explicitly prohibited (Article 13 (2) CPR), as are civil status, family situation, genetic heritage, reduced capacity to work, disability or chronic disease, nationality, ethnic origin, or membership in a trade union (Article 24(1) of the Labour Code). Furthermore, in the area of employment, the Labour Code explicitly prohibits discrimination on the ground of gender identity and of gender reassignment in Article 24 (1).

The scope of this prohibition is also rather wide, including direct or indirect discrimination, harassment, and instructions to discriminate. The possibility to adopt positive action measures in respect to racial or ethnic origin, religion or belief, disability, age, or sexual orientation is also provided for in Portuguese law.

In spite of this rather wide and consistent legal framework, the enforcement of antidiscrimination law has not always accompanied this trend. There still remain numerous cases of discrimination and inequality. However, the political powers have been trying to identify and combat these cases, and the situation has been deeply improving in the last two years. For instance, in the area of gender equality in decision-making, there is a growing intervention, especially related to the presence of women on company boards.

References

Correia FA (2016) Justiça Constitucional. Almedina, Coimbra
Gomes Canotilho JJ (2003) Direito Constitucional e Teoria da Constituição, 7th edn. Almedina, Coimbra
Gomes Canotilho JJ, Moreira V (2006) Constituição da República Portuguesa Anotada, vol I, 4th edn. Wolters Kluwer/Coimbra Editora
Guerra Martins AM (1999) L'interdiction des discriminations raciales en droit portugais. Eur Rev Public Law 11:901–917
Guerra Martins AM (2010) A igualdade e a não discriminação dos nacionais de Estados terceiros legalmente residentes na União Europeia – da origem na integração económica ao fundamento na dignidade do ser humano. Almedina, Coimbra
Guerra Martins AM (2011) Does the treaty of Lisbon really implement equal and non-discriminatory treatment of third-country nationals (TCN)? – the case of legally resident TCN within a member state of the Union. In: Beneyto JM, Pernice I (eds) Europe's constitutional challenges in the light of the recent case law of national constitutional courts – Lisbon and beyond, Baden-Baden, Nomos, pp 327–352
Guerra Martins AM (2012) A interdição de partidos políticos contrários ao princípio democrático. In: Estudos em homenagem ao Professor Doutor Jorge Miranda, vol I. Coimbra Editora, Coimbra, pp 185–214
Guerra Martins AM (2013) A Portuguese perspective of the accession on the European Union to the European Convention of human rights. In: Iliopoulos-Strangas, Pereira da Silva, Potacs (eds) The accession of the European Union to the ECHR. Nomos, Baden-Baden, pp 201–225
Guerra Martins AM (2015) Constitutional judge, social rights and public debt – the Portuguese constitutional case-law. Maastricht J Eur Comp Law 22:678–705
Guerra Martins AM (2017) Manual de Direito da União Europeia, 2nd edn. Almedina, Lisbon
Guerra Martins AM, Roque MP (2013) Chapter 18 – Universality and binding effect of human rights from a Portuguese perspective. In: Arnold R (ed) The Universalism of human rights. Springer, Dordrecht, pp 201–225
Guerra Martins AM, Roque MP (2015) Judicial dialogue in a multilevel constitutional network – the role of the Portuguese constitutional court. In: Andenas M, Fairgrieve D (eds) Courts and comparative law. OUP, Oxford, pp 297–324
Medeiros R (2015) A Constituição Portuguesa num Contexto Global. UCP, Lisbon
Miranda J (2013) Manual de Direito Constitucional, vol VI, 4th edn. Coimbra Editora, Coimbra
Miranda J (2014) Manual de Direito Constitucional, vol IV, 5th edn. Coimbra Editora, Coimbra
Miranda J, Medeiros R (2010) Constituição Portuguesa Anotada, vol I, 2nd edn. Coimbra Editora, Coimbra
Otero P (2010) Direito Constitucional Português - Organização do Poder Político, vol I, Coimbra, Almedina

Ana Maria Guerra Martins is a Professor of Law at the University of Lisbon—School of Law where she obtained all academic degrees—Aggregation, PhD, Master and Graduation in Law. She mainly teaches and researches in the field of EU Law, International Law, and International and European Human Rights Law. She served as Justice at the Portuguese Constitutional Court (2007–2016) and as General Inspectorate of Justice (2006–2007). She is a member of many scientific organizations and networks (ECLN, EPLO), is a Researcher at Lisbon Centre for Research in Public Law (CIDP), and was an invited researcher at the Max-Planck-Institute for Comparative and International Law in Heidelberg (1997–1999). She is the author of many books, articles, chapters in books and commentaries in English, French and Portuguese.

Romania

Irina Moroianu Zlătescu and Petru Emanuel Zlătescu

1 Is Antidiscrimination Law Enforced?

The numerous conflicts that occurred in the course of history and which, unfortunately, were not kept as mere conflicts of ideas, came out from or were based on discrimination.[1] These conflicts were caused by restriction or exclusion on reasons of discrimination based on race, colour, gender or sexual orientation, descent, ethnic, linguistic origins, religious beliefs, culture, intelligence, physical affiliation, civil or social status, political convictions, or any other situation of the kind. Such conflicts reflect the total or partial, *direct*[2] or *indirect*[3] failure to acknowledge the equal position of certain persons in enjoying or exercising their human rights and fundamental freedoms enshrined in the international law.

---

[1] In its 2014 edition The European Semester provides a framework for the coordination of economic policies across the European Union. It allows EU countries to discuss their economic and budget plans and monitor progress at specific times throughout the year. Le petit Larousse dictionary defines discrimination as "the act of differentiating between and treating differently certain individuals or a group as a whole as compared to the rest of the collectivity." See Le petit Larousse, Paris, 2013.

[2] Treating a person unfavourably as compared to others in the same situation. See Moroianu Zlătescu (2015), p. 308 et seq. See Asztalos (2015), p. 15.

[3] As shown on other occasions, legal provisions, neutral criteria or practices, putting certain persons at disadvantage, based on criteria protected by other persons, are an indirect discrimination. See Moroianu Zlătescu (2015) and Asztalos (2015).

I. Moroianu Zlătescu (✉)
National University of Political Studies and Public Administration, School of Law, Bucharest, Romania
e-mail: irina.zlatescu@administratiepublica.eu

P. E. Zlătescu
Member of the European Law Institute, Vienna, Austria

So far there is no generally accepted definition of discrimination in international law. As shown by the doctrine, the principle of non-discrimination imposed itself in the framework of the efforts taken by the international community and by the States to create the necessary conditions for the observance of human rights.[4] It was pointed out that non-discrimination is the negative form of equality of rights, which makes that the two notions are often defined in relation to each other or that one of them is defined relating to the other one.[5]

The artisans of modern thinking in the international law of human rights, fathers of the United Nations Charter and the Universal Declaration of Human Rights,[6] were driven by their wish to make a contribution to the elimination of the main forms of discrimination in about 100 years.[7] This is obviously an objective hard to reach if we only think of the fact that mankind's entire history, from ancient times to the present day, has unfortunately abounded in such attitudes. The Preamble, Article 1(3) and Article 55 in the United Nations Charter as well as Article 2 of the Universal Declaration of Human Rights refer to equal rights and implicitly non-discrimination. Article 2 of the Universal Declaration of Human Rights expressly provides that "Everyone is entitled to all the rights and freedoms set forth in this Declaration, without distinction of any kind, such as race, colour, sex, language, religion, political or other opinion, national or social origin, property, birth or other status." Provisions referring to equality and non-discrimination are also to be found in Article 7 and Article 22 of the same Declaration. To these provisions, numerous regulations on fighting discrimination have been added with time.

For instance Article 2 of the International Covenant on Economic, Social and Cultural Rights and Article 26 of the International Covenant on Civil and Political Rights lay down that the law shall equally and effectively guarantee everyone's protection against any kind of discrimination.[8]

An other notion that emerged and imposed itself at international level in the last decades is the notion of multiple discrimination, which refers to the situation when a person becomes the victim of two or several types of discrimination at the same time. There are different categories of multiple discrimination. Multiple discrimination can be *additional* or *cumulative discrimination* or *intersectional discrimination;* while within the first two categories the protected grounds keep their individuality, within the intersectional discrimination the interaction of the protected gorunds becomes the reason of discrimination itself, creating thus a new ground.[9] As the

---

[4]See Diaconu (2005), p. 22 et seq.; Moroianu Zlătescu (2006), p. 3 et seq.

[5]See IRDO (2001), p. 5 et seq.; Diaconu (2005), p. 22.

[6]See "Artizanii gândirii moderne a drepturilor omului," documents of the international colloquium organized by the Romanian Institute for Human Rights on 28 November 2003 in "Drepturile Omului" No. 4/2003, Ed. IRDO, Bucureşti, 2003. It should also be mentioned that Romania became a member of the United Nations Organization on 14 December 1955.

[7]This comes out from scrutinizing the United Nations solemn session on the Universal Declaration of Human Rights, as well as the Millennium Declaration and the Agenda 2030.

[8]See Moroianu Zlătescu (2012a), p. 41 et seq.; Moroianu Zlătescu et al. (2007).

[9]See Christine Deliyanni-Dimitrakou (2013), p. 681 et seq.

elimination of all forms of discrimination has been a permanent preoccupation within the United Nations, in time, both the organization and its agencies adopted a number of documents in the field, such as The United Nations Discrimination Employment and Occupation Convention, adopted in 1958[10]; the UNESCO Convention against discrimination in Education, adopted in 1960; the UN international Convention for elimination of all forms of racial discrimination, adopted by the General Assembly by Resolution 1904 (XVIII) of 20 November 1963; the Convention on the Elimination of All Forms of Discrimination Against Women, adopted by the United Nations General Assembly on 18 December 1979, was ratified by Romania under Decree No. 342 of 28 November 1981; also, the United Nations Convention on the Rights of Persons with Disabilities, adopted in 2006 under Resolution A/RES/61/106 on 13 December 2006—the first international treaty that explicitly makes reference to multiple discrimination—was ratified by Romania under Law No. 221/2010.[11] These provisions remain nevertheless the starting point for defining and establishing the hierarchy of the main categories of international norms in the field.[12] There are also other fundamental documents combating discrimination on regional level which belong to the European system of human rights. Thus, the European Convention on the Defence of Human Rights and Fundamental Freedoms (the European Convention on Human Rights—ECHR[13]) provides in its Article 14 that "The enjoyment of the rights and freedoms set forth in this Convention shall be secured without discrimination on any ground such as sex, race, colour, language, religion, political or other opinion, national or social origin, association with a national minority, property, birth or other status." However, Art. 14 ECHR is an accessory prohibition of discrimination, which can only be invoked in conjunction with other provisions of the Convention. Provisions against discrimination can also be found in Protocol 12 to the European Convention (adding an autonomous prohibition of discrimination, independent from the ambit of other Convention's rights), as well as in Article 20 and Article E in Part V of the revised European Social Charter (the principle of non-discrimination being considered a fundamental principle).

---

[10]ILO Convention No. 111/1958, ratified by Romania under Decree No. 284 of 11 May 1973.

[11]In order to comply with the standards set forth by the Convention on the Rights of Persons with Disabilities, Romania modified its domestic legislation, adopting for this purpose Law No. 448/2006, published in the Official Gazette of Romania No. 1006 of 18 December 2006, republished in the Official Gazette of Romania No. 1 of 3 January 2008.

[12]See Moroianu Zlătescu (2011), p. 25 et seq.

[13]Romania became a member of the Council of Europe on 7 October 1993, ratified the European Convention on Human Rights on 18 May 1994, and acknowledged the jurisdiction of the European Court of Human Rights. Romania also ratified Additional Protocols 1–15 and signed Additional Protocol 16. By way of consequence, the Convention gained direct applicability in the domestic law, while knowing the jurisprudence of the European Court became an obligation since the Court is the control mechanism for the application of the Convention. The Court is competent to solve the complaints filed by natural persons and, of late, also legal persons from Romania.

At the level of the European Union,[14] the notion of discrimination is defined and explained by the European Commission in its policies on the implementation of the principle of non-discrimination.[15]

The Charter of Fundamental Rights of the European Union[16] provides in its Title III *Equality* (Article 21) that "Any discrimination based on any ground such as sex, race, colour, ethnic or social origin, genetic features, language, religion or belief, political or any other opinion, membership of a national minority, property, birth, disability, age or sexual orientation shall be prohibited." It is worth mentioning that the Treaty on the Functioning of the European Union institutes in its Article 18 (1) (former Article 12 in the Treaty Establishing the European Economic Community), generally prohibits discrimination based on citizenship or nationality, as a general principle of the European Union law. This provision is further developed in various other provisions of the same Treaty.

The conditions for the application of Article 18 of TFEU have a direct effect upon national legislation. It should be mentioned that this Article is only applied in cases where an inequality of treatment occurs. It should be not interpreted as a mere inconsistency between two national regulations. It is also worth mentioning that Article 18(1) shall only be applied if no infringement is inflicted upon the special provisions. It is interesting to note that the principle of non-discrimination based on citizenship or nationality was re-iterated and further enshrined in a number of other provisions. Of course, if the special provisions take into account the objectives of Article 18(1) of the Treaty, then Article 18 is no longer applicable. However, the importance of this limitation is not quite clear and perhaps this is the reason why the jurisprudence is not self-consistent. We believe that in practice, special provisions can be considered similar to other legal provisions taking into account the nationality criterion and including a prohibition of discrimination, such as the fundamental freedoms. To the extent a special provision is applied, we share the opinion of those specialists who affirm that Article 18(1) in the TFEU cannot be invoked. This Article prohibits as a matter of fact any discrimination based on nationality or citizenship, no matter whether it is a direct or an indirect one, while such a prohibition can only be invoked "in the treaties' sphere of applicability."[17] Current European legislation refers to direct and indirect discrimination. The European Union Racial Equality Directive (Directive 2000/43/EC)[18] "implementing the principle of equal treatment between persons irrespective of racial or ethnic origin" provides that direct discrimination occurs when a person is treated less favourably than another in a similar situation, based on racial or ethnic origin. It provides that indirect discrimination occurs where a seemingly neutral provision might put at disadvantage persons of a certain racial or ethnic origin as compared to other persons, unless the provision is

---

[14]Romania became a member of the European Union on 1 January 2007.

[15]See Moroianu Zlătescu and Mihaela Mandrea (2008), p. 16.

[16]The Charter became an official document of the European Union when the Treaty of Lisbon was signed on 13 December 2007.

[17]Epiney et al. (2010), p. 7 et seq.; also see Moroianu Zlătescu (2012b), p. 11 et seq.

[18]Published in OJ L 180 of 19 July 2000.

objectively justified by a legitimate purpose and the means for the achievement of that purpose are adequate and necessary. Another Directive is 2000/78,[19] which refers to equal opportunities with employment and professional competencies. We should also mention Directive No. 86/378/CEE,[20] with the amendments introduced by Directive No. 96/97/CEE[21] on the scope and ways of applying the principle of equal treatment for men and women in occupational social security schemes, as well as Directive 2010/41/EU on the application of the principle of equal treatment between men and women engaged in an activity in a self-employed capacity and repealing Council Directive 86/613/EEC. We should also mention Directive 2002/73,[22] which refers to sexual harassment as gender based discrimination. This Directive was transposed without amendments,[23] which was expected to replace the European provisions in force after 15 August 2009 with regard to equality of opportunities between employed men and women. This ensemble of European regulations proves the European Union's commitment to build a discrimination free society. It is worth mentioning that the two Directives describe in their Preambles the tradition with the European law to combat multiple discrimination.[24]

Romania transcribed a large part of the European Directives provisions into its domestic legislation. For this purpose, new normative acts were adopted so that all discrimination criteria and all fields of social life be covered.

As far as the legal order in Romania is concerned, in its capacity as part of the international and European legal order, including the fight against discrimination and the promotion of the principle of equality of opportunities, the concept of discrimination and the fight against it is to be found in the Constitution[25] in the first place, but it is also present in various laws and ordinances adopted on a later date: Article 11(1) and (2)[26] corroborated with Article 20(1) and (2)[27] and Article 148(2)[28]; also

---

[19]Published in OJ L 303 of 2 December 2000.

[20]In OJ L 225 of 12 August 1986.

[21]OJ L 46 of 17 February 1997.

[22]In OJ L 269 of 5 October 2002, p. 15.

[23]In OJ L 204 of 5 July 2006, p. 23.

[24]Zlătescu (2015).

[25]The Constitution of Romania of 1991 was amended and supplemented under the Romanian Constitution Revising Act No 429/2003, published in the Official Gazette of Romania, Part I, No. 758 of 29 October 2003. Also see, Moroianu Zlătescu (2013), pp. 24, 113, 126.

[26]Article 11 of the Romanian Constitution reads as follows: "(1) The Romanian State pledges to fulfil as such and in good faith its obligations as deriving from the treaties it is a party to. (2) Treaties ratified by Parliament, according to the law, are part of national law."

[27]Article 20 of the Romanian Constitution reads as follows: "(1) Constitutional provisions concerning the citizens' rights and liberties shall be interpreted and enforced in conformity with the Universal Declaration of Human Rights, with the covenants and other treaties Romania is a party to. (2) Where any inconsistencies exist between the covenants and treaties on the fundamental human rights Romania is a party to, and the national laws, the international regulations shall take precedence, unless the Constitution or national laws comprise more favourable provisions."

[28]Article 148 (2) of the Romanian Constitution reads as follows: "As a result of the accession, the provisions of the constituent treaties of the European Union, as well as the other mandatory community regulations shall take precedence over the opposite provisions of the national laws, in compliance with the provisions of the accession act."

Article 4(2); Article 6(2); Article 16; Article 23(8); Article 32(3) Article 32(7); Article 53(2); Article 62; Article 120(2); Article 128. It is worth mentioning that, according to Article 142 of the Constitution, the Constitutional Court is the guarantor of the Constitution's supremacy.

Based on the Constitution, a large number of normative acts were adopted. Let us first mention the new Civil Code that came into force on the 1st of October 2011[29] which takes into account the spirit and the letter of the European Convention on Human Rights and the jurisprudence of the European Court of Human Rights. Mention should also be made of the new Civil Procedure Code adopted in 2010,[30] where the lawmaker bore in mind the most important international documents as well as the principles laid down in the European Convention.[31]

Also, a new Criminal Code and a new Criminal Procedure Code were adopted. As was mentioned in the doctrine, in order to create a legislative system where the criminal trial might take place rapidly and efficiently, where there might be a conceptual harmonization with the provisions of the new Criminal Code adopted under Law No. 286/2009 and implemented under Law No. 187/2012,[32] a new Criminal Procedure Code was adopted in 2009, which was later amended under Law No. 255/2013[33] for the implementation of Law No. 135/2010 through the new Criminal Procedure Code,[34] under which even Law No. 135/2010 was amended. Also, Government Emergency Ordinance No. 3/2014 was adopted.[35]

Special laws and government ordinances with special provisions on discrimination were also adopted. Such an ordinance is Government Emergency Ordinance 137/2000 approved under Law No. 48/2002,[36] which specifies that it is discrimination when a person is treated differently as compared to other persons in the same situation and the respective person is in one of the situations considered as being generated on reasons of discrimination in accordance with international regulations.[37] Government Ordinance

---

[29] Adopted on 1 October 2009, under Law No. 287/2009 and implemented under Law No. 71/2011, amended and supplemented under Government Emergency Ordinance No. 79/2011, republished in the Official Gazette of Romania No. 505/2011, approved under Law No. 60 of 10 April 2012, updated and consolidated under Law No. 138/2014.

[30] In force since 15 February 2013, amended under Government Emergency Ordinance 4/2013 and Law No. 2/2013. The most recent amendment was introduced under Government Emergency Ordinance No. 1/2016 published in the Official Gazette of Romania, Part I, No. 85 of 4 February 2016.

[31] See Leş (2013), p. 1.

[32] See Buneci (2014), pp. XI–XII; also, the Official Gazette of Romania, Part I, No.757 of 12 November 2012.

[33] Official Gazette of Romania, Part I, No. 515 of 14 August 2013.

[34] Official Gazette of Romania, Part I, No. 486 of 15 July 2010.

[35] Official Gazette of Romania, Part I, No. 98 of 7 February 2014.

[36] Official Gazette of Romania, Part I, No. 431 of 2 September 2000, republished in the Official Gazette of Romania No. 99 of 8 February 2007.

[37] See Moroianu Zlătescu (2014), p. 3 et seq.; Moroianu Zlătescu and Zlătescu (2014), p. 1 et seq.

No. 77/2003,[38] approved under Law No. 27/2004, introduced the notion of indirect discrimination in the form provided for by the European Directives.

The regulations in our country worth mentioning here include: Government Ordinance No. 137/2000, which approaches the non-discrimination principle as an instrument for the exercise of the rights. Article 1(2) shows that, in the exercise of the human rights and fundamental freedoms, the principle of equality among citizens and exclusion of privileges and discrimination shall be guaranteed. Therefore, non-discrimination appears to be the actual way of exercising the other rights and freedoms. The Ordinance was approved under Law No. 215/2001,[39] the Local Public Administration Act, Law No. 202/2002[40] on equality of opportunities and treatment between men and women, which in its Article 9(1) prohibits discrimination consisting in the employer's use of practices that put at disadvantage persons of a certain gender. Nevertheless, the Law provides for some exceptions too. These are related to those workplaces where, due to the respective professional activity or to the framework where the labour is performed, a gender related characteristic feature is a genuine and essential professional requirement provided that the objective pursued be legitimate and the requirement be proportional. Next would be Government Emergency Ordinance 31/2002 on the prohibition of organizations and symbols of a fascist, racist, or xenophobic nature and promotion of the cult of persons guilty of crimes against peace and mankind.[41]

We believe that the antidiscrimination legislation is implemented in Romania. Thus, as shown before, the antidiscrimination legislation of Romania corresponds to the international and the European standards in the field. As such, they provide for mechanisms of prevention and control monitoring for all possible violations of the norms. The Romanian legislation in force covers all discrimination criteria provided for in the international documents with universal and regional applicability.

2 How Is Antidiscrimination Law Enforced?

The implementation of legislation is one of the main challenges faced by lawmakers and practitioners. The Government Ordinance No. 137/2000 establishes the four big landmarks for the application of the antidiscrimination legislation. The lawmaker is provided with legal instruments for solving the cases involving discrimination, as well as with the necessary legal instruments to assist the victims of discrimination and to provide evidence, while the jurisprudence is compliant with the European standards in the field. As was shown in the doctrine, the evidence has an important

---

[38] Official Gazette of Romania, I, No. 619 of 30 August 2003.
[39] Published in the Official Gazette of Romania No. 204 of 28 April 2001, republished in the Official Gazette of Romania No. 123 of 2 February 2007.
[40] Republished in the Official Gazette of Romania, I, No. 326 of 5 June 2013.
[41] Official Gazette of Romania, No. 214 of 28 March 2002.

function and it varies, depending on the branch of law. For instance, with civil lawsuits related to labour and the administrative field, the system of providing evidence functions on the basis of severe standards that impose proving the guilt of the accused person that allegedly committed the crime of discrimination.[42]

According to Article 6 of the Government Ordinance No. 137/2000, it constitutes offense to condition the participation in economic activities of any individual or to impede the free choice and exercise of a profession due to the fact that the respective person belongs to a certain race, nationality, ethnicity, religion, or has a certain social origin. It is also a violation of the rights of a person to hire or not to hire someone based on convictions, gender or sexual orientation, age or affiliation to a disadvantaged category.

Also according to this Ordinance it represents an offence to discriminate a person on the ground of belonging to a certain race, nationality, ethnicity, religion, social or disadvantaged category, namely because of their beliefs, age, gender or sexual orientation.

Equally it is an offence to discriminate persons on the above-mentioned reasons when concluding a working contract. It is also an offence to discriminate a person with respect to social protection, except on the following cases as provided by law: the conclusion, suspension, or modification of the labour relation; the establishment and modification of job-related duties, the choice of the work place or the establishment of the wages.

Discrimination between persons should be avoided by employers when granting social rights other than the wages, when offering training and retraining, in professional re-conversion, or in promotion. Discrimination might occur in the enforcement of disciplinary measures; in denying a person the right to join a trade union and to access all the facilities it offers; or to refuse a person any other conditions of work performance, according to law.[43]

Under Government Ordinance No. 137/2000, a legal refusal to hire a person on the ground that they belong to a particular race, nationality, religion, social or disadvantaged category or, convictions, age, gender or sexual orientation, is considered as an offense, unless required by law.

Conditionally filling a job through advertisement or contest, initiated by the employer or its representatives, requiring belonging to a certain race, nationality, ethnicity, religion, and social category or to a disadvantaged category, age, gender or sexual orientation, convictions of candidates, with the exception provided by the Ordinance, constitutes an offense.

Individuals and legal entities involved in mediation and in distributing jobs will treat equally and ensure free equal access to consultation of to the offer and demand on the labour market to all people looking for a job. They will advise on employment opportunities and obtaining a qualification and will refuse to support discrimination against employees. Employers will assure the confidentiality of the data related to

---

[42] See Asztsalos (2013), p. 15 et seq.
[43] See Article 7, Government Ordinance No. 137/2000.

race, nationality, ethnicity, religion, gender, sexual orientation or other private information regarding persons seeking jobs.

According to article 9 of the same Government Ordinance, it constitutes an offense of discrimination of employees by employers when social benefits are not granted because employees belong to a certain race, nationality, ethnic origin, religion, social category or to a disadvantaged category, or on age, gender, sexual orientation or beliefs.[44]

Observance of the right to non-discrimination as a fundamental human right remains one main objective with the legislative and the institutions having powers in the field. As shown in the World Economic Forum report, discrimination is still a problem in Romania, this country being on position 70 out of 134 countries.[45] At the same time, according to the Eurobarometer regarding the authorities' efficiency with combating all forms of discrimination, 26% of the population believes that they are completely inefficient, 29% partly efficient, and 27% totally efficient.

In terms of the legislative, alongside the juridical commissions, the commissions on equal opportunities play an important role and the subcommissions tasked with ensuring regulations are compliant with the international standards. They monitor the situations occurring in practice to increase the applicability of laws.

As far as the executive is concerned, we should mention the National Agency for Equal Opportunities, the National Authority for Persons with Disabilities and the National Agency for the Roma, function under the authority and coordination of the Government.

Finally, the independent national institutions include (in order of establishment): the Romanian Institute for Human Rights (RIHR), established under Law No. 9/1991, the Advocate of the People, established in conformity with Article 58 in the Constitution of Romania, and the National Council for Combating Discrimination (NCCD), established under Ordinance No. 137/2000 on preventing and punishing all forms of discrimination.

While the Advocate of the People has powers in terms of discrimination issues in the administration-citizen relationship, and the RIHR has powers in terms of training, information, research and documentation in the field of human rights, both institutions accomplishing their mandate by specific means, the NCCD has exclusive powers in terms of discrimination.

An important role is also played by the civil society in terms of antidiscrimination education and publicizing cases of discrimination.

---

[44]See Article 9, Government Ordinance No. 137/2000.
[45]World Economic Forum, The Global Gender Gap Report, 2013, p. 11.

3 Who Enforces Antidiscrimination Law?

An important role regarding the application of the legislation in the field is played, alongside the judicial, by the legislative institution (Parliament, Parliamentary Commissions), by the executive (e.g. the Ministry of Labour, Family, Social Protection and Elderly through its National Agency for Equal Opportunities for Men and Women, the National Authority for Persons with Disabilities, National Agency for the Roma etc.), as well as by the independent national human rights institutions—the National Council for Combating Discrimination,[46] the Advocate of the People and the Romanian Institute for Human Rights—through their specific means. The civil society also plays an important role with making cases of discrimination known, combating them, and preventing them.

4 Who Benefits from the Enforcement of Antidiscrimination Law?

Generally speaking, the persons belonging to those categories mentioned above are most likely to be discriminated. This is the reason why we believe that, alongside the above-mentioned institutions, an essential role lies within the media. The media is the first to trigger an alarm signal in relation to cases of intolerance.[47] However, the immediate beneficiaries are the victims.

Ordinance No. 137/2000 admits at the same time the need to make the principle of equality observed in practice, not only by prohibitive means. In this respect, it mentions the possibility for positive measures to be adopted to prevent or to compensate the (historical) disadvantages suffered by certain groups.[48]

The Ordinance offers several blueprints to better clarify the fields where protection against discrimination is offered. Thus, it refers to equality in the economic activity and in terms of employment and profession, access to public services, access to education, freedom of movement (free choice of domicile and free access to public places), and the right to personal dignity.

Regarding the way citizens perceive discrimination, it should be pointed out that, according to the 2010 Social Inclusion Barometer, 78% of Romania's population believes that discrimination on the labour market is quite widespread. At the same time, it comes out that the population is familiar with the legislation in the field and the fact that the legislation provides for employment discrimination based on such

---

[46]The activity of the National Council for Combating Discrimination is regulated by Government Ordinance No. 137/2001, Government Decision No. 1196/2002.

[47]The extent to which the media fulfill their responsibilities of promoting human rights depends on the journalists' professionalism, the publishers' and their employers' availability, and the public's activism as well.

[48]See Government Ordinance No. 137/2000, republished.

criteria as gender, age, ethnicity, civil status, etc.[49] It is interesting to mention that, according to the Eurobarometer regarding the perception of discrimination at the level of the European Union, only 37% Romanians are familiar with their rights in case they become victims of discrimination or harassment.

According to a study, 51% Romanians largely and very largely believe that the discrimination is a current issue in Romania.[50]

On the other hand, when considering women, age is also to be taken into account since the EU Commission recommendations refer to the employment of both youth and older persons.

According to the European Commission, "age discrimination towards older people in employment is becoming increasingly relevant due to the demographic changes in Europe which are at the root of most of the recent age-related legislation such as the abolition of or increase in mandatory retirement ages, disincentives for early retirement and other measures to keep older workers in the labor market."[51]

This aspect is reflected in the recommendations made to several states, Romania included, to keep older people active for longer periods of time by, among other measures, increasing the retirement age. The recommendation makes no gender specification, referring to both men and women.

However, youth unemployment rate remains high across the EU. Young people are excluded from the labor market or, if they are not entirely excluded, the quality of their employment is frequently low. This affects young people's eligibility for social benefits, sick leave, maternity leave, and healthcare, and negatively influences their access to pension schemes.

Some measures to address the social and economic consequences of an ageing population and persisting youth unemployment were proposed in the context of the European Semester.[52]

The recommendations for Romania refer to aspects regarding young people under the age of 25, for whom good-quality job offers should be ensured. They should also benefit from continued education and/or an apprenticeship or traineeship within the first 4 months after completing their studies so that unemployment can be avoided.[53]

Ethnic, racial, religious minorities, and groups of immigrants are the most likely groups to be exposed to discrimination. Persons belonging to these categories also encounter difficulties integrating into the labour market or obtaining public benefits.

---

[49] See the 2010 Social Inclusion Barometer.

[50] Report by the National Council for Combating Discrimination—Perceptions and attitudes vis-à-vis discrimination in Romania, 2012, p. 8.

[51] See European Commission (2015), Joint Report on the application of the Racial Equality Directive (2000/43/EC) and the Employment Equality Directive (2000/78/EC).

[52] The European Semester provides a framework for the coordination of economic policies across the European Union. It allows EU countries to discuss their economic and budget plans and monitor progress at specific times throughout the year.

[53] See Fundamental Rights Report 2016, European Union Agency for Fundamental Rights, p. 62.

5 Who Is Harmed by the Enforcement of Antidiscrimination Law?

Persons who are responsible for discriminating actions, irrespective of their social position are the first to suffer the consequences of the implementation of the antidiscrimination law. For example: it often happens that, when a complaint or a lawsuit is initiated for violation of the principle of equality and non-discrimination, the group or the community to which the perpetrator belongs, try to create a hostile, degrading, humiliating atmosphere or one having a negative impact upon the working and living conditions of the victim in response to the victim's action of turning to the authorities as a result of a discrimination. This is a case of victimization. In case the perpetrator is a public servant or a representative of a State authority, of course any discriminatory action on his/her part is an aggravating circumstance and is treated as such by the legislation and the jurisprudence.

6 What Remedies Are Provided by the Enforcement of Antidiscrimination Law?

The legislation restores the situation preceding the discriminatory action for the persons discriminated against. Sometimes, the courts may order compensation for moral damages.

7 Who Supports the Enforcement of Antidiscrimination Law?

The national human rights institutions, the union trades, the non-governmental organizations, the religious cults etc.

8 Who Opposes the Enforcement of Antidiscrimination Law?

Persons or groups of persons with behaviour deviations and with extremist attitudes.

9 How Broad Is the Coverage of Antidiscrimination Law?

As shown from the very beginning, the Romanian legislation is consonant with the international and the regional-European legislation in the field.

10 Does the Enforcement of Antidiscrimination Law Vary According to the Ground of Discrimination?

Obviously, The European Semester provides a framework for the coordination of economic policies across the European Union. It allows EU countries to discuss their economic and budget plans and monitor progress at specific times throughout the year.

There is Specific legislation in terms of categories of discrimination. For instance, racial discrimination, discrimination based on religious criteria, gender discrimination, labour discrimination, inequality of opportunities in education and the educational system, etc., have different legal regulations.

11 What Is the Relationship Between the Enforcement of Antidiscrimination Law and the Quest for Equality on Both an Individual and Systemic Level?

It is our belief that there is no discrimination at the level of the system; discrimination occurs only at the level of the individual and sometimes at the level of a group.

12 Is the Enforcement of Antidiscrimination Law Regarded as Different from the Enforcement of Other Laws?

Given the fact that the democratic Romanian society regards discrimination as a most serious crime, the most severe measures are taken to combat it.

13 What Does the Enforcement of Antidiscrimination Law Reveal About the Nature of Your Legal System or About the Enforcement of Laws in Your Legal System?

Romania's position with regard to the issue of discrimination is to have all forms of racism, intolerance and xenophobia blamed on the State authorities, for they are considered serious violations of the fundamental human rights. In this respect, Romania joined the international community in its efforts to combat all forms of discrimination in an attempt to promote the values of tolerance and dialogue as a constant partner of international and regional organizations. Our country adopted legislation meant to facilitate the implementation of the provisions of the international and regional conventions and treaties where Romania is a party, to favour the promotion of gender equality, to contribute to the promotion of equality of opportunities between men and women and to combat sexist mentalities and practices. Also, Romania takes efforts to provide an integrated approach to gender issues in various fields of activity, emphasizing the strengthening of the legislative framework, on justice, local administration, culture, education, the rights of persons belonging to any minorities, the rights of migrants, observance of the rights of the child and the young, the rights of elderly persons, women's rights; also on social cohesion, fighting corruption, against trafficking in human beings and abuse of drugs, etc., to provide a sustainable development in an adequate environment. For the achievement of the purposes set forth, such actions should be taken as to promote awareness about equality of opportunities between men and women, eliminate stereotypes from the educational system and education, combat the discourse motivated by hatred, identify and present positive practices in the media, and monitor and point out the progress achieved with fighting discrimination so as to achieve a world based on the respect for diversity and solidarity.

14 Conclusions

Romania, as a democratic state governed by the rule of law, lays more and more emphasis on raising the citizen's level of juridical conscience and on the juridical culture. This can be achieved in the framework of the formal educational process, in the public and private systems, based on a formula of continuous training and also with the contribution of the media, the civil society, etc. This is a way to contribute to the prevention and combat of any form of discrimination.

The juridical education, as a constitutive part of the juridical culture, is a well-defined process of actions and influences upon the conscience and the culture of the members of society who have to reach the habit of respecting the laws and the rights of others based on inner conviction.

The measures that are taken in the legislative or judicial, although largely aimed at protecting victims, always involve time and money, while most victims lack such resources, especially when they come from disadvantaged backgrounds.

Also it has been shown that judicial protection is occasional and random and also that repairs concern only the actual damage.[54]

We believe that new solutions must be found at legal and judicial level to promote and protect human rights in order to ensure the principles of equality and non-discrimination. Special attention should be given to human rights education, both formal and informal, and in particular to continuing education. Because, as it has been often stated, at any given time there is the danger of indifference.

It is known that human rights education, including education against racism, is a broad concept that cannot be reduced to the study of texts of laws and constitutional provisions, or even of the respective mechanisms. In our opinion, the entire activity in this field must be conducted in the spirit of peace, democracy, and the rule of law.[55]

In this context the national institutions for human rights and the collaboration between them would still have an important role to play.[56]

The Romanian Institute for Human Rights, in its capacity as a national institution for human rights, according to the Paris Principles on the establishment of national institutions for the promotion and protection of human rights, plays a significant role in ensuring better understanding by the public institutions, NGOs and individuals of human rights issues and the way they are approached in different countries, in compliance with the provisions of the international covenants and treaties where Romania is a party.

References

Asztalos CF (2015) Nedeş. Editura Pro Universitaria, Bucureşti, p 15
Asztsalos CF (2013) Probele în materia nediscriminării în dreptul românesc, în NEDES 2013. Editura ProUniversitaria, Bucureşti, p 15 et seq
Buneci P (coord.) (2014) Noul Cod de procedură penală. Editura C.H. Beck, Bucureşti, pp XI–XII
Deliyanni-Dimitrakou C (2013) Égalité multidimensionnelle et discriminations multiples en droit comparé. In: Revue internationale de Droit Comparé, no 3/2013, p 681 et seq
Diaconu I (2005) Discriminarea rasială. Editura Lumina Lex, Bucureşti, p 22 et seq
Epiney A, Mosters R, Progin-Teuerkauf S (2010) Droit européen II. Les libertres fondamentales de l'Union Européenne. Editura Stampfli, Bern, p 7 et seq
IRDO (2001) Lupta împotriva rasismului, discriminării rasiale, xenofobiei şi intoleranţei. Editura IRDO, Bucureşti, p. 5 et seq
Leş I (2013) Noul Cod de procedură civilă. Editura C. H. Beck, Bucureşti, p 1
Moroianu Zlătescu I (2006) Racial discrimination. Editura IRDO, Bucureşti, p 3 et seq
Moroianu Zlătescu I (2011) Protection against Racism and Discrimination. Editura IRDO, Bucureşti, p 25 et seq
Moroianu Zlatescu I (2011) Protection against Racism and discrimination. IRDO, Bucharest, p 86 et seq

---

[54] See also Deliyanni-Dimitrakou (2013), p. 682 et seq.
[55] See also Moroianu Zlatescu (2011), p. 86 et seq.
[56] See also Moroianu Zlatescu (2013), p. 92 et seq.

Moroianu Zlătescu I (2012a) Equality and nondiscrimination. In The exercise of the right to nondiscrimination and equal opportunities in the contemporary society. Editura Pro Universitaria, Bucureşti, p 41 et seq

Moroianu Zlătescu I (2012b) Drept European. Editura Pro Universitaria, Bucureşti, p 11 et seq

Moroianu Zlătescu I (2013) Constitutional law in Romania. Wolters Kluwer, Alphen aan den Rijn, pp 24, 113, 126

Moroianu Zlatescu I (2013) 20 de ani de la adoptarea principiilor de la Paris. In: Drepturile Omului, no. 3/2013, IRDO, p 92 et seq

Moroianu Zlătescu I (2014) Fighting multiple discrimination. In: The exercise of the right to non-discrimination and equality of opportunities in the contemporary society. Editura Pro Universitaria, Bucureşti, p 3 et seq

Moroianu Zlătescu I (2015) Human rights: a dynamic and evolving process. Pro Universitaria, Bucuresti, p 308 et seq

Moroianu Zlătescu I, Mihaela Mandrea M (2008) Egalitate. Nediscriminare. Bună administrare. Editura IRDO, Bucureşti, p 16

Moroianu Zlătescu I, Zlătescu PE (2014) Discriminarea şi discriminarea multiplă. INFO-IRDO No. 9/2014, p 1 et seq

Moroianu Zlătescu I, Marinache E, Şerbănescu R (coord.) (2007) Principalele instrumente internaţionale privind drepturile omului la care România este parte, vol I – Instrumente universale. ediţia a IX-a, Editura IRDO, Bucureşti

Zlătescu PE (2015) Multiple discrimination in international and European law. The Juridical Current, Târgu-Mureş

Irina Moroianu Zlătescu is a Titular Member of the International Academy of Comparative Law (IACL), a Titular Member of the Romanian Academy for Legal Sciences, Professor of Law at the National University of Political Studies and Public Administration of Bucharest. She is a Member of the Management Board of the European Union Agency for Fundamental Rights (FRA).

Petru Emanuel Zlătescu is a PhD Candidate and a Member of the European Law Institute (ELI).

South Africa

Debbie Collier

South Africa is one of the world's major social laboratories[1].

1 South African Antidiscrimination Law in Context

Colonial rule and apartheid policy underpin the systemic discrimination, uneven human development and high levels of income inequality still experienced in modern-day democratic South Africa.[2] While a comprehensive and laudable antidiscrimination law framework is in place (see Fig. 1); its gains have been modest and unevenly distributed. At a systemic level, deep and pervasive inequality remains the lived experienced for many South Africans.

Apartheid laws entrenched 'white' racial dominance in all spheres of life, and as a result race is a particularly salient ground of discrimination in South Africa. There are four population groups that are commonly referred to in South Africa: white, coloured, Indian/Asian, and African. The term 'black people' is used as a generic or composite term for the latter three population groups (i.e. coloured, Indian, and

---

[1] Report of the Ministerial Committee on Transformation and Social Cohesion and the Elimination of Discrimination in Public Higher Education Institutions, 30 November 2008, p. 6.
[2] For historically complex reasons, exacerbated by high levels of unemployment and wage distribution weighted in favour of top-end earners, South African society remains notoriously unequal.

D. Collier (✉)
Department of Commercial Law, University of Cape Town, Cape Town, South Africa
e-mail: debbie.collier@uct.ac.za

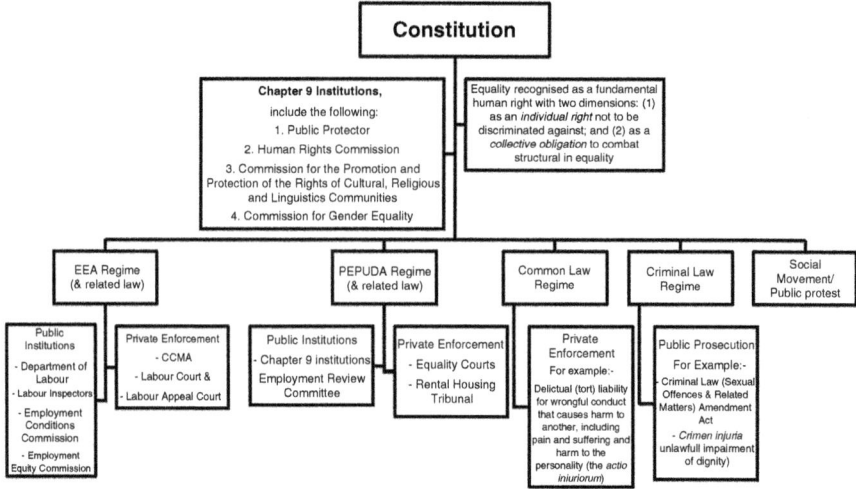

Fig. 1 Regulatory regimes for the enforcement of antidiscrimination law in South Africa

African).[3] In terms of population distribution, recent statistics break down the Economically Active Population (EAP) as follows: African (76.2%); Coloured (10.6%); Indian (2.8%); and White (10.3%).[4] In addition to racial discrimination, conservative and patriarchal values still dominate many decisions and social interactions and result in discrimination on grounds such as gender, sex, pregnancy, disability, HIV Aids, religion, culture, and sexual orientation.

Committed to being a more just society, antidiscrimination law naturally plays a central role in democratic South Africa and derives its force from the Bill of Rights in the Constitution[5] and, importantly, the subsidiary legislation[6] designed and enacted to give effect to these rights (see Fig. 1). Human dignity[7] and the achievement of equality are articulated both as values[8] as well as rights in the Constitution, adopted in 1996 explicitly to '[h]eal the divisions of the past and establish a society based on

---

[3]Section 1 Employment Equity Act 55 of 1998.

[4]Statistics South Africa, (QLFS 3rd Quarter 2014) published in Department of Labour, 'Commission for Employment Equality Annual Report 2014–2015', p. 13.

[5]Constitution of the Republic of South Africa, Act 108 of 1996.

[6]Primarily the Employment Equity Act 55 of 1998 (the EEA) and the Promotion of Equality and Prevention of Unfair Discrimination Act 4 of 2000 (PEPUDA), and related legislation.

[7]In South Africa dignity is central to the interpretation of the right to equality (see for example Ackermann, L *Human Dignity: Lodestar for Equality in South Africa* (2012)), although the centrality of dignity has been questioned (see Fagan (1998), p. 220.

[8]Section 1(a) of the Constitution.

democratic values, social justice and fundamental human rights.'[9] The *equality clause* is set out in § 9 of the Constitution and provides as follows (bold my emphasis):

(1) Everyone is equal before the law and has the right to equal protection and benefit of the law.
(2) Equality includes the full and equal enjoyment of all rights and freedoms. **To promote the achievement of equality, legislative and other measures designed to protect or advance persons**, or categories of persons, disadvantaged by unfair discrimination **may be taken.**
(3) **The state may not unfairly discriminate** directly or indirectly against anyone on one or more grounds, including race, gender, sex, pregnancy, marital status, ethnic or social origin, colour, sexual orientation, age, disability, religion, conscience, belief, culture, language and birth.
(4) **No person may unfairly discriminate** directly or indirectly against anyone on one or more grounds in terms of subsection (3). National legislation must be enacted to prevent or prohibit unfair discrimination.
(5) **Discrimination on one or more of the grounds listed in subsection (3) is unfair unless it is established that the discrimination is fair.**

Curiously, the Constitution (and subsidiary legislation) formulates the right to equality as a right not to be *unfairly* discriminated against; an aspect of our equality law where we deviate, in terminology rather than substantive interpretation, from international and comparative norms in the articulation of the right.[10] The following principles have emerged from the interpretation of § 9 by the Constitutional Court:

1. The Constitutional Court embraces an egalitarian ('substantive') understanding of the concept of equality, which unequivocally extends beyond the traditional, 'formal,' approach to equality that would require only that likes be treated alike. The substantive notion of equality seeks to achieve 'equality of outcomes' by permitting special treatment (including 'affirmative action') and targeted measures to advance persons or groups that are disadvantaged by discrimination.[11] In this regard, black people, women and people with disabilities are designated as vulnerable groups for the purposes of being beneficiaries of affirmative action measures in the workplace.
2. Consequently, the *equality clause* supports a legal framework that upholds both: (a) an '*individual right*' to equal treatment; and (b) a '*collective obligation*' to combat structural inequality promoting equality through restitutionary measures such as affirmative action in the context of employment.

---

[9]See the *Preamble* of the Constitution.
[10]See generally Du Toit (2006), p. 1311.
[11]This is in terms of § 9(2) of the Constitution, interpreted in *Minister of Finance v Van Heerden* 2004 (6) SA 121 (CC); [2004] ZACC 3 and *South African Police Service v Solidarity obo Barnard* 2014 (6) SA 123 (CC).

3. Notwithstanding a *collective obligation* for the redress of systemic discrimination, the Constitutional Court has confirmed that rigid quotas, in the employment context and in relation to the distribution of economic activity more generally, are neither mandated by the Constitution, nor permissible.[12]
4. Increasingly, the 'cross-cutting categories of disadvantage'[13] and the uneven impact of discrimination resulting from the intersectionality of multiple grounds of discrimination are recognized as justification for a more nuanced analysis of equality and discrimination related disputes.[14]
5. The principle of subsidiarity requires that where there is antidiscrimination legislation in place (such legislation is required by § 9(4)), and provided that it is not in conflict with the Constitution, a complainant must utilise the provisions of the subsidiary legislation and may not rely directly on the provisions of the Constitution.[15]
6. The *equality clause* applies both vertically and horizontally and therefore binds not only the state, but also private individuals and organizations (§ 9(4)). Likewise, the subsidiary legislation in place, to the extent that it is applicable, binds both the state and private persons.
7. Differentiation on any of the grounds listed in § 9(3) is presumed to be discrimination that is unfair, and the burden is on the defendant to establish that the discrimination is fair (justified). However, where differentiation is on an unspecified ground, discrimination is the first enquiry, and unfairness must then be established. Whereas unfairness is presumed when the ground is a specified one, if discrimination is alleged on an unspecified ground, unfairness will have to be established by the complainant. 'The test of unfairness focuses primarily on the impact of the discrimination on the complainant and others in his or her situation.'[16]

---

[12]See *SAPS v Barnard* and *South African Restructuring And Insolvency Practitioners Association v Minister of Justice And Constitutional Development and Others; In Re: Concerned Insolvency Practitioners Association NPC and Others v Minister of Justice And Constitutional Development and Others* 2015 (2) SA 430 (WCC). Although, in the context of quotas for the admission of students to university see *Motala v University of Natal* 1995 (3 BCLR 374 (D).

[13]Crenshaw (1991), p. 1241 cited in *South African Restructuring and Insolvency Practitioners Association v Minister of Justice and Constitutional Development and others; Concerned Insolvency Practitioners Association NPC & others v Minister of Justice and Constitutional Development & others* 2015 (4), fn. 151.

[14]In *South African Police Service v Solidarity obo Barnard (Police and Prisons Civil Rights Union as* amicus curiae) 2014 (10) BCLR 1195 (CC) the Constitutional Court recognizes (at para [153]) the flip-side too, observing that '[p]rivilege often manifests in an individual in a multiplicity of different, intersecting and mutually constructive or destructive ways.'

[15]*Minister of Health and Another v New Clicks South Africa (Pty) Ltd & others* [2005] ZACC 14; 2006 (2) SA 311 (CC) paras [96] and [434–437]; de Vos and Freedman (2014), p. 452.

[16]*Supra.* See for example *Larbi-Odam v Members of the Executive Committee for Education (North-West Province)* 1998 (1) SA 745 (CC) involving a challenge of unfair discrimination on the basis of citizenship that was successfully instituted by foreign citizens, who were teachers, in respect of a Regulation governing the employment of teachers in permanent teaching posts: the

Establishing discrimination on an 'unlisted' or unspecified ground is therefore possible, but places a greater evidentiary burden upon the complainant. Figure 1 illustrates the core components of South Africa's Equality Law which consists of various 'enforcement regimes.'

2 Is Antidiscrimination Law Enforced?

Yes, antidiscrimination law (A-D law) is enforceable and is enforced in South Africa although more actively and more successfully in certain contexts than in others. There is no one overarching legal regime for the enforcement of A-D law in South Africa; and Fig. 1 reflects the various regulatory regimes that may be invoked in the context of equality and discrimination. The enforcement route(s) available in any particular scenario involving the right to equality will depend on the facts and also whether there is a transgression that involves a breach of the *individual right to equality* or whether the concern is more accurately described as a failure in relation to the *collective obligation* to combat structural inequality in pursuit of large scale social change or transformation. The various regulatory regimes for the enforcement of A-D law that appear in Fig. 1 may be listed as follows:

1. *The Employment Equity Act (EEA) and related law*—this is the regulatory regime that applies in the realm of employment and related economic activities;
2. *The Promotion of Equality and Prevention of Unfair Discrimination Act (PEPUDA) and related law*—this is the regulatory regime that applies in all contexts except where the EEA applies;
3. *The Common Law Regime*—in addition to having access to the regulatory regimes mentioned in 1 and 2 above, complainants who have been subjected to discrimination may, provided the requirements for liability have been met, have a (concurrent) claim in the civil courts (the High Courts) where the discriminatory act constitutes an actionable wrong in the common law, for example in terms of the law of delict (tort);
4. *Criminal Law Enforcement*—certain acts of discrimination, such as hate speech and sexual assault constitute criminal offences for which a perpetrator may be prosecuted;
5. *Public Protest*—in South Africa, the 'protest capital of the world,'[17] service delivery protests are a common occurrence, and in 2015 and 2016, the public protest phenomenon expanded in scope from being largely about informal housing and poor service delivery (the 'rebellion of the poor'),[18] and about public

---

Regulation largely prohibited the appointment of non-South African citizens to permanent teaching posts, even if the foreigners had permanent residence.

[17]It is reported that there are approximately 15 protests each day largely as a result of poor service delivery. http://www.spotnews.co.za/index.php/news/153-s-a-protest-capital-of-the-world.

[18]Alexander (2012).

corruption and employment and wages,[19] to include University student protests about the lack of transformation on campuses (#RhodesMustFall) and about the cost of higher education (#FeesMustFall).

In addition to these enforcement regimes, organizations that are compliant with the King Code of Governance for South Africa (the 'King Code') ('King IV' was released in November 2016) will be compliant with their obligations in terms of A-D law. Although the King Code has no enforcement mechanism, it is mandatory for companies that are listed on the Johannesburg Stock Exchange (JSE).

3 How Is Antidiscrimination Law Enforced?

In view of the multiple regulatory regimes available for the enforcement of A-D law, the question of *how* A-D law is enforced will be answered by briefly outlining three contexts: (1) *education*; (2) *employment* and *economic empowerment*, and (3) *housing* and *access to public accommodation*.

3.1 Antidiscrimination Law in the Context of Education

Under apartheid, black people received inferior schooling and 'the education system was used to maintain racial and gender prejudices and stereotypes, and to perpetuate inequalities'.[20] As a consequence, significant efforts to address this legacy are underway and although gains have been made, statistics show that white students still have the highest success rates in public higher education institutions (HEIs)[21] and that less than half of all instruction and research staff employed at public HEIs are black.[22]

The right to education is enshrined in § 29 of the Constitution, which provides, inter alia, that

1. Everyone has the right:

---

[19]See generally Alexander and Pfaffe (2014), pp. 204–221.

[20]Department of Basic Education *Action Plan to 2014: Towards the Realisation of Schooling 2025* (Full version, October 2011), p. 16.

[21]In public higher education institutions, the success rate for white students in 2013 was 88.2%, while the success rate for African students was 78.9%, for colour students was 81.8% and for Indian/Asian students was 84.8%. Department of Higher Education & Training *Statistics on Post-School Education and Training in South Africa: 2013* (March 2015), pp. 18–19.

[22]Department of Higher Education & Training *Statistics on Post-School Education and Training in South Africa: 2013* (March 2015), p. 20.

(a) to a basic education, including adult basic education; and
(b) to further education, which the state, through reasonable measures, must make progressively available and accessible.

The Department of Basic Education (DBE) governs all aspects of the two stages of schooling in South Africa; namely primary school (grades R to 7) and secondary school (grades 8 to 12), and also has oversight of early childhood development (ECD) centres and special needs schools. Primary and secondary schooling is provided by public schools and private (independent schools).[23] A second department, the Department of Higher Education and Training (DHET) has oversight of tertiary and vocational training which is provided by further education and training (FET) colleges and higher education (HE) institutions, as well as adult basic education and training (ABET) centres. Both DBE and DHET play a role in transforming education although neither are directly involved in enforcement.

In the context of schooling, the South African Schools Act 84 of 1996 expressly acknowledges in its preamble that 'this country requires a new national system for schools which will redress past injustices in education provision' and it sets out the framework to achieve this. To expedite remedial efforts that would begin to address systemic discrimination in the schooling system, the South African Schools Act was amended in 2007 to include specific provisions for the identification and remediation of 'underperforming schools', which are the most vulnerable public schools.

In terms of enforcement through social movements or activism in the context of access to education at school level, Equal Education,[24] a Public Benefit Organization (PBO) and a Non-Profit Organization (NPO) plays an important role. Equal Education describes itself as a 'movement of learners, parents, teachers and community members working for quality and equality in South African education through analysis and activism.'

At tertiary education level, the November 2008 publication of the Report of the Ministerial Committee on Transformation and Social Cohesion and the Elimination of Discrimination in Public Higher Education Institutions[25] signaled high levels of discomfort at the lack of substantive transformation in these institutions. Although the Committee found that 'in legal and regulatory terms, the higher education system is in a good state' it went on to conclude that 'compliance does not necessarily signify progress in substantive terms. In fact, more often than not, institutional responsiveness to compliance measures remains little more than a paper exercise

---

[23]There are approximately 25,000 ordinary public schools and 1200 independent schools in South Africa. DBE *Action Plan*, p. 12.

[24]See www.equaleducation.org.za.

[25]Ministerial Committee on Transformation in Higher Education, 'Report of the Ministerial Committee on Transformation and Social Cohesion and the Elimination of Discrimination in Public Higher Education Institutions' Final Report (30 November 2008).

with policies and plans submitted and then regularly filed away.'[26] Therefore it should come as no surprise that South African students would subsequently engage in widespread protest action.

3.2 A-D Law in the Workplace and in the Context of Economic Empowerment

The Employment Equity Act[27] 55 of 1998 (EEA) sets out to achieve substantive equality by requiring the elimination of unfair discrimination and also the implementation of affirmative action measures by designated employers. A justiciable *individual right* not to be discriminated against in any employment policy or practice (which is broadly defined and open-ended) is established by the EEA and may be enforced by the alternative dispute resolution processes in the Commission for Conciliation, Mediation and Arbitration (CCMA) and/or by litigation in the Labour Court, depending on the facts. In addition, designated employers are required to implement affirmative action measures—an obligation that does not create an 'individual right' to affirmative action but which has an enforcement mechanism involving the Department of Labour Inspectors or the Director-General of the Department of Labour that may be invoked in cases of non-compliance.

In addition to the more conventional 'command-and-control' obligations and justiciable A-D law, voluntary mechanisms to promote black economic empowerment are enabled by the Broad-Based Black Economic Empowerment Act[28] (BBBEE Act). The objective of the BBBEE Act is to increase economic participation of black people, in particular black women, largely through incentivising skills development and the ownership and control of businesses. Businesses that score high on an empowerment scorecard are rewarded by qualifying for commercial contracts with the State.

3.3 A-D Law in the Broader Social Context Including Access to Housing and Other Public Accommodation

Outside of the employment relationship, discrimination disputes may be resolved in terms of the provisions of the Promotion of Equality and Prevention of Unfair Discrimination Act (PEPUDA). The objectives of PEPUDA are numerous and include the prohibition of unfair discrimination and also 'the advocacy of hatred,

---

[26]Report of the Ministerial Committee on Transformation and Social Cohesion, p. 40.

[27]Other applicable legislation includes the Labour Relations Act 66 of 1995 which prohibits automatically unfair dismissals, which includes 'discriminatory' dismissals and unfair labour practices.

[28]Act 53 of 2003.

based on race, ethnicity, gender or religion, that constitutes incitement to cause harm'.[29] PEPUDA provides procedures and remedies for breaches of the right to equality that manifest as discrimination, hate speech or harassment, and seeks also to 'educate the public and raise public awareness on the importance of promoting equality and overcoming unfair discrimination, hate speech and harassment.'[30]

PEPUDA provides the legislative framework for the equality courts, which are mandated to 'hold an inquiry'[31] when proceedings are instituted for discrimination, hate speech or harassment, and to make an appropriate order in the circumstances. Prior to hearing the matter however, the presiding officer must 'decide whether the matter is to be heard in the equality court or whether it should be referred to another appropriate institution, body, court, tribunal or other forum.'[32]

In a Schedule to PEPUDA, the following 'unfair practices' involving 'Housing, accommodation, land and property' are listed:

(a) Arbitrary eviction of persons on one or more of the prohibited grounds.
(b) 'Red-lining' on the grounds or race and social status.
(c) Unfair discrimination in the provision of housing bonds, loans or financial assistance on the basis of race, gender or other prohibited grounds.
(d) Failing to reasonably accommodate the special needs of the elderly.

However, enforcement in the context of rental housing and access to rental housing disputes is not limited to the provisions in PEPUDA. In this regard the Rental Housing Act 50 of 1999 which regulates the landlord tenant relationship and establishes the Rental Housing Tribunal to mediate disputes between the parties. § 4 (1) of the Rental Housing Act provides that: 'In advertising a dwelling for purposes of leasing it, or in negotiating a lease with a prospective tenant, or during the term of a lease, a landlord may not unfairly discriminate against such prospective tenant or tenants, or the members of such tenant's household or the visitors of such tenant, on one or more grounds, including race, gender, sex, pregnancy, marital status, sexual orientation, ethnic or social origin, colour, age, disability, religion, conscience, belief, culture, language and birth.'

Anyone who fails to comply with § 4 is guilty of an offence and liable on conviction to a fine or imprisonment not exceeding 2 years.[33]

---

[29] Section 1 of PEPUDA.
[30] Section 1(e) of PEPUDA.
[31] This is significant given the adversarial nature of the South African legal system.
[32] Section 20(3)(a) of PEPUDA.
[33] Section 16 of the Rental Housing Act.

4 Who Enforces Antidiscrimination Law?

Enforcement of A-D law is achieved through the actions of (1) public institutions and processes, (2) judicial or quasi-judicial bodies, and (3) private persons and organizations (including voluntary compliance and corporate governance, see also Fig. 1).

4.1 Public Institutions and Processes Involved in Enforcing Antidiscrimination Law

4.1.1 Chapter 9 Institutions

Various public institutions, the so-called 'Chapter 9 institutions,' are established by the Constitution and mandated to perform functions intended to strengthen the protection of human rights and develop a human rights culture in South Africa. These institutions include, among others: (1) the *public protector*,[34] empowered to investigate complaints and to endeavour to resolve any dispute by mediation, conciliation or negotiation, or by advising a complainant regarding appropriate remedies or any other means;[35] (2) the *South African Human Rights Commission*, empowered, inter alia, 'to investigate any alleged violation of fundamental rights and to assist any person adversely affected thereby to secure redress,'[36] and specifically to conduct any investigation and try to resolve any dispute or rectify an act or omission arising in the context of a violation of a fundamental right by mediation, conciliation or negotiation,[37] (3) the *Commission for the Promotion and Protection of the Rights of Cultural, Religious and Linguistics Communities*[38] and (4) the *Commission for Gender Equality (CGE)*,[39] mandated to fulfill information and education programs, evaluate law, and investigate any gender-related issues or complaints received endeavouring to resolve the dispute or rectify any act or omission by mediation, conciliation or negotiation.

---

[34]See also the Public Protector Act 23 of 1994. See generally http://www.publicprotector.org.

[35]Section 6(4) of the Public Protector Act; see generally § 6 on the powers of the Public Protector.

[36]*Preamble*, Human Rights Commission Act 54 of 1994. See generally http://www.sahrc.org.za/home.

[37]Section 9 of the Human Rights Commission Act.

[38]See generally the Commission for the Promotion and Protection of the Rights of Cultural, Religious and Linguistic Communities Act of 2002; and http://www.crlcommission.org.za/.

[39]Commission on Gender Equality Act 39 of 1996; and see http://cge.org.za/.

4.1.2 Education

In the context of education, the processes and ongoing functions of the Department of Basic Education (DBE) and the Department of Higher Education (DHET), although not traditional 'law enforcement agencies,' are intended to have the general effect of transforming South African society. A 2007 amendment[40] to the South African Schools Act is intended to expedite remedial efforts by requiring provincial education departments to identify 'underperforming schools,' to report annually to the minister of basic education on these schools, and to require the underperforming school to provide the head of department with a plan for correcting the underperformance with reasonable steps, and to assist the school in addressing the underperformance.[41]

At tertiary level, the DHET, although it also has no specific enforcement mechanism, takes on the role of monitoring and reporting on the success or otherwise of the policies and practices within higher education institutions that are intended to transform these spaces and making recommendations in this regard.[42]

4.1.3 Employment and Economic Opportunities

The following public institutions, among others, play a role in influencing compliance with the provisions of the EEA:

1. The Employment Conditions Commission[43] (the ECC), established by the Basic Conditions of Employment Act 77 of 1997 (BCEA) largely plays a research, monitoring and advisory role rather than an enforcement role, and also has the power to advise on measures that should be taken to address a disproportionate wage gap.[44]
2. The labour inspectors,[45] also established by the BCEA, are employees in the public service appointed to 'promote, monitor and enforce compliance with an employment law.'[46] The EEA empowers a labour inspector, among other things, to issue a compliance order for non-compliance with the EEAs affirmative action obligations.

---

[40] Act 31 of 2007.

[41] Section 58B (3)-(4).

[42] See for example the Ministerial Committee on Transformation in Higher Education, 'Report of the Ministerial Committee on Transformation and Social Cohesion and the Elimination of Discrimination in Public Higher Education Institutions' Final Report (30 November 2008); and the Department of Higher Education & Training *Statistics on Post-School Education and Training in South Africa: 2013* (March 2015).

[43] The ECC is established by Chapter 9 of the BCEA.

[44] Section 27 of the EEA.

[45] Section 63 of the BCEA.

[46] Section 64(1) of the BCEA.

3. The Commission for Employment Equity (the CEE),[47] established by the EEA, plays a role in researching and reporting equity norms and benchmarks and in the determination of policy and codes of good practice and is also empowered to 'make awards recognizing achievements of employers in furthering the purposes of the Act.'[48]
4. The EEA incentivises compliance by providing that in order to conclude an agreement with the state to supply goods or services, or for the letting and hiring of anything, an employer must provide a certificate as evidence of compliance with the provisions of the EEA.[49]

More broadly, an additional public institution in the context of economic transformation is the newly established BBBEE Commission, whose role it is to oversee adherence with the BBBEE Act and to receive and investigate (in response to a complaint or of its own initiative) any matter concerning BBBEE.[50]

4.2 Judicial Processes (Courts and Tribunals) Enforcing Antidiscrimination Law

The civil law courts have largely retained their inherent jurisdiction in the case of discriminatory practices where the facts are such that a common law claim arises in the circumstances. For example, sexual harassment in the workplace, depending on the facts, may give rise to either a claim under the EEA or a civil law claim in delict.[51]

Where the complainant is an employee who alleges breach of the individual right to equality, the complainant may refer the discrimination to the CCMA for conciliation. In the event that conciliation fails, the dispute may be referred either to the Labour Court for adjudication or, in certain circumstances, to the CCMA for arbitration.[52] On the other hand, where the complaint involves a failure on the part of the employer to implement affirmative action measures, there is no individual remedy *per se* as a 'fundamental feature of the EEA, ... [is] its underlying policy decision that affirmative action is to be collective in nature, that it is to be participating and programmatic, and that it is to be essential self-regulatory. There are targets, there are categories, there are dates and there are numbers. That is its working vocabulary. Its antithesis is an ad hoc adjudication of the kind that the

---

[47]The CEE is established by Chapter 4 of the EEA.

[48]Section 30(2) of the EEA. In 2015 the Department of Labour inaugurated the EE Awards System to recognize employers that have embraced the spirit of Employment Equity.

[49]Section 53 of the EEA.

[50]The functions of the Commission are set out in § 13F of the Act.

[51]See for example *Media 24 Ltd & Another v Grobler* 2005(6) SA 328 (SCA).

[52]Section 10 of the EEA.

applicant seeks to enforce in this matter, on the basis that there is an independent and individual right to affirmative action. It is an approach that the legislature has eschewed.'[53]

4.3 The Triggering of Judicial Enforcement

In the absence of voluntary compliance with the provisions of antidiscrimination law, enforcement may be triggered either by the victim(s) of the alleged discrimination or by public or private actors acting on their behalf. Although the law expressly provides that class action proceedings may be instituted as a method of enforcement in South Africa,[54] class actions were not a feature of our common law[55] and remain a novel and largely untested method of enforcement of antidiscrimination law.

In terms of PEPUDA, the institution of proceedings in terms of the Act may be triggered by: (1) any person acting in their own interest; (2) any person acting on behalf of another person who cannot act in their own name; (3) any person acting as a member of, or in the interests of a group or class of persons; (4) any person acting in the public interest; (5) any association acting in the interests of its members; and (6) the South African Human Rights Commission or the Commission for Gender Equality.

Various court cases in which the proceedings were instituted by Equal Education (EE)[56] or in which EE joined in a case as a 'friend of the Court' provide interesting examples of the enforcement of A-D law through social activism. Equal Education has instituted court proceedings in numerous matters, including cases involving discrimination against Rastafarian learners by prohibiting the wearing of dreadlocks as a hairstyle, discrimination against pregnant learners, and around the question of who has final decision making power about the admission of learners to public schools.

---

[53]Tip AJ para [68] in *Dudley v City of Cape Town* (2004) 25 ILJ 305 (LC).

[54]Section 38 of the Constitution provides for the enforcement of rights and indicates that the persons who may approach a court include 'anyone acting as a member of, or in the interest of, a group or class of persons.' See *Trustees for the time being of Children's Resource Centre Trust and Others v Pioneer Food (Pty) Ltd and others* 2013 (2) SA 213 (SCA) for a discussion of the requirements for the commencement of a class action.

[55]See the South African Law Commission, Project 88: The Recognition of Class Actions and Public Interest Actions in South African Law' Report, August 1998.

[56]See https://www.equaleducation.org.za/campaigns/legal for more detail.

5 Who Benefits from the Enforcement of Antidiscrimination Law?

Three categories of 'beneficiary' of antidiscrimination law are discussed in this section: (a) the *individual* complainant who has been unfairly discriminated against and who, together with proximate individuals, benefits from enforcement; (b) the *designated groups* that are beneficiaries of affirmative action measures; and (c) the *individual* complainant who is in a position of relative *privilege* and who, notwithstanding such privilege, benefits from enforcement.

In category (a), the efficient and effective enforcement of antidiscrimination law will benefit *individual complainants* who are the victims of discriminatory practices, for example the victims of sexist or racist practices in the workplace. Interventions that have the effect of compensating such victims and eliminating such practices will benefit these individuals and are also likely to benefit those in proximate relations to the victims who, but for the enforcement of antidiscrimination law, would also have been victims of such practices. Two case examples demonstrate this:

- *Ekhamanzi Springs (Pty) Ltd v Mnomiya* (2014) 35 ILJ 2388 (LAC). In this case, a pregnant employee was denied access to the workplace by the employer's landlord (a church mission) on the basis of a code of conduct that prohibits 'amorous relationships between any two persons outside of marriage.' The Labour Appeal Court concluded that the employer's failure to intervene in its landlord's discriminatory practice of denying the pregnant employee access to the workplace amounts to a repudiation of the employment contract on the basis of pregnancy and marital status, and that this was unfair and the employee had therefore established an 'automatically' (discriminatory) unfair dismissal and was entitled to compensation.

    This outcome has benefited not only the *individual* complainant, but will also likely have the effect of preventing future discriminatory employment practices of a similar nature from occurring.
- *Biggar v City of Johannesburg, Emergency Management Services* [2011] 6 BLLR 577 (LC). In this case a black employee who lived in a residential complex provided by the employer was subjected to egregious racial harassment perpetrated against him and his family by white colleagues and their families. The Labour Court found that the employer had failed to take action to prevent or alleviate the discriminatory conduct and tailored a remedy that would compensate the employee but would also require the employer in the future to investigate any new complaints that may arise and to take disciplinary action against perpetrators in the future. Thus, the *individual* complainant and other employees, current or future, in a similar position to the complainant, are likely to benefit from the enforcement in favour of the *individual* complainant.

Category (b) is the *designated groups* that are beneficiaries of affirmative action measures. For the purposes of the EEA, these designated groups are defined as citizens of South Africa by birth or, in some instances, by naturalization who are suitably qualified 'black people, women and people with disabilities.' Chapter III of the EEA outlines the *collective obligation* to implement such affirmative action measures. Change is slow, but recent trend analysis in terms of race, gender and disability for the top four occupational levels (top management, senior management, professionally qualified and skilled technical levels), although still reflecting a 'white male' dominance at the top end, does reflect some gradual improvement in certain areas of representativity of the designated grounds between 2010 and 2014. Still, there is much room for improvement.[57]

Category (c) is the *individual* complainant who is in a position of relative *privilege* and who benefits from enforcement. Because there is no 'right to affirmative action'[58] individuals from the designated groups cannot rely on the collective obligation to implement affirmative action. For example, in *Minister of Safety and Security v Govender* (2011) 32 *ILJ* 1145 (LC), Govender who had been overlooked for promotion on three occasions and would have been promoted if the employment equity plan was properly implemented, was without a remedy in the Labour Court in view of the *Dudley* decision.[59] However, an 'overlooked', privileged individual may have a remedy in the event of the unlawful implementation of affirmative action. As Rycroft indicates: 'It is unavoidable to comment that in the 40-odd cases that have been accessed, the vast majority of litigants are white males'. The implications of this are that adjudicators are generally interpreting the law with one sort of applicant in mind and acting, by and large, to protect this group.[60]

6 Who Is Harmed by the Enforcement of Antidiscrimination Law?

Unfortunately, there are 'casualties' that may result from the enforcement of antidiscrimination law. Even those who have potentially benefitted from the law may experience harm. For example, *designated groups* that are beneficiaries of affirmative action measures may be vulnerable to harm as a result of being subjected to, or feeling subjected to, and labelled by, the so-called 'affirmative action' stigma that gives rise to an inference of incompetence contrary to a working environment in which employees feel that individual merit is recognized.[61] At the same time,

---

[57] See generally the trend analysis in the Department of Labour 'Commission for Employment Equity Annual Report 2014–2015' (2015).
[58] *Dudley v City of Cape Town* (2008) ILJ 2685 (LAC).
[59] See further the discussion in Fergus and Collier (2014), pp. 489–492.
[60] Rycroft (1999), p. 1415. Original footnotes omitted.
[61] See for example Op't Hoog et al. (2010), pp. 61–83.

members from the non-designated groups, according to certain studies, are left feeling like 'second-class citizens.'[62]

The emphasis on racial representation (a 'race-based' model of affirmative action) and the emergence of complexities around a 'hierarchy' of disadvantage[63] and the complexities of provincial and national demographic profiles[64] generates suspicion and controversy around the implementation of affirmative action in the workplace that has the potential to divide the workforce and fuel racial tensions in South Africa. Suggestions for less complex 'socio-economic' models of affirmative action[65] do surface from time to time, however the emphasis on race as the foundation for past discriminatory practices remains a compelling argument for retaining the status quo for the time being.

Further harm is caused by the problem of mechanical or 'ritual' compliance.[66] A cautionary observation by the Labour Court judgment in *Director-General, Department of Labour v Win-Cool Industrial Enterprise (Pty) Ltd* (2007) 28 ILJ 1774 (LC) states that '[m]echanical compliance with the prescribed processes is not genuine compliance with the letter and spirit of the EEA. Compliance is not an end in itself. The employer must systematically develop the workforce out of a life of disadvantage. Disadvantage of all kinds is targeted by the EEA.'[67]

7 What Remedies Are Provided by the Enforcement of Antidiscrimination Law?

The provisions of the antidiscrimination law regulatory framework give extensive scope to adjudicators to craft innovative remedies as may be required by the circumstances. For example, where a discrimination dispute has been determined by the equality court, § 21(2) of PEPUDA empowers the equality court to make an appropriate order including:

(a) an interim order;
(b) a declaratory order;
(c) an order making a settlement between the parties to the proceedings an order of court;

---

[62]According to Dirk Hermann, a 2004 study by Prof du Toit of the University of Stellenbosch reveals that 71.4% of non-designated groups feel this way. Herman (2013), p. 114.

[63]See for example *South African Police Service v Solidarity obo Barnard* 2014 (6) SA 123 (CC).

[64]See *Solidarity and Others v Department of Correctional Services and Others* 2015 (4) SA 277 (LAC).

[65]See for example Dirk Herman *Affirmative Tears*.

[66]On the danger of pure 'mechanical' or 'ritual' compliance, see for example Haines (2011) cited in Fergus and Collier (2014), p. 505.

[67]At para [108].

(d) an order for the payment of any damages in respect of any proven financial loss, including future loss, or in respect of impairment of dignity, pain and suffering or emotional and psychological suffering, as a result of this unfair discrimination, hate speech or harassment in question;
(e) [...] an order for payment of damages in the form of an award to an appropriate body or organization;
(f) an order restraining unfair discriminatory practices or directing that specific steps be taken to stop the discrimination [...];
(g) an order to make specific opportunities and privileges unfairly denied in the circumstances, available to the complainant in question;
(h) an order for the implementation of special measures to address the unfair discrimination [...];
(i) an order directing the reasonable accommodation of a group or class of persons by the respondent;
(j) an order that an unconditional apology be made;
(k) an order requiring the respondent to undergo an audit of policies or practices as determined by the court;
(l) an appropriate order of a deterrent nature, including the recommendation to the appropriate authority, to suspend or revoke the licence of a person;
(m) a directive requiring the respondent to make regular progress reports to the court or to the relevant constitutional institution regarding the implementation of the court's order;
(n) an order directing the clerk of the equality court to submit the matter to the Director of Public Prosecutions [...] for the possible institution of criminal proceedings in terms of the common law or relevant legislation;
(o) an appropriate order of costs against any party to the proceedings;
(p) an order to comply with any provisions of the Act.

In addition, § 21(4) of PEPUDA provides that, particularly if the unfair discrimination is persistent or systemic, the equality court may refer the matter to any relevant constitutional institution to investigate further; or may refer the dispute to such institution, or other appropriate body, for mediation, conciliation or negotiation (ADR mechanisms).

In the context of workplace-based discrimination, the EEA provides a similarly extensive range of remedies that may be awarded by the Labour Court. The powers of the Labour Court are set out in § 50 of the EEA. In addition, the EEA in Schedule 1 establishes the maximum permissible fines (that were increased by amendment in 2013) that may be imposed by the Labour Court for the contravention of certain provisions of EEA by employers.

8 Who Supports the Enforcement of Antidiscrimination Law?

The enforcement of antidiscrimination law is supported by both public institutions and by private organizations that recognize the intrinsic value of diversity and representativity. As Rycroft documents:

> Even before the Employment Equity Act, it had become an accepted corporate norm that there should be an affirmative action policy; the earlier debates on the ideology, difficulties and merits of these policies had given way to a widely held perception that it was now an *economic* imperative for an institution or corporation to have a functioning and effective affirmative action policy. [...] Moral imperatives may well fuel the introduction of such policies, but it is economic imperatives which drive it.[68]

In terms of the public institutions supporting the enforcement of A-D law, the so-called 'Chapter 9 institutions'[69] discussed above play an important role. In addition to these institutions, § 32 of PEPUDA establishes an Equality Review Committee, an advisory committee on equality laws, while the above-mentioned Employment Conditions Commission and Employment Equity Commission also play supporting roles in the enforcement of equality law in the employment context.

§ 20(9) of PEPUDA also provides that 'the State and constitutional institutions must, as far as reasonably possible, assist any person wishing to institute proceedings in terms of or under this Act, amongst others, by ensuring that the person is directed to the appropriate functionary in order to take the necessary action in the furtherance of the matter in question.'

In the context of gender equality, institutions collectively referred to as the National Gender Machinery (NGM)[70] exist at national and provincial levels and play a role in supporting the enforcement of antidiscrimination law. In addition, numerous NGOs, Civic organizations and think-tanks monitor the enforcement of the antidiscrimination laws in South Africa and constitute a network of support structures girding efforts to achieve gender equality in all sectors of the society.

---

[68]Rycroft (1999), p. 1413. Original footnotes omitted.

[69]These include (1) the public protector; (2) the South African Human Rights Commission; (3) the Commission for the Promotion and Protection of the Rights of Cultural, Religious and Linguistics Communities; (4) and the Commission for Gender Equality.

[70]See African Development Bank 'South Africa: The National Gender Machinery, Gender Mainstreaming and the Fight against Gender Based Violence' (September 2009).

9 Who Opposes the Enforcement of Antidiscrimination Law?

There is general consensus on the desirability of an *individual right to equality* and a prohibition against unfair discrimination and therefore only muted, if any, opposition in this regard. There is less agreement, however, when it comes to South Africa's regulatory framework for black economic empowerment[71] and the idea of an enforceable *collective obligation* to implement a race-based model of affirmative action.[72] Brassey gives voice to this opposition and he explains that at the root of his opposition is the fact that enactment of the EEA is a 'watershed' moment 'signifying the perpetuation of precisely the institutionalized race consciousness that has already proved so divisive and destructive in our country.'[73] The requirement for racial classification in order to implement affirmative action is a matter that gives rise to much debate in South Africa.[74]

In 2015, the trade union Solidarity drafted a complaint about affirmative action for submission as a shadow report to the United Nations Committee on the Elimination of All Forms of Racial Discrimination (CERD).[75] Solidarity claims that the sole focus on race representivity in South Africa extends beyond the affirmative action measures permitted by international law and that '[t]he problem [of preferment of black people] permeates every facet of the regulatory framework in South Africa' and 'is nothing less than institutionalized racism.'[76]

10 How Broad Is the Coverage of Antidiscrimination Law?

Antidiscrimination law coverage in South Africa is both extensive and open-ended. The right to equality is enforceable against the state (vertical application) and against private individuals and organizations (horizontal application). By way of example,

---

[71] See for example Dr. Anthea Jeffery *BEE: Helping or Hurting* (2014).

[72] See for example Dr. Herman (2013).

[73] Brassey (1998), p. 1359.

[74] For a critique of racial classification and race-based affirmative action see Benatar (2008), p. 274.

[75] Solidarity Trade Union's Centre for Fair Labour Practices 'Constructing a future based on race: 'racial representivity' through affirmative action and broad-based black economic empowerment in South Africa' Response to the Fourth to Eighth Periodic Reports of the Republic of South Africa to the Committee on the Elimination of Racial Discrimination under article 9 of the Convention on the Elimination of All Forms of Racial Discrimination. Accessed online at https://solidariteit.co.za/wp-content/uploads/2015/05/Solidariteit-VN-Skaduverslag-Mei-2015.pdf.

[76] Solidarity 'Constructing a future based on race', p. 2.

the prohibition against discrimination on the basis of sexual orientation binds both the State[77] and private organizations, including the church.[78]

A-D law is open-ended in the sense that § 9 of the Constitution prohibits unfair discrimination on *any* ground *including* the specific grounds that are listed in the section.[79] Similar provisions appear in PEPUDA and the EEA. Section 6 of the EEA provides that '[n]o person may unfairly discriminate, directly or indirectly, against an employee, in any *employment policy or practice*, on one or more grounds, including race, gender, sex, pregnancy, marital status, family responsibility, ethnic or social origin, colour, sexual orientation, age, disability, religion, HIV status, conscience, belief, political opinion, culture, language, birth or on any other arbitrary ground.'

There are 19 listed grounds, to which is added 'any other arbitrary ground' and *employment policy and practice* is broadly defined and open-ended.[80] The EEA expressly provides however that it is not unfair discrimination to implement lawful affirmative action measures or to 'distinguish, exclude or prefer any person on the basis of an inherent requirement of a job.'[81]

In PEPUDA, in addition to a *general* prohibition of unfair discrimination;[82] unfair discrimination on the grounds of race (§ 7); gender (§ 8); and disability (§ 9) is expressly prohibited and elaborated provisions are provided and the Act requires that special consideration be given to discrimination on the grounds of HIV/AIDS status; socio-economic status; nationality; family responsibility; and family status (s 34). PEPUDA prohibits hate speech (§ 10); harassment (§ 11); and the dissemination and publication of information that unfairly discriminates (§ 12).

---

[77]See *Satchwell v President of the Republic of South Africa and Another* (CCT48/02) [2003] ZACC 2; 2003 (4) SA 266 (CC) in which government regulations that conferred certain benefits upon the spouses of judges but not on the permanent same-sex life partners of judges was declared unconstitutional.

[78]See *Strydom v Nederduitse Gereformeerde Gemeente Moreleta Park* (2009) 30 ILJ 868 (EqC) where the equality court ordered compensation and an apology to a complainant who had been working as an independent contractor teaching music to students and whose contract was terminated by the church on the ground of his sexual orientation.

[79]However, in instances where the ground of discrimination is not listed, the onus to prove the unfair discrimination lies with the applicant. On the burden of proof generally see *Harksen v. Lane* [1997] ZACC 12; 1998 (1) SA 300 (CC).

[80]Section 1 of the EEA.

[81]Section 6(2) of the EEA.

[82]Section 6 of PEPUDA.

11 Does the Enforcement of Antidiscrimination Law Vary According to the Ground of Discrimination?

The enforcement of A-D law is context specific and will depend on the facts of the case and the ground of discrimination. Furthermore, the burden of proof that must be discharged in an A-D dispute will vary depending on the facts and the ground of discrimination (i.e. whether it is a specified/listed or unspecified/unlisted/arbitrary ground). In this regard, the basic principles regarding the burden of proof and the stages of enquiry (set out in the applicable statutes)[83] are worth noting. The various stages are comprehensively explained in *Harksen v Lane NO & Others* 1998 (1) SA 300 (CC) at para [54] as follows:

> ... it may be as well to tabulate the stages of enquiry which become necessary where an attack is made on a provision in reliance on section 8 of the interim Constitution [now § 9 of the final Constitution]. They are (bold my emphasis):
>
> (a) Does the provision **differentiate** [stage 1] between people or categories of people? If so, does the differentiation bear a **rational connection to a legitimate** government **purpose**? If it does not then there is a violation of section 8(1) [now § 9(1)]. **Even if it does bear a rational connection, it might nevertheless amount to discrimination.**
> (b) Does the differentiation amount to unfair discrimination? This requires a two stage analysis:
>
>   (b)(i) Firstly, does the differentiation amount to "**discrimination**" [stage 2]? If it is on a **specified ground**, then discrimination will have been established. **If it is not on a specified ground**, then whether or not there is discrimination will depend upon whether, objectively, the ground is based on attributes and characteristics which have the **potential to impair the fundamental human dignity** of persons as human beings or to affect them adversely in a comparably serious manner.
>
>   (b)(ii) If the differentiation amounts to "discrimination", does it amount to "**unfair** [stage 3] discrimination"? If it has been found to have been on a **specified ground**, then unfairness will be presumed. If on an **unspecified ground,** unfairness will have to be established by the complainant. The test of unfairness focuses primarily on the **impact of the discrimination on the complainant and others in his or her situation.**
>
>   If, at the end of this stage of the enquiry, the differentiation is found not to be unfair, then there will be no violation of section 8(2).
> (c) If the discrimination is found to be unfair then a determination will have to be made as to whether the provision can be **justified** [stage 4] . . . .

Although *Harksen v Lane* involved an allegation that a certain legislative provision was discriminatory (i.e. vertical application involving the State), the basic principles may be adjusted for horizontal application.

Additional points of variation in enforcement include the fact that certain (but not all) grounds of discrimination may give rise to criminal as well as civil enforcement. Enforcement may also be asymmetrical depending on whether or not the ground relied upon by the complainant in fact placed the complainant in a vulnerable group

---

[83] Section 11 of the EEA and chapter 3 of PEPUDA.

or in a more powerful, dominant position.[84] Where it is alleged that the discrimination is indirect, the complainant may be under a greater burden to discharge his or her burden of proof.

12 What Is the Relationship Between the Enforcement of Antidiscrimination Law and the Quest for Equality on Both an Individual and Systemic Level?

Although progressive and extensive in scope, South Africa's antidiscrimination laws have had limited effect in transforming the lived experience of the many South Africans who remain poor. Income inequality remains pervasive and continues to undermine the achievement of social justice in South Africa. Even in contexts (like employment) where a comprehensive enforcement regime enabled by the EEA is in force, there is evidence of the limited impact of the law. For example, notwithstanding their inclusion in statutory protection, it is reported that 'lesbian, gay, bisexual, transgendered, queer and intersex people ... face discrimination and harassment in the workplace.'[85] More generally, there are high levels of workplace hostility and bullying reported for South Africa.[86] The successive Annual Reports of the Commission of Employment Equity (CEE) reveal high levels of frustration with the limited extent to which South Africa's legal system is capable of delivering on the constitutional promise of social justice.

However, the burden to transform South Africa's unequal society does not lie solely with the equality law framework. As Hepple points out, '[t]he law cannot be expected to remove the power that privileged elites exercise over disadvantaged groups, "but it can help to direct that power into legitimate procedures which recognize their interests."'[87]

---

[84]This is illustrated by the (controversial) Constitutional Court decisions in the *Barnard* case and in *President of the Republic of South Africa v Hugo* 1997 (4) SA 1 (CC) in which the court maintained that it was not unfair discrimination to exercise the power of pardon in relation to a category of female prisoner (those with minor children under the age of 12 years) and to omit to do so in the case of male prisoners in the same category. See also *Co-operative Worker Association v Petroleum Oil & Gas Co-operative of SA* [2007] 1 BLLR 55 (LC).

[85]United Nations Development Programme (UNDP) (2015), p. 38.

[86]Ibid.

[87]Hepple (2014), p. 228. Hepple points out (at pp. 227–228) the two 'reasons why the cycle of disadvantage and social exclusion cannot be remedied solely by legislation relating to status equality', namely, that 'Law is both too *specific* and too *selective* in its choice of the causes in the "cycle of disadvantage" to be capable, in itself, of delivering real substantive equal rights.'

13 Is the Enforcement of Antidiscrimination Law Regarded As Different from the Enforcement of Other Laws?

In some respects, the enforcement of antidiscrimination law that protects the *individual right to equality* aligns with the prevailing enforcement mechanisms of similar (human rights) laws providing an adjudicative route involving an individual right.

For example, in the employment context, an employee who resigns because the employer has discriminated against the employee and has made continued employment intolerable for the employee, may have an enforceable claim both in terms of the right not to be unfairly dismissed (a claim in terms of the Labour Relations Act) and a claim in terms of the right not to be discriminated against (a claim in terms of the Employment Equity Act). Although the requirements that need to be proved in each claim may differ, the claims will be based on the same facts and, in both cases, the employee will be entitled to bring the claim before the CCMA and/or the Labour Court.

Where enforcement of A-D law does differ from the enforcement of other laws is the extent to which the relevant tribunal (for example the CCMA and the Equality Court) is empowered to adopt a more inquisitorial role than is traditionally permitted by the common law courts, although there are limits to this. Adjudicators of A-D disputes are also mandated to craft awards and orders that will not merely punish perpetrators but will also contribute toward the achievement of transformed spaces.

The role of social movements, public institutions and administrative agencies also play a role in differentiating the enforcement of A-D law from the enforcement of other laws. Focusing in particular on public enforcement, Shavell makes an interesting distinction between law enforcement that is achieved through *specific enforcement effort* and enforcement that is achieved through *general enforcement effort*[88] that perhaps deserves further reflection in the context of A-D law. Enforcement is by *specific effort* if it involves 'activity devoted to apprehending and penalizing a *single* type of harmful act identified by its degree of harmfulness, among its other characteristics.'[89] On the other hand, '*general* enforcement effort is activity affecting the likelihood of apprehension of individuals who have committed any of a *range* of harmful acts [...].' Whenever an enforcement agent's activity involves monitoring that naturally allows him to detect different types of violators, or violators who do different amounts of harm, enforcement activity is what is called here general.[90]

---

[88] Shavell (1991), pp. 1088–1108.
[89] Shavell (1991), p. 1088.
[90] Shavell (1991), p. 1089.

14 What Does the Enforcement of Antidiscrimination Law Reveal About the Nature of Your Legal System or About the Enforcement of Laws in Your Legal System?

South Africa is a fledgling democracy with a legal system in transition from an oppressive to a transformative system, and the enforcement of A-D law should be understood within this context. Changing South Africa's legal culture is a Herculean task.[91] In addition to this, as Hepple advises, '[n]o one should pretend that all inequality can be remedied by law.'[92]

What is concerning in the South African context is the slow pace of transformative change in the social and economic dimensions of our lives. A-D law has not (yet) achieved its goal of transforming 'the hearts and minds' and the lived experience of all. Even where there is commitment and, at least, 'paper' compliance, there is a groundswell of dissatisfaction with the extremes of inequality experienced in South Africa. A striking example of a context in which there is wide-spread compliance with the law, at least with the letter of the law, but where the effectiveness and efficiency of the law remains elusive is in higher education.[93] As a result, a tipping point was reached in 2015 when frustration and anger with the slow pace of transformation in higher education institutions boiled over into protest action across the country. The national student protest movements, #RhodesMustFall and #FeesMustFall waged campaigns not only for transformation in all aspects of higher education and against the rising cost of tertiary education, but also for the rights of outsourced workers employed in higher education institutions. In essence, movement toward a more equal reality ('enforcement') was achieved, not through sustained dialogue, sensitization and proactive and incremental moves toward a more just and equal environment, but rather through confrontational public protest, often involving the threat or use of violence. Violence and intimidation are used as tools in the struggle to dismantle the structural inequality that is preventing South African society from achieving freedom.

---

[91]See Klare (2008), pp. 146–188 and, for a more recent account of transformative law in the context of PEPUDA, and proposals for reform in this regard, see Kok (2008), pp. 445–471.

[92]Hepple (2014), p. 229.

[93]Ministerial Committee on Transformation in Higher Education, 'Report of the Ministerial Committee on Transformation and Social Cohesion and the Elimination of Discrimination in Public Higher Education Institutions' Final Report (30 November 2008).

15 Conclusion

Antidiscrimination law in South Africa is unequivocally ambitious and, at its core, seeks to transform South African society.[94] Although the state of inequality and racial tension in South Africa suggests that our equality law has failed in this regard, it should be borne in mind that all law has its limitations, particularly antidiscrimination law. More importantly, democracy in South Africa, although 20 years in the making, is a mere adolescent struggling to come to terms with an oppressive and racially divisive history.

Acknowledgement I would like to thank Ms. Abigail Osiki for her assistance in researching aspects of this report.

References

Alexander P (2012) The South African Police Service's crown management statistics show that South Africa really is the protest capital of the world. Mail and Guardian, 13 Apr 2012. http://mg.co.za/article/2012-04-13-a-massive-rebellion-of-the-poor

Alexander P, Pfaffe P (2014) Social relationships to the means and ends of protest in South Africa's ongoing rebellion of the poor: the Balfour insurrections. Soc Mov Stud 13(2):204–221

Benatar D (2008) Justice, diversity and racial preference: a critique of affirmative action. S Afr Law J 125:274

Brassey M (1998) The employment equity act: bad for employment and bad for equity. Ind Law J 19:1359

Crenshaw K (1991) Mapping the margins: intersectionality, identity politics, and violence against women of color. Stanf Law Rev 43:1241

de Vos P, Freedman W (eds) (2014) South African constitutional law in context. Oxford University Press, Oxford, p 452

Du Toit D (2006) The evolution of the concept of "Unfair Discrimination" in South African labour law. Ind Law J 27:1311

Fagan A (1998) Dignity and unfair discrimination: a value misplaced and a right misunderstood. S Afr J Human Rights 14:220

Fergus E, Collier D (2014) Race and gender equality at work: the role of the judiciary in promoting workplace transformation. S Afr J Human Rights 30:484

Haines F (2011) The paradox of regulation: what regulation can achieve and what it cannot. Edward Elgar, Cheltenham

Hepple B (2014) Equality: the legal framework, 2nd edn. Hart, p 228

Herman D (2013) Affirmative tears: why representivity does not equal equality. Kraal Uitgewers, Pretoria, p 114

Klare K (2008) Legal culture and transformative constitutionalism. S Afr J Human Rights 14:146–188

Kok A (2008) The promotion of equality and prevention of unfair discrimination Act 4 of 2000: proposals for legislative reform. S Afr J Human Rights 24:445–471

---

[94]For a comprehensive discussion on the concept of 'transformative law' in the South African context, see Kok (2008), p. 445.

Op't Hoog CA, Siebers HG, Linde B (2010) Affirmed identities? The experience of black middle managers dealing with affirmative action and equal opportunity policies at a South African mine. S Afr J Labour Relat 34(2):61–83

Rycroft A (1999) Obstacles to employment equity? The role of judges and arbitrators in the interpretation and implementation of affirmative action policies. Ind Law J 20:1411–1429

Shavell S (1991) Specific versus general enforcement of law. J Polit Econ 99(5):1088–1108

United Nations Development Programme (UNDP) (2015) Human Development Report 2015: Work for Human Development, p 38

Debbie Collier is Associate Professor in the Department of Commercial Law and former Deputy Dean at the University of Cape Town (UCT), and is an associate of the Institute of Development and Labour Law. She holds a PhD and an LLM from UCT and an BA, LLB from Rhodes University. Her core teaching responsibilities, and primary field of research and publication, is in employment law and development, with a focus on workplace discrimination and the law.

Spain

María José Gómez-Millán Herencia

1 Introduction

In the last 40 years, antidiscrimination law has become one of the most important pillars of social policies in Spain. Public and private bodies collaborate in extending antidiscrimination law in different manners, although public and private companies have developed practical criteria to enforce antidiscrimination law, especially in the workplace, where the impact has been extensively studied from a legal, economic, and social point of view.

Nevertheless, the enforcement of antidiscrimination law has some clear limits, because it only operates when laws or practices violate the test of proportionality, which depends of the grounds of discrimination and the type of treatment. Indeed, the influences of the test of proportionality on the scope of antidiscriminatory law enforcement depends on the overall ground covered (although levels of protections vary). In this sense, many factors have influenced the definition of antidiscriminatory law and the different levels of coverage. If the target group has (or does not have) a history of past discrimination, the factors and range of social exclusion and the number of people included in each ground, among other social and economic factors, are often used to determine the different levels of protection of the Spanish Antidiscrimination Legal System.[1] Therefore, some grounds were more covered by a developed antidiscriminatory law (direct and indirect) than others (reverse, association and arising discrimination). Moreover, affirmative action operates on some grounds more than on others.

---

[1] Gómez-Millán Herencia (2011), pp. 42–50.

M. J. Gómez-Millán Herencia (✉)
Pablo Olavide University, Labor Law and Social Security, Seville, Spain
e-mail: mjgommil@upo.es

It is also important to notice that the enforcement of antidiscrimination law is connected with a fundamental right in Spain, so that the law and the claims have more guarantees than other rights and principles of social policies, as it will be explained in this book chapter. In spite of that, the grounds of discrimination and the level of protection make it more or less difficult to get equality from an individual and systemic perspective. All of these characteristics are combined in the Spanish legal protection system, which is formed by the influence of other antidiscrimination legal systems, especially the International Labor Organization (ILO) and the European Union, with the idea of providing equality for all the citizens.[2]

2 Is Antidiscrimination Law Enforced?

Spain has belonged to the EU since 1986, where there is an Equality Framework imposed by Directive 78/2000/UE, of 27 November 2000, establishing a general framework for equal treatment in employment and occupation. However, it is not a general provision, because it only covers the relationship between employers and employees. Other provisions aim at racial and gender equality in the workplace.[3]

Discrimination is recognized as a fundamental right by the Spanish Constitution of 1978, in which Article 14 prohibited discrimination by birth, race, sex, religion, opinion, or other conditions, or another's personal or social circumstances. This fundamental right has been developed by some specific antidiscrimination laws on the grounds of gender equality, disability and residence of citizenship. These laws are usually enacted by the State, although regional governments enforce such antidiscriminatory laws also, especially on gender and disability grounds, as we can see in Andalusia, Catalonia, Extremadura, or Navarra's Equality Laws.[4]

Article 14 of the Spanish Constitution of 1978 mentions that all are equal in the eyes of the law. Consequently, antidiscrimination law has been enforced in public and private relationships. The *Drittwirkung* theory has been applied by Courts in order to resolve lawsuits between private persons, even in the pre-contractual phase.[5] In this way, the European Union and Spain applied antidiscrimination law in private

---

[2] Gómez-Millán Millán Herencia (2010), pp. 74–83.
[3] Such us Directive 43/2000/UE, of 29 June 2000, implementing the principle of equal treatment between persons, irrespective or racial or ethnic origin; Directive 73/2002/UE, of 23 September, of the implementation of the principle of equal treatment for men and women regarding access to employment, vocational training and promotion, and working; Directive 113/2004/UE, of 13 December 2004, implementing the principle of equal treatment between men and women in access to and supply of goods and services; Directive 41/2010/UE, of 7 July 2010, on the application of the principle of equal treatment between men and women engaged in an activity in a self-employed capacity.
[4] Gómez-Millán Herencia (2011), pp. 91–93 and 176.
[5] Alameda Castillo (2013), pp. 75–90.

relationships, especially at work; such can be tested in the mentioned Directives and in the Spanish Antidiscriminatory Law framework. Therefore, antidiscrimination law is enforced in the access to goods and services, in the education system, transport, work, and mass media, each other's. But the antidiscrimination principle is enforced more or less strictly depending on the ground covered (gender, disability, age, race, religion) and the type of relationship settled (civil, labor, administrative, commercial). Because this fundamental right has been developed only in some cases, usually in connection with the target groups as exposed in question 4, and the Spanish Government (and Public Administrations) have more responsibility to enforce equality than private actors. Both must provide a reasonable reason to justify unfavorable or less favorable treatment. Moreover, reasonable accommodations are compulsory in the ground that we are going to study in the following questions, but a high cost can be an exception to this obligation in private relationships.

3 How Is Antidiscrimination Law Enforced?

Antidiscrimination fundamental rights are enforced by law, where definitions of direct, indirect and reverse discrimination are provided, but these laws only 7 cover some grounds (gender, disability, race or ethnic origin, religion or convictions, age or sexual orientation reasons at work), in spite of the general provision of Article 14 of Spanish Constitution.[6] In addition, multiple factors of discrimination are usually taken into account at the intersection of gender and disability. However, laws have been extended to other groups by state aids, especially in the past,[7] and to other intersections by some scholars[8] and by the Spanish Proposal of Equality Law 2011. Finally, affirmative action, as a right to be treated different, which must been provided by State,[9] and to get different conditions, only functions on certain grounds.[10]

---

[6]Direct discrimination is less favoured treatment based on sex (Article 6 Fundamental Gender Equality Law 3/2007, 22 March 2007), based on disability (Article 2.c Disability Law 1/2013, 29 November), based on race or ethnic origin, religion or convictions, age or sexual orientation reasons at work (Article 28.b Law 62/2003, 30 December, fiscal, administrative and social measure). Second, indirect discrimination is an apparently neutral law, criteria or repetitive behavior which produces a specific disadvantage in comparison with the other sex (Article 6 Fundamental Gender Equality Law 3/2007), or because of disability (Article 2.d Disability Law 1/2013); it is also an apparently neutral collective bargain or agreement, individual contract or unilateral decision that creates a particular disadvantage because of race or ethnic origin, religion or convictions, age or sexual orientation at work (Article 28.c Law 62/2003). Moreover, discrimination by association only applies to disabled people (Article 2.e Disability Law 1/2013) as a result of EU influences, in spite of the fact that its extension to other grounds has been supported by the Spanish Proposal of Equality Law 2011.

[7]Gómez-Millán Herencia (2011), p. 108 in contrast to pp. 292 and 320–321.

[8]VVAA (2013).

[9]Machado Ruiz (2002), p. 85.

[10]In this sense, affirmative action is a different treatment in order to get equality, which is fair when the measure is reasonable and proportionate with the aims of getting gender equality (Article

In addition, some of measures have been developed in workplaces, such as the duty of negotiation of Gender Equality Plans in medium sized companies (more than 250 employees)[11] and the certification in gender matters for companies with outstanding results (Article 45.3 and Article 50 Fundamental Gender Equality Law 3/2007). To sum up, Gender Audit at work, in connection or not with Equality Plans, has been promoted by the Spanish Labour Audit Association,[12] but there are no mandatory obligations, unlike with accounting audits.

4 Who Enforces Antidiscrimination Law?

Antidiscrimination law has been ruled by different legislators in Spain. On the one hand, the State provides the general framework, determining the type and the ground covered, taking into account Articles 9 and 14 of Spanish Constitution 1978. For example, the Fundamental Gender Equality Law 3/2007, the Disability Law 1/2013 and Law 62/2003 were produced by the State. On the other hand, devoted and local governments have power to enforce antidiscrimination law, because devolved powers, in connection with protecting target groups in their territories, have been recognized by Articles 137 and 148 Spanish Constitution 1978.[13] Indeed, many antidiscriminatory laws were produced by a devoted government, especially regarding gender and disability discrimination, as revealed in question 1.

The enforcement of antidiscrimination law by the legislature is necessary and convenient, but it is not enough. Political parties, trade unions and associations of target groups and third sector groups encourage general opinion about the negative effect of discriminatory practices for society. Also, independent Defenders of fundamental rights and public freedom—one in the state and one for each devoted governments—are elected by the Spanish General Congress and have power to control public decision, under Spanish Law 3/1981 of 6 April, Ombudsman.

Moreover, antidiscrimination law is also enforced by judicial and extrajudicial mechanisms. There are several Courts in Spain that resolve antidiscrimination law claims. As a maximun judge of Spanish Constitution 1978, the Spanish Constitutional Court resolves lawsuits where equality and fundamental rights involving non-discrimination are discussed, taking an important role in the application of antidiscrimination law. On the other hand, the Spanish Supreme Court, divided in different sections depending on the matter discussed (civil, penal, administrative,

---

[11] Fundamental Gender Equality Law 3/2007), trying to avoid or compensate disability disadvantages, or to get equality for disability people (Article 2.g Disability Law 1/2013), or trying to avoid or compensate, only at work, racial or ethnic origin, religion or convictions, age or sexual orientation (Article 28.c Law 62/2003).

[11] So that only a few employers were compelled to negotiate Equality Plans at the end. Vid. Grau Pineda (2014), pp. 272–273.

[12] Del Bas Marfá et al. (2015), p. 257.

[13] Gómez-Millán Herencia (2011), p. 101.

labour and military), has less power in the enforcement of antidiscrimination law than the Spanish Constitutional Court. In any case, the Spanish Supreme Court is the supreme judge of the general rules. Other Courts, such as the Superior Court of Justice or Trial Courts, which are divided in special sections, also enforce antidiscrimination law, following the Spanish Constitutional and Supreme Court criterion. Concerning extrajudicial mechanisms, interprofessional collective bargaining and Equality Plans (ruling the functions and the process of Equality Commissions[14]) can set up compulsory extrajudicial mechanisms for antidiscrimination issues in collective and individual disputes.

5 Who Benefits from the Enforcement of Antidiscrimination Law?

Some specific groups usually need the antidiscrimination laws and affirmative action in order to participate in equal conditions as others. It is clear that the target groups are directly or indirectly benefitting by the enforcement of antidiscrimination law, because they are so often at social risk and suffer from discriminatory practices and behavior.

In the same way, it can be supported that antidiscriminatory law should promote an equal participation for other target groups. Indeed, many associations were created in the last year with the aim of promoting sex equality and to promote antidiscriminatory law and practices against same sex married, or more generally, against homosexual, lesbian and transgender persons.

Apart from the obvious benefits for the target groups protected as mentioned above, or for others target groups who are also protected by antidiscriminatory law, everybody gets better social conditions if antidiscrimination law is enforced on a country-wide scale, because equality allows a fair society to develop, in which each person can participate with no limit or obstacle because of their personal or social characteristics. In this sense, one of the benefits of antidiscriminatory law is that people feel safer in general, because they know that equality law protects them against any kind of personal or social discrimination, and they can trust that affirmative action will support their participation in society and many measures will cover their basic needs. Moreover, people probably feel safer when their relatives or their friends are under the protective umbrella of antidiscrimination law and affirmative action.

Therefore, a plural society is a direct or indirect consequence of antidiscrimination law enforcement and equality law, among other factors. For these reasons, the enforcement of antidiscrimination is one of the most outstanding aims of Welfare States, in which Spain is included, according to Article 1 of the Spanish Constitution of 1978, as a Mediterranean model.[15] After of all, this allows

---

[14]Gómez-Millán Herencia (2014).

[15]Ferrera (1995), p. 85; Gómez-Millán Millán Herencia (2010), p. 71.

public and private bodies (on different levels, such as individual and collective relationships) to avoid unfair laws and practices. In this sense, Governments and political parties get direct or indirect benefits for implementing and promoting the enforcement of antidiscrimination law, because it is usually easier to manage public polices when people feel that they will be treated under the same conditions.

6 Who Is Harmed by the Enforcement of Antidiscrimination Law?

The enforcement of antidiscrimination law is not easy to implement, and it is not absolutely free in terms of economic cost. On the one hand, theoretical antidiscrimination law schemes can be analyzed and understood by scholars, lawyers, judges and others specialists in law. But Spain has little experience in how to implement reasonable accommodation, and there is no executive order or a body of guidelines about how to do it. Therefore, public bodies, which must implement it in the context of public spaces, do not know their legal obligations. In the same way, they usually struggle to implement it properly, because there are different cases and different options; a specific rule about how to implement it has not been provided yet. In all of these senses, there is a lot of discussion about how to implement antidiscrimination law and reasonable accommodation at schools, especially around if the segregation of children by sex is fair or unfair,[16] if it is constitutional or not to publicly fund these schools (STC 30 of November 2015, rec. 255/2015), if it is convenient or not that disabled people attend the same school as other children and when integration in a special school is justified (STC 27 of January 2014, rec. 6868/2012), and what are appropriate limits on affirmative action for minorities or immigrants.

On the other hand, problems also emerge when there are not enough public or private resources. Ownership assembly, which it not funded by public budgets and is not a private company generating economic resources, must facilitate owners' access to community services, despite economic cost. This can be seen in STS 10 October 2010 (rec. 1161/2011). In the same way, a private company must contribute to the enforcement of antidiscrimination law in order to achieve equality, and this is not easy, because economic cost can be too high and because in some cases it is too difficult or impossible to implement reasonable accommodation. In this sense, insurance companies usually offer to men and women different prices for the same coverage in Spain, but the European Union Directive does not regard this as unequal treatment based on sex.[17] Unisex premiums and benefits are being discussed, and some European decisions resolved in favour of consumers (STJUE 1 March 2011 (C-236/2009)). Regarding labour law, Directive 78/2000/UE and Spanish Disability Law 1/2013, on the one hand, and Spanish Labour Risk Prevention 31/1995,

---

[16]González-Varas Ibáñez (2013), pp. 1–27.

[17]Aguilera Ruiz (2014), p. 19.

8 November, on the other, ruled on compulsory reasonable accommodation for disabled people and for other target groups in society and in the workplace, respectively. Here the basic problem is that there is no guidance for implementation and the limits are not clear enough. In both senses, private companies can be harmed by antidiscrimination law enforcement.

7 What Remedies Are Provided by the Enforcement of Antidiscrimination Law?

The most common remedies are thawing of unlawful law, contract or collective bargaining, and injunctions against unlawful treatment (Article 10 Fundamental Spanish Gender Equality Law and Article 17 Spanish Labour Law) or the indemnity clause for claims (Article 24 Spanish Constitution 1978, Article Fundamental Spanish Gender Equality Law and Article 75.3 Spanish Disability Law 1/2013). Moreover, some provisions set up sanctions and compensation (patrimonial, moral and punitive damage), although employers' sanctions for violations on gender grounds can been replaced by a negotiated Equality Plan. Article 78–93 Spanish Disability Law 1/2013 set up sanctions from 301 euros to 1,000,000 euros, depending on culpability level and other factors (typically less than 30,000 euros for mild sanctions and 90,000 euros for serious sanctions). Moreover, Article 15.3 Spanish Executive Order 5/2000 ruled that serious sanctions are warranted for employers who did not comply with compulsory quotas for those with disabilities, and Article 8 Spanish Executive Order 5/2000 set up very serious sanctions for direct and indirect discrimination for disability. In the same way, Article 46 and 46 Fundamental Spanish Gender Equality Law 3/2007, in connection with Article 13 and Article 8 Spanish Executive Order 5/2000, set up very serious sanctions for employers who did not comply with Equality Plans or who commit a direct or an indirect discrimination by sex. Furthermore, Article 8 Spanish Executive Order 5/2000 set up very serious sanctions for employers who directly or indirectly discriminate by sexual orientation, age, religion or belief, political ideas, trade unions freedom, and others. According to Article 40 Spanish Executive Order 5/2000, very serious sanctions consist of a fine from 300 euros to 3000 euros. Moreover, discrimination victims in workplaces (Article 183 Spanish Law of Social Procedure 36/2011, 10 of October) and in the access of goods and services (Articles 10 and 69 Fundamental Spanish Gender Equality Law 3/2007) can claim damages. To sum up, Article 75.2 Spanish Disability Law 1/2013 ruled that there is no limit for compensatory and moral damages, whether or not there are economic damages. Discriminatory behaviour can also be prosecuted by penal remedies. For example, on the access of goods and services, there is a special legal protected interest for those who commit or fail to prevent prevent discrimination.[18]

---

[18] Machado Ruiz (2002), p. 85.

In private relationships, legal remedies consist of the duty of doing a contract if there is a public offer (Article 69.2 Fundamental Spanish Gender Equality Law 3/2007), ceasing the behaviour (Article 75 Spanish Disability Law 1/2013),[19] refunding back pay or awarding seniority rights in gender gaps, the null dismissal (Articles 53 and 55 Spanish Labour Law), the reinstatement order of employees when there is a change in working conditions (Article 17 Spanish Labour Law), or the loss of state aid following gender-based violations (Article 46 and 46 Fundamental Spanish Gender Equality Law 3/2007).

8 Who Supports the Enforcement of Antidiscrimination Law?

As a Mediterranean Welfare State Model in which Spain is included, there are a lot of supporters of Equality Law. First of all, Mediterranean Welfare State means that the State must guarantee goods and services for the entire of population, especially for citizens and legal residents, so everyone can participate under equal conditions. Political parties, as representative of state power, support the enforcement of antidiscrimination law in different manners, such as trying to detect the lack of antidiscrimination law and to promote new laws.

Secondly, trade unions assume the role of increasing labour and social conditions after Spanish Constitution 1978,[20] as we can found in Article 4 of the Fundamental Spanish Gender Equality Law 3/2007, in connection with the encouragement of antidiscrimination law through collective bargaining and corporate responsibility. Besides, the social dialogue can play an outstanding role, as we can see through the Spanish Committee of racial and ethnic discrimination.[21], the Observatory of gender equality,[22] the Forum for social integration of aliens and the Triparties Committee of non-Spaniards,[23] among others.

---

[19]Infante Ruiz (2014), pp. 234–235.

[20]González Ortega (2004), p. 701.

[21]Article 13 Directive 43/2000/UE was formed by different public bodies (state, devoted and local governments), representative workers, employer associations and racial and ethnic discrimination associations, in order to help victims of racial and ethnic discrimination in claims for direct and indirect discrimination, to study and research this ground of discrimination, to enforce antidiscrimination law in racial and ethnic discrimination matters, etc. (Article 34 Spanish Law 62/2003 and Spanish Order 1262/2007, 21 of September, Committee of racial and ethnic discrimination).

[22]Formed by representative executive power from different Government Departments (state, devoted and local governments) and non-governmental associations, in order to pick up information, to carry out research, to propose gender indicators and to analyse the impact of gender politics, among others (Spanish Executive Order 1686/2000, 6 of October, about Observatory of gender equality).

[23]Article 70 and 72 of Fundamental Law 4/2000, of 11 of January, about rights and freedoms of aliens in Spain and their social integration.

Thirdly, one of the best-known benefits of the Mediterranean Welfare State, in comparison with Corporative or Social-democratic Welfare State, is the development of state structure and the broad scope of social protection. Families and the non-governmental sector emerge to protect the less favoured groups, who often suffer discrimination.[24] Some national associations (in the matter of gender, gender violence and disability), with political parties and trade unions, participate in the enforcement of antidiscriminatory law in Spain. This role was developed with their participation in social dialogue, in meeting with political parties or specialist in this area, attending to the less-favoured population, and in increasing access to public information by publishing on their websites.

9 Who Opposes the Enforcement of Antidiscrimination Law?

It is possible to find some critical opinions about implementation, based on the ground of discrimination and the type of antidiscrimination. Not all grounds, as it will be explained in question 10, get the same treatment in Spain. Differing treatment between non-European citizenship and European-citizenship, which is a consequence of European Union migratory policies, is a clear example of permitted different treatment (in connection to unemployment pension and others benefits like healthcare, Articles 14 and 36.5 Fundamental Spanish Law 4/2000, Article 1.2 Spanish General Law 14/1986 of 25 April, of healthcare). This does not mean that there is no conflict around this issue, or around the enforcement of antidiscrimination law on gender or disability grounds. But on other grounds (like age or illness), the enforcement is more flexible, with fewer opponents, as it will be exposed in question 10.

Focusing on the type of discrimination, the prosecution of direct and reverse discrimination is not controversial for scholars, but there are more doubts about others types. First, indirect discrimination is necessary in order to get equality, because discrimination practices are sometimes intentional. But in other cases, the challenge is to control and correct non-intentional practices, especially whether a law, a collective bargaining, a criterion or a practical behaviour introduces a barrier for a target group. In all of these senses, it is not easy for legislators, negotiators or active subjects (who commit discrimination) to take into account all the situations and all the groups. Second, affirmative action is largely discussed in many countries,[25] particularly when the different treatment is too strong, such as in quotas, or when affirmative action introduces the risk of generating a negative effect in the target groups protected.[26]

---

[24]Ferrera (1995), p. 85; Gallie and Paugam (2000), p. 17; Gómez-Millán Millán Herencia (2010), p. 71.
[25]Reyna et al. (2005), pp. 667–682.
[26]Gómez-Millán Millán Herencia (2010), pp. 62–68.

Affirmative action is particularly strong for women and disabled persons in Spain. Quotas were only ruled permissible for disabled people by law and admitted by Courts without discussion, but the second final provision Fundamental Spanish Gender Equality Law 3/2007 has introduced preferences, in order to increase the number of women in the workforce. Nevertheless, the letter of this provision is not clear enough, so there is an ongoing debate about preferences and gender quotas in Spain.[27] In the EU as well, the proposal for a Directive of the European Parliament and the Council on improving the gender balance among non-executive directors and companies listed on stock exchanges and related measures, which it tried to introduce a compulsory preference for women in big companies, has being blocked since 2012, for the same reasons. As a result, the boundaries between affirmative action and reverse discrimination have more shadows than light[28]; there is not a large tradition of or experience with its implementation.

10 How Broad Is the Coverage of Antidiscrimination Law?

The scope of antidiscrimination law usually depends on the grounds of discrimination. Article 14 Spanish Constitution 1978 only mentioned sex—which is the most developed ground of discrimination in Spain. Nevertheless, Spanish Gender Equality Law 3/2007 is a broader concept.[29] Indeed, some legislators and negotiators have confused the protection of pregnancy and parenthood, and in spite of some judicial solutions (such as Lommers, STJUE of 19 of March of 2002 (C-476/99)) insisted on differences between the two.[30] Indeed, there are a lot of differences in family responsibility protection in Spain, depending on maternity or paternity, natural or adoptions, etc.[31] This is in the same way that European Court of Justice 18 of March 2014 (C- 167/12) provides antidiscrimination law guarantees. On the other hand, the concept of disability is narrow and only protects permanent illness. Thus, temporary illness and chronic illness are not included and these conditions have no real protection by antidiscrimination law in Spain.[32] Similarly, antidiscriminatory law in Spain only protected obesity when it was a disability (STSJ Valencia of 9 of May

---

[27]Gómez-Millán Herencia (2011), pp. 122–132.

[28]Giménez Gluck (1999).

[29]Gómez-Millán Herencia (2008), pp. 849–866.

[30]Second and third provision of Spanish Law of General Budgets for 2016.

[31]Moreno Márquez (2013).

[32]In spite of the fact that the Spanish Constitutional Court has recognized its coverage, STC 26 of May of 2008 (RTC 62/2008) addressed objective dismissal for absences in the case of illness, ruled by Article 52.c Spanish Labour Law and in the judicial solutions (STS 3 of May 2016, rec. 3348/2014). Vid. Gómez-Millán Herencia (2013), pp. 66–77; Gómez-Millán Herencia (2014), pp. 66–77.

2012, rec. 823/12).[33] Also, antidiscrimination law covers age, but the different treatment is usually justified.[34]

Finally, the equality class of sexual orientation has a lot of difficulties in their implementation, and gender identity has no found a strong legal framework in Spain.[35] Furthermore, the intersection between women and religion usually causes many doubts among judges and scholars, for example in connection with wearing a burqa or niqab in public spaces.[36]

11 Does the Enforcement of Antidiscrimination Law Vary According to the Ground of Discrimination?

As addressed in question 2, Spanish Constitution 1978 only mentions some grounds of discrimination: birth, race, sex, religion or convictions, ending with an open clause, where age and disability,[37] identity gender[38] and illness[39] have been included by judges and scholars, because the discrimination is based on mutable characteristics.[40]

In addition, the boundaries of each ground can introduce other important differences regarding scope, as was shown in question 9. Gender and disability discrimination grounds are the strongest protected and are covered by antidiscrimination law and affirmative action measures, but disabled people were protected with stricter measures than women.[41] Nevertheless, other classes of discrimination are less protected, such as age or nationality discrimination, where different treatment usually is deemed fair, as was discussed in questions 8 and 9.

---

[33] In the same way as the European Court of Justice, 18 of December 2014 (C- 354/13), in spite of the fact that article 4.c Spanish Law 17/2011, 5 of July, of foods and nutrition, ruled that obesity was protected by antidiscrimination law. Vid. Rivas Vallejo (2015), p. 25.

[34] González Ortega (2011), p. 93.

[35] E.g. different treatment between civil marriages and non-civil marriages (STC 7 of April 2014, RTC 44/2014, in spite of the European Court of Human Rights, 8 of December of 2009, Muñoz Díaz v. Spain), different-sex marriages and same-sex marriages (STC 14 of February 2013, RTC 41/2013), transgenders (STC 8 of April 2013, RTC 77/2013) and other common cases of allowed different treatments. Vid. Cabeza Pereiro and Lousada Arochena (2014), pp. 23 and 54.

[36] Cuesta López and Santana Vega (2014), pp. 149–154.

[37] Gómez-Millán Herencia (2011), p. 46.

[38] Cabeza Pereiro and Lousada Arochena (2014), p. 11.

[39] Rodríguez-Piñero and Bravo-Ferrer (2008), p. 61.

[40] Fernández López (2009), p. 11.

[41] E.g. in quotas (Article 42 Spanish Disability Law 1/2013 and article 59 Spanish Basic Law of servant employee 5/2015) in contrast to preferences (Article 75 and second additional provision Fundamental Spanish Gender Equality Law 3/2007). Vid. Gómez-Millán Herencia (2011), p. 409 and pp. 110–169 in contrast pp. 193–242.

Age discrimination is sometimes protected by affirmative action, but the key point is that antidiscrimination law is so narrow, as we can see evidenced in the social security system[42] and in the use of a compulsory retirement clause.[43] In the same way, the requirements of residence and birth in a specific place is another allowed basis for difference in treatment, as it was revealed in question 8, in spite of Fundamental Law 4/2000 allowing promotional measures and where it can be included affirmative actions (Article 30 Public Polices of Employment Law 3/2015, 23 of October). In contrast, other grounds of discrimination are only protected by the most classical type of antidiscriminatory law (direct and indirect), such as opinion or physical appearance when it is not connected with a disability. And others (such as religion, convictions or geographical languages) are only covered by the most classical type of antidiscrimination law mentioned before, and by the least strong type of affirmative action (reasonable accommodation). To sum up, discrimination by illness can find some protection in Labour Law, where there are some provisions, although Courts usually permit different treatment.

12 What Is the Relationship Between the Enforcement of Antidiscrimination Law and the Quest for Equality on Both an Individual and Systemic Level?

The enforcement of antidiscriminatory law prevents not only individual discrimination, but also systematic discrimination, which involves societal attitudes and prejudices. In this sense, antidiscriminatory law tries to prevent and to punish discriminatory laws and practices, including direct, indirect and reverse discrimination. The aims of all of them are to prevent unfair and different treatments, especially when those different treatments cause negative effects to a person who belongs to a target group. This means that the enforcement of antidiscrimination law tries to achieve equality at the individual and the systemic level, especially with indirect discrimination, where the claim must be supported by societal stereotypes or attitudes, based on statistic proofs, generally.[44] In the same way, affirmative action's aim is to achieve equality at the individual and the systemic level, as seen in STS 4 of February of 2002 (rec. 2620/1996) or STC 13 of April of 2015 (rec. 66/2015), where judges admit that an employer can break a contract with a disabled person (even if that extinction caused a breach on mandatory quotas) and an employer can use age in order to select workers (in both cases on the framework of a collective dismissals), because the protection is not individual but collective. In all

---

[42]González Ortega (2011), pp. 133–119.

[43]Only allowed (for a transitory period) in private companies when the clause is in a collective bargaining agreement before 2012 (additional Article 10 Spanish Labour Law) and for public servants (Article 7 Spanish Basic Law of servant employee 5/2015), although compulsory retirement was largely used in Spain, García Muñoz (2016), pp. 1–7.

[44]Lousada Arochena (2005), p. 11.

of these senses, some scholars support penalties for discrimination are justified in compelling collective interest cases.[45] They can also be justified given the role that Governments, public bodies, trade unions, associations and others assume on the enforcement of antidiscrimination law.

On the other hand, a plaintiff for discrimination can be an individual victim or focus on a collective subject. First, a law can be unconstitutional or can give rise to a constitutional question. A constitutional question must be addressed in a Constitutional Trial, by Judges or Trial Courts (Article 35 Spanish Fundamental Law 2/1979, 3 of October, Constitutional Trial). Second, focusing on judicial mechanisms, claims of gender discrimination can be interposed by physical and juridical persons who have a legitimate interest (public bodies in equality gender matters, most representative trade unions and state associations in gender matters), except in sexual harassment, where only the victim can make the claim (Article 12 Fundamental Spanish Gender Equality Law 3/2007 and Article 11 Spanish Law 1/2000, 7 of January, Civil Procedure). Moreover, claims of racial and ethnic discrimination can be interposed by juridical persons when they try to protect a collective and legitimate interest (Article 31 Spanish Law 62/2003). Finally, trade unions can support a victim in the judicial process and they also can claim collective damages, when the lawsuit is connected with a labour conflict (Articles 17, 20 and 177 Spanish Law of Social Procedure 36/2011). Therefore, the enforcement of antidiscrimination law in Spain has many mechanisms in order to get equality at an individual and systemic level.

13 Is the Enforcement of Antidiscrimination Law Regarded As Different from the Enforcement of Other Laws?

Equal treatment is a fundamental right in Spain, so that means that the enforcement of antidiscrimination law is strongly protected by the Spanish Constitution of 1978—the maximum level of guarantee. This is in contrast to other rights of Title I, chapter 2, section 2 (property, succession, labour law) and to principles of public polices of Title I, chapter 3 (health, social protection, full employment, housing), as we can see in Article 53 Spanish Constitution 1978.[46] Therefore, equal treatment and enforcement of antidiscrimination laws have the same level of protection as other fundamental rights (dignity; privacy; freedom of thought, belief, opinion and expression; assembly; association). Indeed, as a fundamental right, antidiscriminatory laws can modify other rights (non-fundamental) and principles of public policies, when they arise as part of a claim. This can be seen in lawsuits about the obligations of public and private bodies, especially in the cases where the freedom to do business conflicts with the right of non-discrimination (e.g. STC 13 of April of 2015 (RTC 66/2015)).

---

[45] Machado Ruiz (2002), pp. 94–115.
[46] Gómez-Millán Millán Herencia (2010), pp. 86–98.

Strong protections consist on the following guarantees. First, equal treatment and antidiscrimination law only can be developed by a "fundamental law," which requires more votes in the parliamentary procedure of approval. As it is said in Article 81 of the Spanish Constitution of 1978, this procedure requires a total majority of the Congress in the final vote on the entire proposal of law. Second, discrimination lawsuits are preferred to address non-fundamental rights, and its deadlines are shorter, according to Article 53 of the Spanish Constitution of 1978. Third, the lawsuit can be interposed in a special procedure at Constitutional Court, in coherence with Article 53 Spanish Constitution of the 1978, which adds one judicial step more compared to the rights of Title I, chapter 2, section 2 and the principles of public polices of Title I, chapter 3.

In addition, some specific grounds of discrimination, such as gender and disability, are strongly connected with all public policies. For example, regarding gender discrimination grounds, the concept of mainstreaming inspired all laws and public polices, so that all public measures must take into account gender in their design (public contracts, annual budgets, state aids, public reports) and must have an evaluation about their impact on men and women. Also, an annual review is mandatory (Article 15 Fundamental Spanish Gender Equality Law 3/2007). In contrast, mainstreaming was not being implemented for other grounds of discrimination and for other fundamental rights. Regarding disability, reasonable accommodations also inspired public measures and private decisions; this is the only way to guarantee that disabled people will have access to goods and services (Article 1 and 2 Spanish Disability Law 1/2013). There are also rulings in connection with safety and health at work, and on other grounds, such as special target groups of labour risks, although this is less compulsory than in disability cases.[47]

14 What Does the Enforcement of Antidiscrimination Law Reveal About the Nature of Your Legal System or About the Enforcement of Laws in Your Legal System?

The enforcement of antidiscrimination law reveals that Spain is included in Mediterranean Welfare State Model. First of all, Government rules antidiscrimination law with many articles and provisions.[48] Indeed, there are some general provisions, two specifics laws for the principal grounds (gender and disability) and some specific provisions in labour laws, which concur with some executive orders. These regulations are set up by state, devoted and local governments.

---

[47] Moreno Solana (2010), pp. 72–76.

[48] Many of them with the aim of protecting jobs, because employment is the most important way of social participation in Welfare State, vid Gómez-Millán Millán Herencia (2010), pp. 55–112; Gómez-Millán Herencia (2013), pp. 1–6.

Second, the enforcement of equality combines antidiscriminatory law and affirmative action, in spite of their different levels of development. In this sense, antidiscriminatory law is less complete in Spain than in a Liberal Welfare State Model,[49] because some of types and grounds of discrimination were excluded (in practice) in Spain (e.g. illness), and the test of proportionality was implemented less strictly on some grounds (e.g. nationality and age). At the same time, many types of affirmative action were used to encourage equality in Spain, in the same way as Corporate and Social-democratic Welfare State Models, although it is less developed, as affirmative action usually is the same for all the target groups in Spain.[50] In contrast, Spanish affirmative action is stronger than in Liberal, and it was been largely developed on gender (as a consequence of the outstanding role of women and family in Mediterranean[51]), and disability grounds.

Finally, judicial[52] and extrajudicial[53] remedies are provided by law. But the most important aspect is that a lot of extrajudicial remedies were set up on gender and disability grounds, in contrast to other issues or matters in Spain. This brings Spain closer to Liberal and Social-democratic Welfare State Models, although discrimination victims use judicial remedies more than extrajudicial in practice.[54] Trade unions, associations, and NGOs play an outstanding role, in the same way as in the Corporate and Social-Democratic Welfare State Model.

15 Conclusions

15.1 The Enforcement of Antidiscriminatory Law Is at the Center of Public Policies and Private Decisions

As a country that has adopted the Welfare State Model, Spain regards equality as central to its public policies, promoting equality through the enforcement of antidiscriminatory laws and specific measures of affirmative action, in which Government (state, autonomous and local), public administrations, public bodies and the third sector usually participate. Indeed, the Spanish Constitution provides that equality is a fundamental right, so that antidiscrimination principles regulate and inform the relationship among public/private and physical/juridical persons.

---

[49] Gómez-Millán Herencia (2014), pp. 66–77.
[50] Gómez-Millán Herencia (2011), p. 411.
[51] Martín Castro (2012), p. 187.
[52] Article 12 Fundamental Spanish Gender Equality Law 3/2007, Article 64 and 75 Spanish Disability Law 1/2013.
[53] Article 74 Spanish Disability Law 1/2013, Article 63, 82 and 181 Spanish Law of Social Procedure 36/2011, 10 of October.
[54] Álvarez Ramírez (2013), pp. 290–292.

15.2 The Enforcement of Antidiscriminatory Law Tries to Get Social Participation in Equal Conditions

Spanish Equality Law has connected antidiscrimination law with affirmative action measures in order to get social participation in equal conditions. In this sense, the enforcement of antidiscriminatory law operates at different levels. On the one hand, the scope of antidiscriminatory law is so wide, especially in gender discrimination, from the point of view of mainstreaming policies, because it includes protection in the access to goods and services, and it operates in public and private relationships. On the other hand, claims interposed by an individual victim, and also an antidiscriminatory lawsuit, can pursue equality at the individual and the systematic level. It is important to value the role of trade unions, associations and more generally the third sector, who usually support claims and who promote equal laws.

15.3 The Enforcement of Antidiscriminatory Law Relies on Different Levels of Protection Depending on the Ground

Equality law's scope depends on the ground of discrimination, because societal attitudes and prejudices operate strongly only in some of them. Thus, the enforcement of antidiscriminatory law is harder for some specific grounds (gender connected with discrimination against women and disability related with permanent illness) than in others (e.g. age, nationality, illness or obesity). In the same way, Courts are more concerned about the most protected ground. Therefore, they usually apply the test of proportionality, so as to admit the different treatment for the less protected grounds. To sum up, affirmative action really operates on the most protected grounds (gender and disability), although state aids that compensate for social barriers have been used for all the grounds. Indeed, their existence and their intensity usually depend on autonomous states and local governments, because they can regulate affirmative action measures in order to remove specific socio-economic barriers, which only impacts their territories. Thus, the State assumes the role of promoting a general framework for all citizens.

References

Aguilera Ruiz A (2014) Primas distintas en función del sexo en la contratación de seguros: ¿método natural de cálculo de riesgos o discriminación? In: Mesa Marrero C (ed) Mujeres, contratos y empresas desde la igualdad de género. Tirant lo Blanch, Valencia, pp 17–36
Alameda Castillo MT (2013) Estadíos previos al contrato de trabajo. Aranzadi, Navarra

Álvarez Ramírez G (2013) Discapacidad y sistemas alternativos de resolución de conflictos. Cinca, Madrid. http://www.fderechoydiscapacidad.es/wp-content/uploads/2011/06/Discapacidad-y-sistemas-alternativos-de-resoluci%C3%B3n-de-conflictos-3.pdf

Cabeza Pereiro J, Lousada Arochena JF (2014) El derecho fundamental a la no discriminación por orientación sexual e identidad de género en la relación laboral. Bormazo

Cuesta López V, Santana Vega DM (2014) Estado de Derecho y discriminación por razón de género, orientación sexual e identidad. Tirant Lo Blanch, Valencia

Del Bas Marfá E, Calvo R, García MA (2015) Auditoría socio-laboral: teoría y práctica de una herramienta para la gestión de los RRHH. Tirant Lo Blanch, Valencia

Fernández López MF (2009) Las causas de la discriminación o la movilidad de un concepto. Temas Laborales 98:11–57

Ferrera M (1995) Los Estados del Bienestar del Sur en la Europa Social. In: Sarasa S, Moreno L (Coord.) El Estado del Bienestar en la Europa del Sur. Consejo Superior de Investigaciones Científicas, Madrid

Gallie D, Paugam S (2000) Welfare regimes and the experience of unemployment in Europe. Oxford University Press, Oxford

García Muñoz M (2016) La jubilación forzosa como medida de reparto del empleo y su incidencia en la sostenibilidad del sistema de seguridad social. Revista Internacional y Comparada de Relaciones Laborales y Derecho del Empleo 4(1):185–201

Giménez Gluck D (1999) Una manifestación polémica del principio de igualdad. Acciones positivas moderadas y discriminación inversa. Tirant lo Blanch, Valencia

Gómez-Millán Herencia MJ (2008) Políticas selectivas de empleo para personas responsables del cuidado familiar. In: XVIII Congreso Nacional de Derecho del Trabajo y de la Seguridad Social, published in VV.AA.: Estrategia Europea de Empleo, Estado Autonómico y Políticas de empleo. XVIII Congreso Nacional de Derecho del Trabajo y de la Seguridad Social, Ministerio de Trabajo e Inmigación, Madrid, pp 849–866

Gómez-Millán Herencia MJ (2010) Políticas selectivas de empleo: colectivos destinatarios y transiciones en el mercado de trabajo. memoria de Tesis Doctoral, ejemplar multicopiado, depositado en la Universidad Pablo de Oiavide

Gómez-Millán Herencia MJ (2011) Colectivos destinatarios de las políticas selectivas de empleo. Laborum, Murcia

Gómez-Millán Herencia MJ (2013) Employment policies for target groups in the context of economic crisis. In: Inagural conference of labour law research network, from 13 to 15 of June of 2013, Barcelona (Spain). https://www.upf.edu/gredtiss/_pdf/2013-LLRNConf_Gomez-Millan.pdf

Gómez-Millán Herencia MJ (poster) (2014) Equality plans on the framework of legal and extralegal remedies against discrimination. In: XI European regional congress of labour law, 17 of September to 19 of September of 2014. Dublin, Ireland

Gómez-Millán Herencia MJ (2014) Discapacidad, estados de salud y discriminación en el marco jurídico de la igualdad de Reino Unido. Revista de información laboral 4:41–78

González Ortega S (2004) Los sindicatos y la (nueva) cuestión social en la Constitución. In: Peces-Barba Martínez G, Ramiro Avilés MA (eds) La Constitución a examen: Un estudio académico 25 años después. Marcial Pons, Madrid

González Ortega S (2011) La discriminación por razón de edad. Temas Laborales, pp 93–124

González-Varas Ibáñez A (2013) Régimen jurídico de la educación diferenciada en España. Revista General de Derecho Canónico y Derecho Eclesiástico del Estado, Nº 31

Grau Pineda C (2014) Los planes de igualdad como ¿nueva técnica? para la consecución de la igualdad en las empresas. In: Cuesta López V, Santana Vega DM (eds) Estado de Derecho y discriminación por razón de género, orientación e identidad sexual. Aranzadi

Infante Ruiz FJ (2014) Igualdad, diversidad y protección contra a discriminación en el derecho privado. In: Mesa Marrero C (ed) Mujeres, contratos y empresas desde la igualdad de género. Tirant lo Blanch, Valencia, pp 191–250

Lousada Arochena JF (2005) La prueba de la discriminación y del acoso sexual y moral en el proceso laboral. http://www2.ccoo.es/comunes/recursos/1/643395-La_prueba_de_la_discriminacion..._Jose_Fernando_Lousada.pdf

Machado Ruiz MD (2002) La discriminación en el ámbito de los servicios públicos: análisis del artículo 551 CP. Tirant Lo Blanch, Valencia

Martín Castro MB (2012) Reformas en el Estado del Bienestar Mediterráneo: especial referencia al caso español en la época de crisis. Revista de la Facultad de Ciencias Sociales y Jurídicas de Elche I(8). https://revistasocialesyjuridicas.files.wordpress.com/2012/02/08-tm-11.pdf

Moreno Márquez A (2013) Discriminación y paternidad. http://www3.uah.es/congresoreps2013/Paneles/panel3/ANA%20MARIA%20MORENO%20MARQUEZ(mmarquez@der-pr.uc3m.es)/TCDISCRIMINACIONYPATERNIDAD.pdf

Moreno Solana A (2010) La prevención de riesgos laborales de los trabajadores especialmente sensibles. Tirant Lo Blanch, Valencia

Reyna C, Tucker A, Korfmacher W (2005) Searching for common Ground between supporters and opponents of affirmative action. Polit Psychol 26(5):667–682

Rivas Vallejo P (2015) ¿Es la obesidad causa de discriminación tutelable en el ámbito laboral? IUSLabor, N° 1

Rodríguez-Piñero Y, Bravo-Ferrer M (2008) Despido por enfermedad y discriminación. Relaciones laborales: Revista crítica de teoría y práctica 2:61–81

VVAA (2013) La discriminación múltiple en los ordenamientos jurídicos español y europeo. Tirant Lo Blanch, Valencia

María José Gómez-Millán Herencia is a Contract Doctorated Professor in Labour Law and Social Security at Pablo Olavide University. She earned a Degree in Law from the University of Seville in 2000, Extraordinary Prize of Doctorated in 2012 for Pablo Olavide University (Seville, Spain) and Prize of Real Maestranza de Caballería in 2013. Ms. Gómez-Millán is author of the book Policy of Employment for Target Groups (published in 2011), and she also wrote several journal articles and book chapters about social protection and unemployment, the protection of ill workers, and the labour law treatment of some excluded workers.

Turkey

Nurhan Süral

1 Introduction

In developing Turkish antidiscrimination law, Turkey has been influenced both by its own legal tradition as a civil law country and its relationship with the European Union. National political and social forces and domestic law have influenced Turkey's legal framework, but also by EU law and human rights obligations specified in international treaties to which Turkey is a party.

Until April 2016, antidiscrimination law in Turkey was piecemeal and responsive to particular forms of inequality. Article 5 of the Labour Law[1] was the most extensive general provision on the prohibition of discrimination in employment. It outlawed discrimination on the basis of sex, race and ethnicity, religion and sect (religious denomination), language, colour, disability, political belief, philosophical belief and similar grounds (Labour Law, Article 5(1)). It also prohibited employment-related discrimination on the basis of an employee's fixed-term or part-time work, and on the basis of an employee's union membership and/or involvement in trade union activities (Labour Law, Article 5(2), Unions and Collective Labour Agreements Law, Article 25). Listing in Article 5 of the Labour Law is non-exhaustive covering forms of discrimination deemed 'similar' to those listed above. A separate law, the Law on the Disabled,[2] prohibited discrimination on the basis of disability.

---

[1] Labour Law (*İş Kanunu*), Law No. 4857, Official Gazette 10 June 2003, no. 25134.
[2] Law no. 5378, Official Gazette 7 July 2005, no. 25868.

N. Süral (✉)
Faculty of Economics and Administrative Sciences, Middle East Technical University, Ankara, Turkey
e-mail: sural@metu.edu.tr

A new law, passed in 2016, consolidated many areas of Turkish antidiscrimination law. The Law on Human Rights and Equality Institution of Turkey was submitted to the Parliament by the Government on 28 January 2016, adopted on 6 April 2016, and published in the Official Gazette on 20 April 2016.[3] Characteristics protected by the Treaty on the Functioning of the European Union (TFEU) are sex, racial or ethnic origin, religion or belief, disability, age and sexual orientation (Article 10). Apart from sexual orientation, all these grounds are specified in the Law on Human Rights and Equality Institution of Turkey (Article 3(2)). Grounds not existing in the TFEU but expanded by Turkey are philosophical and political belief, colour, language, property, birth, marital status and health conditions.

2 How Is Antidiscrimination Law Enforced?

The primary means of enforcement of antidiscrimination law is by individual complaint to a court. The procedure is essentially adversarial, processing the case as a dispute between two parties. The burden of proof is shifted to the respondent once the applicant has made out a prima facie case of discrimination (Labour Law, Article 5(7); Law on Human Rights and Equality Institution, Article 21). This principle was first developed by the Court of Justice of the European Union (CJEU) in relation to sex discrimination and then extended to racial discrimination (Race Directive, 2000/43/EC, Article 8), and to disability, age, sexual orientation, religion and belief (Employment Directive, 2000/78/EC, Article 10).

Another way to enforce antidiscrimination law is through representative action, where a trade union brings an action on behalf of a member-worker, upon a written request by the worker (Unions and Collective Labour Agreements Law, Article 26 (2)). While a representative action cannot form the basis of a fully fledged class, it is possible to use one case as a "pilot case" before the court. If the case is won, then the others who have been simultaneously affected by the same issue can apply to the courts and have the decision of the pilot case serve as precedent.

After the first instance court renders a decision, there is also the possibility of judicial review by the high court, the Court of Appeals. In parallel to this appellate court hierarchy is the Constitutional Court.

The Constitutional Court examines the constitutionality, in both form and substance, of laws, decrees having the force of law, and the Rules of Procedure (Standing Orders) of the Parliament (Grand National Assembly of Turkey). The Constitutional Court also decides on individual applications (Constitution, Article 148(1)). The Constitutional Court consists of two sections and the General Assembly. The sections convene under the chairpersonship of the deputy president with the participation of four members. The General Assembly must have the participation of

---

[3]Law on Human Rights and Equality Institution of Turkey (*Türkiye İnsan Hakları ve Eşitlik Kurumu Kanunu*), Law no. 6701, Official Gazette 20 April 2016, no. 29690.

at least ten members, convened under the chairpersonship of the President of the Constitutional Court or a deputy president designated by the President. The sections and the General Assembly make decisions by absolute majority. Committees may be established to examine the admissibility of the individual applications (Constitution, Article 149(1)).

Any person may apply to the Constitutional Court on the grounds that one of the fundamental rights and freedoms within the scope of the European Convention on Human Rights (ECHR), which are guaranteed by the Turkish Constitution,[4] has been violated by public authorities. In order to make an application, ordinary legal remedies must be exhausted. Parties who ultimately wish to reach the European Court of Human Rights (ECtHR) must first file an individual action in the Constitutional Court (Addendum, 2010[5]).

Criminal sanctions for discrimination offenses are provided by Criminal Law.[6] A person who discriminates as a result of hatred stemming from differences in language, race, nationality, sex, disability, political thought, belief or other considerations and accordingly hinders the employment of a particular person, or the sale, transfer or lease of any object to a person, or prevents someone from using a public service, will be punished by between 1 and 3 years' imprisonment (Criminal Law, Article 122). The Criminal Law regulates four types of crimes under the title "Crimes against sexual inviolability": Sexual assault, sexual exploitation of children, sexual intercourse with an under-aged person, and sexual harassment. Sexual harassment is defined as when acts of a sexual nature sexually disturb the victim, thereby violating the moral decency (but not the physical inviolability) of the victim. This behaviour may be verbal (remarks about one's figure/looks, crude sexual jokes, verbal sexual advances/offers, unwanted messages or emails) or non-verbal (staring, whistling, indecent exposure) but not physical. Acts involving physical contact, such as patting, kissing, fondling, hugging, grabbing, and rape constitute types of sexual assault. Additionally, a person's unlawful or forceful interventions in the another's personal lifestyle choices arising from their ideas, beliefs or convictions is criminalized under Law no. 6529,[7] amending Article 115 of the Criminal Law. Similarly, it is illegal to prevent another, either by force or by another illegal act, from using their freedom to announce their religious beliefs, opinions and convictions. Such acts are punishable by imprisonment for between 1 and 3 years. For all of these violations of criminal law, there must be an individual complaint by the victim filed in a criminal court against the perpetrator on the basis of Articles 105, 115 and 122.

All these remedies require an individual applicant/victim to first bring forward a claim. In the adversarial judicial procedure, it is not possible to challenge a

---

[4]Law no. 2709, Official Gazette 9 November 1982, no. 17863.

[5]Law no. 5982 amending the Constitution, Official Gazette 13 May 2010, no. 27580. This amending law was approved through a referendum held on 12 September 2010.

[6]*Türk Ceza Kanunu*, Law No. 5237, Official Gazette 12 October 2004, no. 25611.

[7]*Temel Hak ve Hürriyetlerin Geliştirilmesi Amacıyla Çeşitli Kanunlarda Değişiklik Yapılmasına Dair Kanun*, Law no. 6529, Official Gazette, 13 March 2014, no. 28940.

discriminatory rule/practice unless there is an applicant who can challenge it. Besides this adversarial method, a new approach to enforcement is outlined in the Law on Human Rights and Equality Institution of Turkey (Law no. 6701). Under this new law, discrimination can now be investigated based on a complaint or ex-officio to the Human Rights and Equality Board, the decision-making body of the Institution (Articles 9(1)(g) and 11(1)(b)). To initiate an ex-officio investigation the consent of the victim(s) have to be taken if identifiable (Article 17(6)).

The Human Rights and Equality Board investigates discrimination based on a complaint and ex-officio and is permitted to fine individuals or entities if discrimination is found. The Board can also help guide victims through administrative and legal procedures (Articles 9(g-ğ) and 11(b)). The Human Rights and Equality Institution has a broader authority than its predecessor, the Human Rights Institution.

The Human Rights and Equality Institution is tasked with three functions (Article 1):

1. Protection and enhancement of human rights;
2. To ensure the right to equal treatment and to prevent discrimination in the use of people's rights and freedoms; and,
3. To serve as national prevention mechanism in the framework of the Optional Protocol to the Convention against Torture and other Cruel, Inhuman or Degrading Treatment or Punishment (OPCAT).[8]

The Human Rights and Equality Board convenes upon a call by its President (Article 12(1)). The Board convenes with at least 7 members and arrives at a decision with at least 6 votes in agreement. There cannot be votes of abstention (Article 12 (3)). It is possible for the Board to establish commissions of 3 members for each of its functions (Article 12(4)). The Board can also establish 5-member chambers to discuss and arrive at decisions on complaint applications.

Both natural persons and legal entities can file complaints of discrimination. Applications can be made directly to the Human Rights and Equality Institution or through governors in towns and sub-governors in sub-towns. Applications are free of charge (Article 17(1)). Before an applicant can file a complaint with the Institution, the applicant must apply first to the perpetrator for a correction of the problem. If the application is rejected or not responded to within a period of 30 days, then the applicant can apply to the Institution. The Institution can accept a claim of discrimination when the applicant has not completed the first step only if there is the possibility of occurrence of damages impossible or very difficult to be compensated (Article 17(2)). Applications to the Institution suspend the terms of litigation and prescription (Article 17(3)). In individual applications, the identities of children, people under guardianship or protection, and victims will be kept secret from the public upon request (Article 17(6)). For the Institution to initiate an ex-officio

---

[8]This third task was first entrusted on the predecessor body, the Human Rights Institution with the Governmental Decree of 9 December 2013 (Official Gazette, 28 January 2014, No. 28896).

investigation in cases where the victim could personally be identified, the victim or the victim's representative must approve the investigation first (Article 17(5)).

The Institution will settle complaints within 3 months of receipt of the individual application or following the Institution's decision to initiate an ex-officio investigation. This period can be extended, for at most 3 months, by the President of the Institution (Article 18(1)). The alleged perpetrator will be asked to submit his/her testimony in written form. Upon request, the parties can be called to make oral statements separately before the Board (Article 18/2). In individual complaints, the burden of proof shifts to the respondent when there is a prima facie case of discrimination (Article 21). The Board is to provide for effective, proportionate and dissuasive penalties in cases of the breaches of the antidiscrimination law.

At its own initiative or upon request, the President of the Institution may bring the victim and perpetrator to a settlement discussion first, and if this fails, the Board will arrive at a decision based on the testimony of the parties and the accounts of witnesses. Settlement terms can include ways to avoid the practice that is claimed to be discriminatory, solutions leading to termination of such a practice, and/or payment of a certain amount of compensation. Declarations, explanations and statements made during the settlement process cannot be used as evidence in legal proceedings (Article 18(3)). Upon failure of the settlement attempt, the Board decides whether there has been discrimination or not (Article 18(4)). If the Board determines that the discriminatory act constitutes or involves a crime, it will report it to the authorities (Article 18(5)).

In imposition of an administrative fine, the Board considers aggravating factors, which include the gravity of the violation, the perpetrator's economic status, and multiple instances of discrimination. Public and private bodies, public professional organizations or natural persons held responsible for a violation will face fines between TL 1188 (€237) and TL 17,235 (€3447) in 2018 (Article 25(1)). The Board also has the option to convert the administrative fine into a warning. If a warning is issued and there is a recurrence of the violation by the same perpetrator, then the administrative fine will be increased by 50% (Article 25(4)). Perpetrators can challenge the administrative fine in court (Article 25(6)).

Additionally, the Human Rights and Equality Board shall, upon request, inform judicial bodies, public bodies and relevant persons of its views and considerations on issues within its mandate (Article 11(1)(d)).

3 Who Enforces Antidiscrimination Law?

As described above, the complaints-led model focuses on determination of fault and punishing discriminatory conduct. Besides the complaints-led model, there are also affirmative duties to promote equality. Certain groups and offices are tasked with this duty, including public bodies, private employers, service providers, trade unions and employers' associations, political parties, public professional organisations and NGOs (Law no. 6701, Articles 3(3)-(4) and 5).

The recent establishment of an equality body will now provide for a synthesis in antidiscrimination law enforcement, which was lacking in the adversarial process before the courts. Besides the individual applications to the Human Rights and Equality Institution, there can also be ex-officio investigations initiated by the Institution. The personnel of the Institution, with the permission of its President, may conduct investigations to find out if there are violations of human rights and discriminatory acts and actions. The results of their investigation are to be specified in a report (Law no. 6701, Article 19). Administrative measures and fines may follow the report (Article 25).

The Ministry of Family and Social Policies, established in 2011, is a government ministry responsible for women's issues, family affairs and social services.[9] Before 2011, the portfolio of women and family affairs was executed by a state minister in the cabinet. The new Ministry features the following branches:

- Status of Women
- Family and Public Services
- Children Services
- Disabled and Elderly Services
- Social Aids
- Services for Casualty Victims' Relatives and Veterans

The Ministry has the responsibility to execute antidiscrimination legislation with the support/help of relevant ministries and public bodies. On gender equality issues, the Ministry coordinates the policies and strategies aimed at preventing discrimination against women, protecting and promoting women's human rights and social status, and ensuring that women become active in all fields of social life. The Ministry implements, monitors and assesses these identified policies and strategies. The legislation on women's rights is revised in cooperation with the relevant public institutions and agencies, NGOs and the opinions are presented at the parties concerned and efforts are made to consolidate gender equality in the legal field (Statutory Decree on Establishment and Duties of the Ministry of Family and Social Affairs, Articles 2, 9). There is a General Directorate on the Status of Women attached to the Ministry of Family and Social Policies.

A Prime Ministerial circular[10] on enhancement of female employment and the provision of equality of opportunities envisages gender equality mainstreaming. To implement these polices, the government established a Female Employment National Monitoring and Coordination Board. In all ministries, an assistant undersecretary is to be tasked to monitor implementation of all regulations on equality of opportunities as regards female employment in the public sphere. A unit in each

---

[9]Statutory Decree on Establishment and Duties of the Ministry of Family and Social Affairs *(Aile ve Sosyal Politikalar Bakanlığının Teşkilat ve Görevleri Hakkında Kanun Hükmünde Kararname),* Decree no. 633, Official Gazette, 8 June 2011, no. 27958bis.

[10]*Başbakanlık Kadın İstihdamının Artırılması ve Fırsat Eşitliğinin Sağlanması Genelgesi,* Official Gazette 25.5.2010, no. 27591.

ministry is to be tasked with "Female-Male Equality of Opportunities." One regulation, Capital Markets Board Communiqué no. 57 on Determination and Application of Corporate Government Principles[11] requires companies listed on the Istanbul Stock Exchange to attempt to have at least one female member in their five-member executive committees. Companies must comply with this requirement or explain why they cannot.

In addition to these departments, there is the Ombudsman Institution,[12] which provides some oversight functions. The Ombudsman Institution examines, investigates and submits recommendations on all sorts of acts and actions, as well as attitudes and behaviours of the administration with the purpose of creating an independent and efficient complaint mechanism in the functioning of public services. The Institution is linked to the parliamentary speaker's office. The Institution has a Chief Ombudsperson and five ombudspersons elected by the Turkish Parliament, a secretary general and staff, and a separate budget. One of the ombudspersons is tasked with complaint applications on women and children's rights. When there are such complaints, ombudspersons inquire into the issue and try to help the parties reach an amicable solution. If this is not possible, then there will be a judicial settlement. The judge who hears the case will consider the ombudsperson's report, though it's not binding.

Complaint petitions may be delivered by hand to the Ombudsman Institution or its offices, as well as via mail, email or fax. Complaints may also be lodged through the Institution's electronic system. In addition, the complaints may be lodged by hand or via mail through governorates in provinces and district governorates in districts. Governorates and district governorates shall send the complaints and their annexes to the Institution within three working days. For complaints regarding human rights, fundamental rights and freedoms, women's rights, children's rights, and general issues of interest to the general public, "violation of interests" shall not be sought.

There are also other antidiscrimination related legislative provisions such as those on violence, public/private employers' obligation to hire the disabled/ex-convicts/veterans/relatives of casualty victims/terror victims, equal treatment of women with headscarves and women without headscarves in the public domain, and trade unions' and employers associations' duty to observe the principle of equality and prohibitions of discrimination among their members and the duty to consider the gender equality in their activities. There are national action plans on employment of women and combatting violence.

Turkey proactively addresses gender equality objectives when drawing up and implementing legal rules, policies and activities. Internationally, Turkey played an

---

[11] *Kurumsal Yönetim İlkelerinin Belirlenmesine ve Uygulanmasına İlişkin Tebliğde Değişiklik Yapılmasına Dair SPK Tebliği*, Official Gazette 11 February 2012, no. 28201.

[12] The Law on the Ombudsman Institution (*Kamu Denetçiliği Kanunu*), Law no. 6328, Official Gazette 29 June 2012, no. 28338; Regulation on Procedures and Principles Concerning the Implementation of Law on the Ombudsman Institution, Official Gazette 28.03.2013, No. 28601 (official website http://www.kamudenetciligi.gov.tr).

important role in the drafting of the Istanbul Convention, as the then-Chair of the Committee of Ministers of Council of Europe. Turkey became the first country to ratify the Istanbul Convention and the first country to adopt a new law in compliance with the Convention. Under the leadership of the Turkish G20 Presidency, the G20 members agreed to establish the Women-20 (W20) at the Izmir Sherpa Meeting on 26–27 March 2015. With the aim of promoting women's leadership in business, entrepreneurship, and the public sector, the W20 will work to further advance the commitments of the G20 Leaders. The W20 was launched as a full-fledged G20 engagement group in Ankara on 6 September 2015 under the Turkish G20 Presidency.[13]

4 Who Benefits from the Enforcement of Antidiscrimination Law?

It is mainly workers, women, first entrants, the elderly and the disabled benefitting from the enforcement of discrimination law.

5 Who Is Harmed by the Enforcement of Antidiscrimination Law?

Perpetrators of discrimination are those most harmed by the enforcement of antidiscrimination law. Employers who discriminate are most impacted by these laws; in practice, lawsuits on the basis of discrimination are usually against an employer upon an employee's termination. While there is no research on the issue, theoretically it is possible for some employers to feel harmed as a result of the duties imposed under antidiscrimination law (i.e. the obligation to hire certain categories of people, the obligation to create a harassment-free work environment). This may also be true for service providers, who must similarly make adjustments to comply with antidiscrimination law.

In lawsuits based on claims of violence against women, it is the perpetrator/stalker who is harmed by the enforcement of antidiscrimination law. A party found at fault is required to pay compensation.

---

[13]See https://g20.org/the-women-20-official-launch-event-took-place-in-ankara-under-the-turkish-presidency/; http://w20turkey.org/the-w20-has-been-officially-launched/, accessed 26 October 2015.

6 What Remedies Are Provided by the Enforcement of Antidiscrimination Law?

Remedies focus on the individual who was harmed by the discrimination. The primary remedy available is monetary compensation. The mediators/courts award compensation when there is proof of discrimination, even if the worker was not financially harmed. Starting on 1 January 2018, mediation became a compulsory prejudicial settlement procedure for the majority of labour disputes. If no settlement is reached in mediation, only after then there may be recourse to adjudication. A worker with a discrimination claim can seek as a remedy pay amounting to 4 months' basic wages (Labour Law, Article 5(6)). This is referred to as "discrimination pay." Discrimination pay can exceed 4 months wages, and the EU requires that no upper ceiling be placed on the allowable amount.

Mediators/courts also have the power to order employee reinstatement in discrimination cases. Workers who are employed under open-ended labour contracts either have regular job security or increased job security. Workers with increased job security are entitled to greater protections against dismissals. A worker who has been working under an open-ended labour contract for more than 6 months at a workplace where at least 30 (50 in agriculture) workers are employed is entitled to increased job security if he/she is not in the position of an employer's representative, managing the whole business or workplace with authority regarding recruitment and dismissal. Where the employer owns more than one workplace in the same industry, the total number of workers shall be considered in assessing whether employees should receive increased job security (Labour Law, Article 18(1)). The 30-worker threshold was developed to avoid imposing administrative, financial and legal constraints in a way that would hinder the creation and development of small and medium-sized businesses (SMEs).

Employers may not terminate employees on the basis of sex, pregnancy and maternity, family responsibilities, race, colour, civil status, religion, political belief, other similar grounds, trade union membership and involvement in trade union activities (Article 18(2)). If a worker with enhanced job security is dismissed on any of these grounds, then the mediator/court shall rule for reinstatement. If the employer does not reinstate the concerned worker, then the employer must pay compensation related to the employee's job security status. For example, if a female worker employed under an open-ended labour contract is dismissed due to her pregnancy, she will be compensated according to whether she is a worker with regular or increased job security. If she has regular job security and is dismissed due to her pregnancy, this will be deemed an "abusive dismissal" entitling the worker to severance pay (corresponding to her seniority) and "bad-faith pay," equalling to thrice the amount of pay corresponding to the worker's notice period. Notice periods vary between 2 and 8 weeks, based on the period of employment in that particular place of work. In dismissing a worker with regular job security, the employer has to present the termination in writing but there is no legal obligation for him/her to specify the reason for the dismissal clearly and precisely (Article 17). In contrast, when a worker with increased job security is dismissed, the employer has the legal obligation to specify the reason of dismissal clearly and precisely (Article 19(1)).

The worker has to be provided with an opportunity to defend himself/herself when the allegations are related to his/her capacity or conduct (Article 19(2)). Where no reason is specified or the reason specified is not valid, the worker can pursue legal action to protect his/her rights and can be reinstated by the mediator/court (Article 20). If the employer does not reinstate the employee, the worker is entitled to severance pay and "job security pay." The minimum amount of job security pay corresponds to the worker's 4 months' basic wages and the maximum corresponds to the worker's 8 months' basic wages.

When discrimination amounts to a crime, there will be criminal sanctions for the perpetrator as detailed above.

Sexual harassment constitutes discrimination. Sexual harassment is defined as any disturbing behaviour with a sexual aim/overtone that does not amount to a sexual assault or sexual exploitation.[14] In sexual harassment, the perpetrator and the victim may be of different sexes or the same sex, and can be single or married. Under Article 417, "Protection of the worker's personality" of the new Obligations Code (effective on 1 July 2012), employers are required to take the necessary measures to prevent sexual harassment in the workplace and to prevent further damage to those who have already been victims of sexual harassment.[15] The employer has to "provide an environment compatible with morals" in the workplace. This is beyond encouragement of employers to take preventative actions. The Directive 2006/54 does not legally require individual employers to take preventative action; it merely encourages such activities on the part of employers.

The only reference to workplace sexual harassment in the Labour Law states that it is regulated as a ground for the perpetrator to face instant contract termination (summary termination; termination for a just cause). This category includes "immoral behaviour/conduct by the employer/worker or similar behaviour," where "similar behaviour" implies that the listing is non-exhaustive and that harassment or mobbing may be interpreted as also barred under the law.

Sexual harassment is a crime under Article 105 of the Criminal Law, but "mobbing" has not been specified as a crime. "Mobbing" is defined as deliberate and systematic behaviour, during which an employee is humiliated, degraded, socially excluded, intimidated, has his or her personality and dignity violated, and is subjected to hostile/ill treatment.[16] Previously, moral harassment (mobbing) was not a recognized claim in labour relations, but in recent years it has become an increasingly frequent workplace violence complaint, although it has not been described as a crime in the Criminal Law.

The primary remedies available under the Law on Human Rights and Equality Institution of Turkey are compensation and administrative sanctions.

---

[14] Constitutional Court 25 February 2010, Case No. 2008/55, Decision No. 2010/41 (Official Gazette 22 June 2010, no. 27619).

[15] Official Gazette 4 February 2011, no. 27836.

[16] Official Gazette 19 March 2011, no. 27879.

7 Who Supports the Enforcement of Antidiscrimination Law?

The state, the relevant ministries, public bodies, courts, the Human Rights and Equality Institution, ombudsmen, employers, associations, foundations, trade unions, employers' associations, political parties, public professional organisations and NGOs hold the legal burden of supporting the enforcement of antidiscrimination law.

8 Who Opposes the Enforcement of Antidiscrimination Law?

So far, there has not been an open, general opposition to the enforcement of antidiscrimination law. But in specific individual complaints of discrimination, the perpetrator will object the enforcement of antidiscrimination law to that specific case.

9 How Broad Is the Coverage of Antidiscrimination Law?

Article 10 of the Turkish Constitution reads: "All individuals are equal without any discrimination before the law, irrespective of language, race, colour, sex, political opinion, philosophical belief, religion and sect, or any such considerations." (Addendum, 2004)[17] Under the Constitution, men and women have equal rights. The State shall have the obligation to ensure that this equality exists in practice. (Addendum, 2010[18]) When the state takes affirmative steps to boost women's rights, these actions (known as positive discrimination) cannot be considered violations of the principle of equality.

Since Article 90 of the Constitution was amended in 2004,[19] ratified international agreements on fundamental rights and freedoms now take precedence over national laws. This means, for example, the United Nations Convention on the Elimination of All Forms of Discrimination against Women (CEDAW) or the Istanbul Convention, will be directly applicable even if a related national law could also apply.

Under Article 70 of the Constitution, every Turkish citizen has the right to work in the public service. Unless there is a genuine and necessary occupational

---

[17]Law no. 5170, Official Gazette 22 May 2004, no. 25469.
[18]Law no. 5982 amending the Constitution, Official Gazette 13 May 2010, no. 27580. This law was approved through a referendum held on 12 September 2010.
[19]Law No. 5170, Official Gazette, 22 May 2004, no. 25469.

requirement, job notices by public bodies and organisations cannot specify the sex of applicants.

In the past, women wearing headscarves could not take up public posts. The democratization package introduced on 30 September 2013 spoke of the removal of legal barriers for women with headscarves to take up public posts, the intention to increase penalties for hate crimes, and the intention to criminalise illegal force and intervention in personal life styles. Accordingly, the By-law on the Garments of Public Personnel[20] was amended[21] and women with headscarves may now hold public offices.

Article 5 of the Labour Law, a non-exhaustive provision, lists the protected characteristics as sex, race and ethnicity, religion and sect (religious denomination), language, colour, disability, political belief, philosophical belief, fixed-term or part-time nature of work and union membership and/or involvement in trade union activities. The Law on the Disabled[22] as amended by Law no. 6518[23] protects against direct and indirect discrimination against the disabled (Article 3(a)-(b)). Direct discrimination occurs when a disabled person, in the exercise of their rights and freedoms, is treated less favourably because of their disability. Indirect discrimination occurs where an apparently neutral provision, criterion or practice would put disabled persons at a particular disadvantage that cannot be justified by a legitimate aim. Notably, the Law on the Disabled also speaks of dual discrimination; if the disabled individual is female she may suffer from discrimination on the grounds of both sex and disability and attempts will be made to prevent disabled females from suffering dual discrimination (Article 4(h)).

Characteristics protected by the Law on Human Rights and Equality Institution of Turkey are sex, racial or ethnic origin, religion or belief, sect, disability, age, philosophical and political belief, colour, language, property, birth, marital status and health conditions. This is an exhaustive list of thirteen grounds that cannot be extended by the judiciary, but through legislation alone. However, this does not mean that courts have no role. Under the law, sex is protected but not sexual orientation, gender reassignment or transsexuality. When the courts want to intervene to protect gay or transgender individuals, they can easily re-characterize "sex" in order to bring these groups within the scope of protection. Courts may turn to the leading decisions of the European Court of Justice, where the court applied the prohibition of sex discrimination to discrimination arising from the gender reassignment of a person or transsexuality.

The Law on Human Rights and Equality Institution of Turkey defines direct discrimination, indirect discrimination, harassment, mobbing, multiple discrimination, segregation, instruction to discriminate and implementation of such an

---

[20]*Kamu Kurum ve Kuruluşlarında Çalışan Personelin Kılık ve Kıyafetine Dair Yönetmelik*, Official Gazette, 25 October 1982, no. 17849.
[21]Official Gazette, 8 October 2013, no. 28789.
[22]Law no. 5378, Official Gazette 7 July 2005, no. 25868.
[23]Official Gazette 19 February 2014, no. 28918.

instruction, reasonable accommodation in line with the EU acquis, mainly the Recast Directive 2006/54/EC. Discrimination includes segregation, direct discrimination, indirect discrimination, harassment, mobbing, multiple discrimination, instruction to discriminate, not affording reasonable accommodation and wrongful treatment of those who have initiated proceedings against discrimination, those who have been engaged in these proceedings and their representatives (Article 4).

In case of violation of the prohibition of discrimination, public bodies oversight responsibilities must take measures to end the violation, to prevent its reoccurrence, and to allow for pursuit of claims in judicial and administrative proceedings (Article 3(3)). Natural persons and private legal entities under an obligation regarding prohibition of discrimination have to take measures within their mandate for determination of discrimination, its avoidance and provision of equal treatment (Article 3 (4)).

Discrimination also takes place outside of the labour market. Antidiscrimination law also protects access to and the supply of goods and services. Article 5 of the Law on Human Rights and Equality Institution of Turkey (the Turkish version of the EU Council Directive 2004/113/EC) requires equal treatment between men and women in the access to and supply of goods and services. Public and private bodies will not be allowed to discriminate against citizens who want to obtain information about or access to services such as education, training, justice, police, health, transportation, communication, social security, social services, social aid, sports, accommodations, culture, tourism, and similar services. This provision applies also to access facilities associated with such services. Those that run these services and facilities have to consider reasonable accommodations for the disabled. There can be no discrimination in the processes of lease, sale, or transfer of property. Associations and other organizations cannot discriminate in membership acquisitions and terminations, elections, membership rights, and participation in the group's activities, unless there are exceptions described in the relevant laws or the group's internal regulations.

In the public and private sectors, discrimination is prohibited in access to employment and practical work experience, obtaining information about a workplace or work, job selection criteria and recruitment conditions, employment and working conditions, and in employment termination (Article 6(1)). This includes job notifications, access to all types and to all levels of vocational guidance and training, promotions, access to all levels of professional hierarchy, in-service training, social benefits and similar issues (Article 6(2)). Employers and their representatives cannot deny an application on the grounds of pregnancy, maternity or childcare responsibilities (Article 6(3)). Discrimination is also prohibited in access to self-employment, licensing, registration or similar issues (Article 6(4)). All types of work and labour contracts, whether they are covered by the Labour Law or other laws, are subject to the provisions of this article (Article 6(5)).

There cannot be a claim of discrimination where there is (Article 7):

1. A genuine and determining occupational requirement, provided that the objective is legitimate and the requirement is proportionate;

2. Sex is a determining factor;
3. The fixing of a minimum or maximum age for requirement in recruitment and in employment, provided that the objective is legitimate and the requirement is proportionate;
4. Special measures and preventive measures for children and other people;
5. Employment of people of a particular religion to serve or to provide education or training in religious institutions;
6. Membership requirements in accordance with purpose, principles and values laid down in the relevant legislation or internal regulations by associations, foundations, trade unions, employers' associations, political parties and professional organisations;
7. Positive (affirmative) action;
8. Differences of treatment based on nationality, where rules would govern an employee's entry, residence, and legal status.

The Human Rights and Equality Institution shall inform the Parliamentary Commission of Equal Opportunities for Women and Men and the Parliamentary Commission of Investigation of Human Rights at least once a year on its mandate and authorities (Article 9(3)).

10 Does the Enforcement of Antidiscrimination Law Vary According to the Ground of Discrimination?

Enforcement of antidiscrimination law varies according to the ground of discrimination. The Law on Human Rights and Equality Institution of Turkey is a recent development, and awareness of antidiscrimination law is not high. Typically, antidiscrimination suits concentrate in employment dismissals and (domestic) violence.

11 What Is the Relationship Between the Enforcement of Antidiscrimination Law and the Quest for Equality on Both an Individual and Systemic Level?

Remedies focus on the individual. The party found at fault must pay compensation. Compensation is individualised. The purpose of compensation—whether it is deterrent or compensatory, or both—is open to discussion. When compensation is ordered, it may deter the employer from repeated behaviour. Compensation may also create an incentive for the employer to reach a compromise with others who are adversely affected simultaneously. The employer may feel the need to develop an antidiscrimination policy to avoid future claims for compensation. This is important, because the court is not empowered to recommend/require action to change discriminatory practices or impose a mandatory injunction for the benefit of others.

The quest for equality on both an individual and systemic level has been enhanced by the Law on Human Rights and Equality Institution of Turkey, which now includes rules on affirmative duties to promote equality with a focus on systemic discrimination.

12 Is the Enforcement of Antidiscrimination Law Regarded as Different from the Enforcement of Other Laws?

The enforcement of antidiscrimination law is different from the enforcement of other laws in the sense that besides the complaints-led model (adversarial structure deviating from the individualism of the judicial procedure), there is also focus on systemic discrimination and the creation of institutional mechanisms for the elimination of discrimination.

13 What Does the Enforcement of Antidiscrimination Law Reveal About the Nature of Your Legal System or About the Enforcement of Laws in Your Legal System?

Turkey needed a special body promoting equality, assisting victims of discrimination, monitoring and reporting on discrimination issues, and addressing systemic discrimination. There are no specific guidelines by the EU on how these special bodies should operate. The Human Rights and Equality Institution of Turkey will operate not only in the fields of race and ethnic origin and gender, but covers all 13 grounds of discrimination specified in the Law. It is hoped that the Institution will be an effective body in promoting equality and curbing discrimination.

In drafting the Law on Human Rights and Equality Institution of Turkey, Paris principles were closely followed and the Law prioritizes cooperation and collaboration with the NGOs, universities, occupational organizations, and other public bodies with similar tasks (Articles 9(1)(n), 14(4), 22(1)-(2)). This interaction will add to the assets of the Board, the decision-making body of the Institution. The Board will also build on the experience of its predecessor, the Human Rights Institution. It is likely that the claimants may find recourse to this body easier, simpler, more efficient and faster when compared to judicial proceedings. Also, claims that cannot be made issues of judicial proceedings may easily be brought to this newly established body.

14 Conclusion

The transposition of the Racial Equality and Employment Equality Directives increased legal protection on the grounds of racial and ethnic origin, religion and belief, age, disability and sexual orientation in the EU Member States. Antidiscrimination law is currently developing in Turkey. Turkey screens its own national legislation for compliance with the international treaties to which it is a party. Turkey is levelling up protections across the various grounds of discrimination. Currently, awareness of antidiscrimination law is not high; victims have difficulty in recognising a discriminatory situation and understanding their rights to have the situation addressed.

An important challenge is the application of antidiscrimination law in practice, which used to be quite narrow. Until the enactment of the Law on Human Rights and Equality Institution of Turkey, antidiscrimination cases were mainly addressed through the complaints-led model, requiring the victim to identify a discriminatory act and bring a complaint to a court. The complaints-led model focuses on a determination of fault and punishing discriminatory conduct. This model applies mainly to complaints arising from labour contract terminations, where employees seek to be awarded compensation from the employer. Apart from labour contract disputes, the other area of concentration was (domestic) violence. Many other forms of discrimination were infrequently addressed under the old legal system.

Significant gaps and shortcomings of the old Turkish antidiscrimination law have been improved by the Law on Human Rights and Equality Institution of Turkey. Besides the complaints-led model, there is enhancement of affirmative duties to promote equality with a focus on systemic discrimination. The state, the relevant ministries, public bodies, courts, the Human Rights and Equality Institution, ombudsmen, employers, associations, foundations, trade unions, employers' associations, political parties, public professional organisations and NGOs have the legal burden of supporting the enforcement of antidiscrimination law. Already, Turkey has seen notable political commitment in the promotion of gender equality, especially in efforts to increase the female workforce and to combat violence, domestic violence and workplace sexual harassment.

References

Relevant National Regulations

Constitution (*Anayasa*), Law No. 2709, Official Gazette 9 November 1982;
Law on Human Rights and Equality Institution of Turkey (*Türkiye İnsan Hakları ve Eşitlik Kurumu Kanunu*), Law no. 6701, Official Gazette 20 April 2016;
Law of Obligations (*Borçlar Kanunu*), Law No. 6098, Official Gazette 4 February 2011;

Statutory Decree on Establishment and Duties of the Ministry of Family and Social Affairs (*Aile ve Sosyal Politikalar Bakanlığının Teşkilat ve Görevleri Hakkında Kanun Hükmünde Kararname*), Official Gazette 8 June 2011;
Labour Law (*İş Kanunu*), Law No. 4857, Official Gazette 10 June 2003;
The Law on the Disabled (*Engelliler Hakkında Kanun*) Law no. 5378, Official Gazette 7 July 2005;
Criminal Code (*Türk Ceza Kanunu*), Law No. 5237, Official Gazette 12 October 2004;
The Law on the Ombudsman Institution (*Kamu Denetçiliği Kanunu*), Law no. 6328, Official Gazette 29.06.2012;
The Law on the Parliamentary Commission of Equal Opportunities for Women and Men (*Kadın Erkek Fırsat Eşitliği Komisyonu Kanunu*), Law no. 5840, Official Gazette 24.03.2009;
The Law on the Parliamentary Commission of Investigation of Human Rights (*İnsan Haklarını İnceleme Komisyonu Kanunu*), Law no. 3686, Official Gazette 05.12.1990;
The Law on the Protection of the Family and the Prevention of Violence Against Women (*Ailenin Korunması ve Kadına Karşı Şiddetin Önlenmesine Dair Kanun*), Law no. 6284, Official Gazette 20 March 2012;
By-Law on the Implementation of the Law on the Protection of the Family and the Prevention of Violence Against Women (*6284 Sayılı Ailenin Korunması ve Kadına Karşı Şiddetin Önlenmesine Dair Kanuna Ilişkin Uygulama Yönetmeliği*), Official Gazette 18 January 2013;
By-Law on the Establishment and Functioning of Guest Houses (*Kadın Konukevlerinin Açılması ve Işletilmesi Hakkında Yönetmelik*), Official Gazette 5 January 2013;
By-Law on the Working Conditions for Pregnant or Nursing Workers, and Nursing Rooms and Day Nurseries (*Gebe veya Emziren Kadınların Çalıştırılma Şartlarıyla Emzirme Odaları ve Çocuk Bakım Yurtlarına Dair Yönetmelik*), Official Gazette 16 August 2013;
By-law on Birth Allowance (*Doğum Yardımı Yönetmeliği*), Official Gazette 23 May 2015;
The Prime Ministry circular on the deterrence of mobbing in public bodies and institutions and private workplaces (*İşyerlerinde Psikolojik Tacizin [Mobbing] Önlenmesi Başbakanlık Genelgesi*), Official Gazette 19 March 2011;
Capital Markets Board Communiqué no. 57 amending the former Communiqué on Determination and Application of Corporate Government Principles (*Kurumsal Yönetim İlkelerinin Belirlenmesine ve Uygulanmasına İlişkin Tebliğde Değişiklik Yapılmasına Dair SPK Tebliği*), Official Gazette 11 February 2012.

Nurhan Süral is a Professor of Law at the Middle East Technical University, Ankara, Turkey. She holds an LLB and LLD from Ankara Law School. Ms. Süral writes and teaches in the field of Labor Law and Social Security Law and works in various international projects. She serves as a member of the European Network of legal experts in Gender Equality and Non-discrimination. Her research interests span comparative studies on EU and Turkey's labor laws, gender equality and non-discrimination in the labor market and unionization.

United Kingdom

Colm O'Cinneide

1 Is Antidiscrimination Law Enforced?

1.1 Introduction

Yes. United Kingdom antidiscrimination law is enforced—albeit primarily by means of private individuals bringing tort-style claims against alleged discriminators under the relevant provisions of the UK's antidiscrimination legislation rather than by enforcement action initiated by NGOs or public bodies such as the Equality and Human Rights Commission (EHRC).

More detail follows on this below, as well as on recent developments that may be having a negative impact on enforcement of the law in this area. However, to provide some context for this information, it is necessary to outline some of the key features of antidiscrimination law in the UK.

1.2 The Legislative Framework

The framework of legal norms that make up British antidiscrimination law has been laid down in progressive stages, from the enactment of the (limited) Race Relations Acts 1965 and 1968 to the much more comprehensive Equal Pay Act 1970 (covering

---

C. O'Cinneide (✉)
University College London, Faculty of Laws, London, UK
e-mail: c.o'cinneide@ucl.ac.uk

pay differentials linked to gender), the Sex Discrimination Act 1975 and the Race Relations Act 1976, and subsequently through to the enactment of the Disability Discrimination Act 1995, the implementation via regulations in 2003 and 2006 of the EU Framework Equality Directive 2000/78/EC which prohibited for the first time discrimination in employment on the grounds of age, religion or belief and sexual orientation, and ultimately to the enactment of the comprehensive and codifying Equality Act 2010. Direct and indirect discrimination, victimisation, and harassment on the basis of a number of "protected characteristics," namely age, disability, gender reassignment, marital status, religion or belief, race and ethnicity, sex and sexual orientation, are prohibited by the 2010 Act.[1] (A different legislative framework applies to Northern Ireland, whose broad contours are nevertheless similar to that applying to Britain but with the significant exception that discrimination on the basis of political opinion is also prohibited.) Supplementary legislation regulates matters such as maternity, paternity and paternal leave, and associated rights.

Legislation is thus the primary source of UK antidiscrimination law. In contrast, the common law has played little or no meaningful role in this regard. However, the provisions of the European Convention on Human Rights (ECHR), as interpreted by the Strasbourg-based European Court of Human Rights (ECtHR) and/or the UK courts giving effect to the Human Rights Act 1998 which have made Convention rights enforceable in national law, have plugged some gaps in protection—as in the "gays in the military" case of *Smith and Grady v UK*, where the ECtHR held that the UK's ban on gays serving in the armed forces breached the right to private life as protected by Article 8 ECHR.[2] More significantly, the requirements of EU law have played an important role in extending protection against discrimination in the UK: all UK legislation pending Brexit has to be interpreted with reference to the non-discrimination provisions of the EU treaties and antidiscrimination directives as interpreted by the Court of Justice of the EU (CJEU). CJEU's purposive approach to the interpretation of these EU norms has resulted in various aspects of UK law being struck down or re-interpreted to ensure conformity with their requirements.[3]

---

[1] For the scope of the 2010 Act, see below.

[2] (1999) 29 EHRR 493. The UK is obliged under Article 46 of the ECHR to give effect to judgments of the Court. This international law obligation has significant normative force in the European context.

[3] See, e.g., Case C-303/06, *Coleman v Attridge Law* [2008] IRLR 722. The influence of EU law over UK antidiscrimination law will presumably be cut off when the process of "Brexit" from the EU is completed.

1.3 Awareness of the Law

Thanks to the influence of EU law, and the manner in which the Equality Act 2010 standardised key elements of the legislative framework, UK antidiscrimination law is now comparatively detailed, clear and well-developed. It also enjoys a high profile. Private employers, service providers, trade unions, legal advice centres and public authorities will, in general, have some awareness of the basic requirements of antidiscrimination law, in particular as it relates to employment. Antidiscrimination cases are regularly appealed to the superior courts, including the UK Supreme Court (which, for example, heard two high-profile actions relating to the scope of indirect discrimination in November 2016). Antidiscrimination law is often taught as a core element of EU law, employment law, and human rights law courses in UK law schools, and activist NGOs and other campaigning groups regularly invoke its provisions. Furthermore, the UK media also regularly run stories about particularly important or controversial cases.

1.4 Patterns of Individual Enforcement

As a consequence, antidiscrimination law generates a relatively high level of litigation—in particular in the employment context—and has done so for several decades now. For example, 34,606 discrimination claims were initiated before employment tribunals in England and Wales in 2012–2013.[4] Gender-related cases made up the clear majority of these claims, followed by disability, age and race claims in descending order, with religion/belief and sexual orientation claims bringing up the rear.[5] These figures are broadly consistent with data from previous years, dating back to the 1980s and early 1990s when UK antidiscrimination law first "bedded down" and became influenced by the more expansive scope of EU equality law.

Claimants bringing discrimination claims face considerable hurdles. Many employment discrimination claims are often withdrawn before a final judicial determination (30% according to a 2014 survey).[6] Furthermore, the success rate in employment discrimination cases is notoriously low: the 2014 survey concluded that only 22% of claims that proceed to a full hearing before an employment tribunal

---

[4]This set of statistics from 2012 to 2013 is used as it predates the introduction of tribunal fees in 2013 (see below).

[5]In 2012–2013, 17,406 sex discrimination claims, together with 451 maternity/paternity-specific cases, were initiated, compared to 6985 disability claims, 4679 age claims, 2523 race claims, 948 religion or belief claims, and 614 sexual orientation claims. See Ministry of Justice, *Tribunal Statistics*, Annex C: Management Information on Employment Tribunal Receipts, 2012–15, available at https://www.gov.uk/government/statistics/tribunals-and-gender-recognition-certificate-statistics-quarterly-january-to-march-2015.

[6]Department of Business Innovation and Skills (2014) ("SETA 2014"), p. 181, Table 5.2.

were successful.[7] A 2012 study concluded that only 3% of all discrimination claims initiated in the employment sphere resulted in a positive finding by a tribunal that discrimination had taken place.[8] Tight time limits are imposed, giving claimants only 3 months to initiate an employment claim and 6 months to initiate a goods and services claim. Legal aid is not available in employment claims: claimants are supposed to be able to represent themselves before the employment tribunals, which adopt simplified rules of proceeding as opposed to courts. But in practice, litigating discrimination claims can be difficult to do without legal assistance. Furthermore, as discussed in detail below, class actions in the US sense of the term cannot be initiated in UK law. This means that discrimination claims must be brought on an individualised basis, which in turn means that individuals who lack access to legal advice and support, or who are particularly vulnerable to retaliatory action and/or to being depicted as "troublemakers" in their field of employment, may be deterred from initiating claims.

However, despite these problems, it is widely accepted that UK antidiscrimination law in general has real enforcement "teeth." This is due to the frequency with which individuals (often supported by trade unions, legal advice centres or the equality commissions[9]) have been prepared to bring actions against employers and service providers for apparent breaches of the legislation. A legal culture has been established in which discrimination claims are relatively common-place—as a consequence, discrimination law has acquired real regulatory influence. An important factor in this regard is the adverse media attention that a finding of discrimination will often attract: this embarrassment factor plays a significant role in encouraging compliance with the legislation.

In this respect, it is significant that employment cases could, until recently, be initiated and litigated without claimants having to pay a fee or (in general) run the risk of having costs awarded against them.[10] This ensured that the employment tribunal system was accessible, which in turn generated a steady supply of enforcement actions. Furthermore, while as noted above, the success rate of discrimination

---

[7]Ibid.

[8]According to figures gathered by GQ Employment Law, just 710 out of 3210 discrimination cases that were heard and determined by an employment tribunal were successful in 2014. In contrast, 18,847 out of 30,498 "other" non-discrimination employment law claims succeeded before a tribunal in the same year. However, the figures do not reveal the number of claims that were settled. See "Low Rate of Success for Discrimination Claims," *New Law Journal*, 27 Nov 2014. In part, this low success rate may reflect the complexity of discrimination claims and the difficulty in proving that a protected characteristic was a "ground" of unequal treatment. Anecdotal evidence also suggests that a certain proportion of discrimination claims are initiated as a way of putting pressure on employers to settle employment-related disputes which may have at best a tangential relationship with "discrimination" as defined under law; the absence of a cap on damages in discrimination cases, and the extra moral opprobrium associated with discrimination as distinct from other forms of employment actions may encourage this tendency.

[9]In 2012, 61% of persons bringing a discrimination claim received "assistance" (broadly defined) on a day-to-day basis with the claim process. See SETA (2014), p. 131, Table 3.14.

[10]Costs can be awarded where a claim is deemed to be "vexatious."

claims litigated to trial is very low, the employment tribunal system has historically still generated positive outcomes for many claimants. In this respect, it is significant that many discrimination claims are settled pre-trial: 58% of initiated discrimination claims in 2012.[11] Anecdotal evidence from leading practitioners in this field suggests that it is common for "clear cut" cases of discrimination to be settled in favour of the claimant rather than litigated to trial.

The situation is a little different when it comes to discrimination in access to goods and services, housing, education and other non-employment areas of activity. Such claims are processed by the ordinary court system, where legal costs can be awarded against a complainant. This possibility appears to seriously limit the number of enforcement actions brought in this context. As a result, the volume of claims is low—usually in double or low triple figures annually.[12] However, NGOs and the equality commissions in Britain and Northern Ireland play an important role in helping to correct for this low volume of individual enforcement actions, generally through their support of test cases or targeted legal action. As a consequence, it is relatively common for discriminatory policies and practices to be challenged even outside of the employment sphere, especially when public authorities are involved.

1.5 Recent Developments

Given the UK's reliance on individual enforcement, in particular in the employment context, it is significant that a requirement was introduced in 2013 that complainants must pay a fee of up to £950 to access the employment tribunal system.[13] These fees could be remitted where individuals receiving forms of welfare support, but fees were incurred in the clear majority of cases (an estimated 75%). Their imposition generated a significant decrease in discrimination claims brought before employment tribunals, amounting to a drop of 68% in England and Wales in the first 2 years after they were introduced, with the number of sex discrimination claims being particularly affected.[14]

---

[11] SETA (2014), p. 181, Table 5.2. Only 11% go to a full hearing. See p. 184, Table 5.4.

[12] There is a paucity of statistics on the volume of non-employment discrimination claims. However, it seems as if 111 such cases were initiated in 2014. See the discussion by Pulley (2015).

[13] For details, see the guidance available at https://www.gov.uk/employment-tribunals/make-a-claim.

[14] In 2014–2015, a total of 11,224 discrimination claims were initiated in England and Wales, compared to 34,606 in 2012–2013, as mentioned above. More specifically, sex discrimination claims have fallen by 75%; sexual orientation and religion or belief claims by 71% and 66% respectively; race, disability and age claims by 58%, 59% and 61% respectively; and pregnancy and maternity claims by 49%. See Ministry of Justice, *Tribunal Statistics*, Annex C: Management Information on Employment Tribunal Receipts, 2012–15, Table C.4, available at https://www.gov.uk/government/statistics/tribunals-and-gender-recognition-certificate-statistics-quarterly-january-to-march-2015. Evidence from the Advisory, Conciliation and Arbitration Service (ACAS), who play an important role in resolving discrimination claims, suggests that the single most important

The imposition of these fees was highly controversial and was challenged before the courts on the basis that they interfere with access to justice contrary to the requirements of the common law, EU law and the ECHR.[15] In July 2017, in the case of *R(Unison) v Lord Chancellor*, the UK Supreme Court concluded that the imposition of these fees breached the common law right of access to the courts and was consequently unlawful. As a result, this fee requirement has now been lifted—and fees paid previously are being refunded. It remains to be seen how this will impact on the number of employment discrimination cases being brought by individual complainants.[16]

These concerns have been amplified by recent cuts of 25% or more to the budget of the EHRC, who plays a residual role in enforcing antidiscrimination law by supporting individual cases, intervening in ongoing legal actions, and using their (infrequently deployed) investigative and inquiry powers (discussed below). These budget cuts have substantially limited the ability of the EHRC to provide legal support to all but a handful of individual cases.[17]

1.6 An Alternative Model? Positive Duties

Academic experts have for some time now identified this reliance on individual enforcement as a structural weakness of this area of UK law. In response, a range of positive duties have been imposed on public authorities, requiring them to (1) take steps to promote equality of opportunity and (2) to consult and publicise the measures they are taking to give effect to this obligation.[18] A public authority's failure to comply with these obligations can be judicially reviewed. This has allowed NGOs and trade unions to challenge decisions by public authorities which neglected to give due weight to the requirements of these duties, thereby opening up a new enforcement route.

However, these positive duty requirements are ultimately procedural in nature[19] and generally only apply to the public sector. The exceptions are the positive duty imposed on public and private employers in Northern Ireland to take steps to promote equality of opportunity between Catholics and Protestants[20] and a new

---

reason given by claimants for not pursuing their claim was the costs imposed by tribunal fees. See ACAS (2015), pp. 96–98, which suggests that 26% of claimants were deterred by the new fee system.

[15]*R (Unison) v Lord Chancellor (No 2)* [2017] UKSC 51.

[16]For an overview of the political debate about the imposition of these fees, see House of Commons Library, Briefing Paper No. 7081, *Employment Tribunal Fees*, 22 June 2016. The Scottish Government had previously announced that it was going to abolish this fee requirement in Scotland.

[17]See the Early Day Motion 382, *Budget for Equality and Human Rights Commission*, House of Commons Session 2016-7, 21/07/2016, available at https://www.parliament.uk/edm/2016-17/382.

[18]Section 149 of the Equality Act 2010; section 75 of the Northern Ireland Act 1998.

[19]McColgan (2015), p. 453.

[20]See the Fair Employment and Treatment Order (Northern Ireland) 1998.

equal pay reporting duty imposed on large employers requiring them to publish their average mean and media gender pay gaps from 2018.[21]

As a consequence, the positive duty model remains a supplement to individual enforcement, notwithstanding the possibility that the latter mode of enforcement may in the future prove less effective than it has been in the past.

1.7 Conclusion

In general, it remains to be seen whether UK antidiscrimination law will continue to be as effectively enforced as it has been over the last few decades. The introduction of employment tribunal fees, coming on top of other access to justice barriers, risked undermining the UK's comprehensive antidiscrimination legal framework by deterring the individual litigants who bear the burden of its enforcement—but for now these fees have been abolished following the Supreme Court's 2017 judgment in the *Unison* case.

2 How Is Antidiscrimination Law Enforced?

As the above analysis makes clear, UK antidiscrimination law is primarily enforced by individuals bringing tort-style claims under the Equality Act 2010 and associated legislation, in which they seek compensation and/or declaratory relief for alleged acts of unlawful discrimination that they have suffered. Such claims can be initiated before employment tribunals or county courts, depending on whether they relate to employment or other areas of social activity coming within the scope of discrimination law. But no class actions in the US sense of the term are possible in UK law, meaning that discrimination claims must be lodged and litigated on an individual basis. Such claims may, however, be grouped together and adjudicated on a combined basis, as happens in particular with equal pay claims.

In such individual enforcement claims, UK legislation in line with the requirements of EU law provides for a shift of the burden of proof: if a claimant establishes facts on the balance of probabilities from which a court or tribunal could, in the absence of any other explanation, conclude that unlawful discrimination occurred, then the court or tribunal must conclude that discrimination did occur unless the alleged discriminator can prove otherwise.[22] This shift is designed to ensure more effective enforcement of discrimination law in recognising that proof of discrimination can be notoriously difficult to obtain.

---

[21]See Government Equalities Office, *Mandatory Gender Pay Gap Reporting*, Consultation Paper, February 2016, available at https://www.gov.uk/government/uploads/system/uploads/attachment_data/file/504398/GPG_consultation_v8.pdf.
[22]See section 139 of the Equality Act 2010: also *Igen Ltd & Ors v Wong* [2005] EWCA Civ 142.

Claimants also used to be able to require that alleged discriminators answer a questionnaire relating to the facts at issue in their claim, and courts and tribunals could draw negative inferences from evasive or incomplete answers. This procedure was controversially abolished in 2014 as part of a government assault on "red tape." However, guidance provided by the Advisory, Conciliation and Arbitration Service (ACAS) indicates that claimants are still entitled to ask detailed questions of alleged discriminators, and that courts and tribunals may continue to draw negative inferences from inadequate answers.[23]

Compliance by public authorities with antidiscrimination law—or associated norms of human rights and (for now) EU law, as well as the requirements of the positive equality duties discussed above—can also be enforced via judicial review proceedings by individuals or NGOs with an interest in the matter at hand. The UK's equality commissions—the EHRC in Britain, and the Equality Commission for Northern Ireland (ECNI)—can also initiate judicial review proceedings. The equality commissions can "support" individual actions by providing claimants with legal support and assistance or by "intervening" in ongoing cases to advocate a particular interpretation or application of the legal framework.[24]

Equality commissions also have the power to initiate "investigations" into whether particular public or private bodies are complying with antidiscrimination law when they find that evidence exists that a particular body is failing to comply with its obligations under antidiscrimination law. The investigating commission will then conduct a fact-finding exercise, in the course of which it can require alleged discriminators to give evidence, and which may lead to a commission finding non-compliance with the requirements of antidiscrimination law.[25]

However, these findings are not legally binding: if the alleged discriminator refuses to accept the commission's findings or give effect to any recommended remedial action, the commission will have to seek a court order upholding its determination. Furthermore, the procedural requirements of this process are relatively onerous, and a failure by a commission to comply with these requirements will expose it to legal challenge. When the UK equality commissions first began to exercise this power in the mid to late 1970s, they ran into numerous legal hurdles and faced judicial hostility directed at what one prominent judge described as the "inquisitorial" nature of this process. As a consequence, the investigative powers of the equality commissions never assumed the central role in enforcing antidiscrimination law that the original architects of the UK's 1970s antidiscrimination legislation wanted them to play.[26]

Instead, the equality commissions have tended to make use of their power to launch more wide-ranging "inquiries" into how antidiscrimination law is being enforced and applied in particular areas of social or economic activity. Unlike

---

[23] ACAS (2014).
[24] See in general O'Cinneide (2007), pp. 141–162.
[25] O'Cinneide (2007).
[26] O'Cinneide (2007).

investigations, such inquiries cannot lead to a finding of discrimination being made against a particular discriminator; instead, they serve as vehicles for highlighting the existence of compliance gaps in specific areas of business or public sector activity. This inquiry mechanism is therefore not an enforcement power as such. However, in tandem with NGO activism and media reporting, it can be effective in encouraging employers and service providers to comply with antidiscrimination law.

3 Who Enforces Antidiscrimination Law?

As outlined above, UK antidiscrimination law is primarily enforced by individual claimants alleging they were subject to discrimination in the course of employment. NGOs, trade unions, the equality commissions and other associations may provide legal advice and support, but may not initiate claims on behalf of alleged individual victims of discrimination, unless the dispute in question involves the exercise of public power by a public authority. Then they can bring a judicial review action to challenge such discrimination if they are deemed to have a "sufficient interest" in the matter at hand.

As a result, the equality commissions play at best a residual role in enforcing antidiscrimination law by supporting or intervening in individual actions or through the (very occasional) exercise of their investigative and inquiry powers as discussed above. However, the commissions, along with the unions, NGOs and other civil society associations, often provide claimants with legal assistance and advice.

Individual claimants come from a wide variety of backgrounds. Historically disadvantaged groups such as women and persons from black and minority ethnic (BME) groups are the prime "users" of the law, as might be expected. But the picture is a little complicated by regional variations. For example, a significant proportion of race discrimination cases initiated in Scotland are brought by persons of English ethnicity alleging discrimination on that basis.[27] Older men are more likely to bring age discrimination claims than other groups, while members of minority religious groups such as Muslims and Sikhs are proportionately more likely to bring religious discrimination claims than Christians/non-believers. There are some indications that public sector workers are more likely to bring discrimination claims than their private sector counterparts, perhaps reflecting higher levels of unionisation.

In contrast to many European states, ombudsmen do not play a significant role in enforcing antidiscrimination legislation. There exist several different ombudsmen offices in the UK, dealing with various types of issues, but their profile is relatively low, and their focus is on redressing administrative injustices rather than securing compliance with the law as such. As a result, it is very rare for them to adjudicate discrimination issues in the UK.

---

[27]See, e.g., *BBC v Souster* [2001] IRLR 150.

4 Who Benefits from the Enforcement of Antidiscrimination Law?

Different groups are viewed as benefiting from the enforcement of UK antidiscrimination law, depending upon the grounds of claim at issue. Race discrimination law has provided "visible" black and minority ethnic groups with a shield against prejudice—but the Irish, Poles and other white European minorities have also benefited. Sikhs and Muslims have brought many of the most prominent religious discrimination cases, but evangelical Christians have also invoked the protection of the law in a number of recent very high-profile cases (often however without much success). Older persons have been the prime beneficiary of age discrimination claims, in particular older male middle-class employees working in relatively high-earning professions such as law, and in general, younger workers are proportionately less likely to initiate discrimination claims.[28] Trade union members are proportionately more likely to initiate discrimination claims, as are women and members of religious and (in particular) ethnic minorities.[29]

LGBT persons have benefited considerably from the enforcement of antidiscrimination law over the decades, in particular via the quasi-constitutional protection afforded by the ECHR. Women—in particular pregnant women or mothers and women employed in occupationally segregated parts of the labour force—have benefited from some high-profile and high-value equal pay claims over the years (usually involving the public sector). However, concern remains that pregnancy discrimination remains all too common and that the law in this regard is insufficiently enforced.[30]

Disability discrimination law has been invoked by a range of different groups of persons with disabilities, including individuals with mental health problems. Many disability claims fail on the basis that the claimant is insufficiently disabled to qualify for protection under the legislation, mainly because their impairment is deemed to not to impair their day-to-day functioning to a substantial degree or is not "long term" in nature. This has raised concerns that the "moderately" disabled may, perhaps paradoxically, be excluded from the protection of the legislation.

In Northern Ireland, members of the Catholic/Nationalist minority are viewed as the major beneficiaries of the fair employment legislation in place there. They benefit, in particular, from the positive duties it imposes on employers to take

---

[28] In 2012, only 5% of discrimination claims were initiated by persons 24 and younger: in contrast, 17% were initiated by persons in the 55–64 age range.

[29] In 2012, 73% of initiators of discrimination claims were of "white" ethnicity: in contrast, 90% of British employees are "white"; 13% were of minority religious faith, as compared to 9% of employees; 54% were female, in contrast to 51% of all employees; 44% were members of trade union or staff association, as compared to 27% or so of all employees. See SETA (2014).

[30] See EHRC, *Pregnancy and Maternity Discrimination Research Findings* 21 October 2016, available at https://www.equalityhumanrights.com/en/managing-pregnancy-and-maternity-workplace/pregnancy-and-maternity-discrimination-research-findings.

steps to promote equality of opportunity, which appear to have played a significant role in closing the sizeable gap that used to exist between the two communities when it came to employment and earning opportunities.

The enforcement activities of equality commissions, in tandem with their promotional work, is generally focused on securing greater equality of opportunity and equal treatment for members of disadvantaged groups such as women, BME and LGBT persons, and people with disabilities. However, the commissions have been at pains to emphasise that everyone is potentially a beneficiary of the protection afforded by antidiscrimination law, pointing to the scope of age and disability discrimination law in particular.

5 Who Is Harmed by the Enforcement of Antidiscrimination Law?

Responses to this question will differ greatly, depending on how one defines "harm." Certain disadvantaged groups appear to benefit less than others from enforcement of antidiscrimination law than perhaps they should, such as pregnant women and persons with "moderate" disabilities as discussed above. Other groups struggle to obtain what they would regard as favourable outcomes from discrimination law litigation—evangelical Christians would be a good example, again as previously noted.

Under-use of antidiscrimination law might also be viewed as a species of "harm." As noted above, younger workers bring proportionately much fewer age discrimination claims than their older counterparts. Members of the white English ethnic majority also invoke race discrimination law to a comparatively lower degree than other ethnic groups, although as noted above, the situation is more complicated in Scotland.

The operation of the positive duties in Britain—and the equal opportunities duty in Northern Ireland—seems to favour disadvantaged groups, as was their intention. From the perspective of traditionally dominant groups such as Protestant/Unionists in Northern Ireland, or white males across the UK, this may qualify as "harm" if one adopts a zero-sum perspective on the matter. However, it should be noted that the UK and EU courts have adopted a largely symmetrical interpretation of antidiscrimination law, and UK law provides limited scope for positive action measures that favour disadvantaged groups.[31]

---

[31] Sections 158–159 of the Equality Act 2010.

Public sector employers attract proportionately higher levels of discrimination claims.[32] So do large employers.[33] In both cases, this may reflect the higher levels of unionisation in the public sector and in larger workplaces, which may help to generate a more protective environment for employees who bring a discrimination claim.

6 What Remedies Are Provided by the Enforcement of Antidiscrimination Law?

Under §§ 119 and 124 of the Equality Act 2010, courts and employment tribunals may, if they find that unlawful discrimination has occurred, make a declaration as to the rights of the claimant and order the payment of appropriate compensation. Courts can also grant injunctive relief, requiring discriminators to refrain from engaging in ongoing or future unlawful conduct.[34] Employment tribunals do not have this power but can make recommendations to what a discriminating employer should do in the future to avoid any further breaches of the rights of the claimant. (The 2010 Act had originally given employment tribunals the additional power to make recommendations relating to how employers were treating their workforce at large, but this power was controversially removed by subsequent legislation in 2015.[35])

Damages may be awarded for direct discrimination, harassment, and victimisation, irrespective of intention. In the case of indirect discrimination, if the defendant proves that the act of discrimination at issue was unintentional, then a tribunal or court must consider the adequacy of alternative remedies before deciding to award damages.[36]

The compensation awarded under antidiscrimination legislation can include both pecuniary loss (e.g. non-payment of wages, loss of future earnings) and non-pecuniary loss (e.g. hurt to feelings, psychiatric harm). Compensation awards are governed by broadly the same legal principles that apply to other employment or tort claims. This means that the award of aggravated or punitive damages is rare, and awards in general remain relatively low, at least compared to the size of US claims. This is not specific to the field of discrimination law or even to employment law in general, but a general feature of British tort law.

---

[32]In 2012, 56% of claims were initiated against private employers and 30% against public sector employers, which compares with 70% and 19% respectively of unfair dismissal claims. (Claims made against voluntary sector employees make up the rest.) SETA (2014), p. 259, Table 8.6.

[33]SETA (2014), p. 88.

[34]Discriminatory decisions by public authorities can also be overturned by judicial review, with the exception of Acts of Parliament. See, e.g., section 6 Human Rights Act 1998.

[35]Section 2 Deregulation Act 2015.

[36]Section 119(5)-(6) of the Equality Act 2010.

In 2012, monetary compensation was awarded in 80% of all successful claims, with £18,667 the mean award.[37] However, high awards are possible depending upon the circumstances of a particular case, including in particular the salary of the claimant and the extent of any aggravated damages awarded. Compensation awards in excess of £1,000,000 are not unknown.[38] In line with the requirements of EU law, there is no cap on the damage award following a finding of unlawful discrimination: this is important, as it gives real teeth to discrimination law and ensures that it "bites" even in areas such as financial services, whereas a system of capped awards might deprive the legislation of any real effect. Consequently, monetary compensation awards are on average notably higher in employment discrimination cases than for other types of employment law claims.[39]

In general, UK antidiscrimination law does not provide that employers and service providers be excluded from public procurement tendering for breaches of antidiscrimination law. However, employers in Northern Ireland who fail to comply with their reporting and monitoring obligations imposed by the fair employment legislation can be barred from tendering public authority contracts—a sanction which is regarded as having considerable dissuasive effect.[40]

7 Who Supports the Enforcement of Antidiscrimination Law?

The application of antidiscrimination law is generally quite uncontroversial in the UK, which contrasts interestingly with the highly charged political debates that surround other areas of human rights law such as the ECHR and HRA. While certain aspects of the legislation and the outcome of particular cases attract criticism (as noted in the following section), all mainstream British political parties would claim to be supportive of the Equality Act 2010 and committed to ensuring that its provisions are effectively enforced.

This reflects the fact that antidiscrimination legislation has come to be viewed as an essential regulatory tool in an increasingly multicultural state; politicians from both the left and right of the political spectrum acknowledge both the importance of the right to non-discrimination and the key role played by the legislation in securing this right. Support for the effective enforcement of antidiscrimination legislation is

---

[37]SETA (2014), Tables 5.5 and 5.9, pp. 186 and 190. However, this mean of £18,000 is notably higher than other types of employment awards: for example, by way of contrast, £11,000 is the mean in unfair dismissal actions.

[38]See Cox (2015).

[39]Ministry of Justice, Tribunal and Gender Recognition Certificate Statistics Quarterly, April–June 2016, Employment Tribunal Tables E.1–E.11, available at https://www.gov.uk/government/statistics/tribunals-and-gender-recognition-certificate-statistics-quarterly-april-to-june-2016.

[40]See generally McCrudden et al. (2004), pp. 363–415.

particularly strong on the left of British politics, in particular within the Labour and Liberal Democratic parties. But the centre-right Conservative party claims to support full enforcement of the legislation, notwithstanding its support for the introduction of employment tribunal fees in 2013.

Similarly, trade unions tend to be particularly vocal supporters of the antidiscrimination legislation and place great emphasis on the need to secure its effective enforcement. Employer organisations are also generally supportive of the legislation and its various enforcement mechanisms, although, as noted in the following section, they are critical of what they would see as the potential for the employment tribunal system to be abused. The legal profession is also supportive of the enforcement of antidiscrimination law, with the leading professional bodies such as the Law Society and Bar Council being highly critical of the recent imposition of employment tribunal fees.

There is little hard evidence of general attitudes amongst the general public. However, it is widely assumed that women, disabled persons, members of minority, non-Christian religious groups, and persons of BME ethnicity are particularly supportive of the effective enforcement of the legislation—an assumption that tends to be reflected in the reluctance of mainstream politicians to criticise antidiscrimination law and the necessity of its enforcement in a direct manner.

8 Who Opposes the Enforcement of Antidiscrimination Law?

At the political level, only the hard-right UK Independence Party has queried the need for antidiscrimination legislation. However, members of Parliament from the centre-right Conservative and Unionist parties have periodically expressed concern about what they see as the excessively far-reaching and onerous requirements imposed on employers, service providers, and public authorities by the legislation and, in particular, the manner in which it is applied and enforced. Certain media organs—in particular the right-wing newspapers *The Daily Mail* and *Daily Express*—have also occasionally criticised the implementation of the legislation as contributing to a culture of "political correctness gone mad."

Employer organisations have at times been critical of the general functioning of the employment tribunal system, which in their view is too accommodating of "weak" or poorly supported claims. These concerns influenced the introduction of tribunal fees in 2013, a policy measure implemented by the then Conservative-Liberal Democrat coalition government out of a desire to cut costs by making the tribunal system recoup its own costs of functioning from users of the system. Although this view is not usually publicly articulated, many employers view the imposition of fees as a mechanism for deterring uncertain or borderline claims.

Concern about the regulatory impact of antidiscrimination legislation has also made successive governments reluctant to impose positive equality duties on the private sector or to expand the enforcement powers of the equality commissions. Some high-profile policy advisers linked to the Conservative party have argued for radical reforms to employment law, including the abolition of maternity leave.[41] Leading Conservative politicians, including the current Prime Minister Theresa May MP, have called for repeal of the HRA and even UK withdrawal from the ECHR, which would weaken protection against discrimination and limit the scope of available remedies against public authorities.

Concerns that the enforcement of antidiscrimination legislation imposes undue constraints upon religious freedom have also surfaced in public debate: conservative Christian groups have been particularly critical of how the legislation has been interpreted and applied in a number of cases involving clashes between the right to non-discrimination on grounds of sexual orientation and the right to express one's religious beliefs.[42]

As yet, these critical perspectives have not exerted much impact on the national policy agenda in the field of equality and non-discrimination. However, it remains to be seen how the situation will develop over the next few years, especially now the UK will be exiting the EU and presumably will thus no longer be subject to any legal requirement to give effect to the requirements of EU equality law.

9 How Broad Is the Coverage of Antidiscrimination Law?

As outlined above, UK antidiscrimination legislation in the form of the Equality Act 2010 covers the "protected characteristics" of age, disability, gender reassignment, marital status, religion or belief, race and ethnicity, sex and sexual orientation. Northern Irish legislation also covers political opinion. Supplementary rights are secured by the legislation regulating maternity leave and associated matters, with the HRA providing a quasi-constitutional layer of protection for the right to non-discrimination set out in Article 14 ECHR.

The 2010 Act and its Northern Irish counterparts prohibits direct and indirect discrimination, harassment and victimisation throughout all sectors of private and public employment, and employment and occupation including: military service, contract work, self-employment, and the discharge of statutory office.[43] This prohibition on discrimination in employment and occupation covers access (including selection criteria and recruitment conditions), promotion at all levels, employment and working conditions (including pay and dismissals), occupational benefits

---

[41] See, e.g., *Daily Telegraph*, "David Cameron's Senior Adviser Steve Hilton Suggests UK Should Abolish Maternity Leave," 28 July 2011, http://www.telegraph.co.uk/news/politics/david-cameron/8667058/David-Camerons-senior-adviser-Steve-Hilton-suggests-UK-should-abolish-maternity-leave.html.
[42] See, e.g., *Bull v Hall* [2013] UKSC 73.
[43] See, e.g., sections 39–83 Equality Act 2010.

(including pensions and social security), access to vocational training and guidance, and membership of unions and other employment-linked organisations.

Certain limited statutory exceptions exist to this general prohibition of discrimination in employment and occupation. For example, the prohibition of age and disability discrimination does not apply to the armed forces.[44] Occupation in a purely voluntary capacity, as when a person volunteers to work for a NGO, falls outside the scope of the antidiscrimination legislation—as confirmed by the UK Supreme Court in *X v Mid-Sussex Citizens Advice Bureau*.[45] Furthermore, in the case of *Jivraj v Hashwani*,[46] the Supreme Court ruled that arbitrators were not "employed," on the basis that they were not employed or otherwise in a position of subordination to the parties involved in the arbitration. The scope of this "non-subordinate" exception is not clear and may be clarified by further litigation.

The legislation also applies to the provision of goods and services, education, housing (including rental arrangements), transport, membership of associations, and the performance of public functions. The latter including matters such as policing, social security, health care, and related governmental activities performed by or on behalf of the state.[47] The UK legislation thus replicates and goes beyond the provisions of the key EU non-discrimination directives: it covers most forms of social activities.

Again, however, some limited exceptions exist relating to certain protected characteristics to the otherwise comprehensive and wide-ranging scope of this legislation. They concern issues such as national security and border control, the entitlement of bodies possessing a particular "religious ethos" to protect this ethos, genuine occupational requirements and so on.[48] Schedules 22 and 23(1) of the Equality Act 2010 also clarify that antidiscrimination legislation does not make unlawful something permitted by another statute: discriminatory provisions in other statutes can only be challenged via the HRA and ECHR, or (for now) by reference to EU law.

10 Does the Enforcement of Antidiscrimination Law Vary According to the Ground of Discrimination?

As noted above, data from 2012 indicate that sex discrimination and related issues (maternity leave, for example) accounted for the majority of antidiscrimination claims brought in that year, reflecting a general pattern which has been consistent

---

[44] Sch.9, para 4(3) Equality Act 2010, and equivalent provisions in the Northern Irish legislation.

[45] [2013] UKSC 59. This restriction may not conform to the requirements of EU law. See UK National Report 2015–2016, EU Network of Discrimination Law Experts.

[46] [2011] UKSC 40.

[47] See generally 28-31, 32-38, 84-107160-187.

[48] See, e.g., Schedules 3, 5, 9, 11, 16 and 23 of the Equality Act 2010.

for many years now. Disability and age discrimination are the next biggest categories, followed by race, and then by religion or belief and sexual orientation.[49] However, it should be noted that there are also regional variations in these patterns, particularly BME settlement patterns across the UK.

In general, a similar approach is adopted by courts and tribunals in applying antidiscrimination law across the different protected grounds: key concepts such as the definitions of direct and indirect discrimination are applied on a more or less consistent manner throughout the case law.[50] Concern has, however, been expressed that the courts have adopted a narrower approach to the interpretation of the prohibition on direct discrimination on the basis of religion or belief than they do in other contexts.[51]

Furthermore, the success rate in race and religious discrimination cases tend to be significantly less than for certain other types of antidiscrimination claims. For example, in 2010–11, only 16% of race discrimination claims and 18% of religious discrimination claims that received a full hearing before an employment tribunal were successful, as compared to 37% of sex discrimination claims.[52] The low rate of success for religious discrimination claims is widely attributed to the complex nature of such claims and the currently unsettled state of the case law in this regard. However, in contrast, the case law in respect of race discrimination claims is relatively settled and clear-cut—which has led some commentators to suggest that the low number of successful claims in this context can instead be attributed to a "culture of disbelief" among judges and tribunal members in relation to such claims.[53]

Interestingly, however, the median awards in race discrimination claims tend not to vary to a significant degree from the median awards for other types of claim. In 2015–2016, the median award for race discrimination cases was £13,760. In contrast, for sex discrimination it was £13,500; £11,309 for disability discrimination; £8417 for age discrimination; £16,174 for religious discrimination; and £20,192 for sexual orientation discrimination.[54]

---

[49] As also noted above, the sharp decrease in the number of claims brought following the introduction of tribunal fees particularly impacted on the numbers of sex discrimination claims—but this down-turn has also impacted across the full range of discrimination claims.

[50] See, e.g., *Bull v Hall* [2013] UKSC 73.

[51] McColgan (2009), pp. 1–29.

[52] 780 sex discrimination claims received a full hearing, with 290 (37%) being successful. 84 sexual orientation claims were heard, with 22 (26%) being successful. 830 disability claims were heard, with 190 (23%) being successful. 410 age claims were heard, with 90 (22%) being successful. 147 religion or belief claims were heard, with 27 (18%) being successful. 950 race claims were heard, with 150 (16%) being successful. See *Employment Tribunals and EAT Statistics, 2010–2011* (London: HM Courts & Tribunals Service, 2011), p. 8. This reflects a set annual pattern. Aston et al. (2006).

[53] See Renton (2013).

[54] Ministry of Justice, *Tribunal and Gender Recognition Certificate Statistics Quarterly, April–June 2016*, Employment Tribunal Tables E.6–E.11, available at https://www.gov.uk/government/statistics/tribunals-and-gender-recognition-certificate-statistics-quarterly-april-to-june-2016.

11 What Is the Relationship Between the Enforcement of Antidiscrimination Law and the Quest for Equality on Both an Individual and Systemic Level?

UK antidiscrimination legislation is primarily structured around a symmetrical and individualist model of equality. Some scope exists for positive action,[55] and the positive duties discussed above impose certain positive obligations upon public authorities (and, in Northern Ireland, private employers). The 2010 Act imposes express reasonable accommodation requirements upon employers and service-providers in respect of disability, and similar obligations can arise as a side effect of the prohibition on indirect discrimination.[56] However, in general, the legislation is focused on prohibiting unequal treatment on the basis of protected grounds as between individual employees, service users and so on. While the legislation can be effective in combating certain forms of group disadvantage, it remains largely wedded to a "formal equality" model of regulation.

The reliance placed on individual enforcement in the UK system reflects this orientation. Victims of discrimination are supposed to seek a remedy on an individualised basis through the ordinary court and tribunal processes, without having the benefit of class actions. Furthermore, the equality commissions have limited enforcement powers and cannot bring actions on behalf of individual victims, as is also the case with trade unions and other bodies. As discussed in depth above, individuals face substantial obstacles in securing a remedy for discriminatory treatment, and the imposition of employment tribunal fees has worsened the situation. If this erodes the culture of compliance that has evolved in the UK over the last few decades, it will be interesting to see whether this will generate pressure for a shift to a more asymmetrical, substantive equality model of regulation.

12 Is the Enforcement of Antidiscrimination Law Regarded as Different from the Enforcement of Other Laws?

In general, the enforcement of antidiscrimination law is viewed as being analogous to the enforcement of other forms of civil law regulation. Employment discrimination cases are processed in a similar manner as other types of employment law claims. Similarly, discrimination claims brought in relation to access to goods and services are processed through the county court system like other forms of tort claims.

Some concessions are made to the particular problems associated with discrimination claims—in particular, the provision for a shift of the burden of proof (albeit

---

[55] See, e.g., sections 158-9 of the Equality Act 2010.
[56] *London Underground Ltd v Edwards (No 2)* [1997] IRLR 157.

this was introduced to conform with the requirements of EU law), the introduction of the positive duties, and the limited special enforcement powers given to the equality commissions. However, in the main, the enforcement of antidiscrimination law is channelled through the standard legal routes through which other types of claims are processed.

Academic commentators and NGOs are at times critical of this, arguing that the importance of the interests at stake in discrimination claims should entail the adoption of more specific arrangements, similar to the burden of proof shift. In particular, they tend to call for the enforcement powers and resources of the equality commissions to be beefed up and for existing positive duties to be extended to the private sector. However, these criticisms often fail to achieve much purchase in policy debates. For example, there has been little or no discussion in recent years of whether US-style class actions might have a useful role to play in enhancing compliance with antidiscrimination legislation or whether specialist tribunals with particular expertise in discrimination law could be established to adjudicate other employment and service provision claims (as was done in Ireland in the late 1990s).

13 What Does the Enforcement of Antidiscrimination Law Reveal About the Nature of Your Legal System or About the Enforcement of Laws in Your Legal System?

The reliance placed on individual enforcement in the UK in this context highlights the manner in which the UK legal system is reluctant to embrace class actions or other forms of collective action, or to give statutory bodies such as the equality commissions wide regulatory powers. Instead, considerable faith is vested in the ability of individuals to assert their legal rights before courts and tribunals. Furthermore, there is a reluctance to expose employers and service providers to "undue" regulation and a desire to minimise the costs of litigation to the public purse, which was reflected in the attempt to introduce employment tribunal fees. There also exists complacency about the functioning of the legal system that presumes that norms like antidiscrimination law will continue to be effectively enforced via individual claims even as access to justice becomes more difficult. These traits are not just confined to the discrimination law context—but they perhaps are highlighted here.

References

ACAS (2014) Asking and responding to questions of discrimination in the workplace. ACAS. http://www.acas.org.uk/media/pdf/m/p/Asking-and-responding-to-questions-of-discrimination-in-the-workplace.pdf. Accessed 12 Oct 2016

ACAS (2015) Research paper: evaluation of ACAS Early Conciliation 2015. ACAS, London, pp 96–98. http://www.acas.org.uk/media/pdf/5/4/Evaluation-of-Acas-Early-Conciliation-2015.pdf

Aston J et al (2006) The experience of claimants in race discrimination employment tribunal cases. Employment Relations Research Series No. 55. Department of Trade and Industry/Institute for Employment Studies

Cox S (2015) £3m sex discrimination case winner: 'Everyone Loses'. BBC Radio 4, 30 April 2015. http://www.bbc.co.uk/news/business-32514908

Department of Business Innovation and Skills (2014) Findings from the Survey of Employment Tribunal Applicants, June 2014. https://www.gov.uk/government/uploads/system/uploads/attachment_data/file/316704/bis-14-708-survey-of-employment-tribunal-applications-2013.pdf ("SETA 2014")

McColgan A (2009) Class wars? Religion and (in) equality in the workplace. Ind Law J 38:1–29

McColgan A (2015) Litigating the public sector equality duty: the story so far. Oxf J Leg Stud 35:453

McCrudden C et al (2004) Legal regulation of affirmative action in Northern Ireland: an empirical assessment. Oxf J Leg Stud 24(3):363–415

O'Cinneide C (2007) The commission for equality and human rights: a new institution for new and uncertain times. Ind Law J 36(2):141–162

Pulley D (2015) Disability discrimination: number of cases, 22 October 2015. https://www.kingqueen.org.uk/disability-discrimination-number-of-cases/

Renton D (2013) A culture of disbelief. Institute for Race Relations, 24 January 2013. http://www.irr.org.uk/news/culture-of-disbelief-why-race-discrimination-claims-fail-in-the-employment-tribunal/

Colm O'Cinneide is Professor of Constitutional and Human Rights Law at University College London. He is a graduate of the universities of Cork and Edinburgh, and a member of the Irish Bar. He has published extensively in the field of comparative constitutional, human rights and antidiscrimination law. He has also served as specialist legal adviser to the Joint Committee on Human Rights and the Women & Equalities Committee of the UK Parliament, has advised a range of international organisations including the UN, ILO and the European Commission, and between 2006 and 2016 was a member (and Vice-President 2008–14) of the European Committee of Social Rights in Strasbourg.

The United States

Julie C. Suk and Fred L. Morrison

1 Introduction

The United States' history of protection against discrimination is a study in contradictions. Its Declaration of Independence of 1776 begins, "We hold these truths to be self-evident, that all men are created equal, that they are endowed by their Creator with certain unalienable Rights."[1] Those lofty principles were attenuated by the acceptance of human slavery[2]—the most extreme form of inequality—that continued in parts of the country until 1865.[3] Even after the abolition of slavery, its legacy of low literacy, inadequate education, limited economic resources, and limited employment opportunities for former slaves perpetuated discrimination.

American antidiscrimination law today is a variegated body of law. Some is federal law, operative throughout the country; other provisions are enacted by state and local governments. Some antidiscrimination law is directly based on the Constitution, but other parts are statutory or regulatory. The constitutional limitations primarily prohibit only discrimination by governmental units and officers,[4] but statutory and regulatory measures apply more broadly. Most federal antidiscrimination laws are sectoral, each applying only to housing, employment,

---

[1] U.S. Declaration of Independence.
[2] U.S. Constitution, art. IV, sec. 2, para. 3.
[3] U.S. Constitution, Amendment XIII.
[4] Civil Rights Cases, 109 U.S. 3 (1883), *but see* Jones v. Alfred H. Mayer Co., 392 U.S. 409 (1968).

J. C. Suk (✉)
Yeshiva University, Benjamin N. Cardozo School of Law, New York City, NY, USA
e-mail: jsuk@yu.edu

F. L. Morrison
University of Minnesota, School of Law, Minneapolis, MN, USA
e-mail: morrison@umn.edu

or educational programs, often with exceptions, or providing protection only for one class of persons.[5] They generally enumerate the prohibited grounds for discrimination (e.g., race, gender), but these classes may differ among the statutes. There is no central authority enforcing all of these laws; each statute identifies an agency and approach to enforcement, although the Equal Employment Opportunity Commission (EEOC) has a significant role. Federal laws are supplemented by state and local laws, which are administered by state and local agencies.

Modern American antidiscrimination jurisprudence began with the 1954 decision of the Supreme Court in *Brown v. Board of Education*,[6] which interpreted the Equal Protection Clause of the 14th Amendment to the Constitution to prohibit racial segregation of public schools. This decision triggered a general effort to eliminate other aspects of racial discrimination. Later, gender was added as another protected class.[7] Other protected classes followed. In the 1960's a number of new federal laws were enacted. Each of these laws included its own standards, its own agencies, and its own limitations. Some of the laws provide for private enforcement through litigation. Others contemplate that the Department of Justice will initiate litigation on behalf of the injured party. Still others establish administrative processes and agencies to impose administrative remedies. Some use the threat of disqualification from receipt of federal grants or benefits as an inducement for compliance. Over the past half-century, these laws have been amended and interpreted creating a complex body of technical rules that pursue a goal of elimination of discrimination. This proliferation of institutions and standards makes the United States an ideal locus for studying the relative efficacy of differing enforcement mechanisms.

2 Is Antidiscrimination Law Enforced?

Yes, it is enforced in a variety of ways at the federal, state, and local levels.

3 How Is Antidiscrimination Law Enforced?

There are a wide variety of enforcement measures. Some of the antidiscrimination law is enforced by private litigation. The person who has suffered discrimination brings a lawsuit against the party who has discriminated. This gives the affected individual control of the presentation of the case but has disadvantages of cost, which must ordinarily be borne by the litigant, and possible delay in the adjudication. In a limited class of cases, the United States Department of Justice can also

---

[5]E.g., the Age Discrimination in Employment Act only protects workers over the age of 40 years.
[6]347 U.S. 483 (1954).
[7]Equal Pay Act, Public Law 88-38 (1963); Civil Rights Act of 1964, Public Law 88-354 (1964).

initiate suits to protect against discrimination, but this takes control of the strategy and direction of the case away from the complainant.

Some antidiscrimination law is enforced by administrative agencies, which receive and investigate complaints and sometimes make a decision requiring the rectification of the discrimination, and also imposing restitution requirements on the offender. The administrative agency may also be able to negotiate a settlement of the controversy without taking formal action. One interesting variant of this approach is the procedure in Title VII of the Civil Rights Act of 1964, which requires the party injured by the discrimination to file a complaint with the Equal Employment Opportunity Commission (EEOC), but permits the affected individual to begin private litigation if the Commission fails to reach a timely resolution of the matter.

Some antidiscrimination law is also enforced by compliance requirements attached to federal grants, contracts, and other benefits. A person or institution that has illegally discriminated may be disqualified from receiving future government contracts or grants. Many federal agencies have an "Office of Civil Rights" or a compliance office to enforce these rules.

In only a very small number of cases is criminal prosecution sought.[8]

4 Who Enforces Antidiscrimination Law?

There is a wide variety of "enforcers."

- The *individual who suffered the discrimination* may bring civil litigation. Some such cases may involve multiple plaintiffs and indeed be "class action suits." In these cases the ultimate enforcer is the court that provides a remedy.
- In a limited range of cases, the *United States Department of Justice* or the *Equal Employment Opportunity Commission* may bring civil litigation on behalf of the party suffering discrimination.
- In a broad range of cases, other *federal administrative agencies* have authority to resolve cases brought to their attention. The injured individual brings a complaint to the agency, which then conducts an investigation and in some cases may impose a remedy. A contested case hearing may be required before the remedy is provided.
- *State and local administrative agencies* also provide remedies. These bodies are created by state or local law and have varying powers and authority.
- In another group of situations, departmental *contracting officers* may bar an offender from receiving federal contracts or grants.

---

[8]There must be a specific intent to deprive the injured party of a constitutional right to warrant prosecution. Screws v. United States, 325 U.S. 91 (1945).

5 Who Benefits from the Enforcement of Antidiscrimination Law?

It may appear that everyone benefits. The individual who was injured receives justice. Members of society at large receive the satisfaction of that individual's participation in the community. Even the offender may be helped in understanding that equal opportunity is valuable for all.

Antidiscrimination law has been expanded to encompass an increasing number of groups and claims have always been open not only to individuals belonging to traditionally excluded groups, but also to individuals belonging to majority groups that are traditionally advantaged. For example, opponents of affirmative action programs use antidiscrimination enforcement to challenge efforts to promote equal opportunity, framing such programs as discriminatory preferences for members of groups that have historically been subject to discrimination.[9] As these suits have had some success, antidiscrimination enforcement in the United States is now benefiting different groups from those who initially pioneered antidiscrimination enforcement.

6 Who Is Harmed by the Enforcement of Antidiscrimination Law?

In cases involving specific discriminatory acts, the only harm is to the individual or institution that committed the act. If, however, the question is rephrased to be "who perceives themselves to be harmed," there is a broader answer:

- Employers, even those who are strongly opposed to discrimination, may believe that the burden of compliance with regulatory requirements is excessive.
- Individuals who are adversely affected by affirmative action programs may perceive themselves to be harmed. (Affirmative action programs are efforts to offset the lingering effects of past discrimination against a racial or other group by giving preference to current members of that group in an effort to produce a more egalitarian society. Pursuant to these programs, institutions may seek to favor minority individuals with lower formal qualifications over individuals with higher formal qualifications who are members of the majority group in order to remedy the effects of past discrimination against the racial group as a whole.) The individuals from the majority group who are thus denied admission to an educational institution or the award of a public contract or other benefit may then claim that they are themselves the victims of discrimination.
- Religious organizations may argue that antidiscrimination laws interfere with their religious freedom.

---

[9] See the discussion of Fisher v. University of Texas in section 11, infra.

- Some conservative social groups have opposed the extension of protection against discrimination to additional "protected classes." In 2015 in Houston, Texas, the nation's fourth largest city, the City Council's adoption of an ordinance that included transgender individuals as a protected class led to a referendum in which the city's entire human rights ordinance was repealed.[10]

7 What Remedies Are Provided by the Enforcement of Antidiscrimination Law?

Each statute specifies its own remedies.

In civil litigation, the plaintiff can obtain money damages and an injunction. The injunction will require the defendant to do (or not to do) some specified things. In some cases, the injunction may also provide for the appointment of monitors to oversee the defendant's compliance with the order. In a lawsuit brought against a state or local official or a local unit of government alleging discrimination, a successful plaintiff may also recover attorneys' fees.[11] This has led to the emergence of groups of private lawyers who are willing to take on these cases on a contingent fee basis, without cost to the plaintiff.

In EEOC cases, the agency may investigate the claim, and may be able to secure a settlement of it. The Commission can also initiate litigation on behalf of the injured individual, but is in fact able to do so only in a small portion of the cases. Otherwise, it issues a "right to sue" letter that allows the individual to initiate litigation. In other administrative proceedings, the remedy is usually to order the offending party to take action to correct the discrimination. In an employment case, for example, the offending employer might be required to employ the complaining party and to provide back pay from the time of the violation.

Contract compliance review is more complex. Once the administering office determines that the party has violated the antidiscrimination rules, it will remove that party from the group of eligible bidders, although administrative appeals are available. If the charged party has a large volume of contracts, the effects may be so severe that it will find it necessary to comply with the order.

---

[10] "Houston Voters Repeal Measure Ensuring Rights," *New York Times,* November 5, 2015, p. A1.
[11] 42 U.S.C. 1988.

8 Who Supports the Enforcement of Antidiscrimination Law?

Almost everyone supports the enforcement of antidiscrimination law in principle. They oppose it when it impinges on their own activities or beliefs. Antidiscrimination legislation is, however, sometimes in collision with other fundamental constitutional rights, like the freedom of religion, the freedom of association (including the right not to associate), or the freedom of expression.

9 Who Opposes the Enforcement of Antidiscrimination Law?

The primary opposition to the enforcement of antidiscrimination law has come from defendants and potential defendants in employment discrimination litigation, specifically corporate employers and interest groups defending large corporations. These include the U.S. Chamber of Commerce, the Society for Human Resource Management, various employers' associations, and large national corporations like Wal-Mart, the United States' largest employer. The opposition to antidiscrimination enforcement has been expressed in litigating positions in significant cases with wide-ranging consequences for the landscape of antidiscrimination enforcement. These groups have favored (1) enforcing arbitration clauses in employment contracts, in which employees agree not to litigate their causes of action against the employer (including discrimination) in courts; (2) limiting the scope of the class action rule; and (3) heightening the pleading standard. In the case of the heightened pleading standard, government defendants have also taken successful litigating positions in favor of "plausibility" pleading in discrimination cases, which chills the enforcement of antidiscrimination law through civil litigation.

Many claims of discrimination against employers are unenforceable in courts because the employee has signed an arbitration agreement on the job application or upon accepting the job which binds the worker to settle any job dispute with the help of an arbitrator designated in that employment contract and commonly chosen by the employer.[12] In 2001, the U.S. Supreme Court upheld the validity of arbitration clauses in employment contracts in *Circuit City v. Adams*.[13] When attempting to enforce discrimination claims before arbitrators, employees often find that rules of evidence and procedure are streamlined to favor the employers, whom the arbitrators may come to regard as their client.[14] Nonetheless, the U.S. Chamber of Commerce,

---

[12]See, e.g., Sherry (2016).

[13]See Circuit City Stores v. Adams, 532 U.S. 105 (2001).

[14]See Silver-Greenberg and Corkery (2015). For a recent empirical study of employment discrimination arbitration affirming this finding, see Gough (2014), p. 91.

the Society for Human Resource Management, and various associations of employers have promoted arbitration in lieu of judicial enforcement of employment discrimination laws on the grounds that judicial enforcement is unduly burdensome for employers and courts.[15]

These same groups, as well as the defense bar, filed amicus curiae briefs in *Wal-Mart v. Dukes*,[16] in which the Supreme Court invalidated the certification of the largest-ever employment discrimination class action suit, holding that the women plaintiffs did not have enough in common to proceed as a class. The Wal-Mart plaintiffs had demanded, in addition to money damages, injunctions requiring the United States' largest corporate employer to change a range of employment policies and practices that allegedly disadvantaged women in hiring and promotion. The inability to proceed as a Title VII class undermines the power of litigation to achieve institutional reform on a national scale.

In 2007 and 2009, the Supreme Court decided two cases that heightened the pleading standard for civil plaintiffs.[17] Complaints that lack sufficient factual detail to allege a non-conclusory legal violation may be dismissed for failure to state a claim. Discrimination plaintiffs typically lack access to such factual detail, as evidence revealing such information is usually in the hands of the alleged discriminator. The heightened pleading standard has created new opportunities for the defense bar to get discrimination complaints dismissed before the merits can be reached through the process of enforcement through litigation.[18]

10 How Broad Is the Coverage of Antidiscrimination Law?

Antidiscrimination statutes typically define and limit eligible plaintiffs and defendants even while articulating a generally applicable norm. Employment discrimination law, both state and federal, for instance, only covers employers who have a certain number of employees. To be subject to liability under Title VII of the Civil Rights Act, for instance, the employer must employ at least 15 employees.[19] State antidiscrimination statutes typically have a lower employee threshold, and are thus broader in coverage. To give a few examples, the New York state employment discrimination law imposes liability on employers with four or more employees,[20] and California's Fair Employment and Housing statute defines "employer" as a

---

[15]These groups submitted amicus briefs in Circuit City Stores v. Adams, 532 U.S. 105 (2001), as well as Wal-Mart Stores, Inc. v. Dukes, 564 U.S. 338 (2011).
[16]See Wal-Mart Stores, Inc. v. Dukes, 564 U.S. 338 (2011).
[17]Bell Atlantic v. Twombly, 550 U.S. 544 (2007); Ashcroft v. Iqbal, 556 U.S. 562 (2009).
[18]See Brescia (2011), p. 235.
[19]Title VII of the Civil Rights Act of 1964, 42 U.S.C. § 2000e(b).
[20]New York State Human Rights Law, § 292.2 (2016).

person who regularly employs five or more persons.[21] The federal Fair Housing Act, prohibiting discrimination in housing, does not apply to small owner-occupied buildings in which there are fewer than five units.[22] Under the Age Discrimination in Employment Act, only persons age 40 and over have a cause of action.[23]

Some antidiscrimination laws limit their coverage to recipients of funds. In the education context, Title VI of the Civil Rights Act of 1964 prohibits discrimination on the basis of race, color, and national origin by recipients of federal funds.[24] Title IX of the Educational Amendments of 1972 prohibits discrimination on the basis of sex by recipients of federal funds.[25] Section 504 of the Rehabilitation Act prohibits disability discrimination by recipients of federal funding.[26] Educational institutions that do not receive federal funding are thus outside the scope of these antidiscrimination mandates.

In the employment context, however, it should be noted that even when antidiscrimination statute does not cover a small employer, other sources of law in the common law system could intervene to hold small employers liable. For example, in California, an employer with four employees was held liable for sex discrimination pursuant to the tort of wrongful discharge against public policy.[27] When strong public policies against sex discrimination are grounded in statutory and constitutional law, antidiscrimination enforcement may bleed beyond the statute's definition of coverage.

Finally, an interesting and highly controversial fact about the coverage of antidiscrimination law in the United States is the religious organization exemption. By statute, religious organizations are exempt from the prohibition of religious discrimination,[28] and the Court has further shielded some religious organizations' employment decisions from the coverage of other antidiscrimination laws based on the employer's constitutional right to religious freedom. In *Hosanna-Tabor Evangelical Lutheran Church and School v. EEOC*,[29] the EEOC had attempted to sue a religious school under the Americans with Disabilities Act for its termination of a disabled teacher. The Supreme Court recognized a "ministerial exception," grounded in the First Amendment, to the application of antidiscrimination statutes such as Title VII and the ADA. The "ministerial exception" exempts religious organizations' employment decisions regarding "ministers" from scrutiny under these statutes. In applying the "ministerial exception" to a lay teacher, the

---

[21] Cal. Gov. Code. § 12926(d).
[22] Fair Housing Act of 1968, 42 U.S.C. § 3603(b).
[23] Age Discrimination in Employment Act, 29 U.S.C. § 631.
[24] Title VI of the Civil Rights Act of 1964, 42 U.S.C. § 2000(d).
[25] Title IX of the Education Amendments Act of 1972, 20 U.S.C. § 1681.
[26] Rehabilitation Act of 1973, 29 U.S.C. § 701.
[27] E.g. Badih v. Myers, 36 Cal. App. 4th 1289 (1995).
[28] Title VII, 42 U.S.C. § 2000e-1(a).
[29] See Hosanna-Tabor Evangelical Lutheran Church and School v. EEOC, 132 S.Ct. 694 (2012).

Hosanna-Tabor decision exempts a broad array of employment decisions by religious organizations from the application of employment discrimination laws.

11 Does Enforcement of Antidiscrimination Law Vary According to the Ground of Discrimination?

As a matter of enforcement, the *McDonnell Douglas* framework has been used across all the different grounds of discrimination to allocate the burdens of the parties of proof and production in litigation. Under the *McDonnell Douglas* scheme, the plaintiff must establish four factors: (1) she is a member of the protected class; (2) she was qualified for the job or promotion; (3) she suffered an adverse employment action (i.e., not hired, not promoted, terminated); and (4) the job remained open or went to someone else.[30] Typically, the plaintiff relies on this framework to make out a circumstantial case of discrimination (though other modes of establishing discrimination are also available), and the burden of production (though not proof) shifts to the employer to articulate certain nondiscriminatory reasons for the employment action, including defenses based on the lawfulness of the differential treatment complained of in the prima-facie case.

Courts have developed different doctrinal mechanisms for proving and establishing discrimination, which vary depending on the grounds of discrimination. In 1991, Congress authorized liability with limited remedies for "mixed-motive" race or sex discrimination under Title VII. Pursuant to that statutory amendment, a complainant can prevail by showing that "race, color, religion, sex, or national origin was a motivating factor for any employment practice, even though other factors also motivated the practice."[31] In 2009, the Supreme Court held that this "mixed-motive" mode of establishing unlawful employment practice could not be used by age discrimination complainants.[32] While the Court justified this difference in approach between race and sex on the one hand and age on the other by pointing to the separate statutory regimes, the Court has chosen to unify these disparate statutory regimes on other doctrinal questions in the past, including, for example, the decision to transplant disparate impact theory from Title VII to the Age Discrimination in Employment Act.[33]

Another important difference between the various grounds of discrimination is the availability of the bona fide occupational qualification defense. Title VII exempts differentiation based on prohibited grounds when "religion, sex, or national origin is a bona fide occupational qualification reasonably necessary to the normal operation of that particular business or enterprise."[34] Notably, race is excluded and can never

---

[30]McDonnell Douglas Corp. v. Green, 411 U.S. 792 (1972).
[31]Title VII of the Civil Rights Act of 1964, 42 U.S.C. 2000e-2(m).
[32]Gross v. FBL Financial Services, 557 U.S. 167 (2009).
[33]Smith v. City of Jackson, 544 U.S. 228 (2005).
[34]42 U.S.C. § 2000e-2(e).

be a bona fide occupational qualification under Title VII. The Age Discrimination in Employment Act also makes the bona fide occupational qualification defense available to employers.[35]

Finally, the Americans with Disabilities Act (ADA) specifically and uniquely defines discrimination to include a failure to reasonably accommodate the disabled employee.[36] This definition of discrimination does not operate in other statutory non-discrimination schemes.[37]

12 What Is the Relationship Between the Enforcement of Antidiscrimination Law and the Quest for Equality on Both an Individual and Systemic Level?

Ideally, U.S. antidiscrimination law, which originated in judicial interpretations of the constitutional guarantee of Equal Protection, should be compatible with public policies that promote equality by integrating historically disadvantaged groups into mainstream social institutions. However, antidiscrimination law, as interpreted by the U.S. Supreme Court, is increasingly in tension with quests for equality on both an individual and systemic level.

For example, when a fire department attempted to rethink it test-score-based promotion policy to avoid the exclusion of African Americans from promotion, the Supreme Court held that this race-conscious attempt at integration constituted discrimination in violation of Title VII.[38] Even though the employer intended to avoid liability for disparate impact discrimination against African Americans, the Court held that a race-conscious attempt at doing so constituted disparate treatment discrimination against white firefighters, and was thus prohibited unless the employer had a strong basis in evidence showing that it would lose a disparate-impact lawsuit. Similarly, the Supreme Court has enforced the Equal Protection Clause to invalidate public school districts' race-conscious attempts to integrate primary and secondary schools.[39] The school districts had attempted to achieve racial balance in the composition of the student body of these schools, but the Supreme Court held such racial balancing to be racially discriminatory in violation of Equal Protection.

---

[35] 29 U.S.C. § 621(f)(1).

[36] Americans with Disabilities Act, 42 U.S.C. § 12112(b)(5).

[37] Note, however, that Title VII defines "religion" to include "all aspects of religious observance and practice, as well as belief, unless an employer demonstrates that he is unable to reasonably accommodate to an employee's or prospective employee's religious observance or practice without undue hardship on the conduct of the employer's business." 42 U.S.C. § 2000e(j).

[38] Ricci v. DeStefano, 557 U.S. 557 (2009).

[39] Parents Involved in Community Schools v. Seattle School District No. 1, 551 U.S. 701 (2007).

In a similar vein in the context of higher education, the U.S. Supreme Court requires lower courts to apply strict scrutiny in lawsuits challenging the validity of race-conscious affirmative action programs. In *Fisher v. University of Texas*, decided in 2016, the Court upheld the University of Texas's affirmative action programs in a 4-3 decision, but imposed very strict limits on the use of race as a factor in university admissions decisions.[40] It held that higher education institutions could legitimately take race into account in attempting to achieve diversity in the student body in order to achieve educational objectives. It cautioned that the decision to take race into account would be subject to strict judicial scrutiny. These conflicts stem from deep disagreements about how discrimination should be defined. In Michigan, an amendment to the state constitution explicitly prohibited "discrimination on the basis of race, sex, color, ethnicity, or national origin in the operation of public employment, public education, or public contracting." The amendment was intended to ban race-conscious affirmative action in these domains. The state constitutional amendment was challenged in litigation, wherein pro-affirmative action groups invoked the federal U.S. Constitution's Equal Protection Clause. It was argued that banning affirmative action discriminated against African Americans in the political process by imposing unique burdens on them. The Supreme Court rejected this argument, and upheld the affirmative action ban as a legitimate antidiscrimination law.[41]

13 Is the Enforcement of Antidiscrimination Law Regarded as Different from the Enforcement of Other Laws?

Empirical studies have identified hostility by federal courts towards antidiscrimination plaintiffs as compared to other claimants and causes of action.[42] One effect of this hostility is that, over time, plaintiffs' rate of filing has declined. Judicial hostility to employment discrimination plaintiffs—expressed in higher rates of granting defendants' motions to dismiss[43] or motions for summary judgment[44]— may be driven by the complex and time-consuming nature of employment discrimination cases. Most of these cases are individual cases alleging intentional discrim-

---

[40]Fisher v. University of Texas, 136 S. Ct. 2198 (2016).

[41]Schuette v. Coalition to Defend Affirmative Action, 134 S.Ct. 1623 (2014).

[42]See Clermont et al. (2003), p. 547; Clermont and Schwab (2009), p. 103; Schneider (2010), p. 517.

[43]See Brescia (2011), p. 235.

[44]See Memorandum from Joe Cecil & George Cort, Fed. Judicial Ctr., to Judge Michael Baylson, U.S. Dist. Court for the E. Dist. of Pa. 7 tbl.4 (Nov. 2, 2007), http://www.fjc.gov/public/pdf.nsf/lookup/insumjre.pdf/$file/insumjre.pdf (showing 74–77% summary judgment grant rate in employment discrimination cases, higher than other types of cases included in study).

ination, which involve highly fact-specific inquiries, which, if they progress, require the processing of voluminous conflicting evidence.[45]

The administrative agencies that enforce antidiscrimination laws have a range of different powers. By comparison to agencies that have both rulemaking and adjudicatory power, the Equal Employment Opportunity Commission (EEOC) is weaker and lacks the full range of regulatory tools to enforce the federal employment discrimination statutes with which it is tasked. Under all of these statutes, a litigant is not permitted to proceed in bringing a civil lawsuit unless and until they have first complained to the EEOC and received a right to sue letter from the agency. The agency litigates a very small percentage of the complaints it receives on behalf of the complainants, and its primary power to enforce these statutes lies in its role in investigating some of these claims and litigating civil lawsuits. Unlike many other agencies, the EEOC does not enjoy the rulemaking or adjudicatory power to formulate regulatory standards and then enforce them thorough an administrative judiciary authorized to issue orders and fines. The EEOC adopts guidelines interpreting the statutes that it enforces. But most of these guidelines, particularly those interpreting Title VII, are not binding, and courts are not required to defer to the EEOC's interpretations of Title VII.[46] The Department of Housing and Urban Development (HUD), by contrast, has both rulemaking and adjudicatory power to enforce the antidiscrimination provisions of the Fair Housing Act. However, because HUD is a large agency tasked with enforcing many regulatory norms other than non-discrimination in housing, it is regarded as a weak antidiscrimination enforcer.[47]

14 What Does the Enforcement of Antidiscrimination Law Reveal About the Nature of Your Legal System or About the Enforcement of Laws in Your Legal System?

It is extremely pluralistic and complex. Multiple sovereigns—local, state, and federal governments—enforce antidiscrimination law. Different branches of government enforce it: courts and administrative agencies. Some of the administrative agencies that enforce antidiscrimination laws are specialized on issues of equality and non-discrimination; other agencies are specialized in an entire sector of social life (such as education, labor, or housing) and the prohibition of discrimination is one of many norms enforced by these agencies. Within the various bodies of antidiscrimination law, the prohibition of discrimination extends to many different grounds of discrimination—race, color, sex, sexual orientation, gender identity,

---

[45] See Reeves (2008), p. 481.

[46] Gilbert v. General Electric Co., 429 U.S. 125 (1976) (declining to defer to EEOC's interpretation of Title VII's prohibition of sex discrimination as encompassing pregnancy discrimination). See generally Suk (2006), p. 405.

[47] See Johnson (2012), p. 1339.

pregnancy, national origin, religion, age, disability, genetic information and other factors. Within this pluralistic regime, conflict is inevitable. Thus, discrimination claims by white plaintiffs complaining of race-conscious measures to promote integration come into conflict with discrimination claims by individuals belonging to traditionally disadvantaged groups complaining of facially neutral practices that in fact disproportionately exclude them.

Within this system, the formal enforcement of antidiscrimination laws—primarily through civil litigation by individuals and by the EEOC—catalyzes and incentivizes informal regulation by both public and private entities. Some of these behaviors which can be described as voluntary compliance may further the goals and purposes of antidiscrimination law, whereas others might not. For example, case law offering employers an affirmative defense for adopting internal grievance procedures for sexual harassment and other forms of discrimination incentivizes companies to self-regulate to prevent behaviors that expose them to liability. Similarly, the Department of Education's Office of Civil Rights makes recommendations to federal funding recipients in "Dear Colleague" letters regarding changes thought necessary to comply with Title IX. Scholarly critics in each of these contexts have suggested that this incentivizes companies and educational institutions to over-regulate legal behavior in ways that are undesirable and unconnected to the promotion of women's equal opportunities.[48]

In addition, efforts to strengthen antidiscrimination enforcement may produce some unintended consequences that weaken the operation of antidiscrimination norms. For example, in 1991, Congress authorized punitive damages in Title VII suits for intentional discrimination claims.[49] This incentivized the private bar, working on contingency, to represent discrimination plaintiffs. It also created the financial incentive to frame the facts of every discrimination case as intentional discrimination, even when the facts may more apparently support a disparate impact theory.[50] As a consequence, employment discrimination claims are heavily skewed towards intentional discrimination claims. Today, intentional discrimination rarely takes the form of obvious racism, and thus, complex methods of indirect proof, using circumstantial evidence and burden-shifting doctrines, have been developed as enforcement schemes. Discrimination cases are thus complex and time-consuming to litigate, and shortcuts (early dismissals, summary judgment) have become especially attractive to judges in discrimination cases. Because there is an incentive to pursue unmeritorious claims of intentional discrimination, there is an increased perception that many discrimination claims are unmeritorious, which fuels the use of shortcuts. These dynamics of antidiscrimination enforcement undermine public perceptions of antidiscrimination law's legitimacy.

---

[48] See, e.g., Schultz (2003), p. 2061.

[49] Civil Rights Act of 1991, Pub. L. 102–166, § 1977A, codified at 42 U.S.C. § 1981(a).

[50] For an account of the dynamics between the new remedies in 1991 and the litigation behaviors they incentivized, see Donohue III and Siegelman (2005).

15 Conclusion

In the United States, civil litigation in state or federal courts has long been the most important enforcement system for antidiscrimination law. Victims of discrimination are authorized, under most antidiscrimination statutes, and under a federal civil rights statute, to seek injunctions and damages if they can prove that they were discriminated against. For the most part, discrimination claims are litigated in courts of general jurisdiction according to transsubstantive rules of civil procedure.

The enforcement of antidiscrimination law has generated sufficient resistance so as to influence the evolution of civil procedure rules, and broader changes in civil procedure (which have emerged through the enforcement of other substantive areas of law) are now influencing the enforcement of antidiscrimination law. The federal courts, under the Supreme Court's guidance, now require plaintiffs in civil lawsuits to plead sufficient facts, independent of conclusory allegations, to make out a plausible claim of discrimination. If a defendant's motion to dismiss is granted because the plaintiff has failed to allege sufficient factual detail, the plaintiff will not get the opportunity, through discovery, to demand evidence of discrimination, which is in the hands of the alleged discriminator. Furthermore, as of December 2015, the scope of discovery has been narrowed under the Federal Rules of Civil Procedure. Parties are no longer entitled to discover any matter that is relevant to a claim or defense; rather, they must now establish that such relevant matter is also proportional to the needs of the case. Also, in recent years, the Supreme Court has applied more stringent requirements of commonality to certify class actions. The Supreme Court's repeated approval of arbitration clauses, over the objections of state courts that have held them to be unconscionable or unenforceable, has also made it less likely that meritorious claims of discrimination will be evaluated by the judiciary at all.

Given the new barriers to enforcing antidiscrimination law through the traditional means of civil litigation, strengthening the role of administrative agencies at both the federal and state level will be important to the effectiveness of antidiscrimination law. Such enforcement need not focus on obtaining the remedies traditionally available in civil litigation, such as damages. Agencies might be better equipped to require the production of information that could reveal patterns and practices of discrimination, even in the absence of a real individual victim. For example, in New York City, a new municipal law adopted in April 2015 requires the New York City Human Rights Commission to undertake at least five situation testing investigations of employers in the city and report its findings to the city within a set time frame.[51] Under the new law, the agency must send "testers"—actors of different races who are assigned the same qualifications—to apply for jobs to determine if applicants of different races are treated differently.

In the pluralistic society of the United States, antidiscrimination enforcement has had the double effect of changing employers' practices to include more women and

---

[51]New York Local Law 33, April 20, 2015, available at http://www.nyc.gov/html/cchr/html/law/amendment_4_2015_b.shtml.

minorities over time, while also engendering resistance and hostility to further expansion of antidiscrimination norms. Thus, it is not surprising that the initial channels of enforcement are being undermined, and opportunities to innovate in antidiscrimination enforcement are being sought in other corners of the multi-level administrative state.

References

Brescia RH (2011) The Iqbal effect: the impact of new pleading standards on employment and housing litigation. Kentucky Law J 100:235
Clermont K, Schwab S (2009) Employment discrimination plaintiffs in federal courts: from bad to worse? Harv Law Policy Rev 3:103
Clermont K, Eisenberg T, Schwab S (2003) How employment discrimination plaintiffs fare in federal courts of appeals. Empl Rights Employ Policy J 7:547
Donohue JJ III, Siegelman P (2005) The evolution of employment discrimination law in the 1990s: a preliminary empirical investigation. In: Nielsen LB, Nelson RL (eds) Handbook on employment discrimination: rights and realities. Springer, New York
Gough MD (2014) The high costs of an inexpensive forum: an empirical analysis of employment discrimination claims heard in arbitration and civil litigation. Berkeley J Employ Lab Law 35:91
Johnson O (2012) Beyond the private attorney general: equality directives in American law. N Y Univ Law Rev 87:1339
Reeves L (2008) Pragmatism over politics, recent trends in lower court employment discrimination jurisprudence. Mo Law Rev 74:481
Schneider E (2010) The changing shape of federal pretrial civil practice: the disparate impact on federal civil rights and employment discrimination cases. Pa Law Rev 158:517
Schultz V (2003) The sanitized workplace. Yale Law J 112:2061
Sherry M (2016) A colleague drank my breast milk and other wall street tales. New York Times, January 13
Silver-Greenberg J, Corkery M (2015) A privatization of the justice system. New York Times, November 2
Suk JC (2006) Antidiscrimination law in the administrative state. Univ Illinois Law Rev 2006:405

Julie C. Suk is a Professor of Law at Yeshiva University's Benjamin N. Cardozo School of Law. She holds a J.D. from Yale Law School, a D.Phil. in Politics from Oxford University, and an A.B. in English and French Literature from Harvard University. She is the author of numerous law review articles and book chapters on comparative equality law, including "Are Gender Stereotypes Bad for Women? Rethinking Antidiscrimination Law and Work-Family Conflict" in Columbia Law Review, and "Gender Parity and State Legitimacy: From Public Office to Corporate Boards" in I*CON. She serves as Chair of the European Law Section of the Association of American Law Schools. She writes and teaches in the areas of comparative law, employment law, antidiscrimination law, and civil procedure.

Fred L. Morrison is the Popham Haik Schnobrich/Lindquist & Vennum Professor of Law at the University of Minnesota. He holds an A.B. from the University of Kansas, a B.A. in Jurisprudence and an M.A. from Oxford University, a Ph.D. in Politics from Princeton University, and a J.D. from the University of Chicago. He teaches in the fields of Constitutional Law and International Law and also writes in the field of Comparative Constitutional Law.

Part III
Regional Reports

European Convention of Human Rights/ Council of Europe

Mathias Möschel

1 Introduction

This report will try to describe and assess the enforcement of antidiscrimination law at the level of the European Convention of Human Rights (ECHR). This instrument, adopted within the Council of Europe (CoE) framework, is interpreted by the European Court of Human Rights (ECtHR). Article 14 is the central provision prohibiting discrimination. It states that: *"The enjoyment of the rights and freedoms set forth in this Convention shall be secured without discrimination on any ground such as sex, race, colour, language, religion, political or other opinion, national or social origin, association with a national minority, property, birth or other status."* This article has long been seen as a Cinderella provision[1] because a violation of Article 14 could only be claimed in conjunction with a violation of another right or freedom contained in the ECHR. In other words, Article 14 is only an accessory and not self-standing provision.

To some extent, the limits of Article 14 are overcome by Protocol No. 12 to the ECHR, which allows plaintiffs to simply claim that they have been discriminated against by a public authority on one of the prohibited grounds without needing to claim any other violation of the ECHR. This protocol entered into force in 2005 but has been ratified by only 20 out of 47 Member States of the CoE. Countries such as Denmark, France, Poland, Sweden and Switzerland have not even signed it.

The ECtHR used to be quite reticent to use Article 14 in its case law, preferring to decide the cases under other provisions and often holding that it was unnecessary to enter into the non-discrimination analysis of cases. That changed to some extent

---

[1] See on this expression: O'Connell (2009), p. 211.

M. Möschel (✉)
Department of Legal Studies, Central European University, Budapest, Hungary
e-mail: moschelm@ceu.edu

starting in the early 2000s with some landmark cases, especially those on race, gender and sexual orientation discrimination. However, when looking at the enforcement of some judgments these developments look slightly less ground breaking.

2 Is Antidiscrimination Law Enforced?

The short answer to this question is yes, via the generic enforcement mechanism of ECtHR's judgments established in the European Convention on Human Rights (ECHR). In fact, Article 46(2) of the ECHR provides that "[t]he final judgment of the Court shall be transmitted to the Committee of Ministers, which shall supervise its execution." Some of the shortcomings of this enforcement mechanism will be detailed in the answers below.

3 How Is Antidiscrimination Law Enforced?

This answer describes the principal enforcement mechanism of ECtHR's judgments and therefore also of antidiscrimination law under the ECHR. As we have seen, pursuant to Article 46(2) of the ECHR, it is up to the Committee of Ministers of the CoE to oversee implementation of the ECtHR's judgments and, pursuant to Article 39 of the ECHR, also of the terms of friendly settlements that the parties to a case may have entered into. If and when the ECtHR finds an Article 14 violation (separately or in conjunction with other human rights violations) or that the parties entered a friendly settlement, the judgment or the friendly settlement are transmitted to the Committee of Ministers.

The Rules of the Committee of Ministers for the supervision of the execution of judgments and of the terms of friendly settlements establish that such supervision gets inscribed into the agenda of special human rights meetings. During such meetings, the Committee of Ministers invites the Contracting Party against whom the violation has been declared to inform it of the measures which this Contracting Party has taken or intends to take in consequence of the judgment. In particular, the Committee looks into whether the damage award has been paid, and whether/which individual or general measures have been adopted. Especially in cases where structural and general measures need to be taken, the Committee demands an action plan and the case remains on the agenda of the human rights meetings until the Contracting Party shows that it paid the damage award or that the possible individual or general measures have been adopted. Similarly, the Committee of Ministers examines whether the terms of the friendly settlement, as set out in the Court's decision, have been executed. During this process, the Committee can adopt interim resolutions and supervision is closed by a final resolution.

Since 2004, priority is given to supervision of the execution of judgments in which the Court has identified what it considers a systemic problem or those it defines as pilot judgments.² This enhanced supervision is also extended to judgments requiring urgent individual measures, interstate cases, and other judgments that for special reasons require such supervision.

Article 46(3) and (4) of the ECHR establish rules for situations in which cases are referred back to the ECtHR if the supervision of the execution of the judgment is hindered by a problem of interpretation or where the Committee of Ministers sees that a Contracting Party refuses to abide by a final judgment.

4 Who Enforces Antidiscrimination Law?

As we have seen, the main body involved in the enforcement of judgments of the ECtHR and by consequence of antidiscrimination law is the Committee of Ministers. It is the CoE's decision-making body that is (in theory) composed of the foreign ministers of all 47 CoE Member States. In practice, the foreign ministers appoint a Deputy who is usually a Permanent Representative of the respective Member State in Strasbourg. So, ultimately, the enforcement is mainly delegated to a political body.

However, over the past years, other bodies have been increasingly involved in the execution of the ECtHR's judgments. First of all, the ECtHR itself has started to suggest a number of cases in which the Contracting States should adopt individual or general measures in order to conform to its judgments.³

Second, to some extent, the Parliamentary Assembly of the Council of Europe also plays an increasing role in the enforcement mechanism of ECtHR's judgments. The Parliamentary Assembly is the deliberative body of the CoE. Parliamentarians are appointed by the national parliaments of the 47 Member States. Its involvement in the enforcement of judgments has increased inasmuch as it monitors the activities of the Committee of Ministers and adopts reports and resolutions dealing *inter alia* with the issue of (non-)enforcement of ECtHR judgment,⁴ thus highlighting potential shortcomings at the Committee of Ministers level.

Third, the Commissioner of Human Rights of the CoE also plays a certain, albeit even more marginal, role in the enforcement by intervening before the Committee of Ministers, publishing reports and making country visits.

---

²Resolution *Res (2004) 3* of the Committee of Ministers on judgments revealing an underlying systemic problem *(adopted by the Committee of Ministers on 12 May 2004, at its 114th Session)*, accessible at: https://search.coe.int/cm/Pages/result_details.aspx?ObjectId=09000016805dd190.

³See more in detail on this point: Sicilianos (2014), pp. 285–315.

⁴See e.g. Parliamentary Assembly Resolutions 1516 (2006), 1787 (2011), 1955 (2011) and 2075 (2015) on the implementation of judgments of the European Court of Human Rights.

5 Who Benefits from the Enforcement of Antidiscrimination Law?

That usually depends on the judgment and how broadly it is framed. In the narrower cases, it is "only" the applicant-victims. However, if the ECtHR also suggests broader measures, the beneficiaries might be a whole group or minority within one given national system. For instance, in the landmark Roma desegregation case, *D.H. and Others*,[5] the beneficiaries of enforcement are not just the applicants in Ostrava schools but Roma children throughout the Czech Republic.

Given the role of the ECtHR, sitting at the apex of all 47 Council of Europe Member States, a judgment finding a violation on a specific issue can potentially have repercussions beyond the borders of the defending State. Indeed, other judgments on similar issues in other countries, such as Greece,[6] Croatia,[7] and Hungary[8] followed *D.H. and Others*, meaning that potentially the ultimate circle of beneficiaries might be broader than expected.

6 Who Is Harmed by the Enforcement of Antidiscrimination Law?

Under the ECHR (and according to classical international law), the defendant is always a State Party. Discrimination claims are brought directly against the State because it discriminated against the applicant. In other words, if a violation of Article is found, it is the State and its agents that are harmed. A typical example of discrimination cases before the ECtHR are the numerous police violence cases where the claim was that the police discriminated against Roma individuals or other racial minorities on the grounds of race.[9]

Via the doctrine of positive obligations, the ECtHR also extended certain provisions to apply to violations committed by private parties. For instance, in a number of race discrimination cases involving violence committed by private parties against Roma or other racial minorities, the ECtHR has found procedural violations of Articles 2 (right to life) and 3 (protection against inhuman and degrading treatment) in conjunction with Article 14, meaning that the State failed to effectively investigate whether the violence had been racially motivated or failed to prosecute the

---

[5]*D.H. and Others v. Czech Republic* [GC], Application no. 57325/00, 13 November 2007.

[6]*Sampanis and Others v. Greece*, Application no. 32526/05, 5 June 2008 and *Sampani and Others v. Greece*, Application no. 59608/09, 11 December 2012.

[7]*Oršuš and Others v. Croatia* [GC], Application no. 15766/03, 16 March 2010.

[8]*Horváth and Kiss v. Hungary*, Application no. 11146/11, 29 January 2013.

[9]See e.g. *Petropoulou-Tsakiris v. Greece*, Application no. 44803/04, 6 December 2007 and *Stoica v. Romania*, Application no. 42722/02, 4 March 2008.

perpetrators of the violence.[10] Nevertheless, one can see that even in this type of situation, the ultimate addressee and harmed actor is and remains the State and its agents.

7 What Remedies Are Provided by the Enforcement of Antidiscrimination Law?

As a general rule, the ECtHR establishes whether a human rights violation has taken place or not. In many cases, the victim of discrimination has the *moral satisfaction* of his or her right being officially acknowledged.

Beyond that, the ECtHR can also grant monetary damage awards for both pecuniary and non-pecuniary damages suffered by the victims. No punitive damages are awarded because the scope of such awards is to put the applicant into the position he or she would have been in without the violation. This explains why damage awards are often quite limited, especially when seen from the American point of view. The average award lies somewhere between 2000 and 8000 euro.

As mentioned, there is a recent trend by which the ECtHR involves itself in the enforcement process under Article 46 by indicating not only a monetary damage award but also specific measures that the defending State could or should take in addressing or remedying the violation. This is particularly true in pilot judgment procedures that address structural human rights problems arising from (recurrent) facts of a case. So far this mechanism has not been used to address Article 14 violations.

However, the ECtHR started providing suggestions as to which structural measures could or should be adopted also in non-pilot judgment cases. Thus, we have Article 14 cases in which the ECtHR has indicated concrete remedies. For example, in a recent Roma education segregation case against Greece, the ECtHR recommended that, beyond the monetary damages awarded, those applicants who were still of school age be enrolled at another State school and that those who had reached the age of majority be enrolled at "second chance schools" or adult education institutes set up by the Ministry of Education under the Lifelong Learning Programme.[11]

Last but not least, a number of antidiscrimination cases have been resolved via friendly settlements and unilateral declaration[12] pursuant to which the State government will need to indicate—in an action plan or not—the measures it will take in order to address and redress some of the issues raised. In the context of the *Moldovan* cases dealing yet again with anti-Roma violence cases in Romania (described further

---

[10] See e.g. *Šečič v. Croatia*, Application no. 40116/02, 31 May 2009 and *Abdu v. Bulgaria*, Application no. 26827/08, 11 March 2014.

[11] *Sampani and Others v. Greece*, Application no. 59608/09, 11 December 2012, para. 128.

[12] See for more details on these *infra* at point 8.

under point 8), the general measures proposed and taken were aimed at fighting discrimination, preventing intercommunity conflicts and improving the economic, social, educational and housing situation of the Roma community in Hadareni.

Thus one can see that some of these cases also lead to change in legislation and practice.

8 Who Supports the Enforcement of Antidiscrimination Law?

In my opinion, the main supporters of enforcement of antidiscrimination law are NGOs.[13] They do so by bringing strategic litigation in the first place and also by providing updates on the (lack of) enforcement of ECtHR's judgments. For example, a number of NGOs including the European Roma Rights Centre (ERRC), the Open Society Foundations, the Romani CRISS, and the local chapters of the Helsinki Committee for Human Rights are very active in fighting racial discrimination against Roma individuals and groups.

As mentioned above, the Parliamentary Assembly and the Commissioner of Human Rights also play a certain monitoring role in enforcement of ECtHR judgments. Thus, they contribute to and support the enforcement of antidiscrimination law by monitoring the Committee of Ministers.

Another interesting development in the enforcement of antidiscrimination law is that the European Commission threatened to start infringement proceedings under Article 258 of the Treaty on the Functioning of the European Union against the Czech Republic, Slovakia and Hungary for their racially segregated schools against Roma. In part, this is linked to the already mentioned ECtHR's 2007 Grand Chamber judgment, *D.H. and Others*,[14] where enforcement is still not complete, in spite of the judgment being granted enhanced supervision. The Committee of Ministers examined the case again in its 1222nd human rights meeting in March 2015. In spite of several action plans being adopted, the State's progress was slow and the Committee decided that by May 2015 the Czech Republic should "provide an update with the most recent statistics concerning the education of Roma pupils in groups/classes for pupils with 'mild mental disability'" and that "[t]hey should also respond to other concerns raised by the Committee, in particular about the functioning of the testing system and effective supervision of the use of diagnostic tools; and the follow-up for pupils recommended for transfer to mainstream education."

Even though the European Commission is not in a strict sense enforcing any of the ECtHR education segregation judgments, such decisions certainly play a role in the European Commission's decision alleging a violation of the EU's Article 21 of

---

[13]See e.g. the Monitoring Handbook issued in 2011: https://ecthrproject.files.wordpress.com/2011/07/monitoringhandbook_calibruch1.pdf.

[14]*D.H. and Others v. Czech Republic* [GC], Application no. 57325/00, 13 November 2007.

the Charter of Fundamental Rights as well as of the Race Equality Directive 2000/43/EC. So far, the Czech Republic, Slovakia and Hungary have only received formal notice assessing the situation.[15] But it should be noted that the EU law enforcement mechanism is stronger and to some extent less political than that of the Committee of Ministers. If the EU does not stop these infringement proceedings, this would be an interesting case of complementarity of enforcement mechanisms.

9 Who Opposes the Enforcement of Antidiscrimination Law?

Given that the addressees of the ECHR are the States, they are the ones that "naturally" oppose the enforcement of antidiscrimination law. As stated earlier, the CoE's Committee of Ministers primarily runs the enforcement mechanism. This is a political body in which the diplomats of the CoE Member States supervise the execution of the ECtHR's judgments. So ultimately, the watchdog is composed of those that are being watched, which poses a certain problem when it comes to the enforcement not only of antidiscrimination law.

A concrete example of how slow and ineffective the enforcement of antidiscrimination law can be is the *Moldovan* judgment.[16] This 2005 judgment involved racially-motivated violence that occurred between 1990 and 1993 against villagers of Roma origin, the destruction of their homes and the ensuing improper living conditions in which they were left, as well as the incapacity of the authorities to put an end to the violations of their rights (Articles 3, 6, 8, 13 and 14 in conjunction with Articles 6 and 8). The fact pattern of this judgment gave rise to a number of other unilateral declarations,[17] friendly settlements,[18] and follow-up judgments.[19] In its 2014 annual report, the Committee of Ministers expressed the following concern:

> [N]otwithstanding the call made by the CM more than a year ago, the authorities have still not succeeded in putting in place the organizational and budgetary framework for the general measures which remain to be adopted for the implementation of the judgments Moldovan

---

[15] See: https://www.opensocietyfoundations.org/press-releases/european-commission-targets-slovakia-over-roma-school-discrimination; https://www.opensocietyfoundations.org/press-releases/brussels-takes-action-against-czech-republic-over-roma-school-discrimination and http://www.equineteurope.org/European-Commission-targets-school-segregation-of-Roma-children-in-Hungary-with.

[16] *Moldovan and Others v. Romania (No. 2)*, Applications no. 41138/98 and 64320/01, 12 July 2005.

[17] *Kalanyos and Others v. Romania*, Application no. 57884/00, 26 April 2007; *Tanase and Others v. Romania*, Application no. 62954/00, 26 May 2009.

[18] *Moldovan and Others v. Romania (No. 1)*, Applications no. 41138/98 and 64320/01, 12 July 2005.

[19] *Lăcătuş and Others v. Romania*, Application no. 12694/04, 13 November 2012.

and Others (Nos. 1 and 2) and Lăcătuș and Others. Therefore, the CM exhorted the authorities to urgently adopt this framework and to implement without further delay the remaining general measures. Resuming its examination at its December meeting, the CM deplored the significant and persistent delay in the adoption and the implementation of the general measures which remain to be taken for the execution of the judgments Moldovan and Others (Nos. 1 and 2) and Lăcătuș and Others, and strongly urged the authorities to submit, by 1 April 2015 at the latest, a detailed action plan for the full execution of these judgments, with precise and short deadlines for all the measures that are still required.[20]

As one can see, the active or passive opposition of a State to the execution of a judgment for facts that have taken place almost 25 years ago and a judgment that took place 10 years ago do not entail many sanctions.

As to the possibility of private individuals, groups or social movements opposing the enforcement of judgments on non-discrimination, so far there are little indications that a "conservative" backlash as one can observe in the United States is occurring. Nevertheless, in the Roma segregation cases mentioned above, it is possible that non-Roma parents might oppose the integration of school classes, thus opposing and slowing down enforcement of ECtHR's judgments.

10 How Broad Is the Coverage of Antidiscrimination Law?

As stated in the introduction, there have been certain limitations to Article 14 as a self-standing non-discrimination provision that have only been partially overcome by Protocol No. 12. However, beyond this ambit limitation, Article 14 is an open model of non-discrimination.[21]

First of all, Article 14 does not distinguish between direct and indirect discrimination. In earlier cases, the ECtHR recognized certain Article 14 violations in situations of indirect discrimination but without explicitly referring to this term.[22] That changed in the landmark Grand Chamber decision, *D.H. and Others*,[23] in which the ECtHR explicitly acknowledged indirect discrimination and thus expanded the coverage to situations where seemingly neutral provisions or practices have a discriminatory effect or impact.

Secondly and most importantly, Article 14 prohibits discrimination based on "sex, race, colour, language, religion, political or other opinion, national or social origin, association with a national minority, property, birth *or other status*." This means that there is an open list of grounds on the basis of which the ECtHR can find

---

[20] 8th Annual Report of the Committee of Ministers, *Supervision of the Execution of Judgments of the European Court of Human Rights*, 2014, p. 188, available at: http://www.coe.int/t/dghl/monitoring/execution/Source/Publications/CM_annreport2014_en.pdf.

[21] See in this sense Arnardóttir (2015), pp. 224–225.

[22] See e.g. *Thlimmenos v. Greece*, Application no. 34369/97, 6 April 2000 and *Zarb Adami v. Malta*, Application no. 17209/02, 20 June 2006.

[23] *D.H. and Others v. Czech Republic* [GC], Application no. 57325/00, 13 November 2007.

an Article 14 violation. And indeed under the "other status," the ECtHR has included things as different as sexual orientation,[24] HIV status,[25] birth out of wedlock,[26] trade union membership,[27] marital or civil partnership status,[28] and collaboration with secret services,[29] just to name a few.

As a comparison, EU non-discrimination law is a closed model of non-discrimination where the distinction between direct and indirect discrimination is clearly spelled out and where the grounds of discrimination are explicitly limited. Moreover, looking at the case law, many decisions of the Court of Justice of the European Union (CJEU) deal with age discrimination. This criterion is so far almost absent in the ECtHR's case law,[30] where one rather finds many cases dealing with race/Roma discrimination.

11 Does the Enforcement of Antidiscrimination Law Vary According to the Grounds of Discrimination?

At the ECHR level, the variation is not necessarily related to the grounds of discrimination but rather occurs along the lines of whether the discrimination is a punctual one which can be solved by payment of damages or a simple measure or whether we are dealing with structural problems of discrimination. As an example of a punctual type of violation, in *Todorova Paskareva v. Bulgaria*, the ECtHR held that a Bulgarian judge's refusal to suspend a sentence on the grounds that the applicant was a Romani woman was discriminatory.[31] Obviously, in this case the fact of awarding 5000 euro for non-pecuniary damages and 2218 euro for costs and expenses plus the indication that reopening of the criminal proceedings would be the most appropriate form of redress. Similarly, it is much easier to address issues of removal of discrimination against children born out of wedlock (e.g. in inheritance matters) by changing the rules in the national civil code.[32]

On the contrary, as we have already seen in *D.H. and Others* but also in the *Moldovan* case,[33] the situation is quite different when structural issues of

---

[24]*Identoba and Others v. Georgia*, Application no. 73235/12, 12 May 2015.

[25]*Kiyutin v. Russia*, Application no. 10 March 2011.

[26]*Fabris v. France* [GC], Application no. 16574/08, 7 February 2013.

[27]*Danilenkov v. Russia*, Application no. 67336/01, 30 July 2009.

[28]*Petrov v. Bulgaria*, Application no. 15197/02, 22 May 2008.

[29]*Zickus v. Lithuania*, Application no. 26652/02, 7 April 2009.

[30]The one exception being *Schwizgebel v. Switzerland*, Application no. 25762/07, 10 June 2010 where the ECtHR nevertheless found no violation.

[31]*Paraskeva Todorova v. Bulgaria*, Application no. 37193/07, 25 March 2010.

[32]See e.g. *Mazurek v. France*, Application no. 34496/07, 1 February 2000 and *Fabris v. France* [GC], Application no. 16574/08, 7 February 2013.

[33]See *supra* points 7 and 8.

discrimination are involved. This could also include the 21 cases dating from 2004 to 2012[34] (whose enforcement has been grouped under the *Barbu Anghelescu* case[35]) involving police violence in general but also against Roma individuals in Romania.

In conclusion, rather than observing a difference amongst the grounds of discrimination, the difficulty revolves around whether a judgment deals with isolated and punctual forms of discrimination or broader structural issues. Either way, it should be noted that amongst these there is an uncanny presence of cases dealing with discrimination against Roma.

12 What Is the Relationship Between the Enforcement of Antidiscrimination Law and the Quest for Equality on Both an Individual and Systemic Level?

As stated above, enforcement of individual cases and punctual violations is easier than the cases dealing with systemic issues of discrimination. In the former situation, the victim obtains money and that closes the case.

However, in the latter, such as *D.H. and Others* and the *Moldovan* cases that have been described above, the enforcement takes a lot of time and really calls into question the effectiveness of enforcement and ultimately also the (merely) symbolic value of ECtHR judgments finding an Article 14 violation.

13 Is the Enforcement of Antidiscrimination Law Regarded as Different from the Enforcement of Other Laws?

Obviously, with the ECHR we are not speaking about enforcement of antidiscrimination laws but only of one provision—Article 14—once the ECtHR has found a violation.

That being said, I do not have the sense that the enforcement of Article 14 judgments is any different than that of any other violation found by the ECtHR. The differences or perceived differences were rather inserted into the text of the ECHR itself by limiting the ambit of Article 14, as described in the introductory comments. But at the enforcement level, there neither seems to be any qualitative or quantitative difference between (non-)enforcement of Article 14 claims and other claims. If anything, the differences might be more country-related, where some countries are better than others at enforcing ECtHR judgments. Italy, Turkey, the Russian Federation, Ukraine, Greece, Romania, Poland, Hungary and Bulgaria are the countries

---

[34]See http://www.coe.int/t/dghl/monitoring/execution/Reports/pendingCases_en.asp?CaseTitleOrNumber=&StateCode=ROM&SectionCode=.

[35]*Barbu Anghelescu v. Romania (No. 1)*, Application no. 46430/99, 5 October 2004.

that have been identified as having the most difficulties in implementing the ECtHR's judgments.[36]

14 What Does the Enforcement of Antidiscrimination Law Reveal About the Nature of Your Legal System or About the Enforcement of Laws in Your Legal System?

In my opinion, it reveals the general limits of the CoE enforcement mechanism for ECtHR's judgments. The political process at the Committee of Ministers level re-gives control to States and governments over the proceedings, which heavily limits the outcome both in terms of transparency and of efficiency.

15 Conclusion

Antidiscrimination law is definitely being enforced once the ECtHR finds an Article 14 violation. The enforcement mechanism of its judgments has been described as one of the most advanced for any human rights court, and there is a particularly high success rate when it comes to punctual, individual measures and payment of damages.

However, the limits of the process come to the fore when general and structural deficiencies of a national system need to be addressed. Here, the political process and the length of implementation of ECtHR's judgments show quite clearly.

References

Arnardóttir OM (2015) Cross-fertilization, clarity and consistency at an overburdened European Court of Human Rights—the case of the discrimination grounds under Article 14. Nordic J Hum Rights 33(3):224–225

O'Connell R (2009) Cinderella comes to the ball: Art. 14 and the right to non-discrimination in the ECHR. Leg Stud 29:211

Sicilianos LA (2014) The role of the European Court of Human Rights in the execution of its own judgments: reflections on Article 46 ECHR. In: Seibert-Fohr A, Villiger ME (eds) Judgments of the European Court of Human Rights—effects and implementation. Nomos, Baden Baden, pp 285–315

---

[36]See the 8th Report by Mr. Klaas de Vries on the implementation of judgments of the European Court of Human Rights, Doc. 13864 | 09 September 2015, available at: http://assembly.coe.int/nw/xml/XRef/Xref-XML2HTML-en.asp?fileid=22005&lang=en.

Mathias Möschel is Associate Professor in Comparative Constitutional Law and Human Rights Law at Central European University of Budapest. He holds a Ph.D from the European University Institute in Florence, an LLM from Berkeley School of Law and a law degree from the State University of Milan. He is the author of "Law, Lawyers and Race: Critical Race Theory from the United States to Europe" and his research and teaching focuses on comparative law and antidiscrimination law.

The Inter-American Court of Human Rights

Anne-Claire Gayet

1 Introduction

Antidiscrimination law has been part of the Inter-American Human Rights system from its beginnings: the 1948 *American Declaration of the Rights and Duties of Man* provided for the equal protection of the law of all persons and the right to enjoy the rights and duties of the Declaration "without distinction as to race, sex, language, creed or any other factor." Now, the principle of non-discrimination is guaranteed in several other regional Human Rights instruments. In particular, the *American Convention on Human Rights* (hereafter the American Convention, adopted in 1968 and entered into force in 1978) is the most exhaustive human rights instrument of the region, and is enforced by the Inter-American Court of Human Rights (hereafter the IACHR), along with the Inter-American Commission on Human Rights (hereafter the Commission).

Although the IACHR interpreted the principle of non-discrimination in 1984,[1] it is only since 2005 that it has found violations of the obligation to not discriminate in contentious cases. Since then, the enforcement of antidiscrimination law by the IACHR has contributed to addressing discrimination suffered by certain individuals and traditionally marginalized groups. This has benefited both the victims identified in these cases and the broader population, including by way of the large scope of remedies ordered by the IACHR. The enforcement of antidiscrimination law by the IACHR has garnered international and domestic support from actors concerned with human rights. However, as antidiscrimination law often disrupts the status quo, its

---

[1]Advisory Opinion OC-4/84, "Proposed Amendments to the Naturalization Provisions of the Constitution of Costa Rica" (1984) [Advisory Opinion OC-4/84].

A.-C. Gayet (✉)
La Cimade, Rhône-Alpes Auvergne, Bourg-en-Bresse, France

enforcement has also given rise to resistance from some domestic actors.

The coverage of antidiscrimination law in the Inter-American Human Rights system is quite broad. Not only does it apply to the rights guaranteed in the American Convention, but also to the domestic legislation and policies of State Parties. The protection afforded by antidiscrimination law has also broadened over the years as a result of the inclusive and evolving interpretation of the prohibited grounds and some provisions of the American Convention by the IACHR.

2 Is Antidiscrimination Law Enforced?

The IACHR is charged with interpreting and applying a number of regional human rights instruments, including the American Convention. The American Convention contains two antidiscrimination provisions, Articles 1(1) and 24. Article 1(1) provides for a general non-discrimination obligation according to which the State must respect and guarantee "non-discrimination" in the enjoyment of the rights enshrined in the American Convention, whereas Article 24 protects the right to "equal treatment before the law," prohibiting discrimination in domestic law. Hence, if the State discriminates in its enforcement of conventional rights, then Article 1(1) and the substantial right involved would be violated. Contrarily, if the discrimination arises from unequal protection under domestic law, there would be a violation of Article 24.[2]

These two provisions include at least two conceptions of non-discrimination or equality. These are formal equality and substantive equality, which both belong to *jus cogens*.[3] The right to *equality before the law*, expressly protected by Article 24 and implicitly by Article 1(1), amounts to formal equality. This conception of non-discrimination guarantees that all individuals are treated alike, disregarding their personal situations, and ensuring that the differences in treatment of the law are not arbitrary but are reasonable and objective. However, there is a presumption of arbitrariness if the classification is based on suspicious categories, listed in Article 1(1).[4]

The right to *equal protection of the law* without discrimination, explicitly protected by both provisions, provides for protection for historically disadvantaged groups, who share one or several aspects of their identities protected by the non-discrimination principle (being race, color, sex, language, religion, political or other opinion, national or social origin, economic status, birth, or any other social

---

[2]*Caso Gonzales Lluy y otros vs. Ecuador. Excepciones Preliminares, Fondo, Reparaciones y Costas* [in Spanish only]. Judgment of September 1, 2015. Ser C No 298, para 243.

[3]Advisory Opinion OC-18/03, "Juridical Condition and Rights of the Undocumented Migrants" (2003), para 101.

[4]*Caso Gonzales Lluy y otros vs. Ecuador. Excepciones Preliminares, Fondo, Reparaciones y Costas* [in Spanish only]. Judgment of September 1, 2015. Ser C No 298, paras 256 and ff.

condition). This more substantive conception of equality allows and requires States to both take positive actions for and treat historically disadvantaged groups differently, in order to guarantee their equal enjoyment of the rights and freedoms provided for by both the American Convention and domestic law. This conception of non-discrimination has the most transformative potential and reflects the evolution of international human rights law. Indeed, more recent group-specific regional instruments aim at guaranteeing equal protection of the law to specific vulnerable groups. For example, the *Inter-American Convention on the Prevention, Punishment and Eradication of Violence against Women* (hereafter the Convention of Belem, adopted in 1994 and entered into force in 1995) aims at preventing, punishing, and eradicating all forms of violence against women including discrimination and provides for the equal protection of the law in Article 4. Article 6 specifies that the right of every woman to be free from violence includes "[t]he right of women to be valued and educated free of stereotyped patterns of behavior and social and cultural practices based on concepts of inferiority or subordination." The *Convention on the Elimination of All Forms of Discrimination Against Persons with Disabilities* (adopted in 1999 and entered into force in 2001) aims at preventing and eliminating all forms of discrimination against persons with disabilities and promoting their full integration into society (Article II). It is the only regional instrument that defines the concept of discrimination in Article I.2.a). Antidiscrimination law will be further enforced regionally with the entry into force of the *Inter-American Convention Against All Forms of Discrimination and Intolerance* (A-69) and the *Inter-American Convention Against Racism, Racial Discrimination and Related Forms of Intolerance* (A-68).

3 How Is Antidiscrimination Law Enforced?

As of November 2016, 22 Latin American States have ratified the American Convention and thereby accepted the binding jurisdiction of the IACHR on matters relating to the interpretation or application of the American Convention, in accordance with Article 62(1). The IACHR can apply and interpret the American Convention and more specifically its antidiscrimination provisions through two functions: a judicial function, governed by Articles 61, 62, and 63, and an advisory function, governed by Article 64.

Regarding the IACHR's judicial function, only the Commission and the State Parties to the American Convention are authorized to submit a case regarding the interpretation or application of the American Convention to the IACHR, on condition that the procedure before the Commission (described in Articles 48 to 50) has been exhausted, as provided by Article 61. The Commission is vested with authority to receive communications from groups and individuals alleging a violation of human rights contained in the American Convention. After investigating the allegations of violations, the Commission guides the claimants and the State towards a friendly settlement. If that fails, the Commission issues a report in which it advises the State to take certain actions. If the State does not comply, the Commission may refer the case to the IACHR. In accordance with Article 25 of the *Rules of Procedure* of the IACHR, the alleged victims or their representatives can participate in the proceedings before the IACHR autonomously, alongside the Commission.

The enforcement of the non-discrimination provisions through the judicial function of the IACHR extends beyond the rulings of the IACHR. The IACHR monitors States compliance with its rulings, asking them to report on a regular basis about the implementation of the IACHR's remedial orders. The Commission and the victims have the opportunity to review and respond to those self-reports. The IACHR then usually issues its own compliance report, in which it lists the things the State must do. The IACHR retains jurisdiction over the case until it deems there has been full compliance with all its demands.

The judicial function of the IACHR also extends to other regional human rights treaties. Article 12 of the Convention of Belem allows individuals, groups of persons, and NGOs to lodge petitions with the Commission containing complaints of violations of Article 7 of the Convention of Belem by a State Party. The Commission can then bring a complaint before the IACHR following the same procedure of the American Convention.

The advisory function of the IACHR under Article 64 of the American Convention allows the thirty-five Member States of the Organization of American States (hereafter OAS) to consult the IACHR regarding the interpretation of the American Convention or other regional Human Rights treaties or to obtain its opinion regarding the compatibility of their domestic laws with these instruments. Several advisory opinions of the IACHR concern the application and scope of the non-discrimination principle.[5] Article 11 of the Convention of Belem also allows State Parties to request advisory opinions on the interpretation of this Convention.

4 Who Enforces Antidiscrimination Law?

Article 33 of the American Convention provides that both the IACHR and the Commission have competence with respect to matters relating to the fulfilment of the commitments made by State Parties. Therefore, there are the two main organs in charge of enforcing antidiscrimination law in the Inter-American Human Rights system. Both the IACHR and the Commission can interpret the American Convention and determine the specific content of each provision, including the equality and non-discrimination provisions. Their interpretations of the American Convention are equally important, although the IACHR's rulings and the Commission's reports are not equally binding. Also, regarding individual complaints, both the IACHR (in virtue of Article 61) and the Commission (under Article 51) can render final decisions under the American Convention. The IACHR enforces antidiscrimination

---

[5]Including: Advisory Opinion OC-18/03, *supra* note 3; Advisory Opinion OC-4/84, *supra* note 1.

law in its binding decisions when it makes a finding of discrimination. Enforcement is also guaranteed—at least on paper—through the IACHR's monitoring of compliance with its decisions. From its very first case in 1989,[6] the IACHR has monitored States' compliance with the remedies it ordered by requiring States to submit periodic reports on the steps taken to redress the human rights violations. Since 1989, the IACHR has closed files only when all the remedies it ordered had been complied with. Once the IACHR has ordered the State to make changes to its laws and/or in the practices of some of its domestic actors, the national legislator, courts and other public officials have a responsibility to enforce antidiscrimination law as ordered by the IACHR. Very often, the IACHR issues equitable remedies that require action from the executive, the legislator, the judiciary, and sometimes other domestic actors. In the case of *Yean and Bosico*,[7] the IACHR found that the State's refusal to issue birth certificates for children who were born in the Dominican Republic but were of Haitian origin was discriminatory. It ordered the State to modify the norms of late birth registration in the civil status registry in order to make late birth registration accessible "irrespective of [the children's] parentage or origin," and to implement "a program to provide training on human rights, with special emphasis on the right to equal protection and non-discrimination, to the State officials responsible for registering births."[8] Not only did the enforcement of these orders require the involvement of the executive, but also that of the legislator and the public administration. Other actors in the enforcement of antidiscrimination law are the victims' lawyers and counselors involved in the litigation of discrimination cases before the Commission and the IACHR. By advancing discrimination violation arguments in their briefs and oral pleadings before the IACHR, they contribute to bringing international attention to domestic discriminatory situations, propelling change.

5 Who Benefits from the Enforcement of Antidiscrimination Law?

The direct beneficiaries from the enforcement of antidiscrimination provisions are the injured parties. *Atala*[9] was the first case in which the Court dealt directly with a situation of structural discrimination based on sex orientation, cultivated by deeply

---

[6]*Case of Velásquez-Rodríguez v. Honduras, Reparations and Costs*. Judgment of July 21, 1989, Ser C No 7 at para 60(5): "The Court [...] [d]ecides that the Court shall supervise the indemnification ordered and shall close the file only when the compensation has been paid."

[7]*Case of the Girls Yean and Bosico v. Dominican Republic*. Judgment of September 8, 2005. Ser C No 130 at paras 236–240.

[8]Case of the Girls Yean and Bosico v. Dominican Republic. Judgment of September 8, 2005. Ser C No 130 at paras 236–240, paras 241–242.

[9]*Case of Atala Riffo and daughters v. Chile. Merits, Reparations and Costs*. Judgment of February 24, 2012 Ser C No 239 [*Atala*].

rooted societal and institutional stereotypes against homosexual individuals. The victims were offered psychological rehabilitation and a public act acknowledging international responsibility from the State. "The victims" families and broader communities can also benefit from the enforcement of antidiscrimination laws when recognizing the discrimination suffered results in symbolic reparations. In *Cotton Field,* a case related to the death of three women in the context of widespread violence against women in the Mexican State of Chihuahua, the IACHR ordered the State to organize a public act to acknowledge international responsibility for the human rights violations and to erect a monument "to commemorate the women victims of gender-based murder in Ciudad Juárez, [. . .] as a way of dignifying them and as a reminder of the context of violence they experienced, which the State undertakes to prevent in the future."[10]

The enforcement of antidiscrimination law by the IACHR often also benefits other current or potential victims of discrimination through its transformative remedies. Transformative remedies aim at changing the underlying structures that are at the origin of the discrimination. Such remedies were ordered in *Xákmok Kásek,* a case in which the IACHR found the Republic of Paraguay responsible for failing to ensure the right of the Xákmok Kásek Indigenous Community and its members to their ancestral property. The IACHR ordered the State to establish an effective system for *all* indigenous peoples in Paraguay to claim their ancestral lands as well as a judicial authority that is competent to decide the disputes that arise between the right to property of private entities and the rights of the indigenous peoples. It also infused structural changes in the relationships between the State and the indigenous communities by imposing to redefine the right to property as to include a collective dimension. More specifically, the IACHR imposed a shift in the criteria used by the State's authorities when deciding land claims and, by implication, expropriation cases. While before the judgment expropriation cases in Paraguay were decided by considering whether the land that was claimed was privately owned and rationally exploited, the IACHR ordered the State to take into account, in its expropriation decisions, the indigenous peoples' attachment to their ancestral lands, given its fundamental link to their cultural subsistence and their food supply.[11]

The enforcement of antidiscrimination law by the IACHR also impacts all Member States through the Convention control. Due to the Convention control, the interpretation given by the IACHR of the American Convention becomes as binding as the American Convention itself on all State Parties. For example, the sexual orientation of persons has become a protected ground under the prohibited grounds of discrimination of "any other social condition" of Article 1(1). This more inclusive interpretation applies not only to Chile from which the case *Atala* emerged, but also to all the Member States' domestic legislation and policies. The Convention

---

[10]*Case of González et al ("Cotton Field") v. Mexico. Preliminary Objection, Merits, Reparations and Costs.* Judgment of November 16, 2009. Ser C No 205 [*Cotton Field*], para 471.

[11]*Case of Xákmok Kásek Indigenous Community v Paraguay. Merits, Reparations and Costs.* Judgment of August 24, 2010. Ser C No 214, paras 276 and ff.

control has also broadened the right to property under Article 21 to encompass, in addition to private property, the indigenous peoples' communal conception of property, recognizing their traditional connections to their lands as an essential part of their cultures, their spiritual life, their integrity, and their economic survival, thanks to the *Xákmok Kásek* case.[12]

6 Who Is Harmed by the Enforcement of Antidiscrimination Law?

Enforcing antidiscrimination law questions privileges and inequality, and tends to disrupt the status quo. In that sense, it can "harm" traditionally privileged groups in society, at least from their points of view. The evolving and inclusive interpretation of the American Convention by the IACHR can be seen as contesting the historical superiority of some economically privileged groups. For example, the interpretation of the right to property of Article 21 now includes—in addition to the conception of indigenous communal property and cultural identity—the rights of indigenous peoples to be consulted prior to the exploitation of their lands since the *Kichwa Indigenous People of Sarayaku v. Ecuador* in 2012.[13] Therefore, the enforcement of antidiscrimination law in relation to the right to property and to indigenous peoples limits the State's and private landowners' ability to contract over the lands of indigenous populations, which can be seen as a serious inconvenience.

The IACHR's inclusive interpretation of the American Convention has also contested the views of historically culturally dominant groups. For example, public opinion, which was widely influenced by the Catholic religion, was largely against the annulation of the prohibition of in vitro fertilization in Costa Rica[14] and the inclusion of sexual orientation among the prohibited grounds of discrimination in Chile. In *Atala*, the proceedings at the national level showed that both the Chilean society and the judiciary shared the view that a family could only be composed of a heterosexual couple, and by no means could a homosexual mother keep the custody of her children. On the contrary, the IACHR affirmed that the American Convention does not define a limited concept of family, nor does it only protect a 'traditional'

---

[12] Case of Xákmok Kásek Indigenous Community v Paraguay. Merits, Reparations and Costs. Judgment of August 24, 2010. Ser C No 214, paras 85–87.

[13] *Case of Kichwa Indigenous People of Sarayaku v. Ecuador, Merits and reparations.* Judgment of June 27, 2012. Series C No. 245 [*Sarayaku*]. The IACHR held, unanimously, that the State of Ecuador was responsible for the violation of the rights to consultation, to indigenous communal property, and to cultural identity, in the terms of Article 21, in relation to Articles 1(1) and 2 thereof, to the detriment of the Kichwa Indigenous People of Sarayaku, for granting a permit to a private oil company to carry out oil exploration activities in its territory from the late 1990s, without previously consulting the Sarayaku.

[14] *Case of Artavia Murillo et al. v. Costa Rica. Preliminary Objections, Merits, Reparations and Costs.* Judgment of November 28, 2012. Series C No. 257 [*In Vitro Fertilization*].

model of the family. The Court found that "the language used by the Supreme Court of Chile regarding the girls' alleged need to grow up in a 'normally structured family [...],' and not in an 'exceptional family,' reflect[ed] a limited, stereotypical perception of the concept of family," which was irreconcilable with the Convention.[15]

Domestic actors having to implement the IACHR's orders can also be "harmed" by the enforcement of antidiscrimination law when they have to direct some of their limited resources to address human rights violations that they sometimes endorsed initially. The IACHR often orders remedies that the executive cannot implement single-handedly, thus domestic actors can delay the implementation of these remedies. For example, in *Cotton Field*, it was only in 2013—four years after the judgment—that the IACHR considered that the State had complied with the orders of providing gender-sensitivity training to numerous public officials and a program of education for the general public; these remedies necessarily required the collaboration of other state institutions at the local level.[16]

7 What Remedies Are Provided by the Enforcement of Antidiscrimination Law?

The American Convention gives broad remedial jurisdiction to the IACHR; in accordance with Article 63, the IACHR can order measures that ensure that the victims enjoy future respect of the rights that were violated, remedy the consequences of the violations, and compensate for the harm. According to the IACHR, the enforcement of antidiscrimination law requires a different kind of reparation than the traditional restitution; instead of re-establishing the previous situation in cases of discrimination, the reparations "must be designed to change th[e] situation, so that their effect is not only of restitution, but also of rectification."[17] Consequently, the IACHR orders two types of remedies in such cases: individual remedies and transformative reparations. Individual remedies include monetary and non-monetary compensations, symbolic reparations and restitution of rights. In the *In Vitro Fertilization* case, the IACHR ordered financial compensation and measures of psychological rehabilitation for the victims who were persons with reproductive disabilities and women and couples who did not have the financial resources to undergo IVF abroad, because the IACHR found that the absolute prohibition of IVF in Costa Rica had a disproportionate impact on these groups.[18] In the *Xákmok Kásek* case, the failure of Paraguay to ensure the right of an indigenous community to their

---

[15]*Atala, supra* note 9 at paras 142 and 145.

[16]*Cotton Field, supra* note 10 at paras 541–543. Some orders were still not complied with in 2013 (See Resolution from the IACHR of May 2013 on the compliance with the judgment, at para 111: http://www.corteidh.or.cr/docs/supervisiones/gonzález_21_05_13.pdf).

[17]*Cotton Field, supra* note 10 at para 450.

[18]*In Vitro Fertilization, supra* note 14 at para 381.

ancestral property led to the privatization of their lands and the maintenance of this group in a vulnerable situation with regard to food, medicine, and sanitation. The IACHR ordered the State to address the immediate and very basic needs of the community by establishing a permanent health clinic with the necessary medications and supplies to provide adequate health care to the community.[19] In *Gonzalez Lluy*, a 3-year old girl contracted HIV as a result of a contaminated blood donation. This led to her and her family experiencing discrimination at school, work, in housing, etc. The IACHR ordered the State to provide and pay for immediate medical and psychological treatment through public health institutions or the private sector, as well as a scholarship towards undergraduate university studies, and another scholarship to complete her graduate studies "at any university in the world where [the victim] is accepted."[20] The State was also charged with providing the family with decent housing.[21] Additionally, the State was obliged to pay $50,000 USD to each victim for pecuniary damage,[22] $350,000 USD to the contaminated girl, $30,000 USD for her mother and $25,000 USD for her brother for non-pecuniary damage.[23]

Transformative remedies include: training for public officers (e.g. *Cotton Field*) and health practitioners (e.g. *Gonzales Lluy*),[24] legal reforms (e.g. *In Vitro Fertilization*), creation or reform of institutions (e.g. *Xákmok Kásek*), and raising social awareness (e.g. *Cotton Field*). In the *In Vitro Fertilization* case, the IACHR ordered the State to annul the prohibition to practice IVF and to regulate this practice, and to implement permanent education and training programs on human rights, reproductive rights, and non-discrimination for judicial employees "in all areas and at all echelons of the Judiciary".[25]

---

[19] *Xákmok Kásek, supra* note 11 at paras 2 and 306.

[20] Caso Gonzales Lluy y otros vs. Ecuador. Excepciones Preliminares, Fondo, Reparaciones y Costas [in Spanish only]. Judgment of September 1, 2015. Ser C No 298, paras 359–360 and 372–373.

[21] Caso Gonzales Lluy y otros vs. Ecuador. Excepciones Preliminares, Fondo, Reparaciones y Costas [in Spanish only]. Judgment of September 1, 2015. Ser C No 298, para 377.

[22] Caso Gonzales Lluy y otros vs. Ecuador. Excepciones Preliminares, Fondo, Reparaciones y Costas [in Spanish only]. Judgment of September 1, 2015. Ser C No 298, paras 407–409.

[23] Caso Gonzales Lluy y otros vs. Ecuador. Excepciones Preliminares, Fondo, Reparaciones y Costas [in Spanish only]. Judgment of September 1, 2015. Ser C No 298, paras 412–416.

[24] Caso Gonzales Lluy y otros vs. Ecuador. Excepciones Preliminares, Fondo, Reparaciones y Costas [in Spanish only]. Judgment of September 1, 2015. Ser C No 298, para 386.

[25] *In Vitro Fertilization, supra* note 14 at para 341.

8 Who Supports the Enforcement of Antidiscrimination Law?

Various domestic and international actors support the enforcement of antidiscrimination law in the Inter-American Human Rights system. The IACHR supports the enforcement of antidiscrimination law by monitoring the States' compliance with its orders. By requesting that the States submit periodic reports on the progress of their remedial actions, the IACHR reminds them of their international obligations on a regular basis. Since its 2005 judgment in *Yean and Bosico*, the IACHR has issued four resolutions monitoring the Dominican Republic's compliance (2007, 2009, 2010, and 2011); the State is still being monitored. The Commission also supports antidiscrimination law by contributing to the supervision of the compliance by submitting its own reports (see question 2).

International and domestic civil society, including legal clinics, also contribute to support the enforcement of antidiscrimination law. One important way to do so is by submitting *amicus curiae* to the IACHR. For example, the IACHR received nine *amici curiae* for the *Nadege* case related to the Dominican Republic's responsibility for the death and bodily injuries of Haitian migrants by military agents.[26] Several of them pushed for IACHR's recognition of the context of structural discrimination against persons of Haitian origin in the Dominican Republic. Another way for civil society to support the enforcement of antidiscrimination law is to support the victims—or even represent them—in the proceedings before the Commission and the IACHR. For example, the victims in *Nadege* were represented by the *Groupe d'Appui aux Rapatriés et Réfugiés* of Haiti, the *Centro Cultural Dominico-Haitiano* of the Dominican Republic and *La Clinique internationale des Droits humains de l'Université du Québec à Montréal* from Quebec, Canada, which documented in their briefs systemic racism against Haitians in the Dominican Republic's history as well as discrimination in the particular facts of *Nadege*.[27]

Civil society also plays a key role in supporting the enforcement of antidiscrimination law outside the international legal proceedings, since they can diffuse in their networks the IACHR's decisions and reach a population that would otherwise be unaware of the rulings made by the IACHR. Similarly, scholars who write on the discrimination cases of the IACHR contribute to strengthening the IACHR's analysis and informing the public and academia about the human rights questions decided by the IACHR. The media also contributes to support the enforcement of antidiscrimination law when they publish the judgments prepared by the IACHR. So doing, they contribute to implementing the IACHR's remedies. Indeed, the IACHR very often orders the publication of the official summary of its judgment,

---

[26]Case of *Nadege Dorzema et al v Dominican Republic. Merits, Reparations and Costs.* Judgment of October 24, 2012. Ser C No 251 [*Nadege*] at para 9.

[27]See the *Escrito sobre Argumento y Pruebas* submitted by the representatives of the victims in *Nadege* at para 1.

both in the Official Gazette of the State and in a national newspaper with widespread circulation.[28]

Government representatives, who may want to comply with the IACHR's orders to enhance their international reputation among other reasons,[29] sometimes support antidiscrimination law enforcement by recognizing and documenting discrimination in their briefs,[30] and/or by supporting the remedial actions. Other state institutions that support the enforcement of antidiscrimination law include Ombudsman offices, which can take part in litigation before the IACHR and promote its holdings.

9 Who Opposes the Enforcement of Antidiscrimination Law?

Contrary to the Commission whose mandate includes encouraging friendly settlements, the IACHR is obliged to rule on contested cases. Its rulings, which are implemented less than the friendly settlements designed under the Commission's auspices,[31] necessarily give rise to resistance from some domestic actors. In a couple of extreme cases, they even led to the States' denunciation of the American Convention (Venezuela, Trinidad and Tobago). Regarding the enforcement of antidiscrimination law, the opposition can be particularly strong as measures to remedy discrimination of historically disadvantaged groups often disrupt the societies' equilibrium and question longstanding discriminatory practices and policies.

Status quo supporters include some executives themselves. The case of the Dominican Republic is telling: despite an extensive documentary, testimonial, and expert evidence regarding the existence of widespread discrimination against persons of Haitian origin in the country and evidence of discrimination against the victims in three different cases,[32] the State constantly denied the presence of discrimination in the country. The Dominican Republic even rejected the last judgment of the IACHR in this matter.[33]

The legislature is another body that can effectively oppose the enforcement of antidiscrimination law, particularly in countries where the majority's view is that there is no discrimination. It can do so by refraining from adopting or transforming the legislative measures ordered by the IACHR. That was the case in the Dominican

---

[28]See, for example, *Case of Expelled Dominicans and Haitians v. Dominican Republic. Preliminary Objections, Merits, Reparations and Costs.* Judgment of August 28, 2014. Series C No. 282 [*Case of Expelled Dominicans and Haitians*] at para 460.

[29]Huneeus (2011), p. 513.

[30]*Cotton Field, supra* note 10 at para 27.

[31]Basch et al. (2010), pp. 25–26.

[32]The three cases are: *Yean and Bosico, supra* note 7; *Nadege, supra* note 26; *Case of Expelled Dominicans and Haitians, supra* note 28.

[33]See Commission (2014).

Republic; more than 6 years after *Yean and Bosico*, the legislature—in line with the executive's denial of the situation—had not yet reformed the late registration of birth to prevent future discrimination against children of Haitian descent.[34]

The judiciary can also oppose the enforcement of non-discriminatory measures ordered by the IACHR by not enforcing the rulings. The judiciary can do so as it is not accountable before the IACHR; it is generally independent and it may not agree with the IACHR's finding of discrimination (as in *Atala*). An extreme manifestation of opposition to the IACHR's rulings from the judiciary is the decision of the Constitutional Court of the Dominican Republic declaring unconstitutional the instrument accepting the jurisdiction of the IACHR.[35] This happened two months after the IACHR ruled in the *Case of Expelled Dominicans and Haitians* that the State's attempt to deny citizenship to Dominicans of Haitian ancestry violated articles 3, 18, 20 and 24 of the American Convention.[36]

Finally, the media and civil society can also oppose rulings and contribute to increasing the gaps between the population's majority and traditionally discriminated and marginalized groups.

10 How Broad Is the Coverage of Antidiscrimination Law?

The principle of non-discrimination of the American Convention, interpreted by the IACHR both in its consultative opinions and its binding decisions, has a broad scope of application; it is *erga omnes*, its grounds have recently been expanded, and it applies both to the rights and freedoms guaranteed by the American Convention and to domestic legislation and policies.

The IACHR broadened the scope of the non-discrimination principle by considering it a *jus cogens erga omnes* principle.[37] This means that the obligations that derive from this principle, which are of a peremptory character, bind all States and give rise to effects with regard to third parties, including individuals. The obligation to ensure the principle of the right to equal protection and non-discrimination is "irrespective of a person's migratory status in a State."[38]

The prohibited grounds of discrimination listed in Article 1(1) are composed of race, color, sex, language, religion, political or other opinion, national or social origin, economic status, birth, or any other social condition. As a result of the open nature of the last ground, the protected grounds have been expanded to encompass

---

[34]*Yean and Bosico, Monitoring Compliance with Judgment, Order of the IACHR of October 10, 2011* at p. 7.

[35]In the judgment TC-0256-14: see Commission (2014).

[36]*Case of Expelled Dominicans and Haitians, supra* note 28 at para 512(13).

[37]Advisory Opinion OC-18/03, *supra* note 3 at paras 100–101, 110.

[38]*Yean and Bosico, supra* note 32 at para 155.

sexual orientation,[39] HIV/AIDS and disability,[40] and more categories could be protected in the years to come. In *Atala,* to determine that the sexual orientation of a person was protected under the ground of "any other social condition," the IACHR referred to the broader international human rights context. In particular, it focused on the European Court of Human Rights' interpretation of the ground "another condition" of Article 14 of the *European Convention on Human Rights,* which includes "sexual orientation" among the forbidden categories of discrimination.

Regarding the scope of Articles 1(1) and 24 of the American Convention, an important quality of the American Convention is its applicability beyond the rights and freedoms guaranteed in the Convention. On one hand, Article 1(1) guarantees non-discrimination for all the provisions of the Convention. Therefore, "[r]egardless of its origin or the form it may assume, any treatment that can be considered to be discriminatory with regard to the exercise of any of the rights guaranteed under the Convention is *per se* incompatible with that instrument."[41] On the other hand, Article 24 extends the prohibition of discrimination to all domestic law and policies that the States approve and apply, under the concept of equality before the law.[42] This moves the reach of antidiscrimination law well beyond the American Convention, in contrast with its European counterpart. Also, to guarantee and ensure the enjoyment of rights without discrimination, States have both negative and positive obligations: they must refrain from discriminating (by adopting discriminatory laws or practices for example) but they must also take positive measures to reverse instances of discrimination and ensure substantive equality for traditionally disadvantaged groups.[43]

11 Does the Enforcement of Antidiscrimination Law Vary According to the Grounds of Discrimination?

The principle of non-discrimination is a *jus cogens* principle, and all the grounds of discrimination listed in Article 1(1) are equally prohibited. Therefore, the enforcement of antidiscrimination law should not vary according to the grounds of discrimination in the Inter-American Human Rights system. This being said, it seems that some discriminatory practices in relation to certain grounds (including when

---

[39] *Atala, supra* note 9 at paras 86–91.
[40] *Gonzales Lluy, supra* note 2 at para 255.
[41] Advisory Opinion OC-4/84, *supra* note 1 at para 53.
[42] *Case of Yatama v. Nicaragua. Preliminary Objections, Merits, Reparations and Costs.* Judgment of June 23, 2005. Series C No. 127 [*Yatama*] at para 186; Advisory Opinion OC-4/84, *supra* note 1 at para 54.
[43] *Yean and Bosico, supra* note 32 at para 173; *Yatama, supra* note 42 at para 185.

discrimination involves various prohibited grounds) tend to aggravate the importance of the violation, and lead to stronger obligations of the States. For example, *Miguel Castro Castro Prison v. Peru* is related to the State's responsibility for the excessive use of force resulting in the death of dozens of prisoners as well as many injured inmates.[44] The IACHR made a number of considerations specific to female inmates and pregnant inmates. The IACHR highlighted that the violations of the right to humane treatment were exacerbated by the fact that some inmates were pregnant and concluded "the acts of violence had a greater effect on them."[45] The IACHR also gave specific consideration to the treatment the women received in the prison and later in the hospital, saying that this treatment violated their personal dignity, and that some amounted to sexual violence.[46] Although the IACHR did not find that the attacks to physical integrity were a violation of the obligation not to discriminate on the ground of sex provided by Article 1(1), it was clearly concerned by the gender dimension of the violence that occurred, and also the greater vulnerability of pregnant women to violence.[47] In addition to the general obligation to investigate and prosecute possible acts of torture and other cruel, inhuman or degrading treatment, the IACHR ordered the State to fulfil a more stringent obligation to investigate the violent acts against women in the case in accordance with two other human rights treaties ratified by Peru, namely, the Convention of Belem and the *Inter-American Convention to Prevent and Punish Torture*.[48]

In the case of *Gonzales Lluy*, the IACHR found that the victim's discrimination based on her HIV-positive condition was aggravated by other factors such as being a girl, then a woman, disabled, and from a poor family. The IACHR noted that this compounded discrimination made the victim even more vulnerable and increased the damage she and her family suffered in education, medical care, work, social life, and housing.[49]

Therefore, it seems that the prohibition of discrimination is even stronger when it involves certain grounds and intersectional discrimination, especially when the victims are socially and economically marginalized, and more vulnerable to violence and exclusion.

---

[44]*Merits, Reparations and Costs*, Judgment of November 25, 2006, Series C No. 160.
[45]*Ibid* at para 293.
[46]*Ibid* at para 306.
[47]See also *Gonzales Lluy, supra* note 2 at para 288.
[48]*Ibid* at paras 344–346.
[49]*Gonzales Lluy, supra* note 2 at paras 285–291.

12 What Is the Relationship Between the Enforcement of Antidiscrimination Law and the Quest for Equality on Both an Individual and Systemic Level?

For the IACHR, it is clear that enforcing antidiscrimination law is not limited to abstaining from adopting discriminatory laws or policies, which would amount to formal equality; rather, it usually aims at achieving substantive equality on an individual and systemic level by repairing the harm suffered by the victims of discrimination and transforming underlying structural discrimination. The jurisprudence of the IACHR mentions that in addition to the general obligations to protect the exercise and enjoyment of the rights of the American Convention under Articles 1(1) and 2, some "special obligations" can derive from these general obligations "based on the particular needs for protection of the holders of the right, due either to their personal status or to the specific situation in which they find themselves."[50] In the case of disability, these special obligations imply that "States are obliged to facilitate the inclusion of persons with disabilities by means of equality of conditions, opportunities and participation in all spheres of society" and they "must promote social inclusion practices and adopt measures of positive differentiation" to remove the barriers persons with disabilities face.[51] The elimination of discrimination based on disability is therefore linked to the enjoyment of individual equality and inclusion in the society.

Also, the States are obliged "to take affirmative measures to reverse or change discriminatory situations that exist in their societies to the detriment of a specific group of persons."[52] When enforcing the right to non-discrimination, particularly in cases where discrimination is widespread in the society, the IACHR aims not only at full restitution, which "entails the re-establishment of the previous situation," but also "rectification," to change the context of structural discrimination.[53] Rectification involves law reforms, such as allowing the practice of IVF in *In Vitro Fertilization*, reform to birth registration, such as in *Yean and Bosico*, and education through training for public officials and educational programs for the general public such as in *Cotton Field*.

Although the IACHR has showed great interest in ensuring equality at the individual and systemic level while it enforces antidiscrimination law, it is limited in what it can order by the evidence it receives and by the remedies the Commission and the representatives of the victims request. In *Atala*, while the facts of the case indicated homophobia among part of the society and the domestic judicial

---

[50] *In Vitro Fertilization, supra* note 14 at para 292; *Sarayaku, supra* note 13 at para 244.
[51] *Ibid* at para 292.
[52] Advisory Opinion OC-18/03, *supra* note 3 at para 104; *Atala, supra* note 9 at para 80.
[53] *Cotton Field, supra* note 10 at para 450.

proceedings, the Commission and the representatives requested the Court to order the State to adopt legislation, public policies, programs and initiatives to prohibit and eradicate discrimination based on sexual orientation in all areas of the exercise of public power, including the administration of justice.[54] However the IACHR considered that they "did not provide sufficient facts that would suggest that the violations resulted from a problem with the laws per se" and therefore, it did not order this remedy,[55] limiting the systemic impacts of this antidiscrimination decision.

13 Is the Enforcement of Antidiscrimination Law Regarded as Different from the Enforcement of Other Laws?

The enforcement of antidiscrimination law by the IACHR seems to have been regarded as different from the enforcement of other components of the American Convention.[56] One initial observation is that findings of discrimination are much more recent than other provisions of the Convention. Whereas the IACHR's first judgments date back to 1989, it was only in 2005 that the IACHR found a violation of the right to equal protection of the law and non-discrimination under Article 24 in *Yatama v. Nicaragua*,[57] a case dealing with indigenous communities that were forced to create political parties to participate in municipal elections contrary to their customs, organization, and culture.

The second observation is that, even after 2005, the enforcement of antidiscrimination law seems less systematic than other components of the American Convention. In some cases, although the IACHR did refer to the situation of discrimination that the victims suffered from, it did not find a violation of the non-discrimination provisions of the American Convention. This was to the detriment of historically disadvantaged groups, who would have, on the contrary, benefited from a more systematic denunciation of the structural disadvantages they have faced. For example, in *Moiwana Community v. Suriname*,[58] in which soldiers killed more than 40 members of the Maroons community and many others had to flee, the IACHR briefly mentioned that the Maroon community might have felt

---

[54]*Atala, supra* note 9 at paras 273–274.

[55]But it did order the State to continue implementing trainings related to discrimination, overcoming gender stereotypes of LGBTQI persons and homophobia, at paras 271–272.

[56]Several ideas of this answer are taken from González Le Saux and Parra Vera (2008), pp. 151–152 [Le Saux and Parra Vera].

[57]*Yatama, supra* note 42 at para 229.

[58]*Preliminary Objections, Merits, Reparations and Costs*. Judgment of June 15, 2005. Series C No. 124.

discriminated against,[59] but it did not find discrimination. In the *Case of the Yakye Axa Indigenous Community v. Paraguay*,[60] which dealt with the State's failure to ensure the ancestral property rights of the indigenous community, the IACHR recalled that, pursuant to Articles 24 and 1(1), to effectively ensure the rights to equality and non-discrimination to indigenous populations, both the State and the IACHR must take into account the specific characteristics of the indigenous peoples that differentiate them from the general population, and treat them differently accordingly. However, the IACHR did not find that there was discrimination. It found that the State violated the right to property under Article 21 in combination with the obligation to respect and guarantee Article 1(1). Yet, it failed to find that this violation was also in combination with the obligation not to discriminate. However, the violation of the right to property resulted from the State's preference for a rational exploitation of the lands over the community's needs and ancestral relationship with the lands. This impacted this entire group that has been traditionally disadvantaged, and it was discriminatory.

The third observation is that transformative remedies after findings of discrimination generally give rise to more resistance from domestic actors, and are overall less implemented than monetary orders. Enforcing antidiscrimination law often confronts widely shared views in the society, which is not necessarily the case of other components of the American Convention.[61]

14 What Does the Enforcement of Antidiscrimination Law Reveal About the Nature of Your Legal System or About the Enforcement of Laws in Your Legal System?

The enforcement of antidiscrimination law by the IACHR reveals that the American Convention and the other human rights treaties enforced by the IACHR are applied contextually. The IACHR is sensitive to the social and historical context of cases, particularly when they relate to longstanding practices of exclusion, exploitation or discrimination. For example, the historical background in *Xákmok Kásek* shows longstanding exclusion of the indigenous populations.[62] The case of *Cotton Field* was not only about three women who were killed: it was decided against a background of widespread violence against women in the region as well as deeply ingrained gender stereotypes held by society and the police.[63]

---

[59] *Ibid* at para 94.

[60] *Merits, Reparations and Costs*. Judgment of June 17, 2005. Series C No. 125 at para 51.

[61] Basch et al. (2010), p. 21. This study analysed all the holdings of the IACHR between 2001 and 2006, and surveyed all the resolutions supervising compliance with the remedies ordered up until June 30, 2009. Non-compliance was observed in 50% of awareness raising measures, 57% of training measures, 84% of institutional strengthening measures, and 93% of legal reforms measures.

[62] *Xákmok Kásek, supra* note 11 at paras 56–84.

[63] *Cotton Field, supra* note 10 at paras 113 and ff.

The American Convention's interpretation is evolutive. Antidiscrimination law has gained greater authority over the years as the grounds of discrimination are expanded to include new categories under "any other social condition." This is exemplified by the inclusion of the indigenous conception of property under the right to property. The IACHR's interpretation of the American Convention is in part inspired by other human rights tribunals, and in particular its European counterpart. The IACHR's interpretation of the American Convention is also partly based on the written submissions and the oral pleadings of the Commission and the representatives of the victims, as well as by the *amici curiae* that it receives. Therefore, the future evolution of antidiscrimination law requires both new cases with a discrimination dimension, as well as civil society to support and inform the work of the IACHR.

Remedial actions ordered by the IACHR often implicate many domestic actors, who are not directly accountable to the IACHR, and who do not necessarily have incentives to comply with the orders. In addition, despite the fact that the IACHR's rulings are binding on the State Parties, and that the IACHR monitors compliance with its judgments, no sanctions are imposed for a lack of compliance, barring a potential impact on the States' international reputation. These are weaknesses that limit the enforcement of the IACHR's rulings, and more specifically, the actual impact of its transformative remedies.

More generally, given the overall low compliance with the transformative remedies ordered by the IACHR, and the fact that the IACHR does not use the non-discrimination provisions as often as it could, one can see a discrepancy between the high value given to the principle of non-discrimination in the Inter-American Human Rights system (part of the *jus cogens*, the IACHR considers it is *erga omnes*) and its enforcement.

15 Conclusion

The enforcement of antidiscrimination law by the IACHR has been an important part of the work done by the IACHR in the field of human rights in the Latin American region, especially in recent years. However, antidiscrimination law needs to be more systematically addressed by the IACHR. This must be done in order to make human rights a reality for historically marginalized groups in the region such as indigenous peoples, groups traditionally disadvantaged such as women, and groups historically invisible, but whose discrimination is now recognized and fought against (at least by the IACHR), such as persons with disabilities and LGBTQI persons.

It is also important that the IACHR clarifies its use of the non-discrimination provisions of Articles 1(1) and 24 of the American Convention.[64] Although Article 1(1) can be interpreted as including both the obligation to respect and guarantee the

---

[64]On these aspects, see Le Saux and Parra Vera (2008).

rights of the American Convention and the obligation not to discriminate, this second dimension has to be more clearly denounced by the IACHR to ensure that situations of (especially structural) discrimination do not continue. Indeed, Article 1 (1) is always read in combination with the violations of other rights guaranteed by the Convention, as a subordinate clause, and it is not always clear when the IACHR finds that, in addition to the violation of the substantive right, the violation also implied discrimination against a group or members of a group traditionally disadvantaged. Also, the IACHR should clarify the use of Article 24 as an autonomous provision, guaranteeing non-discrimination in domestic laws and policies.

The IACHR is innovative in the reparations it orders, taking into account the personal situation of the victims and their special needs (e.g. decent housing, scholarship, etc.), and is more generous than the European Court of Human Rights in its monetary damages for discrimination-related findings. It is also aware of the impacts of intersectional discrimination and has aimed in recent rulings to address the particular vulnerability and needs of the victims in these cases.

Nevertheless, there are limits to the great transformative potential of the IACHR's rulings. One of these limits is the IACHR's difficulty in achieving compliance with its rulings because of the limited leverage it has in the domestic sphere. Another limit is linked to the fact that its remedies target disparate actors with different interests and ideologies, and sometimes with very little knowledge of the IACHR.[65] Ultimately, it is the States' responsibility to enforce antidiscrimination law in their respective countries and to comply with their international Human Rights obligations.

This being said, by enforcing antidiscrimination law, the IACHR contributes to enforcing equality at both an individual and systemic level in the Latin American region, and is an example of a proactive international Human Rights Court.

References

Basch FF et al (2010) The effectiveness of the Inter-American system of human rights protection: a quantitative approach to its functioning and compliance with its decisions. Int J Human Rights (English Version) 7(12):9

Commission (2014) IACHR Condemns Judgment of the Constitutional Court of the Dominican Republic. Commission's Press Release (6 November 2014). http://www.oas.org/en/iachr/media_center/PReleases/2014/130.asp

Huneeus A (2011) Courts resisting courts: lessons from the Inter-American Court's struggle to enforce human rights. Cornell Int Law J 44:493

Le Saux MG, Parra Vera Ó (2008) Concepciones y cláusulas de igualdad en la jurisprudencia de la Corte Interamericana. A propósito del Caso Apitz. Revista IIDH 47:127

---

[65] Huneeus (2011), p. 495.

Anne-Claire Gayet is a legal expert in French Migration Law and International Human Rights Law. She holds a LL.M. and M.Sc. from Université de Montréal, and a LL.B. and B.C.L. from McGill University (Canada). She completed an internship at the Inter-American Court of Human Rights in 2012 and researched and wrote on the concept of systemic discrimination. She works as project manager for the European project UPRIGHTS for the capacity building of professionals assisting unaccompanied minors in asylum applications within the French NGO Forum réfugiés-Cosi. She is also an elected member of La Cimade's Rhône-Alpes Auvergne regional board. La Cimade is a French NGO defending foreigners' rights and dignity.

Appendix A: Questionnaire

The 29 reports included in this volume were guided by the following 13 questions, which were submitted to the authors as the basic organizing tool for their reports.

1. Is antidiscrimination law enforced?
2. HOW is antidiscrimination law enforced?
3. WHO ENFORCES antidiscrimination law?
4. WHO BENEFITS from the enforcement of antidiscrimination law?
5. WHO IS HARMED by the enforcement of antidiscrimination law?
6. WHAT REMEDIES are provided by the enforcement of antidiscrimination law?
7. WHO SUPPORTS the enforcement of antidiscrimination law?
8. WHO OPPOSES the enforcement of antidiscrimination law?
9. HOW BROAD is the coverage of antidiscrimination law?
10. DOES ENFORCEMENT OF ANTIDISCRIMINATION LAW VARY according to the ground of discrimination?
11. WHAT IS THE RELATIONSHIP between the enforcement of antidiscrimination law and the quest for equality on both an individual and systemic level?
12. IS THE ENFORCEMENT OF ANTIDISCRIMINATION LAW REGARDED AS DIFFERENT from the enforcement of other laws?
13. WHAT DOES THE ENFORCEMENT OF ANTIDISCRIMINATION LAW REVEAL about the nature of your legal system or about the enforcement of laws in your legal system?

Appendix B: Meet the Editors

Marie Mercat-Bruns
Marie Mercat-Bruns is an Affiliated Professor at Sciences Po Law School and a tenured Associate Law Professor at the Conservatoire National des Arts et Métiers and co-pilot of the Gender Program (LISE,CNRS). She holds an LLM (University of Pennsylvania Law School) and a comparative prize winning PhD on Law and Aging (University of Paris West Nanterre).

She is a member of the scientific board of Presage (Sciences Po Gender program) and conducted in June 2016 a 2-year study for the French Ministry of Justice and the Defender of Rights on discrimination law in France and the Netherlands, co-heading a team of researchers from the University of Paris-Assas-La Sorbonne and Sciences Po (CEVIPOF).

In 2015, appointed with David Oppenheimer as one of the general reporters of the International Academy of Comparative Law, she prepared the 2016 Thematic Congress on the "Enforcement and Effectiveness of Antidiscrimination Law". In 2009, she helped create with students a public interest law clinic on access to justice at Sciences Po Law School she currently supervises. It is focused on discrimination law, women's rights, poverty law, and street law.

Her recent books on discrimination include: *Discrimination at Work: Comparing European, French, and American Law*. University of California Press, 2016; *Discriminations en droit du travail : dialogue avec la doctrine américaine* Dalloz 2013; Articles include: Le droit de la non-discrimination : une nouvelle discipline en droit privé ? Rec. Dalloz, 2017, p. 224 ; Racisme au travail : les nouveaux modes de détection et les outils de prévention Droit social, 2017, p. 361 ; L'identification de la discrimination systémique, *Rev. Droit du Travail*, 2015, p. 672 ; Discriminations multiples et identité au travail au croisement des questions d'égalité et de liberté, *Rev. Droit du Travail*, 2015, p. 28 ; Age and disability differential treatment in France – Contrasting EU and national court's approaches to the inner limits of antidiscrimination law, *International Journal of Discrimination and the law*, Nov. 12 2014, (Sage online).

David B. Oppenheimer

David B. Oppenheimer is a Clinical Professor of Law at the University of California, Berkeley, School of Law. He graduated from the University Without Walls (Berkeley) and Harvard Law School. He clerked for California Chief Justice Rose Bird, and thereafter worked as a staff attorney for the California Department of Fair Employment and Housing, and as Director of the Boalt Hall Employment Discrimination Clinic, before entering full time teaching.

He is a co-author of Comparative Equality & Antidiscrimination Law: Cases, Codes, Constitutions & Commentary (Foundation Press 2012, Second Edition 2017 Comparative Equality Press) (co-authored with Sheila Foster, Sora Han and Richard Ford), the first U.S. textbook on comparative antidiscrimination law. His co-authored book, Whitewashing Race: The Myth of a Color-Blind Society (with M. Brown, M. Carnoy, E. Currie, T. Duster, M. Schulz & D. Wellman) (University of California Press 2003) won the 2004 Benjamin L. Hooks outstanding book award. Other recent books include an edited volume on the importance of dissenting opinions in the jurisprudence of the California Supreme Court, and teaching materials for Civil Procedure and Trial Advocacy.

Professor Oppenheimer has presented scholarly papers on discrimination law and on legal education at numerous universities, including Berkeley, Harvard, Yale, Stanford, Columbia, UCLA, Duke, Oxford, Sciences-Po Paris, Heidelberg, the European University Institute (Florence), Kings College London, the Free University of Brussels, Humboldt University Berlin, the University of Valencia, Bucerius Law (Hamburg), the University of Lyon and the University of Paris (I and X), and at the Indian Law Institute and the annual meetings of the Association of American Law Schools and the American Political Science Association.

Professor Oppenheimer has published articles on discrimination law and on legal education in the *Pennsylvania Law Review*, the *Cornell Law Review*, the *Journal of Legal Education*, the *American Bar Association Journal*, the *Columbia Journal of Human Rights Law*, the *Berkeley Women's Law Journal*, the *Berkeley Journal of Employment and Labor Law*, the *European Antidiscrimination Law Journal*, *Droit et Cultures*, *Revue de Droit Travail*, and many others, and was a contributor to MacKinnon and Siegel's Directions in Sexual Harassment Law (Yale University Press 2003), Friedman's Employment Discrimination Stories (Foundation Press 2006), and Mercat-Bruns' Discriminations en droit du travail (Dalloz 2013, UC Press 2016). He is an active member of the American Law Institute.

For more information on the Berkeley Study Group and Professor Oppenheimer's work on comparative antidiscrimination law, see https://www.law.berkeley.edu/research/berkeley-comparative-equality-antidiscrimination-law-study-group/ and www.comparativeequality.org.

Cady Sartorius

Cady Sartorius is an attorney with the California Civil Rights Group. She is a 2017 graduate of the University of California, Berkeley, School of Law. During law school, in addition to working on this project with Professors Mercat-Bruns and Oppenheimer, she interned in the Disability Rights section of the ACLU, the San

Francisco District Attorney's Office, and the U.S. Attorney's Office for the Northern District of California. She was also on Berkeley Law's Alternative Dispute Resolution (ADR) team and competed on Berkeley Law's Mock Trial team. She worked as a teaching assistant for Professor Oppenheimer for both Evidence Law and Federal Civil Procedure.

After graduating *summa cum laude* from the University of New Mexico and prior to studying law, Ms. Sartorius worked as a freelance sign language interpreter. That, and her volunteer work for the disabled led to her interest in civil rights law. She now practices law at the California Civil Rights Law Group—a plaintiff-side firm fighting for those who experience sexual harassment or discrimination in the workplace on the basis of race, gender, age, disability, sexual orientation, national origin, or religion.